THE ENCYCLOPEDIA OF
MODERN AIRCRAFT

FROM CIVILIAN AIRLINERS TO MILITARY SUPERFIGHTERS

GENERAL EDITOR:
JIM WINCHESTER

THUNDER BAY
P · R · E · S · S

San Diego, California

Thunder Bay Press
An imprint of the Advantage Publishers Group
5880 Oberlin Drive, San Diego, CA 92121-4794
www.thunderbaybooks.com

All notations of errors or omissions should be addressed to Thunder Bay Press,
Editorial Department, at the above address. All other correspondence (author inquiries,
permissions) concerning the content of this book should be addressed to
Amber Books Ltd., Bradley's Close, 74–77 White Lion Street, London N1 9PF,
United Kingdom. www.amberbooks.co.uk.

ISBN-13: 978-1-59223-628-2
ISBN-10: 1-59223-628-6

Library of Congress Cataloging-in-Publication Data available upon request.

Printed in Singapore

1 2 3 4 5 10 09 08 07 06

PICTURE CREDITS
All photographs and illustrations provided by Art-Tech/Aerospace Publishing,
except the following:
6–7, 9, 10: U.S. Department of Defense
278: Getty Images

CONTENTS

*U.S. Air Force F-16 Fighting Falcons are refuelled midair by a
USAF Boeing KC-135 Stratotanker. Nearly all internal fuel can
be pumped through the tanker's flying boom. A special
shuttlecock-shaped drogue, trailed behind the flying boom,
is used to refuel aircraft fitted with probes.*

Introduction

The civil and military aircraft in service today represent a range of technologies dating as far back as the 1930s and 1940s, and include features such as stressed alloy construction and electro-mechanical instrumentation to exotic composites and computerized 'glass' cockpits in use since the 1980s and 1990s.

IN THE POST-WAR YEARS, combat aircraft designs have tended to last longer in active use than commercial airliners. The U.S. Phantom and Skyhawk, and the Russian MiG-17 and MiG-21 and derivatives are among those designs still going strong five decades after their first flights. Most individual surviving examples of these classics were built in the 1970s and have been upgraded at least once since.

When the older aircraft in this book entered service, the

The F-117A Nighthawk was the world's first operational aircraft designed to exploit stealth technology. The aircraft was first used in combat in the Gulf War (1990–91), where F-117s made direct hits on more than 1600 ground targets.

world was a different place, largely divided into two camps. Those nations aligned with NATO bought their combat aircraft from the major U.S. and European makers, such as McDonnell Douglas, Northrop and Dassault, while the Soviet bloc and its client states took the output of the great design bureaux, Mikoyan and Sukhoi. The same was true to some extent in the civil market, with Boeing and BAC products plying the skies of the Western developed nations, while Tupolevs and Ilyushins served routes where customers had no choice. The above is a simplification, but illustrates the contrast with the current environment, where the former Soviet giants are having trouble selling aircraft even to their own governments and have to

compete for sales on equal terms with Western manufacturers. Export sales of combat aircraft, particularly in Asia, have just kept Sukhoi and MiG afloat and funded new development, although true replacements for the MiG-29 and Su-27 have yet to appear.

New competition

Non-aligned nations like Sweden, India and Brazil developed their own combat aircraft programmes. These nations, exemplified by Saab, had limited success in the export market mainly for domestic political reasons, achieving sales of Draken fighters only to Finland, Denmark and Austria. The Gripen, however, has found favour in markets such as Eastern Europe and South

Africa. India has been trying to replace some of its European and ex-Soviet purchases with an indigenous combat aircraft design for some years, but has achieved limited success so far, having flown a few prototypes of its Tejas light combat aircraft, which it has stated will not enter service.

China in turn is moving slowly away from armed forces dominated by Soviet-designed aircraft and local adaptations to one at least partially equipped with the indigenous Chengdu J-10 and the FC-1, developed with Pakistan.

In the 1990s, mergers and acquisitions robbed the aerospace industry of some famous names such as McDonnell Douglas. Northrop and Grumman also merged, as did Lockheed and Martin,

subsuming General Dynamics and other manufacturers along the way. GD had itself swallowed Convair in the 1960s. Boeing's 'legacy products' now include aircraft once sold by North American, Rockwell and McDonnell and Douglas, although such abominations as 'Boeing DC-3' and 'Boeing Mustang' have yet to catch on.

Other manufacturers, such as British Aerospace (now BAE Systems) no longer make new civil airliners altogether, although their structures divisions contribute large parts to the two remaining large 'airframers' – Boeing and Airbus.

Global village
Large aircraft programmes are increasingly multi-national affairs. Companies like Airbus and EADS are organized as cooperative ventures with component and subassembly manufacture located in several countries, and even U.S.-based Boeing outsources much of its production overseas. Large parts of the 767 and the upcoming 787 are made in Japan, for example.

This internationalism is taken to extreme lengths with the NH 90 utility helicopter, which has completion lines in four European countries for the ten European customers to date. Further lines may be commissioned for Asia-Pacific customers.

The stressed-skin metal construction methods perfected in the 1940s and used for the primary structures of most airliners and combat aircraft for the following three decades have progressively given way to non-metallic composites. Glass-fibre panels and fillets have been used for non load-bearing parts for many years, but modern carbon fibre can now be moulded into major airframe sections, saving weight, parts and complexity. Some issues with composite outer surfaces such as lightning strike resistance and detection of damage from minor impacts remain to be fully addressed, however.

Today's commercial airliner market is buoyant for the large manufacturers and their suppliers, but the direction of the large orders has changed. Several state airlines in Europe are struggling, and some (such as Sabena and Swissair) have gone under or been taken over (for example, KLM).

A number of U.S. carriers have also merged out of existence (like TWA) or are kept afloat only by U.S. bankruptcy laws (such as United and Delta). The growth in airliner sales is coming on one hand from the Middle East where airlines like Emirates are growing at a colossal rate and even start-ups like Abu Dhabi's Ethihad are near the top of the queue for the Airbus A380 super jumbo. Low-cost airlines such as Ryanair and Easyjet in the UK, Southwest in the U.S. and Kingfisher in India are ordering huge numbers of New Generation 737s and A320s to satisfy a seemingly insatiable demand for cheap air travel.

Latest developments
In the world of general aviation, the litigation problems that beset the main US makers in the 1980s have been resolved, and new Cessna and Piper single-engined private and training aircraft are rolling off the lines again after a long hiatus, while the courts decided the limits of corporate liability. The gap in the light aircraft market was

*Launched in 2002, the Brazilian-made **EMBRAER** 170 is one of a new breed of high-speed commercial jetliners designed to carry up to 70 passengers to short-haul destinations.*

largely filled in the interim by kitplanes such as the Lancair, and by new entrants such as Diamond and Cirrus, whose SR22 features a ballistic parachute to bring the whole aircraft down gently if the engine stops. It has been used in several emergencies to date, allowing the occupants to walk away and even for the aircraft to fly again in some cases.

Composites and new avionics technologies have allowed private owners to enjoy performance, navigation and communications capabilities once only available to corporations and very wealthy businessmen. The first decades of the twenty-first century will see even greater advances as new technology crosses over between civil and military programmes and seeps down to even the humblest private aviator.

Jim Winchester, *Editor*

Military Aircraft

Today, only a few nations can afford the 'superfighters' offered by the last remaining manufacturers of state-of-the-art combat aircraft. The cost of procuring and maintaining jet fighters has grown exponentially to the point where the $100 million 'sticker price' has been reached by a few examples, such as the Lockheed Martin F/A-22A and Japanese Mitsubishi F-2.

Some nations, including New Zealand and the Philippines, have disbanded their air combat arms or let them wither, ostensibly for budgetary reasons. Others make do with 'legacy' aircraft like the MiG-21, F-5 and the early F-16. In the future, Unmanned Air Vehicles (UAVs) will take over many of the functions of fighter, attack and electronic warfare aircraft, but for most of the world's governments, manned combat aircraft are fielded as much for domestic and political reasons as for their military utility in time of war. Despite the advent of the latest generation 'superfighters', such as the Eurofighter 2000 and the Sukhoi Su-37, conventional fighters and their associated trainers and transports will continue to have a place for the foreseeable future.

A United States Air Force pilot climbs into the cockpit of an A-10 Thunderbolt, prior to flying a mission over the former Yugoslavia, 1999. The ground-attack aircraft features titanium armour plating, to protect it against heavy anti-aircraft fire.

Ilyushin Il-28 'Beagle' Light bomber

The bomb bay of the Il-28R was modified to carry photographic equipment and additional fuel. The additional weight required larger mainwheel tyres, which were later to become standard on the bombers.

A pioneering turbojet-powered tactical light bomber, the **Il-28**, ASCC/NATO reporting name **'Beagle'**, was developed in competition with the Tu-73/78. The first prototype of the Il-28 recorded its initial flight on 8 July 1948.

The all-metal aircraft accommodated a three-man crew in separate positions in its circular-section fuselage. This also carried the twin-wheel nose unit of the tricycle landing gear, the fuel and the weapons bay. The tail unit comprised swept vertical and horizontal surfaces, but the wing was straight and carried two underslung nacelles for the powerplant of two Klimov VK-1A turbojets, as well as the landing gear's single-wheel main units. The VK-1A turbojet was a Soviet development of the RD-45, itself a Soviet copy of the Rolls-Royce Nene, and was one of the keys to the Il-28's excellent performance.

'Beagle' into service

In October 1948 the Il-28 was evaluated successfully against the Tupolev Tu-78 and rushed into production for service from September 1950. Production is thought to have totalled some 3000 aircraft, of which more than half were exported to the USSR's Warsaw Pact allies, China, and many other countries. The Il-28 was also

licensed for production in China, and in Czechoslovakia as the **B-228**. Despite its obsolescence in the basic light bomber role, the Il-28 remains in limited service.

The Il-28 was also developed into a three-seat tactical reconnaissance variant, as the **Il-28R**, the erstwhile weapons bay being revised for the carriage of between three and five cameras or, in an alternative radar reconnaissance form, replaced by a large radar installation. The **Il-28RTR** featured an electronic reconnaissance package with a radome under the rear fuselage. The **Il-28REB**

A typical bomb load for the Il-28 generally comprised one 3000-kg (6,614-lb) FAB-3000 free-fall bomb, four 500-kg (1,102-lb) FAB-500 free-fall bombs or eight 250-kg (551-lb) FAB-250 free-fall bombs.

was an electronic warfare jamming platform, with antennas under the fuselage and in tip 'tanks'. Other baseline models were adapted for the target-towing (**Il-28B**), nuclear detonation atmospheric sampling (**Il-28ZA**), and unmanned missile target roles. The swept-wing **Il-28S** was never completed.

SPECIFICATION	
Ilyushin Il-28 'Beagle'	21,200 kg (46,738 lb)
Type: three-seat light bomber	**Dimensions:** wing span 21.45 m
Powerplant: two Klimov VK-1A	(70 ft 4½ in) without tip tanks;
turbojet engines each rated at	length 17.65 m (57 ft 11 in) for
26.48 kN (5,952 lb st)	fuselage excluding tail cannon;
Performance: maximum speed	height 6.7 m (21 ft 11¾ in); wing
902 km/h (560 mph) at 4500 m	area 60.8 m² (654.47 sq ft)
(14,765 ft); cruising speed 876 km/h	**Armament:** two 23-mm Nudel'man-
(544 mph) at optimum altitude;	Rikhter NR-23 fixed forward-firing
initial climb rate 900 m (2,952 ft)	cannon in the lower nose and two
per minute; service ceiling 12,300 m	NR-23 trainable rearward-firing
(40,350 ft); range 2400 km (1,491	cannon in the tail turret, plus up to
miles) at 10,000 m (32,810 ft)	3000 kg (6,614 lb) of disposable
Weights: empty 11,890 kg	stores carried in a lower-fuselage
(28,417 lb); maximum take-off	weapons bay

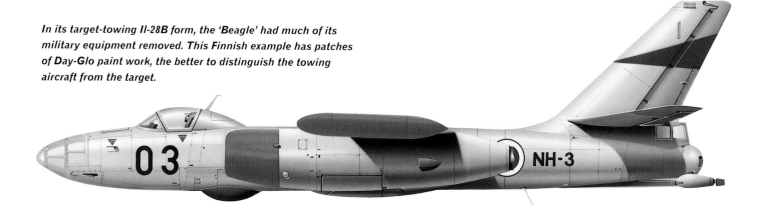

In its target-towing Il-28B form, the 'Beagle' had much of its military equipment removed. This Finnish example has patches of Day-Glo paint work, the better to distinguish the towing aircraft from the target.

Tupolev Tu-16 'Badger' Nuclear/conventional medium bomber

Originally designated **'Aircraft N'** or **Tu-88**, the **Tupolev Tu-16 'Badger'** was developed as a twin-jet medium bomber to complement the strategic Myasishchev M-4 and Tupolev Tu-95, with a design team headed by Dmitri S. Markov. The aircraft's bomb bay was sized to accommodate the USSR's largest bomb, the 9000-kg (19,840-lb) FAB-9000; this allowed the use of a fuselage shortened from, but closely based on, that of the Tu-85 bomber prototype (itself derived from the Tu-4 'Bull'). The basic requirement, however, was to carry a load of 5000 kg (11,020 lb) over 5000 km (3,100 miles). The central part of the fuselage was waisted rather than circular, minimizing cross-sectional area where the engines joined the fuselage (the powerplant location was formulated by the legendary Tupolev himself), reducing drag considerably. The swept wing was based on that of the proposed Tu-82, and incorporated huge integral fuel tanks. The wing proved too thin to accommodate the bogie undercarriage, which retracted into streamlined pods projecting from the trailing edge, designed by A. A. Judin. Such undercarriage pods subsequently became a Tupolev trademark.

The Tu-88 prototype made its maiden flight in April 1952, powered by AM-3A engines, while the second AM-3M-engined prototype flew later the same year. Evaluation against

Ilyushin's conservative Il-46 only served to underline the larger Tu-88's incredible performance, and the latter aircraft was

ordered into production as the Tu-16. Limited production with the RD-3 engine began at Kazan in late 1953. Nine aircraft were available for the 1954 May Day flypast over Red Square, while 54 were in the 1955 Aviation Day flypast 15 months later. About 1520 of all variants were built before production ceased, excluding production in China, where the aircraft is designated **Xian H-6**, and remains in front-line service.

Nuclear bomber

The production RD-3M-powered **Tu-16A 'Badger-A'** nuclear bomber dispensed with the pressurized tunnel between the cockpit and the rear gunner's

compartment, necessitating the provision of separate entry hatches for the rear fuselage. The undernose radome for the

In its initial 'Badger-A' guise, the Tu-16A (Atomnyi) employed a weapons bay configured for five types of free-fall nuclear bomb, or other loads of up to 9000 kg (19,840 lb). Conventional weapons options included the FAB-9000 'demolition aerial bomb', with a nominal weight of 9000 kg.

Rubin navigation/bombing radar was deepened slightly and the overwing fences lengthened. A glazed nose station housed

SPECIFICATION

Tupolev Tu-16 'Badger-A'
Type: twin-jet medium bomber and maritime reconnaissance aircraft
Powerplant: two MNPK 'Soyuz' (Mikulin) AM-3A turbojets each rated at 85.22 kN (19,185 lb st) or, in later aircraft, two AM-3M-500 turbojets each rated at 93.16 kN (20,944 lb st)
Performance: maximum level speed 'clean' at 6000 m (19,685 ft) 992 km/h (616 mph); maximum rate of climb at sea level 1250 m (4,101 ft) per minute; service ceiling 12,300 m (40,355 ft);

range 5925 km (3,682 miles) with a 3800-kg (8,377-lb) warload
Weights: empty equipped 37,200 kg (82,012 lb); maximum take-off 75,800 kg (167,110 lb)
Dimensions: wing span 32.93 m (108 ft ½ in); length 36.25 m (118 ft 11¼ in); height 14 m (45 ft 11½ in); wing area 164.65 m² (1,772.34 sq ft)
Armament: bombload of up to 9000 kg (19,800 lb), plus forward and rear ventral barbettes each containing two 23-mm NR-23 guns and two similar weapons in a tail position

14

The underwing pylons on this 'Badger' carry FAB-250 250-kg (551-lb) freefall bombs. Surprisingly, the nose-mounted thimble radome suggests the aircraft is actually a Tu-16P 'Badger-L' EW version.

the navigator/bombardier on an armoured seat, and behind the side-by-side pilots sat the radist (Rubin radar operator), while the dorsal gunner managed electrical systems and signals. In the tail of the aircraft was a ventral gunner, provided with lateral blisters, and a tail gunner in the rear turret.

Several versions of the basic bomber were produced, including the AV-MF's **Tu-16T 'Badger-A'**, which was equipped to carry four 533-mm (21-in) torpedoes or mines. A number of these aircraft was later converted to **Tu-16S 'Badger-A'** SAR standard, with a Fregat radio-controlled para-dropped rescue boat under the fuselage.

Most Tu-16As were rebuilt for other purposes after 1960, although Egypt received 20 of the approximately 700 built,

most of which were destroyed in the 1967 Six-Day War.

Modernized version

The Tu-16N conversion was developed as a tanker for other Tu-16s, using a modernized version of the wing tip-to-wing tip refuelling system used on the Tu-4 'Bull'. Many redundant 'Badger-As' were also converted to serve as missile carriers, recce platforms, EW aircraft and **Tu-16Sh** crew trainers for the Tu-22. Other Tu-16 variants which retain the 'Badger-A'

reporting name include the **Tu-16LL**, a dedicated testbed able to carry a variety of test engines on a semi-retractable cradle under the fuselage. The 'Badger-A' reporting name also applied to a pair of slightly modified aircraft referred to as **Aircraft No. 14** and **Aircraft**

No. 16, which set a number of world payload-to-height and speed with payload records during February to October 1991. The **Tu-16 Tsyklon** weather recce version was converted from 1977, and the **M-16** designation refers to unmanned target conversions.

The first major production version, built from late 1954, the Tu-16A 'Badger-A' was equipped with the PV-23 fire control system, linked to the PRS-1 Argon tail radar under the rudder. The PU-88 portside nose installation, with a single long-barrel AM-23 23-mm cannon with 100 rounds, was aimed by one of the pilots by reflector sight, and was common to the 'Badger-A' and the Tu-88.

Tupolev Tu-22 'Blinder' Inadequate medium bomber

The need for a supersonic bomber that could outrun the new generation of supersonic interceptors then being developed resulted in the Tupolev design bureau putting forward its **Samolet 105** design, built as the **Tu-22 'Blinder'**.

The configuration of the aircraft was unusual compared to contemporary bombers, its engines being mounted above the fuselage at the base of the tail. Little thought had been given to the consequences for engine maintenance once in service, and this would later become a nagging problem with the design.

The basic configuration of the aircraft was optimized for subsonic cruise speeds, with dash capability up to Mach 1.5 when the aim was penetrating enemy air defences.

The type first flew on 21 June 1958 and many types of engine were considered, including Kuznetsov NK-6s and the VD-7M, which was chosen to

power the second prototype, the **Samolet 105A**. Production aircraft were given VD-7Ms and, later, RD-7Ms.

Free-fall bomber

The Tu-22 was originally designed to be a free-fall bomber, but the increase in the sophistication of SAMs coupled with the threat of interceptors led bomber designers in the 1960s to look at ways of producing a stand-off capability. Thus, only 15 **Tu-22B 'Blinder-B'** aircraft were built as such, and were used mainly for training. The only export customers, Iraq and Libya, also received -22Bs, but these examples were late-build Tu-22R aircraft modified as free-fall bombers.

The **Tu-22R 'Blinder-C'** was oriented towards naval reconnaissance, but did retain a bombing capability. A total of 127 was built, making it the most common 'Blinder' model manufactured. Aircraft fitted with inflight refuelling probes

An aesthetically pleasing design, the Tu-22 was widely dreaded by its crews, who nicknamed it 'Shilo' (awl). The bomber was pronounced 'unflyable' by some pilots and featured downward-firing ejection seats.

SPECIFICATION	
Tupolev Tu-22R 'Blinder-C' **Type:** supersonic maritime reconnaissance aircraft **Powerplant:** two RD-7M2 turbojets each rated at 161.77 kN (36,376 lb st) with afterburning **Performance:** maximum speed 1510 km/h (938 mph) or Mach 1.42 at 12,000 m (39,370 ft); service ceiling 13,300 m (43,635 ft); combat radius 2200 km (1,367 miles)	**Weights:** maximum take-off 84,000 kg (185,185 lb) **Dimensions:** wing span 23.65 m (77 ft 6⅞ in); length 41.60 m (136 ft 5¾ in) excluding probe; wing area 162.25 m² (1,746.5 sq ft) **Armament:** one 23-mm AM-23 cannon in tail, otherwise unarmed; Tu-22B could carry up to 12,000 kg (26,455 lb) of stores in weapons bay, or Kh-22 ASM in Tu-22K

The Tu-22P was the final production version of the 'Blinder' and was intended to serve chiefly alongside the Tu-22K as an escort jammer. One squadron of 'Blinder-Es' was generally allocated to each Tu-22K regiment. The Tu-22P played a small but important role during the final years of its frontline career in the Soviet Union, when it escorted Tu-22M-2 'Backfires' on bombing missions over Afghanistan.

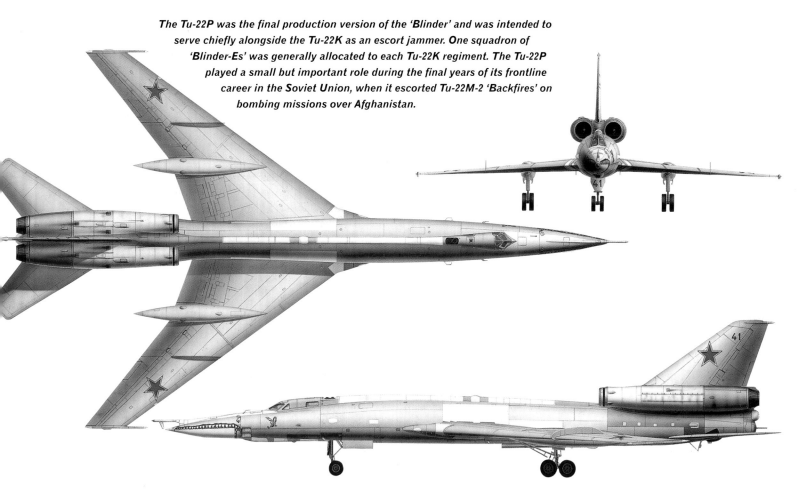

Libya received between seven and 18 Tu-22s, at least four of them being lost in combat over Chad. Few Libyan crews became proficient, the aircraft most likely being flown by foreign mercenaries.

were redesignated as **Tu-22RD** machines. Adding improved Elint gear to the aircraft produced the **Tu-22RK**, or **Tu-22RKD** if equipped with a probe. Another upgrade of the reconnaissance equipment on the Tu-22RD in the early 1980s produced the **Tu-22RDM**.

'Blinder' trainer

The Tu-22 was a difficult aircraft to fly, being very different from the subsonic 'Badger' from which most crews were converting. A dedicated trainer version was required because the aircraft possessed only a single cockpit. To overcome this problem, the **Tu-22U ('Blinder-D')** was produced to a total of 46 examples.

Missile carriers

In the early 1960s the Tu-22 was redesigned to carry the Kh-22 cruise missile. Taking to the air for the first time in early 1961, a total of just 76 **Tu-22K** missile carriers (also **'Blinder-B'**) was built. These included the improved **Tu-22KD** with upgraded engines. Tu-22Ks built to use an anti-radar version of the Kh-22 missile were designated **Tu-22KP**. ARM carriers with a refuelling probe were designated **Tu-22KPD**. An electronic warfare version, the

Tu-22P 'Blinder-E', was built in the early 1960s.

A total of 47 **Tu-22P-1** and **Tu-22P-2** aircraft was built, the two versions varying in the precise configuration of their electronics. As was the case with the other Tu-22 variants, the aircraft were upgraded with the RD-7M-2 engines and refuelling probe from 1965 onwards, and were redesignated **Tu-22PD**.

Eventually, the EW package was improved, leading to the **Tu-22P-4**, **Tu-22P-6** and **Tu-22P-7** variants. The Tu-22PD was usually issued on the basis of one squadron per regiment of Tu-22K missile carriers, to provide EW support to the attack aircraft.

Boeing B-52 Stratofortress Strategic bomber

This Seymour-Johnson-based B-52G shows the two-tone green and grey over anti-flash white scheme that was used in the 1980s. The IR part of the ALQ-151 system was housed in the fairing visible beneath the nose.

The **B-52 Stratofortress** design life began in 1948 as a turboprop successor to the B-50. The design team realized that the turbojets of the period were so thirsty that a huge airframe would be needed to carry the fuel necessary for the required range. The turboprop was more economical than the turbojet, but was less reliable. Then, in 1949, Pratt & Whitney brought out its efficient J57 turbojet.

Beating the YB-60

Boeing and Convair fought bitterly to win the contract for the new USAF bomber. Convair had already provided the mammoth B-36, but its proposed YB-60, though cheaper than the competing B-52, could not equal the latter's performance, and Boeing won the day.

The **XB-52 (Model 464-67)** prototype took to the air for the first time on 15 April 1952. Its technology was based on that of the B-47, so it therefore had a similar wing, with eight engines in podded pairs, and the same undercarriage arrangement. Both the XB-52 and **YB-52** second prototype offered tandem seating for the pilots.

The first three production aircraft were designated **B-52A (Model 464-201-0)**, and they remained with Boeing for testing. The first USAF version of the aircraft was the **B-52B (Model 464-201-3)**. Of the 50 built, 27 were converted as **RB-52B** recce aircraft.

The **B-52C (Model 464-201-6)** was substantially improved in performance and equipment. It was succeeded by the **B-52D**

An important sideline to the B-52G's force-projection role was maritime operations. The aircraft regularly carried AGM-84 Harpoon AShMs, as illustrated by this 42nd BW aircraft out of Loring Air Force Base, Maine. Anti-ship mines were also a regular payload.

SPECIFICATION

Boeing B-52G Stratofortress
Type: six-crew long-range strategic bomber
Powerplant: eight Pratt & Whitney J57-P-29WA turbojets each rated at 53.73 kN (12,1000 lb st)
Performance: maximum speed 668 km/h (415 mph) at low level; cruising speed 893 km/h (555 mph) at altitude; operating altitude 152 to 13,716 m (500 to 45,000 ft); range 11,861 km (7,370 miles)

Weights: empty typically 85,730 kg (189,000 lb); maximum take-off 204,120 kg (450,000 lb)
Dimensions: wing span 56.39 m (185 ft); length 47.73 m (156 ft 7 in); height 14.72 m (48 ft 3¾ in), wing area 371.6 m² (4,000 sq ft)
Armament: four 0.5-in (12.7-mm) trainable rearward-firing machine guns in remotely controlled tail turret, plus up to 27,215 kg (60,000 lb) of bombs

(**Model 464-201-7**), of which 170 examples were built with an improved fire-control system for the tail armament. B-52 improvement continued with the **B-52E** (**Model 464-259**), the 100 examples of which had a more advanced navigation and weapons delivery system.

Continuing weight increases naturally called for more power, especially at take-off, and the **B-52F** (**Model 464-260**), of which 89 were built, had a later, more powerful version of the J57, which was fitted like earlier versions with water injection to boost power on take-off.

Final variant?

The **B-52G** (**Model 464-253**), which was planned initially as the final version pending arrival of the B-70, brought along a

Demonstrating the tall fin that was standard on B-52 models up to and including the F, this aircraft is one of the relatively rare RB-52B machines. These aircraft had provision for a two-man pressurized capsule in their bomb bays, along with camera or ECM mission equipment. With the capsule removed, they became standard bombers.

host of major improvements. The airframe was substantially redesigned to save weight and to make it safer; integral wing-tanks greatly increased the aircraft's fuel capacity; the tail gunner was relocated in the crew compartment; the fin was shortened; and provision was made for launching ECM decoys and stand-off missiles. B-52G production totalled 193 aircraft.

Service use

In 1963 the B-52D was studied as a CBC (conventional bomb carrier) and in the following year the process of rebuilding of B-52D bombers began at Wichita. This permitted the type to carry 105 340-kg (750-lb) bombs and to become embroiled in the Vietnam War.

When deliveries of the troubled B-1 finally began in July 1985, it was clear that the limited number of these penetration bombers meant that the veteran B-52 would still have a great deal of strategic responsibility.

This fact was reflected in the very large sums that were and are still being spent on programmes to improve and update the B-52 force. The Offensive Avionics System (OAS) was implemented to update the navigation and weapons delivery systems of B-52G and B-52H aircraft in USAF service. With the completion of the programme in the early 1980s, the entire surviving fleet had an improved low-level penetration capability. Other new systems included the ALQ-151 EVS (Electro-optical Viewing System) with low-light-level TV and forward-looking IR in undernose turrets.

In the early 1990s, 98 B-52Gs were modified to carry AGM-86B cruise missiles, while the remaining 69 were earmarked for the force-projection role with free-fall weapons.

As more updated B-52Hs became available, the nuclear-tasked B-52Gs were reassigned to the force-projection role, and the last of the B-52Gs had finally been retired from service by the end of 1994.

Although it initially retained white undersurfaces to proof it against nuclear flash, the B-52H soon acquired a tactical upper surface camouflage more in keeping with the role facilitated by the EVS system.

Defensive systems

During the Vietnam War it had been realized that modern bombers were most at threat from enemy SAM and AAA defences. The best defence against such systems was a comprehensive ECM system, and in December 1971 development of the next stage in an ongoing B-52 upgrade programme, the Phase IV ECM Defensive Avionics System, was begun. Such was the complexity of the new system that the last B-52Gs did not emerge with the full 'kit' until late in the 1980s. In fact, the 'kit' consisted of several systems working in harmony, these including countermeasures receivers, radar warning receivers and tail radar warning receivers. In its defence, a modified B-52G could employ active ECM, a false target generating system, jamming across a range of systems, 192 flares and 1125 bundles of chaff.

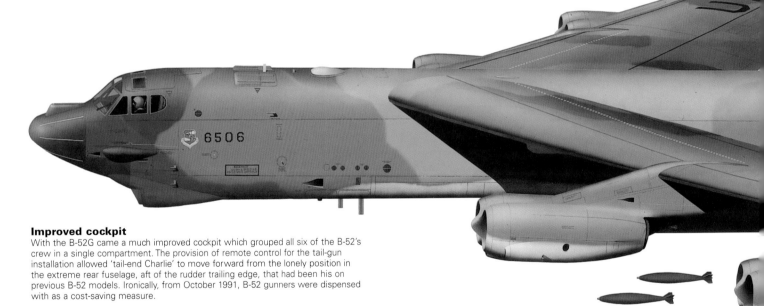

Improved cockpit

With the B-52G came a much improved cockpit which grouped all six of the B-52's crew in a single compartment. The provision of remote control for the tail-gun installation allowed 'tail-end Charlie' to move forward from the lonely position in the extreme rear fuselage, aft of the rudder trailing edge, that had been his on previous B-52 models. Ironically, from October 1991, B-52 gunners were dispensed with as a cost-saving measure.

B-52G Stratofortress

Generally known as the 'BUFF', or 'Big Ugly Fat F***er', the B-52 was built in surprisingly few variants during its production life. The most prolific of these variants was the B-52G, of which 193 were built. This B-52G served with SAC's 2nd Bombardment Wing and is illustrated prior to its conversion to a cruise-missile carrier (CMC). The 2nd BW was based at Barksdale Air Force Base, Louisiana, and comprised the 62nd and 596th Bombardment squadrons. Today, the 2nd BW operates the B-52H on behalf of Air Combat Command.

DESERT STORM: BOMBING IRAQ

DEFENSIVE SYSTEMS: TAIL GUNS

Desert Storm allowed the B-52G to exercise its new-found offensive muscle, as well as its upgraded ECM systems. As many as 80 of the bombers were eventually involved in attacks which mainly focused on Iraq's much-feared Republican Guard units. Flying from bases in Egypt, the Indian Ocean, Saudi Arabia, Spain and the United Kingdom, the B-52s toted some 51 340-kg (750-lb) M117 bombs each per raid and kept up constant pressure on the Republican Guard emplacement. Bombing was conducted in three-aircraft cells, as it had been over Vietnam, although now the tactic was used to ensure maximum destructive power, rather than maximum ECM power. Some 35 AGM-86C CALCMs (Conventional Air-Launched Cruise Missiles) were also fired.

When the B-52A entered service, it retained one throwback to the World War II era – a tail turret. Various fire-control systems have been used by the B-52; however, for the majority of variants, the standard gun fit comprised four 0.5-in (12.7-mm) M3 machine guns. Some B-52Bs possessed twin 20-mm M24A1 cannon, while the B-52H introduced the M61A1 Vulcan cannon (illustrated). Between 1991 and 1994, these were removed in favour of defensive ECM equipment.

Checking on 'Cruise'

From 1982, the B-52G became operational with the AGM-86B ALCM. This missile and similar weapons in the Soviet inventory became the subject of much concern and following the SALT (Strategic Arms Limitation Talks) II treaty it was decided that those aircraft capable of carrying cruise missiles should be clearly identifiable. The B-52Gs equipped for AGM-86B were therefore given additional wing root fairings. These had no aerodynamic function, were engineered in such a way that they were very difficult to remove and were clearly visible to Soviet reconnaissance satellites.

USAF
76506

Weapons

This aircraft is depicted dropping 227-kg (500-lb) Mk 82 bombs. A bewildering array of weapons was associated with the B-52G, the most potent of which were undoubtedly the AGM-86B nuclear cruise missile and the AGM-69 SRAM (Short-Range Attack Missile). Missiles could be accommodated on a rotary launcher within the bomb bay, as well as under the wings. A maximum load of 20 ALCMs or SRAMs could be carried, each of the former packing a 200 kT warhead and each of the latter a 170 kT warhead. This was a far cry from the two Hound Dogs that had been the bomber's warload earlier in its career. Each of these weapons boasted a 4 MT warhead. Just as the Cold War was drawing to a close and the B-52G was bowing out of service, the stealthy 200-kT AGM-129 became operational on the B-52H.

'Buff' upgrades

Having already served for five decades by the beginning of the twenty-first century, the B-52 has undergone a mass of upgrades and modifications to keep it viable.

WEAPONS:
CONVENTIONAL WEAPONS

When the B-52 entered service, no one could foresee a role for the aircraft other than that of the nuclear bomber. Various cruise missiles might come along, but essentially the B-52 was a nuclear delivery platform. The escalating conflict in Vietnam changed that thinking overnight and soon showed that the 27-bomb conventional capability of the B-52F was lacking. Eventually, 'Big Belly' B-52Ds were modified for a huge 31,750-kg (70,000-lb) bomb load. In the post-Vietnam era, the B-52's conventional capabilities became increasingly important, although the type was also the primary carrier of the US cruise missile fleet, employing weapons such as the AGM-86 (right). During the early 1990s, all surviving B-52Gs were eventually assigned to the force-projection role. In this, they used free-fall M117, Mk 80-series (above right) and cluster bombs, AGM-84 Harpoon AShMs, AGM-142 Have Nap AGMs and a vast range of other ordnance.

By the late 1970s, it had become clear that the B-52 had very little chance of successfully attacking the Soviet Union unless penetration to within striking range could be made at ultra-low level. A comprehensive avionics upgrade was required to allow the giant bomber to perform in such a manner and this was embodied in the ALQ-151 EVS (Electro-optical Viewing System). Added to

LOW-LEVEL OPS: ALQ-151 EVS

B-52G and B-52H airframes, ALQ-151 consists of a low-light-level TV scanner in an undernose faring to port and a FLIR to starboard. These sensors feed cockpit displays which allow the crew to fly low and accurately at night.

General Dynamics F-111 Aardvark Swing-wing striker

The major advantages offered by variable-geometry (VG) wings are high supersonic performance with the wing swept back, economical subsonic cruising speed with the wing fully spread, a long operational or ferry range, and relatively short take-off and landing runs at very high weights. So when in 1960 the USAF's Tactical Air Command was seeking a strike and inter-diction warplane to replace the F-105 Thunderchief, it was very interested in VG experiments that had been conducted by NASA. At the same time the US Navy was looking for a fleet air-defence fighters to succeed the McDonnell F4H Phantom II, and eventually the Department of Defense decreed that the two requirements should be combined as the TFX (Tactical Fighter, Experimental).

Secretary of Defense Robert McNamara stuck to this decision despite strong objections from both services, and this led to the **F-111 Aardvark**, the last a long-standing nickname that was formally adopted at the time of the F-111's disappearance from US service. On 24 November 1962 a development contract for 23 aircraft was awarded to General Dynamics, for 18 **F-111A** tactical warplanes for the USAF and five **F-111B** aircraft developed primarily by Grumman for the USN. The F-111B began to run into trouble almost immediately, and despite a long and intensive flight development programme the type was cancelled in July 1968.

Unhappy Aardvark

The F-111A, on which all subsequent models were based, had an almost equally unhappy early history after its first flight on 21 December 1964. It was eventually cleared for service, with deliveries of 141 production examples beginning in October 1967 to the 474th TFW at Nellis AFB, Nevada. On 15 March 1968 the 428th TFS detached six of its F-111As to Thailand for operational deployment over Vietnam, losing three of them in four weeks; groundings and modifications followed. When 48 more F-111As were sent to Vietnam in 1972–73, they flew more than 4000 combat sorties in seven months for the loss of only six aircraft. The F-111 subsequently emerged as arguably the world's best long-range interdictor of the 1980s.

Both the extended Pave Tack pod and Paveway III LGB are notable features on this 48th TFW F-111F. The 48th's F-111s notched up an impressive combat record during Desert Storm.

When it worked, the F-111D's avionics system made it the most capable of all the F-111s. The model was based at Cannon AFB throughout its career.

The F-111A, powered by two 82.29-kN (18,500-lb st) TF30-P-3 turbofan engines, was followed by the second production variant, the **F-111E**, of which 94 were completed with improved air inlets and slightly upgraded avionics. Then came the **F-111D**, of which 96 were built with more powerful 87.19-kN (19,600-lb st) TF30-P-9 engines and a radically updated avionics system, which proved over-ambitious. The F-111D was retired in 1992.

Strategic Air Command purchased the **FB-111A**, which was equipped for strategic nuclear missions. This featured a 2.13-m (7-ft) increase in wing span for additional fuel- and weapons-carrying capability. When the survivors of these 76 aircraft, which also had

strengthened landing gear and 89.63-kN (20,150-lb st) TF30-P-7 engines, were retired, some 51 of them were reworked for the 27th TFW as **F-111G** machines, and these served in a training role until 1993.

Aussie Aardvarks

Export sales were limited to Australia, although the RAF ordered (and subsequently cancelled) the **F-111K**. Australia's

24 **F-111C** aircraft were delivered in 1973 and featured the long-span wing of the FB-111A and the lower-powered engines and avionics of the F-111A. Four ex-USAF F-111As were purchased as attrition replacements and modified to F-111C standard, and in the early 1990s the RAAF purchased 15 F-111Gs. Four of the RAAF aircraft operate in **RF-111C** reconnaissance form with a multi-sensor reconnaissance pallet mounted in the former weapons bay.

The final F-111 production variant was the **F-111F**, and was also the last in operational USAF

service, flying until 1996. Production of the F-111F totalled 106 aircraft, and between 1977 and 1992 the force was deployed to Lakenheath, UK, with the 48th TFW. By far the most important improvement introduced by the F-111F was its uprated powerplant. It was built (like all Aardvarks except the FB-111A) with provision for a 20-mm cannon in the weapons bay, but this was never used. The F-111F's weapons bay was used primarily for the carriage of the AVQ-26 Pave Tack pod, which incorporates a FLIR sensor and bore-sighted laser rangefinder/designator.

With a SRAM nestling in its weapons bay, this FB-111A demonstrates its long-span wings.

SPECIFICATION	
General Dynamics F-111F Aardvark **Type:** two-seat long-range multi-role interdiction and attack warplane **Powerplant:** two Pratt & Whitney TF30-P-100 turbofan engines each rated at 111.65 kN (25,100 lb st) with afterburning **Performance:** maximum speed 2655 km/h (1,650 mph) or Mach 2.5 at 10,975 m (36,000 ft); cruising speed 919 km/h (571 mph) at high altitude; service ceiling 18,290 m (60,000 ft); range more than 4707 km (2,925 miles) with internal fuel	**Weights:** empty 21,537 kg (47,481 lb); maximum take-off 45,360 kg (100,000 lb) **Dimensions:** wing span 19.20 m (63 ft) spread and 9.74 m (31 ft 11½ in) swept; length 22.40 m (73 ft 6 in), height 5.22 m (17 ft 1½ in); wing area 48.77 m² (525 sq ft) swept and 61.07 m² (657.07 sq ft) swept **Armament:** provision for one 20-mm General Electric M61A-1 Vulcan fixed forward-firing six-barrel rotary cannon in an optional weapons bay installation, plus up to 14,228 kg (31,500 lb) of disposable stores

Tupolev Tu-95 Strategic bomber

About 70 Tu-95s of both variants are based with heavy bomber regiments at Engels and Ukrainka. This total includes three aircraft formerly held in Ukraine. Russia plans to add the Kh-101 ALCM and Kh-SD ASM to the inventory of the Tu-95MS to improve their conventional long-range precision strike capability. The air force also operates some earlier-model Tu-95KUs as trainers.

Variants of the turboprop-powered **Tu-95 'Bear'** strategic bomber have been in service since 1956, with an advanced development of the design remaining an important part of Russia's long-range air power. Having already developed the superlative Tu-142MK for the ASW role, Tupolev began working on a cruise missile-carrying variant of the aircraft in the 1970s.

The machine was intended to take on a role similar to that of the B-52, with several missiles being carried on rotary launchers. Designed for the Kh-55 (AS-15 'Kent') missile, 12 of which were to be carried on two launchers, the **Tu-142MS** proved capable of carrying only six missiles due to centre-of-gravity concerns.

It was decided that the production of the **Tu-142MS** would take place alongside that of the Tu-142MK, and it would be designated as the Tu-95MS. In the meantime, however, an experimental **Tu-95M-55** was built as a test platform, aimed at proving the various systems of the new missile-carrier. This test aircraft made its initial flight on 31 July 1978 and it had accomplished a huge amount of useful test flying before unfortunately suffering a fatal crash on 28 January 1982.

Tu-95MS 'Bear-H'

Given the NATO designation **'Bear-H'**, the new bomber was based on the airframe of the **Tu-142MK**, but with a shorter fuselage ahead of the wing. It features a redesigned cockpit section and a new nose profile which accommodates a totally new radar, along with other missile-guidance and navigation-related equipment. The compact nature of this new installation, combined with centre-of-gravity considerations, resulted in the shorter forward fuselage.

A prototype for the new series was produced by modifying a production Tu-142MK and this aircraft was to complete its first flight in September 1979. Other features of the aircraft to become clear at this stage were its revised powerplant of four more-powerful NK-12MP engines and seven-person crew.

The Tu-95MS 'Bear-H' went into production during 1983 and it soon became clear to NATO observers that, like 'Bear-F Mod 4', 'Bear-H' had a long cable conduit running externally along the left side of its fuselage, one end disappearing into the nose and the other into the rear pressure cabin. The fuselage had a small ram air inlet on each side, but no large Elint blisters or camera ports, as had been seen on previous 'Bears'. In fact, apart from the aft ADF sensor strake, almost the only bulge was a small flat-topped dome above the forward fuselage. At the rear, the extended-chord rudder was common to all Tu-142M/Tu-95MS variants.

As there were no remotely controlled turrets, the lateral sighting blisters were no longer needed; however, the tail gunner and turret were retained. The turret was of a totally new

---

SPECIFICATION	
Tupolev Tu-95MS-6 'Bear-H'	185,000 kg (407,850 lb)
Type: eight-crew strategic bomber	**Dimensions:** wing span 50.04 m
Powerplant: four KKBM (Kuznetsov)	(164 ft 2 in); length 49.13 m
NK-12MA turboprops each rated at	(161 ft 2¼ in); height 13.30 m
11033 ekW (14,795 ehp)	(43 ft 7¾ in); wing area 289.90 m²
Performance: maximum level speed	(3,120.50 sq ft)
'clean' at 7620 m (25,000 ft) 925	**Armament:** GSh-23L tail gun
km/h (575 mph); cruising speed at	installation. MKU-6 internal rotary
optimum altitude 711 km/h	launcher for six Kh-55/AS-15 '
(442 mph); service ceiling 12000 m	Kent-A' or Kh-55SM/ AS-15 'Kent-B'
(39,380 ft); unrefuelled operational	long-range ALCMs, with range of
radius 6400 km (3,977 miles) with	2400–3000 km (1,491–1,864
11340-kg (25,000-lb) weapon load	miles); Kh-35/AS-20 'Kayak' AShMs
Weights: empty 91,800 kg	of Tu-142MZ have range of 81 miles
(202,380 lb); maximum take-off	(130 km)

The first Tupolev Tu-95 variant to carry a missile was the Tu-95K 'Bear-B' of 1960, which carried a single Kh-20 (AS-3 'Kangaroo') nuclear weapon.

origin, never seen previously. The central power-aimed section had an increased arc of fire and carried a pair of GSh-23L guns. In fact, this turret was identical to that which was employed by the Tu-22M-2.

'Bear-H' nominally became operational in 1982, before series production was properly under way. The type was built in two basic variants: the **Tu-95MS-6 'Bear-H'**, which as armed with up to six RKV-500A (Kh-55/AS-15 'Kent') cruise missiles on a rotary launcher in the bomb bay, and the **Tu-95MS-16**, with the rotary launcher of the MS-6 and the

capacity to carry up to 12 additional weapons underwing. This gave the MS-16 a truly awesome weapon load of up to 18 'Kents', although a load of 16 was probably more normal.

Later, in accordance with the SALT-2/START armament-limitation treaties, the MS-16s were reduced to MS-6 standard and in 2002 this type continued to form the backbone of the Russian bomber force.

This Soviet Tu-95MS-6 'Bear-H' was photographed from a Canadian Armed Forces CF-188. Russia continues to operate around 60 Tu-95MSs.

Tupolev Tu-22M 'Backfire' Medium strategic bomber

Tu-22M-3 is capable of carrying as many as three supersonic Kh-22M (AS-4 'Kitchen') nuclear-tipped guided missiles, intended for use against ships, as well as against land targets. In the event of a major conflict during the 'Backfire's' Cold War heyday, US Navy carrier battle groups would have been primary targets for the big Tupolev bomber.

The **Tu-22M** was developed from the earlier Tu-22, incorporating variable-geometry outer wing panels. The first **Tu-22M-0** prototype flew in 1969. Powered by a derivative of the engine originally designed for the Tu-144 supersonic airliner, the **'Backfire'** is extremely fast, even at low level. The **Tu-22M** lacks sufficient range for truly strategic missions and is classified as a medium bomber. The first series production model was the **Tu-22M-2**

Raked rectangular intakes make the Tu-22M-3 'Backfire-C' easy to identify. The type remains in extensive use with both Russia and Ukraine.

'Backfire-B' (211 examples built) for the VVS and the AV-MF. Normally armed with a single Kh-22 stand-off missile

Tupolev Tu-22M-3 'Backfire-C'
Type: medium-range bomber, maritime attack and recon aircraft
Powerplant: two NK-25 turbofans each rated at 245.20 kN (55,115 lb st)
Performance: maximum level speed at 11,000 m (36,090 ft) 2000 km/h (1,242 mph); unrefuelled combat radius 1850 km (1,150 miles)

Weights: basic empty 54,000 kg (119,048 lb); maximum take-off 130,000 kg (286,596 lb)
Dimensions: wing span 34.30 m (112 ft 6½ in) spread; length 39.60 m (129 ft 11 in); wing area 170 m² (1,829.92 sq ft) spread
Armament: one GSh-23 23-mm cannon in tail; maximum weapon load 24,000 kg (52,910 lb)

(although up to three can be carried), this variant became operational with 185 GvTBAP in 1978, and also served in the Soviet conflict in Afghanistan.

Ultimate version

The ultimate bomber/missile carrying variant is the **Tu-22M-3 'Backfire-C'** (268 built). The M-3 features strengthened wings and raked rectangular intakes serving more powerful engines.

This variant also possesses an increased weapons load.

In 2005 the M-3 remained numerically the most important bomber in the Russian air force's Long-Range Air Army inventory, serving with seven regiments (one of which also operates M-2s). The AV-MF has about 80 Tu-22Ms, mostly M-3s, split equally between divisions subordinated to the Northern and Pacific fleets. The AV-MF

has 12 M-3s converted as **Tu-22MR** reconnaissance aircraft, and reportedly also operates limited numbers of recce-configured **Tu-22M-2R** aircraft. Because of delays in the development of the Sukhoi T-60, the Tu-22M-3's intended replacement, 'Backfire', is to be upgraded. The Tu-22Ms of both the Air Force and Naval Aviation will be upgraded to **Tu-245** standard, with a new radar, new

missile systems and an automatic terrain-following capability. Some redundant Tu-22M-3 airframes were converted as **Tu-22MP** prototypes of a planned EW/ escort jammer variant. The other operator of the 'Backfire' is Ukraine, which gained former Black Sea Fleet regiments of Tu-22M 'Backfires'. About 50 bombers equip three air force heavy bomber regiments.

Tupolev Tu-160 'Blackjack' Heavy strategic bomber

Early in the twenty-first century the 'Blackjack' remains in very limited Russian service. Funding problems continue to limit the aircraft's operational capabilities in the same way that they have limited its production. The star markings beneath the cockpit of this aircraft probably denote live missile firings.

The **Tu-160 'Blackjack'** is the world's largest operational bomber. Dwarfing the similar-looking American B-1B, it is the heaviest combat aircraft ever built. Unlike the Lancer, the Tupolev Tu-160 is designed for both low-level penetration (at transonic speeds) and high-level penetration at speeds of about Mach 1.9.

Although the aircraft has an FBW control system, all cockpit displays are analogue and there is no HUD. The long pointed

radome houses a terrain following and attack radar. Below this is a fairing for a forward-looking TV camera which is used for visual weapon aiming.

The development programme for the Tu-160 was very protracted; the prototype Tu-160 first flew in 1981 and the second aircraft was lost in 1987. Series production was at Kazan and continued until January 1992, when President Yeltsin announced that no further strategic bombers would be

SPECIFICATION
Tupolev Tu-160 'Blackjack'

Tupolev Tu-160 'Blackjack'
Type: long-range strategic bomber
Powerplant: four NK-321 turbofans each rated at 137.20 kN (30,843 lb st) dry and 245.16 kN (55,115 lb st) with afterburning
Performance: maximum level speed at 12,200 m (40,000 ft) 2220 km/h (1,380 mph); service ceiling 15,500 m (49,200 ft);

unrefuelled range 12,300 km (7,640 miles)
Weights: empty 118,000 kg (260,140 lb); maximum take-off 275,000 kg (606,261 lb)
Dimensions: length 54.10 m (177 ft 6 in); wing area 360 m² (3,875.13 sq ft)
Armament: up to 12 Kh-55 series ALCMs or 24 Kh-15P SRAMs

built. It is believed that production totalled no more than 39 'Blackjacks'.

Even after the aircraft entered service, problems continued to severely restrict operations and

production of the Tu-160 began before a common standard and configuration were agreed. Thus wingspans, equipment fit, and intake configurations differ from aircraft to aircraft.

Eight Tu-160s of 19 left behind in Ukraine after the collapse of the Soviet Union in 1991 were returned to Russia in late 1999, along with 564 Kh-55 missiles.

Boeing B-52H Stratofortress Strategic bomber

In the 11 years since the 1991 Gulf War, in which the B-52 was a key participant, the USAF's B-52Hs have seen action over the Balkans and, recently, against terrorist targets in Afghanistan from October 2001.

Although by normal standards it is long since obsolete, thanks to its huge radar cross-section and vulnerability to surface-to-air missiles, the mighty **Boeing B-52** remains a frontline weapon half a century after its first flight. In the process, it has seen two much more advanced would-be successors fall by the wayside. It remains a major element in the 'Triad' of US strategic deterrents and will continue to give valuable service until well into the twenty-first century.

The B-52 'BUFF' ('Big Ugly Fat Feller' in polite form) began in 1948 as a turboprop successor to the B-50 Superfortress. In 1949 it was decided to incorporate eight of the new Pratt & Whitney J57 turbojets, and the XB-52 prototype made its maiden flight on 15 April 1952. The B-52 evolved through progressively improved **B-52A** to **B-52G** models, the latter remaining in service to late 1994.

Re-engined 'H'

There are two major changes which characterize the ultimate **B-52H**: introduction of TF33 turbofans that give greater thrust in concert with a much reduced specific fuel consumption, and structural changes which permit the big bomber to fly at low altitudes without excessive fatigue problems.

The final B-52H was rolled out in June 1962 and, with the B-1B and B-2A entering service in only limited numbers, the B-52H has been constantly upgraded. As the B-1B has increasingly assumed the free-fall nuclear role of the B52-H, the 'Cadillac' (as the H-model is nicknamed) has been handed the force projection role, with weapons now including the AGM 86C conventionally armed variant of

Right: B-52 crews are quite often younger than the aircraft they fly! The 'Cadillac's' left-hand seat is occupied by the aircraft's commander.

Below right: B-52s have been able to carry cruise missiles since 1981; since B-52Gs were retired in the 1990s, the H-model has assumed the ALCM-carrier role.

the nuclear cruise missile and Have Nap missiles. The B52H's importance lies in its ability to meet the USAF's continued need for warplanes with global reach while carrying very heavy warloads. That importance is demonstrated by the fact that

upgrades for the remaining aircraft, both in terms of avionics and weapons systems, are still planned and, although a re-engining programme appears to have lost momentum, the type is still scheduled to remain in service until at least 2040.

SPECIFICATION

Boeing B-52H Stratofortress
Type: five/six-crew long-range strategic bomber
Dimensions: wing span 56.39 m (185 ft); length 49.05 m (160 ft 10⁹⁄₁₀ in); height 12.40 m (40 ft 8 in); wing area 371.60 m² (4,000 sq ft)
Weights: maximum take-off 229,088 kg (505,000 lb)
Powerplant: eight Pratt & Whitney TF33-P-3 turbofans each rated at 75.62 kN (7,000 lb st)
Performance: maximum speed 958 km/h (595 mph) at optimum altitude; service ceiling 16,765 m (55,000 ft); range over 16,093 km (10,000 miles) without inflight refuelling
Armament: one 20-mm Vulcan six-barrelled cannon in tail turret housing, plus up to 22,680 kg (50,000 lb) of ordnance including AGM-86C conventional-warhead cruise missiles, B61 or B83 free-fall thermonuclear bombs, AGM-142 Have Nap (Rafael Popeye) stand-off precision-guided attack missiles and up to 51 340-kg (750-lb) Mk 117 or 454-kg (1,000-lb) Mk 83 conventional free-fall bombs

Rockwell B-1B Lancer Strategic bomber

Studies initiated in 1962 led, during 1965, to the USAF's Advanced Manned Strategic Aircraft requirement for a low-altitude penetration bomber. The **B-1B Lancer** can trace its origins to the **B-1A**, which in June 1970 emerged as the winner of a competition for a new strategic bomber. The first of four B-1A prototypes flew on 23 December 1974. At that time Strategic Air Command hoped for 250 B-1As to replace its ageing B-52s, but congressional opposition and a new administration culminated in the B-1A's downfall. President Carter announced in June 1977 that testing of the four proto-types would continue only as a

form of 'insurance' and that no production would follow.

Wind of change

In 1981 President Reagan was taking a much more hardline attitude towards the USSR. An immediate beneficiary was SAC, which was informed in September 1981 that it would at last receive the long-overdue new bomber in the form of the much altered **B-1B**, of which only 100 were to be completed.

The B-1B has a blended body/low-wing configuration with variable geometry on the outer wing panels. To the rear of the titanium wing pivots are overwing fairings blended into

This B-1B is illustrated as it appeared when on the strength of the 37th Bomb Squadron of Air Combat Command's 28th Bomb Wing. It was based at Ellsworth Air Force Base (hence the 'EL' tailcode), South Dakota, in the late 1990s.

the wing trailing edges and the engine nacelles. Four turbofan engines are mounted in pairs beneath and aft of the fixed centre section of the wing. All flying controls are operated by an electro-hydraulic system, with the exception of the two outboard spoilers on each wing, which are fly-by-wire.

High-lift devices were incorporated to ensure that the B-1B could take off from shorter runways than the B-52, and would also be capable of

deploying quickly in times of crisis to more austere forward operating bases. The B-1B is fitted with a nose-mounted refuelling receptacle.

Major airframe improvements were introduced on the B-1B, including strengthened landing gear, a movable bulkhead in the forward weapons bay to allow for the carriage of a diverse range of weapons, optional weapons bay fuel tanks for increased range, and external underfuselage stores stations for additional fuel or weapons. The reduction in the B-1A's Mach 2.5 dash capability at high altitude led to the replacement of the variable engine inlets by fixed-geometry inlets.

Careful use of 'stealth' technology has given the B-1B a radar cross-section at least an order of magnitude smaller than that of the B-52, despite the fact that the B-1B is only marginally smaller in size.

Offensive radar

The primary offensive avionics systems is the APQ-164 multi-mode radar system derived from the F-16's APG-66. Self-defence is provided by the much troubled ALQ-161 system. This can detect, locate and classify

As a type of crucial importance to the US military machine, the B-1B Lancer is heavily involved in Operation Enduring Freedom, flying missions against the Taliban regime in Afghanistan.

The B-1B effects the low-altitude, high-speed penetration role against sophisticated air-defence systems. It is aided by electronic jamming, IR countermeasures, radar location and warning systems, and the application of 'low observables' technology.

signals from hostile emitters transmitting simultaneously. The system is also able to establish priority in dealing with these threats and automatically initiates countermeasures.

The first production B-1B flew on 18 October 1984; deliveries began on 27 July 1985 at Offutt Air Force Base, Nebraska. Since this time the B1-B's career has been coloured by controversy and interrupted by frequent lengthy grounding orders, and several highly publicized losses. Problems were caused by false alarms from the computerized self-diagnostic systems, non-

functioning terrain-following radar, and repeated failure of the ALQ-161. Engine problems were also a significant factor in the

type's grounding, and perhaps some of the losses.

Future plans for the B1-B include the addition of GPS,

a MIL-1760 databus, ECM improvements and advanced weapons capability. In this last capacity, the **Block C** standard provided for the carriage of cluster bombs, and the current **Block D** standard adds the capability for internal carriage of up to 24 GBU-35 Joint Direct-Attack Munitions, a new countermeasures system and communications/navigation system.

The **Block E** standard was introduced in 2002 with extra capabilities and in 2003 the **Block F** standard featured improved defensive systems.

Had the relatively-clean B-1B ever flown operationally with external pylons, its outright performance and stealth capabilities would have been compromised.

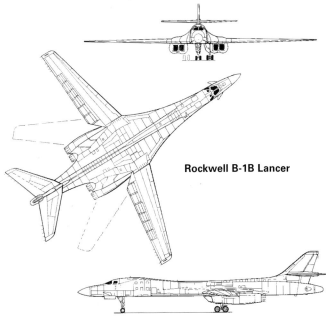

Rockwell B-1B Lancer

SPECIFICATION

Rockwell B-1B Lancer
Type: four-seat strategic penetration bomber and missile launch platform
Powerplant: four General Electric F101-GE-102 turbofan engines each rated at 64.94 kN (14,600 lb st) dry and 136.92 kN (30,780 lb st) with afterburning
Performance: maximum speed 1324 km/h (823 mph) or Mach 1.25 at high altitude; service ceiling more than 15,240 m (50,000 ft); range about 12,000 km (7,455 miles)
Weights: empty 87,091 kg (192,000 lb); maximum take-off 216,365 kg (477,000 lb)

Dimensions: wing span 41.67 m (136 ft 8½ in); length 44.81 m (147 ft); height 10.36 m (34 ft 10 in); wing area about 181.16 m² (1,950 sq ft)
Armament: up to 34,019 kg (75,000 lb) of disposable stores carried internally and 26,762 kg (59,000 lb) externally; weapons include B61 and B83 thermonuclear bombs; AGM-69A Short-Range Attack Missiles; AGM-86B Air-Launched Cruise Missiles and a maximum of 84 227-kg (500-lb) Mk 82 bombs or 227-kg (500-lb) Mk 36 mines internally

Rockwell B-1B Lancer
US Strategic bomber

Cockpit
Inside, everything is modern, airy and ergonomic; light grey panels, beautifully designed instruments, and dominated by the large colour CRT displays which have become de rigueur in today's combat aircraft. The cockpit is big enough to accommodate two instructors as well as the crew of four, and includes a toilet and galley. The pilots' windscreens are exceptionally large but sharply raked, and meet severe birdstrike specifications. Each rear crew station has a small window. An EPS (environmental protection system) protects the forward and main side windows against ice, misting and rain, and heats the dual pitot heads under the nose.

Radar
The B-1B has a single radar, with a single antenna, which incorporates attack and terrain-following functions. The APQ-164 was developed by Westinghouse from the Common Improved version of APG-66 radar used in the F-16. It has a fixed phased array (electronically scanned) antenna, which is mounted at an angle to reflect enemy radar emissions downwards. It can operate in any of 11 modes, and is optimized for use in single sweeps or partial sweeps to minimize both emissions and the risk of detection. In many modes the radar switches constantly between different kinds of operation. The TFACU (Terrain-Following Avionics Control Unit) figuratively 'draws a line' parallel to the terrain profile seen by the radar, and the aircraft flies this line. Over the sea or flat desert radar scans may be several seconds apart, but in hilly terrain the scans will be in rapid succession. The terrain-following software can be configured by the crew to command a soft ride with a gentle profile in the vertical plane, or a hard ride in which the terrain profile is followed more precisely. This latter option can impose violent vertical accelerations.

CMUP: NEW ROLES FOR THE 'BONE'

In order to enhance the B-1B's conventional capability and fill a recognized void in its bomber force, the USAF began a complex series of Lancer upgrades in 1993, referred to as the Conventional Munitions Upgrade Program (CMUP). Adding to the Lancer's Mk 80-series bomb capability (above and above left) the CMUP was designed to be incorporated in blocks, with each improvement building on the previous upgrade. All B-1Bs existing prior to the CMUP were designated as Block A models. Block B saw the addition of an improved synthetic aperture radar (SAR). Block C added CBU submunitions capability, Block C allowed the delivery of cluster bombs (left) such as the CBU-87B/B Combined Effects Munitions (CEM), the CBU-89 Gator area denial munition and the CBU-97 Sensor Fuzed Weapons (SFW). Block D added precision strike capability with the GBU-31 JDAM, while Block E – which achieved initial operating capability in 2003 – included modified avionics to provide true precision strike capability.

Fan blade failures

On 14 October 1990, a B-1B was in the course of a training mission when, as engines went to MIL power (afterburner) to start a climb, there was a loud explosion, and the crew became aware of an orange glow. Several Master Caution lights lit, and a blue flame was seen streaming from the left side. After shutting down No. 1 engine and pressing that engine's fire push-button, a night landing was made. Uncontained failure of No. 1 engine fan had caused severe local damage. The engine had broken completely away from the aircraft, fortunately without hitting anything. Just over two months later, on 19 December 1990, another B-1B was engaged in night touch-and-gos when, on engines going to MIL power, the crew felt a sharp jolt and again became aware of an orange glow. Engine No. 3 was shut down, and its fire button pushed. Again, the cause was uncontained fan failure. Such engine problems have since been overcome.

AN/ALQ-161A

The trailing edge of the fin cap houses receivers for the AN/ALQ-161A defensive avionics system. A high-intensity strobe light is located immediately below the antennas.

Protective coatings

Only before it is painted does a B-1B reveal how far it is from being a conventional aluminium aircraft. Grey strips at the wingroots are Teflon protective coatings over the areas that rub against the overwing fairing as the wing is swept. Darker areas are RAM (radar absorbent material), but these disappear as the finish camouflage is applied.

Nuclear weapons

For the former nuclear role, the B-1B's bomb bays could be configured to carry a Multi-Purpose Launcher (MPL) for up to eight nuclear weapons or up to eight Boeing AGM-69A Short-Range Attack Missiles (SRAMs) per bay. By reconfiguring the intermediate bulkhead, the B-1B could also carry the Cruise Missile launcher (CRM) with eight longer ranged AGM-86B Air Launched Cruise Missiles (ALCMs). External weapons (up to eight B28 nuclear gravity bombs or up to 12 other weapons, totalling 26,762 kg (59,000 lb) could theoretically be carried, but were prohibited under the START II agreements.

Undercarriage

The aircraft's landing gear has a lower footprint than a B-52, allowing the B-1B to operate from more primitive runways. The hydraulically steerable nose gear has twin wheels. The main gears have twin tandem wheels. Each leg has multi-disc carbon brakes. All landing gears have an emergency extension system using high-pressure nitrogen.

With the B-1B remaining a platform of primary strategic importance for US strategy makers, the type is subject to a constant test effort aimed at proving new systems and 21st-century weapons. This 37th Bomb Squadron, 28th Bomb Wing, was engaged in a weapons test mission from Edwards Air Force Base, California.

SPECIFICATION

B-1B Lancer
Manufacturer: Rockwell (Boeing North American)
Type: supersonic strategic penetration bomber and missile launch platform
Crew: four

Powerplant

Four General Electric F101-GE-102 turbofan engines each rated at 64.94 kN (14,600 lb st) dry and 136.92 kN (30,780 lb st) with afterburning

Performance

Maximum speed at high altitude: 1324 km/h (823 mph) or Mach 1.25
Penetration speed at approximately 61 m (200 ft): 965 km/h (600 mph) or Mach 0.92
Service ceiling: more than 15,240 m (50,000 ft)
Range: 12,000 km (7,455 miles)

Dimensions

Overall length: 44.81 m (147 ft)
Height: 10.36 m (34 ft 10 in)

Span (maximum sweep): 23.84 m (78 ft 2½ in)
Span (minimum sweep): 41.67 m (136 ft 8½ in)
Wing area: 181.16 m² (1,950 sq ft)
Aspect ratio (fully spread): 9.58
Aspect ratio (fully swept): 3.14
Tailplane span: 13.67 m (44 ft 10 in)
Wheel track: 4.42 m (14 ft 6 in)
Wheelbase: 17.53 m (57 ft 6 in)

Weights

Empty: 87,091 kg (192,000 lb)
Maximum take-off: 216,365 kg (477,000 lb)

Armament

Up to 34,019 kg (75,000 lb) of disposable stores carried internally and 26,762 kg (59,000 lb) carried externally; weapons include B61 and B83 thermonuclear bombs; AGM-69A Short-Range Attack Missiles; AGM-86B Air-Launched Cruise Missiles and a maximum of 84 227-kg (500-lb) Mk 82 bombs or 84 227-kg (500-lb) Mk 36 mines internally

'Bone' in combat

Rockwell's B-1B, or 'Bone', as its crews prefer to call it, received its belated combat debut in 1998 during Operation Desert Fox.

Although deployed and ready to support the near-attack against Saddam Hussein's forces in November 1998, the B-1B would have to wait another month for its chance to enter combat. Four B-1Bs were forward-deployed in Oman in November; two more B-1Bs were diverted inflight at the last minute when President Clinton cancelled the strikes.

Operation Desert Fox saw the B-1B make its combat debut on 17 December 1998, when two of the six deployed Block C B-1Bs attacked Iraq. The aircraft attacked separate targets in the Al Kut barracks complex in northwest Iraq from approximately 6100 m (20,000 ft). Flying six-hour, night-time missions, each B-1B carried a total of 63 227-kg (500-lb) bombs. A total of six B-1B Desert Fox missions was flown to drop 57,154 kg (126,000 lb) of Mk 82s. Capt Jeff Taliaferro, a B-1B co-pilot, later stated that, 'Most of our missions lasted over six hours and were attacks against

fielded forces, to include military barracks. The B-1B is well suited for large-area targets and, in our case, the missions were incredibly effective.' Commenting on the B-1B's overall performance during the operations, Lt Col Garrett Harencak, commented, 'Desert Fox proved what those of us in the B-1B programme have always known – the B-1 is the premier strike aircraft in the world today.'

Allied Force

Operation Allied Force began on 24 March 1999, with B-1Bs flying their first missions out of RAF Fairford, United Kingdom, beginning 1 April, just 14 hours after the first bombers arrived in theatre. Initial strikes were against Serbian army staging areas in Kosovo. All B-1Bs participating

Both the B-1B and F-15E Eagle have been involved in Operation Enduring Freedom. These aircraft were photographed on a pre-strike training mission, the F-15Es bombing Afghanistan being home based at RAF Lakenheath.

originated from Ellsworth AFB's 28th BW; in total, the aircraft launched over 100 combat sorties and amassed over 700 flight hours in Allied Force. All missions saw the bomber loaded with 84 Mk 82 bombs and some CBUs, although the latter were not dropped.

Targets during the 72-day campaign included airfields, ammunition and storage facilities, armour and troop staging areas, aircraft revetments and vehicle convoys. Most missions were flown by two-ship formations, although there was a limited number of four-ships. On many

missions, B-1Bs would strike multiple targets, and all missions involved tanking. The decision to forward-deploy the B-1B rather than stage from the United States was welcomed by crews who still flew missions of up to seven hours' duration, almost all of which were at night. According to sources, the B-1Bs at RAF Fairford could have flown a higher number of missions had NATO been less restrictive in its employment of air power.

Enduring Freedom

On 7 October 2001 a US-led alliance began strikes against Taliban and Al-Qaeda targets in Afghanistan in the wake of the terrorist attacks on the World Trade Center in New York on 11 September 2001. B-1Bs flying from Diego Garcia in the Indian Ocean were involved in this first attack and up to 10 machines remained bombing on an almost daily basis into December.

Desert Fox marked the delayed baptism of fire for the B-1B. Two aircraft flew a long dumb bombing mission (with Mk 82 bombs) against a Special Republican Guard barracks. Here, two aircraft from the 28th Bomb Wing are seen at their temporary base in Oman.

Northrop Grumman B-2A Spirit 'Stealthy' strategic bomber

The B-2A's 'stealthy' features include S-curved engine inlets and dielectric panels covering the APQ-181 radar. These prevent its antenna from reflecting hostile radar waves while allowing the aircraft to function normally.

The **B-2A Spirit** flying wing was developed as a 'stealthy' strategic bomber for the Cold War mission of attacking Soviet targets with nuclear bombs and stand-off weapons. The B-2 began as a 'black' programme, known in its infancy as **Project Senior C. J.** and later as the **ATB (Advanced Technology Bomber)**. At the Cold War's height the USAF expected to procure some 132 B-2s.

Collaboration

Drawing heavily on its previous flying wing designs, Northrop was aided extensively by Boeing, Vought and General Electric, using a three-dimensional computer-aided design and manufacturing system to create the B-2's unique 'blended wing/double-W' shape. Northrop is responsible for the forward sections and cockpit, Boeing the aft centre and outboard sections, and Vought for the mid-fuselage sections and aluminium,

titanium and composite parts.

Graphite/epoxy composites are extensively used to provide a radar-absorbent honeycomb structure. To reduce infra-red signature, the engines exhaust through V-shaped outlets set back and above the trailing edges to hide these heat sources from the ground. Chlorofluoro-sulphonic acid is injected into the exhaust plume to suppress the formation of contrails. The B-2's swept leading edge and saw-tooth trailing edge configuration trap radar energy.

The cockpit is equipped for two, with ACES II ejection seats, and there is room for a third crew member. The aircraft has a quadruply redundant digital fly-by-wire system, actuating movable surfaces on the wing trailing edges. A beaver tail acts as a pitch-axis trimming surface and helps in gust alleviation.

To verify targets at the last moment, the B-2 briefly activates its APQ-181 radar, spotlighting only a small area, then attacks. The aircraft is equipped with an electronic warfare system which includes the highly classified ZSR-62 defensive aids system.

The B-2 was envisaged as a high-level penetrator, but, when its design was frozen in 1983, a low-level role had been assumed and this necessitated extensive modifications to the design.

Roll out

The first machine was rolled out from USAF Plant 42 at Palmdale, California, on 22 November 1988. The B-2's first flight took place on 17 July 1990, when AV-1 (Air Vehicle One) was delivered to Edwards Air Force Base for the start of the test programme.

In July 1991 deficiencies were revealed in the B-2's stealth profile. It has been admitted that the aircraft can be detected

by some land-based high-powered early warning radars. The USAF therefore implemented a 'set of treatments' to reduce the type's signature across a range of frequencies.

Problems with the B-2's performance, however, did not aid the new bomber's battle for funding. Although the original target had been a fleet of 132 aircraft, this number was steadily reduced to 15, before rising to the 2001 total of a mere 21 aircraft.

The first B-2A, to the initial **Block 2** standard, for the USAF, was AV-8, named *Spirit of Missouri*, which was delivered to the 509th Bomb Wing at Whiteman Air Force Base, Missouri, on 17 December 1993. The 20th and 21st aircraft were completed to the definitive **Block 30** standard, to which all 19 other aircraft are to be upgraded; this standard includes extended weapons capabilities and the definitive 'stealth' suite.

SPECIFICATION	
Northrop Grumman B-2A Spirit **Type:** two-seat long-range strategic bomber **Powerplant:** four General Electric F118-GE-100 turbofan engines each rated at 84.52 kN (19,000 lb st) **Performance:** maximum speed about 764 km/h (475 mph) at high altitude; service ceiling 15,240 m (50,000 ft); range 12,223 km (7,595 miles) with eight AGM-129 missiles and eight B61 bombs on a hi-hi-hi mission or 8334 km (5,178 miles) with the same weapons load on a hi-lo-hi mission; endurance more than 36 hours **Weights:** empty 69,717 kg (153,700 lb); typical take-off 152,635 kg (336,500 lb) **Dimensions:** wing span 52.43 m (172 ft); length 21.03 m (69 ft);	height 5.18 m (17 ft); wing area about 490.05 m² (5,275 sq ft) **Armament:** up to 18,144 kg (40,000 lb) of disposable stores carried in two weapons bays in the underside of the centre section, and generally comprising up to 16 AGM-129 missiles, or 16 B61 or B83 nuclear free-fall bombs, or 80 227-kg (500-lb) Mk 82 or 254-kg (560-lb) Mk 36 bombs, or 80 Mk 62 sea mines, or 36 340-kg (750-lb) M117 fire bombs or CBU-87/89/97/98 cluster bombs, or 16 Joint Direct Attack Munitions or 907-kg (2,000-lb) Mk 84 bombs, or eight 1996-kg (4,400-lb) GBU-28 deep-penetration bombs, or (to be retrofitted) varying numbers of the Joint Air-to-Surface Stand-off Missile and Joint Stand-off Weapon

*The first production B-2A was named **S**pirit of **T**exas when it was handed over to the 509th Bomb Wing at Whiteman Air Force Base in September 1994. The B-2A has been committed to Operation Enduring Freedom, flying nonstop missions from the United States.*

Dassault Mirage 2000N Nuclear penetrator

With the Mirage 2000N-K2 comes the ability to deliver the nuclear ASMP and conventional ordnance. The Mirage 2000N is France's primary air-launched nuclear weapons platform.

When the **Mirage 2000** was being designed, one of its envisaged roles was that of a nuclear penetrator. The aircraft would be used to deliver the new Aérospatiale tactical stand-off weapon known as the ASMP (*Air-Sol Moyenne Portée* – air-to-ground medium-range) missile. Originally, this weapon was carried by the Mirage IVPs of the Strategic Air Forces and the navy's carrier-based Super Etendards. However, due to the age of the Mirage IVP, Dassault received a contract for two prototypes of an interdictor version of the new Mirage 2000, to be designated **2000P** ('P' for **Pénétration**). The designation was changed to **Mirage 2000N** ('N' for **Nucléaire**) to avoid confusion with the Mirage IVP.

Two-seater

Due to the high pilot workload encountered during an interdiction mission at low-level, it was decided that a weapons system officer would be needed to undertake radar navigation, control the ECM equipment and manage the armament. The 2000N was based on the 2000B trainer, but the airframe was strengthened to withstand the stresses of high-subsonic, low-level flight. Some internal equipment was also modified from the original Mirage 2000C interceptor, reflecting the need for greater positional accuracy.

New radar

In the nose the RDM/RDI was replaced by a Dassault Electronique/Thomson-CSF Antilope V radar featuring terrain-following, air-to-air, air-to-sea, air-to-ground, ground-mapping and navigation-updating modes. The 2000N carries Magic 2 AAMs and Dassault Electronique

Sabre jammers for self-defence, plus a Serval radar warning receiver. Since 1989 the MATRA Spirale integrated decoy system has been fitted to all aircraft.

The initial requirement was for 100 Mirage 2000Ns, which would be allocated 75 ASMP missiles. However, delays with the Dassault Rafale programme and the need for an interim replacement for the Mirage IIIE meant that a further 70 Mirages were added for the conventional attack role, with the ASMP interface deleted. Generally regarded as 'non-nuclear' aircraft, they were given the designation **Mirage 2000N'** (**N Prime**). A reassessment of nuclear requirements resulted in later changes to the number of Ns and N's and, to simplify the distinction between the two, the latter was designated **Mirage 2000D** in 1990.

The first 2000Ns with ASMP capability were **K1** sub-types. Provision is also made for a pair of 2000-litre (528-US gallon) drop tanks underwing. From the 32nd 2000N onwards, the designation **K2** was used and these aircraft are capable of carrying conventional ordnance or a guided nuclear payload.

In service

In late 2001, six Escadres de Chasse flew the Mirage 2000 in its 'D' or 'N' form. Mirage 2000Ds are part of the *Commandement de la Force Aérienne de Combat* (CFAC), which controls air defence,

*Just visible on the centreline station of this aircraft is its **ASMP** missile. **ASMP** has a ramjet powerplant and solid rocket booster, giving a Mach-2 top speed.*

conventional ground-attack and tactical reconnaissance missions. Three squadrons fly from Nancy. Mirage 2000Ds are expected to serve well into the twenty-first century and will be the last of France's current warplane fleet to be replaced by Rafale. It is estimated that France's air force will have a fleet of 300 Rafales and Mirage 2000Ds by 2015.

Mirage 2000Ns operate as part of the Commandement des Forces Aériennes Strategiques (CFAS). The main mission of the

strategic air forces is to provide a nuclear deterrent. Since the withdrawal of the Mirage IVP and the phase-out of the ballistic missiles at the Plateau d'Albion, the CFAS nuclear deterrent rests solely with the three Mirage 2000N units. Equipped with the ASMP missile they, together with the French navy's ballistic missile submarines, provide France with its nuclear strike capability. Tanker support for the 2000Ns is provided by Istres-based C-135FRs.

SPECIFICATION	
Dassault Mirage 2000N **Type:** two-seat multi-role fighter **Powerplant:** one SNECMA M53-P2 turbofan engine rated at 95.12 kN (21,384 lb st) with afterburning **Performance:** maximum level speed 'clean' 2338 km/h (1,453 mph) at 11,000 m (36,090 ft); penetration speed at 60 m (200 ft) 1112 km/h (691 mph); initial climb rate 17,070 m (56,000 ft) per minute; service ceiling 16,460 m (54,000 ft); range 3333 km (2,071 miles) with drop tanks or 1850 km (1,151 miles) on hi-hi-hi mission	**Weights:** empty 7500 kg (16,534 lb); maximum take-off 15,000 kg (33,069 lb) **Dimensions:** wing span 9.26 m (30 ft 4½ in); length 14.55 m (47 ft 9 in); height 5.15 m (16 ft 10¾ in); wing area 41.00 m² (441.33 sq ft) **Armament:** two 30-mm DEFA 554 fixed forward-firing cannon in the lower part of the forward fuselage, plus up to 6300 kg (13,889 lb) of disposable stores carried on five underfuselage and four underwing hardpoints

Dassault Mirage III/5/50 family
Delta-winged fighters

Serving with l'Armée de l'Air's EC 3/10 'Vexin' at BA 188 in Djibouti, this Mirage IIIC is illustrated as it appeared in 1980. The camouflage scheme shown was officially described as sand and chestnut.

Designed in response to a 1954 Armée de l'Air requirement, the **M.D.550 Mystère-Delta** prototype first flew on 25 June 1955. As then flown, this single-seat machine had a delta wing set low on the fuselage, a triangular vertical tail surface, retractable tricycle landing gear, and two Dassault M.D.30 (Armstrong Siddeley Viper) turbojets. The prototype was later revised as the **Mirage I**.

Later evaluation led to the conclusion that the Mirage I was too small to carry a significant military load. This in turn led to consideration of larger **Mirage II** version with increased power from two Turboméca Gabizo turbojets. Both the Mirage I and Mirage II were then abandoned in favour of the **Mirage III**.

Mirage III legend

The success of this later design was legendary; the prototype Mirage III first flew on 17 December 1956, but the last of 1422 related Mirage III, **Mirage 5** and **Mirage 50** warplanes was not completed until 1992. Even then, several air forces had just completed or were in the process of upgrading their Mirage IIIs.

Discounting some anomalies, the designation Mirage III covers aircraft equipped with nose radar, the first of which for the Armée de l'Air were 10 **Mirage IIIA** pre-production machines and, entering service in July 1961, 95 **Mirage IIIC** interceptors. These had an auxiliary rocket motor in the rear fuselage for high-altitude missions, although the facility was little used. Variants of the Mirage IIIC and its two-seat **Mirage IIIB** equivalent were also exported widely.

Advanced Mirage III

The second phase of Mirage III development was represented by the **Mirage IIIE**, which first flew on 5 April 1961 and was optimized for strike and attack, as well as interception. France received 183 such aircraft, as well as 20 of the **Mirage IIIBE** trainer. With a camera nose, the Mirage IIIE became the **Mirage IIIR**, of which 70 were delivered to the French air force, the last 20 to **Mirage IIIRD** standard with Doppler navigation. Again, Mirage IIIE-based export variants sold well.

SPECIFICATION

Dassault Mirage IIIE
Type: single-seat strike and attack fighter with interception capability
Powerplant: one SNECMA Atar 9C-3 afterburning turbojet engine rated at 60.80 kN (13,668 lb st), and provision for one jettisonable SEPR 844 rocket booster rated at 14.71 kN (3,307 lb st)
Performance: maximum speed 2350 km/h (1,460 mph) or Mach 2.21 at 12,000 m (39,370 ft); initial climb rate more than 5000 m (16,405 ft) per minute; service ceiling 17,000 m (55,775 ft) with turbojet or 23,000 m (75,460 ft) with turbojet and rocket; combat radius 1200 km (746 miles) on a hi-hi-hi mission with a very small warload
Weights: empty 7050 kg (15,542 lb); maximum take-off 13,700 kg (30,203 lb)
Dimensions: wing span 8.22 m (26 ft 11¾ in); length 15.03 m (49 ft 3½ in); height 4.5 m (14 ft 9 in); wing area 35 m² (376.75 sq ft)
Armament: two 30-mm DEFA 552 fixed forward-firing cannon in the underside of the forward fuselage, plus up to 4000 kg (8,818 lb) of disposable stores

Mirage 5 for Israel

In 1966 the Israeli air force asked Dassault to build a simplified Mirage IIIE optimised for daytime ground-attack. The basic changes implemented in the development of this Mirage 5 were the movement of the avionics racking from its original location behind the cockpit to the nose – which was now largely unoccupied after the removal of the radar – the reprofiling of the nose, and the addition of additional fuel tankage in the fuselage volume freed by the movement of the avionics racking. At the same time, two outward-canted underfuselage weapons pylons were added.

The prototype first flew on 19 May 1967, but delivery of the 50 **Mirage 5J** aircraft, ordered by Israel, was embargoed by President de Gaulle. The stored aircraft were finally delivered to the Armée de l'Air for service as **Mirage 5F** warplanes. Following this initial order, the Mirage 5 proved popular with many customers requiring a cheap but potent fighter-bomber. Dassault also produced **Mirage 5D** two-seat trainer, and **Mirage 5R** reconnaissance aircraft.

Mirage 50

A derived programme resulted in the **Mirage 50**, which introduced the Atar 9K-50 turbojet as developed for the Mirage F1. The greater thrust of this unit endows the aircraft with better runway performance, faster acceleration, larger weapon load, and improved manoeuvrability. The Mirage 50 prototype made its maiden flight on 15 April 1979, and Chile was the first customer with an order for 16 aircraft (four **Mirage IIIR2Z** had already been delivered to South Africa with the 9K-50 engine). The Mirage 50 package was also made available as a conversion of Mirage III/5 aircraft, and the complete avionics/ weapons range of the Mirage III/5 was available on the Mirage 50. Considerable numbers of Mirage 50s were built for export.

A Chilean Mirage 50C of Brigada Aérea IV lands at Punta Arenas. Chile is one of many countries to have opted for extensive Mirage upgrade programmes.

Mikoyan-Gurevich MiG-17 'Fresco'
Improved MiG-15 development

The MiG-17, including PFs such as this Bulgarian example, was widely exported to countries which included Albania, Bangladesh, Sri Lanka, Sudan and Zimbabwe.

Combat experience in Korea had highlighted the MiG-15's major shortcoming, in which a tight high-speed turn initiated a snap roll resulting in an uncontrollable spin. Redesign was initiated to eliminate this problem, the resulting **I-330** prototype, known also as the **MiG-15bis-45°**, having a completely redesigned wing incorporating 45 degrees of sweep and flying for the first time on 13 January 1950. At the same time, the fuselage was lengthened to reduce drag, the tail unit was revised and the opportunity was taken to improve internal layout and systems. Following completion of official tests, the aircraft was ordered into production in mid-1951 under the designation MiG-17, and production deliveries to the VVS began in late 1952.

Allocated the ASCC/NATO code name **'Fresco'**, the **MiG-17** was built in variants that included the original MiG-17 production version which retained the VK-1 turbojet of the MiG-15, followed by the **MiG-17F 'Fresco-C'** day fighter, which was the main production version and introduced an afterburning VK-1F engine. The **MiG-17P 'Fresco-D'** added night- and all-weather capability to the MiG-17, while the **MiG-17PF 'Fresco-D'** combined this capability with the VK-1F engine. The **MiG-17PFU 'Fresco-E'** had its gun armament deleted in favour of RS-2US (AA-1 'Alkali') AAM armament, making it the first missile-armed interceptor in production in Europe.

Although considered virtually obsolete by the Soviet Union in the mid-1960s, MiG-17s saw considerable and effective use in operations over Vietnam, where it was flown by North Vietnamese pilots.

Massive production

Production in the Soviet Union probably exceeded 8900 aircraft by the time manufacture was terminated in the late 1950s, this total not including aircraft built under licence in Poland as the **LIM-5** (MiG-17), **LIM-5M** (MiG-17F) and **LIM-5P** (MiG-17PF), and in Czechoslovakia as the **S-104** (MiG-17PF). The MiG-17 was also built in China, the basic Chinese-built MiG-17F being produced by the Shenyang Aircraft Factory, but later derivatives being developed and built by Chengdu. The first such development was the **J-5A**, basically a Chinese-built MiG-17PF

with AI radar in a larger, longer, forward fuselage. Relatively small numbers were produced, and none is known to have been exported. The prototype first flew on 11 November 1964.

More successful was the **JJ-5**, a two-seat trainer derivative of the J-5. This had a slightly lengthened fuselage, and the nose intake and jetpipe were refined. Development began in 1965, when it was becoming clear that the MiG-15UTIs then in use lacked performance and had some unacceptable handling characteristics. The JJ-5 first flew on 8 May 1966, and 1061 had been built by 1986, when production ceased. The JJ-5 was exported (as the **FT-5**) to a number of customers, most notably Pakistan, which, in 2003, still used the aircraft as its standard advanced jet trainer. Interestingly, Mikoyan-Gurevich itself never designed a two-seat MiG-17 variant.

China's locally developed two-seat version of the MiG-17, the Chengdu JJ-5/FT-5 was believed to be still in use in China, North Korea, Pakistan and Sudan in 2003. The aircraft shown here are Pakistani examples.

SPECIFICATION	
Chengdu JJ-5 **Type:** two-seat advanced jet trainer **Powerplant:** one Xian (XAE) Wopen WP-5D rated at 26.48 kN (5,952 lb st) **Performance:** normal operating speed 'clean' at optimum altitude 775 km/h (482 mph); maximum rate of climb at sea level 1620 m (5,315 ft) per minute; service	ceiling 14,300 m (46,915 ft); maximum ferry range 1230 km (764 miles) **Weights:** empty equipped 4080 kg (8,995 lb); maximum take-off 6215 kg (13,701 lb) **Dimensions:** wing span 9.63 m (31 ft 7 in); length 11.5 m (37 ft 9 in); height 3.8 m (12 ft 5¾ in); wing area 22.6 m² (243.27 sq ft)

Mikoyan-Gurevich MiG-19 'Farmer'/Shenyang J-6
Supersonic fighter

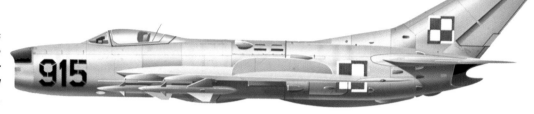

Poland operated large numbers of MiG-19s, including the MiG-19PM, although the latter had a relatively small production run.

Although successful, the MiG-17 was little more than an improved version of the MiG-15, and in the late 1940s the MiG bureau initiated design of a completely new fighter at the request of the Kremlin. The MiG bureau was instructed to use the Mikulin AM-5 powerplant, and this was flown in the **I-360** prototype on 24 May 1952. Subsequent development led to the AM-9-engined **SM-9/1**, which, with modifications, was ordered into production as the **MiG-19** on 17 February 1954. The MiG-19 (ASCC/NATO **'Farmer'**) entered service from March 1955, but, despite having supersonic capability in level flight, it was withdrawn because of its difficult handling. The major change in the **MiG-19S**, which resulted from a redesign to eliminate stability problems, was the incorporation of an all-moving tailplane and refinements to the flying controls and systems.

'Farmer' variety

About 2120 examples of the highly successful MiG-19S 'Farmer-C' were built, along with a number of **MiG-19P** **'Farmer-B'** aircraft with radar to provide all-weather capability, and the AAM-armed **MiG-19PM** and **MiG-19PMU 'Farmer-D'**. A limited number of high-altitude **MiG-19SV** interceptors was produced in an effort to counter high-flying Western spyplanes and balloons. In addition, small numbers of the **MiG-19R** recce

aircraft were built and just six **MiG-19UTI** two-seaters. Aircraft from Soviet production were supplied to Czechoslovakia and Poland, where they operated under the designations **S-105** and **LIM-7** respectively and, in addition, the type was exported to countries that included Albania, Bangladesh, Egypt, Kampuchea, Tanzania and Vietnam.

Chinese production

China began assessment of the supersonic MiG-19 during the late 1950s and it was selected for production under the second Five Year Plan. Design drawings were supplied to the Shenyang Aircraft Factory, which produced a copy of the basic MiG-19P under the designation **J-6**. The first Chinese-assembled aircraft made its maiden flight on 17 December 1958, and the first Chinese-built aircraft followed it into the air on 30 September 1959.

Licence-production of the MiG-19 and MiG-19PM was also assigned to the Nanchang Aircraft Factory. Seven MiG-19Ps were built, while five MiG-19PMs were assembled from Soviet kits and another 19 were built at the factory, these apparently being designated **J-6B**. Unfortunately, quality-control problems meant that between 1958 and 1960 not one J-6 from Shenyang or Nanchang was accepted by the PLA air force. Many were scrapped after failing post-production inspections; others were rebuilt before

delivery. The programme to build the MiG-19 began again in 1961 using Soviet-supplied drawings and technical documents. Production was of the basic MiG-19S, although small numbers of the MiG-19P and the MiG-19PM may also have been built. The first 'second batch' J-6 flew in December 1961. The aircraft began to enter service in significant numbers in 1964–65.

Chinese variants

By 1973, the prevailing political situation had improved sufficiently for development of new variants. The most important of these was the **JJ-6** trainer, but this was accompanied by the **JZ-6**. Handfuls of J-6s had been built

for medium-level and low-level recce duties from 1967, under the JZ-6 designation, but a requirement for an entirely new JZ-6 was issued in January 1976, and construction of a prototype/demonstrator began in April.

Production of the JJ-6 totalled 634 examples, and many were exported under the designation **FT-6** to serve as conversion and continuation trainers for export **F-6** aircraft and A-5s.

Frequently misidentified as the **J-6Xin**, the **J-6III** was actually a high-speed day fighter. A prototype flew on 6 August 1969, but the J-6III was plagued by handling and quality control problems. The more modest **J-6C** variant was more successful.

SPECIFICATION

Shenyang J-6/F-6 'Farmer'
Type: single-seat fighter and attack aircraft
Powerplant: two Liming (LM) Wopen-6 (Tumanskii R-9BF-811) turbojets each rated at 25.49 kN (5,730 lb st) dry and 31.87 kN (7,165 lb st) with afterburning
Performance: maximum level speed 'clean' at 10,975 m (36,000 ft) 1540 km/h (957 mph); maximum rate of climb at sea level more than 9145 m (30,000 ft) per

minute; service ceiling 17,900 m (58,725 ft); combat radius 685 km (426 miles) with two 760-litre (201-US gal) drop tanks
Weights: nominal empty 5760 kg (12,698 lb); maximum take-off about 10,000 kg (22,046 lb)
Dimensions: wing span 9.2 m (30 ft 2¼ in); length 14.9 m (48 ft 10½ in); height 3.88 m (12 ft 8¾ in); wing area 25 m² (269.11 sq ft)
Armament: maximum ordnance 500 kg (1,102 lb)

As the United States was working on the F-100 Super Sabre, it had no idea that the Soviet answer to the F-100 was already well into its test programme. The MiG-19 'Farmer' and the Chinese-built J-6 became true global warriors, seeing action with a large number of air arms, and spawning many variants. These Pakistani F-6s are armed with AIM-9 AAMs.

Mikoyan-Gurevich MiG-21 'Fishbed' Early versions

The first 'Fishbed' version in service with the enlarged nose cone, necessitated by the larger R1L radar, was the MiG-21PF, built in vast numbers in the 1960s to equip the air defence regiments of the Soviet Union.

The original concept of the **Mikoyan-Gurevich MiG-21** was for a simple, lightweight fighter, in which sophistication and considerations of endurance and firepower were sacrificed for outright performance.

Prototypes

As usual, the production MiG-21 was preceded by a series of prototypes. Some of these had swept wings, while others had the delta-wing planform which was eventually chosen. The 40 pre-production **MIG-21F** (**Ye-6T** or **Type 72**) fighters, which attained limited service in 1959, were allocated the ASCC/NATO reporting name **'Fishbed-B'**; however, the first full production version was the **MIG-21F-13 'Fishbed-C'**, or **Type 74**.

Into service

Initial operational capability came in January 1963, with the 28th Regiment based at Odessa, and the first export sales being made to Finland. The first 114 MiG-21F-13s had a narrow-chord vertical tail, and all had their armament reduced from two to one NR-30 cannon, on the starboard side, with underwing pylons for two AA-2 'Atoll' heat-seeking AAMs or rocket pods. The aircraft's fuel capacity was increased from 2280 litres (502 Imperial gallons) to 2550 litres (561 Imperial gallons). China was to build a copy of this original production MiG-21 as the Shenyang J-7, or F-7 for export.

The **MiG-21P 'Fishbed-D'** dispensed with cannon entirely.

The large inlet centrebody of the fighter housed a TsD-30T R1L 'Spin Scan' radar. The canopy and spine were modified, with a bulge immediately aft of the cockpit. Internal fuel capacity was increased to 2750 litres (605 Imperial gallons).

More power

The MiG-21P was followed by the R11F2-300-engined **MiG-21PF (Type 76)**, which had the pitot probe relocated to the top of the nose and was equipped with the improved RP-21 Sapfir radar. NATO allocated these aircraft the reporting name **'Fishbed-E'**.

SPECIFICATION

Mikoyan-Gurevich MiG-21PFM 'Fishbed-F'
Type: single-seat multi-role fighter
Powerplant: one MNPK Soyuz (Tumansky) R-11F2S-300 turbojet rated at 38.26-kN (8,600-lb) dry thrust and 60.57-kN (13,613-lb) afterburning thrust
Performance: maximum level speed 'clean' 2125 km/h (1,320 mph) at 11,000 m (36,090 ft); maximum rate of climb at sea level with two missiles and 50 per cent fuel more than 7500 m (24,600 ft) per minute; service ceiling 19,000 m (62,335 ft); ferry range more than 1300 km (808 miles) with an 800-litre (176-Imp gal) drop tank
Weights: empty 5350 kg (13,670 lb); normal loaded 7960 kg (11,795 lb); maximum take-off 9080 kg (20,018 lb)
Dimensions: wing span 7.15 m (23 ft 5¾ in); length 15.76 m (51 ft 8½ in) including probe; height 4.13 m (13 ft 6¼ in); wing area 23 m² (247.5 sq ft)
Armament: one 23-mm GSh-23 cannon, plus up to 500 kg (1,102 lb) of ordnance

Above: Czechoslovakia received large numbers of MiG-21s up to the MF model. The Aero factory also produced 195 MiG-21F-13s locally, as the S.107 (illustrated).

Below: Finland was the first export customer for the MiG-21, receiving 22 MiG-21F-13 aircraft like this one, plus two MiG-21U two-seaters. Later, the country also used the MiG-21bis and MiG-21UM, retiring its last machine in 1998.

The **MiG-21FL** was externally identical to the late MiG-21PF. Intended for export, it had less powerful R-2L radar and the original engine. About 200 of these were built under licence in India. The **Type 94** subvariants, known in production as the **MiG-21PFS** and the **MiG-21PFM 'Fishbed-F'**, had two-piece canopies with fixed windscreens, blown flaps, a cruciform brake 'chute, R-11F2S-300 engines and RP-21M radar. They could fire semi-active radar-homing RS-2US (K-5M) air-to-air missiles.

'Fishbed-D' dispensed with cannon armament to become an all-missile-armed, radar-equipped interceptor. Note the revised pitot tube position.

Cockpit
Many Indian pilots dismissed the MiG-21F-13 as a 'Supersonic Sportsplane'. The later MiG-21FL had rather better range and endurance characteristics, but retained the same exhilarating handling characteristics and was much closer to being a viable operational fighter aircraft.

Armament
The K-13A missile, dubbed AA-2 'Atoll' by NATO, had many shortcomings, just like the early Sidewinder from which it was copied. It had virtually no all-aspect capability, and the seeker head could easily lose its lock-on if the target aircraft flew across the sun, or dumped flares. The two missiles were augmented by a GP9 cannon pod on the centreline. The cannon was an outstanding weapon with a long range and a powerful punch.

MiG-21FL
This MiG-21FL was built in India by Hindustan Aeronautics Ltd and served with No. 1 Squadron 'Tigers', Indian Air Force, until 1973. MiG-21s, in various forms, have had a long and glorious career with the IAF and early variants, such as the MiG-21FL, still remained in service with a number of squadrons in 2003, although No. 1 Squadron had converted to the rather more capable Mirage 2000H.

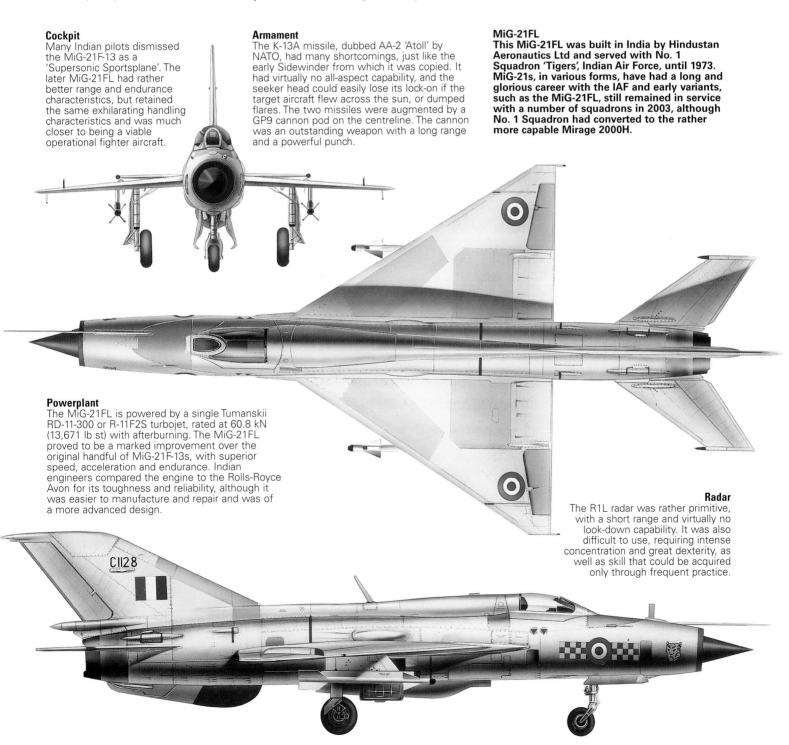

Powerplant
The MiG-21FL is powered by a single Tumanskii RD-11-300 or R-11F2S turbojet, rated at 60.8 kN (13,671 lb st) with afterburning. The MiG-21FL proved to be a marked improvement over the original handful of MiG-21F-13s, with superior speed, acceleration and endurance. Indian engineers compared the engine to the Rolls-Royce Avon for its toughness and reliability, although it was easier to manufacture and repair and was of a more advanced design.

Radar
The R1L radar was rather primitive, with a short range and virtually no look-down capability. It was also difficult to use, requiring intense concentration and great dexterity, as well as skill that could be acquired only through frequent practice.

Panavia Tornado ADV Air defence Tornado

The multinational **Tornado** remains one of Europe's most important combat aircraft. Developed from the Tornado Interdictor/Strike (IDS) variant for a wholly RAF requirement, the **Tornado ADV (Air Defence Variant)** is optimized for long-range interception. Key features comprised installation of

Foxhunter radar and a lengthened fuselage for carriage of semi-recessed Sky Flash AAMs.

The interim **Tornado F.Mk 2** was soon replaced by the definitive **Tornado F.Mk 3**. The RAF received its first of 152 production F.Mk 3s in 1986 and these have since had several updates. The 'Stage 1' upgrade

The Tornado F.Mk 3 has come in for considerable criticism owing to its shortcomings as a close-in fighter. The aircraft was designed as a bomber interceptor, however, a job at which it excels.

included HOTAS controls, RAM coating, and flare dispensers, while 'Stage 2' enhances the computer and radar imagery and adds the JTIDS data-link. As an interim measure while the RAF

waits for Eurofighter Typhoon, 100 F.Mk 3s are passing through a Capability Sustainment Programme. This adds AMRAAM and ASRAAM capability (albeit

As Tornado F.Mk 3s are replaced by Typhoons, they may become available for a variety of combat support roles. These could include lethal SEAD with ALARM anti-radar weapons. The aircraft illustrated is a No. 29 Sqn machine.

not exploiting the full potential of these weapons), a multiple target engagement capability for the radar and improved defensive aids. The Common Operational Value (COV) modification features some structural rework, an NVG-compatible cockpit with new displays, GPS and Have Quick secure radios. The first CSP/COV aircraft were redelivered to RAF units in 2000 and towed radar decoys are also now in use.

Foreign service

Saudi Arabia received 24 new ADVs to F.Mk 3 standard, while Italy leased 24 upgraded, ex-RAF F.Mk 3s from 1995, pending arrival of its Typhoons. ADVs have seen combat with all three nations, during Desert Storm, over the former Yugoslavia and in other NATO peacekeeping actions.

SPECIFICATION	
Panavia Tornado F.Mk 3	**Weights:** empty operating
Type: two-seat all-weather	14,502 kg (31,970 lb); maximum
interceptor	take-off 27,986 kg (61,700 lb)
Powerplant: two Turbo-Union	**Dimensions:** wing span 13.91 m
RB.199-34R Mk 104 turbofans each	(45 ft 7½ in) spread, 8.6 m (28 ft
rated at 40.48 kN (9,100 lb st) dry	2½ in) swept; length 18.68 m
and 73.48 kN (16,520 lb st) with	(61 ft 3½ in); height 5.95 m (19 ft
afterburning	6¼ in); wing area 26.6 m²
Performance: maximum level speed	(286.33 sq ft)
'clean' at 10,975 m (36,000 ft)	**Armament:** one 27-mm Mauser
2238 km/h (1,453 mph), operational	fixed forward-firing cannon, plus a
ceiling 21,335 m (70,000 ft),	usual load of four Sky Flash AAMs,
combat radius more than 556 km	plus four AIM-9 Sidewinder,
(345 miles) supersonic	ASRAAM, or AIM-120 AAMs

Dassault Mirage F1C All-weather interceptor

The **Mirage F1** was Dassault's successor to its Mirage III and Mirage 5. Employing a high-mounted swept wing and conventional tail surfaces, the private-venture prototype first flew on 23 December 1966. With greater power available from the Atar 9K-50 afterburning turbojet, the Mirage F1 easily outperformed the Mirage III.

Interceptor

To meet the French air force's primary requirement for an all-weather interceptor, the **Mirage F1C** initial production model was equipped with a Thomson-CSF Cyrano IV monopulse radar, the later Cyrano IV-I standard adding limited look-down capability. The Mirage F1C was eventually armed with two internal 30-mm cannon, R530 medium-range and short-range, IR-homing R550 Magic AAMs.

The Armée de l'Air acquired 83 basic Mirage F1Cs. Another 79 aircraft, delivered between March 1977 and December 1983, were of the **Mirage F1C-200** subvariant with a fixed inflight-refuelling probe. Provision for the probe required a very small 'plug' in the forward fuselage, increasing the aircraft's length by 7 cm (2¾ in).

South Africa used its F1CZ aircraft in combat and also armed them with indigenous missiles. The aircraft were retired, however, in favour of the Cheetah.

Variants and exports

The **Mirage F1B** two-seat operational conversion trainer has a lengthened fuselage and cockpit, carries less fuel and has no cannon. Exports of the Mirage F1C were made to six countries. South Africa received the **Mirage F1CZ**, Morocco the **Mirage F1CH**, Jordan the **Mirage F1CJ** and Kuwait the **Mirage F1CK** and **Mirage F1CK-II**. Greece took delivery of 40 **Mirage F1CG** fighters from August 1975, while

Below: Spain's C.14A aircraft have an important secondary ground-attack role. For many years a C.14A detachment was maintained for the air defence of the Canary Islands.

Spain bought 45 **Mirage F1CE** fighters with the local designation **C.14A**. Like the majority of export customers, Spain also bought its own version of the F1B, in this case the trainer order taking the form of six **Mirage F1BE** aircraft.

As soon as it had become clear that the Mirage F1 would support a major production run, Dassault studied a dedicated tactical reconnaissance version.

The first of the resulting Mirage F1CR-200 aircraft completed its maiden flight on 20 November 1981. The later Mirage F1CT derives its designation from being a tactical (tactique) air-to-ground version of the Mirage F1C-200. The two prototypes were conversions. The Mirage F1CT programme upgraded the Mirage F1C interceptor to a standard similar to that of the Mirage F1CR.

SPECIFICATION

Dassault Mirage F1C
Type: single-seat fighter and attack warplane
Powerplant: one SNECMA Atar 9K-50 turbojet rated at 70.21 kN (15,785 lb st) with afterburning
Performance: maximum speed 2335 km/h (1,451 mph) or Mach 2.2 at 11,000 m (36,090 ft); initial climb rate 12,780 m (41,930 ft) per minute; service ceiling 20,000 m (65,615 ft); combat radius 425 km (264 miles) on a hi-lo-hi attack mission with 14 250-kg (551-lb) bombs

Weights: empty 7400 kg (16,314 lb); maximum take-off 16,200 kg (35,715 lb)
Dimensions: wing span 8.4 m (27 ft 6¾ in) without tip stores; length 15.3 m (50 ft 2½ in); height 4.5 m (14 ft 9 in); wing area 25 m² (269.11 sq ft)
Armament: two 30-mm DEFA 553 fixed forward-firing cannon in the underside of the forward fuselage, plus up to 6300 kg (13,889 lb) of disposable stores

IAI Kfir and F-21A Lion Israeli Mirage III derivative

Israel was the first export customer for the Dassault Mirage III, and used the type to great effect during the 1967 and 1973 Arab-Israeli wars. Despite the Mirage's success, Israel was aware of its shortcomings, which included very fast take-off and landing speeds (requiring long take-off and landing runs), lack of thrust and primitive avionics. This obvious need for improvement, coupled with arms embargoes, forced Israel first to upgrade its Mirages, then to build its own improved derivatives.

This process resulted in Project Salvo, under which Israel's Mirage IIICJs were rebuilt and upgraded, then in the Nesher, and eventually in the **Kfir** (lion cub). Israel powered the Kfir with the J79 engine that was also installed in its F-4 Phantoms, necessitating the provision of enlarged air intakes and extensive heat shielding of the rear fuselage. A large air scoop was added to the tailfin's leading edge for afterburner cooling. Other airframe changes included a strengthened undercarriage.

This aircraft was the first Kfir-C2 to be publicly displayed – at Hatzerim air base in 1976. The aircraft is armed with a pair of Shafrir 2 AAMs and has 500-litre (110-Imp gal) drop tanks underwing, with a 1300-litre (286-Imp gal) tank on the centreline. The large black-outlined orange triangles on the wings and fin were applied to avoid confusion with Arab-operated Mirages.

Production variants

The basic **Kfir-C1** was produced in small numbers (27) and most were later upgraded with small narrow-span fixed canards on the intakes and rectangular strakes behind the ranging radar, on the sides of the nose. Twenty-five survivors were later

lent to the US Navy and US Marines for adversary training (between 1985 and 1989), as the **F-21A Lion**.

The **Kfir-C2** was the first full-standard variant, equipped with nose strakes and large fixed canard foreplanes from the outset. The new variant also had a dogtooth wing leading edge.

The Kfir-C2 also introduced new avionics, including an ELTA M-2001B ranging radar. Other equipment includes a twin-computer flight control system, angle-of-attack sensor vane on the port side of the forward fuselage (retrofitted to early aircraft), Elbit S-8600 multi-mode navigation and weapons delivery system (alternatively Elbit/IAI WDNS-141), Taman central air data computer and Israel

Electro-Optics HUD. Some 185 C2s and **Kfir-TC2** trainers were built, and many Kfirs remained in storage in Israel in 2004.

Exports and C7

After long delays in gaining US approval to re-export the J79, 12 Kfir-C2s were sold to Ecuador in 1982, and another 11 went to Colombia in 1988–89. Both customers also took a pair of Kfir-TC2s. Virtually all surviving Israeli Kfir C2s and TC2s were

SPECIFICATION
IAI Kfir-C7
Type: single-seat fighter-bomber
Powerplant: one IAI Bedek Division-built General Electric J79-J1E turbojet rated at 52.89 kN (11,890 lb st) dry and 83.40 kN (18,750 lb st) with afterburning
Performance: maximum level speed more than 2440 km/h (1,516 mph) 'clean' at 10,975 m (36,000 ft); maximum rate of climb 14,000 m (45,930 ft) per minute at sea level; stabilized supersonic ceiling 17,680 m (58,000 ft); combat radius 776 km (482 miles) on a hi-hi-hi

interception mission with two Shafrir AAMs, one 825-litre (181-Imp gal) and two 1300-litre (286-Imp gal) drop tanks
Weights: empty about 7285 kg (16,060 lb); maximum take-off 16,500 kg (36,376 lb)
Dimensions: wing span 8.22 m (26 ft 11¾ in); length 15.65 m (51 ft 4¼ in) including probe; height 4.55 m (14 ft 11¼ in); wing area 34.8 m² (374.6 sq ft)
Armament: up to 6085 kg (13,415 lb) of US and Israeli-made bombs and missiles

Left: IAI flew the first Kfir-T in February 1981. The two-seater TC2 seen at left was based on the fuselage of the C2, but with a considerably longer nose. The trainer's longer nose houses repositioned avionics and an air-conditioning plant.

Below: A brightly marked No. 144 Sqn C7 touches down with the aid of its brake 'chute. Landing and take-off performance were greatly increased, compared to the Mirage 5 and Mirage III, through the installation of wide-span canards.

upgraded to **Kfir-C7** and **Kfir-TC7** standards, but it is uncertain as to whether any were built as new airframes.

The C7 designation is applied to upgraded aircraft delivered from 1983 onwards. These incorporate a number of avionics improvements, and have what is effectively a HOTAS cockpit. The only external difference in comparison to the C2 is the provision of an extra pair of hardpoints under the engine intakes.

The US Navy and Marine Corps used the Kfir for dissimilar air combat training in the late 1980s. The aircraft flew in a number of colour schemes, some in two-tone grey, and others in Israeli camouflage.

McDonnell Douglas F-110/F-4 Phantom II
Multi-role warplane

Above: The Israeli Defence Force/Air Force first used the F-4E in an air-to-air role during the 1969–71 war of attrition. Later, the aircraft adopted multi-role tasking.

When production of the **McDonnell Douglas F-4 Phantom II** ended in October 1979, a total of 5195 had been built. This remarkable total is challenged only by the MiG-21. The Phantom II's history began 26 years earlier when, in September 1953, McDonnell began studies for a twin-engine

Right: Wearing TAC badges, these two USAF F-110A Phantoms are actually Navy F4H-1s. The USAF's Phantoms were delivered in a similar scheme until camouflage was adopted.

While US Navy F-4s were primarily used for air-to-air work over Vietnam, USAF Phantoms, such as this F-4C, were increasingly employed on 'mud-moving' operations.

all-weather fighter to supersede the F3H Demon. However, the F8U Crusader promised to fulfil the fighter role, and eventually McDonnell was encouraged to undertake an all-weather attack/fighter instead, and in July 1955 the company received a contract covering two **YF4H-1 Phantom II**.

First flown on 27 May 1958, the Phantom II soon proved that it offered completely new capability, being the first aircraft which could detect, intercept and destroy any target within its radar range without assistance from surface-based radar. Such capability meant that the US Navy lost little time in ordering the initial **F4H-1** production version, redesignated **F-4A** in September 1962. The USAF also bought the aircraft and Phantoms saw extensive use in Southeast Asia, and subsequently played a significant first-line role in service with Greece, Iran, Israel, Japan, South Korea, Spain, Turkey, the UK, the United States and West Germany; the type also served temporarily with the Royal Australian Air Force pending delivery of General Dynamics F-111s.

Long service

The earliest Phantom model still in service is the **F-4D**, while the **F-4E** multi-role fighter remains the most widespread Phantom in service. The latter model resulted from experience gained in air-to-air engagements over North Vietnam. It was first flown

Although the F-4 was foisted on the RAF by political events, it went on to be the stalwart of the air force for more than 20 years. It was respected by its crews and foes alike for its exceptional weapon system, good performance and undeniable strength.

on 30 June 1967 and entered service in 1968. With 1397 examples manufactured, the F-4E was also the most numerous version and remains the subject of various upgrades for continued service.

The F-4E also served as the basis for the **Mitsubishi F-4EJ** dedicated interceptor built under licence in Japan, and for West Germany's **F-4F**. The F-4EJ, of

SPECIFICATION

McDonnell Douglas F-4E Phantom II
Type: two-seat multi-role fighter
Powerplant: two General Electric J79-GE-17A turbojets each rated at 52.53 kN (11,810 lb st) dry and 79.62 kN (17,900 lb st) with afterburning
Performance: maximum level speed 'clean' at 10,975 m (36,000 ft) 2390 km/h (1,485 mph); maximum initial climb rate 18,715 m (61,400 ft) per minute; service ceiling 18,975 m (62,250 ft);

area interception combat radius 1266 km (786 miles)
Weights: basic empty 13,757 kg (30,328 lb); maximum take-off 28,030 kg (61,795 lb)
Dimensions: wing span 11.71 m (38 ft 5 in); length 19.2 m (63 ft); height 5.02 m (16 ft 5½ in); wing area 49.24 m² (530 sq ft)
Armament: one M61 20-mm cannon, plus maximum ordnance load of 7258 kg (16,000 lb)

which 140 were completed, lacked ground-attack capability and, as delivered, inflight-refuelling capability. The F-4F was originally intended to be a lightweight single-seat version of the F-4E, but emerged as a very similar machine.

Deliveries amounted to 175 aircraft. Both the F-4EJ and the F-4F have been subject to upgrade.

Photo Phantoms

The reconnaissance version of the Phantom made its maiden flight when the first of two **YRF-4C** aircraft took off on 8 August 1963. The first production **RF-4C** soon followed. Production totalled 503 aircraft, in which optical, radar, electronic and IR recce equipment was housed in a modified nose. The RF-4C has a much revised avionics fit

and was exported to South Korea and Spain (as the **CR.12**).

Other F-4 variants included the **F-110A** (later **F-4C**) fighter/attack version based on the Navy's **F-4B** but for the USAF; the **EF-4C** redesignation of a number of F-4Cs following conversion to Wild Weasel configuration; the **F-4D** USAF production version; the **EF-4D** Wild Weasel conversion; the

RF-4E export tactical recce version; the JASDF's **RF-4EJ**; the USAF's **F-4G** Wild Weasel; the **F-4J(UK)** conversion of 15 ex-US Navy F-4J aircraft for the RAF and the **F-4K Phantom FG.Mk 1** revised version of the F-4J for the Royal Navy, and powered by Rolls-Royce Spey turbofans; and the **F-4M Phantom FGR.Mk 2** version of the F-4K for the RAF.

Northrop F-5 Freedom Fighter, Tiger II and T-38 Talon Light fighter and training aircraft

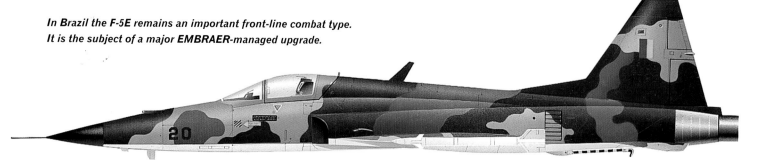

Canada designated its indigenous CF-5A aircraft the CF-116A in service. No. 434 Sqn was the first to receive the CF-116A, on 5 November 1968.

The first **F-5A Freedom Fighter** single-seat light-fighter prototype flew in May 1963 and went on to form the basis of a major warplane family. Canadair built **CF-5A/D** single- and two-

seat warplanes and **NF-5A/B** aircraft for the Canadian and Dutch air force respectively; the survivors of these later found a ready resale market to countries including Botswana, Turkey and

Venezuela. In addition, Iran, Morocco, the Philippines, Saudi Arabia, South Korea, Spain, Thailand, Turkey, Venezuela and Yemen all have first-generation F-5s on strength today. Venezuela's **VF-5A/D** aircraft have been the recipients of a limited upgrade by Singapore Technologies Aerospace.

Tiger II

The improved **F-5E/F Tiger II** was developed from the F-5A/B as an International Fighter Aircraft for sale to US allies. The F-5E prototype first flew in August 1972 and was followed by 1300 production F-5Es and two-seat F-5Fs for sale to 20 air forces. The F-5E was also assembled under licence in

Taiwan and South Korea.

Tiger IIs remain in widespread service with Bahrain, Brazil, Chile, Honduras, Indonesia, Iran, Jordan, Kenya, Malaysia, Mexico, Saudi Arabia, Singapore, Switzerland, Taiwan, Thailand, Tunisia, the US Marine Corps, the US Navy and Yemen. Inevitably, a wide range of update programmes has become available.

Upgrades and Talons

These upgrades offer a mix of new avionics and structural refurbishment of the airframe. Chile operates F-5Es upgraded with Israeli assistance to **Tigre III** standard; their advanced avionics – including Elta 2032 radar and HOTAS controls – give

SPECIFICATION	
Northrop F-5E Tigre III **Type:** single-seat lightweight tactical fighter **Powerplant:** two General Electric J85-GE-21B turbojet engines each rated at 15.57 kN (3,500 lb st) dry and 22.24 kN (5,000 lb st) with afterburning **Performance:** maximum speed 1700 km/h (1,056 mph) at 10,975 m (36,000 ft); initial climb rate 10,455 m (34,300 ft) per minute; service ceiling 15,550 m	(51,800 ft); combat radius 1405 km (875 miles) with two AIM-9 AAMs and maximum fuel **Weights:** empty 4349 kg (9,558 lb); maximum take-off 11187 kg (24,664 lb) **Dimensions:** wing span 8.13 m (26 ft 8 in); length 14.45 m (47 ft 4¾ in) including probe; height 4.08 m (13 ft 4½ in); wing area 17.28 m² (186 sq ft) **Armament:** two 20-mm cannon in nose, plus up to 3175 kg (7,000 lb) of disposable stores

In Brazil the F-5E remains an important front-line combat type. It is the subject of a major EMBRAER-managed upgrade.

a level of combat capability matching that of F-16s. The FIAR Grifo F/X Plus multi-mode radar has been fitted to Singapore's **F-5S** aircraft and has also been selected for Brazil's F-5Es. US-based TCA has offered to remanufacture existing F-5s to

two-seat F-5F configuration in order to meet a projected need for cost-effective lead-in fighter trainers.

From the original **N-156** concept that led to the F-5 family, Northrop also developed the **T-38 Talon** tandem two-seat,

supersonic advanced trainer. Flown for the first time on 10 April 1959, the first of 10 **YT-38** prototypes was followed by 1187 **T-38A Talon** trainers. Conversion programmes have resulted in the **AT-38A** weapons trainer, **NT-38A** research aircraft,

DT-38A drone director and **QT-38A** drone, while upgraded aircraft are designated **T-38C**. The Talon remains a major USAF type with several hundred scheduled to undergo an upgrade programme for service into 2040.

Mikoyan-Gurevich MiG-21 'Fishbed' Second generation

This Soviet MiG-21MF 'Fishbed-J' flew with the 5th Frontal Aviation Army in the Kiev Military District in the 1973-74 period. It is armed with AA-2 'Atoll' AAMs and rocket pods underwing and carries a typical MiG-21-style drop tank on the centreline.

The first of the new generation was the MiG-21R 'Fishbed-H' reconnaissance aircraft. The **MiG-21S** was a fighter based on the MiG-21R, but with RP-22 radar and a ventral GP-9 cannon pod. It was followed by the **MiG-21SM** with the 63.66-kN (14,307-lb) thrust R-13-300 and GSh-23L cannon recessed into the belly. The **MiG-21M** was an export version of the MiG-21SM with the older R-11F2S-300 engine: this variant was also built under licence in India. The **MiG-21MF 'Fishbed-J'** was a MiG-21M derivative for Soviet use with the R-13-300 engine, RP-22 radar and AAM capability on all four underwing pylons. The **MiG-21MT** introduced the more powerful R-13F-300 engine, but only 15 examples were built.

The **MiG-21SMT 'Fishbed-K'** was fitted with a huge dorsal spine, but this reduced stability so much that the aircraft's fuel capacity had to be reduced by 50 per cent.

Third-generation

The third-generation **MiG-21bis** was the most advanced variant to enter production, but was notable for its lack of BVR missile capability, limited radar

range, mediocre low-speed handling and poor endurance. The MiG-21bis was developed as a multi-role fighter for Frontal Aviation, with better close combat capability through improved avionics, the ability to carry the new R-60 AAM, and enhanced ground-attack capability. Other features of the MiG-21bis included the improved Sapfir-21 radar, the R-25-300 engine, and a completely redesigned dorsal spine which looks little different from that fitted to most second-generation 'Fishbeds', but holds almost as much fuel as the huge spine of the MiG-21SMT.

The **MiG-21bis 'Fishbed-L'** entered service in February 1972, while the reporting name **'Fishbed-N'** was applied to later

The last of Hungary's final 12 MiG-21bis air-defence aircraft was retired in September 2000.

aircraft with undernose 'Swift Rod' ILS antennas and improved avionics. 'Fishbed-N' was built under licence in India between 1980 and 1987. Another version of the MiG-21bis was optimized for the nuclear strike role. In 2003 the MiG-21bis continued in widespread service. It soon became apparent that the MiG-15UTI would be inadequate for MiG-21 conversion training. MiG

accordingly developed a scheme for a two-seater trainer based on the MiG-21F-13. The new trainer first flew on 17 October 1960, and it entered production as the **MiG-21U 'Mongol-A'**.

Early production aircraft had the original narrow-chord fin, while the **MiG-21US 'Mongol-B'** introduced the broader-chord fin

SPECIFICATION	
Mikoyan-Gurevich MiG-21bis 'Fishbed-L' **Type:** single-seat multi-role tactical fighter **Powerplant:** one MNPK 'Soyuz' (Tumanskii) R-25-300 turbojet engine rated at 40.2 kN (9,038 lb st) dry and 69.65 kN (15,653 lb st) with afterburning **Performance:** maximum speed 2230 km/h (1,386 mph) or Mach 2.1 at 13,000 m (42,650 ft); initial climb rate 11,700 m (38,385 ft) per minute with two missiles and 50 per cent fuel; service ceiling	17,500 m (57,415 ft); range 1470 km (913 miles) with two AAMs and one drop tank **Weights:** empty 5895 kg (12,996 lb); maximum take-off 10,420 kg (22,972 lb) **Dimensions:** wing span 7.15 m (23 ft 5¾ in); length 14.7 m (48 ft 2¾ in); height 4.13 m (13 ft 6¼ in); wing area 23 m² (247.58 sq ft) **Armament:** one 23-mm Gryazev-Shipunov GSh-23L fixed forward-firing twin-barrelled cannon in lower fuselage, plus up to 1500 kg (3,307 lb) of disposable stores

MiG-21MF 'Fishbed-J'

Belonging to No. 7 'Battle Axes' Squadron of the Indian Air Force, this MiG-21MF made up part of the IAF's significant MiG force. Although No. 7 Squadron now flies the Mirage 2000, two other squadrons still operate the Mig-21MF, which was once the most numerous MiG-21 variant operated worldwide. Since its first deliveries, India has flown nearly 700 MiG-21s, either supplied from the Soviet Union or built by HAL (Hindustan Aeronautics Limited) at Nasik. The M, FL and U variants also continue to be operated.

Fin
The streamlined fairing at the top of the fin houses an RWR (radar warning receiver) which signals to the pilot if the MiG is caught in the beam of an enemy radar. Some MiG-21s also have IFF (identification friend or foe) aerials above the fin. Immediately above the rudder is a static wick, which disperses static electricity, and the white tail navigation light which faces aft. The top of the fin is made of glassfibre dielectric material so that radio aerials can be housed in it.

Powerplant
The MiG-21MF is equipped with the Tumanskii R-13-300 afterburning turbojet engine, which was designed to be easily interchangeable with the earlier R-11 in the MiG-21. The compressor was redesigned to give a higher work rate and greater airflow, and the HP (high-pressure) spool was given five stages, giving a substantial increase in ratings to 39.92 kN (8,972 lb st) and 63.66 kN (14,037 lb st) with maximum afterburner. These advances were accompanied by almost unchanged fuel consumption, such was the increased efficiency of the compressor and afterburner. The use of titanium instead of steel in many larger engine components meant that there was a significant reduction in engine weight.

Airbrakes and wheelbrakes
Twin forward airbrakes open out and down diagonally, under the thrust of hydraulic rams, to slow the aircraft. A third airbrake is mounted further aft. Opening the airbrakes causes no change in aircraft trim. The rear airbrake, on the centreline, is bulged and perforated. Like the two forward ones, it opens forward against the airflow under the force of a hydraulic jack. A circular canopy braking parachute, housed below the rudder, can supplement the wheel brakes upon landing, whereupon twin pointed doors open to eject the canopy. The parachute is normally used to reduce wear on the expensive wheel brakes.

Before its break-up, Yugoslavia had long been a major user of the MiG-21, taking delivery of variants from all three generations of the type. After the break-up, Croatia remained the only one of the former republics to fly the aircraft; it is believed to have initially operated two dozen MiG-21 fighters, which flew combat missions over the Krajina region during 1995 (one was shot down during a raid on the Bosanska Gradiska road bridge in May 1995). A possible 1998 deal for an Elbit upgrade package would seem to have come to nothing, following the 2002 signing of a deal with Aerostar which has included the purchase of more airframes.

The large number of MiG-21s used by India includes 580 built or assembled by HAL. Variants used have included the MiG-21F, MiG-21FL, MiG-21PFMA, MiG-21M, MiG-21MF, MiG-21U/UM and MiG-21bis (illustrated). In 2001 the latter were in the early stages of an upgrade programme, two MiG-21bis-UPG prototypes having flown, with the programme continuing into 2003.

Radome
The conical centrebody of the engine inlet is mounted on rails and can be slid in and out hydraulically to three positions: retracted (normal), part extended (Mach 1.5+) and fully extended (Mach 1.9+). Inside is the R2L 'Jay Bird' radar. This radar suite is not sophisticated enough to guide the AA-7 AAM, but it does provide a target-illuminating function for the AA-2-2 Advanced 'Atoll' semi-active radar-homing missile which cannot be carried by earlier MiG-21 models.

Fuselage
One of the features introduced to the MiG-21MF was a pair of aerodynamic fences which were added below the auxiliary inlets to prevent disturbance when the gun is fired. The fences force the airflow to remain smooth-flowing despite the sudden cloud of hot gas generated by the gun immediately below. Further aft, under the wing, is a large hinged door that covers the retracted main landing gear. The door is bulged to accommodate the large 800-mm (31½-in) diameter tyres, larger than those fitted to early MiG-21 versions. These tyres enable the heavier versions of the aircraft to operate from unpaved airstrips.

Armament
Indian MiG-21MFs were equipped to carry a wide range of weaponry, reflecting their multi-role capability. For air-to-air combat, the Indian Air Force uses the Soviet K-13A ('Atoll') and R-60 ('Aphid'), as well as the French Matra R550 Magic, as shown here. Most MiG-21 fighters are armed with the GSh-23L cannon, with a pair of 23-mm calibre barrels, recessed into the bottom of the fuselage. For close support, MiG-21s can carry many types of rocket launchers. The most common is the Soviet UV-16-57 as shown here, which incorporates tubes for 16 rockets, each of 57-mm (2.24-in) calibre. Other configurations for the MiG-21MF include the carriage of the R3S or RS-2US AAM and FAB 250, or 500, free-fall bombs.

East Germany was once a major operator of the MiG-21 – more than 200 aircraft served with three regiments based at Cottbus, Drewitz and Marxwalde. With the end of the Cold War and the reunification of Germany, the Luftwaffe inherited a number of MiG-21s from the former East German air force. Unlike their newer counterparts such as the MiG-29 and Su-22, however, the type was soon retired and most were scrapped.

Mikoyan-Gurevich MiG-23 'Flogger'
Variable-geometry interceptor

Above: Libya retained a sizeable fleet of 'Flogger' variants in 2003. This aircraft is a MiG-23MS 'Flogger-E'.

Right: Hungary withdrew its MiG-23MF force in 1997. Here one of the machines is shown with potential air-to-air and air-to-ground weapons, including Kh-23 and R-23.

Development of the MiG-23 'Flogger' began during the early 1960s as a replacement for the MiG-21. Two concepts were explored: the **Model 23-01** had a fixed wing and two dedicated lift engines, while the **Model 23-11** had a variable-geometry wing and just one engine. The Model 23-11 made its maiden flight on 10 April 1967, and was

Poland's MiG-23MFs were retired in September 1999. The aircraft will be replaced by F-16s.

later ordered into production as the **MiG-23S**. Fifty were built for operational trials before production switched to the **MiG-23M 'Flogger-B'**.

This featured Sapfir-23 pulse-Doppler radar and R-23 'Apex' AAMs and new avionics. The new 122.63-kN (27,557-lb st) R-29-300 engine was also fitted. The downgraded **MiG-23MS 'Flogger-E'** and **MiG-23MF 'Flogger-B'** were built for export.

The **MiG-23ML 'Flogger-G'** was revised for improved handling, with more power

coming from the R-35-300 engine. The very similar **MiG-23P** interceptor could be automatically steered onto its target from the ground.

'Flogger-K'

The MiG-23ML also served as the basis for the **MiG-23MLD 'Flogger-K'**, reportedly produced as MiG-23ML conversions

with greater manoeuvrability. Further changes included swivelling pylons under the outboard wing panels.

The **MiG-23UB 'Flogger-C'** tandem two-seat trainer prototype made its maiden flight in May 1969. Although it lacked radar, the MiG-23UB was always supposed to be used for both pilot conversion and weapons training: a separate guidance and illuminator pod for the

'Apex' was therefore fitted in a conical fairing on the starboard wing root. Production aircraft all had wing slats, and the two tandem cockpits were covered by separate upward-hinging canopies.

All MiG-23 operators use the MiG-23UB, and the type, which was phased out of production at Irkutsk in 1978, also served with many Soviet MiG-29 and Su-27 units.

SPECIFICATION	
Mikoyan-Gurevich MiG-23ML 'Flogger-G' **Type:** single-seat multi-role tactical fighter **Powerplant:** one MNPK 'Soyuz' (Tumanskii/Khachaturov) R-35-300 turbojet engine rated at 83.88 kN (18,849 lb st) dry and 127.48 kN (28,660 lb st) with afterburning **Performance:** maximum speed 2500 km/h (1,553 mph) or Mach 2.35 at 11,000 m (36,090 ft); service ceiling 18,500 m (60,695 ft); range 1960 km (1,212 miles) with internal fuel	**Weights:** empty 8200 kg (18,078 lb); maximum take-off 17,800 kg (39,242 lb) **Dimensions:** wing span 13.97 m (45 ft 9¾ in) spread and 7.78 m (25 ft 6½ in); length 16.7 m (54 ft 9½ in) including probe; height 4.82 m (15 ft 9¾ in); wing area 37.35 m² (402.05 sq ft) spread and 34.16 m² (367.71 sq ft) swept **Armament:** one 23-mm Gryazev-Shipunov GSh-23L twin-barrelled cannon in a ventral pack; up to 3000 kg (6,614 lb) of disposable stores

Mikoyan MiG-25 'Foxbat' Interceptor

Development of this Mach 3-capable interceptor was initiated in 1958, in order to counter the threat posed by the B-58A (development was later spurred by the emergence of the XB-70 and A-12 programmes). From the outset, the aircraft was intended to meet requirements for interceptor, strategic reconnaissance and strike versions (the latter was originally to be armed with an air-launched ballistic missile).

The Ye-155P prototype interceptor's first flight was in September 1964, six months

after that of the recce-configured Ye-155R. Both aircraft incorporated a number of radical features in order to allow prolonged high-speed high-altitude operations, and their construction, although mainly of welded steel, included eight per cent heat-resistant titanium alloy.

Seven Ye-155P development prototypes were followed by the **MiG-25P ('Foxbat-A')**, which became operational in 1973, equipped with the Smerch-A1 radar (with a limited look-down capability) and fire-control system and four R-40 (AA-6 'Acrid')

The MiG-25PD's Sapfir-25 radar was almost certainly developed from the MiG-23ML's Sapfir-23 set. This radar introduced a true look-down/shoot-down capability and an improved 115-km (71-mile) detection range.

SPECIFICATION	
MiG-25PD 'Foxbat-E' **Type:** all-weather interceptor **Powerplant:** two Tumanskii R-15BD-300 turbojets rated at 11,200 kg (24,691 lb) thrust with afterburning **Performance:** maximum speed limited to 3000 km/h (1,864 mph); maximum speed at sea level 1300 km/h (808 mph); climb to 20,000 m (65,617 ft) in 8.9 minutes; service ceiling 20,700 m	(67,915 ft); range with external fuel tank 2400 km (1,491 miles) **Weights:** empty 20020 kg (44,136 lb); maximum take-off 36,720 kg (80,952 lb) **Dimensions:** span 14.02 m (45 ft 11¾ in); length 21.67 m (71 ft 1 in); wing area 61.40 m² (660.9 sq ft) **Armament:** four R-40TD/RD (AA-6 'Acrid') AAMs, or two R-40TD/RD and four R-60 (AA-8 'Aphid') AAMs

AAMs. A typical load comprised a pair of IR-guided R-40Ts and a pair of radar-guided R-40Rs. Despite its interim radar, the MiG-25P version was built in the greatest numbers (around 600) and was exported to Algeria (20), Iraq (20), Libya (65) and Syria (30). According to the PVO, the MiG-25P's weapons system was capable of engaging the SR-71A, but orders were never given to fire upon these aircraft.

In 1978 production switched to the **MiG-25PD ('Foxbat-E')**

with uprated R-15BD engines, and a retractable inflight refuelling probe on some aircraft. This variant also incorporated a new Sapfir-25 pulse-Doppler radar with improved look-down capability and IRST, and added R-60 (AA-8 'Aphid') and upgraded R-40TD/RD AAM capability. In 1990, 27 of these remained operational in Ukraine. Export interceptors were known as the MiG-25PD, but they were much closer to the MiG-25P, with Smerch radar, although they did have provision for the R-60 dogfight AAM. Between 1979 and 1984 around 370 Soviet MiG-25Ps were upgraded to PD standard, receiving the designation **MiG-25PDS**. Developed from 1968, the **MiG-25PU ('Foxbat-C')**, was an unarmed pilot trainer with a new front cockpit for an instructor, and the radar deleted. Underwing pylons were retained for dummy AAMs.

The late production MiG-25P introduced the definitive R-15BD-300 turbojet engine.

Atlas Cheetah South African Mirage III upgrade

This Cheetah C served with No. 2 Sqn at AFB Louis Trichardt during the late 1990s. Note the aircraft's large nose radome and Kfir-style undercarriage.

A November 1977 UN weapons embargo forced the South African Air Force (SAAF) to place a high priority on a midlife upgrade of its surviving Mirage III fighters and related types. The upgrade was revealed on 16 July 1986 with the unveiling of a two-seat Mirage IIID2Z converted to the new **Atlas Cheetah** standard that benefited from Israeli technology and closely resembled the Kfir.

Aerodynamic modifications include Kfir-type small nose side-strakes, dog-toothed outboard leading-edge extensions, short fences replacing leading-edge slots, canard foreplanes, and fixed droop on the wing leading edges. The converted two-seaters also have curved strakes below the cockpit along the lower fuselage.

The conversions from two-seat and Mirage IIIR2Z standards are powered by Atar 9K50 turbojets, for which Atlas had a manufacturing licence. Other conversions retain the original Atar 9C or 9D turbojets. Another improvement was the addition of an inflight-refuelling probe, which permits take-off with a lower fuel load and a correspondingly higher warload.

Cheetah systems

Performance improvements include reductions in take-off distance, minimum speed and climb, and sustained turn rate. The avionics upgrade allows the HUD, computer terminal unit and armament control and display panel to function via a MIL-1553B databus, and facilitates for pre-flight programming and HOTAS operation. The nav/ attack system includes an INS and options include a helmet-mounted sight (of indigenous or Israeli origin) and a radar altimeter. The Kfir-type drooped nose houses an ELM-2001B radar ranging unit. Like the Kfir, the Cheetah features a fuselage plug ahead of the windscreen designed to accommodate the extra avionics.

SPECIFICATION

Atlas Cheetah C
Type: single-seat multi-role fighter
Powerplant: one SNECMA Atar 9K50 turbojet engine rated at 49.03 kN (11,023 lb st) dry and 70.61 kN (15,873 lb st) with afterburning
Performance: maximum speed 2338 km/h (1,453 mph) or Mach 2.2 at 12,000 m (39,370 ft); maximum cruising speed 956 km/h (594 mph) at 11,000 m (36,090 ft); service ceiling 17,000 m (55,775 ft)
Dimensions: wing span 8.22 m (26 ft 11¾ in); length 15.65 m (51 ft 4¼ in) including probe; height 4.55 m (14 ft 11¼ in); wing area 34.8 m² (374.6 sq ft)
Armament: two 30-mm fixed forward-firing cannon and up to 4000 kg (8,818 lb) of disposable stores carried externally

---

The Cheetah's fixed armament comprises two 30-mm DEFA cannon. Other weapons include many of South African manufacture, such as the the V3B Kukri/V3C Darter dogfight missile. Ordnance is carried on the hardpoints the Cheetah inherited from the Mirage III, supplemented by two hardpoints (like those of the Kfir-C7) fitted directly ahead of the wing/engine inlet trunking.

Cheetah conversions

The first Cheetah conversions comprised eight Mirage IIID2Z trainers adapted to two-seat **Cheetah D** standard. These were declared operational in 1987 as trainers with a possible first-line role as pathfinders for **Cheetah E** single-seaters. The

SAAF had a total of 16 Mirage IIIDZ and D2Z two-seaters available for conversion; however, at least another four aircraft have been produced as conversions from two-seat Mirage IIIs secured from an undisclosed source, but possibly from Israeli stocks.

Cheetah D also differs from the Cheetah E in having a longer nose, like that of the Kfir-T, with more pronounced droop and accommodating avionics displaced from the spine. An undernose fairing to the rear of the pitot boom contains two radar warning antennas and a large cooling intake.

Cheetah E was the original single-seat version of the family, and more than 26 such aircraft were produced as conversions from 21 SAAF Mirage III aircraft, as well as at least five machines secured from an undisclosed source. The aircraft apparently retain their original engines, and the Mirage IIIRZ and Mirage IIIR2Z conversions retained

No. 2 Squadron decorated this Cheetah C to celebrate the 75th anniversary of the SAAF. The aircraft was soon nicknamed 'Spotty' by SAAF personnel.

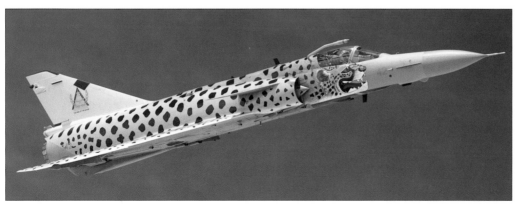

their original photo-recce nose configurations. Cheetah E has been phased out of service, leaving the Atar 9k950-engined **Cheetah C** as the SAAF's primary single-seat warplane. The aircraft most likely has an Elta EL/M-2032 radar with full air-to-air capability. The type will continue to serve alongside Cheetah D until both are replaced by Saab Gripens.

IAI Kfir Upgraded Kfirs

Ecuador's Kfir-C2 (illustrated) and TC2 fleet have been the subject of an IAI upgrade which adds Elta 2034 radar, other new avionics, HOTAS controls, a pair of colour cockpit display screens and provision for Python 4 AAMs. The upgraded aircraft fly in the attack role alongside Jaguar ES warplanes.

Ecuador received its Kfirs in two batches from Israeli stocks. Along with the country's Mirage F1s, the Kfirs have notched up at least three kills against Peruvian aircraft.

With a large number of Kfirs remaining available for Israeli service and with several exported, a clear need for upgrade packages emerged. While the use of radar-nosed Kfirs by Israel is unlikely, later upgrades to Ecuadorian Kfirs added Elta 2034-5 radar to produce the **Kfir CE** to a standard known by IAI as **Kfir 2000**.

During 1993, Israel began seeking export customers for its surplus Kfir-C2/C7s, and to this end IAI proposed a further upgrade as the **Kfir-C10**. This version includes a new cockpit fit, new radar in an enlarged radome, more external fuel and provision for an IFR probe. In 2004, the Kfir was in service with Colombia (C7 and TC7), Ecuador, Israel and Sri Lanka (C2, C7 and TC7). Israel has large numbers of Kfir-C7 and TC7 aircraft in storage and seems likely to retain the TC7 in active service.

Below: Sri Lanka uses its Kfir-C2 aircraft as interceptors, while the Kfir-C7 flies attack missions. Around eight C2s and two C7s were available in 2004.

Dassault Mirage III/5/50 Upgraded Mirage deltas

With a huge fleet of Mirage III/5/50 aircraft in service, the type has been a prime candidate for upgrade. In South America, Argentina has upgraded its **Mirage IIIEA** interceptors, while Brazil acquired 16 **Mirage IIIEBR** aircraft and, from 1988, six ex-French aircraft upgraded with foreplanes and new avionics, to which standard 10 older aircraft were raised. The machines are locally designated **F-103**.

More III upgrades

Four more countries chose extensive Mirage III update programmes, but that for Spain's Mirage IIIEE aircraft fell victim to funding cuts in 1992, and they were withdrawn. South Africa eventually upgraded its surviving Mirage IIIs to Cheetah standard. Switzerland received 36 **Mirage IIIS** and 18 **Mirage IIIRS** aircraft, which were later fitted with new avionics and canards. During its service, the Mirage IIIS was fitted with the Hughes TARAN 18 radar and navigation suite for compatibility with the Falcon AAM. Lastly, Venezuela bought seven Mirage IIIEVs, followed by Mirage 5s, all of which have been upgraded to **Mirage 50EV** configuration.

With Brazil's F-X new fighter competition bogged down in a mire of delay and the F-103E due for retirement in 2004, used fighters will have to be leased. These might well turn out to be upgraded Kfirs.

Mirage 5 and 50

Argentina received **Mirage 5P** interceptors in addition to IAI Daggers, and these aircraft have been updated with a laser rangefinder, HUD and IFR probe. Some 15 of Belgium's Mirage 5BA and five of its Mirage 5BD aircraft were being upgraded with HUD, laser rangefinder and canards when the type was retired in December 1993.

Chile then bought the aircraft as **Mirage 5MA/MD Elkan** warplanes. Chile also took delivery of the Mirage 50C and Mirage 50DC and, with IAI assistance, ENAER upgraded these to **Mirage 50CN Pantera** standard, with canards and Israeli avionics. Colombia received Mirage 5COA, 5COR and 5COD aircraft. IAI later converted the Mirage 5CODs with some Kfir avionics and 50 per cent canards, while the remainder of

the fleet was converted with 75 per cent canards to become **Mirage 50M** warplanes.

Egypt has completed a minor update programme on some of its Mirage 5s, while Pakistan's Mirage 5s have been upgraded with new avionics; aircraft in service in mid-2003 include various standard Mirage III models as well as **Mirage 5PA** interceptor and attack aircraft, plus **Mirage 5DPA** conversion trainers. Peru has upgraded its Mirage fleet with inflight refuelling probes and laser rangefinders. Its handful of aircraft probably

includes **Mirage 5P-IV** and **Mirage 5DP-IV** machines.

Venezuela has re-engined both single- and two-seat aircraft with the Atar 9K50 – raising their designation to **Mirage 50EV** and **Mirage 50DV** respectively – for service

alongside new-build aircraft of both variants and second-hand aircraft upgraded to Mirage 50EV standard. Features of the Venezuelan aircraft include canard foreplanes, an inflight refuelling probe, Cyrano IVM-3 radar and Exocet capability.

Switzerland's Mirage IIIRS aircraft boast an impressive RATO capability. Note the canards on this upgraded IIIRS. The type is due for retirement in 2006.

SPECIFICATION	
Dassault Mirage 50M	AAMs and three drop tanks
Type: single-seat multi-role fighter	**Weights:** empty 7150 kg (15,763 lb);
Powerplant: one SNECMA Atar	maximum take-off 14,700 kg
9K50 turbojet rated at 70.82 kN	(32,407 lb)
(15,873 lb st) with afterburning	**Dimensions:** wing span 8.22 m
Performance: maximum speed	(26 ft 11¾ in); length 15.55 m
2335 km/h (1,451 mph) at	(51 ft ¼ in); height 4.5 m
12,000 m (39,370 ft); initial climb	(14 ft 9 in); wing area 35 m²
rate 11,160 m (36,614 ft) per	(376.75 sq ft)
minute; service ceiling 18,000 m	**Armament:** two 30-mm DEFA 552A
(59,055 ft); combat radius 1315 km	cannon in the undersides of the
(817 miles) on a hi-hi-hi	inlets, plus up to 4000 kg (8,818 lb)
interception mission with two	of disposable stores

ADA Light Combat Aircraft (LCA)
Indigenous Indian fighter

Faced with Pakistan and China as potentially dangerous enemies, India maintains a large and effective air force. Since the time of India's defeat in skirmishes with Chinese forces in 1962, the Indian Air Force (IAF) has relied heavily on the Soviet Union as its major supplier of warplanes and ground equipment. By the early 1980s the most important of the Soviet-supplied warplanes, constituting more than 50 per cent of the IAF's strength, was the MiG-21 'Fishbed' in both Soviet-supplied and Indian licence-manufactured forms. This type was already obsolescent, however, and from 1981, in the face of Pakistani and Chinese efforts to modernize their air forces, the Indian defence ministry planned to start the process of acquiring a successor to the MiG-21.

Indigenous fighter

The course to proceed selected was based on the desire to exploit the country's developing aircraft design and production capabilities by creating an Indian solution to the IAF's needs. An indigenous design would also ensure full role optimization and reduce the flow of Indian financial resources out of the country. At the same time, India's dependence on imports from the increasingly troubled USSR would be diminished.

Clearance for the project was given in 1983 and in June 1984 the Aeronautical Development Agency (ADA) was established in Bangalore to undertake design for the project. The ADA grouping combined the Indian Gas Turbine Research Establishment and Hindustan Aeronautics Ltd, which were respectively allocated the tasks of developing an indigenous engine (the GTX-35VS Kaveri turbofan that was designed with the aid of the French company SNECMA) and of undertaking the actual production of the new fighter aircraft.

A feasibility study completed in 1985 envisaged the primary task of the **Light Combat Aircraft** (**LCA**) to be air superiority, with close support and interdiction as important secondary roles. Dassault was brought in to serve as consultant during the project definition phase, which extended from the spring of 1987 to late 1988.

This allowed the completion of the basic design by 1990, when the LCA was revealed as a lightweight, single-seat, all-weather, multi-role fighter of control-configured (negative stability) configuration. The aircraft has been optimized for key features such as agility, rapid acceleration, good field performance and the carriage of a weapons load more than double that of the MiG-21.

The LCA's airframe is based on an oval-section fuselage with a shoulder-set delta wing. All control surfaces are operated via a full quadruplex digital fly-by-wire control system, designed jointly by Lockheed Martin Electronics and the Indian Aeronautical Development Establishment.

Cockpit

The cockpit is equipped with HOTAS (Hands On Throttle And Stick) controls, a HUD and two Sextant Avionique colour multi-function CRTs compatible with night-vision goggles. These avionics are integrated with other elements of the electronic suite such as the INS via a central computer and three MIL STD 1553B databuses.

The LCA's sensors include a HAL/Electronics Research & Development Establishment multi-mode pulse-Doppler radar and a FLIR. The aircraft's RWR provides data for the in-built defensive system. The LCA's radar has had a troubled

India could not fly its LCA until 2001, despite assistance from American, French and Israeli manufacturers. The aircraft represents an ambitious attempt to develop and produce a next-generation combat aircraft by an industry more familiar with the licensed production of foreign designs.

development and was the subject of an Indian request for assistance from Israeli radar firms in March 1995.

Composite materials and advanced alloys such as aluminium-lithium alloys are used extensively throughout the LCA's airframe, keeping weight to a minimum. Composite materials amount to more than 30 per cent of the structure weight, and extensive use is made of CFRPs (carbon-fibre reinforced plastics) in the wings, control surfaces and vertical tail. Aluminium-lithium alloy is used in the rest of the airframe with the exception of hot areas near the engine, where titanium alloy is employed.

Fixed armament planned for the LCA comprises a Russian-sourced 23-mm GSh-23L twin-barrelled cannon, mounted internally and supplied with 220 rounds of ammunition. Stores may be carried on seven external hardpoints, one under the fuselage and three under each wing. Primary air-to-air armament comprises two beyond-visual-range weapons of unspecified type, and two short-range missiles, also of unspecified type, but which are most likely the highly manoeuvrable Vympel R-73 (AA-11 'Archer').

The LCA is to be powered by a single Kaveri turbofan. The Kaveri programme has suffered considerable delay, however, and 11 General Electric F404-GE-F2J3 turbofans were purchased from the United

SPECIFICATION
ADA Light Combat Aircraft **Type:** single-seat multi-role fighter **Powerplant:** (prototype) one General Electric F404-GE-F2J3 turbofan rated at 80.50-kN (18,097-lb) thrust with afterburning; production aircraft are to be fitted with one Kaveri GTX-35VS turbofan rated at 51.30-kN (11,533-lb) thrust dry and 80.20-kN (18,030-lb) thrust with afterburning **Performance:** maximum speed 1700 km/h (1,056 mph) or Mach 1.6 at high altitude; initial climb rate 12,000 m (39,370 ft) per	minute; service ceiling more than 15,250 m (50,035 ft) **Weights:** empty about 5500 kg (12,125 lb); maximum take-off 13,000 kg (28,660 lb) **Dimensions:** wing span 8.2 m (26 ft 10¾ in); length 13.2 m (43 ft 3¾ in); height 4.4 m (14 ft 5¼ in); wing area about 37.5 m² (403.66 sq ft) **Armament:** one 23-mm Gryazev-Shipunov GSh-23L fixed forward-firing twin-barrelled cannon, and more than 4000 kg (8,818 lb) of stores

States for installation in the prototypes and development aircraft. The aircraft's fixed geometry engine air intakes restrict its maximum speed to about Mach 1.6, but avoid extra design complexity.

An internal fuel capacity of 3000 litres (660 Imperial gallons) can be augmented by a fixed inflight-refuelling probe. The centreline hardpoint and two inner hardpoints under each wing are 'plumbed' for the carriage of external fuel tanks.

Programme progress

In November 1996 the first LCA prototype was rolled out, but development problems delayed its first flight until 4 January 2001. Such problems have continued and, although test flying was continuing at a slow rate in early 2004, no firm service date can be given, with HAL suggesting an entry into series production could be possible in 2007, while other sources claim an in-service date of between 2006 and as late as 2015.

The IAF has a requirement for some 200 such aircraft, but is also reported to have requested information of fighter purchases in the LCA class, while MiG-21 upgrading continues at a pace. Developments of the LCA are planned, including a two-seat model for operational conversion, weapons and continuation training roles. A maritime strike variant was also planned for use by the Indian naval air arm; however, the latter's recent purchase of the MiG-29K must now make the future of this variant somewhat unsure.

BAe Systems Hawk Mk 200 Single-seat multi-role fighter

The international success of the Hawk's two-seat models persuaded BAe to develop a single-seat variant which would attract new customers, particularly smaller air arms requiring a relatively cheap fighter and ground-attack aircraft. The resulting **British Aerospace** (now **BAe Systems**) **Hawk Mk 200** is far more cost-effective in the long term, when compared to the short-term option of continual refurbishment of older aircraft. Moreover, a single-seat type is more practical and desirable in some respects, not least because there is simply not a ready pool of trained navigators to occupy second seats.

In redesigning the Hawk's forward fuselage to accommodate a single cockpit, BAe also provided the volume for the incorporation, to customer requirement, of a modern radar and, under the cockpit floor, an inbuilt pair of 25-mm ADEN cannon that represents a significant increase

in combat capability. The provision of seven hardpoints (including wing-tip AAM launchers) enables the carriage of up to 3000 kg (6,614 lb) of stores, the same as the load of the Hawk Mk 100. Constructed of conventional aluminium alloy and having about 80 per cent commonality with the two-seat models, the Hawk Mk 200 is also powered by a single Adour Mk 871 turbofan. Even with

Above: Malaysia's Hawk Mk 203s feature Northrop Grumman AN/APG-66H radar, wing-tip Sidewinder launch rails, tail-mounted RWR and a removable refuelling probe.

Here, a Malaysian Hawk Mk 208 shows off the type's unusual wing planform when the wing-tip missile rails are fitted.

SPECIFICATION	
BAE Systems Hawk Mk 200 **Type:** single-seat air superiority and ground-attack warplane **Powerplant:** one Rolls-Royce/ Turboméca Adour Mk 871 turbofan engine rated at 26 kN (5,845 lb st) **Performance:** maximum speed 1017 km/h (632 mph) at sea level; cruising speed 796 km/h (495 mph) at 12,495 m (41,000 ft); initial climb rate 3508 m (11,510 ft) per minute; service ceiling 13,715 m (45,000 ft); range 3610 km (2,244 miles) with three drop tanks; radius 945 km (587 miles) on a hi-lo-hi mission	with a 1361-kg (3,000-lb) warload **Weights:** empty 4450 kg (9,810 lb); maximum take-off 9100 kg (20,061 lb) **Dimensions:** wing span 9.39 m (30 ft 9¾ in) with normal tips or 9.93 m (32 ft 7 in) with missile-carrying tips; length 11.33 m (37 ft 2 in) excluding probe; height 4.16 m (13 ft 8 in); wing area 16.69 m² (179.6 sq ft) **Armament:** two 25-mm ADEN fixed forward-firing cannon in the lower part of the forward fuselage, plus up to 3000 kg (6,614 lb) of disposable stores carried externally

In 1990 Oman (illustrated) became the Hawk Mk 200 launch customer, followed since by Malaysia, Indonesia and Saudi Arabia.

additional equipment to tailor it for a multi-mission combat task, the aircraft has a maximum take-off weight of less than 9527 kg (21,000 lb).

Multi-mode radar

The Northrop Grumman APG-66H radar is a multi-mode equipment modified from that which was fitted in the Lockheed Martin F-16. With the pilot's seat set farther aft than the forward position of other Hawks, the pilot faces a main instrument panel which includes a comms/navigation integration panel, HUD, multi- function CRT display, radar display configured for the most modern symbology, and a RHAW receiver.

On 19 May 1986, the Hawk Mk 200 demonstrator made its maiden flight; it was later lost in an accident. The second Hawk Mk 200 flew on 24 April 1987 and, unlike the first aircraft, was fitted with full avionics but no radar and, later, a number of small but significant airframe revisions were made.

To counteract any tendency for the tailplane of the Hawk Mk 200 to stall, a condition which was belatedly revealed on the trainer in 1975, the aircraft eventually received the fuselage-mounted tailplane vanes, or SMURFs (side-mounted under root fins), that were developed for the US Navy's T-45 Goshawk trainer. These vanes throw a vortex over the tailplane to prevent undue travel caused by downwash from the flaps when the aircraft is in the low-speed configuration. In addition, an RWR was fitted to the fin leading edge, and the rear fuselage brake chute 'box' was deepened to house a chaff/flare

Issues surrounding alleged violations of human rights surrounded Indonesia's Hawk Mk 209 order.

dispenser and rearward-facing RWR antenna. The first APG-66 equipped **Hawk 200RDA (Radar Development Aircraft)** flew on 13 February 1992.

Customers

The country of Oman became the launch customer for the Hawk Mk 200 when it ordered 12 **Hawk Mk 203** aircraft

on 31 July 1990, primarily as replacements for its ageing Hawker Hunters. Malaysia followed on 10 December 1990 with an order for 18 **Hawk Mk 208** aircraft. It was at one time thought that Saudi Arabia's Al Yamamah II order might have included an unconfirmed number of APG-66H equipped **Hawk Mk 205** machines within

an overall buy of approximately 60 Hawks, but no such aircraft has been built.

The Indonesian Hawk purchase of June 1993 combined both Hawk Mk 109 two-seaters and **Hawk Mk 209** single-seat machines, the order for the latter eventually being finalised as 32 aircraft, of which 30 were in service in 2004.

Mikoyan-Gurevich MiG-21 'Fishbed'
Lancer and other upgrades

Above: This Lancer A is armed with a pair of Opher IR-guided bombs and Python III AAMs.

Right: The 25 Lancer C air-defence versions represent the ultimate evolution of the upgraded MiG-21 in Romanian service, and are capable of carrying both Russian R-73 and Israeli Python III AAMs.

Below: The ten Romanian Lancer Bs (ex-MiG-21UM/US aircraft) have a secondary combat role and frontline standard defensive aids.

The MiG-21 is the world's most widely produced jet fighter, and it continued to serve in 2003 in significant numbers with in excess of 30 air arms. The market for upgrades is therefore substantial. Many of the proposed retrofit programmes for the MiG-21, promoted by companies such as Elbit, IAI and MiG-MAPO, are applicable mainly to late variants.

The most comprehensive recent upgrade that has been applied in quantity concerns 100 single-seat MiG-21MF and 10 twin-seat MiG-21UM/US Romanian aircraft. These underwent extensive systems and digital avionics modernization by a combined Aerostar/Elbit team. Procurement comprises **Lancer A** dedicated ground-attack aircraft, two-seat **Lancer B** conversion trainers and **Lancer C** dedicated interceptors.

New equipment includes Elta EL/M-2032 multi-mode radar for Lancer Cs and EL/M-2001B ranging radar for Lancer A/Bs, DASH helmet sights, Litening targeting pods, advanced cockpit displays and a comprehensive EW suite. Aerostar and Elbit are offering the **Lancer III** upgrade for MiG-21bis customers.

Indian upgrade

The Indian air force has been by far the largest export MiG-21 customer, having received nearly 1000 aircraft, more than 700 of which were built under licence by HAL. India's air force susbesequently has a pressing requirement to upgrade its massive MiG-21bis fleet pending the arrival of the much-delayed indigenously developed Light Combat Aircraft. India selected MiG MAPO's **MiG-21-93**

The MiG-21-93 is being produced in India as the MiG-21I. The programme has been severely delayed, however, by problems on both the Russian and Indian sides of the deal.

programme in 1994, and the first upgraded aircraft made its maiden flight in October 1998. Continuing delays, however, meant that the first 12 **MiG-21I** aircraft did not become operational until late 2002.

At the heart of the upgrade is a Kopyo multi-mode radar. Developed from the Zhuk radar installed in the MiG-29M fighter, Kopyo is compatible with BVR weapons including R-27RI SARH

and RVV-AE (R-77) active-radar missiles, as well as PGMs such as the kh-31P and kh-25MP high-speed anti-radar missiles, kh-31A and kh-35 anti-ship missiles and KAB-500 Kr television-guided bombs.

Several Western avionics systems have been incorporated on Indian MiG-21-93s, including a ring laser-gyro INS with satellite correction, and a lightweight RWR.

SPECIFICATION	
Mikoyan-Gurevich MiG-21MF Lancer A **Type:** single-seat multi-role tactical fighter **Powerplant:** one MNPK 'Soyuz' R-13-300 turbojet rated at 39.92 kN (8,972 lb st) dry and 63.66 kN (14,307 lb st) with afterburning **Performance:** maximum level speed 'clean' 2178 km/h (1,353 mph) at 11,000 m (36,090 ft); maximum initial climb rate 7200 m (23,622 ft) per minute; service ceiling 18,200 m (59,711 ft); combat radius 370 km (230 miles) on a hi-lo-hi attack	mission with four 250-kg (551-lb) bombs and centreline tank **Weights:** empty 5843 kg (12,880 lb); maximum take-off 9400 kg (20,723 lb) **Dimensions:** wing span 7.15 m (23 ft 5¾ in); length 14.7 m (48 ft 2¾ in); height 4.13 m (13 ft 6¼ in); wing area 23 m² (247.58 sq ft) **Armament:** one 23-mm Gryazev-Shipunov GSh-23L two-barrel cannon; maximum weapon load 2000 kg (4,409 lb); including Russian and Israeli ordnance

Mikoyan-Gurevich MiG-23 'Flogger' 'Flogger' survivors

The 'swing-wing' **MiG-23 'Flogger'** was developed in the 1960s to replace the MiG-21. It combined greater payload, range and firepower with BVR intercept capability from more powerful onboard sensors. The **Model 23-11** prototype first flew in 1967. The production **MiG-23M 'Flogger-B'** introduced BVR capability with Sapfir-23 ('High Lark') pulse-Doppler radar and R-23 (AA-7 'Apex') semi-active air-to-air missiles.

Later variants

Two downgraded export versions of the MiG-23M were produced, while the **MiG-23ML 'Flogger-G'** was intended to have improved handling especially at high angles of attack, enhanced manoeuvrability and higher 'g' limits. It featured a lightened airframe, a more powerful R-35-300 engine, improved, lightweight Sapfir-23L radar adding a new dogfight mode,

more capable defensive avionics and a new IRST. It formed the basis for the **MiG-23MLD 'Flogger-K'** that had a number of aerodynamic modifications to increase high angle-of-attack capability and controllability.

By 1999 the MiG-23 had been phased out of frontline service from Russian PVO interceptor and VVS units, and by 2003 it had also disappeared from reserve and training units. However, MiG-23 fighters remain in widespread service with export customers. The basic MiG-23M serves with the

Turkmenistan PVO and Cuba, while Algeria and Libya operate the MiG-23MS. MiG-23MFs serve with India and Romania, while MiG-23MLs may serve with Angola and almost certainly remain on strength in North Korea. A combination of MiG-23MF/ML/MS aircraft constitutes the backbone of the air defence forces of Syria. Bulgaria has operated a mix of MF/ML/MLD aircraft, but by 2003 may have only the MF still in service. MiG-23MLDs also equip fighter units in Belarus. The **MiG-23UB 'Flogger-C'** is

the two-seat trainer and operational conversion variant and remains active with all MiG-23 operators.

Upgrades

With a large fleet of MiG-23s in service worldwide, the type remains an attractive upgrade possibility. Phazotron offers a MiG-23 upgrade based around its N019M Topaz multimode radar compatible with R-77 BVR active radar AAMs. MiG offers **MiG-23-98**, which has much in common with the above and is based on the MiG-23MLD.

In 1982, Bulgaria received the MiG-23ML. It allowed Bulgarian pilots to engage targets head-on at BVR using AA-7 'Apex' radar-/IR-guided AAMs.

Mikoyan MiG-31 'Foxhound' MiG-25 evolution

The **MiG-31 'Foxhound-A'** was developed as part of an overall programme to provide Soviet air defences with the ability to meet the threat posed by NATO low-level strike aircraft and cruise missiles. The new interceptor

was the **Ye-155MP** development of the **Ye-155M** experimental development of the MiG-25, and was a two-seater featuring new landing gear with side-by-side nose wheels and offset tandem main wheels. New airbrakes were

fitted ahead of the landing gear. The wing planform was subtly changed, with small leading-edge root extensions and no wingtip anti-flutter weights.

The Ye-155MP made its maiden flight on 16 September

1975. Production of the MiG-31 began in 1979, the new designation having been adopted to acknowledge that this was a new aircraft with new capabilities, and the type entered service during 1982 incorporating changes from prototype standard that included refined leading-edge slats and relocated airbrakes.

MiG-31 radar

At the heart of the MiG-31 lies the N-007 Zaslon radar (ASCC/NATO) 'Flash Dance'. This uses a unique, fixed phased-array antenna, which points its beam electronically. Groups of four MiG-31s can operate together, with only the leader linked to the AK-RLDN ground-based automatic guidance network but joined to his wing men by datalink and covering a swathe of territory 900 km (560 miles) across. MiG-31 also has an IRST sensor.

Some improvements were added during the course of production of 280 aircraft, and later MiG-31s are fitted with a semi-retractable inflight-

In comparison to the MiG-25, the MiG-31 is strengthened for supersonic operations at low level and also has an increased fuel load.

refuelling probe, while the number of underwing pylons has been increased from two to four.

Improved MiG-31M

The **MiG-31M** (possibly **'Foxhound-B'**) was an improved interceptor variant built only in prototype form (eight aircraft). The variant features Zaslon-M radar, in a revised radome.

The radar can detect fighter-sized targets at a claimed range of 360 km (224 miles), and can control six simultaneous engagements. The new variant also has two additional underfuselage missile stations, increasing the total to six, but no internal cannon. It also has provision for a fixed IRST and laser rangefinder in a fairing below the nose. The first of the MiG-31Ms was delivered for flight trials in March 1984.

Other changes include a redesigned rear cockpit with three colour CRT displays. MiG-31M features a host of aerodynamic and structural refinements, which increase

maximum take-off weight to 52,000 kg (114,638 lb). Handling at high angles of attack has been improved and the aircraft reportedly features a new digital flight control system. It also has increased fuel capacity, smaller windows for the rear cockpit and a one-piece canopy and a new one-piece windscreen for the pilot.

Other variants

MiG-31D retained the original nose and had large winglets above and below the wingtips. This variant, of which only two were completed, was intended for the anti-satellite role. Other variants of the MiG-31 include

Although China, India and some other potential customers have been shown the downgraded MiG-31E, no orders have resulted.

the **MiG-31B** with enhanced radar, ECM and EW equipment, as well as upgraded R-33S missiles; **MiG-31BS** conversion from MiG-31 to MiG-31B standard; **MiG-31E** proposed export model with downgraded radar; **MiG-31F** proposed long-range fighter-bomber; **MiG-31BM** Wild Weasel version of the MiG-31B that reached the prototype stage; and **MiG-31FE** proposed export variant of the MiG-31BM.

SPECIFICATION	
Mikoyan MiG-31 'Foxhound-A' **Type:** two-seat long-range interceptor **Powerplant:** two PNPP Aviadvigatel (Soloviev) D-30F6 turbofans each rated at 93.19 kN (20,944 lb st) dry and 152.06 kN (34,171 lb st) with afterburning **Performance:** maximum speed 3000 km/h (1,865 mph) or Mach 2.83 at 17,500 m (57,400 ft); cruising speed 2500 km/h (1,553 mph) of Mach 2.35 at high altitude; climb to 10,000 m (32,810 ft) in 3 minutes; service ceiling 20,600 m (67,585 ft); combat radius 720 km	(447 miles) with standard fuel **Weights:** empty 21,825 kg (48,115 lb); maximum take-off 46,200 kg (191,851 lb) **Dimensions:** wing span 13.46 m (44 ft 2 in); length 22.69 m (74 ft 6 in); height 6.15 m (20 ft 2¼ in); wing area 61.6 m² (663.08 sq ft) **Armament:** one 23-mm Gryazev-Shipunov GSh-23-6M six-barrel cannon in the starboard lower side of fuselage; up to four R-33 (AA-9 'Amos') AAMs carried under fuselage and two R-60T (AA-6 'Acrid') plus four R-60 (AA-8 'Aphid') AAMs carried on four underwing hardpoints

Below: Had it not fallen foul of the crisis which followed the break-up of the Soviet Union, the MiG-31M would have been one of the world's finest interceptors.

McDonnell Douglas F-4 Phantom II Upgrades

With a large fleet of Phantoms in operation worldwide, the type is an obvious candidate for upgrading. Many companies offer upgrade packages for the aircraft and by early 2003 these had been taken up as follows.

Germany – F-4F ICE

Work started in 1983, by MBB (then Daimler Chrysler Aerospace, now part of EADS (European Aeronautic and Space Company), on a Kampfwertsteigerung (KWS) or **Improved Combat Effectiveness** (**ICE**) project aimed at conferring BVR lookdown/shoot-down capabilities to 110 air defence F-4Fs. A new, licence-built Hughes APG-65GY pulse-Doppler radar was installed and Hughes AIM-120 AMRAAMs supplemented the original IR-homing AIM-9 Sidewinder capability. For ground-attack roles, another 37 German F-4Fs received similar avionics and structural improvements, but retained the original radar. Initial deliveries were made in April 1992; the last example was redelivered during 1998. In service the aircraft are generally referred to by the designation **F-4F ICE**. They fly alongside MiG-29s and will eventually be replaced by the Eurofighter.

Greece – DASA F-4E

The Phantom is planned to serve in the Greek air force at least until 2015. Some 70 F-4Es are undergoing a Service-Life Extension Programme (SLEP) at Hellenic Aerospace Industries, while the air force is upgrading

the first two of 39 'SLEPed' F-4Es at DASA (now EADS) to a similar standard as the German air force F-4F ICE. Modernization (costing about US $8 million per aircraft), includes APG-65 radar, which is able to support AIM-120s. The remaining 37 F-4Es will undergo the modification at HAI. In the autumn of 1999 the first DASA Phantom was redelivered. Externally, the DASA F-4E can be identified by the small IFF antenna on top of the nose radome.

Israel – Kurnass 2000

In the mid-1980s, the IDF/AF instigated an ambitious programme to upgrade 130 of its original F-4E Kurnass (Heavy Hammer) and RF-4E aircraft to

Kurnass 2000, or **Phantom 2000**, standard for service into the next century. Airframe reinforcements were made to the fuselage and hydraulic and fuel systems were modified.

The core of the Phantom 2000 avionics package is Elbit's ACE-3 mission computer (which was developed for the IDF/AF's F-16s), integrated with a

This F-4EJ Kai was marked for the 10th anniversary of the 306th Hiko-tai in 1991. The F-4EJ Kai is slowly giving way to the F-15J, with which the 306th has now re-equipped.

Norden/UTC APG-76 synthetic-aperture multi-mode radar. Initial IDF/AF deliveries followed in 1989, although the new radar installations were not started until 1992. IAI planned a re-engined **Super Phantom 2000**, with 92-kN (20,600-lb st) thrust PW1120 turbofans, but no orders were won.

Iran – F-4D and F-4E

Local upgrading of the IRIAF's surviving Phantoms has improved the detection range of the radars of both F-4Ds and F-4Es, as well as added defensive countermeasures.

Several 'new' weapons have been integrated on the IRIAF F-4s, including the Chinese YJ-1/C-801 anti-ship missile, which was test-fired in 1997.

Photographs also depict Iranian Phantoms launching what appears to be a TV-guided missile, and carrying a Standard missile. The latter, in its AGM-78 form, is an anti-radar missile, but Iranian weapons may have

Below: The utility of Israel's Kurnass 2000 aircraft has been limited by the United Kingdom's reluctance to supply important spare parts for the type.

Mitsubishi/McDonnell Douglas RF-4EJ Kai Phantom II
Type: two-seat tactical reconnaissance aircraft
Powerplant: two General Electric J79-GE-17A turbojets each rated at 52.53 kN (11,810 lb st) dry and 79.62 kN (17,900 lb st) with afterburning
Performance: maximum level speed 'clean' at 10,975 m (36,000 ft) 2390 km/h (1,485 mph); maximum

climb rate at sea level 14,630 m (48,000 ft) per minute; service ceiling 18,105 m (59,400 ft); combat radius 1353 km (841 miles)
Weights: basic empty 12,826 kg (28,276 lb); maximum take-off 26,308 kg (58,000 lb)
Dimensions: wing span 11.71 m (38 ft 5 in); length 19.17 m (62 ft 11 in); height 5.03 m (16 ft 6 in); wing area 49.24 m² (530 sq ft)

been modified to have an air-to-air or air-to-ground role.

The IRIAF is expected to retain the Phantom in frontline service as long as it can be viably supported.

Japan – F-4 Kai

Around 90 RF-4E/F-4EJ Phantoms have been upgraded for continued JASDF service, the F-4EJs being redesignated **F-4EJ Kai**. Airframe life is extended to 5000 hours and the aircraft are fitted with an all-new avionics suite, including the APG-66J radar, with much improved look-down/shoot-down capability.

The F-4EJ Kai can be identified by its distinctive twin RWR fairings on the fin and wing tip, by a taller blade antenna for its AC-164 UHF and by small conducting strips on the radome.

The aircraft is compatible with the ASM-1 anti-ship missile, and some may be used in the maritime strike role. In addition, 13 RF-4Es have been similarly upgraded (with the exception of the radar) as **RF-4E Kai** aircraft. These examples serve alongside the **RF-4EJ Kai**, 17 of which were produced by conversion from F-4EJ standard. These have digital avionics, APQ-120 radar, retain their Vulcan cannon and carry a variety of podded sensors.

Spain – RF-4C SARA

'Have Quick' digital UHF/VHF communications radios, Itek AN/ARL-46 RWRs, Tracor AN/ALE-40 chaff/flare dispensers and AIM-9L Sidewinder AAM capability were standardized throughout the Spanish RF-4C Phantom II fleet in the late 1980s. In late 1996, the **SARA (Sistema Avanzado de Reconocimiento Aéreo)** upgrade programme was announced, including a Texas Instruments AN/APQ-172 terrain-following radar, ring laser-gyro INS and provision for an inflight-refuelling probe.

Turkey – 2020

In this two-part F-4E upgrade programme, structural upgrading is carried out, as is the fitting of a new avionics package, broadly based on that of the Phantom 2000. In 1996 IAI was selected to upgrade 26 F-4Es in Israel and supply kits for another 28 F-4Es, to be upgraded by the Turkish air force. In some respects, including its 'glass' cockpit displays, the THK Phantom upgrade is more advanced than the IDF/AF version, with an Elta Electronics EL/M-2032 radar developed for the IAI Lavi, instead of the Norden APG-76. The prototype of the so-called **Phantom 2020** flew on 11 February 1999, and initial deliveries of the aircraft commenced in 2000.

Germany's primary interceptor type will remain the F-4F ICE until some time after the first of the country's Eurofighters are delivered in the period 2003–2005. Belonging to the ETD.61 test unit, this F-4F ICE was engaged in AMRAAM trials at NAS Point Mugu, California, during 1992. Four AMRAAMs and four AIM-9s is the type's design AAM loadout.

McDonnell Douglas F-15 Eagle Air superiority fighter

The **F-15 Eagle** programme dates from 1965 when the USAF issued its FX requirement for a long-range tactical air superiority fighter to replace the F-4. Vietnam experience pointed towards the need for twin engines, two crew (eventually not adopted) and an internal gun. McDonnell Douglas won the competition to build the F-15 and initially produced 10 single-seat development **F-15A** and two **TF-15A** development aircraft. The first F-15 made its maiden flight on 27 July 1972. A total of 355 production F-15As was eventually built, together with 57 two-seat **F-15B** trainers.

The Eagle's large wings give a remarkably low wing loading and confer a surprising degree of agility, while the F-15A was delivered with an advanced and sophisticated avionics system, based around the APG-63 radar.

Driving the Eagle

The F-15 pilot sits high up and well forward under a large

Japan's F-15 fleet includes a number of specially finished F-15DJ 'Aggressor' aircraft. JASDF machines have an indigenous ECM system.

Some F-15A aircraft fly on with the Air National Guard in 2003, although this 128th TFS, 116th TFW machine is shown as it appeared with the Georgia ANG in the early 1990s.

blown canopy with excellent all-round view. The original cockpit was well laid out, but equipped only with analogue instruments. A HUD and a variety of control column- and throttle-mounted controls give true HOTAS operation of all important systems. The operational career of the Eagle began with the first delivery of an F-15A to TAC's 1st TFW at Langley AFB, VA, on 9 January 1976.

The first Eagles to see combat were blooded by Israel on 27 June 1979 when they claimed five Syrian MiG-21s. On 7 June 1981, Israeli Eagles escorted F-16 Fighting Falcons on the long-range strike against Iraq's Osirak nuclear reactor, and were heavily involved in the 1982 'turkey shoot' which took place over the Bekaa.

Further variants

During the 1980s, the F-15A was to have been the carrier aircraft for the ASAT (anti-satellite) weapon, although development of the latter was cancelled. In addition, the original Eagle two-seater was modified to become the SMTD (STOL/Maneuver Technology Demonstrator), equipped with two-dimensional Pratt & Whitney nozzles that could vector through 20 degrees up and down, and provide reverse thrust. The SMTD Eagle made its 138th and final flight on 12 August 1991.

In the 1990s, the USAF improved its F-15A/Bs through an ambitious MSIP (Multi-Stage Improvement Program). This followed a far more modest

These F-15C Eagles hail from the 199th Fighter Squadron of the Hawaii Air National Guard, based at Hickam AFB on Oahu.

MSIP of the early 1980s. The 1990s F-15A/B MSIP (carried out in conjunction with an F-15C/D MSIP) replaces the APG-63 with the more advanced APG-70 look-down/shoot-down radar and introduces new avionics and digital central computers.

F-15A/Bs emerging from MSIP differ from F-15C/D models only in lacking the latter's radar warning receiver antenna located next to the horizontal stabilizer and the 907 kg (2,000 lb) of extra fuel carried by the F-15C.

The **F-15C** followed the F-15A on the St Louis production line and made its first flight on 26 February 1979. The two-seat **F-15D** similarly succeeds the F-15B trainer. F-15C/Ds came off the production line with the improved, lightweight APG-63 X-band pulse-Doppler radar with reprogrammable signal processing, and with provision for 2389-litre (750-US gallon) CFTs (conformal fuel tanks) on the sides of the intakes.

Formerly known as FAST (fuel and sensor, tactical) packs, the CFTs cannot be jettisoned and the fuselage AIM-7 Sparrow AAM stations they displace are duplicated on the outside of the pack itself. CFTs have not been used operationally on USAF F-15C/Ds.

The F-15C was intended to be powered by the more powerful F100-PW-220 engine, although

SPECIFICATION

McDonnell Douglas F-15C Eagle
Type: single-seat air superiority fighter
Powerplant: two Pratt & Whitney F100-P-220 turbofans each rated at 65.26 kN (14,670 lb st) dry and 106 kN (23,830 lb st) with afterburning
Performance: maximum level speed 'clean' at 10,975 m (36,000 ft) over 2655 km/h (1,650 mph); maximum initial climb rate over 15,240 m (50,000 ft) per minute; service ceiling 18,290 m (60,000 ft); combat radius 1967 km (1,222 miles)

on an interception mission
Weights: operating empty 12,793 kg (28,600 lb); normal take-off 20,244 kg (44,630 lb) on an interception mission
Dimensions: wing span 13.05 m (42 ft 10 in); length 19.43 m (63 ft 9 in); height 5.63 m (18 ft 5½ in); wing area 56.48 m² (608 sq ft)
Armament: one M61 Vulcan 20-mm cannon with 940 rounds; maximum ordnance 7257 kg (16,000 lb), including AIM-120 AMRAAM, AIM-7M Sparrow and AIM-9M AAMs

---

early aircraft retained the -100. Initial F-15C deliveries were made in September 1979, the first F-15C victories coming when two Saudi aircraft shot down two Iranian F-4E Phantoms over the Persian Gulf on 5 June 1984.

During Operation Desert Storm, no F-15C/D Eagles were lost in scoring 32 aerial victories. Later, four AMRAAM kills

against Serb MiG-29s were scored during Operation Allied Force in 1999. The USAF's F-15s have undergone staged improvements into 2003, with advanced datalinks being added to some aircraft.

The F-15C/D has also been sold to Japan, **F-15J** (single seat) and **F-15DJ** aircraft being built under licence by Mitsubishi with some local avionics content.

Lockheed Martin F-16 Fighting Falcon
Air defence/interceptor aircraft

The **Lockheed Martin F-16A ADF (Air Defense Fighter) Block 15** was assigned to the air defence of North America during the last years of the Cold War. In October 1986 the US Air Force announced the conversion of 270 (later changed to 241) aircraft, consisting of 217 F-16As and 24 F-16Bs, to ADF standard.

The interceptor role had not been foreseen when the Fighting Falcon was developed, and the ADF conversion was centred primarily on upgrading the existing AN/APG-66 radar to improve small target detection and to provide continuous-wave illumination (thus giving the aircraft the ability to launch AIM-7 Sparrows).

Further modifications included a night identification light in the port forward fuselage, advanced IFF, high frequency, single side-band radio, improved ECCM and provision for GPS and AIM-120 AMRAAM missile datalink. The F-16 ADF is capable of carrying up to six AIM-7 or AIM-9 AAMs, and retains the internal 20-mm M61 cannon of the F-16A. Conversion of the F-16 ADFs was completed in early 1992 using General Dynamics-sourced modification kits.

Changes brought about by the collapse of the Soviet Union led to a wave of drastic military cuts throughout the US armed forces. Among the ranks of the USAF, the ADF-equipped squadrons were to suffer heavily as a result of these cuts. From an original frontline strength of 11 interceptor squadrons, by early 2004 the ADF equipped just two ANG fighter squadrons.

This F-16A ADF wears the markings of the 178th FS, 119th FG, North Dakota ANG.

Export ADFs

The resulting large quantities of surplus USAF ADF airframes have resulted in the aircraft being heavily marketed to foreign operators as an 'off-the-shelf' cheap alternative to new F/A-18 Hornets and MiG-29s.

First among the foreign operators to acquire the interceptor was Portugal. A total of 17 F-16As and three F-16Bs was delivered to ADF standard to 201 Esquadra under the Peace Atlantis programme. Intended originally for the air defence mission, they are armed with AIM-7Fs. Latterly,

however, these Portuguese aircraft adopted a secondary ground attack role, resulting in participation in NATO operations over the former Yugoslavia. Portugal is expected to purchase a second batch of 25 aircraft in view of the retirement of the A-7P Corsair from the ground-attack role.

Jordan, a new customer for the F-16, received 25 ADF aircraft, along with other Fighting Falcon models, under the Peace Falcon (lease) agreement.

Surplus ADFs have also been offered on lease to Britain, Spain and Italy, among other countries,

Both the European MLU and further work have greatly increased the air-to-air capabilities of many European F-16s. Some, including this Dutch machine, now have HMCS compatibility.

Portugal's ADF F-16s have a primary air defence tasking, but can be armed with AGM-65 Mavericks for secondary ground-attack duties. Clearly visible in this picture is the ADF's distinctive bulged fin base, which houses its relocated rudder actuators.

in this case as a stopgap until Eurofighter Typhoon entered service. However, the RAF opted against a lease, Spain purchased further F/A-18s and Italy initially opted to lease Tornado F.Mk 3s from the RAF. Interestingly, these Tornados are now being returned, with Italy leasing 34 F-16A/B ADF aircraft instead. In addition, former Warsaw Pact countries including Poland, Hungary and the Czech Republic were offered ADFs, but only Poland has opted for the F-16, albeit in more advanced C/D Block 52 form.

Other customers

While the ADF conversion resulted in a specialized interceptor F-16, the standard models also have a formidable air-to-air capability. Thus, countries including Bahrain, Taiwan, Thailand (which ordered additional F-16s, in ADF form, in 2000) and Venezuela all fly standard F-16A/B/C/D aircraft in primary air-to-air roles.

Lockheed Martin F-16 Fighting Falcon
'Big spine' multi-role variants

Israel has the most diverse 'mix' of Fighting Falcons of any operator. Its unique F-16 configurations include the F-16D Block 30 Brakeet.

Fitting the F-16 with an enlarged fuselage spine to increase the available space for mission systems without consuming weapons pylons is by no means a new concept. The 'big spine' fit was pioneered by Israel on its **F-16D Block 30 Brakeet** aircraft, the new appendage being rumoured to house everything from fuel to undisclosed avionics. In fact, it seems most likely that it is associated with defence suppression Wild Weasel avionics, possibly including the Elta SPS 300 ECM jamming system.

Singapore also opted for the 'big spine' fit on some of its F-16Ds and, while they almost certainly accommodate extra avionics, the exact nature of these is open to question.

Later, as Lockheed Martin strove to keep the F-16 competitive in an evolving marketplace which included Dassault's Rafale, Eurofighter Typhoon and advanced F-15, MiG-29 and Su-30 variants, it turned to the 'big spine' as a major feature for new export F-16 developments.

Advanced orders

While the manufacturer and the UAE wrangled over the exact details of the latter's eventual 80-aircraft order, work was going on to develop a slightly revised 'big spine' and to

The first Greek aircraft built to advanced Block 52 standard was initially flown without paint and remained in the United States into 2003 for training purposes.

integrate conformal fuel tanks onto the F-16. The first of the UAE's **F-16E/F Block 60** aircraft was scheduled for delivery in 2004, with avionics including APG-80 radar and an integral IRST. Power is provided by the 142.31-kN (32,000-lb) thrust F110-GE-132 engine.

The UAE deal was concluded finally in 2000, as was a deal with Israel for the eventual supply of up to 102 **F-16I Soufa** (storm) aircraft to a so-called **advanced F-16D Block 52** standard. The aircraft have APG-68(V)9 radar and other advanced systems. The initial two machines arrived in Israel on 19 February 2004. Finally, in 2001, Greece ordered some 50 **F-16C/D Block 52+** aircraft with options for 10 more. The aircraft have much in common with the Soufa, Greece wanting the F110-GE-132 engine but being denied this and taking the 124.52-kN (28,000-lb) thrust F100-PW-229 engine of the Israeli machine instead. The first Greek aircraft was received in the country in April 2003.

General Dynamics F-16C Fighting Falcon

Among the broad spectrum of roles undertaken by the F-16 across the globe, no mission is more specialized than that flown by the F-16s of the 52nd Tactical Fighter Wing at Spangdahlem in Germany. Defence suppression is their task, equipped with the F-16C/D block 30/32. This variant introduced the ability to launch the Shrike and HARM anti-radiation missiles, which home in on hostile air defence radars. The 52nd TFW was the first unit to deploy the F-16 in this role, initially using it as a 'shooter' to augment the dedicated F-4G 'Wild Weasel', while other USAF 'Wild Weasel' units continued to use the F-4E/F-4G pairing.

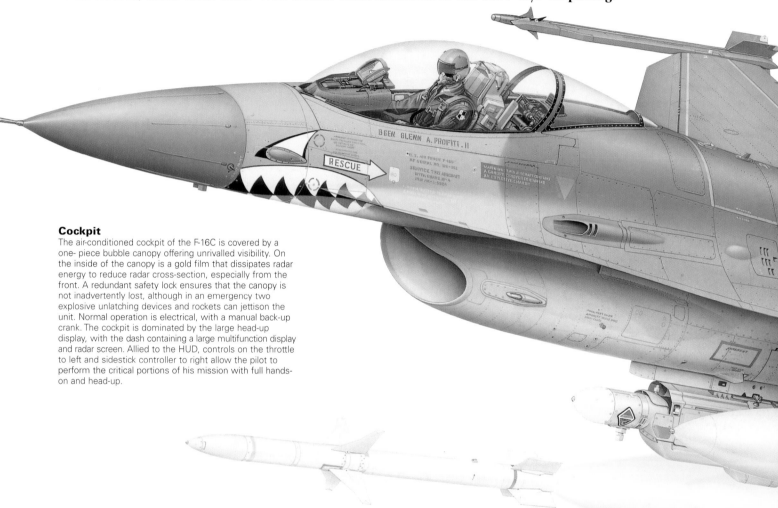

Cockpit

The air-conditioned cockpit of the F-16C is covered by a one-piece bubble canopy offering unrivalled visibility. On the inside of the canopy is a gold film that dissipates radar energy to reduce radar cross-section, especially from the front. A redundant safety lock ensures that the canopy is not inadvertently lost, although in an emergency two explosive unlatching devices and rockets can jettison the unit. Normal operation is electrical, with a manual back-up crank. The cockpit is dominated by the large head-up display, with the dash containing a large multifunction display and radar screen. Allied to the HUD, controls on the throttle to left and sidestick controller to right allow the pilot to perform the critical portions of his mission with full hands-on and head-up.

Cold War 'Wild Weasel' tactics

The 52nd TFW began F-16 operations on 4 July 1987, and at the end of the Cold War had 36 Falcons assigned. Twelve served with each of three squadrons (23rd, 81st and 480th Tactical Fighter Squadrons) which formed the wing's complement. Completing each squadron were 12 McDonnell Douglas F-4Gs, making the 52nd TFW unusual amongst tactical units for operating two frontline types side-by-side. For the defence suppression mission, an F-4G/F-16 pair was the basic operating formation, although two pairs often flew missions so that the enemy radars could be engaged by the second pair while the first regrouped for further attacks. Operating close to the battle front, the 'Weasel' pair set up an 'EOB' (electronic order of battle) orbit. During runs parallel to the front line the F-4G would pop up above the terrain to allow its sophisticated APR-38 RHAWS equipment to pinpoint and classify enemy radars. Either the F-4G itself could launch a missile or it could pass target information to the F-16 to launch an attack. When the radars had been destroyed and the area was deemed safe enough, the F-16 could go in to attack the enemy SAMs with cluster bombs. Replacing F-4Es in this role with F-16s considerably enhanced the attack capability of the 'Weasel' pairing, especially in the anti-radiation missile launch role as the F-4Es were restricted to Shrike launches only. Furthermore, the F-16 offered the pair far better protection should hostile fighters intervene.

HARM

Although the AGM-45 Shrike continued to be used into the early 1990s, the Texas Instruments AGM-88 HARM (High-speed Anti-Radiation Missile) is the principal weapon of the USAF defence suppression forces. Measuring some 417 m (13 ft 8 in) in length and weighing 361 kg (796 lb) at launch, the HARM has fixed rear fins and controllable mid-set fins. A fixed seeker in the nose has a digital passive antenna which covers radar frequencies across a wide band, including high I-band (8-10 GHz). It can be programmed before launch to attack a specific target, or it can be launched 'blind' at longer range to acquire a target during its flight. A laser proximity fuse detonates a 66-kg (145-lb) high-explosive fragmentation warhead.

The United Arab Emirates' F-16 Block 60 Desert Falcon was chosen after evaluation against the Eurofighter Typhoon, Rafale and F-15E. The Desert Falcon, of which 80 are on order, features conformal fuel tanks for extended range, new cockpit displays, a new internal sensor suite, mission computer and Northrop Grumman Agile Beam Radar for improved tracking of multiple targets.

An F-16 Fighting Falcon of the 416th Flight Test Squadron drops a Joint Direct Attack Munition (JDAM) equipped with the Direct Attack Munition Affordable Seeker (DAMASK). Released from several miles away, the weapon – set in GPS-denied mode – punched a hole in a target nearly dead centre, relying only on JDAM's inertial navigation system and DAMASK's template-matching capability.

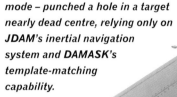

Armament

The basic defensive armament of the F-16 comprises the internal M61A1 20-mm six-barrel rotary cannon with 515 rounds of ammunition, and two infrared air-to-air missiles on wingtip rails. These are usually Sidewinders (AIM-9M shown), but Pakistan and Belgium have utilized MATRA Magic 2s. Today, post-Block 40 USAF F-16s usually carry AIM-120 AMRAAMs on the wingtip rails. One fuselage and six underwing hardpoints can carry fuel tanks and additional weapons. At 5.5 g manoeuvring, the fuselage point is stressed for 998 kg (2,200 lb), inboard pylons for 2041 kg (4,500 lb), centre for 1587 kg (3,500 lb) and the outboard for 318 kg (700 lb). At 9 g manoeuvring these figures fall to 544 kg (1,200 lb), 1134 kg (2,500 lb), 907 kg (2,000 lb) and 204 kg (450 lb) respectively. A huge variety of weapons can be carried, from rocket pods to the Penguin anti-ship missile. Guided weapons include additional air-to-air missiles, anti-radiation missiles and Maverick precision attack weapons.

ECM

Carried under the fuselage of this F-16 is the Westinghouse AN/ALQ-131 ECM pod, the standard unit for USAF tactical aircraft. Of modular design, the pod can be reconfigured for up to 16 different mission requirements, covering from one to five frequency bands with both noise and deception jamming. Contained within the pod is its own digital computer, which can be reprogrammed on the flightline to match the nature of the threat to be encountered on the mission.

Dassault Mirage 2000 Multi-role fighter family

This Mirage 2000C flew with EC 2/5, based at Al Ahsa AB, Saudi Arabia, during Operation Daguet, the French contribution to Operation Desert Storm. The French 2000s flew CAPs and escort missions for French Jaguars. Abu Dhabi's Mirage 2000RADs flew recce missions, while its 2000EADs flew air defence missions.

For the third generation of its Mirage warplane series, Dassault returned to the delta configuration. It used negative longitudinal stability and a fly-by-wire flight control system to eliminate many of the shortcomings of a conventional delta. The **Mirage 2000** was designed with its predecessor's large high-lift wing, considerable internal volume (for fuel and avionics) and low wave drag, but had the improved agility, low-speed handling and more docile landing speed available from a computer-controlled, naturally unstable aircraft.

Taiwan flies 48 Mirage 2000-5EI fighters alongside the F-16 and Ching Kuo. The Mirages are equipped for air defence duties, with EADS Magic 2 and MICA missiles.

Cancelled ACF

Conceived in 1972 as the low-key **Delta 1000** project, the type moved up several gears from December 1975, when cancellation of the projected **Dassault Avion de Combat Futur** left the Armée de l'Air without a new in-development interceptor. In March 1976 the official specification was written for the aircraft, and a high-priority development programme was launched to ensure a service debut in 1982.

The Mirage 2000 has a large and lightly loaded wing fitted

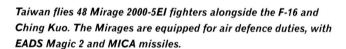

with powerful lift-enhancing and control surfaces. The air inlets for its M53 turbofan are of the traditional Mirage type, with, on the outside, small vortex-generating strakes. Construction is largely of traditional alloys with sparing use of carbon fibre. The first of five **Mirage 2000** prototypes became airborne on 10 March 1978.

A fin of broader chord with less complex leading-edge shape and trailing-edge root fairings was introduced during the test programme. It also characterized the first production-standard **Mirage 2000C** on its initial flight on 20 November 1982. As with the 36 machines which followed, power was increased to 88.26 kN (19,842 lb st) through installation of the uprated M53-5 engine.

Among its initial batch of Mirage 2000s, Abu Dhabi received six 2000DAD trainers. Export 2000 trainers have the generic designation Mirage 2000ED.

Delivery of the Mirage 2000C single-seat interceptor began in April 1983. Eventually, three squadrons of EC 2 were equipped with early production aircraft fitted with the M53-5 engine and Thomson-CSF RDM (Radar Doppler Modulations) radar; some 37 of these early aircraft were upgraded to **Mirage 2000-5** standard in 1994–97. The 38th Mirage 2000C introduced the definitive initial standard with a 95.12-kN (21,384-lb st) M53-P2 engine and the Thomson-CSF/Dassault Electronique RDI (Radar Doppler Impulsions) radar optimized for look-down/

SPECIFICATION	
Dassault Mirage 2000-5	**Weights:** empty 7500 kg (16,534 lb)
Type: single-seat multi-role fighter	maximum take-off 15,000 kg (33,069 lb)
Powerplant: one SNECMA M53-P20 turbofan engine rated at 98.06 kN (22,046 lb st) with afterburning	**Dimensions:** wing span 9.13 m (29 ft 11½ in); length 14.36 m (47 ft 1¼ in); height 5.2 m (17 ft ¾ in): wing area 41 m² (441.33 sq ft)
Performance: maximum speed 2335 km/h (1,451 mph) or Mach 2.2 at high altitude; initial climb rate 17,070 m (56,000 ft) per minute; service ceiling 16,460 m (54,000 ft); range 1850 km (1,151 miles) on a hi-hi-hi mission	**Armament:** two 30-mm DEFA 554 fixed forward-firing cannon in the lower part of the forward fuselage, plus up to 6300 kg (13,889 lb) of disposable stores

France will rely on the Mirage 2000C for its air defence until the Rafale enters widespread service. Mirages have served over the former Yugoslavia and over Afghanistan.

shoot-down intercepts with Super 530D SARH AAMs.

Exports

Total production of the Mirage 2000C for France was 121. Similar aircraft were also manufactured for export with the combination of the M53-P2 and the RDM radar modified for compatibility with the Super 530D. Abu Dhabi, Egypt, Greece, India and Peru all received early-model Mirage 2000 fighters; Abu Dhabi's order included **Mirage 2000R** recce aircraft. In 1986 a programme to enhance the Mirage 2000 was launched, ultimately resulting in the **Mirage 2000-5** multi-role warplane.

From 1992, customers for the 2000-5 have included Taiwan and Qatar. In addition, the Armée de l'Air's first 37 Mirage 2000Cs were upgraded to -5 standard. In 1999, Greece ordered 15 improved **Mirage 2000-5 Mk II** aircraft – a redesignation of the **Mirage 2000-9** – with the M53-P2 engine. The UAE purchased Mk IIs to complement existing aircraft converted to the same standard. The Greek Mk IIs were supplemented by the conversion of 10 **Mirage 2000EG** machines.

A two-seat conversion trainer, the **Mirage 2000B**, has been produced for France, with similar aircraft being widely built for export customers.

Dassault Rafale Fifth-generation multi-role fighter

The **ACX** (**Avion de Combat Experimentale**) was designed by Dassault in the early 1980s (before France's August 1985 withdrawal from the multinational European Fighter Aircraft (EFA) project) as a technology demonstrator for a national combat aircraft programme. France's withdrawal from the EFA was prompted ostensibly because the French forces, especially the navy, wanted a smaller and lighter design. The ACX demonstrator, first flown on 4 July 1986, helped to establish the basic aerodynamic design, configuration, performance, fly-by-wire control system, and composite-based structure of the planned **ACT** (**Avion de Combat Tactique**) that became the **Dassault Rafale**.

ACX becomes Rafale

The ACX, later renamed **Rafale A**, was initially powered by two 68.6-kN (15,422-lb st) General Electric F404-GE-400 turbofans, but after initial tests, including touch-and-go deck landings on *Clemenceau*, the port F404 was replaced by a 73.5-kN (16,523-lb st) flight-development M88-2 engine.

The **Rafale C** single-seat prototype first flew on 19 May 1991, revealing a supercruise capability in the course of this sortie. The **Rafale B** two-seat dual-control prototype made its first flight on 30 April 1993 with the Thomson- CSF/ Detexis RBE2 multi-mode radar and Thomson-CSF/MATRA Spectra defensive aids package. Originally envisaged as a combat-capable conversion trainer, the two-seater is now being developed as the principal operational variant of the Armée de l'Air.

Definitive variants

In its definitive production forms, which entered service from 2002, the Rafale multi-role warplane will replace up to half a dozen French air force interceptor, strike/attack and reconnaissance types.

The generic **Rafale D** (**Discret**, or stealthy) prototype for the Armée de l'Air versions is slightly smaller and lighter than ACX. Changes to reduce the radar cross-section include more rounded wingroot fairings, an internally gold-coated canopy, radar-absorbing dark grey paint and a reprofiled rear-fuselage/fin junction. The fin itself is lower and topped by an ECM fairing and lateral IR missile launch detector windows. The Rafale D's canard foreplanes are linked with landing gear extension to tilt 20 degrees upwards to provide extra lift for landing and are larger than those of the ACX.

Five of the aircraft's 14 stores stations are plumbed for drop tanks. Among the advanced weapons that can be carried are the MICA medium-range AAM, AS30L ASM, Scalp stand-off

Rafale B, to Rafale D standards, will be the Armée de l'Air's primary equipment. In 2003, France will purchase 46 B/Cs, plus a further 13 Rafale Ms. By 2003, French commitments will stand at 120 aircraft, with more orders to come.

Rafale M's nosewheel unit has a catapult bar, and a 'jump-strut' for automatic unstick rotation on launch.

SPECIFICATION

Dassault Rafale D
Type: single-seat multi-role warplane
Powerplant: two SNECMA M88-2 turbofan engines each rated at 72.9 kN (16,400 lb st) with afterburning
Performance: maximum speed 1913 km/h (1,189 mph) or Mach 1.8 at 11,000 m (36,090 ft); maximum climb rate at sea level 18,290 m (60,000 ft) per minute; service ceiling 16,765 m (55,000 ft) radius of action on a low-level penetration mission with 12 250-kg (551-lb) bombs, four MICA AAMs and three

drop tanks 1055 km (655 miles)
Weights: empty equipped 9060 kg (19,973 lb), maximum take-off 19,500 kg (42,989 lb) increasing to 24500 kg (54,012 lb) in later-production aircraft
Dimensions: wing span 10.8 m (35 ft 5¼ in) with tip-mounted AAMs; length 15.27 m (50 ft 1¼ in), height 5.34 m (17 ft 6¼ in); wing area 45.7 m² (491.93 sq ft)
Armament: one 30-mm GIAT/DEFA M791B fixed forward-firing cannon in the starboard side of the forward fuselage, plus up to 9500 kg (20,944 lb) of disposable stores

munitions dispenser, ASMP nuclear missile, and AM39 Exocet AShM.

Advanced avionics

Rafale's advanced avionics include a wide-angle Sextant HUD, a head-level tactical awareness display, and two head-down multifunctional displays in a cockpit with HOTAS controls and a pilot's helmet with sight and display. Voice command capability will be added at a later stage.

The Armée de l'Air is scheduled to receive at least 234 Rafales, including about 130 two-seater Rafale Bs, the remainder being Cs. The first production machine was delivered in December 1998. The early aircraft are to the air-to-air optimized **Rafale B/C F1** standard, but later, more fully equipped standards include the **F2**, for delivery from about 2003. The definitive **F3**, will have improved radar able to undertake simultaneous air search and terrain following. The 93-kN (20,907-lb st) M88-3 will become standard later in the programme.

Rafale M

Originally known as the **ACM** (**Avion de Combat Marine**), the first prototype **Rafale M** single-seat multi-role carrier-borne warplane made its initial flight on 12 December 1991. Rafale M has reinforced landing gear, just 13 hardpoints, and a reduced maximum take-off weight. The Aéronavale will receive 60 single-seat Rafale Ms, with delivery beginning in 2001. By late 2002, the Aéronavale had around 10 Rafale Ms in service aboard *Charles de Gaulle*. The navy will also take the two-seat **Rafale N**.

France expects to achieve IOC with its air force Rafales around 2005, at which point the last of the country's Jaguar strike/attack aircraft will be retired. A Rafale C, with wingtip Magic missiles, is illustrated here.

AIDC F-CK-1 Ching-Kuo Taiwanese superfighter

Taiwan's ambitious programme to develop an advanced fighter to replace its F-5s and F-104s began in 1982, after the US government placed an embargo on the sale of the Northrop F-20 and any comparable fighter. The same restrictions were not placed on technical assistance, however, and US aerospace companies have collaborated closely with AIDC to develop an indigenous fighter and weapons system. The overall programme, code-named An Hsiang (Safe Flight), was managed through four subsidiary programmes for airframe, engines, avionics and armament systems.

Ying Yang

The airframe was developed with assistance from General Dynamics in the Ying Yang (Soaring Eagle) programme, and the prototypes and first 160

production aircraft were to be powered by two AlliedSignal/ Garrett TFE-1042-70 (F125) turbofans. These are afterburning versions of the Garrett TFE731, developed under the Yun Han (Cloud Man) programme. More powerful versions of the F125 or General Electric J101 were considered for later aircraft. Avionics were developed by a team led by Smiths Industries under a programme code-named Tien Lei (Sky Thunder); the primary missile armament was developed in the Tien Chien (Sky Sword) programme. The aircraft is equipped with a Golden Dragon GD-53 multi-mode pulse-Doppler radar based on the GE AN/APG-67M developed for the F-20, but incorporating some technology from the Westinghouse AN/APG-66 (used by the F-16A Fighting Falcon).

SPECIFICATION

AIDC F-CK-1A Ching-Kuo
Type: single-seat multi-role fighter
Powerplant: two Honeywell/ AIDC TFE-1042-70 (F125) turbofans each rated at 6,060 lb st (26.80 kN) dry and 9,460 lb st (42.08 kN) with afterburning
Performance: maximum level speed 'clean' at 10975 m (36,000 ft) more than 1275 km/h (792 mph); maximum rate of climb at sea level 15,240 m (50,000 ft) per minute,

service ceiling 16,760 m (55,000 ft)
Weights: normal take-off 9072 kg (20,000 lb)
Dimensions: wing span over wing tip missile rails 8.53 m (28 ft); length including probe 14.21 m (46 ft 7½ in); height 4.65 m (15 ft 3 in); wing area 24.26 m² (261.10 sq ft)
Armament: one M61A1 cannon, plus Sky Sword 1 and Sky Sword 2 AAMs; and Hsiung Feng 2 AShMs

Of conventional all-metal construction (with an increasing proportion of composites being introduced on the production line), the **F-CK-1A Ching-Kuo** is of conventional configuration, albeit with wing/fuselage blending. The pressurized cockpit is fitted with a sidestick controller, a wide-angle HUD, and three multifunction look-down displays The aircraft has an internal

20-mm M61A1 cannon beneath the port leading-edge root extension, and has two under-fuselage and two underwing hardpoints, in addition to its wingtip missile launch rails.

Ching-Kuo in the air

The first prototype made its maiden flight on 28 May 1989, while the first two-seat **F-CK-1B Ching-Kuo** prototype first flew

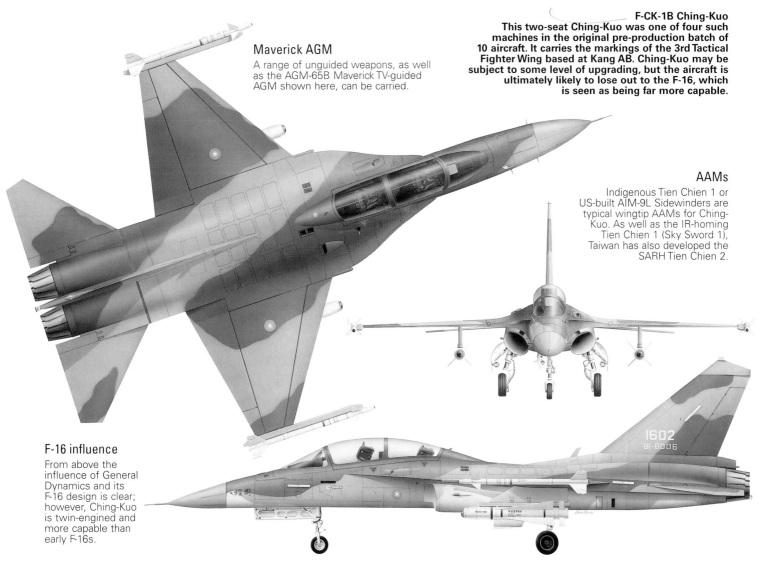

F-CK-1B Ching-Kuo
This two-seat Ching-Kuo was one of four such machines in the original pre-production batch of 10 aircraft. It carries the markings of the 3rd Tactical Fighter Wing based at Kang AB. Ching-Kuo may be subject to some level of upgrading, but the aircraft is ultimately likely to lose out to the F-16, which is seen as being far more capable.

Maverick AGM
A range of unguided weapons, as well as the AGM-65B Maverick TV-guided AGM shown here, can be carried.

AAMs
Indigenous Tien Chien 1 or US-built AIM-9L Sidewinders are typical wingtip AAMs for Ching-Kuo. As well as the IR-homing Tien Chien 1 (Sky Sword 1), Taiwan has also developed the SARH Tien Chien 2.

F-16 influence
From above the influence of General Dynamics and its F-16 design is clear; however, Ching-Kuo is twin-engined and more capable than early F-16s.

Although the Taiwanese government saw fit to curtail Ching-Kuo production, the country can feel proud that it developed a fighter with similar capabilities to the JAS 39 Gripen.

on 10 July 1990. The aircraft is named after a former President of Taiwan, Chiang Ching-Kuo.

Deliveries to the Taiwanese air force began in February 1993, when No. 7 'Seed' Squadron publicly unveiled its first aircraft. In March 1993, after a deal for F-16s had finally been signed in late 1992, Taiwan's legislature announced that procurement would be limited to only 130 aircraft, to equip two, instead of the planned four, wings.

Lockheed Martin F-16 Fighting Falcon
Block 50/60 Advanced F-16 developments

In late 1991, General Dynamics began building the **Block 52 F-16 Fighting Falcon**. Since it had first flown in F-16A Block 1 form, the Fighting Falcon had put on some 1406 kg (3,100 lb) in empty weight and was becoming decidedly underpowered in

Above: A long-time F-16 customer, Greece ordered 40 Block 50 aircraft in 1997–98. Unusually, Greece flies its Block 50s with LANTIRN pods, this system not being associated with USAF Block 50/52 F-16s.

SPECIFICATION

Lockheed Martin F-16C Block 50/52
Type: single-seat multi-role fighter
Powerplant: one General Electric F110-GE-129 turbofan rated at 131.48 kN (29,588 lb st) with afterburning (Block 50) or one Pratt & Whitney F100-PW-229 turbofan rated at 129.44 kN (29,100 lb st) with afterburning (Block 52)
Performance: maximum level speed 'clean' at 12,190 m (40,000 ft) more than 2124 km/h (1,320 mph); initial rate of climb more than 15,240 m (50,000 ft) per minute; service ceiling

more than 15,240 m (50,000 ft); radius 1485 km (923 miles) with two 2,000-lb (907-kg) Mk 84 bombs and two AIM-9 Sidewinder AAMs
Weights: empty 8581 kg (18,917 lb); maximum take-off 12,292 kg (27,099 lb)
Dimensions: wing span 10.01 m (32 ft 9¾ in); length 15.03 m (49 ft 4 in); height 5.01 m (16 ft 5¼ in); wing area 28.87 m² (300 sq ft)
Armament: one 20-mm M61A1 Vulcan cannon, plus up to 5443 kg (12,000 lb) of disposable ordnance

With no prospect of a purpose-designed Wild Weasel in sight, the USAF will continue to rely on the F-16CJ for its SEAD needs well into the twenty-first century. The USAF has decided not to buy further F-16s, but is implementing a Common Configuration Implementation Programme to bring 650 Block 40/42 and 50/52 aircraft to an improved standard.

Israel placed 50 F-16D Block 52+ aircraft on firm order for delivery in 2003–2006. The aircraft will have the conformal fuel tanks (CFTs) of the Block 60.

Perhaps most importantly, Block 50/52 aircraft feature a HARM Avionics Launcher Interface Computer and HARM Targeting System equipment, ensuring greater compatibility with the AGM-88 missile than was previously possible. SEAD (suppression of enemy air defences) is therefore an important Block 50/52 role, USAF aircraft employed in this role commonly being referred to as **F-16CJ** warplanes.

Block 60

Block 60 represents the ultimate F-16 configuration and has been developed for export. The UAE was the initial Block 60 customer, and is expecting to take 80 of the advanced aircraft between 2004 and 2006.

some circumstances. Having recognized this situation, the USAF commissioned higher-performance versions of the standard P&W and GE engines under the Increased Performance Engine programme. The resulting GE F110-GE-129 was ready first, with the first Block 50 machine

flying in October 1991, while the PW F100-PW-229-engined Block 52 flew for the first time around one year later.

Other improvements

As well as increased power, which is as much as 33 per cent up at high speed and low level,

the Block 50/52 aircraft feature a new wide-angle HUD and improved APG-68(V)5 radar, along with an Advanced Programmable Signal Processor.

This digitally enhanced image shows a possible Block 60 single-seat configuration. CFTs are a key feature of the design, as is a built-in FLIR above the nose.

Eurofighter 2000/Typhoon European superfighter

Eurofighter built seven EF2000 prototypes, known as DA1 to DA7. The first British prototype, DA2, is illustrated here; the machine made its maiden flight on 6 April 1994 from BAE's Warton airfield.

Known as the **Eurofighter Typhoon** for the RAF and export customers, and variously as the **Eurofighter 2000**, **EF2000** or simply **Eurofighter** by the remaining partner nations, this swing-role warplane is one of the most advanced ever built.

The aircraft is designed to perform air-to-air and air-to-ground roles with equal ability, but is also able to switch role mid-mission – a so-called 'swing-role' capability. A Typhoon loaded with air-to-ground stores is also likely to be carrying a formidable air-to-air loadout, and such are the aircraft's technological and performance advantages that it is fully able to engage and neutralize an aerial threat before continuing on a precision attack mission.

Typhoon has its origins in a European multinational requirement of the early 1970s. Much debate and theorizing, primarily involving parties from Britain, West Germany and France, eventually resulted in the Experimental Aircraft Programme (EAP) demonstrator flying for the first time in 1986.

By this time France had withdrawn from the programme and West Germany's involvement in EAP was minor at this point, too. Nevertheless, by late 1985, the governments of Britain, Italy, Spain and West Germany had agreed to collaborate on a fighter programme.

EFA to EF2000

This new programme began in earnest under the title

The Eurofighter consortium consists of Alenia in Italy, BAE Systems in the United Kingdom, EADS CASA in Spain and EADS Germany. By mid 2002, Eurofighter had flown three instrumented production aircraft, of which this was the third.

Typhoon has a classic fourth-generation fighter layout, with canards forward and a complex wing. The aircraft is inherently unstable, giving it superb manoeuvrability.

Unit), to work up.

The other partner nations will receive their aircraft slightly later than the RAF, which plans to have the Typhoon, in its initial configuration, fully operational by 2006.

Constant updates

Eurofighter is available in single- and two-seat variants, the latter being fully combat capable. Its high-technology systems include Captor radar, voice-activated cockpit systems, IRST and datalink systems. Both of these latter systems allow the aircraft to make air-to-air engagements without using radar, bolstering the design's somewhat limited stealth capabilities.

Eurofighter is mindful that the aircraft must be constantly updated to keep it ahead of its competitors during its 40-year service life. As such, Typhoon is to be delivered in an increasingly sophisticated form, with the ultimate Tranche 3 aircraft being available in 2010.

In 2004, the German, Italian and Spanish air forces all received delivery of single seater versions of the Eurofighter. In December 2005, Saudi Arabia ordered 72 Eurofighter Typhoons as part of an ongoing program to update their air defence systems.

DA2 has latterly been painted in a high-conspicuity black scheme for flight test duties. The aircraft is dedicated to flight envelope expansion and flight control system testing.

European Fighter Aircraft (EFA) and by 1989 the first machines were being built. Political wrangling, delays caused by development problems and a convoluted programme management structure have come to blight the entire Eurofighter programme, and conspired to delay the aircraft's first flight

until 27 March 1994. By mid-2002, however, the programme had advanced sufficiently for Eurofighter to announce scheduled delivery of the first production aircraft to the RAF later in the year. This would allow operational training to begin and preparations to be made for the RAF's Typhoon OCU (Operational Conversion

SPECIFICATION

Eurofighter Typhoon
Type: single-seat swing-role combat aircraft
Powerplant: two Eurojet EJ2000 turbofan engines each rated at about 60 kN (13,490 lb st) dry and 90 kN (20,250 lb st) with afterburning
Performance: maximum speed 2125 km/h (1,321 mph) or Mach 2 at 11,000 m (36,090 ft); climb to 10,670 m (35,000 ft) and Mach 1.5 in 2 minutes 30 seconds; service ceiling 14,500 m (47,570 ft); radius 1390 km (864 miles) on an air-superiority mission with three

drop tanks for a 10-minute combat air patrol
Weights: empty 10,995 kg (24,239 lb); maximum take-off 23,000 kg (50,705 lb)
Dimensions: wing span 10.95 m (35 ft 11 in) over tip-mounted ECM pods; length 15.96 m (52 ft 4¼ in); height 5.28 m (17 ft 4 in); wing area 50 m² (538.21 sq ft)
Armament: One 27-mm Mauser BK27 fixed forward-firing cannon in the starboard side of the forward fuselage, plus up to 8000 kg (17,637 lb) of external stores

Saab/BAE Systems JAS 39 Gripen Swedish superfighter

French Aéronavale service, and none of the other types listed was close to full frontline service.

Gripen was planned from the outset as a replacement for Sweden's fleet of Viggens and a few surviving Drakens. It was to improve upon all of the capabilities offered by the Viggen variants, but in a much smaller and lighter airframe. It had to be rugged and easy to maintain – Sweden's policy of forward-basing aircraft in the field dictated this – but it must also employ the very latest in technology. That it does all of these things phenomenally well is a great credit to the ingenuity of the Saab team and its partners.

FCS problems

Gripen is a single-engined, delta-winged aircraft, displaying high manoevrability thanks to its inherently unstable design and advanced flight control system (FCS). Early, and highly public, failures of the FCS have been overcome and the aircraft is proving remarkably reliable. A key feature of the aircraft is its datalink system, which conveys information from its Ericsson radar and other sensors to other Gripens in its formation, as well as S 101B Argus AWACS aircraft. Indeed, Gripen can fire its AIM-120 AMRAAM missiles against targets that it has never 'seen', the missiles guiding on information downlinked to them by the S 101B. Gripen is also a highly capable attack and reconnaissance platform.

The Swedish government has committed to a purchase of 204 Gripens, the first prototype having completed its maiden flight on 9 December 1988. In 1999, Saab became an element in BAE Systems, Gripen then being offered for export as the Saab/ BAE Systems Gripen. BAE has offered the aircraft alongside the Hawk 100 and Typhoon, as part of the ideal combat aircraft package. The Hawk offers lead-in fighter training and light-attack capabilities, while Gripen and

Sweden employs the single-seat JAS 39A and the two-seat JAS 39B, as illustrated here. The B is a tandem-two seat operational trainer, but retains full combat capability.

Saab designed the **JAS 39 Gripen** as a true fourth-generation fighter. As such, it is the technological equal of the Dassault Rafale, Eurofighter Typhoon, Lockheed Martin F-22 and Sukhoi Su-35. By mid-2002, a large fleet of Gripens was in operational service with the Swedish air force, a handful of Rafale Ms – naval fighters with as yet limited capability – was in

*Gripen's great versatility is reflected in its weapon choices.
Here Sidewinders, Mavericks and RBS 15 missiles make up
a typical anti-shipping loadout.*

SPECIFICATION	
Saab JAS 39A Gripen	(1864 miles) with drop tanks
Type: Single-seat multi-role combat aircraft	**Weights:** empty 6622 kg (14,599 lb); maximum take-off about 13,000 kg (28,660 lb)
Powerplant: one Volvo Aero RM12 turbofan rated at 54 kN (12,140 lb st) dry and 80.51 kN (18,100 lb st) with afterburning	**Dimensions:** wing span 8.40 m (27 ft 6¾ in); length 14.10 m (46 ft 3 in); height 4.50 m (14 ft 9 in)
Performance: maximum speed 2125 km/h (1,321 mph) or Mach 2 at 11,000 m (36,090 ft); service ceiling 20,000 m (65,615 ft); range 3000 km	**Armament:** One 27-mm Mauser BK27 fixed forward-firing cannon in lower forward fuselage; plus up to 6500 kg (14,330 lb) of external stores

*AMRAAM is a weapon of primary importance for Gripen. The missile
is fully integrated into the aircraft's weapons-control systems.*

Typhoon are offered as light and heavyweight fighters, respectively. Some success has come from this venture, as Gripen is to be exported to South Africa in two batches, one of nine two-seaters for delivery in 2007–2009 and a second of 10 single-seaters in 2009–2012. The aircraft will replace the Cheetah in service, while South Africa is also taking Hawks. Hungary is leasing 14 Gripens from Swedish air force stocks and Brazil, the Czech Republic and Poland are all seen as possible future customers.

*Large canards mounted on the air intake trunks help to give
the Gripen its outstanding manoeuvrability. They also help to
shorten its landing run, being angled forwards and down during the
landing roll to act as aerodynamic brakes. Gripen's predecessor, the
Viggen, used thrust reversing to similar effect.*

Gripen and Typhoon

Although the origins of their designs are worlds apart, Gripen and Typhoon have evolved into a complimentary pair of fighters – at least according to the BAE Systems/Saab team marketing the aircraft internationally. It is difficult to imagine any nation acquiring examples of both of these extremely capable types, although both designs have notched up orders outside their home nations. South Africa has made a firm commitment to Gripen, while in late 2003 Austria was so far the only nation to have made a similar commitment to Eurofighter.

Radar and datalink

Although Gripen's PS-05 radar is a capable system, it is often of great use to a fighter to be able to engage a target without alerting the target to its presence by the tell-tale emissions of its radar. In Swedish service Gripen uses the Tactical Information Data Link System (TIDLS, often pronounce 'tiddles') to pass data to and from the ground and other aircraft. Thus, both radar emissions and radio traffic are kept to a minimum, a Gripen being able to launch an Rb 99 missile under the control of an Argus AEW&C aircraft without switching on its own radar.

Armament flexibility

Much of Gripen's operational capability comes from the versatility offered by its armament options. This aircraft has a dual attack/air-to-air loadout of BK 90 (DWS 39) glide weapons and Rb 74 (AIM-9) and Rb 99 (AIM-120) AAMs. BAE Systems is developing a system which will allow weapons to interface with the aircraft via data transfer between the weapon and its pylon, greatly increasing the weapon options available while minimizing the need for new systems to be added to the aircraft.

Ejection seat

Eurofighter's Martin-Baker Mk 16A ejection seat was developed from the same company's lightweight Mk 15. With a moderately raked back, the seat weighs less than 63.5 kg (140 lb), and uses its twin propulsion tubes as load-carrying structures. Tested from 0–1110 km/h (690 mph), and at altitudes of up to 15,240 m (50,000 ft), the seat is actuated using a single seat-pan handle. Operation is computer controlled, with the seat incorporating its own airspeed and altitude sensors, drogue chutes and flip-out aerodynamic surfaces. The rejection of the very steeply raked sitting position pioneered by the F-16 recognizes that the drawbacks (poor rearward view, a likelihood of neck and back problems, limited view downward over the nose of the aircraft, the need for a sidestick, and the need for higher-mounted displays) outweigh the benefit of marginally improved g tolerance. Enhanced g protection is provided through newly designed flying clothing, which incorporates what are called 'full coverage anti-g trousers' and a partial pressure jerkin, together with pressure breathing. This is estimated to increase an individual's g tolerance by about 1g. The seat is offered with an optional harness system, which allows unassisted strapping-in.

Eurofighter DA6

The first two-seat Eurofighter to fly was the second aircraft to be built – the CASA-constructed DA6 (XCE.16-01). DA6 took to the air for the first time on 31 August 1996 and was the second Eurofighter to fly with the EJ.200 engines from the very beginning (Italy's DA3 had the honour of being the first). While flying with a pair of early development engines on 21 November 2002, however, the aircraft suffered a double engine surge and flameout at around 13,716 m (45,000 ft). The crew was unable to relight the engines and both crew members ejected safely.

Canard foreplanes

The use of canard foreplanes contributed to Eurofighter's unstable aerodynamic configuration, with an aft centre of gravity. The use of canard foreplanes also added to total lift on take-off or in a turn (rather than generating downforce, as does a tailplane), and reduced drag. Strakes on the fuselage sides smooth out vortices from the canard foreplanes, and have reportedly been used as footsteps by pilots, indicating their strength. The strakes move through just six degrees in flight, in unison only.

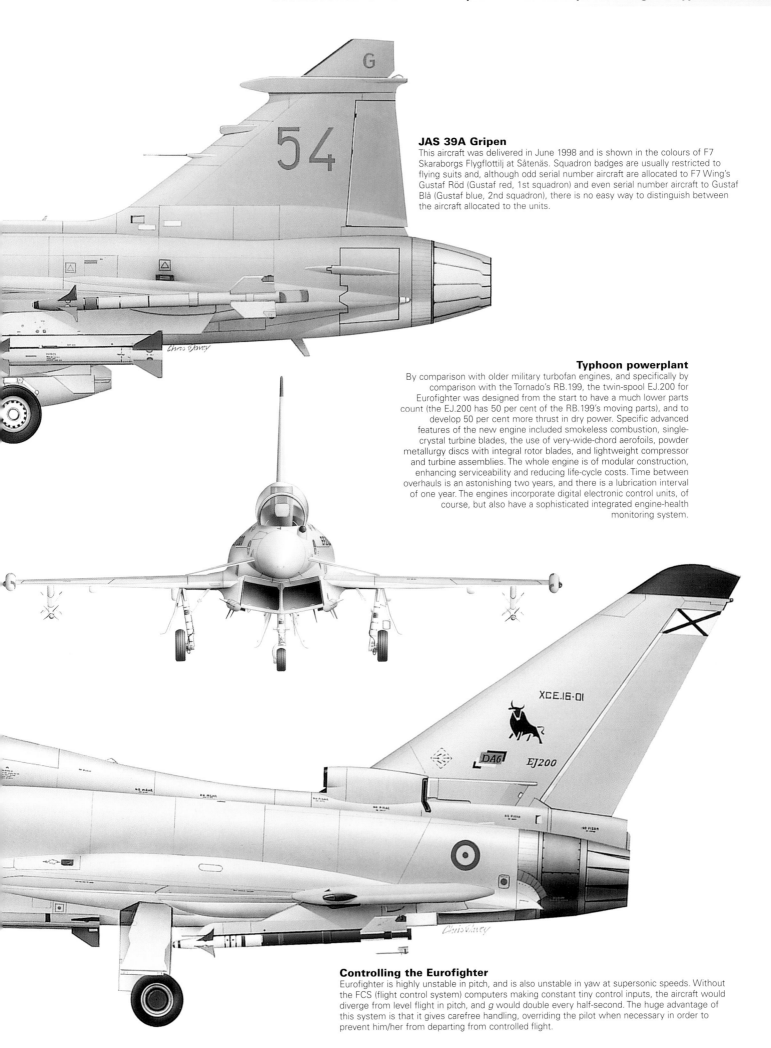

JAS 39A Gripen

This aircraft was delivered in June 1998 and is shown in the colours of F7 Skaraborgs Flygflottilj at Såtenäs. Squadron badges are usually restricted to flying suits and, although odd serial number aircraft are allocated to F7 Wing's Gustaf Röd (Gustaf red, 1st squadron) and even serial number aircraft to Gustaf Blå (Gustaf blue, 2nd squadron), there is no easy way to distinguish between the aircraft allocated to the units.

Typhoon powerplant

By comparison with older military turbofan engines, and specifically by comparison with the Tornado's RB.199, the twin-spool EJ.200 for Eurofighter was designed from the start to have a much lower parts count (the EJ.200 has 50 per cent of the RB.199's moving parts), and to develop 50 per cent more thrust in dry power. Specific advanced features of the new engine included smokeless combustion, single-crystal turbine blades, the use of very-wide-chord aerofoils, powder metallurgy discs with integral rotor blades, and lightweight compressor and turbine assemblies. The whole engine is of modular construction, enhancing serviceability and reducing life-cycle costs. Time between overhauls is an astonishing two years, and there is a lubrication interval of one year. The engines incorporate digital electronic control units, of course, but also have a sophisticated integrated engine-health monitoring system.

Controlling the Eurofighter

Eurofighter is highly unstable in pitch, and is also unstable in yaw at supersonic speeds. Without the FCS (flight control system) computers making constant tiny control inputs, the aircraft would diverge from level flight in pitch, and g would double every half-second. The huge advantage of this system is that it gives carefree handling, overriding the pilot when necessary in order to prevent him/her from departing from controlled flight.

Mikoyan MiG-29 'Fulcrum' Counter-air fighter

Although an outstanding performer, early MiG-29s had notoriously short legs. Mikoyan's first attempt to solve the range problem involved fitting a simple bolt-on refuelling probe to a MiG-29SD.

The **MiG-29** was developed to meet a Soviet air force requirement for a lightweight multi-role fighter, in much the same way that the F-16 was developed in the United States. Larger and heavier than anticipated, yet possessing stunning manoeuvrability, the MiG-29 re-established the Soviet Union's reputation as a producer of 'cutting edge' combat aircraft. Incorporating an advanced aerodynamic design and unmatched agility, the MiG-29 has a N-019 pulse-Doppler radar (NATO 'Slot Back') as its primary sensor; this is allied to an IRST (Infra-Red Search and Track system) for passive tracking of targets.

'9-12' prototype

The prototype, which was given the company designation **9-12**, made its first flight in 1977, and the type entered service with Soviet Frontal Aviation in 1982. Early NATO reports described the new fighter, first seen in satellite photos at the Ramenskoye research facility, as the **Ram-L**. Later given the NATO reporting name of **'Fulcrum'**, the MiG-29 replaced the MiG-23 in Soviet service, and was assigned dual air superiority and ground-attack roles. Certain fighter regiments were also tasked with tactical nuclear strike, using the 30-kT RN-40 free-fall bomb.

The basic MiG-29 has proved

An early single-seat 'Fulcrum-A' escorts a two-seat 'Fulcrum-B' on one of the MiG-29's early visits to the West. Large numbers of these aircraft were sold to former Warsaw Pact air forces, as well as to countries such as India and Cuba.

Cockpit

A redesigned cockpit canopy covered the raised seat position, improving all-round visibility.

Fly-by-wire

An analog fly-by-wire control system was introduced in the MiG-29M, as opposed to the old-fashioned mechanical control connections employed in the original MiG-29.

Engines

The MiG-29M and its naval cousin the MiG-29K were powered by a pair of uprated RD-33K engines. This powerplant is interchangeable with the standard RD-33 fitted in 'Fulcrum-As'.

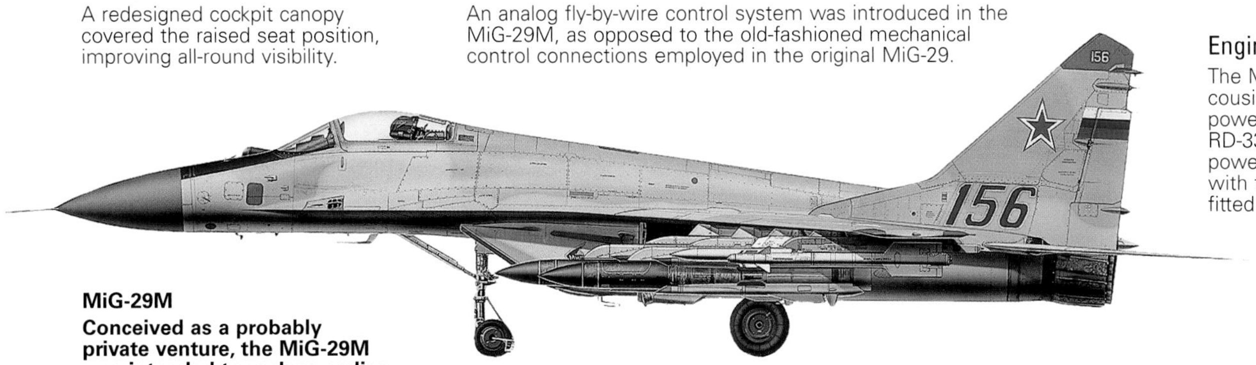

MiG-29M

Conceived as a probably private venture, the MiG-29M was intended to replace earlier MiG-23s and Su-17s in the tactical fighter-bomber role. Political wrangling intervened, however, and no production aircraft were built. Six MiG-29M prototypes were constructed; '156' was the last of these.

Missile armament

Bort '156' is depicted here with a mixed load of R-73 and R-77 air-to-air missiles (outboard pylons) and large Kh-31 anti-radiation missiles inboard.

Radar

Whereas the basic MiG-29 had a dedicated air-to-air radar, the MiG-29M had a more modern multi-mode radar with both air-to-air and air-to-ground modes. The latter included terrain-following and terrain-avoidance.

itself as a formidable close-in dogfighter. The pilot has a helmet-mounted sight to cue missiles onto an off-boresight target, and the very agile R-73 (AA-11 'Archer') missile is widely viewed as the best close combat air-to-air weapon in service today.

However, the 'Fulcrum' is far from perfect. The RD-33 engines suffer from poor service life and low maintainability, and the aircraft is also handicapped by its lack of range and endurance. The MiG-29's primary medium-range weapon, the radar-guided R-27 (AA-10 'Alamo'), is no more than adequate.

Some of the weaknesses of the fighter were addressed by an improved variant (company designation **9-13**) allocated the NATO reporting name **'Fulcrum-C'**. This featured a bulged and extended spine, which houses both fuel and avionics, including an active jammer. Commonly nicknamed **'Gorbatov'** (hunchback), this variant was built alongside the standard 9-12 MiG-29s.

The MiG-29 has been built in substantial numbers and can be found in service all over the world. The Ukraine is the largest operator after Russia, with six regiments (including 'Fulcrum-

Cs'). Other operators of the type include Belarus, Bulgaria, Cuba, Eritrea, Germany, Hungary, India, Iran, Iraq, Kazakhstan, North Korea, Malaysia, Peru, Poland, Romania, Slovakia, Syria, Turkmenistan, Uzbekistan and Yugoslavia. The MiG-29s serve primarily as air defence fighters. All operators have small numbers of MiG-29UB two-seat conversion trainers.

To address the shortcomings of the baseline MiG-29, the design bureau developed two radically improved, multi-role variants. Both the **MiG-29M** and the naval **MiG-29K** became victims of fierce spending cuts

after the end of the Cold War, however, with MiG MAPO choosing to pursue more limited upgrade programmes for more immediate application to Russian and export baseline MiG-29s.

The **MiG-29S** upgrade was applied to a limited number of Russian 9-13 variant MiG-29s, the first phase introducing provision for underwing fuel tanks. It remains unclear if further phased improvements were applied. These included a doubling of the warload, provision for IFR and an upgraded 'Topaz' radar with simultaneous dual target engagement capability. The

Developed as an export variant of the 9-13 model, the MiG-29SE was optimized for air-to-air combat, though it carried an increased bomb load. No sales of the basic model were made, but Bort '999' was used as a testbed for advanced air-to-ground systems incorporated into later variants of the aircraft.

radar would have given compatibility with R-77 BVR AAMs. Such features were then offered for export MiG-29s, along with Western navigation and communications equipment, as well as a bolt-on retractable IFR probe.

The standard export **MiG-29S** was known as the **MiG-29SD** for 9-12 airframes and as the **MiG-29SE** when it was based on the 9-13 airframe.

Malaysia's **MiG-29Ns** are effectively MiG-29SDs. While these versions were marketed

as air superiority fighters, the **MiG-29SM** stressed its multi-role capability with TV- and laser-guided air-to-surface weapons.

Pending the production of a fifth-generation fighter, the Russian air force is upgrading more than 150 9-13 MiG-29 aircraft to a standard comparable to that of the **MiG-29SMT (9-17)**; this first full-standard prototype flew in 1998. The upgrade includes an N-019ME or MP radar, a modern 'glass' cockpit, greatly increased internal fuel capacity, RD-43 engines,

improved serviceability, addition of an IFR system, and increased combat load.

India's acquisition and upgrade of the former RNS carrier *Admiral Gorshkov* has

attracted renewed interest in the MiG-29K. DASA, Romania's Aerostar and Elbit offer the 'Sniper' upgrade, which incorporates elements from the MiG-21 Lancer programme.

SPECIFICATION

Mikoyan MiG-29 (9-12) 'Fulcrum-A'

Type: single-seat tactical fighter
Powerplant: two Klimov/Leningrad RD-33 turbofans each rated at 9.42 kN (11,111 lb st) dry and 81.39 kN (18,298 lb st) with afterburning
Performance: maximum level speed 'clean' at 11,000 m (36,090 ft) 2445 km/h (1,519 mph) or at sea level 1500 km/h (932 mph); maximum initial climb rate 19,800 m (64,961 ft) per minute; service ceiling 17,000 m (55,775 ft); ferry range 2100 km (1,305 miles) with three tanks; range 1500 km (932 miles) with internal fuel

Weights: operating empty 10,900 kg (24,030 lb); normal take-off 15,240 kg (33,598 lb) as an interceptor; maximum take-off 18,500 kg (40,785 lb) in strike configuration
Dimensions: wing span 11.36 m (37 ft 3¼ in); length 17.32 m (56 ft 9½ in); height 4.73 m (15 ft 6¼ in); wing area 38.00 m² (409.04 sq ft)
Armament: one 30-mm GSh-301 cannon, maximum ordnance 2000 kg (4,409 lb), (intercept) two R-27R/R1 or R-27T/T1IR-/radar-guided BVR AAMs and four short-range R-60/60M or R-73RM2D IR-homing missiles

Sukhoi Su-27 'Flanker' Multi-role fighter

Work on the **T-10** design that led to the **Su-27** began in 1969. The requirement was for a highly manoeuvrable fighter with very long range, heavy armament and modern sensors, capable of meeting the F-15 on equal terms. To maximize manoeuvrability, the T-10 was designed from the outset to be unstable, and

required a computer-controlled fly-by-wire control system at least in pitch. The first prototype T-10 made its maiden flight on 20 May 1977, eventually gaining the reporting name **'Flanker-A'**. The early flight development programme revealed serious problems, some insurmountable, leading to a total redesign.

The resulting **T-10S-1** flew on 20 April 1981. The new reporting name of **'Flanker-B'** was subsequently allocated.

The Su-27 finally began to enter operational service during the mid-1980s, variants including the basic Su-27 **'Flanker-B'** with advanced NIIP N-001 pulse-Doppler radar;

Su-27UB 'Flanker-C' trainer with a lengthened forward fuselage and tailfins increased in height and area; the **Su-27M** advanced Su-27 derivative with canard foreplanes, retractable IFR probe, 'glass' cockpit, quadruplex digital FBW FCS, advanced radar and enhanced multi-role capability, which was later redesignated

Su-35 by Sukhoi; and the **Su-33**, which is the new designation for the carrier-based fighter previously known as the **Su-27K**.

Ultra 'Flankers'

The latest 'Flankers' include the **Su-37**, which is the Su-35 revised with thrust-vectoring engines; the **Su-30** (**Su-30K** for export) basic operational long-range/extended endurance two-seat interceptor fighter with IFR probe and second pilot/WSO in rear cockpit; **Su-30M** (**Su-30MK** for export) multi-role two-seater

with provision for TV, radar and IR-guided ASMs and PGMs; **Su-30MKI** definitive multi-role aircraft with canard foreplanes,

Above: Sukhoi has made much of the Su-30MK's multi-role capability. The machine has been ordered by China and India, the latter taking the ultimate, thrust-vectoring Su-30MKK.

thrust vectoring and with option of Western avionics, displays and defensive systems, as ordered by India and China.

Left: A pair of Su-27s, in 'Flanker-B' interceptor form (foreground) and 'Flanker-C' trainer guise.

Below: A pair of Su-35s demonstrates the enhanced weapons capability offered by the 'second generation' 'Flankers'. The lead aircraft carries an air-to-air load, the rear carries air-to-ground stores.

SPECIFICATION

Sukhoi Su-27 'Flanker-B'
Type: single-seat air superiority fighter
Powerplant: two NPO Saturn (Lyul'ka) AL-31F turbofans each rated at 79.43 kN (17,587 lb st) dry and 122.58 kN (27,557 lb st) with afterburning
Performance: maximum level speed 'clean' at 11,000 m (36,090 ft) 2280 km/h (1417 mph); maximum rate of climb at sea level 19,800 m (64,960 ft) per minute; service ceiling 17,700 m (58,071 ft); range at high altitude 3680 km (2,287 miles)

Weights: empty 17,700 kg (39,021 lb); maximum take-off 33,000 kg (72,751 lb)
Dimensions: wing span 14.70 m (48 ft 2¾ in); length 21.94 m (71 ft 11½ in) excluding probe; height 5.93 m (19 ft 5½ in); wing area 46.50 m² (500.54 sq ft)
Armament: one 30-mm GSh-301 cannon with 150 rounds; maximum ordnance 6000 kg (13,228 lb); weapons include up to six medium-range R-27 (AA-10 'Alamo') and four short-range R-73 (AA-11 'Archer') AAMs

The second Su-30MKI prototype, '06 Blue', was converted from the sixth Su-27UB 'Flanker-B' by the addition of thrust-vectoring nozzles for its AL-31 turbofans, canard foreplanes and an extensive suite of avionics. The aircraft became the only Su-30MKI in existence on 12 June 1999, when the first prototype was lost very publicly during a practice display for that year's Paris Air Show. The accident did nothing to dent the formidable reputation of the type or to dampen India's enthusiasm for the Su-30MKI.

Next-generation 'Flankers'

Advanced Su-27 derivatives

Sukhoi has developed a wide range of advanced aircraft based on the Su-27 'Flanker'. They include two-seat interceptors, two-seat interceptors with thrust vectoring, naval fighters and dedicated long-range attack aircraft.

Su-27K (Su-33)

Cutaway key
1 Pitot head
2 Upward-hinging radome
3 Radar scanner
4 Scanner mounting
5 Radome hinge point
6 Infrared search and tracking scanner
7 Refuelling probe housing
8 Radar equipment module; tilts down for access
9 Lower SRO-2 'Odd Rods' IFF aerial
10 Incidence transmitter
11 Cockpit front pressure bulkhead
12 Retractable spotlight, port and starboard
13 Cockpit side console panel
14 Slide-mounted throttle levers
15 Flight-refuelling probe, extended
16 Instrument panel shroud
17 Pilot's head-up display
18 Upward-hinging cockpit canopy

19 K-36MD 'zero/zero' ejection seat
20 Canopy hydraulic jack
21 Dynamic pressure probe, port and starboard
22 Cockpit rear pressure bulkhead
23 Temperature probe
24 Nosewheel door
25 Twin nosewheels, forward-retracting
26 Kh-41 long-range ramjet and rocket-powered anti-shipping missile

27 Missile folding fins
28 Nosewheel hydraulic steering jacks
29 Deck approach 'traffic-lights'
30 Leading-edge flush EW aerial

Of the advanced 'Flanker' fighters, only the Su-30 (illustrated) and Su-33 have reached service status in Russia. In the case of the Su-30, this status is very limited.

SPECIFICATION

Su-35

Powerplant

Two NPO Saturn (Lyul'ka) AL-31FM afterburning turbofans each rated at 125.49 kN (28,218 lb) with full

Performance

Maximum speed at sea level: 1400 km/h (870 mph)
Maximum speed at high altitude: 2500 km/h (1,553 mph)
Limiting Mach number: 2.35
Maximum climb rate: 14,400 m (47,244 ft) per minute
Service ceiling: 17,200 m (56,430 ft)

Weights

Normal take-off: 25,200 kg (55,555 lb)
Normal maximum take-off: 34000 kg (74,955 lb)
Maximum take-off: 38,800 kg (85,538 lb)

Dimensions

Fuselage length (including probe): 22.18 m (72 ft 9 in)
Wing span: 14.7 m (48 ft 2½ in)
Wing aspect ratio: 7.76
Tailplane span: 9.88 m (32 ft 5 in)
Wing area: 62.04 m² (667.8 sq ft)
Horizontal tail area: 12.24 m² (131.75 sq ft)
Height: 6.34 m (20 ft 9½ in)
Wheel track: 4.34 m (14 ft 3 in)
Wheelbase: 5.88 m (19 ft 4 in)
Maximum wing loading: 456.2 kg/m² (93.4 lb/sq ft)afterburning

Range

Range: 3400 km (2,113 miles)
Ferry range: 4200 km (2,610 miles)
Range with one inflight refuelling: 6300 km (3,915 miles)

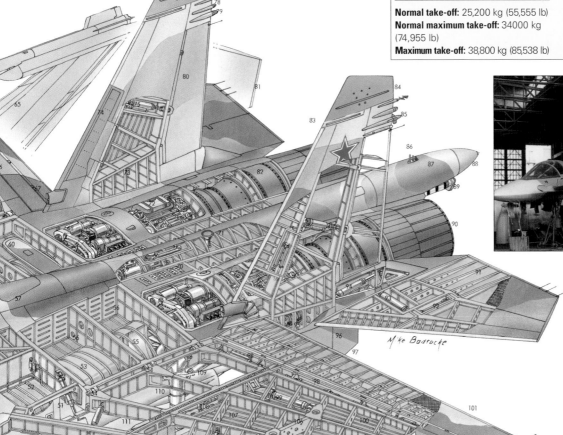

Mike Badrocke

In its Su-34 form, the 'Flanker' is a dedicated long-range attack aircraft, with considerable potential for a wide range of over water operations. The aircraft was designed primarily to replace the Su-24 'Fencer'.

31 Avionics equipment bay
32 Ammunition magazine, 149 rounds
33 HF aerial
34 Starboard fuselage GSh-30-1 30-mm cannon
35 Canard foreplane
36 Starboard wing missile armament
37 Dorsal airbrake
38 Gravity fuel filler cap
39 Centre fuselage fuel tank
40 Forward lateral fuel tanks
41 Kh-41 missile carrier on fuselage centreline station
42 Variable-area intake ramp doors
43 Ramp hydraulic jack
44 Foreplane hydraulic actuator

45 Port canard foreplane
46 Engine air intake
47 Boundary layer bleed air louvres
48 Segmented ventral suction relief doors
49 Retractable intake FOD screen
50 Mainwheel door
51 Door hydraulic jack
52 Port mainwheel bay
53 Intake trunking
54 Wing panel attachment joints
55 Engine compressor face
56 Wing centre-section integral fuel tanks
57 ADF antenna
58 Airbrake hydraulic jack

59 Starboard mainwheel, stowed position
60 Fuel tank access panels
61 Wing-fold hydraulic jack
62 Leading-edge flap, down position
63 Starboard outer, folding, wing panel
64 Outboard plain flap, down position
65 Starboard wing, folded position
66 Inboard double-slotted flap segments
67 Engine bleed air pre-cooler air intake
68 Engine accessory equipment gearbox

69 Central auxiliary power unit
70 Chaff/flare launchers
71 Rear fuselage integral fuel tank
72 Engine oil tank
73 Fin structure
74 Leading-edge HF aerial
75 Rudder hydraulic actuator
76 Fintip UHF/VHF aerial
77 ILS aerial
78 Tail navigation light
79 Radar warning antenna
80 Starboard rudder
81 Starboard tailplane folded position
82 AL-31F afterburning turbofan engine

83 Port tailfin
84 ILS aerial
85 ECM antenna
86 Upper SRO-2 'Odd Rods' IFF aerial
87 Tailcone fairing
88 Rear EW antenna fairing
89 Deck arrester hook
90 Variable-area afterburner nozzle
91 Port tailplane
92 Tailplane fold joint rotary actuator
93 Tailplane pivot bearing
94 Hydraulic actuator
95 Hydraulic accumulator
96 Ventral fin
97 Port inboard double-slotted flap segments
98 Flap hydraulic actuators
99 Wing-fold hydraulic jack
100 Outer wing panel structure
101 Outboard plain flap segment
102 Port navigation light

103 Wingtip missile launch rail
104 Vympel R-73 (AA-11 'Archer') air-to-air missiles
105 Leading-edge flap
106 Pylon attachment hardpoints
107 Port wing integral fuel tank
108 Wing-fold locking mechanism jack
109 Main undercarriage hydraulic retraction jack
110 Mainwheel leg strut
111 Wing-fold hinge joint
112 Leading-edge flush EW aerial panels
113 Missile pylon
114 Vympel R-27 (AA-10 'Alamo-B') IR-homing air-to-air missile
115 Port mainwheel
116 Vympel R-27 (AA-10 'Alamo-C') RHAAM

Sukhoi Su-37 Advanced multi-role fighter

Above: At the heart of the Su-37's unique abilities lie the aircraft's thrust-vectoring nozzles. Their operation is fully integrated into the flight control system software.

Above: Questions have been asked as to the validity of thrust vectoring in a modern BVR air war. Recent experience has shown that modern wars tend to be 'limited', however, and an aircraft such as the Su-37 could offer a decisive advantage in close combat.

The Su-35 formed the basis of the even more advanced **Sukhoi Su-37**. The prototype of this multi-role, all-weather fighter first flew on 2 April 1996. The Su-37's incredible agility made it the star turn at the Farnborough air show five months later.

The Su-37 is powered by two experimental Saturn (Lyul'ka) AL-31FU thrust-vectoring turbofans. The key to the fighter's superb agility is the AL-31FU's axis-symmetric swivelling nozzles which vector thrust in pitch. The nozzles can be deflected together or individually, allowing the aircraft to perform fully controlled manoeuvres well inside the post-stall envelope; backward somersaults and 90-degree changes of heading at 90-degree angle of attack are well within the Su-37's capabilities and are regularly demonstrated.

Systems

In configuration the Su-37 is similar to the Su-35, with control provided by a short-travel side stick, canard foreplanes, a 'glass' cockpit with four wide-screen liquid-crystal displays, and a digital 'fly-by-wire' flight control system; these are

Above: With no money available from the Russian air force and no export customers, the Su-37 seems likely to remain little more than a technology demonstrator for advanced 'Flanker' variants such as the Su-30MKI.

incorporated into an airframe with virtually no angle-of-attack limitations. The Su-37 can locate targets with its radars and bring its weapons to bear from virtually any flight position.

The multifunction phased-array radar can track up to 15 targets, guiding four to six missiles simultaneously.

SPECIFICATION	
Sukhoi Su-37	(56,592 lb); maximum take-off
Type: single-seat multi-role fighter	34,000 kg (74,957 lb)
Powerplant: two Saturn (Lyul'ka)	**Dimensions:** wing span 15.16 m
Al-37F or Al-41F vectored nozzle	(49 ft 8¾ in); length overall 22.2 m
turbofans each rated at 93.10 kN	(72 ft 10 in); height overall 6.36 m
(20,930 lb st) dry and 153 kN	(20 ft 10¼ in); wing area 62 m²
(34,392 lb st) with afterburning	(667.40 sq ft)
Performance: maximum level speed	**Armament:** up to 14 IR-homing
at altitude 2500 km/h (1,555 mph)	and radar-guided air-to-air missiles,
and at sea level 1400 km/h	or a mix of up to 8000 kg
(870 mph); service ceiling 18,800 m	(17,637 lb) of air-to-air, air-to-ground,
(61,680 ft); range 3300 km (2,050	anti-radar or precision- guided
miles) on internal fuel at altitude	munitions on 12 hardpoints, plus
Weights: normal take-off	one GSh-301 30-mm gun in
approximately 25,670 kg	starboard wing root

Boeing F/A-18A/B Hornet

Above: The 'Black Knights' of VMFA-314 was the first frontline Hornet unit, and took the aircraft into action against Libyan targets in 1986, flying from USS Coral Sea. An F/A-18A from VMFA-314 displays the type's responsiveness, despite a load of eight 500-lb (226-kg) bombs.

Spain initially acquired 72 F/A-18A/Bs from the St Louis production line, then augmented its force with 24 ex-US Navy Hornets. They have since been upgraded to near F/A-18C status.

Early F/A-18s were eagerly received into service and soon managed to chalk up several export orders, although they were besieged by a number of problems. A and B models still serve with Australia, Spain and the USMC, among others, despite the fact that the more potent C variant is now in service.

McDonnell Douglas and Northrop were announced as winners of the US Navy's NACF (Navy Air Combat Fighter) programme in May 1975, and the first F/A-18 flew in November 1978. It was a new aircraft, sharing only its general layout with the YF-17. Compared with its predecessor, it was larger and more powerful, incorporating the stronger structure and landing gear that were necessary for carrier operations.

In many respects, the F/A-18 was technologically more advanced than its great rival, the

The US Navy's Blue Angels display team operates eight F/A-18As, from which the six-ship team is drawn. A two-seater F/A-18B is also kept on strength for training and 'media orientation' flights.

F-16A. Its 'fly-by-wire' flight control system used digital rather than analog processors, and it used more composite materials (in the wing skins, for example). It had a multi-mode radar and a cockpit which used cathode-ray tube (CRT) displays in place of conventional dial-and-pointer instruments. It was designed from the ground up to accept pods for electro-optical navigation and targeting aids, and the AIM-7 medium-range air-to-air missile – none of these could be carried on the F-16. McDonnell Douglas touted the new fighter as a true multi-role type, as opposed to the simpler F-16A.

Canada and Australia, both with large fleets of older supersonic fighters, were persuaded by

these arguments, selecting the F/A-18A over the F-16 before the new fighter had finished its flight tests. One of the F/A-18's rivals was Northrop's land-based F-18L, similar in size to the F/A-18, but with an almost completely redesigned structure. Unfortunately for Northrop, the export customers found that the lower risks of the F/A-18A, already in full-scale development for the US Navy, outweighed the higher performance promised by the Northrop design.

Advantages

Canada, with its large expanses of Arctic terrain, and Australia, with its overwater interception mission and the need to overfly the Australian interior (known to pilots as the GAFA, or the Great Australian ****-All), assigned some value to the F-18's twin engines. In fact, the new fighter's General Electric F404 was proving to be trouble-free, in sharp contrast to the F-16's F100 engine.

The F/A-18's new-technology cockpit was also widely acclaimed, and its radar and weapons integration drew no criticism. This was just as well because other important attributes of the new aircraft were. During development, the F/A-18 underwent some major

changes. Dog-teeth disappeared from the wing and stabilizer leading edges. The wing itself was reinforced and the lateral controls were revised because the long, thin wing proved insufficiently stiff – leading to a severe shortfall in roll rate. Long slots in the LERXes were sealed along most of their length, to reduce drag.

Left: F/A-18As and Bs still have a part to play in US Navy aggressor units. Examples serving with VFC-12 'Omars' are used to represent aircraft such as the MiG-29 or Su-27.

Left: F/A-18As and Bs still have a part to play in US Navy aggressor units. Examples serving with VFC-12 'Omars' are used to represent aircraft such as the MiG-29 or Su-27.

Above: Canada was the first and largest customer for the Hornet. In Canadian service, the CF-188 is a true multi-role fighter, employed on a 50/50 basis for air defence and ground attack. The Canadians also pioneered the use of 'fake' cockpits on the underside of their Hornets, with the intention of disorientating an opponent in ACM.

Even these measures, however, barely touched the basic problem. The F/A-18 was failing, by a large measure, to meet its warload and radius specifications. Both of the aircraft which it was supposed to replace (the F-4 and A-7) could carry larger loads over a greater distance. Weight and drag increases also meant that the F/A-18 was limited in its 'bring-back' capability. With normal fuel reserves, the new fighter could not land aboard a carrier at an acceptable approach speed with more than a minimal ordnance load.

In 1982, US Navy test squadron VX-5 recommended that the F/A-18 programme be suspended until some way of alleviating the range shortfall could be found. Among other measures, McDonnell Douglas proposed a thicker wing and an enlarged dorsal spine, which would have improved the aircraft's range at the expense of transonic acceleration and speed.

The US Navy, however, rejected these suggestions and overrode VX-5's recommendations. By that time, the service had other priorities, including development of modernized versions of the A-6 and F-14, and the definition

of a long-range, 'stealthy' bomber to carry the war to the Soviet navy's land bases. All these aircraft were expensive, however, and would not be built soon, or in large quantities. Meanwhile, the US Navy's carrier fleet was expanding, and ageing F-4s and A-7s, dating back to the Vietnam War, had to be replaced. Cancelling or delaying the F/A-18 would leave the US Navy short of modern aircraft, so the USN decided to put the aircraft into production without attempting to solve the range problem. Early F/A-18s were popular and were soon being exported to many destinations, despite some technical problems. A and B models still serve with Australia, Spain and the US Marine Corps, even though the more impressive C variant is now in service.

Basically identical to the F/A-18A, the two-seat F/A-18B was developed alongside the single-seater. In consequence, two examples of the TF-18A (initial designation, later replaced by F/A-18B) featured in the original contract which covered the procurement of a batch of 11 prototype aircraft for RDT&E tasks. The provision of a

second seat in tandem was accomplished at a modest six per cent penalty in fuel capacity. Otherwise, the F/A-18B was unaltered, possessing identical equipment and near-identical combat capability.

Subsequent procurement of the F/A-18B for service with US Navy and Marine Corps units ended with the 40th production example, and this version has never been employed by frontline forces. Apart from a few examples assigned to test agencies, the F/A-18B serves only with VFA-106.

The end of the F/A-18A

The F/A-18A garnered a total of three export customers – Canada, Australia and Spain. They were in a rather better situation than the US Navy because the limitations on the Hornet's range and bring-back capability could be alleviated when it was operated from land bases. Canada, for instance, developed an 1800-litre (480-US gallon) external tank to supplement the 1250-litre (330-US gallon) tanks used by the US Navy. The US Navy did not adopt this external tank because it would not fit on the centreline.

In spite of moves to solve the F/A-18's problems, such as that stated above, the aircraft's deficiencies, combined with the arrival of the F-16C/D, ushered in

a long sales drought.

Pilots were – as always – enthusiastic about the F/A-18A/B when it entered service in 1983. However, historical fact tells a different story. Some 410 of this initial version were built until production switched to the F/A-18C/D in 1987. By 1995, the US Navy had retired most of the A/B models from carrier-based service, the shortest first-line career of any modern fighter. Apart from a small 'top-up' batch of aircraft delivered to Spain from USN stocks in 1995, there are no plans at present to offer these aircraft for export, or to upgrade them – unlike the older and more austere F-16A/B.

The fact was that VX-5 had been right. The F/A-18A/B was a somewhat inadequate aircraft, which validated the adage 'jack of all trades, master of none' in its full and not altogether complimentary sense. It took a series of upgrades to produce a Hornet variant which could be called the master of most of its many missions.

This process started with the first F/A-18C/D, delivered from September 1987. The first F/A-18C/Ds, basically designed to accommodate new technologies and weapons, have formed the basis for a series of Hornets the exterior resemblance of which to the original A/B is entirely deceptive.

Boeing F/A-18C/D Hornet

The F/A-18C represented a major addition to the US Navy's strike force. In fact, the Hornet was considered so important that the USN's tactics were changed to accommodate the aircraft's somewhat limited range.

Despite early teething troubles, the F/A-18 has evolved into the C/D models which, with their new avionics and weapons, far surpass their predecessor.

When the F/A-18A/B entered service in 1983, it was generally greeted enthusiastically. Yet realistically the Hornet proved a somewhat inadequate aircraft, and it took a number of steps to produce a Hornet variant that mastered its various missions. This process started when the first of the F/A-18C/Ds, designed to accommodate new weapons and technologies, were delivered from September 1987.

Airframe development
The F/A-18C/D airframe is not very different to that of the A/B, and has not changed significantly since it entered production. This was not so much because the original design was perfect as it was that it had run into a hard limit on its growth. The F/A-18 had been designed for an approach speed of 125 kt (231 km/h; 143 mph), but development problems raised this to 134 kt

(250 km/h; 155 mph), a respectable speed for a land-based fighter, but a little high for a carrier-based aircraft. This in turn set a cap on the Hornet's maximum landing weight which, coupled with the fact that the navy requires its carrier-borne aircraft to retain large fuel reserves for landings, meant that the Hornet could not undergo major airframe modifications without sacrificing the number of weapons carried or reducing the already limited range of its operations. In fact, the only visible outboard changes to the Hornet have been the addition of antennas and a pair of strakes or 'billboards' above the LERX. These help to break up vortices at angles of attack above 45 degrees. These strakes have been retrofitted to most Hornets.

'Stealthy' Hornet
One significant change is the addition of 'stealthy' materials. During the 1970s and 1980s, new types of RAM (radar-absorbent material) were developed which were lighter and more durable

than their predecessors. As a result, both the navy and air force initiated programmes to reduce the RCS (radar cross-section) of their aircraft. Under the 'Glass Hornet' programme, F/A-18s were given a gold-tinted canopy, coated with a thin layer of indium-tin oxide (ITO) in order to reflect radar signals away from the transmitter. RAM paint on the engines and engine inlets also helped to absorb radar signals. The price of this 'stealthiness' was a weight gain of 113 kg (250 lb), which further reduced the Hornet's bring-back load.

Engine development
Although the Hornet has changed little externally, one significant development has been the

changes to the F/A-18's engines. General Electric's F404 had been free from handling limits and, by 1988, the basic F404-GE-400 engine had accumulated 700,000 flight hours, and reliability and maintainability statistics were good. However, some problems did surface at the million-hour mark. A number of fires broke out in these high-time engines, causing the loss of several aircraft; these fires were attributed to FOD (foreign object damage) eroding the coating on the compressor casing, which resulted in the titanium blades and any debris rubbing together and therefore causing a fire. A number of new safety coatings was developed to cover these blades and to prevent any burning through friction, but the installation of a new engine was inevitable.

To meet Swiss requirements for its Hornets, the F404-GE-402 Enhanced Performance Engine (EPE) was developed and this became the standard powerplant on all Hornets from 1992. Delivering 10 per cent more static sea-level thrust than its predecessor, the EPE also offers 18 per cent more excess power at Mach 0.9 and 10,000 ft (3048 m), and increased transonic acceleration. A typical runway-

The C/D-model Hornets stole back orders from the F-16 on account of their proven ability and sophistication. Meanwhile, the F-14 has been steadily edged off the carrier decks by US Navy Hornets.

The F/A-18 has four fuselage fuel tanks and two wing tanks, and runs on JP-8 aviation fuel. F/A-18C/Ds are fitted with an electronic fuel system that monitors usage and automatically adjusts the aircraft's centre of gravity as fuel is consumed. In the case of damage, all fuel tanks are self-sealing, with a foam infill system.

*Above: **One** of several non-**US** operators of the **F/A-18C/D**, Switzerland decided to purchase the **Hornet** over competing aircraft such as the **Mirage 2000**. **T**his caused a great deal of consternation, and a national referendum was held on whether **S**witzerland had a need for a new fighter at all.*

launched interception profile, from brake release to Mach 1.4 at 50,000 ft (15,240 m), takes 31 per cent less time than before.

Avionics

The F/A-18 was the first true 'digital aircraft'. Many aspects of what the Hornet pilot sees on the cockpit displays are determined by a core mission computer, or by processors built into the other avionics sub-systems. The introduction of new software packages every couple of years has steadily improved the Hornet's capability because of this. The centre of the avionics suite is the mission computer. On the F/A-18C/D, this is the XN-8 system, which is expected to last until 2002/3; the XN-8 will also be the computer system fitted to the first F/A-18E/Fs.

The multi-sensor integration (MSI) system is another important aspect of the C/D-model Hornets. With the MSI, the computer receives inputs from different sensors, correlates them and displays them so that each target appears clearly on the pilot's display. This can be used in an air-to-air or air-to-ground role and is particularly useful in the SEAD (suppression of enemy air defences) mission, where the HARM seeker, radar and RWR can be integrated to locate threats and display them to the crew.

Radar

By 1994, all later-model F/A-18s were fitted with the new APG-73 radar, as opposed to the APG-65 of earlier variants. The -73 uses the same antenna and travelling-wave tube (TWT) transmitter as

its predecessor, but the rest of the hardware is new. The receiver/ exciter unit is more sophisticated and provides much faster analogue-to-digital conversion, allowing the radar to cut the incoming signal into smaller fragments and therefore achieve better range resolution. What is more, air-to-air detection and tracking ranges are up by 7 to 20 per cent. For air-to-ground mapping and bombing modes, the APG-73 also offers higher resolution than before.

Other systems fitted to the later Hornets include NITE Hawk (Navigation IR Targeting Equipment) FLIR, which can track moving targets on the ground and designate them for laser-guided bombs. A new, more reliable Identification Friend or Foe (IFF) system was also incorporated after Kuwait decided upon it for its Hornets; soon after, it was fitted to USN and USMC Hornets.

The Advanced Tactical Air Reconnaissance System (ATARS) fits into the Hornet's nose and incorporates a low- and medium-altitude EO sensor and an infrared linescan imager, all produced by Loral. The first of the ATARS systems was fielded by USMC F/A-18Ds over Yugoslavia in 1999.

Weaponry

Representing a massive leap forward in air-to-air capability over the AIM-7 Sparrow is the AIM-120 AMRAAM. The AMRAAM has its own radar, datalink and inertial navigation system. It is also lighter and

faster (at Mach 4) than the Sparrow, and has been operational on the F/A-18C/D since September 1993. A wide range of stand-off weaponry is also available. This includes the land-attack derivative of the Harpoon missile, the SLAM, and its extended-range variant, the SLAM-ER. For shorter-range stand-off attacks, the AGM-154 Joint Stand-Off Weapon (JSOW) will be used by C/D-model aircraft. The Hornet is also taking over as the main exponent of SEAD missions and of the AGM-88C High-speed Anti-Radiation Missile (HARM).

Operators

Both the US Navy and Marines operate the F/A-18C/D. For the navy, the Hornet is fast becoming its most important aircraft, with most carrier wings operating three F/A-18C/D squadrons. It has taken the place of the Intruder and supplemented the F-14 Tomcat in many areas. Marine Corps D-model Hornets are used for night-attack missions, while single-seat aircraft are used for SEAD and other ground-attack missions.

It was not until the night-attack version of the F/A-18C/D became available that export sales of the later Hornet took off. It was the aircraft's night-attack capability that swayed Kuwait into purchasing 40 C- and D-models. Switzerland, Finland and Malaysia have also purchased varying numbers of the later-model Hornet.

Foreign operators

While not matching its great rival, the F-16, the Boeing (McDD) Hornet has notched up several high-profile export sales.

Australia

Australia selected the Hornet in October 1981 as its next-generation tactical fighter and Mirage III replacement. The US$2,788 million deal included 57 F/A-18As (AF-18As) and 18 F/A-18Bs (AF-18Bs), all but two of which were assembled at Australia's own Government Aircraft Factory. Hornets were delivered to four units between 1985 and 1990 – No. 2 OCU (re-equipped May 1985), No. 3 Sqn (August 1986), No. 77 Sqn (July 1987) and No. 75 Sqn (May 1988). Three of these are based at RAAF Williamtown, NSW, which was refurbished to become the main base of RAAF Hornet operations between 1983 and 1985. No. 75 Sqn is based at Tindal, NT. The Aircraft Research and Development Unit (ARDU), based at Edinburgh, SA, routinely has an AF-18A and an AF-18B on strength for weapons and systems trials. Hornet squadrons regularly make mass deployments to other bases and FOLs, such as Curtin and Schergar. Australian Hornets are being upgraded with APG-73 radar in place of the APG-65, and AIM-132 ASRAAM short-range missiles.

Finland

After a long and exhaustive evaluation of various fighter types, Finland chose the Hornet to replace its elderly Drakens and MiG-21s in April 1992. An order, placed on 5 June 1992, covered 57 F/A-18Cs and seven F/A-18Ds. The two-seaters were all built at St Louis, the first flying there on 21 April 1995. The single-seaters were assembled by Valmet in Finland, the first taking to the air in 1996. All had been delivered by 2000. The Finnish Hornets are fitted with APG-73 radar, ALQ-165 ECM and F404-GE-402 EPE engines, and are armed with AIM-9M Sidewinders and AIM-120B AMRAAMs. They undertake a purely air defence role, and are consequently known as F-18s. Three squadrons fly the type: HävLLv 11 at Rovaniemi, HävLLv 21 at Pirkkala and HävLLv 31 at Rissala, covering the northern, central and southern sectors of the country, respectively.

Kuwait

The Kuwait air force selected the Hornet to replace its A-4KUs and Mirage F1CKs in 1988, placing a September order for 32 F/A-18Cs and eight F/A-18Ds, plus associated AIM-9L, AIM-7F, AGM-65 Maverick and AGM-84 Harpoon missiles. The 1990 invasion of Kuwait affected Hornet deliveries, but the first three arrived in-country on 25 January 1992, with deliveries completed on 21 August 1993. The aircraft are designated KAF-18C/D in service. Initially operating from Kuwait International, the Hornets moved to Ahmed al Jaber AB once it had been rebuilt. The aircraft serve with No. 9 Squadron on air defence tasks and with No. 25 Squadron on attack duties. An option for 38 was cancelled in 1992, and Kuwait is seen as a potential Super Hornet customer.

Land-based Hornets

Such is the capability of the Hornet that it has won a clutch of export orders. It remains the primary combat type with a number of land-based operators.

Right: Malaysia is unique among Hornet operators in buying only the F/A-18D. The Malaysian Hornets are configured primarily for air-to-ground work in a manner similar to those of the US Marine Corps. They are mainly tasked with night/precision attack and anti-shipping work, the latter with AGM-84 AShMs. There is a possibility that Malaysia could trade in some or all of its eight F/A-18Ds for F/A-18Fs.

Right: Kuwait received its first KAF-18C/D aircraft in January 1992, their delivery having been delayed by the 1991 Gulf War. The aircraft are used on air-defence and attack duties. KAF-18Cs are shown here.

Left: Canada's CF-188 fleet has been the subject of much hardship over the years. Some 138 single-seat (illustrated) and 24 two-seat aircraft were ordered, the first entering service in 1982. The aircraft flew combat missions during the 1991 Gulf War, but immediately upon their return defence cuts saw the fleet halved.

Right: Switzerland received the last of its 34 Hornets in 1999. Although designated as F-18A and F-18B (as here) aircraft, they are equipped to a very high standard and have AMRAAM capability.

Left: Spain's single-seat Hornets are known to the manufacturer as EF-18As and to the Spanish air force as C.15s. Similarly, the two-seaters are EF-18Bs to Boeing and CE.15s locally. A fleetwide upgrade programme in the early 1990s brought the Spanish Hornets up to EF-18A+ and EF-18B+ (illustrated) standard, with AIM-120 and Nite Hawk capability, a new central computer, an integrated EW/jamming system and Mil Std 1553 databus. Spain has used its Hornets in combat over Kosovo during Operation Allied Force, where the aircraft employed LGBs against Serb forces.

Lockheed Martin F-35 Joint Strike Fighter
Multi-role tactical fighter family

Above: None of the X-35 aircraft was fully representative of the production-standard F-35. Here, the X-35C shows off the type's general configuration.

Right: The baseline F-35A configuration is represented here by the X-35A. The aircraft will mark a quantum leap in performance over the F-16.

Above: This image gives a good impression of the X-35B's configuration for hovering flight. Note the open upper and lower fuselage doors.

On 26 October 2001 it was announced that Lockheed Martin, with BAE Systems and Northrop Grumman as key partners, had won the Joint Strike Fighter (JSF) competition with its **X-35** design. The competition had been close, but Boeing's X-32 was seen as a less competent package.

Three X-35 variants were built for the evaluation process: the conventional take-off and landing (CTOL) **X-35A**, the short take-off and vertical landing (STOVL) **X-35B** and the carrier-capable (CV) **X-35C**. After down-selection of the X-35, these three variants have continued to be developed as the F-35A, F-35B and F-35C, respectively.

F-35 design features

The F-35A is being developed as a replacement for the US Air Force's F-16 force and looks likely to find export sales with a number of current F-16 operators, especially those within NATO. In addition, Australia has signed up for the aircraft to replace its F/A-18 and F-111 fleets. F-35A is powered by the Pratt & Whitney F135 turbofan, which is based on the F/A-22's F119. The F135 is planned to be ready for CTOL use in July 2005, ready for the first F-35A, and first JSF, flight in October 2005. For STOVL use, the F135 employs an

An X-35B sits on the runway with its upper and lower fuselage doors open.

ingenious lift-fan system designed by Rolls-Royce and Hamilton Sundstrand. For STOVL operations or during transitions from/to wingborne flight from the hover, the aircraft's jet nozzle is directed downwards, while doors above and below the forward fuselage open to allow the passage of air through a horizontally mounted fan. This fan is driven by a shaft from the engine and provides the forward component of the

aircraft's thrust during hovering flight. This technology makes for more efficient hovering performance than that of the Harrier II, as well as allowing the JSF to be firmly supersonic in all its variants.

Lastly, F-35C is the dedicated naval variant for the US Navy. The aircraft will have larger wing surfaces and increased-area tailplanes in order to better suit it to carrier operations. Like the other JSF variants, it carries its

primary AAM or attack load in bays which are located on the fuselage sides.

By late 2003, the joint US and British requirement for the JSF stood at around 3000 aircraft, with Britain having identified a need for 150 F-35Bs to replace its Harrier fleet. JSF flight testing is likely to continue into the second decade of the twenty-first century, with major F-35A flight testing due to continue into 2010.

Lockheed Martin F/A-22 Raptor Low-observable warplane

In 1991, the USAF announced that it had selected the **Lockheed Martin F-22** as the winner in its ATF (Advanced Tactical Fighter) competition to find a replacement for the F-15 Eagle. The aircraft won in the face of stiff competition from Northrop's YF-23, with a pair of

YF-22A prototypes flying evaluation missions until 1997.

Lockheed Martin, with Boeing as its primary partner, has designed the F-22, now officially designated **Raptor**, to satisfy very low observable (VLO) criteria. As such, the aircraft has an unusual configuration, with a

trapezoidal wing whose angles are repeated on other surfaces to reduce radar signature, canted fins and internal weapons carriage. The aircraft has supremely advanced avionics, based on the APG-77 active electronically scanned array radar. Passive sensors, such as

an IRST, are also available, the on-board computer systems switching between passive and active sensor operation as the tactical situation demands. In addition, the avionics allow the fusing of data from the Raptor's own sensors, as well as that from other systems such as AWACS platforms, reducing pilot workload and increasing combat effectiveness.

Raptor testing

Incorporating two-dimensional thrust-vectoring engine nozzles, triplex fly-by-wire controls and a

This image emphasizes the F/A-22's distinctive configuration. The aircraft is not stealthy in the manner of the B-2A, but is sufficiently difficult to detect to give it an engagement-winning advantage.

Around 27 per cent of the F/A-22's empty weight is made up of composite materials. Modern design and materials technology has allowed Lockheed Martin to make the aircraft stealthy, without compromising its aerodynamic or flight performance.

raft of advanced features, the F-22 has, of course, required a lengthy test programme. The Engineering, Manufacture and Development (EMD) contract signed in 1991 originally called for 11, later revised to nine, **F-22A** machines and two **F-22B** two-seaters. The latter were subsequently cancelled on the grounds of cost.

Although the first EMD F-22A completed its maiden flight in 1997, by 2001 the programme was under close scrutiny from US Congress. It was allowed to continue only under strict supervision and with the setting of milestone targets that then had to be met.

In an attempt to emphasize the multi-role potential of the Raptor and also as an indication of its likely long-term use, the US Air Force subsequently redesignated the aircraft as the **F/A-22**. For a possible attack role, the type has been demonstrated with external pylons, but these would seriously compromise its stealth characteristics.

In November 2002, Lockheed Martin delivered the last of five Dedicated Initial Operational Test and Evaluation (DIOT&E)

SPECIFICATION
Lockheed Martin F/A-22 Raptor **Type:** single-seat air-dominance and multi-role fighter **Powerplant:** two Pratt & Whitney F119-PW-100 turbofans each rated in the 155.65-kN (35,000-lb) thrust class with afterburning **Performance:** maximum speed around Mach 2; supercruise speed in excess of Mach 1.5	**Dimensions:** wing span 13.56 m (44 ft 6 in); length 18.92 m (62 ft 1 in); height 5 m (16 ft 5 in) **Armament:** one 20-mm M61A2 Vulcan cannon, plus up to six AIM-120C AMRAAMs in internal weapons bay, or two 454-kg (1,000-lb) GBU-32 JDAMs and two AIM-120Cs, plus provision for stores on external pylons

Raptors (aircraft No. 11) and by June 2003 the 10 flying Raptors had accumulated 3500 hours of flight time. Four DIOT&E aircraft entered operational testing in the autumn of 2003, while the remaining DIOT&E aircraft, plus two other machines, continued tactics development at Nellis. Three more Raptors were delvered to Nellis during summer 2003, for a total of 14 aircraft built. The USAF has a stated requirement for 339 Raptors, with initial operational capability expected by 2006.

Known to Lockheed Martin as Raptor 4011, this machine was the last DIOT&E aircraft. Work to establish the type's initial production configuration continues.

NAMC Q-5/A-5 'Fantan' Attack aircraft

The **Q-5 'Fantan'** is a dedicated attack aircraft loosely based on the airframe of the J-6, the Chinese-built MiG-19. Development began in August 1958, the new aircraft actually sharing only the rear fuselage and main landing gear of the MiG-19 with a new and longer fuselage, area-ruled to reduce transonic drag. The fuselage also has an internal weapons bay and two adjacent weapons pylons. It has a conical nose, giving an improved view forward and downward, and providing a potential location for an attack radar that never materialized. The Q-5 also has a wing of greater area and reduced sweep for more lift and better turn performance. The tailplane was increased in size, necessitating the provision of lateral air intakes. The nose-wheel was also redesigned.

Prototype construction began in May 1960, but was abandoned during the political turmoil of the early 1960s. It was resumed full time in 1963 and the prototype first flew on 4 June 1965, but extensive modifications proved necessary to solve many problems. Two new prototypes flew in October 1969 and the type was ordered into production during 1970 as the Q-5, of which nearly 1000 were built for the Chinese forces in four variants.

This Chinese People's Liberation Army Air Force (PLAAF) Q-5III wears a three-tone camouflage. Such schemes are usually applied only to export aircraft, PLAAF Q-5s being white.

'Fantan' variants

Little is known about a dedicated nuclear-capable version, but the extended-range **Q-5I** has a fuel tank in place of the internal weapons bay and other changes. These modifications meant a 500-kg (1,102-lb) increase in warload and a 35 per cent increase in low-level radius of action. Some Q-5Is were modified to serve with the Chinese naval air force as carriers for the C-801 anti-ship missile or torpedoes.

The **Q-5IA** features two more underwing hardpoints, pressure refuelling, a new gun/bomb sight system and new defensive avionics. Forty examples were delivered to North Korea. The **Q-5II** was basically the Q-5IA revised with an RWR.

Export aircraft

The **A-5C** is the export version of the Q-5IA for Pakistan (52 aircraft). but later ordered by Bangladesh and Burma (24 each), and in fact entered production before the domestic variant. Known in Pakistan as the **A-5-III**, the A-5C has improved avionics, compatibility with various Western weapons including the AIM-9, and the Martin Baker Mk 10L ejection seat. Upgrades with Western avionics resulted in prototypes of the **Q-5K** and **A-5M** with French and Italian systems, respectively, but no orders resulted.

SPECIFICATION	
Nanchang Q-5IA 'Fantan' **Type:** single-seat close air support and ground-attack warplane **Powerplant:** two Liming (LM) (previously Shenyang) Wopen-6A turbojet engines each rated at 29.42 kN (6,614 lb st) dry and 36.78 kN (8,267 lb st) with afterburning **Performance:** maximum speed 1190 km/h (740 mph) at 11,000 m (36,090 ft); maximum rate of climb 6180 m (20,275 ft) per minute with afterburning at 5000 m (16,405 ft); service ceiling 15,850 m (52,000 ft); combat radius 400 km	(249 miles) on a lo-lo-lo mission with maximum external stores and no afterburning **Weights:** empty 6375 kg (14,054 lb); maximum take-off 11,830 kg (38,812 lb) **Dimensions:** wing span 9.68 m (31 ft 9 in); length 15.65 m (51 ft 4¼ in) including probe; height 4.33 m (14 ft 2¾ in); wing area 27.95 m² (300.86 sq ft) **Armament:** two 23-mm Type 23-2K fixed forward-firing cannon in the leading edges of the wing roots, plus up to 2000 kg (4,409 lb) of disposable stores

XAC JH-7/FBC-1 Flying Leopard Interdictor/maritime attacker

The XAC **JH-7** has been in development since the mid-1970s to meet a requirement from the Chinese PLAAF and APN (Aviation of the People's Navy) for an all-weather interdictor. In design, the warplane resembles a scaled-up SEPECAT Jaguar. Its projected performance approaches that of the Tornado IDS, albeit with a reduced payload, but with a longer unrefuelled range.

The JH-7 features a wide range of indigenously developed systems and equipment; these include the JL-10A multi-mode radar, Blue Sky low-altitude radar/FLIR navigation pods and inertial/GPS navigation systems. The Xian WS-9 engines are

An aircraft of impressive appearance, the JH-7 is still probably a little primitive by Western standards. Nevertheless, it is undoubtedly a potent warplane.

licence-manufactured Rolls-Royce Spey turbofans. Although the prototype reportedly made its maiden flight in 1988, the programme was troubled by technical problems throughout the 1990s, leading China to consider alternative combat aircraft from Russia in the form of Sukhoi Su-27s and two-seat Su-30s. Surprisingly, the acquisition of the Sukhois has not ended the JH-7 programme.

It is likely that the JH-7's revival has stemmed from the People's Liberation Army's desire to modernize its air forces and also from the need of the Chinese aerospace industry to be able to offer more modern fighters for export.

Home orders

The decision to feature the JH-7 prominently at the Zhuhai air show in 1998 was accompanied by a modest order for the type. With the PLAAF's acquisition of the Su-30 for the long-range strike role, the JH-7 is being acquired for the APN, with a reported figure of between 25 and 32 aircraft required for a single regiment. The service is gaining a potent long-range maritime attack capability.

Armed with the indigenous C-802 or supersonic KR-1 missiles (the latter a version of the Russian Kh-31P/AS-17 'Krypton') the JH-7 will exert a marked influence on the balance of power in the Taiwan Straits, and beyond into the South China Sea. During China's 1995/96 'exercises' near Taiwan, Chinese television briefly showed a JH-7 dropping a clutch of free-fall general purpose bombs. The JH-7 is being promoted actively for export as the **FBC-1 Flying Leopard**. It was recently offered – unsuccessfully – to Iran. In 2004, the APN had around 20 JH-7s in service, but also seemed likely to purchase attack variants of the Su-30MKK.

SPECIFICATION	
XAC JH-7/FBC-1 Flying Leopard **Type:** two-seat all-weather interdictor and maritime attack aircraft **Powerplant:** two Xian WS9 (Rolls-Royce Spey Mk 202) turbofans each rated at 91.20 kN (20,515 lb st) with afterburning **Performance:** maximum level speed 'clean' at 11,000 m (36,080 ft) 1808 km/h (1,122 mph); service ceiling 'clean' 15,600 m (51,180 ft); combat radius 1650 km (1,025 miles)	**Weights:** maximum take-off 28,475 kg (62,776 lb); maximum landing 21,130 kg (46,583 lb) **Dimensions:** wing span 12.71 m (41 ft 8¼ in); length including probe 22.33 m (73 ft 3 in) including probe; height 6.58 m (21 ft 6¾ in); wing area 52.3 m² (563 sq ft) **Armament:** one twin-barrelled 23-mm cannon; plus maximum ordnance of 14,330 lb (6500 kg), including C-701, C-801 and C-802K AShMs; 500-lb (227-kg) LGBs and short-range PL-5 or PL-9 AAMs

AMX International AMX Light strike aircraft

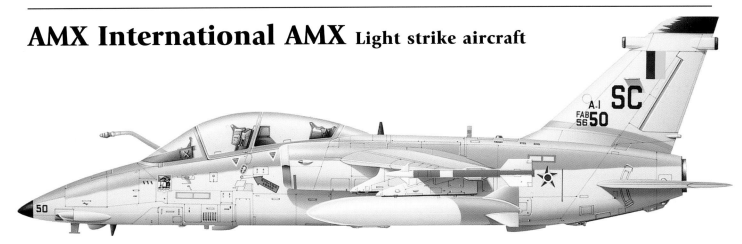

In April 1978, Aeritalia and Aermacchi combined their resources to meet AMI (Italian air force) requirements for an advanced multi-purpose strike/recce aircraft. The programme received extra impetus in 1980 when it was joined by Brazil. A common specification, including good short-field performance, high subsonic operating speeds and advanced nav/attack systems, allowed initial agreement for the procurement of 79 **AMX** aircraft for Brazil and 187 for Italy, plus six prototypes.

The initial AMX prototype flew at Aeritalia's flight-test centre in May 1984, and the first Brazilian-assembled prototype followed in October 1985.

The design

Design features of the AMX include HOTAS, INS, a HUD, HDDs, digital databus, active

Represented here by a Brazilian A-1B, AMX-T forms the basis of Venezuela's AMX-ATA.

and passive ECM, and provision for air-to-air refuelling. By mid-1998, programme totals had increased to 332 aircraft, including 66 two-seat **AMX-T** machines designated **A-1B** in Brazil. The single-seat AMX is

These Italian single-seaters have wingtip Sidewinders and underfuselage recce pods. Note the 'bolt-on' refuelling probes.

SPECIFICATION	
AMX International AMX **Type:** single-seat close air support and reconnaissance aircraft **Powerplant:** one Fiat/Piaggio/Alfa Romeo Avio/CELMA-built Rolls-Royce Spey RB.168 Mk 807 turbofan rated at 49.06 kN (11,030 lb st) **Performance:** maximum level speed 'clean' and maximum cruising speed at 10,975 m (36,000 ft) 1914 km/h (568 mph); maximum rate of climb at sea-level 3124 m (10,250 ft) per minute; service ceiling 13,000 m (42,650 ft);	combat radius 556 km (345 miles) on a lo-lo-lo attack mission with a 907-kg (2,000-lb) warload **Weights:** operating empty 6700 kg (14,771 lb); maximum take-off 13,000 kg (28,660 lb) **Dimensions:** wing span 10 m (32 ft 9 in) over wingtip AAMs, length 13.58 m (44 ft 6 in); height 4.58 m (15 ft); wing area 21 m² (226.05 sq ft) **Armament:** one internal 20-mm M61A1 cannon (or two internal 30-mm DEFA 554 cannon in Brazilian aircraft), plus a maximum ordnance load of 3800 kg (8,377 lb)

flown as the **A-1** in Brazil. In the reconnaissance role, the AMX can either carry external photo or IR pods, or can be equipped with any one of three sensor

pallets for internal carriage in the forward fuselage.
Italian air force pilots began training on the AMX in 1988, with the first operational

squadron receiving its first aircraft on 7 November 1989. The first Brazilian A-1 unit began to receive its aircraft on 17 October 1989. Venezuela

announced its intention to purchase eight of the advanced **AMX-ATA**, a two-seater multi-mission attack fighter version for combat and training, in 1998.

SOKO/IAv Craiova J-22 Orao/IAR-93 Attack aircraft

The **J-22 Orao/IAR-93** is the product of an unlikely collaborative agreement between Yugoslavia and Romania. Both nations had a requirement for a lightweight, robust transonic close-support/ ground-attack aircraft, with secondary interceptor and recce capabilities, to enter service around 1977. Construction was allocated to two companies: Romania's CNIAR (now IAv Craiova) and SOKO in Yugoslavia. The aircraft emerged with a configuration reminiscent of the larger SEPECAT Jaguar.

Both single- and two-seat prototypes were constructed in each country, and these made simultaneous maiden flights on 31 October 1974 and 29 January 1977 (two-seaters). Series production of the Romanian IAR-93 followed in 1979, and of the Yugoslavian J-22 Orao (Eagle) in 1980. Continued non-availability of afterburners meant that the first 20 production aircraft in each country were delivered without reheat. The

first Romanian version of the aircraft was the **IAR-93A**, which made its maiden flight in 1981.

Adding reheat

CNIAR built 26 single-seaters and 10 two-seaters with an extended forward fuselage and sideways-opening canopies. The following **IAR-93B** introduced afterburning Viper Mk 633-41 turbojets. It also featured modified wings.

Romania ordered 165 IAR-93s, including two-seaters. In Yugoslavia, the first production variant was the **Orao 1**,

This is one of the Viper Mk 632-engined IAR-93MBs, which is otherwise similar to the IAR-93B two-seater. This aircraft was later used to test an advanced cockpit.

powered by non-afterburning Vipers. The lack of performance of these early production aircraft was such that they were allocated to the tactical recce role under the designation **IJ-22**. A few of the 20-aircraft batch appeared as trainers with the designation **NJ-22**.

The Orao 1 was followed by the single-seat **Orao 2** or **J-22(M)**, with enlarged integral wing fuel tanks, and with increased capacity in two fuselage tanks. Afterburning Viper 633-41 engines made possible a small increase in payload. The Orao 2 also has a Thomson-CSF HUD. Further problems with the engines, however, meant that these

aircraft did not begin to enter service until 1986.

The two-seat Orao 1 proved to be somewhat underpowered and shortlegged, and SOKO therefore designed a new two-seat trainer incorporating the more powerful engines and the increased-capacity wing tanks of the Orao 2. The first example of the new **Orao 2D**, or **NJ-22(M)**, made its maiden flight on 18 July 1986, and production 2Ds have been augmented by a conversion programme bringing all surviving Orao 1 two-seaters up to the same standard. Like the Orao 2, the 2D has the same wing leading-edge root extensions as are fitted to the IAR-93B.

SPECIFICATION

SOKO/IAv Craiova J-22 Orao/ IAR-93
Type: lightweight close-support and ground-attack aircraft
Powerplant: in most aircraft, two Turbomécanica/ORAO-built Rolls-Royce Viper Mk 633-41 turbojets each rated at 17.79 kN (4,000 lb st) dry and 22.24 kN (5,000 lb st) with afterburning
Performance: maximum level speed 'clean' at 11,000 m (36,090 ft) 1020 km/h (634 mph); maximum rate of climb at sea level 5340 m (17,520 ft) per minute; service ceiling 15,000 m (49,210 ft);

tactical radius 522 km (324 miles) on a hi-lo-hi attack mission with four cluster bombs and one drop tank
Weights: empty equipped 5500 kg (12,125 lb); maximum take-off 11,080 kg (24,427 lb)
Dimensions: wing span 9.3 m (30 ft 6 in); length 14.9 m (48 ft 10 in); height 4.52 m (14 ft 10 in); wing area 26 m² (279.87 sq ft)
Armament: two GSh-23L 23-mm cannon plus a maximum ordnance load of 2800 kg (6,173 lb)

This Romanian IAR-93A features ventral fins as well as underfuselage and underwing pylons.

Panavia Tornado IDS Interdictor and attack aircraft

No. 14 Sqn was the last of the Brüggen-based Tornado units to form. Although the GR.Mk 1 illustrated here is carrying cluster bombs, this squadron was the first to receive the JP233 airfield attack weapon.

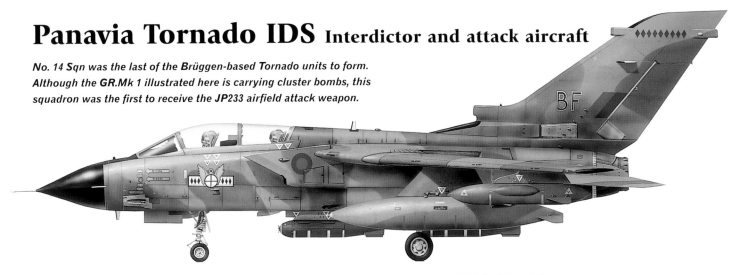

A No. 31 Squadron Tornado GR.Mk 4 (foreground) is joined by a Tornado GR.Mk 4A reconnaissance aircraft of No. II(AC) Squadron for a training sortie in July 2002.

SPECIFICATION	
Panavia Tornado GR.Mk 4	**Weights:** basic empty about
Type: two-seat all-weather attack	13,890 kg (30,620 lb); maximum
and interdiction aircraft	take-off about 27,951 kg (61,620 lb)
Powerplant: two Turbo-Union	**Dimensions:** wingspan 13.91 m
RB.199 Mk 103 turbofans each	(45 ft 7½ in) minimum sweep and
rated at 8,650 lb st (38.48 kN) dry	8.60 m (28 ft 2½ in) maximum
and 16,075 lb st (71.50 kN) with	sweep; length 16.72 m (54 ft
afterburning	10¼ in); height 5.95 m (19 ft 6¼ in);
Performance: maximum speed	wing area 26.60 m² (286.33 sq ft)
2338 km/h (1,453 mph) at	**Armament:** two 27-mm IWKA-Mauser
10,975 m (36,000 ft); climb to 9145	cannon with 180 rpg; maximum
m (30,000 ft) in less than	ordnance load over 9000 kg
2 minutes; service ceiling more	(19,841 lb); current weapons include
than 15240 m (50,000 ft); combat	454-kg (1,000-lb) free-fall bombs,
radius 1390 km (863 miles) with a	CPU-123/B Paveway II LGBs; new
heavy warload on a typical hi-lo-hi	weapons include GBU-28 Paveway
mission	III LGBs and Storm Shadow SMDs

The multi-national **Tornado Interdictor Strike** (**IDS**) aircraft remains one of Europe's most important combat aircraft. Its various attack, reconnaissance and defence suppression versions have played major roles during recent operations in the Balkans and over Iraq. The RAF retains the type in frontline service, primarily in the long-range interdiction/overland attack role. They also have specialized missions that comprise maritime attack (**Tornado GR.Mk 1B**) and reconnaissance (**Tornado GR.Mk 1A**). In 2001 the RAF began using fully operational **GR.Mk 1**s upgraded to **GR.Mk 4** standard with new cockpit displays, full compatibility with the TIALD pod for autonomous PGM delivery, integration of NVGs with an upgraded FLIR and an enhanced self-defence suite. Recce-configured GR.Mk 1As are similarly being upgraded as **GR.Mk 4A**s.

The Luftwaffe had around 270 IDS aircraft in service early in 2001, including a number to **ECR** (Electronic Combat and Reconnaissance) standard. The aircraft underwent a comprehensive MLU similar to the RAF's GR.Mk 4 programme that will also add Litening targeting pods and towed radar decoys. New weapons include BLU-109 and GBU-22 Paveway III LGBs, Taurus tactical cruise missiles and IRIS-T AAMs.

The Marineflieger has a wing with around 50 IDS aircraft assigned conventional attack, anti-shipping (with Kormoran AShMs), defence suppression (with HARMs) and recce missions. The Italian air force has three fighter-bomber IDS groups, one of which is assigned the anti-ship role with Kormoran missiles.

Saudi Arabia is the remaining Tornado operator, with the survivors of 96 aircraft assigned to three units.

McDonnell Douglas/BAe Harrier GR.Mk 5/7
Close support aircraft

The **Harrier GR.Mk 5** was generally similar to the AV-8B for the US Marine Corps, albeit with structural strengthening to suit it to the low-level battlefield support role envisaged by the RAF. A total of 62 GR.Mk 5s was ordered for the RAF, the workshare on these being divided between BAe and McDonnell Douglas. The **Harrier GR.Mk 7** is basically the RAF equivalent of the 'night attack' AV-8B, using similar equipment and avionics. The variant is distinguished from the GR.Mk 5

This No. IV (Army Co-Operation) Squadron Harrier GR.Mk 7 wears a high-conspicuity tailfin for low-level operations over Germany.

by undernose forward hemisphere antennas for the Zeus ECM. The GR.Mk 7 is also NVG compatible and a digital colour map is fitted.

Equipment upgrade

The first GR.Mk 7s ordered as such were 34 aircraft requested during 1988, which took total RAF Harrier II procurement to 94 (plus two prototype/pre-series aircraft). To serve as GR.Mk 7 prototypes, both pre-series aircraft were adapted to accommodate the overnose FLIR and Zeus, the first flying in its new guise in late 1989.

The additional capability offered by the GR.Mk 7 was such that it was soon decided that all RAF Harrier IIs would be retrofitted to this configuration, and to ease this process Harrier IIs Nos 42–60 were completed as **GR.Mk 5A** machines with provision for GR.Mk 7 avionics, and were delivered straight to storage to await conversion. Conversions of these aircraft began in December 1990. From aircraft No. 77 all RAF Harriers were fitted with a LERX (Leading-Edge Root Extension), improving the turn performance.

The first production GR.Mk 7 was delivered in May 1990, with service deliveries beginning in August. However, the GR.Mk 7 had a troubled development, hampered by the non-availability of many important equipment items. The GR.Mk 7 initially lacked a reconnaissance capability and, when the RAF needed to replace Jaguars being used in Turkey to police the

northern 'No-Fly Zone' over Iraq, GR.Mk 7s were selected. In order to give some recce capability, at least nine aircraft were rewired to carry the old Harrier GR.Mk 3 recce pod. Since then the GR.Mk 7 has been given the capability to operate using the Vinten Vicon 18 Series 601 and 603 recce pods.

New cannon

Other important delayed equipment included the Harrier's 30-mm ADEN cannon and MAWS (Missile Approach Warning System). The MAWS automatically activates appropriate countermeasures and augments Zeus. Provision of a dedicated Sidewinder pylon allows adequate defensive capability even when carrying a full offensive load. An integral chaff dispenser in these pylons frees the aircraft from having to carry a Phimat pod.

By late 1992 some aircraft already had their INAS upgraded to FIN1075G standards, with the incorporation of a GPS receiver. The first aircraft so equipped flew with the new kit in late 1992. The presence of GIPS can be discerned by the addition of a small antenna on the spine of the aircraft.

The RAF's No. 1 Sqn received GR.Mk 7s in late 1992, and became the first frontline unit to start night-attack training in earnest. The Harrier is now receiving the TIALD laser designation pod, as well as the Brimstone anti-armour missile and Paveway III LGB.

Seeking to acquire a trainer fully representative of the

Now supplemented by the CRV-7 rocket, the 68-mm SNEB has long been a favoured Harrier weapon. The aircraft can carry four MATRA 155 pods, each containing 19 rockets fitted with various warheads.

SPECIFICATION
McDonnell Douglas/BAe Harrier GR.Mk 7 **Type:** single-seat V/STOL attack and close support warplane **Powerplant:** two Rolls-Royce Pegasus Mk 105 vectored-thrust turbofan rated at 95.6 kN (21,500-lb st) **Performance:** maximum level speed at low altitude 1065 km/h (661 mph); service ceiling over 15,240 m (50,000 ft); combat radius 1101 km (684 miles) on a hi-lo-hi mission after short take-off with seven 227-kg (500-lb) bombs and two drop tanks **Weights:** empty equipped 7050 kg (15,542 lb); maximum take-off	14,061 kg (31,000 lb) after short take-off **Dimensions:** wingspan 9.25 m (30 ft 4 in); length 14.53 m (47 ft 8 in); height 3.55 m (11 ft 7¾ in); wing area 21.37 m² (230 sq ft) excluding LERX **Armament:** two 25-mm ADEN fixed forward-firing cannon in underfuselage pods with 100 rounds, plus up to 3747 kg (8,260 lb) of disposable stores on five external hardpoints; weapons include BL755 and CBU-87 cluster bombs, GBU-16, CPU-123/B and GBU-24/B LGBs, MATRA 155 or CRV-7 rockets pods, AIM-9L/M AAMs and GP bombs of up to 454 kg (1,000 lb)

second-generation Harrier's performance, equipment and capability, the RAF decided to procure a version of the TAV-8B. A decision to proceed with the **Harrier T.Mk 10** was taken in February 1990 and an order for 13 aircraft was confirmed early in 1992.

Powered by the Pegasus Mk 105 engine, the T.Mk 10 retains the standard avionics of the GR.Mk 7 and is thus fully combat capable. The first Harrier T.Mk 10 made its maiden flight on 7 April 1994 and service deliveries began to No. 20 Sqn, RAF, in 1995.

SEPECAT Jaguar Attack and close support aircraft

Both Armée de l'Air and RAF (pictured) Jaguars have seen considerable action over the former Yugoslavia. This example carries a centreline TIALD pod.

SPECIFICATION

SEPECAT Jaguar International
Type: single-seat attack and close support warplane
Powerplant: two Rolls-Royce/Turbomeca Adour Mk 804 turbofans each rated at 23.66 kN (5,320-lb st) dry and 35.75 kN (8,040 lb st) with afterburning
Performance: maximum level speed 'clean' at 10,975 m (36,000 ft) 11699 km/h (1,056 mph); service ceiling 14,000 m (45,930 ft); range 3524 km (2,190 miles) with drop tanks

Weights: empty equipped 7700 kg (16,975 lb); maximum take-off 15,700 kg (34,612 lb)
Dimensions: wingspan 8.69 m (28 ft 6 in); length 16.83 m (55 ft 2½ in) including probe; height 4.89 m (16 ft ½ in); wing area 24.18 m² (260.27 sq ft)
Armament: two 30-mm ADEN fixed forward-firing cannon in the underside of the fuselage, plus up to 4763 kg (10,500 lb) of disposable stores on five external hardpoints

The **SEPECAT Jaguar** resulted from a 1965 Anglo-French specification for a STOL advanced/operational trainer and tactical support aircraft. The RAF and Armée de l'Air agreed to buy 200 aircraft each, the RAF split being 165 and 35 of the single and two-seat models, respectively, the former designated **Jaguar S** (Strike) by the manufacturer and **Jaguar GR.Mk 1** by the RAF. The GR.Mk 1 has a chisel-shaped nose for a Laser Ranger and Marked Target Seeker (LRMTS) and a fin-top RWR pod. As built, RAF aircraft were powered by 32.51-kN (7,305-lb st) Adour Mk 102 engines and were delivered between 1973 and 1978.

The two-seat **Jaguar B** was built with full navigation and attack avionics, but without the LRMTS, IFR probe and RWR, and has only one cannon. RAF aircraft were **Jaguar T.Mk 2** machines, of which 14 were brought up to **T.Mk 2A** standard with the FIN1064 nav/attack unit and Adour Mk 104 engines.

The RAF's GR.Mk 1s were upgraded in 1978–84 with 35.14-kN (7,900-lb st) Adour Mk 104s, and raised further from December 1983 to **GR.Mk 1A**

standard by introduction of the FIN1064. Further upgrades have seen, or will see, introduction of the TIALD targeting pod (in 11 aircraft to create nine **GR.Mk 1B** and two **T.Mk 2B** machines), a new terrain-reference navigation system, a helmet-mounted sight, and an upgraded cockpit (in most operational aircraft to create **GR.Mk 3** and **T.Mk 4** machines) and full TIALD and ASRAAM capability (as a retrofit in most aircraft to produce **GR.Mk 3A** and possibly **T.Mk 4A** machines). Some 96 RAF aircraft are being upgraded offering 10 per cent more thrust but reduced operating costs.

France bought 160 single-seat and 40 two-seat aircraft. Compared with its British equivalent, the French single-seat **Jaguar A** (*Appui*, or attack)

has generally inferior mission avionics. Like the GR.Mk 1, the Jaguar A has a retractable IFR probe and two 30-mm cannon. The last 80 aircraft have an undernose laser ranger and an improved RWR, and the last 30 are able to carry a nose-mounted laser designator. With the temporary exception of the first 10 production aircraft, Jaguar As were fitted with Adour Mk 102s.

Armée de l'Air trainer

France's two-seat aircraft are **Jaguar E** (*Ecole*, or school) machines and lack full nav/attack avionics, but from the 27th aircraft were fitted with a fixed IFR probe. Deliveries of Jaguar A were completed between 1972 and 1981, and the type equipped nine squadrons, two of them tasked with delivering the AN 52 nuclear bomb.

Export Jaguars have been based on the Jaguar B/S airframe. First flown in 1974, the **Jaguar International** prototype was an RAF machine with Adour Mk 104s offering more thrust than original Mk 102s. Ecuador's 10 **Jaguar ES** single- and two **Jaguar EB** two-seat aircraft were delivered in 1977, the seven survivors augmented by three refurbished RAF aircraft during 1991.

From March 1977 Oman took delivery of 10 single-seat **Jaguar OS** and two two-seat **Jaguar OB** aircraft. A similar second batch was delivered in 1983. Second-batch aircraft were powered by 37.37-kN (8,400-lb st) Adour 811s. Oman's fleet was augmented by single ex-RAF one- and two-seat aircraft. Between 1986 and 1989, 21 survivors were upgraded with the FIN1064.

The biggest Jaguar operator is India, which had taken delivery of 131 aircraft (116 **Jaguar IS** single-seat and 15 **Jaguar IT** two-seat machines) by mid-1999, plus 18 on loan from the RAF (now returned). The IAF ordered a further 17 two-seat aircraft from HAL for delivery from 2001, and a further 20 single-seaters in 2000. The second batch (of 35 IS and five IT machines) was assembled by HAL. These were powered by uprated Adour Mk 804 engines and were fitted with the Navigation and Weapons Aiming Sub System. India's third batch consisted of 35 IS and 10 IT machines assembled by HAL; later aircraft were Indian-built. They were fitted with a locally integrated attack and navigation system, and were powered by the Adour Mk 811. For the anti-ship role HAL built the radar-equipped **Jaguar IM**. The final export customer was Nigeria, with 13 **Jaguar SN** and five **Jaguar BN** two-seat aircraft delivered in 1984.

Replacing the nose-mounted LRMTS, the Agave radar gives India's Jaguar IM an anti-ship capability: 10 were delivered for carriage of the Sea Eagle missile.

Mitsubishi F-1 Support fighter

As a country utterly dependent on foreign trade, Japan sees defence of the sea lanes as a high priority. Besides, after Japan lost World War II, Allied strictures, combined with the humiliation of the old military class and the growth of a culture of anti-militarism, made it inevitable that Japan's new armed forces would be overtly defensive in nature. The three arms were even named as 'self-defense forces' and equipped with defensive weapons and systems. Thus the anti-shipping role is known as the 'anti-landing craft' role, and fighter-bombers are known as support fighters.

By the 1970s the Japan Air Self-Defense Force was keen to acquire a dedicated support fighter – a type it had never operated – and also had a pressing need for a supersonic trainer to better prepare pilots for its F-104J Starfighters. So it was decided to combine the SF-X and T-X requirements in a single type.

Initially Japan looked abroad to fufil its needs, the Northrop F-5 and SEPECAT Jaguar being obvious candidates. In the event, a decision to proceed with an entirely indigenous trainer was taken in November 1966, after intensive lobbying by Japanese aircraft manufacturers, and in September 1967 Mitsubishi was awarded a development contract for the T-2, with a basic

*With a striking resemblance to the **SEPECAT** Jaguar, the Mitsubishi F-1 was even powered by the same Adour turbofans as the Anglo-French aircraft.*

design contract following on 30 March 1968.

The T-2 (T-X) prototype made its maiden flight on 20 July 1971 and became Japan's first supersonic trainer on its thirtieth flight. From the start the new trainer was developed with a view to providing the basis for a fighter-bomber, and Mitsubishi continued studies of a fighter-bomber version of the aircraft.

'Single-seat T-2'

A prototype development contract was placed by the Defense Agency in 1973.

Mitsubishi was commissioned to take the sixth and seventh T-2s from the Komaki production line, and to rebuild them as single-seat fighter-bombers. These two aircraft were initially known as Special Spec T-2s, then as T-2(FS)s, before taking the designation FS-T2 Kai.

The seventh T-2 (59-5107) was the first of the two aircraft to fly in single-seat form on 3 June 1975, with the sixth (59-5106) following on 7 June. At the end of the test programme the JASDF placed its first order for 18 of the new aircraft. The

*This aircraft, 70-8203, was the 3rd of 77 production F-1s delivered to the **JASDF**. It carries the panther badge of 8 Hiko-tai (8th Sqn), 3 Kokudan (3rd Air Wing), based at Misawa **AB** on the island of Honshu. It carries the locally designed Type 80 ASM-1 anti-ship missile, which uses inertial guidance and active radar terminal homing, has a range of about 50 km (31 miles) and is fitted with a 150-kg (331-lb) semi-armour-piercing warhead.*

SPECIFICATION

Mitsubishi F-1
Type: single-seat close-support and anti-ship attack fighter
Powerplant: two Ishikawajima-Harima TF40-IHI-801 (Rolls-Royce/Turboméca Adour Mk 801A) turbofan engines each rated at 32.49 kN (7,305 lb st) with afterburning
Performance: maximum level speed 'clean' at 10,975 m (36,000 ft) 1700 km/h (1,056 mph); maximum rate of climb at sea level 10,670 m (35,000 ft) per minute; service ceiling 15,240 m (50,000 ft); combat radius 555 km (345 miles) on a hi-lo-hi attack mission with two AShMs and two tanks

Weights: operating empty 6358 kg (14,017 lb); maximum take-off 13,700 kg (30,203 lb)
Dimensions: wing span 7.88 m (25 ft 10¼ in); length 17.86 m (58 ft 7 in) including probe; height 4.39 m (14 ft 5 in); wing area 21.17 m² (227.88 sq ft)
Armament: one JM61 20-mm rotary cannon; maximum ordnance 2721 kg (6,000 lb) including ASM-1/2 AShMs, AIM-9L AAMs; 227-kg (500-lb) Mk 82 or 340-kg (750-lb) bombs, bombs fitted with the GCS-1 IIR-seeker head (optimized for anti-shipping) and 70-mm (2.75-in) JLAU-3A, or RL-7, or 125-mm (5-in) RL-4 rocket pods

JASDF had wanted to place an initial order for 50 aircraft in Fiscal Year 1976; however, it was unable to do so because of the deteriorating financial situation, and was forced to 'drip-feed' the order over several fiscal years.

Placing a large single order would have allowed more rapid re-equipment of the three-squadron fighter-bomber force, whereas limiting the original order to only 18 aircraft delayed formation of the second and third units by one and two years, respectively. The first true **F-1** prototype, 70-8201, was rolled out at Komaki on 25 February 1977, and made its maiden flight on 16 June 1977. After flight trials, it was handed over to the JASDF on 16 September 1977.

The first JASDF unit to convert to the Mitsubishi F-1 was 3 Hiko-tai at Misawa, which began re-equipment in September 1977, transferring to the control of the 3 Kokudan on 1 March 1978 when conversion was complete. Three Kokudan's second squadron, the 8 Hiko-tai, began conversion to the F-1 on 30 June 1979, and when this was complete the 6 Hiko-tai began transition to the new type, on 11 March 1980. Diminishing airframe numbers and a decision to cut the number of F-1 squadrons in order to increase the number of aircraft allocated to each of the surviving squadrons, led to the re-equipment of 8 Hiko-tai with F-4EJs in the 1980s.

The Mitsubishi F-2 – a modified version of the F-16 –

Japanese air force pilot S/Sgt. J. Yamagishi prepares for take off in a Mitsubishi F-1.

has since been developed as a replacement, and will have replaced all F-1s by 2006.

The Japanese Self-Defense Force's longest surviving fighter squadron, 3 Hiko-tai, made the complete transition to the

Mitsubishi F-2 in 2001, with the last of the unit's F-1s being retired on 20 March.

Mitsubishi F-2 Close support and anti-ship fighter

In October 1987, Japan selected the F-16C Fighting Falcon as the basis for a much developed version to replace the F-1, primarily in the fighter support role. Although a costly and controversial programme – one Mitsubishi F-2 costs at least the same as four Block 50/52 F-16Cs – the F-2 illustrates Japan's commitment to maintaining its high-technology aerospace industry.

The F-2 features a new wing of 25 per cent greater area and all-composite construction, with radar-absorbent material on the leading edges. In order to house

additional mission avionics that include an integrated electronic warfare system, the F-2's fuselage has a lengthened forward section when compared to the F-16C. Other features are a longer nose to accommodate an active phased-array radar, a larger tailplane, a brake chute and a strengthened canopy.

Mitsubishi is the prime contractor responsible for airframe assembly, as well as manufacture of the forward fuselage section, while the other major assemblies are produced by Lockheed Martin, Kawasaki and Fuji. With either

wingtip-mounted AIM-9 or Mitsubishi AAM-3 AAMs, the F-2 still has 11 hardpoints available for other stores, including the ASM-2 anti-ship missile as one of its principal weapons.

Long delays

The F-2 programme has suffered long delays, cost escalation and a number of structural problems including wing cracking and severe flutter. Four prototypes have been built comprising two single-seat **XF-2A** machines and a pair of two-seat **XF-2B** aircraft.

The first XF-2A recorded the type's maiden flight on

7 October 1995. In late 1995 the Japanese government approved a programme for the manufacture of 130 aircraft with an entry into service scheduled for 1999. Delays resulting from modifications to cure structural problems delayed the Mitsubishi F-2's entry into operational service until 2001.

Reduced order

The JASDF had hoped to acquire 141 F-2s, including 58 two-seaters. However, 11 two-seaters originally earmarked for the 'Blue Impulse' aerobatic display team were cancelled in

1997, leaving 130 aircraft planned for, comprising 83 **F-2A** single-seaters and 47 **F-2B** two-seaters.

Retaining full combat capability, the F-2Bs have a fuel capacity which is reduced by 685 litres (151 Imp gallons). The F-2Bs will be used for conversion and proficiency training, replacing the T-2s.

By February 2001 57 production aircraft had been approved, the first of these being delivered to the JASDF in October 2000. Early production aircraft were assigned to No. 1

Technical School at Hamamatsu and Rinji F-2 Hiko-tai (temporary F-2 squadron). The latter unit became 3 Hiko-tai when it reached IOC in April 2001 (replacing the existing 3 Hiko-tai, which was flying F-1s). The remainder of the first 45 aircraft delivered will be allocated to a Matsushima-based Air Training Command OCU.

In 2006, 6 Hiko-tai at Tsuiki will convert from the F-1 to the F-2, with 8 Hiko-tai (currently flying the F-4EJKai) following suit the following year.

SPECIFICATION

Mitsubishi F-2A
Type: single-seat, close-support and anti-ship fighter with secondary defensive counter-air role
Powerplant: one General Electric F110-GE-129 turbofan engine rated at 75.62 kN (17,000 lb st) dry and 131.22 kN (29,500 lb st) with afterburning
Fuel: internal 4637 litres (1,225 US gal) of which 4588 litres (1,212 US gal) are useable and external up to 4542 litres (1,200 US gal) in drop tanks; no provision for in-flight refuelling
Performance: maximum speed 2125 km/h (1,321 mph) or Mach 2.0 at altitude; combat radius more than 834 km (518 miles) on an anti-ship mission

Weights: empty 9527 kg (21,003 lb); maximum take-off 22100 kg (48,721 lb)
Dimensions: wing span 11.13 m (36 ft 6 in) with tip-mounted missile launchers; length 15.52 m (50 ft 11 in); height 4.69 m (15 ft 4¾ in); wing area 34.84 m² (375.03 sq ft)
Armament: one 20-mm JM61A1 cannon, maximum weapon load of 8085 kg (17,824 lb); weapons include ASM-1/2 AShMs, AIM-7F/AIM-7M+ Sparrow AAMs, AIM-9L or AA-3+ AAMs, 227-kg (500-lb) Mk 82 and 340-kg (750-lb) JM117 free-fall bombs with GCS-1 IIR seeker heads, 454-kg (1,000-lb) bombs, CBU-87/B cluster bombs, JLAU-3/A and RL-4 rocket launchers

Powerplant

The F-2 is fitted with a GE F110-GE-129 engine, as used by the F-16C/D Block 50. This improved version of the F110-GE-100 used in F-16C/D Blocks 30/40 offers around 30 per cent extra thrust (131.27 kN/ 29,500 lb in afterburner).

Wing shape

Although based on that of the F-16, the wing shape of the F-2 offers significantly greater area. This is achieved by extending the span, increasing root chord and reducing leading-edge sweepback, and by having a slightly swept forward trailing edge which adds area to the rear of the wing.

Wing structure

The wings were designed by Mitsubishi and employ a co-cured composite structure. Under the workshare agreement, Lockheed Martin builds the port wing and both leading-edge flaps.

XF-2B

This is the fourth F-2 prototype, completed as an XF-2B two-seater and featuring full systems and assigned to the Hiko Kaihatsu Jikken-dan (ADTW) at Gifu Air Base. The aircraft is painted in a blue-grey colour scheme intended for production aircraft. It is shown in typical anti-ship configuration, with four ASM-2 anti-ship missiles (albeit here in dummy form for tests) and two wingtip AAM-3s for self-defence.

Pylons

Weapons are usually carried on Stations 1-4 and 8-11, comprising the three outboard wing stations and wingtips. Stations 4 and 8 are moveable between two hardpoints (4 and 4L, 8 and 8R) depending on the type of store being carried. Air-to-air missiles are carried on Frazer Nash CRLs (Common Rail Launchers), licence-built by Nippi. These can mount AIM-7, AIM-9 or AAM-3 from any station other than the wingtips, which are only AIM-9/AAM-3 capable.

FBW controls

The fly-by-wire system has several advanced features, including decoupled yaw mode, which allows the aircraft to yaw without banking. This is useful for ground attack during gun/rocket attacks when the pilot can 'sweep' the fire accurately through a target.

Fuel

Internal fuel capacity of the F-2B is 3948 litres (1,043 US gal). The centreline (Station 6) and two inboard wing pylons (Stations 5 and 7) are wet, the two wing pylons being able to carry 2271-litre (600-US gal) tanks, while the centreline can mount a 1136-litre (300-US gal) tank.

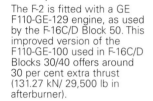

Cannon

The F-2 uses the trusty 20-mm six-barrelled General Electric (now General Dynamics) Vulcan cannon, licence-built in Japan as the JM61A1. It is mounted in the same port wingroot position as in the F-16 and is provided with 512 rounds of ammunition.

Mikoyan-Gurevich MiG-23B and MiG-27 'Flogger'
Attack-dedicated 'Floggers'

Above and right: Like the MiG-23BM/BK, the MiG-27 has a simple two-position afterburner nozzle. However, the latter type also has short-chord splitter plates ahead of its fixed intakes.

The **MiG-23B** was developed from the MiG-23 interceptor in the late 1960s to meet a Frontal Aviation requirement for a tactical attack aircraft. The series production **MiG-23BN 'Flogger-F'** variant proved disappointing in service and was replaced by the more capable **MiG-27 'Flogger-D'**. The upgraded **MiG-23BM** and **MiG-23BK 'Flogger-H'** variants incorporated the improved avionics of later MiG-27s. Many BM/BKs built for export were described as MiG-23BNs. In 2003, operators included Algeria, Angola, Bulgaria, Cuba, Ethiopia, India, Iraq, Libya and Sudan.

MiG-27

The MiG-27 was developed as a fully optimized fighter-bomber based on the MiG-23BM. Along with the Su-17, the MiG-27 formed one half of the main attack force of the Tactical Frontal Aviation armies. Between 1991 and 1994, however, both types were withdrawn from VVS service.

The only current MiG-27 operators are India and Sri Lanka. Both operate the **MiG-27M 'Flogger-J'** variant fitted with the PrNK-23M nav/attack system, Pelenga weapons system giving compatibility with PGMs and guided ASMs and a Klen (maple) laser rangefinder/target tracker. The MiG-27M is capable of automatic night or bad weather blind bombing with a very high degree of accuracy. In India HAL has manufactured 165 MiG-27Ms under licence (these aircraft are designated **MiG-27L** by MiG). Although a MiG-21 upgrade was always a priority,

the Indian air force had intended to keep its MiG-27 force viable until 2020 and HAL's Nasik plant investigated a substantial

MiG-27 upgrade. This would have given the ability to launch stand-off weapons and provided a night-attack capability. New

SPECIFICATION	
Mikoyan MiG-27K 'Flogger-D' **Type:** single-seat tactical fighter-bomber **Powerplant:** one MNPK 'Soyuz' (Tumanskii/Khachaturov) R-29B-300 turbojet engine rated at 78.45 kN (17,637 lb st) dry and 112.77 kN (25,353 lb st) with afterburning **Performance:** maximum level speed 'clean' 1885 km/h (1,170 mph) at 8000 m (26,245 ft); service ceiling 14,000 m (45,930 ft); combat radius 540 km (335 miles) on a lo-lo-lo attack mission with two Kh-29 ASMs and three drop tanks	**Weights:** empty equipped 8200 kg (26,252 lb); maximum take-off 20300 kg (44,753 lb) **Dimensions:** wing span 13.97 m (45 ft 9¾ in) spread and 7.78 m (25 ft 6¼ in); length 17.08 m (56 ft ¼ in) including probe; height 5 m (16 ft 5 in); wing area 37.35 m² (402.05 sq ft) spread and 34.16 m² (367.71 sq ft) swept **Armament:** one 30-mm Gryazev-Shipunov GSh-6-30 six-barrel cannon in a ventral pack, plus up to 4000 kg (8,818 lb) of disposable stores carried on seven hardpoints

equipment would include two MFDs, an updated HUD, HOTAS and a ring laser gyro INS and GPS-based navigation system similar to that fitted to Indian Jaguars. The MiG-27s may also have gained an improved EW suite, inflight refuelling capability, FLIR and a Vicon recce pod in the upgrade. The Indians, however, have now made the decision to retire their remaining 130-plus MiG-27s.

The MiG-23BN has markedly different nose contours to the MiG-27. Note also its much larger splitter plates.

Mikoyan MiG-29 'Fulcrum' Multi-role developments

Designed primarily as an air-defence fighter, the **Mikoyan MiG-29 'Fulcrum'** has generally been developed with new systems and weapons in keeping with this role. Nevertheless, the aircraft clearly has potential in the attack and strike (nuclear attack) roles, as recognized early in its career, when it gained a secondary nuclear strike capability. The left inner wing pylons of Soviet aircraft were reinforced to allow carriage of the 30-kT RN-40 free-fall bomb.

In general service these modifications were as close as

The fourth prototype 9-12 MiG-29, '904', was initially used for structural loads analysis, testing the limits of combat manoeuvrability. Later, it went on to air-to-ground weapons testing.

the MiG-29 came to becoming an attack aircraft, but Mikoyan soon realized that the type would have added export potential if it could be offered as a multi-role warplane. Accordingly, new models were produced, including the **MiG-29SM**, which was categorized as a multi-role

tactical fighter. Planned as a version of the 'fat-backed' 'Fulcrum-C' fighter, the MiG-29SM has failed to find orders, however, and with the 'all new' multi-role **MiG-29M** (and its

MiG-29K naval equivalent) seemingly falling victim to political intrigue and cuts in funding, Mikoyan has instead pursued development of the **MiG-29SMT/ UBT** upgrades.

Armed with Kh-31, R-77 and R-73 missiles, Bort '917', the first full-standard 9-17 MiG-29SMT was previously the MiG-29SE demonstrator Bort '555', the multi-tone blue/grey camouflaged company 'hack'.

Sukhoi Su-7/17/20/22 'Fitter' Attack aircraft family

This Su-17M-4 was operated by the 20 Aviatsionnaya Polk Istrebeitelei-Bombardirovchikov (20th Fighter-Bomber Regiment), based at Gross-Dölln (Templin) in the former East Germany. '27 Yellow' is armed with UB-32-57 57-mm (2¼-in) rocket pods and R-60 self-defence missiles underwing, with Kh-25MP (AS-12 'Kegler') anti-radar missiles under the fuselage.

While the original **Su-7 'Fitter'** probably survives only in limited service with the air forces of Iraq, North Korea and Turkmenistan, its swing-wing derivatives remain in widespread service. The **Su-17M 'Fitter-C'** attack aircraft was the first of these variable-geometry variants, also introducing more power and improved avionics. By 2003, the type appeared to have been phased out of service. The further improved **Su-17M-2D 'Fitter-D'** entered production in 1974 with a slightly lengthened, slightly drooping nose, a revised avionics suite and a laser rangefinder. A slightly sanitized version, with a new dorsal fin fillet and possibly without a laser rangefinder, was built for export under the designation **Su-17M-2K 'Fitter-F'**. Next came the **Su-17M-3 'Fitter-H'** (designated **Su-22M-3** for export) which featured a further modified airframe and wingroot cannon. 'Fitter' trainers include the

Su-17UM-2D 'Fitter-E' and export **Su-17UM-2K**, and the **Su-17UM-3D 'Fitter-G'** (export **Su-22UM-3K**).

Ultimate 'Fitter'

The ultimate 'Fitter', with new avionics and compatibility with an even wider range of weapons, was developed for the Soviet air forces and for export. New avionics included a new CVM 20-22 mission computer and PrNK-54 navigation system (using the LORAN-equivalent RSDN and the TACAN-equivalent A-312), which reduced pilot workload and improved navigational and weapons delivery accuracy. Other avionics

include a DISS-7 Doppler, an ASP-17BC gunsight, an IKV-8 inertial platform, an ARK-22 radio compass, an SRO-2 IFF system, an SO-69 transponder and an SPO-15LE (Sirena) RWR. This **Su-17M-4** (export **Su-22M-4**) **'Fitter-K'** is externally identifiable by a prominent ram-air inlet projecting forward from the finroot and the

aircraft is optimized for high speed at low level.

Aircraft of the Su-17M/Su-22 family remained in service with Angola, Bulgaria, Iraq, Libya, Peru, Poland, Slovakia, Syria, Ukraine, Uzbekistan, Vietnam and Yemen early in 2003. The 'Fitter' has been upgraded with the addition of refuelling probes for the Peruvian air force.

SPECIFICATION

Sukhoi Su-17M-4 'Fitter-C'
Type: single-seat ground attack fighter
Powerplant: one NPO Saturn (Lyul'ka) AL-21F-3 turbojet rated at 76.49 kN (17,196 lb st) dry and 110.32 kN (24,802 lb st) with afterburning, plus provision for two RATO units
Performance: maximum level speed 'clean' at sea level 1400 km/h (870 mph); maximum rate of climb at sea level 13,800 m (45,276 ft) per minute; service ceiling 15,200 m (49,870 ft); combat radius 1150 km (715 miles) on hi-lo-hi attack mission with a 2000-kg (4,409 lb) warload

Weights: normal take-off 16,400 kg (36,155 lb); maximum take-off 19,500 kg (42,989 lb)
Dimensions: wing span 13.8 m (45 ft 3 in) spread and 10 m (32 ft 10 in) swept; length 18.75 m (61 ft 6¼ in) including probes, height 5 m (16 ft 5 in); wing area 40 m² (430.57 sq ft) spread and 37 m² (398.28 sq ft) swept
Armament: two NR-30 30-mm cannon, each with 80 rounds; maximum weapon load 4250 kg (9,369 lb); weapons include guided and unguided free-fall bombs, ASMs, self-defence AAMs, gun and rocket pods

The Su-17M in its latter variants formed an important part of tactical elements of the VVS prior to the collapse of the Soviet Union. The nearest aircraft, an Su-17M-4 '43 Blue', carries a typical ground attack load of a single S-24 240-mm (9.4-in) rocket on the starboard inboard wing station, and a pair of FAB-250 250-kg (551-lb) bombs underfuselage.

Sukhoi Su-24 'Fencer' Tactical attack aircraft

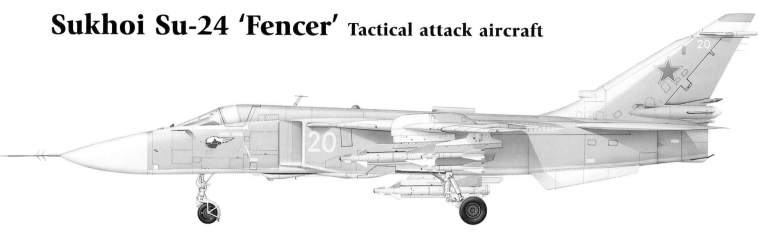

Above: Armed with Kh-29L (AS-14 'Kedge') TV command-guided ASMs and R-60 (AA-8 'Aphid') AAMs, this Su-24M was based in Poland with the 89th BAP, 149th BAD in 1992.

The **Su-24** was developed as a replacement for the Yakovlev Yak-28 'Brewer' in the tactical bomber, reconnaissance and EW roles. Design of the aircraft began in the early 1960s, but Sukhoi abandoned its initial configuration (an enlarged, twin-engined, tandem cockpit design based loosely on the Su-7 layout) in favour of the compound delta **T6**, which also featured fuselage-mounted lift jets for enhanced STOL performance. This design was built and flown, before the T6 was redesigned six months later, with a variable-geometry wing. The lift-jet-equipped **T6-11** made its maiden flight on 2 July 1967, and was followed by the variable-geometry **T6-21** on 17 January 1970.

The Ukrainian air force has more than 200 'Fencers' arranged in two divisions. The 32nd BAD has 'Fencer-B/Cs', while the 289th BAD has Su-24M 'Fencer-Ds' (illustrated). These units also have a few recce Su-24MRs assigned.

Su-24 emerges

This aircraft was ordered into production as the Su-24 in late 1970. The Su-24 entered VVS service (with Frontal Aviation) in 1973, and it rapidly replaced the Yak-28 in the tactical bombing role. It was never intended or used as a strategic bomber, a fact obscured by comparisons with the General Dynamics F-111, which enjoyed a range 1,200 nm (2224 km; 1,382 miles) greater. Western intelligence noted the aircraft's service entry in 1974, allocating the reporting name **'Fencer'** to what it mistakenly thought was designated **Su-19**.

The type entered service with the Group of Soviet Forces in

SPECIFICATION
Sukhoi Su-24M 'Fencer-D'

Type: two-seat variable-geometry attack aircraft

Powerplant: two Perm/Soloviov (Lyul'ka) AL-21F-3A turbojets each rated at 109.83 kN (24,691 lb st) with afterburning

Performance: maximum level speed 'clean' at low altitude 1320 km/h (820 mph); service ceiling 17,000 m (55,775 ft); combat radius at sea level 560 km (348 miles)

Weights: empty 22,300 kg (49,162 lb); normal take-off 36,000 kg (79,365 lb)

Dimensions: wing span 17.64 m (57 ft 10 in) spread and 10.37 m (34 ft) swept; length 22.59 m (74 ft 1 in); height 6.19 m (20 ft 4 in); wing area 55.17 m² (594 sq ft) spread and 51.02 m² (549 sq ft) swept

Armament: one GSh-6-23M 23-mm cannon; maximum ordnance 8000 kg (17,637 lb); weapons include TN-1000 and TN-1200 free-fall nuclear weapons; comprehensive range of semi-active laser and TV-guided PGMs includes Kh-23, Kh-25ML, Kh-29L/T and Kh-59 Ovod ASMs; Kh-25MP, Kh-31P, Kh-29MP and Kh-58 ARMs: Kh-31A and Kh-35 AShMs, KAB-500Kr LGBs, R-60 AAMs

Su-24s based in Europe, such as these 'Fencer-Bs' (background) and 'Fencer-Cs' (foreground) seen here at Osla in Poland, represented the powerhouse of the Soviet forces in Europe. While situated far back from the borders with the West, they were nevertheless close enough to make their considerable presence felt if war ever broke out in Central Europe.

Germany in 1979, and from 1984 the Su-24 saw active service in Afghanistan.

Low-level attack

The Su-24 is fast and stable at low level, and is capable of carrying an impressive warload (though only at the expense of an appreciable reduction in range), but by comparison with Western contemporaries the Su-24 is crude and its avionics are backward and unreliable. The aircraft was thus never as capable as Western attack aircraft such as the Panavia Tornado and F-111, nor even the radar-less SEPECAT Jaguar.

The Su-24 did, however, form the basis of an export fighter bomber, delivered to Iran, Iraq, Libya and Syria (and also, according to some sources, to Algeria), and of recce and EW variants.

The primary 'Fencer' attack variants were the **Su-24 Production Series 2-11 'Fencer-A'**; the **Su-24 Production Series 12-23 'Fencer-B'** with a kinked tailplane leading edge and other changes; **Su-24 Production Series 24-27 'Fencer-C'**; the definitive **Su-24M 'Fencer-D'** with an EO targeting system beneath the forward fuselage plus other changes and the **Su-24MK 'Fencer-D (Mod)'** export version.

Early Su-24s had this unusual 'goose' sensor arrangement on their nose cones.

Sukhoi Su-25 'Frogfoot' Attack aircraft

Su-25UTG was designed as a trainer for the pilots destined to fly Su-33s from Russia's new generation of aircraft carriers.

Development of the **Su-25 'Frogfoot'** began during the late 1960s, parallelling US studies. Sukhoi, like the US firms, was heavily influenced by USAF experience in the Vietnam War. Sukhoi believed that high speed was essential to ensure survivability over the battlefield, and chose to use turbojet engines and relatively little armour. The **T-8** prototype made its first flight on 22 February 1975, but much redesign, including the installation of a new powerplant, was necessary before series production was authorized. Two prototypes were sent to Afghanistan for a combined series of operational and state acceptance trials (Operation Rhombus).

Over Afghanistan

The first 12 Su-25s also served in Afghanistan, where the type received its **'Grach'** (rook) nickname. The Su-25 eventually flew some 60,000 combat sorties in Afghanistan. This experience led to a number of modifications and, during 1987, production aircraft were fitted with the more powerful R-195 engine, which was also fitted to all production 'Frogfoot' two-seaters, as the **Su-25 'Frogfoot-A'**.

R-195-engined Su-25s are self-supporting, thanks to a set of support equipment carried in four underwing pods. A handful of Su-25s has been modified as **Su-25BM** (**Buksir Misheni**, or target tug) machines. The need for an all-weather and night-capable

Su-25 with increased range/ endurance required more airframe space; a new variant, based on the two-seat **Su-25UB 'Frogfoot-B'**, was built. 'Frogfoot-A' aircraft for export were designated **Su-25K**, equivalent two-seaters being **Su-25UBK** machines.

Russia is planning to upgrade some of its early aircraft to **Su-25SM** single-seat and **Su-25UBM** standard, although the exact status of this upgrade is difficult to assess accurately.

Tank killer

The first such **T-81M** prototype made its maiden flight on 17 August 1984, with a 30-mm cannon below the centre fuselage. A preproduction batch of 20 **Su-25T** (**Tankovyi**, or anti-tank) (later **Su-25TM**) aircraft was built and the type has been offered for export as the **Su-25TK**. This latter machine has radar for greater night/all-weather capability. It is marketed by Sukhoi as the **Su-39**. Another derivative of the Su-25UB is the navalized **Su-25UTG** trainer which first flew in 1988. Ten production

Su-25UTGs were built, five of them passing to the Ukraine. A handful of Su-25UBs has been modified to **Su-25UBP** standard for Russia, to make up for the Su-25UTGs lost to the Ukraine.

One other variant of the ubiquitous Su-25 is worthy of mention. In an attempt to provide a replacement for the large fleet of Aero L-29 and L-39 trainers in Soviet service, in 1985 Sukhoi flew an unarmed variant of the Su-25UB. Known as the **Su-28**, it failed to gain any orders.

Unguided rockets, here housed in UB-32M pods, are important Su-25 weapons. The aircraft has great combat persistence, thanks to its heavy ordnance load and multiple pylons.

*When **Czechoslovakia** was divided, the **Czech** Republic received 24 **Su-25Ks** (illustrated) and a single **Su-25UBK**. Slovakia took 11 **Su-25Ks** and a single **Su-25UBK**.*

SPECIFICATION

Sukhoi Su-25 'Frogfoot-A'
Type: single-seat ground attack aircraft
Powerplant: two MNPK 'Soyuz' (Tumanskii) R-195 turbojets each rated at 44.13 kN (9,921 lb st)
Performance: maximum level speed 'clean' at sea level 950 km/h (590 mph); take-off run 600 m (1,969 ft); service ceiling 7000 m (22,965 ft); combat radius 495 km (267 miles) on a hi-lo-hi attack mission with an 4000-kg (8,818-lb) warload and two drop tanks
Weights: empty equipped 9800 kg (21,605 lb); maximum take-off

18,600 kg (41,005 lb)
Dimensions: wing span 14.36 m (47 ft 1¼ in); length 15.53 m (50 ft 11 in); height 4.8 m (15 ft 9 in); wing area 30.1 m² (324 sq ft)
Armament: one internal 30-mm AO-17A cannon; maximum ordnance 4400 kg (9,700 lb) including unguided rockets, free-fall and laser-guided bombs, cluster bombs, incendiary weapons and cannon pods; Kh-23 (AS-7 'Kerry'), Kh-25 (AS-10 'Karen') and Kh-29 (AS-14 'Kedge') ASMs and R-60 (AA-8 'Aphid') AAMs for self-defence

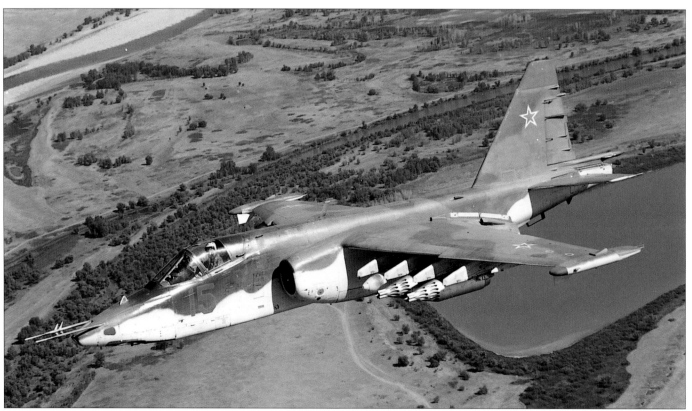

Sukhoi Su-30 family Advanced multi-role combat aircraft

In the 1980s, the PVO expressed a desire to have a dedicated combat version of the Su-27UB that would be used as a long-range interceptor as well as a command post to vector single-seat 'Flankers'. The new aircraft would also provide cover for the Soviet navy as the **Su-27PU**.

However, this aircraft merely served as the basis of the **Su-30**, which would be able to carry basic air-to-ground weapons. It was soon realized that the basic Su-30 would not be capable or versatile enough and so the multi-role, long-range fighter/fighter-bomber **Su-30M** was built. Export aircraft would be designated **Su-30MK**.

Attack weapons

With its modernized radar, the Su-30 enjoyed a degree of latent ground-attack capability and the type was initially offered as a SEAD platform. A TV display was added, for use with the KAB-500kr guided bomb, and Kh-29T missiles, together with provision for the ARK-9 datalink pod. This pod allowed carriage of the Kh-59M (AS-18 'Kazoo') TV-guided missile. The laser-guided Kh-29L (AS-14 'Kedge') could also be used. A weapon offered only with the Su-30MK is the SPPU gun pod.

The Su-30M made its maiden flight on 14 April 1992. It was fitted with an inflight-refuelling probe and offset IRST. The multi-role Su-30M was offered to the Russian air forces as a low-cost alternative to the Su-27IB, but only a tiny number was purchased.

Export aircraft

In late 1996 it was announced that India had signed a $1.5 billion contract for the supply of 40 Su-30MK fighter-bombers. The same contract also covered a licence-production agreement for an eventual total of 100 Su-30 aircraft. India's Su-30s are designated **Su-30MKI** and differ

from the standard MK by means of improved agility achieved through the addition of canards and thrust-vectoring AL-37FU engines. One other feature was that several of the systems, such as the HUD and satellite navigation system, would be built by Sextant Avionique of France, although the all-important fire control system is Russian-built.

The first MKI flew on 1 July 1997 and was equipped with AL-31FP thrust vectoring nozzles. A second prototype flew in the following year. However, India had already received eight Su-30Ks (a designation which was applied to a limited number of **Su-30K** interceptors in Russian service, but described in this case as a 'commercial' version of the Su-30), without canards and thrust vectoring, as a stopgap measure. Later, 10 canard-equipped Su-30MKs were added. Unfortunately, in Indian service the aircraft were beset with problems, to the point that they attracted criticism from India's government auditor. Nevertheless, by September 2002, India had received its first batch of 10 MKIs. These aircraft were not to the full

This unpainted Su-30 demonstrator shows the type's impressive weapons capability, with a load of R-73s, R-77s and Kh-31s. The Su-30 is a capable machine, but is struggling to win export orders.

SPECIFICATION	
Sukhoi Su-30MK **Type:** two-seat multi-role warplane **Powerplant:** two NPO Saturn (Lyul'ka) AL-31F turbofans each rated at 79.43 kN (17,587 lb st) dry and 122.58 kN (27,557 lb st) with afterburning **Performance:** maximum level speed 'clean' at 11,000 m (36,090 ft) 2280 km/h (1,417 mph); maximum rate of climb at sea level 19,800 m (64,960 ft) per minute; service ceiling 17,700 m (58,071 ft);	combat range with two inflight refuellings more than 7000 km (4,350 miles) **Weights:** empty 17,700 kg (39,021 lb); maximum take-off 33,000 kg (72,751 lb) **Dimensions:** wing span 14.7 m (48 ft 2¾ in); length 21.9 m (71 ft 10 in); height 19 ft 5½ in (5.93 m); wing area 46.5 m² (500.54 sq ft) **Armament:** one 30-mm GSh-301 cannon with 150 rounds; maximum ordnance 8000 kg (17,636 lb)

specification, which was later established by a batch of machines delivered in 2004. With these latter machines in service, the remaining Su-30Ks, Su-30KMs and early Su-30MKI will be upgraded.

Su-30KI and MKK

Early in the Su-27's career, Sukhoi marketed export examples as the **Su-27SK**. During the mid-1990s, it was decided to upgrade this aircraft and the result was the **Su-30KI** single-seat tactical fighter. The aircraft is fitted with a retractable refuelling probe and a satellite navigation system. Furthermore, the Su-30KI's

weapons suite has been enhanced through the introduction of R-77 medium-range AAMs and a range of air-to-ground weaponry.

The **Su-30MKK** is a multi-role two-seat fighter, also derived from the Su-27SK. Equipped to perform a range of air superiority and strike missions, the aircraft is fitted with 12 hardpoints for a total of 8000 kg (17,636 lb) of stores with which the Su-30MKK can take off, along with a full load of fuel, a capability not possessed by other 'Flankers'.

The first MKK flew on 19 May 1999 and China is taking 78 aircraft, the first of which was delivered in 2001.

Sukhoi Su-27IB, Su-32FN and Su-34
Advanced long-range attack aircraft

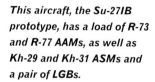

This aircraft, the Su-27IB prototype, has a load of R-73 and R-77 AAMs, as well as Kh-29 and Kh-31 ASMs and a pair of LGBs.

Although Sukhoi's Su-27 has always had a secondary ground-attack capability, Sukhoi chose to develop a dedicated two-seat attack version of the 'Flanker'. This radically rebuilt aircraft was dubbed **Su-27IB** (**Istrebitel** Bombardirovschik/fighterbomber) and had the designation **T10V-1**.

The prototype, which first flew on 13 April 1990, was converted from an Su-27UB trainer, with a new side-by-side armoured cockpit section (including the nose gear) grafted onto the existing fuselage. The Su-27IB has a distinctive long, flattened nose, which led to the nickname 'Platypus'. The aircraft is also fitted with small canards on the long chines running back to the leading edge of the wing.

Western perception of the Su-27IB was muddied when TASS released a photograph of the prototype ('Blue 42') apparently landing on the carrier *Tiblisi*. It was announced that this aircraft was the '**Su-27KU**', a carrier training version – though it had no arrestor hook! The reasons for this 'disinformation' are still unclear. Photographs of the Su-27IB, this time carrying a heavy warload, were released after the aircraft was presented to Russian and CIS air force commanders during the Minsk-Maschulische 'display' in 1992. Later that year the same aircraft flew at the Moscow air show.

Production variants

The designation **Su-34** was applied, by Sukhoi, to the production version of the Su-27IB, for the Russian air force. The first pre-production Su-34 ('Blue 43') was rolled out from Sukhoi's Novossibirsk plant in 1993, making its maiden flight on 18 December.

The full-standard Su-34 (Bureau designation **T10V-2**), is fitted with 12 hardpoints. It is cleared to carry virtually the full range of Russian air-to-surface ordnance. This could include a total of 34 100-kg (220-lb) AB-100 bombs under various pylons, or a triple cluster of 250-kg (550-lb) AB-250s under each hardpoint for a total of 22 bombs, or 12 500-kg (1,100-lb) AB-500 bombs. Alternatively, the Su-34 can carry up to seven KMGU cluster bomb dispensers, a variety of unguided or laser-guided rockets, or a number of precision-guided missiles, such as the KAB-500 or the KAB-1500.

The aircraft's cockpit uses a mix of conventional instruments and multi-function CRT displays (in the central console, shared by the two crew). Only the pilot has a HUD. Both crew are seated on K-36DM ejection seats. The large forward cabin provides the pilots with room in which to move around on long-duration missions. There is also a food heater and even a chemical toilet.

Other strike roles

Although the Su-34 might be considered to be a replacement for the air force's Su-24s in the tactical strike role, it may also replace Tu-16s and Tu-22Ms in

This is the first pre-production Su-34 (Sukhoi Bureau designation T10V-2) which is the Russian air force version of the Su-27IB. The air force itself still appears to use the Su-27IB designation.

Wearing show number 343, Su-32FN '44' takes off at the 1997 Paris Air Show. The naval strike variant of the Su-27IB, the Su-32FN, is described by Sukhoi as a shore-based, long-range all-weather attack aircraft.

some roles, such as that of a long-range stand-off missile carrier. The Su-34 has already been proposed as a potential launch platform for the Novator ASM-MS Alfa long-range hypersonic cruise missile. The Alfa is primarily an anti-shipping weapon and it seems that Sukhoi is now directing its efforts towards earning a maritime strike role for the Su-34.

When Sukhoi first presented the Su-34 at the 1995 Paris Air Show, it did so using the surprise designation **Su-32FN**. The aircraft was described as an all-weather, 24-hour maritime strike aircraft, equipped with the Sea Snake sea-search and attack radar. An (unlikely) anti-submarine capability was even attributed to the aircraft, when Sukhoi stated that it could carry up to 72 sonobuoys and be fitted with a MAD system in the tail 'sting'. The Su-32FN is certainly capable of carrying all existing Russian anti-ship/air-to-surface missiles. The Su-32FN returned to Paris in 1997 when another aircraft took part in the flying display for the first time. The exact status of the Su-27IB/Su-34/Su-32FN is unclear, but the Su-34 is seen as a priority programme in Russia. Nevertheless, the first handful of operational aircraft is unlikely to be in service until 2006.

SPECIFICATION	
Sukhoi Su-34	(39,022 lb), maximum take-off
Type: two-seat long-range	44360 kg (97,800 lb)
interdictor	**Dimensions:** wing span 14.7 m
Powerplant: two NPO Saturn	(48 ft 2¾ in); length 23.3 m (76 ft
(Lyul'ka) AL-31F turbofans each	5¼ in); height 6.5 m (21 ft 4 in);
rated at 74.5 kN (16,755 lb st) dry	wing area 62 m² (667.4 sq ft)
and 122.6 kN (27,557 lb st) with	**Armament:** one 30-mm GSh-301
afterburning	cannon; maximum weapon load
Performance: maximum level speed	8000 kg (17,636 lb); weapons
at altitude 2500 km/h (1,553 mph);	include Kh-25M (AS-10 'Karen'),
service ceiling 19,800 m	Kh-29 (AS-14 'Kedge'), Kh-31A/P
(65,000 ft); range with maximum	(AS-17 'Krypton'), Kh-59M (AS-18
internal fuel 4000 km (2,485 miles)	'Kazoo'), Kh-35 (AS-20 'Kayak') and
Weights: empty 17,700 kg	Kh-41 Moskit ASMs

Lockheed F-117A Nighthawk Stealthy attack aircraft

In 1974 the US Defense Advanced Research and Procurement Agency called for development of a true stealth warplane using a mix of radar-absorbent materials, a radar-reflective internal structure and a similarly 'reflective' configuration to provide a dramatic decrease in radar cross-section. In overall terms, faceting reflects radar energy in all directions, making the aircraft virtually invisible even to AWACS platforms. The concept extends to the wing itself, the aerofoil section of which consists of two flat surfaces on the underside and three on top of the wing. Avoidance of straight lines is continued on access panels and doors, many of which have serrated edges for the same reason. The cockpit transparencies are coated with gold.

Skunk Works

The Skunk Works organization of Lockheed was awarded a development order in April 1976 for two sub-scale technology demonstrators. The first of these flew in 1977, and, although both aircraft were lost, the experience gained was sufficient to win Lockheed a November 1978 contract to develop a full-scale operational tactical warplane. Major changes were introduced, most notably to the configuration of the tail surfaces, which were canted outward rather than

inward. The first of five full-scale development prototypes flew on 18 June 1981; these machines had smaller tail surfaces than the production aircraft.

In October 1983 the first unit was declared operational, with about five **F-117A Nighthawk** and 18 Vought A-7D aircraft, the latter flown for proficiency and as a security 'cover'.

It was not until November 1988 that the F-117A was officially acknowledged by the Pentagon, and on 19 December 1989 the type finally went into action, two aircraft attacking the Rio Hate barracks during the US invasion of Panama. This baptism of fire was overshadowed by the type's contribution to the Desert Storm operation, in which an eventual total of 42 aircraft flew from Khamis Mushait in Saudi Arabia on nightly missions against targets in Iraq and occupied Kuwait. In 1999, the F-117A was also used in attacks on Serbian targets

With stealth as the overriding motivation in its design, the F-117A had to have an internal and hence relatively small weapon load. This load is delivered with devastating accuracy.

during efforts to secure peace in Kosovo. In this campaign the F-117A suffered its first operational loss. Most recently, the F-117A has been in action during Operation Iraqi Freedom.

SPECIFICATION	
Lockheed F-117A Nighthawk	with a 1814-kg (4,000-lb) warload
Type: single-seat stealth attack	**Weights:** empty about 13,608 kg
warplane	(30,000 lb); maximum take-off
Powerplant: two General Electric	23,814 kg (52,500 lb)
F404-GE-F1D2 turbofan engines	**Dimensions:** wing span 13.2 m
each rated at 48.04 kN	(43 ft 4 in); length 20.08 m (65 ft
(10,800 lb st) dry	11 in); height 3.78 m (12 ft 5 in);
Performance: maximum speed	wing area about 105.9 m²
about 1040 km/h (646 mph) at high	(1,140 sq ft)
altitude; cruising speed 904 km/h	**Armament:** up to 2268 kg (5,000 lb)
(562 mph) at 9145 m (30,000 ft);	of disposable stores in two lower-
service ceiling 11,765 m (38,600 ft);	fuselage weapons bays, comprising
radius about 862 km (535 miles)	primarily GBU-28 laser-guided bombs

Lockheed F-117A

This Nighthawk carries the markings of the 49th Fighter Wing, based at Holloman Air Force Base in New Mexico. The unit was established as such on 10 August 1948, and activated on 18 August at Misawa Air Base, Japan, with F-51 Mustangs and F-80 Shooting Stars. It fought with F-84 Thunderjets in the Korean War. In 1953 the unit took its fighter-bombers to France and Germany with, successively, the F-86 Sabre, F-100 Super Sabre, F-105 Thunderchief and F-4 Phantom II. The wing moved to Holloman Air Force Base in 1968, and flew combat missions in Southeast Asia during 1972. In October 1977 the wing began receiving F-15A Eagles, which served with the 7th, 8th and 9th Tactical Fighter squadrons until 1992, when the F-117 arrived.

A hybrid of components
To reduce development risks and maintain security, the F-117 was created, in part, as a hybrid of components from other aircraft types. The cockpit included dials, lights and switches which date to the analog features of the 'Century Series' of fighters. Many of the cockpit systems are derived from the F/A-18 Hornet, including stick grip, throttles, engine instruments, fuel gauge and HUD (head-up display). The F-117 has at least one minor component from each of a dozen aircraft types, including the P-2 Neptune, F-104 Starfighter, T-33, C-130 Hercules and SR-71 Blackbird. The sensor display is provided by Texas Instruments and borrows heavily from the OV-10D Bronco and P-3C Orion programmes.

Stealthy engine exhausts
In order to vastly reduce its infrared signature, the F-117 uses a novel slot exhaust. Jet efflux from the circular-section jetpipe is mixed with cold bypass air to cool it, then widened and flattened to exit the slot in a plume some 100 mm (4 in) deep and 1.5 m (5 ft) wide. A honeycomb sandwich of nickel alloy reshapes the flow of exhaust gases and absorbs much of the heat of the exhaust. Designed by Astech/MCI Manufacturing of Santa Ana, California, the exhausts do not reduce thrust and incorporate an extended lower lip to shield the main heat source from sensors below, a series of guide vanes along the slot to maintain thrust direction, and ceramic heat tiles similar to the re-entry heat shields fitted to the Space Shuttle. The F-117 has 'a very special nozzle' in the back, as described by Lockheed's Jack Gordon: 'It uses a Coanda effect to turn the flow back into the axial direction, but from the waterline of the trailing edge of the aeroplane and below, you cannot look up into the nozzle and into the engines, so it helps very much in controlling the signature.'

Wing and handling characteristics
Aerodynamically the F-117 relies on the many vortices created by its sharp edges to form a lifting airflow pattern. The wing forms a simple aerofoil by having three flat sections above and two below. The flat surfaces underwing blend into the underfuselage surfaces to create a whole lifting surface below the aircraft. Contrary to some press opinion, which gave rise to the 'Wobblin' Goblin' nickname, the F-117 has more than adequate handling characteristics and considerable agility for an aircraft of its size and power. Pilots describe the F-117 as pleasurable and smooth to fly, if not entirely forgiving. Its characteristics are not unlike those of other deltas, such as the F-106. Landing and take-off speeds are quite high (a parachute is always used on landing) and the aircraft flies nose-high at low speeds and decelerates rapidly in a sharp turn.

Keith Fretwell

Stealth features
Apart from the flat facets making up its exterior, the F-117 exhibits many other features for a low radar cross-section, notably in the front hemisphere. The straight line running from nose to wingtip (swept at 67.5 degrees) and similar sharp sweep-back on the fins is a major dissipator of radar energy away from its source. Every door or surface protuberance has diagonal patterns on the fore and aft edges, while the whole airframe is coated with radar-absorbent material (RAM). This was originally applied to the aircraft surface in sheets, but is now available as a spray. Operational alert aircraft are regularly kept in full stealth status with regular visits to the RAM spray facility to maintain the coating in top condition. All glazed panels are coated with gold to conduct radar energy into the airframe. Necessary holes in the overall shape, for the engine intakes and two IRADS sensors, are covered with a grille. This has a fine mesh much smaller than the wavelengths of detection radars, and consequently would appear as another faceted surface. The fins were carefully positioned to keep radar reflections to a minimum, and also to help shield the engine exhausts from infrared sensors, especially those carried by a chasing fighter.

Internal weapons bay
Primary weapon of the F-117A is the laser-guided bomb (LGB), part of the 'smart' family of ordnance known to the USAF as precision-guided munitions (PGMs). The F-117 has a slender, centre-hinged bomb bay with two weapon-bearing hoists, or trapezes, which lift weapons up into the bay. Because the F-117 is directionally unstable over large parts of its operational envelope, it is of interest that opening the weapons bay makes the aircraft more unstable than it is already. The F-117 is fully capable of level, loft, dive, dive toss, and LADD (low-altitude drogue delivery) weapon release manoeuvres, but usually uses straight and level overfly delivery. This Nighthawk is releasing two 907-kg (2,000-lb) GBU-27A/B LGBs, fitted with the hardened BLU-109/B penetrator warhead.

Flight control system

Designing an aircraft with true stealth properties and relaxed stability was deemed virtually impossible, so the F-117 uses a fly-by-wire (FBW) system to maintain stability. This is almost certainly based on the GEC Astronics quadruplex unit employed very successfully on the F-16. Providing precise air data for the system posed Lockheed designers with a problem in maintaining stealth properties. The result is a group of four air data probes projecting from the nose, each being facetted to defeat radar and with multiple ports for taking differential pressure readings. These are heated to prevent ice fouling the ports. Comparison of the readings from each probe gives adequate data for the flight control system.

Cockpit

The original cockpit featured Texas Instruments (TI) monochrome displays surrounded by standard 'off-the-shelf' flight instruments from other aircraft, notably the F/A-18 Hornet. In the centre of the dashboard is a large TV screen which displays imagery from the IRADS, with two smaller multi-function displays on either side for aircraft information. Above the dashboard is a Kaiser head-up display based on the AVQ-18. The new OCIP (Offensive Capability Improvement Programme) cockpit replaces the TI displays with Honeywell full-colour screens, and adds a large colour moving map for improving situational awareness. The pilot sits on a McDonnell Douglas ACES (Aircrew Escape System) II ejection seat under a heavily framed canopy with five flat glazed panes made by Sierracin/Sylmar Corporation. The pilot sits high in the cockpit and has a good view forward, sideways and downward across the sharply sloping nose. However, the view to the rear is virtually nonexistent due to the broad fuselage and engine trunks.

IRADS

The Texas Instruments IRADS (Infra-Red Acquisition and Designation System) is the F-117's primary search and attack sensor and consists of the forward-looking infrared (FLIR) in front of the cockpit, and the downward-looking infrared (DLIR) mounted to the starboard side of the nosewheel bay. Both are mounted in swivelling turrets, which can rotate to the rear when not in use to protect the delicate optics. The IR sensors employ a wide-angle function for initial search and target acquisition, followed by closer target designation using a zoom function. Both turrets also incorporate a laser designator.

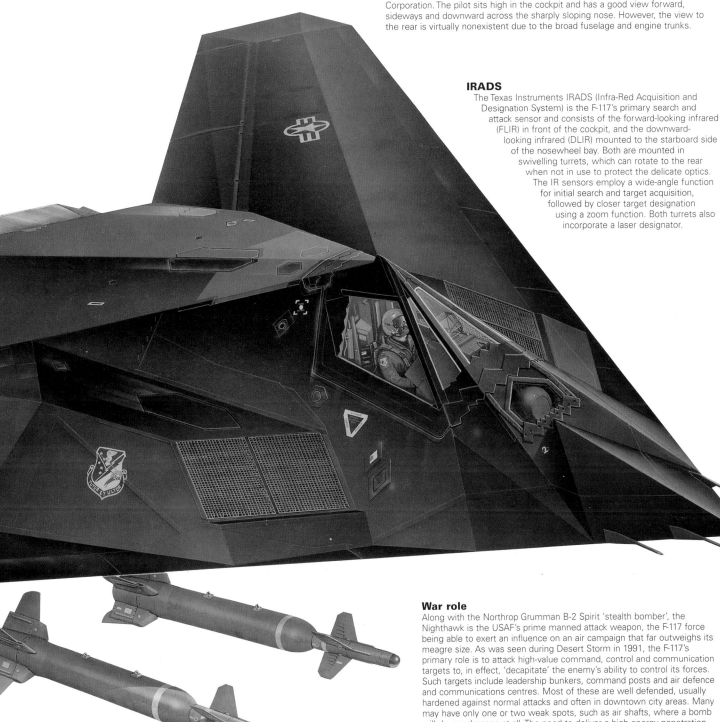

Structure

With its facetted shape, the F-117 required unusual construction techniques. The central carapace and engine trunks are constructed as one unit, with the faceted panels attached to this internal skeleton. The wings are bolted on outboard of the engine trunks.

War role

Along with the Northrop Grumman B-2 Spirit 'stealth bomber', the Nighthawk is the USAF's prime manned attack weapon, the F-117 force being able to exert an influence on an air campaign that far outweighs its meagre size. As was seen during Desert Storm in 1991, the F-117's primary role is to attack high-value command, control and communication targets to, in effect, 'decapitate' the enemy's ability to control its forces. Such targets include leadership bunkers, command posts and air defence and communications centres. Most of these are well defended, usually hardened against normal attacks and often in downtown city areas. Many may have only one or two weak spots, such as air shafts, where a bomb will do any damage at all. The need to deliver a high-energy penetration weapon causing the least-possible collateral damage requires the utmost accuracy and high survivability. By using stealth, the F-117 can cruise into the target area unmolested by hostile air defences, relying on its extensive low-observable properties for protection and achieve the optimum position for an accurate attack. The crew of a conventional aircraft has to fly low and fast while dodging defences to penetrate the target area, leaving them little time to concentrate on accuracy. By contrast, the F-117 pilot can take time to use the sophisticated weapons system to ensure a pinpoint strike. If the strategic targets run out, the F-117 is a valuable weapon in a standard interdiction role, being able to hit bridges, railroad depots, airfields and industrial complexes with ease.

Boeing F-15E Eagle Advanced attack aircraft

It is most likely that the F-15E would rely on precision-guided munitions in combat conditions. However, if the mission scenario allows, the aircraft can deliver cheaper 'dumb' ordnance – represented here by a pair of inert 907-kg (2,000-lb) Mk 84 bombs – with great accuracy.

In 1982, McDonnell Douglas set out to modify its TF-15A demonstrator as a prototype of what it termed the **'Strike Eagle'**. The company had recognized that the USAF would need a replacement for its General Dynamics F-111 strike aircraft in the near- to mid-term, and invested its own money in an effort to provide that replacement.

The Eagle was originally built with a secondary air-to-ground capability, but few units trained in the 'mud moving' role with the aircraft, its primary air-to-air role soon becoming its only duty in service. However, the airframe had much attack potential, with the promise of considerable load-carrying capability, allied to an airframe large enough to accommodate a range of new systems.

F-15E Strike Eagle

The new Eagle variant boasted a powerful APG-70 radar, an AN/AVQ-26 Pave Tack targeting pod, a strengthened airframe and common engine bays for either the Pratt & Whitney F100 or General Electric F110 turbofan. Such were the obvious qualities of the new machine that it was ordered into production in 1984, for first delivery to the USAF on 11 December 1986. The service was scheduled to receive the 237th and last of its **F-15E** Eagles in 2003.

The name 'Strike Eagle' has never been officially adopted by the USAF and the Pave Tack was, likewise, not adopted for service use in its F-15E application. Instead, among the F-15E's primary navigation and targeting equipment is the LANTIRN (Low-Altitude Navigation and Targeting by Infra-Red at Night) system. This

The F-15S is a formidable attack aircraft almost on a par with the F-15E. The Saudi aircraft have the most powerful F100-PW-229 engines as a standard fit.

Israel has received a total of 25 F-15Is and, although little is known of their operational use, these aircraft have almost certainly seen extensive combat since gaining their initial operational capability in 1999.

is housed in two pods, one carried under each intake trunk.

Conformal fuel tanks (CFTs), developed for the F-15C but seldom used (at least in USAF service) are standard fixtures on the F-15E. As well as allowing the aircraft to carry additional fuel, the CFTs also mount six hardpoints, greatly increasing the weapon-loading options.

Combat operations

When the 1991 Gulf War broke out, the F-15E was still a relatively immature system. Nevertheless, the aircraft's performance during the conflict was outstanding.

With few weapons cleared for carriage on the aircraft, air and ground crews did all they could to make do with what they had,

as well as carrying out their own clearance trials in combat! LANTIRN pods were also rare, and the handful that did arrive in theatre before the end of the war were jealously guarded, most especially by those crews which were engaged in 'Scud'- hunting operations.

Since 1991, the F-15E has seen combat over Iraq while policing NATO no-fly zones, over the Balkans and, most recently, over Afghanistan. Should the United States return to combat in its campaign to eradicate terrorism and the supporters of terrorist acts, it is inconceivable that the

On 14 May 2002 an F-15E released five 907-kg (2,000-lb) JDAM munitions in a single sortie. Featuring an inertial/GPS guidance system, JDAM adds to the F-15E's impressive armoury. The aircraft can deploy the majority of USAF weapons, including AIM-7, -9 and -120 AAMs; LGBs; and the GBU-15 EO-guided bomb and its powerful AGM-130 rocket-boosted version.

F-15E would not be committed to combat again.

Eagles abroad

Compared to the lighter, cheaper F-16, Eagle exports have been limited. Orders for F-15E-based aircraft have come from three overseas customers: Israel, Saudi Arabia and South Korea.

Israel's **F-15I Ra'am** (thunder) is virtually identical to the USAF's F-15E. It was delivered with certain functions of the APG-70 radar deleted, but reports suggest that it has now had these reinstated by local modifications. As with the majority of export Eagles, the

aircraft were also delivered without much of the type's sophisticated ECM equipment, but this shortfall has also been made up from local sources.

Saudi Arabia received the first of 72 **F-15S** aircraft in 1995, these machines being all but identical to the F-15E and even including the majority of that machine's ECM fit.

South Korea could turn out to be the last F-15 customer, with F-15 production for the USAF drawing to a close. South Korea's 40 **F-15K** aircraft will be delivered from around 2005 and will have a specification likely to cause a certain amount of

jealousy among USAF F-15E crews. An interesting decision on the part of the Koreans will see the F-15K powered by General Electric F110 engines,

the first time that this powerplant has been specified for an operational Eagle model. F-15K deliveries are scheduled for completion around 2008.

SPECIFICATION
Boeing F-15E Eagle	(60,000 ft); ferry range with
Type: two-seat all-weather attack aircraft	drop tanks and CFTs 5745 km (3,570 miles)
Powerplant: two Pratt & Whitey F100-PW-229 turbofans, each rated at 79.18 kN (17,800 lb st) dry and 129.45 kN (29,100 lb st) with afterburning	**Weights:** empty equipped 14,379 kg (31,700 lb); maximum take-off 36,741 kg (81,000 lb)
Performance: maximum level speed 2655 km/h (1,650 mph) 'clean' at 10,975 m (36,000 ft); maximum rate of climb at sea level 15240+ m (50,000+ ft) per minute; service ceiling 18,290 m	**Dimensions:** wing span 13.05 m (42 ft 9¾ in); length 19.43 m (63 ft 9 in); height 5.63 m (18 ft 5½ in); wing area 56.48 m² (608 sq ft)
	Armament: one fixed forward-firing M61A1 Vulcan rotary cannon, plus up to up to 11,000 kg (24,250 lb) of bombs, fuel tanks and missiles

F-15E Eagle
This aircraft carries the markings of the 391st FS, part of the 366th Wing. The latter is a composite wing, equipped with a range of aircraft types which allow it to fulfil a broad spectrum of roles. The 366th Wing also has an F-15C squadron, the 390th FS. Both Eagle units are based at Mountain Home, Idaho.

LANTIRN pods
The LANTIRN system is always carried as an AN/AAQ-13 navigation pod to starboard and an AN/AAQ-114 targeting pod to port.

Air-to-air missiles
Even when fully equipped for an air-to-ground strike, the F-15E still packs a formidable air-to-air punch. Here the aircraft is shown with two pairs of AIM-9 Sidewinders, but the air-to-air loadout could just as easily consist of four AIM-120 AMRAAMs. Allied to a powerful ECM system, these missiles give the F-15E an awesome self-protection capability.

Fairchild Republic A-10 Thunderbolt II 'Tankbuster'

This A-10A is depicted as it appeared on the strength of the USAFE's 10th TFW based at Alconbury, United Kingdom, in the late 1980s. Some 707 A-10A production aircraft were built.

Originally conceived as a counter-insurgency aircraft to help the US war effort in Southeast Asia, the **A-10A Thunderbolt II** emerged as a dedicated close air support aircraft, with the primary role of destroying enemy armour.

Two **YA-10A** were built for competitive evaluation in the USAF's AX competition. The Fairchild Republic type was judged the winner on 18 January 1973 after evaluation against the Northrop YA-9A. The first development aircraft was subsequently converted into the sole two-seat **YA-10B**, or **N/AW A-10**, intended for the dedicated night/adverse weather role.

'Warthog' is a nickname that has stuck with the A-10, largely as a result of its awkward looks. The design, however, is central to the ability of the A-10 to operate effectively in a lethal battlefield environment. The A-10A also has outstanding agility, enabling it to jink and weave at very low level. Survivability factors were the keys to the design of the A-10's configuration, the widely spaced engines being mounted high on the rear fuselage where they are shrouded from ground fire from most angles by either the

wing or the tailplane. A strong structure and system redundancy ensure that the A-10 is able to stay aloft with large amounts of battle damage, including an engine or fin shot away. A titanium armour 'bathtub' protects both the pilot and the ammunition tank.

Giant cannon

In terms of ordnance, the A-10 is designed around the enormous GAU-8/A cannon, which is the world's most powerful airborne gun. The principal weapon of the A-10, however, is the TV- or IR-guided AGM-65 Maverick ASM.

The basic avionics fit of the A-10 includes a HUD, a Maverick display screen and 'Pave Penny' laser spot seeker. Most current aircraft have received the LASTE (low-altitude safety and target enhancement) modification, which added an autopilot and improves gun accuracy.

Concerns about the A-10A's perceived vulnerability led to

a gradual withdrawal of the type in favour of the F-16, redundant A-10As becoming available for use as **OA-10A** FAC aircraft. However, the 1991 Desert Storm campaign saw the A-10 turning in a remarkable performance, and the aircraft is now likely to remain an important combat type well into the twenty-first century.

SPECIFICATION	
Fairchild Republic A-10A Thunderbolt II **Type:** single-seat close air support and anti-tank warplane **Powerplant:** two General Electric TF34-GE-100 turbofan engines each rated at 40.32 kN (9,065 lb st) **Performance:** maximum speed 706 km/h (439 mph) at sea level; initial climb rate 1829 m (6,000 ft) per minute; radius 1000 km (620 miles) on a deep attack mission	**Weights:** empty 11,321 kg (24,959 lb); maximum take-off 22,680 kg (50,000 lb) **Dimensions:** wing span 17.53 m (57 ft 6 in); length 16.26 m (53 ft 4 in); height 4.47 m (14 ft 8 in); wing area 47.01 m² (506 sq ft) **Armament:** one 30-mm General Electric GAU-8/A Avenger fixed forward-firing seven-barrel rotary cannon, plus up to 7257 kg (16,000 lb) of disposable stores

The AFRES A-10A seen here demonstrates the grey scheme that was adopted later in the type's career.

Lockheed Martin F-16 Fighting Falcon

SPECIFICATION

Lockheed Martin F-16C Block 30 Fighting Falcon
Type: single-seat multi-role tactical warplane
Powerplant: one General Electric F110-GE-100 turbofan engine rated at 128.9 kN (28,984 lb st) with afterburning
Performance: maximum level speed 'clean' at altitude 2124 km/h (1,320 mph); maximum climb rate at sea level 15,240 m (50,000 ft) per minute; service ceiling more than 15,240 m (50,000 ft); combat radius 547 km (340 miles) with

six 2,000-lb (907-kg) bombs on a hi-lo-hi mission
Weights: empty operating 8663 kg (19,100 lb); maximum take-off 19,187 kg (25,071 lb)
Dimensions: wing span 9.45 m (31 ft) without tip-mounted missiles; length 15.03 m (49 ft 4 in); height 5.09 m (16 ft 8½ in); wing area 27.87 m² (300 sq ft)
Armament: one 20-mm M61A1 Vulcan fixed forward-firing six-barrel rotary cannon, plus up to 7072 kg (15,591 lb) of disposable stores

The majority of Belgium's surviving F-16A and F-16B (illustrated) aircraft have been brought up to the MLU standard.

The **Lockheed Martin** (originally **General Dynamics**) **F-16 Fighting Falcon** was conceived as a lightweight air-combat fighter, but has evolved into a versatile and effective multi-role workhorse. First flown on

20 January 1974, the service-test **YF-16** defeated Northrop's YF-17 in a fly-off competition. The first of eight full-scale development **F-16A** airframes flew in 1975. The **F-16B** is a combat-capable two-seat version.

Nicknamed **'Viper'**, the F-16 has its engine air intake located under the forward fuselage. The type's unusual shape features wing/body blending and large

leading-edge root extensions to enhance lift at high angles of attack. The aircraft is statically unstable with a fly-by-wire system for controllability, a zero/zero ejection seat angled back by 30 degrees to improve pilot *g* tolerance, and a side-stick controller in place of a conventional control column. The cockpit has a HUD and MFDs as well as a one-piece frameless canopy with no windscreen. Except for the ADF variants, all surviving US F-16A/Bs have attack as their primary role.

NATO's search for an F-104 replacement led in June 1975 to an agreement whereby Belgium, Denmark, the Netherlands and Norway selected the F-16A/B. Production of these aircraft was split between SABCA in Belgium and Fokker in Holland. Some Dutch **F-16A(R)** aircraft have a centreline tactical recce pod.

Service aircraft

The F-16A/B was built in distinct production blocks numbered **1**, **5**, **10**, and **15**. Block 15 introduced the first important changes, including the extended horizontal stabilator that is now standard. A number of Block 15 aircraft was converted to **F-16A/B ADF (Air Defence Fighter)** standard, with changes including an upgraded APG-66 radar compatible with the AIM-7 Sparrow AAM.

The OCU (Operational Capabilities Upgrade) programme, adopted by Belgium, Denmark, the Netherlands and Norway, improves the F-16A/B's avionics and powerplant. From 1988, exports were to **Block 15 OCU** standard. Further improvements for the F-16A/B came with the European MLU (Mid-Life Update) which brings the cockpit to Block 50 standard. AIM-120 capability is also added

Bought to replace the F-4 and F-106 in the defence of the continental United States, the F-16 ADF is the primary AIM-7 user among F-16 variants. Bulges in the sides of the fin/fuselage fairing were added to house the aircraft's rudder actuators, which were displaced by additional avionics. This aircraft has the early 1990s markings of the 144th FW, California ANG.

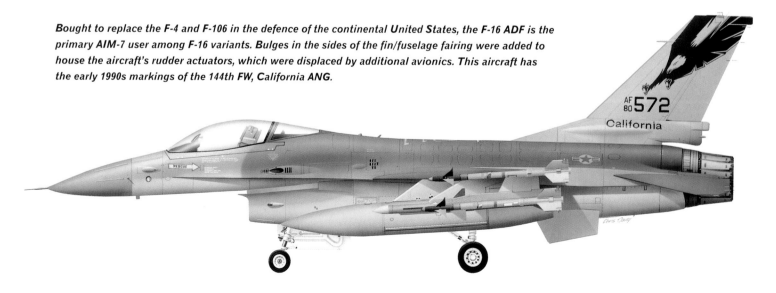

and **F-16 MLU** aircraft are in service with Belgium, Denmark, the Netherlands and Norway. Belgium refers to its MLU aircraft as **F-16AM** (single-seat) and **F-16BM**. Aircraft sold to Taiwan are to a similar standard, known as **Block 20**.

F-16C/D

First flown on 19 June 1984, the **F-16C** single-seater and its

F-16D two-seat counterpart are distinguished by an enlarged base leading up to the vertical fin. Compared with earlier versions, the F-16C/D gives the pilot a wide-angle HUD and employs the considerably more capable APG-68 radar.

The F-16C/Ds introduced progressive changes, some installed at the factory and others as part of MSIPs (Multinational-

Staged Improvement Programs) II and III.

F-16C/D Block 25 aircraft entered production in July 1984. With **Block 30/32** and **Block 40/42** aircraft came the option in the Block 30 for the F110-GE-100 engine or in the Block 32 for the 106.05-kN (23,840-lb st) F100-PW-220. The F110 engine required an enlargement of the air inlet.

Avionics changes were also introduced with Block 30/32. Some Block 30/32 aircraft were used by the US Navy as **F-16N** and **TF-16N** adversary trainers.

Block 40/42 Night Falcon warplanes were built from December 1988. These aircraft included features such as LANTIRN pods, GPS, APG-68(V) radar and automatic terrain-following capability.

Douglas A-4 Skyhawk Lightweight attack aircraft

Malaysia's A-4s were delivered from 1985 for service to 1995. In the event, they were withdrawn early and had been replaced by BAe Hawk Mk 208s by late 1994.

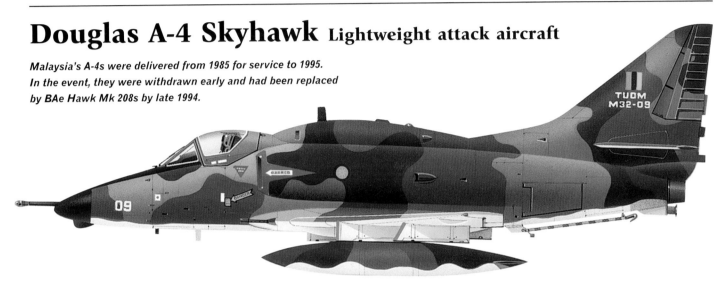

A short-sighted political decision forced the RNZAF to retire its upgraded Skyhawks. In common with other such aircraft, these featured AN/APG-66 radar and HOTAS controls.

The **A-4 Skyhawk** originated as a private venture but, when the US Navy began the search for a turbine-powered successor to the Skyraider, Douglas was able to propose a new attack aircraft

with a gross weight of about half that of the official specification and one which was considerably faster. With a low-set delta wing and a Wright J65 turbojet, the type was ordered during the Korean War. The prototype first flew on 22 June 1954, with initial deliveries in late 1956.

Vietnam action

By the time the US Navy and US Marines became involved in operations in Vietnam, both were able to deploy the Skyhawk with the greatest confidence in its capability. Indeed, such was their effectiveness that steadily improving A-4s remained in

production until February 1979, built to a total of 2960 aircraft including trainers and exported to several armed forces. Variants included the **A-4A**; **A-4B**; **A-4C**; **A-4E**; **A-4F**; **A-4H** for Israel's air force; **A-4K** for the RNZAF; **OA-4M** conversion of **TA-4F** trainers for the USMC fast FAC role; **A-4N Skyhawk II** for the Israeli air force; and the **Singapore Aircraft Industries A-4SU** and **TA-4SU Super Skyhawk** upgraded variants. In 2003, Skyhawks remained in service in a variety of original and upgraded forms with Argentina, Brazil, Indonesia, Israel (many in storage) and Singapore.

SPECIFICATION	
McDonnell Douglas A-4M Skyhawk **Type:** single-seat carrier-based attack-bomber **Powerplant:** one Pratt & Whitney J52-P-408A turbojet rated at 49.8 kN (11,200 lb st) **Performance:** maximum speed 1102 km/h (685 mph) at sea level; maximum rate of climb at sea level 3140 m (10,300 ft) per minute; service ceiling 11,795 m (38,700 ft);	combat radius 547 km (345 miles) with a 1814-kg (4,000-lb) warload **Weights:** empty 4747 kg (10,465 lb); maximum take-off 11,113 kg (24,500 lb) **Dimensions:** wing span 8.38 m (27 ft 6 in); length 12.29 m (40 ft 3½ in); height 4.57 m (15 ft); wing area 24.15 m² (260 sq ft) **Armament:** two 20-mm cannon, plus up to 4153 kg (9,155 lb) of weapons on five external hardpoints

FMA IA-58 Pucará Twin-turboprop COIN aircraft

Armed with Argentinian-built 110-kg (243-lb) bombs, this aircraft is one of the six delivered to the Fuerza Aérea Uruguaya. The bombs are carried in triplets below the fuselage (six weapons) and the wings (three each).

Meeting a Fuerza Aérea Argentina (FAA) requirement for a close air support, reconnaissance and counter-insurgency (COIN) aircraft, the **Pucará** was an indifferent performer in the 1982 Falklands War and consequently suffered a loss of support for its modus operandi.

The aircraft originated in the early 1960s, when anti-guerrilla and COIN were the types of warfare that were anticipated by Argentina. FMA produced the **IA-58** design with twin turboprops and all-metal construction. The prototype flew on 20 August 1969, powered by a pair of Garrett engines; however, the production version utilized the Astazous which powered the second aircraft for its maiden flight on 6 September 1970.

Pucará performance

Named for the indigenous South American stone forts, the Pucará is a manoeuvrable and rugged aircraft able to operate from short, rough airstrips – 80 m (262 ft) is enough when helped by three RATO bottles. A tall, retractable tricycle undercarriage provides ample clearance for weapons and the generous propeller ground clearance necessary for flights from uneven surfaces.

The Pucará's crew is provided with ejection seats, the rear occupant having full dual controls and a raised cockpit floor. In practice, a second crew member is rarely necessary for COIN missions and the aircraft is usually flown with the rear seat empty.

The first production **IA-58A** flew on 8 November 1974 and deliveries began to the FAA in 1976. Early action was seen late in 1976 against rebel forces in northwest Argentina. All 24 of the aircraft deployed to the Falkland Islands in 1982 were lost to sabotage, ground fire and bombing, or were captured by British forces, one of these latter later flying in British markings for evaluation. Nevertheless, a Pucará shot down a Westland Scout.

In October 1981, the first of six aircraft was delivered to Uruguay, while Colombia was presented with three for drugs interdiction operations in late 1989. In late 2002, Argentina had around 37 Pucarás in service, some with the rear cockpit deleted in favour of additional fuel.

Failed variants

IA-58B was the designation for one prototype, flown on 15 May 1979, with two 30-mm DEFA 553 cannon, a deeper forward fuselage and improved avionics, but no production resulted. Taking aboard the lessons of the Falklands War, the **IA-58C 'Pucará Charlie'** was a proposed rebuild of IA-58As with the DEFA 553s in addition to the standard gun fit, the front cockpit faired over, the rear cockpit enlarged and weapon options expanded. One prototype was flown on 30 December 1985. **IA-66** was the designation of a prototype Pucará which flew in 1980, powered by 746-kW (1,000-ehp) Garrett TPE331-11-601Ws.

Four ex-FAA IA-58As were delivered to Sri Lanka in 1993. They have seen some combat, with two remaining airworthy late in 2002.

Still remaining in frontline service with Argentina, the Pucará is undoubtedly a capable type, but was unsuited to operations in the Falklands War.

SPECIFICATION

FMA IA-58A Pucará
Type: two-seat close support and COIN warplane
Powerplant: two Turboméca Astazou XVIG turboprops each rated at 762 kW (1,022 shp)
Performance: maximum level speed 'clean' 500 km/h (311 mph) at 3000 m (9,845 ft); maximum rate of climb at sea level 1080 m (3,543 ft) per minute; service ceiling 10,000 m (32,800 ft); combat radius 225 km (140 miles) on lo-lo-lo attack mission with a 1500-kg (3,307-lb) warload

Weights: empty 4020 kg (8,862 lb); maximum take-off 6800 kg (14,991 lb)
Dimensions: wing span 14.5 m (47 ft 6¾ in); length 14.25 m (46 ft 9 in); height 5.36 m (17 ft 7 in); wing area 30.3 m² (326.16 sq ft)
Armament: fixed armament of two 20-mm Hispano cannon under the nose and four 7.62-mm (0.30-in) Browning machine guns abreast of the cockpit, plus an additional 1500 kg (3,307 lb) of external stores

EMBRAER Tucano Light attack and anti-narcotics aircraft

The Brazilian air force's formation aerobatic team, the Escuadron de Fumaca (smoke squadron), received T-27 aircraft to replace its ageing North American Harvard machines, and has displayed extensively throughout the American continent.

Design of the turboprop-powered **EMB-312 Tucano** (toucan) high-performance trainer started in 1978 in response to a Força Aérea Brasileira (FAB) specification for an indigenously designed type to replace the Cessna T-37. First flown on 16 August 1980 the initial Tucano, of some 133 for Brazil, was delivered in September 1983 for service with the designation **T-27**. Designed from the outset to provide jet-like flying experience, the Tucano has vertically staggered ejection seats and a single power lever governing both propeller pitch and engine rpm.

In September 1983 an order for 134 Tucanos was concluded with Egypt, and all but the first 10 of these were licence-assembled at Helwan. The Egyptian air force operates 54 locally assembled machines, the other 80 going to Iraq. Orders have also come from Argentina, Colombia, Honduras, Iran, Paraguay, Peru, Venezuela and an undisclosed customer. Another major order was placed in July 1990 when France announced its intention to buy Brazilian-built **EMB-312F** aircraft for delivery from July 1993. The EMB-312F has a ventral airbrake and other improvements and is

ALX can be flown as a single-seater, or in the twin-seat form illustrated. The aircraft has a comprehensive range of weapons options for air-to-ground and air-to-air missions.

used for basic training. The Tucano's most notable export success came in March 1985, when it won a hotly contested British order for the RAF. The resulting, much modified **Tucano T.Mk 1** was produced under licence by Shorts, which also built aircraft to a similar standard for Kenya and Kuwait.

Super Tucano

In June 1991 EMBRAER announced the **EMB-312H** (later **EMB-314**) **Super Tucano** with an uprated PT6A engine driving a five- rather than three-bladed propeller. The EMB-312H was planned in three variants: the basic EMB-312H with one 1193-kW (1,600-shp) PT6A-67R engine, the **EMB-312HJ** unsuccessful JPATS (Joint Primary Aircraft Training System)

contender, and the **ALX** border patrol version. To accommodate the longer engine and to preserve the centre of gravity in the correct position, the fuselage has been lengthened by the insertion of 'plugs' forward and aft of the cockpit and strengthened for the incorporation of a centreline hardpoint. Other revisions include a new wing with a fixed forward-firing armament of two 12.7-mm (0.5-in) machine guns, HOTAS controls and a ventral airbrake.

The EMB-312H first flew in May 1996, but in August 1995 the FAB authorized development

of the ALX for delivery from 1999 with the PT6A-68-5 engine. For its Amazon surveillance programme, the Brazilian air force intends to operate some 99 examples of the type in the form of 49 of the single-seat **A-29** for the dedicated attack role with a fuselage 10.53 m (34 ft 6½ in) long, 20 of the two-seat **AT-29** with the full-length EMB-314 fuselage and provision for a FLIR turret for night targeting capability, and 30 of the AT-29 with dual controls, as advanced trainers to replace the EMBRAER Xavante.

SPECIFICATION	
EMBRAER EMB-312 Tucano	(30,000 ft); typical range 1844 km
Type: two-seat basic flying and	(1,145 miles) with internal fuel
armament trainer	**Weights:** empty 1810 kg (3,991 lb);
Powerplant: one Pratt & Whitney	maximum take-off 3175 kg (7,000 lb)
Canada PT6A-25C turboprop	**Dimensions:** wing span 11.14 m
engine rated at 559 kW (750 shp)	(36 ft 6½ in); length 9.86 m (32 ft
Performance: maximum speed 448	4¼ in); height 3.4 m (11 ft 1¾ in);
km/h (278 mph) at 3050 m (10,000	wing area 19.4 m² (208.82 sq ft)
ft); initial climb rate 680 m (2,231 ft)	**Armament:** up to 1000 kg (2,205 lb)
per minute; service ceiling 9145 m	of external stores

Aero L-39, L-59 and L-159 Trainer and light support aircraft

The first step in the L-39's development came with the L-39ZO, which was fitted with four hardpoints for a light attack capability. This pair is from the 3rd Század of the Hungarian air force, based at Kecskemét, and is among the 20 L-39ZOs delivered in 1994 as a gift from the German government.

The experiences of Warsaw Pact and Soviet client air forces with the Aero L-29 highlighted several faults with the type, but despite its shortcomings the L-29's overall success meant that Aero was solely allocated the task of designing a replcement trainer.

The new aircraft was developed primarily to meet a Soviet air force requirement, and the resulting **L-39 Albatros** introduced a much enhanced overall performance, due primarily to the adoption of a more powerful engine, the Soviet AI-25 TL turbofan, known as the Walter Titan.

Albatros on test

The L-39's cockpit was designed to be as similar as possible to that of the Soviet MiG-21 and uses the same gunsight and many of the same instruments. A pre-production batch of 10 aircraft joined the flight test programme in 1971 and series production began the following year. In late 1972, the L-39 was officially selected to replace the L-29 by Czechoslovakia, the USSR and East Germany. Service acceptance trials in Czechoslovakia and the USSR

were successfully undertaken during 1973, and the L-39 began to enter service, initially with the Czech air force, in 1974.

The Albatros made its first appearance in the West at the 1977 Paris Air Show, by which time approximately 1000 examples had been ordered. By early 2003, in excess of 2800 L-39s had been produced.

Albatros variants

The L-39 was widely exported and developed in a bewildering array of variants, including the **L-39C** standard basic and advanced trainer, **L-39V**, **L-39ZO** weapons trainer, **L-39ZA** ground-attack/recce aircraft, L-39ZA/MP multi-purpose variant of the L-39ZA and the **L-39MS** (**L-59**) further developed version of the basic L-39. In addition, the L-59 has been developed into

SPECIFICATION	
Aero L-39ZA Albatros **Type:** single-seat light ground attack/reconnaissance aircraft **Powerplant:** one ZMDB Progress (Ivchyenko) AI-25TL turbofan rated at 16.87 kN (3,797 lb st) **Performance:** (for aircraft with all-up weight of 4570 kg/10,075 lb with empty tip tanks) maximum level speed at sea level 700 km/h (435 mph); maximum rate of climb 1320 m (4,330 ft) per minute; service ceiling 11,500 m (37,730 ft); range at 5000 m (16,404 ft) 1800 km (1,118 miles) with	underwing tanks **Weights:** empty 3565 kg (7,859 lb); maximum take-off 6000 kg (13,227 lb) **Dimensions:** wing span 19.46 m (31 ft ½ in) including tip tanks; length 12.13 m (39 ft 9½ in); height 4.77 m (15 ft 7¾ in), wing area 18.8 m² (202.36 sq ft) **Armament:** one centreline 23-mm Gryazev-Shipunov GSh-23L fixed forward-firing two-barrel cannon with 150 rounds in the lower fuselage, and up to 1100 kg (2,425 lb) of stores

the **L-159** single-seat light fighter aircraft. Despite development, economic and political set backs, the L-159 looks set to become the standard attack and light-fighter

aircraft of the Czech air force. It is armed with both air-to-air and air-to-ground stores (including AGM-65 Maverick) as standard and has an advanced avionics fit.

Following the division of Czechoslovakia, the Slovaks retained a total of 21 L-39s in C, MS, V and ZA variants. Three have been lost in accidents and the remainder are used in the training role, except for the two Vs which are combat support aircraft.

Dassault/Dornier Alpha Jet
Trainer and light-attack aircraft

The **Alpha Jet**, ultimately derived from the Breguet Br.126 and Dornier P.375 projects, has a shoulder-set swept wing and stepped tandem cockpits. The aircraft was primarily delivered to France and West Germany, with considerably different equipment fits. The Luftwaffe wanted a replacement for the Fiat G.91R/3 in the light ground-attack role, while France wanted an advanced trainer.

Alphas into service

The first **Alpha Jet E** (**Ecole**, or school) from the French production line made its maiden flight on 4 November 1977, and the first **Alpha Jet A** (**Appui**, or attack) from the German production line flew on 12 April 1978, and was alternatively called the **Alpha Jet Close Support Version**. From late 1992 the surviving West German aircraft were withdrawn, 50 being delivered to Portugal. The other aircraft were mothballed, and their future remained uncertain until 1999, when Thailand decided to take 50 (soon reduced to 25) machines and the United Kingdom decided to take 12 for experimental work.

In 1980 work began on the **Alpha Jet Alternative Close Support Version**, which first flew on 9 April 1982. In addition to light attack and anti-helicopter roles, the new version had improved potential for the lead-in fighter training role. Customers for this variant were Egypt (with the designation **Alpha Jet MS2**) and Cameroon. As with the **Alpha Jet MS1** trainer Egypt received the first four of its

Germany's Alpha Jet As potentially represent a potent force for any smaller air force looking to purchase a relatively low-houred fleet of light attack aircraft. Thailand is replacing its border patrol OV-10 Broncos with 20 refurbished Alpha Jet As.

SPECIFICATION	
Dassault/Dornier Alpha Jet E (light-attack version) **Type:** light-attack aircraft **Powerplant:** two 13.24-kN (2,976-lb) thrust SNECMA/Turboméca Larzac 04-C6 turbofans **Performance:** maximum speed clean at sea level 1000 km/h (621 mph); radius on a lo-lo mission with four 500-lb (227-kg) bombs 425 km (264 miles) **Weights:** empty 3345 kg (7,374 lb); maximum take-off	8000 kg (17,637 lb) **Dimensions:** wing span 9.11 m (29 ft 10¾ in); length 11.75 m (36 ft 6½ in); height 4.19 m (13 ft 9 in); wing area 17.5 m² (188.37 sq ft) **Armament:** provision for belly pod with 30-mm DEFA (Alpha Jet A 27-mm Mauser) cannon, plus maximum external load of 2500 kg (5,511 lb) on five stations including gun pods, bombs, rockets, missiles, tanks, ECM pods or a reconnaissance pod

MS2s from Dassault and co-produced the remaining 11.

Other variants that reached the prototype stage but did not enter production were the **Alpha Jet NGEA** and the **Alpha Jet 3**. The Alpha Jet NGEA (**Nouvelle Génération Ecole/Appui**), later known as the **Alpha Jet 2**, was a development of the Alpha Jet MS2 and, in addition to new avionics, had provision for Magic 2 AAMs, as well as uprated Larzac 04-C20 engines.

The **Alpha Jet 3 Advanced Training System** (later known as **Lancier**) was derived from the MS2, with revised cockpit displays for mission training with such sensors as Agave or Anemone radar, FLIR, laser, video and ECM systems, plus advanced weapons.

An Alpha Jet, destined for the France Aérienne Togolaise, is seen armed and in French markings prior to delivery.

Fouga CM.170 Magister Trainer and light-attack aircraft

Notable as the first jet trainer to enter service anywhere in the world, and also for its use of a butterfly tail, the **Fouga CM.170 Magister** resulted from a French air force trainer requirement. The aircraft is of light alloy semi-monocoque construction with an oval-section fuselage, which carries the crew in tandem in a pressurized cockpit under a large and heavily framed canopy. The powerplant of two small turbojets is attached to the fuselage sides. The mid-set wing is of high aspect ratio and without dihedral.

Production aircraft

Following the maiden flight of the first of three CM.170 prototypes on 23 July 1952, orders were placed in January 1954 for quantity production. The pre-production type was to the **CM.170-1 Magister** standard that was continued into the early production aircraft, of which the first made its maiden flight on 29 February 1956. Production of the CM.170 in France totalled 622 to meet orders from the French air force (400) and navy (32), as well as export sales to the air forces of Austria, Belgium, Brazil, Cambodia, Congo Léopoldville, Finland, the Federal Republic of Germany, Israel and Lebanon.

In addition, the Flugzeug Union Süd organization in Germany built 188 examples, Valmet in Finland built 62 and IAI in Israel built 36, bringing overall production including prototypes to some 921 aircraft.

The CM.170-1 had a pair of Marboré IIA engines, but these were replaced in the **CM.170-2** by 4.71-kN (1,058-lb st) Marboré VIC engines. Differences that then distinguished the **CM.170-3**,

With almost 1000 produced, the CM.170 Magister was one of the most widely used trainer/light attack aircraft of the 1950s and 1960s. It remained in service with Israel as a trainer early in 2003.

first flown on 8 June 1964 and later redesignated as the **CM.173 Super Magister**, included an enlarged fuel capacity and Martin-Baker ejection seats under a modified canopy. The variant for the Aéronavale was the carrier-capable **CM.175 Zéphyr**, which was based on the CM.170-1, but had an arrester hook among other changes. The first of two prototypes made its maiden flight on 30 May 1959.

Light-attack roles

The withdrawal from service of Magisters by their original purchasers led to the acquisition of small quantities of used CM.170s by several other air forces for use in the basic-training and/or light-attack roles, the latter with an underwing armament of bombs and/or gun and rocket pods. Current or recent among these 'second-hand' operators are Algeria, Bangladesh, Cameroon, Gabon, Ireland, Libya, Morocco,

El Salvador, Senegambia and Togo.

The Israeli Defence Force/Air Force retains the Magister in a training role, after adding nine ex-Belgian and possibly other second-hand examples to its original import purchase and indigenous production of 82 machines. Between 1981 and 1986, some 80 were modernized by Bedek Division of IAI to have uprated Marboré VI engines, new avionics and other upgrades, then renamed **Tzukit** (thrush).

An interesting development of the basic type that proceeded

no further than prototype stage was the **Potez-Heinkel CM.191** that made its maiden flight on 19 March 1962 as a Super Magister development with a revised and wider forward fuselage providing four-seat accommodation under a single-piece canopy. The type was offered in the **CM.191-A** military form for the training, liaison and reconnaissance roles.

Bangladesh had replaced all of its ageing Magisters with another veteran jet trainer – the American Cessna T-37 – by 1997.

SPECIFICATION	
Fouga CM.170-1 Magister **Type:** multi-role flying and weapons training aircraft with light attack capability **Powerplant:** two Turboméca Marboré IIA turbojets each rated at 3.92 kN (882 lb st) **Performance:** maximum speed 715 km/h (444 mph) at 9000 m (29,525 ft); initial climb rate 1020 m (3,346 ft) per minute; service ceiling 11,000 m (36,070 ft); range 1200 km (746 miles) with auxiliary fuel	**Weights:** empty 2150 kg (4,750 lb); maximum take-off 3200 kg (7,055 lb) **Dimensions:** wing span 12.15 m (39 ft 10 in) with tip tanks; length 10.06 m (33 ft); height 2.8 m (9 ft 2 in); wing area 17.3 m² (186.22 sq ft) **Armament:** provision for two fixed forward-firing machine guns in the nose, and up to 100 kg (220 lb) of disposable stores carried on two underwing hardpoints

Aermacchi MB.326 Trainer and light-attack aircraft

Aermacchi began design work on the **MB.326** as a two-seat basic trainer during 1954, and the first of two prototypes flew on 10 December 1957. Following Italian air force acceptance of an initial batch of aircraft, the first of 85 production trainers was received during February 1962. The MB.326 has been built in many variants, and from the beginning of the programme was seen as possessing potential for development with a light attack capability.

Light attack

Such a capability was first offered in the proposed **MB.326A** variant with six underwing hardpoints for a variety of external stores, but the AMI at that time had no requirement for such a type. However, orders for similar aircraft were received from Ghana and Tunisia for nine **MB.326F** and eight **MB.326B** aircraft, respectively.

The **MB.326H**, with full armament capability, was assembled or licence-built in Australia by CAC (Commonwealth Aircraft Corporation) as the **CA-30** for the Royal Australian Air Force and Navy.

The last of the early versions were 135 of a total of 151 **MB.326M** aircraft assembled or licence-built by Atlas for the SAAF, by which the type is known as the **Impala Mk 1**.

More power

The more powerful Viper ASV.20 engine was introduced early in 1967 to create the **MB.326G**: in combination with a strengthened airframe, the uprated powerplant

allowed the carriage of a 1814-kg (4,000-lb) warload, twice the weight of that possible in the earlier variants. The MB.326G was built as the **MB.326GB** for the Argentine navy and the air forces of Zaïre and Zambia, while EMBRAER in Brazil licence-built 182 similar **MB.326GC** aircraft for the air forces of Brazil (as the **AT-26 Xavante**), Paraguay and Togo. Eleven ex-Brazilian EMB.326GBs were later transferred to the Argentine navy air arm in 1983 to help offset its losses in the Falklands War of 1982.

Aermacchi delivered to the AMI six **MB.326E** aircraft with basically the airframe of the MB.326GB but the lower-rated Viper II of the MB.326, and also converted six earlier MB.326s to the same configuration. The final two-seat version was the **MB.326L** advanced trainer that was based upon the single-seat **MB.326K**: two were supplied to

South Africa will in time replace its long-serving Impalas with BAE Systems Hawk LIFT aircraft.

The Ghana air force was one of the earliest MB.326 export operators, receiving a total of nine MB.326Fs from mid-1965 for service with the training school at Tamale.

Dubai and four to the Tunisian air force. The delivery of the final EMB.326 in February 1983 completed production at the 761st aircraft.

By 2003, the MB.326 was rapidly becoming obsolete and had been withdrawn from service by Ghana and Italy. It remained in service with the Argentine navy, Brazil, Congo, Dubai, Paraguay, Togo, Tunisia

and Zambia. The eight survivors of the Australian navy's CA-30s were transferred to the RAAF in mid-1983. By 1985, a total of 82 'Macchis' had been cycled through a life-extension programme, but all had been retired by 2003.

In South Africa, the once-prominent Impala Mk 1 force had been reduced from 115 in 1994 to around 35 in early 2003.

SPECIFICATION	
Aermacchi MB.326GB **Type:** two-seat basic/advanced trainer and light attack aircraft **Powerplant:** one Rolls-Royce Viper 20 Mk 540 turbojet rated at 15.17 kN (3,410 lb st) **Performance:** maximum level speed 'clean' at optimum altitude 867 km/h (539 mph); maximum rate of climb at sea level 945 m (3,100 ft) per minute at maximum take-off weight; service ceiling 11,890 m (39,000 ft) at 4763 kg (10,500 lb); combat radius 648 km (403 miles) on hi-lo-hi attack mission with a 769-kg (1,695-lb) warload	**Weights:** basic operating 2558 kg (5,640 lb); maximum take-off 5216 kg (11,500 lb) **Dimensions:** wing span 10.15 m (33 ft 3½ in) without tip tanks; overall length 10.67 m (35 ft ¼ in); height 3.72 m (12 ft 2 in); wing area 19.35 m² (208.29 sq ft) **Armament:** provision for up to 1814 kg (4,000 lb) of weapons on six underwing hardpoints, including AS11 or AS12 wire-guided ASMs; 500-lb (227-kg) GP bombs; MATRA SA-10 30-mm ADEN cannon pods; machine-gun pods and rocket pods

Aermacchi AM.3 Tactical support/observation aircraft

Intended to replace the ageing Cessna L-19 Bird Dogs then serving with the Italian army, the **AM.3** high-wing observation/liaison aircraft was a joint venture by Aerfer (later Aeritalia) and Aermacchi. Forming the basis of its design were the wings and tailplane of the Aermacchi AL.60, allied to a revised fin and a new narrower, low-drag fuselage built by Aerfer. Two AM.3 prototypes were built; allocated the designation **MB.335A**, the first (assembled by Aermacchi) made its initial flight on 12 May 1967, and was followed by the Aerfer-built second prototype on 12 August 1968. The AM.3 was evaluated extensively by the Italian army, but as no production order was as yet forthcoming, Aefer and Aermacchi began to develop an improved AM.3.

The prototypes were powered by a 254-kW (340-hp) Continental GTSIO-520-C flat-six engine, but were later fitted with the Piaggio-built Lycoming GSO-480B1B6. This was fitted to production standard aircraft, resulting in the redesignation **AM.3C**.

The prototype AM.3C was rolled out almost exactly five years after the initial flight of the first AM.3 prototype. The outer wing panels were lengthened by a total of 0.98 m (3 ft 2½ in), raising gross wing area by 1.32 m² (14.21 sq ft); the nose was lengthened and refined aerodynamically; and new fairings were added under the fuselage to provide attachment points for the wing struts and mainwheel legs. The AM.3C's cabin was optimized to offer good visibility at all times. The Plexiglass windows were bulged laterally and extended very low on the cockpit sides. The nose sloped sharply to give a good forward view even when taxiing. The cabin normally accommodated a pilot and co-pilot in tandem with dual controls. A third seat at the rear could be removed to accommodate a stretcher or freight, with access via three doors in the sides of the cabin.

AM.3C missions

The AM.3C's roles were seen as forward air control (FAC), armed patrol, helicopter escort, liaison and light transport, photo reconnaissance, battlefield illumination and casualty evacuation. The anticipated Italian army order did not materialize, but the provision of a single NATO M-4A stores attachment rack under each wing made the AM.3 suitable as a light tactical ground support aircraft. This feature was almost certainly responsible for sales to two export customers. The South African Air Force bought 40 AM.3Cs, the aircraft being delivered between May 1972 and December 1974, while a further three AM3Cs were delivered to Rwanda.

SPECIFICATION	
Aermacchi AM.3C **Type:** two-seat light tactical support/observation aircraft **Powerplant:** one 254-kW (340-hp) Piaggio-Lycoming GSO-480B1B6 six-cylinder air-cooled piston engine **Performance:** maximum speed 278 km/h (173 mph) at 2440 m (8,005 ft); cruising speed 246 km/h (153 mph) at 75 per cent power at 2440 m (8,005 ft); climb to 3302 m (9,850 ft) in 7 minutes 30 seconds; service ceiling 8400 m (27,560 ft);	maximum range 990 km (615 miles) at cruising speed (with 30-minute reserves) **Weights:** empty 1080 kg (2,381 lb); maximum take-off (with underwing weapons) 1700 kg (3,748 lb) **Dimensions:** wing span 12.64 m (41 ft 5¾ in); length 8.73 m (28 ft 7¾ in); height 2.72 m (8 ft 11 in); wing area 20.26 m² (219.2 sq ft) **Armament:** total weapons load of 340 kg (750 lb) carried on two underwing hardpoints

Atlas Impala COIN/advanced training aircraft

In the mid-1960s South Africa finalized a contract to build the **Aermacchi MB.326M** variant of the MB.326GB, suitable for advanced training and counter-insurgency roles. An initial 16 kits were supplied by Aermacchi, these being assembled by Atlas for a first flight on 11 May 1966. The next 30 kits were less complete, requiring Atlas to fabricate a percentage of the structure before assembly. After this, an additional 105 were built almost wholly by Atlas, the last of these being completed in 1974. These machines entered service with the SAAF under the designation **Atlas Impala Mk 1**, being initially received by the Flying Training School at Langebaanweg, where they were flown by No. 83 Jet Flying School for the streaming of jet- and transport-assigned pilots. The two-seat trainer was also the mount of the 'Silver Falcons', the SAAF's aerobatic display team.

Single-seater

South Africa also acquired a licence for the **MB.326KM** subvariant of Aermacchi's single-seat MB.326. Atlas production began yet again with assembly of Italian-supplied kits, in this instance for seven aircraft, and progressed to almost 90 per cent manufacture in South Africa of a further 93 aircraft. The first of these entered service with the SAAF on 22 April 1974 under the designation **Impala Mk 2**. This type retains the same powerplant as the Impala Mk 1 instead of the more powerful version of the Viper turbojet used in the MB.326K. A mixture of Impala Mks 1 and 2 serve in the COIN/advanced training role, and Impala Mk 2s are also used in the streaming of future Cheetah pilots.

South Africa's surviving Impala Mk 2 (as here) and Mk 1 aircraft will eventually be replaced by Hawk Mk 100-based aircraft.

SPECIFICATION	
Atlas Impala Mk 2 **Type:** single-seat light attack warplane with operational and armament training capabilities **Powerplant:** one Rolls-Royce Viper 20 Mk 540 turbojet engine rated at 15.17 kN (3,410 lb st) **Performance:** maximum speed 890 km/h (553 mph) at 1525 m (5,000 ft); initial climb rate 1981 m (6,500 ft) per minute; service ceiling 14325 m (47,000 ft); radius 268 km (167 miles) on a lo-lo-lo attack mission with a warload of 1280 kg (2,822 lb)	**Weights:** empty 2964 kg (6,534 lb); maximum take-off 5897 kg (13,000 lb) **Dimensions:** wing span 10.15 m (33 ft 3¾ in) without tip tanks and 10.85 m (35 ft 7 in) with tip tanks; length 10.67 m (35 ft ¼ in); height 3.72 m (12 ft 2 in); wing area 19.35 m² (208.29 sq ft) **Armament:** two 30-mm fixed forward-firing cannon, and up to 1814 kg (4,000 lb) of disposable stores carried on six underwing hardpoints

Aermacchi MB.339 Trainer and light-attack aircraft

During the Falklands War, Argentine navy MB.339s were based at Port Stanley for attack missions against British forces. Several were lost.

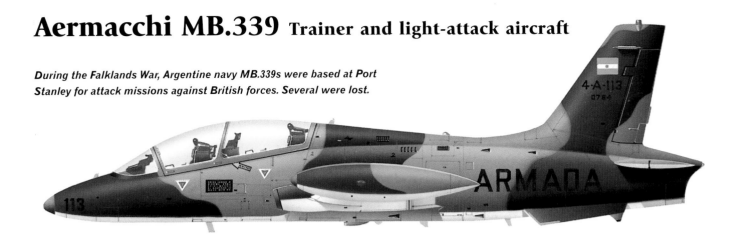

Following prolonged studies, Aermacchi flew the prototype **MB.339** trainer on 12 August 1976. The type was developed from the company's MB.326 design; the chief modification compared with the MB.326 was the redesign of the tandem cockpits to give the instructor a good view ahead over the helmet of the pupil. The aircraft's directional stability was maintained by a larger fin and canted ventral fins, and standard equipment included the Viper Mk 632 engine and Mk 10F zero/zero seats.

Production aircraft

The first of 100 **MB.339A** trainers for the Italian air force was handed over on 8 August 1979. Other AMI variants include the **MB.339PAN** of the 'Frecce Tricolori' aerobatic team and the **MB.339RM** calibration aircraft. In addition, aircraft generally similar to MB.339A standard have been widely exported to customers which include Argentina, Dubai, Ghana, Malaysia, Nigeria, Peru and the UAE. Aermacchi also produced the **MB.339B**, with upgraded attack capabilities, but this was dropped in favour of the even more advanced **MB.339C**. Variants of the MB.339C include the **MB.339CD** for advanced/fighter lead-in training and its **MB.339FD** export equivalent with a fully digital cockpit and the **MB.339CB** which was delivered to New Zealand. Eritrea received six **MB.339E**

non-digital variants of the MB.339C. Developed in 1995 from an MB.339A, the **MB.339AM** is a specialzed anti-ship variant armed with two Marte Mk 2A missiles.

Attack Veltro 2

On 30 May 1980 the prototype **MB.339K Veltro 2** entered flight test. The aircraft's forward fuselage was broadly similar to that of the MB.326K, with a single-seat cockpit and two 30-mm guns below. Advanced avionics, comprehensive weapons compatibility and a rugged airframe failed to tempt customers, however, and the type was dropped.

SPECIFICATION	
Aermacchi MB.339C	a hi-lo-hi attack mission with four
Type: basic and advanced trainer with weapons training and light attack capabilities	Mk 82 bombs and two drop tanks **Weights:** empty equipped 3430 kg (7,562 lb) maximum take-off
Powerplant: one Piaggio-built Rolls-Royce (Bristol Siddeley) Viper Mk 680-43 turbojet rated at 19.57 kN (4,400 lb st)	6350 kg (14,000 lb) **Dimensions:** wing span 10.86 m (36 ft 9¾ in) over tip tanks; length 11.24 m
Performance: maximum level speed 817 km/h (508 mph); combat radius 500 km (311 miles) on	(36 ft 10½ in); height 3.99 m (13 ft 1¾ in); wing area 19.3 m² (207.74 sq ft) **Armament:** up to 1814 kg (4,000 lb) of external stores

Aermacchi S.211 Trainer and light-attack aircraft

Developed as a private-venture basic jet trainer by SIAI-Marchetti, the **S.211** also has a light attack capability, bestowed by four underwing hardpoints. First flown on 10 April 1981, it was adopted by four air forces: Brunei, Haiti, the Philippines and Singapore, with aircraft for the Philippines being assembled locally by PADC. Similarly, Singapore Aerospace was responsible for local assembly of 24 of an initial batch of 30 aircraft for advanced flying training. The Royal Brunei armed forces air wing purchased four. The Haitian air corps ordered a similar number, but, like Brunei, has now disposed of its S.211s. A version of the S.211 with an improved nav/attack system was

planned, as was another version with an uprated JT15D engine and increased fuel capacity.

Aermacchi takes over

Having acquired SIAI-Marchetti in 1997, Aermacchi has plans to make the S.211 competitive with the latest turboprop trainers. The so-called S.211D would have far greater power, a glass cockpit and upgraded avionics. No timescale for development had been announced in mid-2003.

The Grumman-backed S.211 was unsuccessful in its bid to gain orders for a US primary trainer requirement, but several countries bought the original type, including Haiti.

SPECIFICATION	
Aermacchi S.211	(345 miles) on a hi-lo-hi attack
Type: military jet trainer and light-attack aircraft	mission with four rocket launchers **Weights:** empty equipped 1850 kg
Powerplant: one Pratt & Whitney JT15D-4C rated at 11.12 kN (2,500 lb st)	(4,078 lb); maximum take-off 3150 kg (6,944 lb) as an attack warplane
Performance: maximum cruising speed 667 km/h (414 mph) at 7620 m (25,000 ft); maximum rate of climb at sea level 1280 m (4,200 ft) per minute; service ceiling 12,190 m (40,000 ft); combat radius 556 km	**Dimensions:** wing span 8.43 m (27 ft 8 in); length 9.31 m (30 ft 6½ in); height 3.8 m (12 ft 5½ in); wing area 12.6 m² (135.63 sq ft) **Armament:** up to 390 kg (1,455 lb) of disposable stores

Aermacchi SF.260 Basic trainer and light-attack aircraft

Designed by Stelio Frati for the Aviamilano company, the **SF.260** first flew in 1964 as a civil two-/three-seat light aircraft for fully aerobatic use. Subsequently it was developed by the SIAI-Marchetti company for many roles, including civil and military training (including night, navigation and formation instruction), and in two role-equipped forms, as the **SF.260W Warrior** and **SF.260SW Sea Warrior**. Only one Sea Warrior was built, as a surveillance/SAR/supply aircraft, but the Warrior has been sold to air forces and paramilitary customers all over the world.

SF.260 described

The basic SF.260 is an all-metal, fighter-like machine with retractable tricycle landing gear and an enclosed cockpit seating pupil and instructor side-by-side, with a third seat central at the rear. All fuel is in the wings or the fixed wingtip tanks, and there is an extremely wide choice of avionics, equipment and, in the SF.260W models, weapons. The military **SF.260M** aerobatic trainer has been sold to countries including Italy, Belgium, Bolivia, Burma, Ecuador, Libya (160 of whose were assembled in that country), Morocco, the Philippines, Singapore, Thailand, Tunisia, Zaire and Zambia. Zimbabwe's air force received the **SF.260C**.

The SF.260W Warrior is used with various role kits by several countries, including the the Philippines, the Republic of Ireland, Tunisia and Zimbabwe. In July 1980 the SIAI-Marchetti flew the first **SF.260TP** with an Allison turboprop, and this version is available as an alternative to the older piston-engined models, the 261-kW (350-hp) output of the Allison 250 offering useful benefits in the performance/payload mix. In 2003, Aermacchi (which took over SIAI-Marchetti) continued to build and market both piston-engined and turboprop SF.260 models.

SPECIFICATION	
Aermacchi SF.260W **Type:** multi-role trainer and close-support aircraft **Powerplant:** one 194-kW (260-hp) Textron Lycoming O-540-E4A5 piston engine **Performance:** maximum speed 305 km/h (190 mph); mission radius on a 4-hour 54-minute attack mission with 5 minutes over the target and a 20-kg (44-lb) fuel	reserve 556 km (345 miles) **Weights:** empty 770 kg (1,697 lb); maximum take-off 1300 kg (2,866 lb) **Dimensions:** wing span (over tanks) 8.35 m (27 ft 4¾ in); length 7.1 m (23 ft 3½ in); height 2.41 m (7 ft 11 in); wing area 101 m² (108.7 sq ft) **Armament:** up to 300 kg (661 lb) of stores on (when flown solo) including up to four 7.62-mm (0.3-in) gun pods

The SF.260M is a basic military trainer operated by a number of air forces including that of the Philippines. The PAF utilizes both the trainer variant and the dedicated attack version, the Warrior.

Pilatus PC-7 Turbo Trainer, PC-9 and PC-21
Trainer and light-attack aircraft family

Although the **PC-7** directly derives from the early 1950s piston-powered P-3, little of the original design is now retained in the definitive **Turbo Trainer**.

Two P-3s were modified as prototypes, the first suffering a forced landing and the second flying for the first time on the power of a 485-kW (650-shp) PT6A-25 flat-rated to 410 kW (550 shp) on 12 May 1975.

In conjunction with Dornier, Pilatus designed a completely new low-fatigue, one-piece wing. Dornier also helped design an entirely new electrically actuated undercarriage to meet a 57 per cent increase in maximum take-off weight. Flight development with these modifications in the second prototype also resulted in aerodynamic changes to the rear fuselage and tail.

These and other changes, including the bubble canopy for the non-pressurized cockpit, were all embodied in the first production PC-7, which made its initial flight on 18 August 1978.

Delivery of the PC-7

First deliveries were to the Myanmar air force. With the Beech T-34C then its sole production competitor, the PC-7 achieved growing export success, supplemented in June 1981 by a Swiss air force order for 40. For weapons training, six underwing hardpoints can accommodate external stores of up to 1040 kg

A PC-7 Mk II is taken through its paces. The SAAF is one of the largest buyers of the PC-7 Mk II.

SPECIFICATION

Pilatus PC-9
Type: basic and advanced trainer
Powerplant: one 857-kW
(1,150-shp) Pratt & Whitney Canada
PT6A-62 turboprop flat-rated at
708 kW (950 shp)
Performance: maximum speed at
sea level 500 km/h (311 mph);
maximum rate of climb at sea level
1247 m (4,090 ft) per minute;

service ceiling 11,580 m (38,000 ft);
range 1642 km (1,020 miles)
Weights: basic empty 1685 kg
(3,715 lb); maximum take-off
3200 kg (7,055 lb)
Dimensions: wing span 10.12 m
(33 ft 2½ in); length 10.18 m
(33 ft 4¾ in); height 3.26 m
(10 ft 8¼ in); area 16.29 m²
(175.35 sq ft)

PC-21 represents the future of Pilatus' trainer family. The aircraft could later be developed for light attack missions.

(2,293 lb), and PC-7s are believed to have been used operationally by both sides in the Iran/Iraq war. In 1985, Pilatus offered an optional installation of twin Martin-Baker CH.Mk 15A ejection seats, with Iran as the first retrofit customer.

Pilatus later developed the more advanced **PC-7 Mk II**, an aircraft which has been developed into the 2003 production standard **PC-7 Mk II M**. Some 60 of this latter aircraft have been ordered by the SAAF as the **PC-7 Mk II Astra**.

PC-9

The prototype **PC-9** made its first flight on 7 May 1984, powered by a PT6A-62. There is only 10 per cent commonality between the PC-7 and PC-9. The latter is similar but recognizable by its larger canopy, stepped tandem cockpits with ejection seats, ventral airbrake and four-bladed propeller. Development began in 1982; flight testing of many features and components was carried out using a PC-7 test bed before the construction of two pre-production prototypes was initiated.

The PC-9 was one of four shortlisted contenders to meet the RAF's requirement for a Jet Provost replacement, but lost to the Tucano. Nevertheless, Pilatus retained the links with BAe that it had made for the RAF competition. This was a strong factor in securing the initial PC-9 production order, announced only a week later, for 30 aircraft for the RSAF.

Pilatus then switched its marketing effort to Australia, offering offset package deals on both the PC-7 and PC-9 to the Australian government. The PC-9 was subsequently co-produced by Hawker de Havilland in Australia under the designation **PC-9/A**.

A German target-towing version, which is designated **PC-9B**, is operated on behalf of the Luftwaffe. Other PC-9 operators include the air forces of Cyprus, Myanmar, Switzerland and Thailand.

In conjunction with Beechcraft, Pilatus offered the **PC-9 Mk II** as a JPATS (Joint Primary Aircraft Training Programme) contender. This differed substantially from the PC-9, with a 70 per cent redesign, including strengthened fuselage and digital avionics.

At first glance there is little to differentiate between the PC-7 Mk II and PC-9 Mk II (below). However, the PC-9 is a considerably heavier and more powerful machine.

The first Beech-assembled aircraft flew on 23 December 1992, and in 2003 the aircraft was in production as the **Raytheon T-6 Texan II** for the USAF and US Navy (as the **T-6A Texan II**), the NATO Flying Training in Canada programme (as the **T-6A-1** or **CT-156 Harvard II**), and Greece.

PC-21

On 1 July 2002, Pilatus flew the first prototype of its new **PC-21** design. Again a single-turboprop aircraft, the PC-21 has obvious family similarities with the PC-9. However, it is a new design, featuring advanced avionics and design, to produce an aircraft capable of cost-effective training with jet-like performance.

Pilatus is offering the machine as part of a training package, claiming that it will allow the retirement of two trainer types in some air forces, as it is able to take on the basic, advanced and lead-in fighter training roles.

The PC-21 achieved full certification in 2004, when a full production schedule started.

BAC Strikemaster Armed Jet Provost

The **BAC Strikemaster Mk 80** light-attack family traces its history to the Percival P.84 Jet Provost, the jet conversion of the Provost piston-engined trainer, first flown on 26 June 1954 with the 7.29-kN (1,640-lb) thrust Armstrong Siddeley Viper engine. Delivery of the refined Jet Provost T.Mk 3 began in 1959 and this added 201 to the 12 of earlier marks, followed by 198 Jet Provost T.Mk 4s with the 11.12-kN (2,500-lb) thrust Viper 201 and 110 Jet Provost T.Mk 5s with the side-by-side cockpit pressurised. More than 70 Jet Provosts were exported.

Arming the Jet Provost

The Strikemaster uses the same airframe, but with reinforcement for the underwing load given in the specification, and with much special role equipment for operation in harsh climates from rough airstrips. The first aircraft flew on 26 October 1967, and its ability to provide effective close-

The first BAC 167 Strikemaster to be delivered to the Royal New Zealand Air Force undergoes tests while carrying drop tanks and rocket pods, January 1973. Eighteen 68mm (2.7in) rockets are carried in each pod.

support attack firepower at low cost resulted in wide sales, 146 aircraft being exported to Ecuador, Kenya, Kuwait, New Zealand, Oman, Saudi Arabia, Singapore, the South Arabian Federation and the Sudan. The last-named country used the **BAC.145** (**Strikemaster Mk 55**) aircraft, this being an interim machine with four instead of eight hardpoints and retaining the less powerful Viper 201 engine. By 2003, however, the Strikemaster remained in service only with Ecuador.

Seen here in a Kenyan colour scheme, the Strikemaster served with a large number of air forces including those of Ecuador, Kenya, Kuwait, New Zealand, Oman and the Sudan.

SPECIFICATION	
BAC Strikemaster Mk 80 series **Type:** light close-support and weapon-training aircraft **Powerplant:** one 15.17-kN (3,410-lb) thrust Rolls-Royce Viper Mk 535 turbojet **Performance:** maximum speed, 'clean' at 9070 m (20,000 ft) 760 km/h (472 mph); radius with maximum weapons on a hi-lo-hi mission 400 km (250 miles) **Weights:** empty 2810 kg (6,195 lb); maximum take-off	5215 kg (11,500 lb) **Dimensions:** wing span 11.23 m (36 ft 10 in); length 10.27 m (33 ft 8½ in); height 3.34 m (10 ft 11½ in); wing area 19.8 m² (213.7 sq ft) **Armament:** eight hardpoints for 1361 kg (3,000 lb) of stores including all common bombs, rockets and launchers, retarded bombs, tanks and BAe/Vinten camera pod, plus two 7.62-mm (0.3-in) machine-guns, each with 550 rounds, in the fuselage

BAE Systems Hawk Fighter, light-attack and trainer family

After receiving a batch of 29 Hawk Mk 53s beginning in 1980, Indonesia placed orders for eight Mk 109s (one of which is pictured) and 32 Mk 209s. The latter equip Nos 1 and 12 sqns of the Indonesian air force.

Originally designated **Hawker P.1182**, the superlative **Hawk** has been developed into a range of world-beating trainer and combat aircraft. No prototype was built, the first five aircraft off the line being allocated to flight trials, begun on 21 August 1974. Deliveries began in 1976 and in 2003 the **Hawk T.Mk 1** and **T.Mk 1A** weapons trainer remained as the RAF's only basic/advanced jet trainer, although discussions regarding a replacement were under way in the light of rapidly dwindling airframe life among the badly overstretched fleet. It could be that the United Kingdom adds new-build **Hawk Mk 100** aircraft to its fleet, although other trainers are under consideration.

Export Hawks

In November 1981 the US Navy selected the Hawk as its new-generation trainer. The aircraft was ultimately procured as the **T-45 Goshawk**, a machine based on the **Mk 60**. Export two-seat Hawk variants include the **Mk 50** series, based closely on the Hawk T.Mk 1 and exported to customers including Finland, Indonesia and Kenya; the **Mk 60** series with the uprated 25.35-kN (5,700-lb st) Adour Mk 861 engine for customers including Abu Dhabi, Dubai, Kuwait, Saudi Arabia, South Korea, Switzerland and Zimbabwe; and the heavily modified **Mk 100** series. The Hawk Mk 100 features a revised

When the Air Force of Zimbabwe ordered eight Hawk T.Mk 61s, it became the first customer for the uprated Mk 60 series. However, the first four Hawks delivered in July 1982 were damaged by a terrorist attack, one aircraft being destroyed.

wing, with wingtip missile-launch rails, advanced attack avionics and a 'chisel nose' housing optional FLIR or laser sensors. With its advanced/weapons training and formidable attack capabilities, the Mk 100 has been exported to Abu Dhabi, Australia, the NATO Flying Training in Canada organization, Malaysia and Oman. Hawk Mk 100 will also be acquired by South Africa as part of a deal including the Saab Gripen fighter.

SPECIFICATION

BAE Systems Hawk Mk 200
Type: single-seat air superiority and ground-attack warplane
Powerplant: one Rolls-Royce/Turboméca Adour Mk 871 turbofan engine rated at 26 kN (5,845 lb st)
Performance: maximum speed 1017 km/h (632 mph) at sea level; cruising speed 796 km/h (495 mph) at 12,495 m (41,000 ft); initial climb rate 3508 m (11,510 ft) per minute; service ceiling 13,715 m (45,000 ft); range 3610 km (2,244 miles) with three drop tanks; radius 945 km (587 miles) on a hi-lo-hi mission

with a 1361-kg (3,000-lb) warload
Weights: empty 4450 kg (9,810 lb); maximum take-off 9100 kg (20,061 lb)
Dimensions: wing span 9.39 m (30 ft 9¾ in) with normal tips or 9.93 m (32 ft 7 in) with missile-carrying tips; length 11.33 m (37 ft 2 in) excluding probe; height 4.16 m (13 ft 8 in); wing area 16.69 m² (179.6 sq ft)
Armament: two 25-mm ADEN fixed forward-firing cannon in the lower part of the forward fuselage, plus up to 3000 kg (6,614 lb) of disposable stores

---

Hawk Mk 200

A radical and surprising development of the basic Hawk airframe is represented by the Mk 200 series. This single-seat air-superiority and ground-attack aircraft has an APG-66H radar in a revised nose radome and a pair of in-built 25-mm ADEN cannon beneath the cockpit floor. On 13 July 1990, the **Hawk Mk 203** was ordered by Oman to replace its Hawker Hunters, and further exports of the aircraft to Indonesia and Malaysia followed.

With its advanced avionics, powerful radar and extensive weapon options, the Hawk 200 series represents an effective low-cost fighter family. This Sidewinder-armed Mk 208 is shown as it appeared with No. 3 Flying Training Centre of the Royal Malaysian Air Force at Butterworth in 1995.

Beech T-34 Mentor and T-34C Turbo Mentor
Trainer and COIN aircraft family

The T-34C-1 has been sold to a number of air arms. This example, flown by the Moroccan air force, is typical in that provision has been made for underwing hardpoints.

Derived from the Bonanza tourer as a primary and basic trainer, the original **Beech 45 Mentor** undertook its maiden flight on 2 December 1948, employing the 168-kW (225-hp) Continental O-470 piston engine. Selected as the standard US military trainer, it was produced in quantity as the **T-34A** for the USAF (350) and **T-34B** in naval guise (423), overseas licences being granted for manufacture of a further 160 of a military variant in Japan by Fuji; 125 in Canada (100 to the USAF) by CCF; and 75 in Argentina by FMA, in addition to Beech exports.

Turbo Mentor

When the US Navy required a replacement, Beech offered a turboprop version of the design, fitted with modern avionics to conform with current training aircraft standards. The powerplant selected was the popular Pratt & Whitney Canada PT6A, which has been adopted by many similar trainers.

Designated **YT-34C**, the prototype flew on 21 September 1973, a mere six months after the start of design work. Service entry of the **T-34C Turbo Mentor** began in November 1977, and the final delivery against orders for 352 aircraft was made in April 1990.

SPECIFICATION	
Beech T-34C-1 Turbo Mentor **Type:** two-seat armed trainer **Powerplant:** one 410-kW (550-shp) Pratt & Whitney Canada PT6A-25 turboprop derated from 533 kW (715 shp) **Performance:** maximum speed 382 km/h (237 mph); initial climb rate 436 m (1,430 ft) per minute; service ceiling more than 9145 m (30,000 ft); combat radius 555 km (345 miles)	**Weights:** empty 1356 kg (2,990 lb); maximum take-off 2494 kg (5,500 lb) **Dimensions:** wing span 10.16 m (33 ft 4 in); length 8.75 m (28 ft 8½ in); height 2.92 m (9 ft 7 in); wing area 16.69 m² (179.6 sq ft) **Armament:** four underwing pylons for 7.62-mm (0.3-in) Minigun pods, rocket pods, light bombs and flares, up to a maximum weight of 544 kg (1,200 lb)

For greater appeal to the export market, Beech produced the **T-34C-1** with provision for underwing hardpoints and a reflector weapon sight, and capable of being used for armament training or combat COIN missions, together with forward air control. First deliveries were made to Morocco of 12 aircraft, late in 1977, although they appear not to have been used in the Western Sahara operations against Polisario guerrillas. Further deliveries have comprised 23 to Ecuador (three for the navy), six to the Peruvian navy, 15 to the Argentine navy, 25 to Indonesia, three to the Uruguayan navy, four to the Gabonese presidential guard and 44 to Taiwan. More than 300 T-34Cs remain in US Navy service today.

Cessna T-37 and A-37 Dragonfly Trainer/light-attack aircraft

When Cessna Aircraft flew the prototype **Cessna XT-37** on 12 October 1954, it was the first purpose-designed military jet basic trainer in the world apart from the Fouga Magister, and it was also the first use since 1918 of a foreign engine in a production US military type (the same engine as the Magister, installed in the same way in the wing roots). Unlike the French with their trainer, the USAF adopted side-by-side seats, another startling departure from US practice. The **T-37A** entered service in 1957, and has been the standard USAF undergraduate pilot trainer ever since. Following 534 T-37As came 447 **T-37B** aircraft with more power, revised instruments and better navaids.

Dragonfly

The urgent 1960s need for light attack aircraft was met by a modification of the armed **T-37C** export trainer. Via the **YAT-37D** came the very much more powerful **A-37 Dragonfly**, of which 39 **A-37A** machines began life as T-37Bs and 577 more were built as **A-37B** aircraft. Features include a 6-*g* airframe with full load, inflight-refuelling probe, and additional internal and external fuel. A-37s were active in Vietnam and exported to many countries as both new and used aircraft.

Above: After being used successfully in Vietnam, the A-37 found favour with many countries whose major threats to stability came from within. In South America, nations such as Ecuador still flew A-37s on internal security duties in 2003.

Below: Numerous T-37B, T-37C (a variant of the B-model with underwing hardpoints) and A-37B aircraft have been exported. A-37Bs, such as this one, are the primary offensive type of the Fuerza Aérea Uruguaya. Sixteen were acquired from ex-USAF stocks in 1992 and 1993; most remained in use in 2003.

SPECIFICATION	
Cessna A-37A Dragonfly	maximum take-off 6350 kg
Type: light-attack aircraft	(14,000 lb)
Powerplant: two 12.68-kN (2,850-lb)	**Dimensions:** wing span (over tanks)
thrust General Electric J85-17A	10.93 m (35 ft 10½ in); length
turbojets	(excluding probe) 8.62 m (28 ft
Performance: maximum speed,	3¼ in); height 2.8 m (9 ft 2 in); wing
'clean' 843 km/h (524 mph); range	area 17.09 m² (183.9 sq ft)
at high altitude with maximum	**Armament:** one 7.62-mm (0.3-in)
payload (including 1860 kg/4,100 lb	GAU-2B/A7 Minigun in nose, plus
of ordnance) 740 km (460 miles)	up to 1860 kg (4,100 lb) of
Weights: empty 2817 kg (6,211 lb);	disposable ordnance

Cessna O-2 Light-attack, FAC and COIN aircraft

The unusually-configured 'push-pull' **Cessna 336 Skymaster** first flew on 28 February 1961 and was delivered to civilian operators from May 1963 onwards as a four-/six-seat business aircraft. In February 1965, it was replaced on the production line by the **Model 337 Super Skymaster** which introduced, among other features, retractable landing gear.

In parallel, work proceeded on the **Model 337M**, assigned the US military designation **O-2A** when an initial batch of 145 was ordered in December 1966. Deliveries to the USAF eventually totalled 467 for replacement of

the single-engined Cessna O-1 Bird Dog in the forward air control (FAC), target marking and attack coordination roles, notably in Vietnam. Southeast Asia was also the main operational theatre of 31 **O-2B** aircraft likewise ordered in December 1966 and rapidly produced by converting aircraft built for civilian sale. The O-2B was a psychological warfare aircraft, its main 'weapons' being a high-powered loudspeaker system and a leaflet dispenser.

Milirole

In France, Cessna licensee Reims Aviation produced an armed version of the Super Skymaster

The Cessna O-2 series was the main light forward air control platform in Vietnam. By 1969, the USAF was using 'Psy War' O-2Bs fitted with powerful amplifiers and directional loudspeakers.

designated **Reims FTB337 Milirole**, and supplied principally to Portugal and the illegal government of Rhodesia (now Zimbabwe). The latter received 18 with the local name of **Lynx**.

Armed Super Skymasters were also produced in the form of conversions of civil T337s, with two turbocharged 168-kW (225-hp) TSIO-360s, as the **Summit O2-337 Sentry**.

In a country where matters of internal security are generally more pressing than national defence, El Salvador's Cessna O-2s provide a useful observation and light-attack capability.

SPECIFICATION	
Cessna O-2 Super Skymaster **Type:** COIN and FAC aircraft **Powerplant:** two 157-kW (210-hp) Continental TSIO-360A piston engines **Performance:** maximum speed 320 km/h (199 mph) at sea level; initial climb rate 366 m (1,200 ft) per minute; service ceiling 5945 m (19,500 ft); range 1553 km (965 miles)	**Weights:** empty 1204 kg (2,655 lb); maximum take-off 1995 kg (4,400 lb) **Dimensions:** wing span 11.58 m (38 ft); length 9.07 m (29 ft 9 in); height 3.06 m (10 ft); wing area 18.67 m² (201 sq ft) **Armament:** 7.62-mm (0.3-in) Minigun pods, rocket pods, flares and other light ordnance on four underwing strongpoints

Grumman OV-1 Mohawk Armed reconnaissance aircraft

In the mid-1950s both the US Army and US Marine Corps drew up specifications for a battlefield surveillance aircraft. Their requirements were generally similar: to carry a variety of reconnaissance equipment, to have rough-field capability, and to offer STOL capability. It proved possible for both services to agree on a common design, and in 1957 the US Navy, acting as programme manager, ordered nine examples of the **YAO-1A** for testing. The designation was subsequently altered to **YOV-1A**, and the first of the aircraft had its maiden flight on 14 April 1959.

Early evaluation left little doubt as to the design's excellence, but even before the prototype had made its first flight the USMC had withdrawn from the initial

contract, and no examples of that service's **OF-1** variant were built. Instead, the flight-test programme was accelerated, and before the end of 1959 the US Army had placed production contracts for **OV-1A** and **OV-1B** aircraft with the name **Mohawk**. The first turboprop aircraft to enter US Army service, the OV-1 is comparatively slow but highly manoeuvrable and, to help offset its vulnerability as a result of its speed and role, has a well-armoured cockpit.

The OV-1 may be conventional in its basic configuration, but recognition features include the turboprops, one mounted high on each wing with its centreline canted outwards and upwards; a tail unit with three fin-and-rudder assemblies and sufficient

tailplane dihedral for the endplate fins to be inward canted; bulged cockpit sides to provide the two-person crew with the best possible downward fields of vision; and in the OV-1B version an SLAR housed in a long glassfibre container carried on pylons below the fuselage and offset to starboard.

Mohawk service

Although the OV-1s were capable of carrying armament, it was Department of Defense policy from 1965 that the US Army's fixed-wing aircraft should carry no weapons, to avoid conflict and confusion with the USAF's close-support aircraft. However, as with many other US aircraft, a number were

SPECIFICATION	
Grumman OV-1D Mohawk **Type:** two-seat multi-sensor observation aircraft **Powerplant:** two Lycoming T53-L-701 turboprop engines each rated at 1044 kW (1,400 shp) **Performance:** maximum speed 465 km/h (289 mph) at 3050 m (10,000 ft) on a SLAR mission; cruising speed 333 km/h (207 mph) at optimum altitude; initial climb rate 1103 m (3,618 ft) per minute;	service ceiling 7620 m (25,000 ft); range 1519 km (944 miles) on a SLAR mission **Weights:** empty 5468 kg (12,054 lb); maximum take-off 8214 kg (18,109 lb) on a SLAR mission **Dimensions:** wing span 14.63 m (48 ft); length 12.50 m (41 ft); height 3.86 m (12 ft 8 in); wing area 33.44 m² (360 sq ft) **Armament:** provision for up to 1225 kg (2,700 lb) of disposable stores

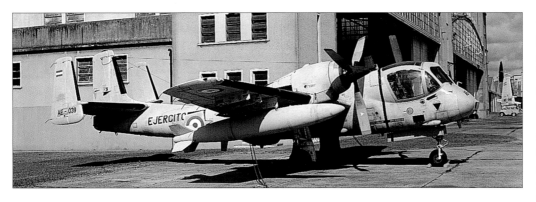

The Argentine army uses the OV-1D Mohawk for reconnaissance missions from Campo de Mayo. The aircraft retain the US Army grey colour scheme in which they were delivered.

deployed to Vietnam with underwing armament.

The basic version of the Mohawk, of which 380 were completed, was the OV-1A for day and night visual or photo reconnaissance, and provided with dual controls. The OV-1B which followed had increased wing span, SLAR and an internal camera with in-flight processor; the dual controls were deleted. The next production version was the **OV-1C**, similar to the late-production OV-1A, but with the AAS-24 infrared surveillance system. The last production model, of which 41 (including four **YOV-1D** service test aircraft) were completed, was the **OV-1D** with side-loading doors to accept a pallet with SLAR, IR, or other sensors; in addition to production aircraft, 80 OV-1B and OV-1C aircraft were converted to OV-1D standard. The designations **RV-1C** and **RV-1D** were applied, respectively, to 31 OV-1C and OV-1D aircraft permanently modified for electronic reconnaissance missions.

The last Mohawks were retired from US Army service in 1997. Israel had retired its last aircraft by this time, leaving Argentina as the world's sole operator of the type during 2003.

Lockheed T-33 Trainer and light attack/COIN aircraft

West Germany's Luftwaffe was one of the many air arms which flew its 'T-Birds' in a warlike camouflage. West Germany purchased 193 T-33As, which served as trainers and courier aircraft.

SPECIFICATION	
Lockheed AT-33A **Type:** tandem-seat armed jet trainer **Powerplant:** one 24.01-kN (5,400-lb) thrust Allison J33-A-35 turbojet **Performance:** maximum speed 966 km/h (600 mph); initial climb rate 1684 m (5,525 ft) per minute; range 909 km (565 miles) **Weights:** empty 3666 kg (8,084 lb);	maximum take-off 6551 kg (14,442 lb) **Dimensions:** wing span 11.85 m (38 ft 10½ in); length 11.51 m (37 ft 9 in); height 3.56 m (11 ft 8 in); wing area 22.02 m² (237 sq ft) **Armament:** two nose-mounted 0.5-in (12.7-mm) machine guns, plus various light bombs, rockets and machine-gun pods

Once the world's most widely employed jet trainer, the **Lockheed T-33** was derived directly from another aircraft of note, the Lockheed F-80 Shooting Star, America's first mass-produced jet fighter. In fact, the T-33 was initially known as the **TF-80C** until assigned the more appropriate designation **T-33A** and universally nicknamed **'T-Bird'**. By August 1959, Lockheed had produced 5691 of the type, including 699 for the US Navy, by which it was known originally as the **TO-2** and later as the **TV-2** (and **T-33B** from 1962 onwards). Also within this total were 1058 supplied to friendly nations under MAP, these subsequently being augmented by numerous others retired from USAF service. Some of these were **RT-33A** tactical reconnaissance versions, with a camera nose

As part of devastating defence cuts which affected the Canadian Armed Forces from 2000, the remaining CAF Silver Stars were retired during 2002. The aircraft were primarily used for ECM training and included some machines in CE-133 form.

and voice-recording equipment occupying the rear cockpit, from 85 of the type converted.

Licence-production

In Japan, Kawasaki built 210 T-33As under licence, while Canadair produced 636 **T-33AN Silver Star** aircraft. The type was designated designated **CT-133** in RCAF/CAF service and Canadian-built 'T-Birds' were non-standard in being powered by a 22.16-kN (5,000-lb) thrust Rolls-Royce Nene turbojet. Of 60 T-33ANs transferred to France, 52 were joined by 31 US-built aircraft in a modification programme undertaken by SFERMA, bringing them to a common standard as the **T-33SF**.

Fitted as standard with two machine guns in the nose, the T-33A could be converted to **AT-33A** standard for counter-insurgency (COIN) missions, carrying ordnance on underwing pylons. A number of T-33s remain in service with air arms including those of Iran, Mexico, Paraguay and South Korea. The aircraft formerly operated by Burma were used against guerrilla forces following their delivery in the late 1960s, a COIN role which the Mexican and Paraguayan AT-33As retain. Most remarkably, the CT-133s serving in Bolivia are solely responsible for the air defence of their country and were augmented by 18 T-33SFs supplied by France.

North American T-6 Texan Trainer, light attack & COIN aircraft

T-6 trainers were used in the attack role by the Armée de l'Air in Algeria. Armament included two Browning machine guns in the wings, as well as underwing rockets and light bombs.

SPECIFICATION	
North American T-6 Texan	**Weights:** empty 1769 kg (3,900 lb);
Type: tandem-seat armed trainer	maximum take-off 2338 kg (5,155 lb)
Powerplant: one 447-kW (600-hp)	**Dimensions:** wing span 12.81 m
Pratt & Whitney R-1340-49 radial	(42 ft ¼ in); length 8.84 m (29 ft);
piston engine	height 3.57 m (11 ft 8½ in); wing
Performance: maximum speed	area 23.57 m² (253.7 sq ft)
338 km/h (210 mph); cruising	**Armament:** one fixed forward-firing
speed 235 km/h (146 mph); climb	machine gun or (T-6G) various
to 3048 m (10,000 ft) in 7 minutes	loads of light ordnance on
24 seconds; service ceiling 7376 m	underwing pylons (typically two
(24,200 ft); range 1012 km	machine-gun pods and six rockets
(629 miles)	on individual rails)

Having flown in prototype form more than 70 years ago, in April 1935, the **North American AT-6 Texan** has, surprisingly only recently passed out of wide-scale military use, although it is more readily identified within the British Commonwealth by its RAF name **Harvard**.

In 10 years, more than 17,000 AT-6s of various subtypes were built by the parent firm, including the **SNJ** series for the US Navy, augmented by another 4500 constructed under licence in four other countries. In 1948 a rationalization of designations resulted in the A (Advanced) being deleted from the USAF nomenclature just as the aircraft was about to take on a fresh lease of life: there being no immediate successor in prospect, 2068 aircraft were remanufactured with a raised instructor's seat, new cockpit layout, additional fuel capacity, propeller spinner, steerable tailwheel and P-51 Mustang-type landing gear and flap actuating levers.

Produced between 1949 and 1953, the 'new' aircraft were designated **T-6G**, many going to NATO for pilot training duties, together with 285 similar **T-6J Harvard Mk IV** aircraft built by CanCar in Canada.

Combat over Korea

Early in the Korean War, lightly armed **T-6F** machines were used for COIN-type missions until replaced by some of the 97 **LT-6G** conversions which had been optimized for forward air control (FAC) and battlefield

*Portugal flew its **T-6Gs** in action over **Mozambique** and **Guinea** in the 1960s; Portugal's **T-6Gs** were supplemented by the **F-84G** from 1964.*

surveillance. LT-6Gs were also supplied to France and Turkey. Like Portugal, France also used the T-6G for policing its overseas colonies, fitting underwing racks for bombs and machine guns, while 120 of the 201 delivered to Spain received the official 'fighter' designation **C.6** for close-support missions armed with two 7.62-mm (0.3-in) guns in the wing and provision for 10 10-kg (22-lb) bombs or 12 rockets.

North American T-28 Trojan Trainer and COIN aircraft

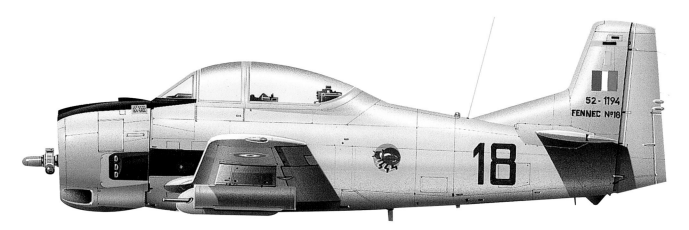

Produced to replace the company's highly successful T-6 Texan as a basic trainer, the prototype **North American XT-28** made its first flight on 26 September 1949, as one of the most powerful aircraft in its class and introducing tricycle landing gear to this stage of the instructional syllabus. USAF contracts covered 1194 **T-28A Trojan** aircraft, while the US Navy bought 489 **T-28B** and 299 arrester hook-equipped **T-28C** aircraft, the two last-mentioned models being powered by the 1063-kW (1,425-hp) Wright R-1820 engine.

Sud-Aviation adopted the Pacific Airmotive Nomad conversion of the T-28A as a powerful attack aircraft. France made good use of the resulting Fennec during the colonial conflict in Algeria. This machine is armed with gun and rocket pods.

Armed options

Production was completed in 1957, but between 1961 and 1969 North American converted 321 T-28As to **T-28D** standard, then passed to Fairchild-Republic the task of producing another 72. The T-28D was fitted with six strongpoints and two guns beneath the wings, the maximum permitted weapon load eventually reaching a very useful 1814 kg (4,000 lb). Another batch of 75 T-28As was

A North American T-28 in flight over the Canal Zone in the late 1960s. With a 1814-kg (4,000-lb) load, the T-28D proved to be among the most capable of all the trainers converted to combat aircraft.

converted to T-28D standard under US Navy auspices.

T-28Ds were mainly for the MAP programme, and were assigned to South Vietnam (where they saw considerable action), Laos, Royal Khmer Aviation and the USAF's Farm Gate detachment out of Bien Hoa AB near Saigon. In Southeast Asia, the T-28Ds replaced T-28As and recce-configured **RT-28B** aircraft which had begun suffering structural failures under the harsh operating conditions in which they were being employed. Among the last frontline T-28s were those of Thailand and the Philippines.

Advanced versions

In Taiwan, 50 T-28As were fitted with 1081-kW (1,450-shp) Lycoming T53-L701 turboprops during 1976–81 as the **AIDC T-CH-1 Chung Hsieng** basic trainer. This followed USAF trials in 1963–64 of three **YAT-28E** conversions with the 1827-kW (2,450-shp) Lycoming T55 turbo-prop and no fewer than 12 wing strongpoints; the variant failed to achieve a production order.

A further military conversion of surplus T-28As, the **PacAir**

T-28R Nomad, was adopted by France as the **Sud-Aviation T-28S Fennec**. Sud-Aviation produced 147 Fennecs between 1960 and 1962 for replacement of the T-6Gs used in the COIN role in Algeria, and, after their withdrawal in the mid-1960s,

63 of the aircraft were sold to the Argentine navy (the 18 survivors being passed to Uruguay's navy in 1980–81) and 25 to Morocco. A US dealer acquired others, of which 10 were refurbished for Haiti in 1973, but apparently not used.

Lockheed AC-130 Gunship Hercules

From early experience in the Vietnam War, the USAF perceived a need for quick-reaction concentrated firepower for use against small targets, especially where defenders of isolated areas were subject to nocturnal attack. The first solution was the gunship AC-47. With a need to improve firepower and equipment, the AC-119 was developed, for use while USAF's Aeronautical Systems Division began converting the 13th production C-130A as a gunship in 1965. This involved installation of four 20-mm Vulcan cannon, four 7.62-mm Miniguns, flare equipment and improved sighting. The aircraft was tested operationally in Vietnam in late 1967; LTV Electrosystems was awarded an immediate contract to modify seven JC-130A missile trackers to **AC-130A** standard.

The first AC-130s

Their weaponry remained the same, but these aircraft were fitted with a range of sensors including radar, a searchlight and target-acquisition and direct-view image intensifiers. Four were in service in Vietnam by the end of 1968. A further C-130 was converted in the Surprise Package project, with two 40-mm cannon replacing two of the 20-mm variety, and with computerized fire control. Nine more C-130A conversions were delivered to the same standards in the Pave Pronto programme, with new sensors including

All of the AC-130's armament projects from the left side of the fuselage, as demonstrated by this AC-130H. The aircraft attacks in a tight left turn, orbiting the target as it delivers fire.

LLTV and a laser designator. So successful was the project that 11 C-130Es were converted to **AC-130E** standard in the Pave Spectre programme.

The aircraft were given heavier armour, better avionics and provision for more ammunition, and, from 1973, the 10 survivors were brought to **AC-130H** standard with the installation of uprated T56-A-15 engines. The final developments for use in Southeast Asia were the fitting of a 105-mm howitzer and laser target designator in the Pave Aegis programme. At the end of the Vietnam War, remaining

AC-130A/H aircraft returned to the United States.

The AC-130Hs have since had their rear Miniguns deleted and do not usually carry forward Miniguns, either. From 1978 onwards, the aircraft were fitted with inflight-refuelling receptacles. The SOFI (Special Operations Force Improvement) programme of the early 1990s upgraded their sensors, fire control computers, ECM and nav/comms suite.

At war again

The AC-130 was once again used operationally with the

US occupation of Grenada in October 1983, and was later involved in operations in Panama (1989) and the Gulf (1991).

Five AC-130Hs were used in Operation Desert Storm to conduct night operations against Iraqi ground targets. One aircraft was lost in the Gulf and another during operations over Somalia in 1994.

AC-130Hs also flew night patrols over Bosnia, covered the evacuation of US personnel from Albania and performed combat missions during Operation Enduring Freedom in 2001–02.

Today, the AC-130H continues to serve alongside the improved **AC-130U** gunship with USAF Special Operations Command.

AC-130U

The AC-130U was produced by conversion from standard C-130H airframes to produce a third-generation gunship for AFSOC. The AC-130U is powered by four 3655-ekW (4,900-shp) Allison T56-A-15 turboprops and has a crew of 13. It has a performance that is generally similar to that of the C-130H transport.

To engage ground targets in a pylon turn, the AC-130U retains the single L-60 40-mm Bofors cannon and M102 105-mm howitzer of earlier C-130 gunships. A single 25-mm GAU-12 cannon with 3000 rounds replaces the AC-130H's two M61 cannon. The new cannon is fitted on a trainable mount, with an autonomous ammunition-handling

and feed system (firing rate 1800 shots/minute) and a stand-off range of 3657 m (12,000 ft). The AC-130U's sensors include a main fire control radar derived from that of the F-15E, FLIR, LLLTV with a laser target designator and rangefinder (mounted in a turret under the fuselage with a 360-degree field of view), and a jammer and expendable countermeasures package. The four mission computers are linked by a 1553B databus. Navigation is greatly facilitated by a combined INS and GPS/Navstar. Fully all-weather capable, the AC-130U is able to engage two targets simultaneously.

The first AC-130U made its initial flight on 20 December

The US Air Force authorized development of the AC-130U in August 1985. The 'U-boat' introduced a host of new sensors to give the aircraft greater stand-off capability while retaining accuracy.

1990. Delivery of the first operational aircraft to Hurlburt Field, Florida, was made in June 1994. The USAF's buy of 13 AC-130Us includes one aircraft bought as a replacement for the AC-130H lost in the Gulf War. The AC-130U was also active in Enduring Freedom.

When they were retired, the AC-130As were the oldest C-130s then in active USAF service. This machine was on strength with the 711th SOS in the early 1990s. Note the chaff/flare dispenser on the outer underwing pylon and twin ECM pod carriage on the inner pylons.

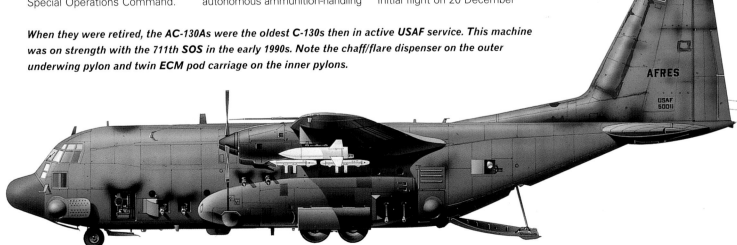

McDonnell Douglas (Hawker Siddeley) AV-8A
Harrier STOVL attack, close-support and air-combat aircraft

SPECIFICATION

McDonnell Douglas (HS) AV-8C Harrier

Type: single-seat ship- or land-based STOVL light attack fighter

Powerplant: one 95.61-kN (21,500-lb) thrust Rolls-Royce Pegasus Mk 103 vectoring-thrust turbofan

Performance: maximum speed over 1186 km/h (737 mph) at low altitude; climb to 12,190 m (40,000 ft) in 2 minutes 22 seconds; service ceiling more than 15,240 m

(50,000 ft); combat radius with 1367-lb (3,000-lb) external stores load 95 km (59 miles) after VTO

Weights: empty 5529 kg (12,190 lb); maximum take-off 7734 kg (17,050 lb) for VTO or 10,115 kg (22,300 lb) for STO

Dimensions: wing span 7.7 m (25 ft 3 in); length 13.87 m (45 ft 6 in); height 3.45 m (11 ft 4 in); wing area 18.68 m² (201.1 sq ft)

Armament: two 30-mm cannon, plus up to 2404 kg (5,300 lb) of disposable ordnance

The US Marine Corps designated its Hawker Siddeley Harriers as the **McDonnell Douglas AV-8A Harrier** (single-seat) and **TAV-8A Harrier** (two-seat), respectively (credit for their origin going to

McDonnell Douglas for political reasons). The aircraft had the Pegasus Mk 103 engine, but lacked several of the nav/attack systems incorporated in the RAF's Harrier GR.Mk 3. Instead

VMA-231 'Aces' was the third and final operational Marine Corps AV–8A squadron. It came closest to seeing actual combat when deployed aboard the USS Tarawa in 1983 for peacekeeping operations over Lebanon.

they carried AIM-9 Sidewinders for air-to-air combat, in which role the USMC pilots added a remarkable new trick to the Harrier's repertoire. Known as 'VIFFing' (Vectoring In Forward Flight), this makes use of the thrust-vectoring facility in dogfighting situations, where it gave the aircraft an unprecedented manoeuvrability that no other warplane could match. The USMC had one training and three operational squadrons equipped with the

AV-8, and in-service AV-8As were later upgraded to **AV-8C** standard with a host of modifications to the airframe and systems.

Other operators

The only other operators of the standard Harrier, equivalent to the USMC versions, have been the Spanish and Thai navies. In Spanish service the type was named as the **Matador**, and nine **AV-8S** single-seat and two **TAV-8S** twin-seat aircraft, known

This USMC AV-8A was flown by VMA-231. The aircraft was primarily operated from assault carriers for support of ground forces.

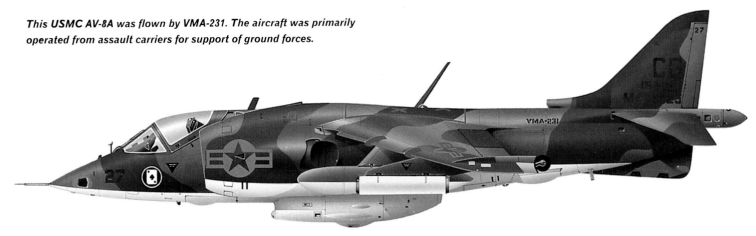

by the local designations **VA.1** and **VAE.1**, respectively, equipped one Spanish squadron based on the light carrier *Dédalo*. With the Spanish navy's purchase of the more advanced McDonnell Douglas/BAe AV-8B Harrier II,

the surviving aircraft were available for export, resulting in the purchase during 1997 of seven single- and two twin-seat aircraft by the Thai naval air service. The aircraft were used to help the naval air service to

acquire experience in the operation of STOVL warplanes on the light carrier *Chakri Naruebet* pending delivery of AV-8Bs. The Thai navy, however, has suffered funding problems which have prevented *Chakri*

Naruebet going to sea for much of the time. In addition, the Harriers are likely to be in poor condition, the lack of funds affecting the supply of spares, as well as making the AV-8B purchase unlikely.

Douglas A4D/A-4 Skyhawk Carrierborne attack aircraft

Wearing the markings of VA-72 'Blue Hawks', this Skyhawk was aboard the carrier USS **Independence** *in the South China Sea during May 1965.*

One of the most successful post–World War II aircraft to serve with the US Navy, the **A-4 Skyhawk** originated as a private-venture design under a team headed by Ed Heinemann.

Thus, when the US Navy began the search for a turbine-powered successor to the Skyraider, Douglas was able to propose a new attack aircraft with a gross weight of about half that of the official specification and one which was considerably faster.

Ordered during the Korean War, the prototype was first flown on 22 June 1954 and the first pre-production aircraft on 14 August 1954, with initial deliveries to US Navy Attack Squadron VA-72 beginning on 26 October 1956. Three months later, in January 1957, VMA-224 became the first US Marine Corps squadron to receive Skyhawks.

Vietnam

It was a fortunate period in which to introduce this sparkling

Two-seat Skyhawks provided carrier-capable training facilities for USN/USMC aircrew from 1966 until 1999, when the last training examples were replaced by T-45A Goshawks.

new attack aircraft, for by the time the US Navy and US Marine Corps became involved in operations in Vietnam, both of these services were able to deploy the Skyhawk with the greatest confidence in its capability; indeed, such was its effectiveness that steadily improving A-4s remained in production until February 1979.

The type was built to a total of 2960 aircraft including trainers, and exported to the armed forces of several nations.

Skyhawks remain in service in a variety of original and upgraded forms with Argentina, Brazil, Indonesia, Israel and Singapore.

Furthermore, Argentina's A-4 fleet has been augmented by 32 radically updated ex-USMC A-4Ms which are known under the designation **A-4AR Fightinghawk**, along with four OA-4M-based **TA-4R** machines. Features of these Lockheed Martin-produced conversions include AN/APG-66 radar and HOTAS controls.

Multiple variants

The Skyhawk was built in a vast number of models, those specifically built for naval use including the first generation **XA4D-1** prototype, powered by a 32.02-kN (7,200-lb) thrust Wright J65-W-2 turbojet; the 19 **YA4D-1** (later **YA-4A**, then **A-4A**) pre-production aircraft; the **A4D-1** (later A-4A) first production aircraft; the **A4D-2** (later **A-4B**) with strengthened rear fuselage, inflight-refuelling equipment, and more power; the **A4D-2N** (later **A-4C**) with terrain-following radar, autopilot, increased power and a number of other improvements; the **A4D-5** (later **A-4E**) improved production version, introducing

the 37.8-kN (8,500-lb) thrust Pratt & Whitney J52-P-6A turbojet and two additional underwing hardpoints to allow a maximum weapon load of 3719 kg

(8,200 lb); the lengthened, tandem two-seat **TA-4F** production trainer; the **A-4F** final attack production version for the US Navy with the J52-P-8A

A late-model A-4M of Marine squadron VMA-324 fires a Zuni air-to-ground unguided rocket at a range in California.

engine and additional avionics in a hump-back fairing on the rear fuselage; the **EA-4F** conversions of four TA-4Fs to carry stores simulating Soviet missile and aircraft signatures for dissimilar air combat training; the **A-4G**, similar to the A-4F but with the

avionics hump removed and built for the Royal Australian Navy; two **TA-4G** trainers for the RAN; the **TA-4J** trainer for the USN; and the **A-4L** conversion of A-4Cs after withdrawal from first-line use and upgrading for use by reserve squadrons – all with J65-W-16C engines. So-called second-generation variants and later conversions included the **A-4M Skyhawk II** production version for the USMC, introducing a number of improvements and the more powerful J52-P-408A engine; the **OA-4M** conversion of the TA-4F for the USMC fast FAC role and the **A-4Q** refurbished ex-USN A-4Bs for service with Argentina's naval air arm.

SPECIFICATION

Douglas A-4M Skyhawk II
Type: single-seat carrier-based attack aircraft
Powerplant: one Pratt & Whitney J52-P-408A turbojet rated at 49.8 kN (11,200 lb st)
Performance: maximum speed, 'clean' at sea level 1078 km/h (670 mph); combat radius with external weapons on a hi-lo-hi mission 620 km (385 miles);

service ceiling 12,880 m (42,250 ft)
Weights: empty 4899 kg (10,800 lb); maximum take-off 11,113 kg (24,500 lb)
Dimensions: wing span 8.38 m (27 ft 6 in); length 12.29 m (40 ft 4 in); height 4.57 m (15 ft); wing area 24.15 m² (260 sq ft)
Armament: two 20-mm cannon, plus up to 4153 kg (9,155 lb) of weapons on five external hardpoints

Vought A-7 Corsair II Navy and Air Force attack aircraft

This highly successful subsonic attack aircraft originated from a US Navy requirement for an aircraft to replace the A-4 Skyhawk. On 19 March 1964 Vought was awarded a contract for three prototypes under the Navy designation **A-7**, the company reviving the name of its most famous wartime fighter in designating this new aircraft **Corsair II**.

One of the requirements of the specification had been that

the new aircraft should be based on an existing design, to keep costs low and to speed delivery, but, while the A-7 was of basically similar configuration to the F-8 Crusader it was, in fact, a completely new design with no large-scale commonality of structural assemblies.

Corsair prototype

The first prototype was flown on 27 September 1965, almost four weeks ahead of schedule,

and initial deliveries to the US Navy began on 14 October 1966. Less than four months later, on 1 February 1967, VA-147 became the first squadron to be commissioned with the Corsair II.

Long before the first A-7 entered US Navy service in December 1965, the USAF had decided to adopt a denavalized version of the aircraft to serve as a tactical fighter. The primary change was the selection of

the Allison-built Rolls-Royce Spey to power it instead of the Pratt & Whitney TF30 turbofan of the Navy's A-7.

Corsair combat

US Navy Corsair IIs equipped 27 squadrons during the Vietnam War, flying more than 90,000 combat missions, and the type was also used by the USAF in that theatre, although to a far lesser extent. After being replaced on active-duty service

These Naval Air Warfare Center A-7Es are seen dropping inert 500-lb (227-kg) retarded bombs on a flight from their China Lake base in California.

development of the **A-7F**, which involved a radical reworking of the ANG machines with afterburning F100 turbofans, a lengthened fuselage and updated avionics. However, the programme was cancelled after two prototype conversions had flown, and the A-7 began a rapid withdrawal from ANG service. The last was retired in 1993.

Exports of the Corsair were limited, sales to Pakistan and Switzerland having been thwarted. Portugal received two batches of aircraft from 1981 onwards, these being rebuilt Navy **A-7A** and **A-7B** aircraft. In service these were designated as the **A-7P**, the **TA-7P** being a two-seat derivative. The primary role of Portugal's Corsairs was maritime strike using AGM-65 Maverick missiles, but the aircraft also had a secondary air-defence role.

Greece purchased 60 **A-7H** and five **TA-7H** aircraft, based on the Navy's TF41-powered **A-7E**. The fleet was bolstered by the transfer of 36 ex-US Navy aircraft, mostly A-7Es, but also including a handful of **TA-7C** trainers. The final operator to receive the A-7 was the Royal Thai Navy, which received 14 ex-USN A-7Es and four ex-USN TA-7Cs in 1995.

SPECIFICATION	
Vought A-7E Corsair II	(19,490 lb); maximum take-off
Type: carrier-based attack bomber	19,051 kg (42,000 lb)
Powerplant: one 64.48-kN (14,500-lb	**Dimensions:** wing span 11.81 m
thrust) Allison TF41-A-2 (derived from	(38 ft 9 in); length 14.06 m (46 ft
the Rolls-Royce Spey) turbofan	1½ in); height 4.9 m (16 ft ¾ in);
Performance: maximum speed,	wing area 34.84 m² (375 sq ft)
clean, 1123 km/h (698 mph) at sea	**Armament:** one 20-mm M61A1
level; tactical radius with typical	six-barrel cannon, plus up to
weapon load 1127 km (700 miles)	6804 kg (15,000 lb) of mixed
Weights: empty 8841 kg	stores carried externally

by the A-10, the USAF's **A-7D** aircraft were issued to ANG units, where the type continued to have a productive career.

In January 1981 the two-seat **A-7K** made its maiden flight, the 31 examples built being issued only to ANG units.

In order to keep the A-7 viable in the 1990s, Vought began

The US Navy's Corsair IIs saw combat for the last time during the 1991 Gulf War, when VA-46 joined VA-72 (illustrated) aboard USS John F. Kennedy.

Dassault Rafale M/N Next-generation naval fighter

Rafale M1, the first navalized production aircraft, maintains 80 per cent structural and systems commonality with the single-seat Rafale C. The initial software standard permits air defence missions against multiple targets, and in 2002 added IR-guided MICA AAMs, and a datalink for communication with the E-2C.

The ACX, later Rafale A, demonstrator flew several hundred test sorties, including touch-and-go deck-landings on the French carrier *Clemenceau*. As such, it proved the basic suitability of the new fighter design for carrier operations, paving the way for the **Rafale M** dedicated multi-role naval fighter.

Naval Rafale

Originally known as the **ACM** (**Avion de Combat Marine**), the first Rafale M prototype made its initial flight on 12 December 1991. The main changes differentiating the Rafale M from its land-based counterparts weigh some 750 kg (1,653 lb)

During Operation Enduring Freedom, the Aéronavale's first Rafale Ms took the opportunity for a little 'cross-deck' practice. Here, USS John C. Stennis experiences a Rafale fly-by on 14 March 2002.

and include major reinforcement of the Messier-Bugatti landing gear (whose nosewheel unit also became the first in France to require attachment of a take-off catapult bar), plus provision of a 'jump-strut' for automatic unstick rotation.

Other changes include 13 rather than 14 hardpoints, and a maximum take-off weight reduced by 2000 kg (4,409 lb) to 19,500 kg (42,989 lb). The Aéronavale's initial requirement for 86 single-seat Rafale Ms is unlikely to be satisfied. Budget

cuts have forced the total buy down to 60 aircraft. In addition, having studied aircraft performance during the 1991 Gulf War and the conflict over Kosovo, the Aéronavale decided that it required a mix of Rafale M and two-seat **Rafale N**

The second naval prototype, M02, is shown here launching from FNS Foch with a typical air-to-air load of MICA and Magic 2 missiles.

laser rangefinder or an Optronique Secteur Frontale IR search-and-track system mounted forward of the cockpit and supplementing the radar for passive multi-target identification and tracking, and the MIDS datalink.

The definitive multi-role **Standard F3**, with improved radar able to undertake simultaneous air search and terrain following should be in service by 2010. Rafale N flew out for the first time in 2005, for delivery in 2007.

In the closing stages of Operation Enduring Freedom during 2002, Rafales flew operationally from *Charles de Gaulle*, but saw no combat.

Procurement of the Rafale M continued with an order for a further 13 machines in early 2003, at which time the final M/N mix had not yet been announced.

SPECIFICATION	
Dassault Rafale M	MICA AAMs and three drop tanks 1055 km (655 miles)
Type: single-seat carrierborne multi-role warplane	**Weights:** empty equipped 9800 kg (21,605 lb); normal take-off 16,500 kg (36,376 lb)
Powerplant: two SNECMA M88-2 turbofan engines each rated at 75 kN (16,861 lb st) with afterburning	**Dimensions:** wing span 10.9 m (35 ft 9 in) with tip-mounted AAMs; length 15.3 m (50 ft 2¼ in); height 5.34 m (17 ft 6¼ in); wing area 46 m² (495.16 sq ft)
Performance: maximum speed 2125 km/h (1,321 mph) 'clean' at 11,000 m (36,090 ft); maximum climb rate at sea level 18,290 m (60,000 ft) per minute; service ceiling 16,765 m (55,000 ft); combat radius on a low-level penetration mission with 12 250-kg (551-lb) bombs, four	**Armament:** one 30-mm GIAT/ DEFA M791 fixed forward-firing cannon in the starboard side of the forward fuselage, plus up to 6000 kg (13,228 lb) of disposable stores

aircraft. In May 2001, Flottille 12F was formed with four Rafale Ms. These early aircraft are equipped to **Standard F1**, optimized for the air-to-air role, and certain systems of the definitive aircraft.

Later standards include **Standard F2**, delivered from 2004, with improved air-to-surface capability. This will include Scalp, a jam-resistant passive optronic surveillance and imaging system with a

Dassault Super Etendard Multi-role carrierborne fighter

A French naval requirement of the early 1970s for 100 new carrierborne strike/attack fighters (for which procurement of the navalized SEPECAT Jaguar M was originally planned) eventually resulted in a 1973 contract to Dassault-Breguet for 60 examples of a development of its current Etendard IV warplane. The upgraded **Super Etendard** (super standard) was planned with the powerplant of one 49.03-kN (11,023-lb st)

The Super Etendard was developed from the 1950s-vintage Etendard IV. A new nav/attack system was installed, but the thirsty SNECMA Atar engine was retained. Despite the aircraft's increased weight, the Super Etendard's new wing does give improved handling.

SNECMA Atar 8K-50 turbojet and some 90 per cent airframe commonality with the Etendard IV. A new wing leading-edge profile and redesigned flaps ensured a mainly unchanged carrier deck performance despite the Super Etendard's heavier operating weights.

Greater capability

To widen its anti-ship attack and air-to-air capabilities, the Super Etendard also featured a new ETNA nav/attack system and an Agave monopulse search and fire-control radar, an SKN602 INS, Crouzet 66 air data computer (and associated Crouzet 97 navigation display and armament system), and

In service the Super Etendard has proved to be a useful type. This pair is taking fuel from a US Navy KA-6D Intruder. Note that the Super Etendards seen here have the post-1984 camouflage scheme.

a HUD. A retractable inflight-refuelling probe was fitted forward of the cockpit.

Three Etendard IVM airframes were converted as prototypes, flying from 29 October 1974. Production of 71 Super Etendards was then undertaken, the first of these aircraft flying on 24 November 1977. The new type began to replace Etendard IVs and some Vought F-8E(FN) Crusader interceptors from June 1978.

Falklands hero

By the time the Falklands War started in April 1982, the Argentine navy (the sole Super Etendard export customer) had received the first five of 14 aircraft on order to equip its air arm's 2ª Escuadrilla, together with five Aérospatiale AM39 Exocet anti-ship missiles. These aircraft made their operational debut on 4 May 1982, sinking HMS *Sheffield* off the Falklands, followed on 25 May by the destruction of the supply ship *Atlantic Conveyor*. The squadron suffered no wartime losses. In October 1983, the Iraqi air force leased five Super Etendards and bought a substantial number of AM39 missiles for use against Iranian tankers in the Iran/Iraq war, scoring many successes. One of the aircraft, however, was lost to an accident.

A mid-1980s upgrade programme was planned to extend the long-range and anti-ship attack capabilities of the Aéronavale's surviving force of nearly 60 Super Etendards (some 53 of which had already been modified to launch the ASMP stand-off nuclear missile). The main changes were: modernization of the avionics, a revised cockpit with new instrumentation and HOTAS controls, and the new Anemone radar – incorporating track-while-scan, air-to-surface ranging, ground mapping and search functions. New systems included a wide-angle HUD with TV or IR imaging, Sherloc RWR and a VCN65 ECM display together with the Barem jammer pod, a more modern INS, a weapons and air data computer with more processing capacity, and provision for night-vision goggles.

Airframe changes, combined with ongoing systems upgrades,

will help to extend the service life of Super Etendard's to about 2011.

The prototype of the upgraded **Super Etendard Modernisé** first flew on 5 October 1990, Dassault modifying two more for operational development.

Following disbandment of Flottille 14F in July 1991, pending its eventual re-equipment as the Aéronavale's first Rafale M unit, its Super Etendards were used to replace the last 11 Etendard

IVP reconnaissance aircraft equipping Escadrille 59S at Hyères. The Super Etendards were used for the operational conversion of French naval pilots after deck-landing training in Aérospatiale Zéphyr aircraft at the same base.

Flottilles 11F and 17F comprised the Aéronavale's remaining frontline Super Etendard squadrons in mid-2003, flying Modernisé aircraft, and will operate the machines until they are replaced by Rafale Ms.

SPECIFICATION	
Dassault Super Etendard **Type:** single-seat carrier-based attack aircraft **Powerplant:** one 49.05-kN (11,023-lb thrust) SNECMA Atar 8K-50 turbojet **Performance:** maximum speed 'clean' at sea level 1380 km/h (857 mph); maximum climb rate at sea level 6000 m (19,685 ft) per minute; service ceiling 13,700 m (44,950 ft); radius on a hi-lo-hi	mission with one AM39 and two drop tanks 850 km (528 miles) **Weights:** empty equipped 6500 kg (14,330 lb); maximum take-off 12,000 kg (26,455 lb) **Dimensions:** wing span 9.6 m (31 ft 6 in); length 14.31 m (46 ft 11½ in); height 3.86 m (12 ft 8 in); wing area 28.4 m² (305.71 sq ft) **Armament:** two 30-mm DEFA cannon plus up to 2100 kg (4,630 lb) of disposable ordnance

The Super Etendard gained fame during the Falklands campaign when Argentinian Super Etendards sank two British ships with Exocet missiles.

Sukhoi Su-27K (Su-33) 'Flanker-D'
Naval Su-27

'Red 64' was assigned to the 1st Squadron of the Severomorsk Regiment, AV-MF, and was one of the aircraft deployed aboard Admiral Kuznetsov for its first operational cruise in 1996.

Service introduction of the Su-27K made it eligible for a separate ASCC/NATO reporting name suffix, and the aircraft is now understood to have been known as 'Flanker-D'. The reporting name saw little use, however, as the aircraft's correct designation (and the OKB's Su-33 designation) became widely known and used.

Development of a navalized, shipborne version of the Su-27 was launched in the early 1980s at the same time as the Soviet carrier programme. The aircraft was seen as a single-role fleet air defence aircraft, which would form one element in a mixed air wing alongside a new AWACS platform and the MiG-29K multi-role strike fighter. As such, the **Su-27K 'Flanker-D'** was developed from the basic Su-27, not the multi-role Su-27M.

Several Su-27s tested different aspects of the intended Su-27K production configuration, including canards for approach handling tests and an arrester hook. Three Su-27 prototypes and an early Su-27UB were used for early take-off trials from a dummy carrier deck. The first 'deck' take-off was made from the dummy deck at Saki on 28 August 1982. The dummy deck was subsequently rebuilt to incorporate a ski-ramp identical to that fitted to the first Soviet carrier, *Tbilisi*, and intended to reduce the take-off run.

Su-27K prototypes

The three modified Su-27s were followed by a batch of **T10K** (Su-27K) prototypes, each of which differed slightly from the others. The first Su-27K prototype made its maiden flight on 17 August 1987. All of the T10Ks featured twin nosewheels, wing and tailplane folding, and double-slotted trailing-edge flaps.

The Su-27K prototypes were also all fitted with abbreviated 'tail stings' and square-section arrester hooks; none had brake 'chutes. Later prototypes also had an extra pair of inboard underwing weapons pylons, raising the total number to 12, including the wingtip stations.

*An Su-27K runs up to full power on **Admiral Kuznetsov**. Early in the Russian carrier programme, it was decided that the development of a steam catapult would not be possible within the timescale set for the first of the new carriers, and that they would be fitted with ski ramps instead. The Su-27K makes unassisted take-offs, using a combination of restrainers and take-off ramps.*

Carrier landing trials began on 1 November 1989, when Victor Pugachev landed the second Su-27K aboard *Tbilisi*, becoming the first Russian pilot to land a conventional aircraft aboard the carrier. The second prototype was the first full-standard Su-27K.

Russian naval pilots began carrier operations on 26 September 1991. Service trials were highly successful and led to State Acceptance Trials, which were successfully passed in 1994.

Carrier fleet?

Had the Soviet Union's ambitious plan to build four aircraft-carriers reached fruition, perhaps as many as 72 production Su-27Ks would have been required simply for their air wings. However, the end of the Cold War led to a massive down-scaling of the Soviet Union's

carrier programme. With the *Admiral Kuznetsov* (formerly the *Tbilisi*, and before that *Brezhnev*) the only carrier left for service with the Russian navy, both the AEW aircraft and the MiG-29K programmes were abandoned.

If only one fixed-wing type was to be procured for the new carrier, logic would have dictated that it should be the multi-role MiG-29K. However, the political influence of Sukhoi's chief designer, Mikhail Simonov, was such that the Sukhoi was selected for production and service, and the Russian navy was forced to accept the aircraft's (and thus the carrier's) more limited role.

The Su-27K does enjoy some significant advantages over the MiG-29K, primarily exceptional range performance. Before entering service, the production

Su-27K was redesignated **Su-33** by the OKB, but the aircraft remains a navalized version of the basic IA-PVO interceptor, with the same basic 'Slot Back' radar and with only a very limited ground-attack capability. It is uncertain whether the AV-MF regularly uses the Su-33 designation.

First cruise

Kuznetsov's first truly operational deployment took place in early 1996, when it spent two months in the Mediterranean. The ship's complement included the Su-27K-equipped 1st Squadron of the Severomorsk Regiment. Although 24 Su-27Ks have been built, *Kuznetsov's* complement for this first cruise included just seven production Su-27K aircraft.

Since that first cruise, which revealed a number of operational

deficiencies in the ship/aircraft combination, Russian defence spending has been even further cut. Only a handful of cruises has therefore occurred, but Su-27K pilots have trained in inflight-refuelling with Il-78 tankers, and live weapons training with AAMs has been accomplished.

With the advent of the two-seat **Su-27KUB**, the Russian navy potentially has a formidable new asset. Originally considered to be a naval Su-32FN/Su-34 derivative by the West, the aircraft combines a two-seat side-by-side cockpit with a conical nose profile. Designed as a trainer, the Su-27KUB also has great potential as an ECM, reconnaissance or AEW platform. Even if funding allows, however, it is likely to be many years before such developments could take effect.

Mikoyan MiG-29K A carrierborne 'Fulcrum'

The **MiG-29K** project was launched to provide a multi-role strike fighter to complement the Su-27K interceptor on the carriers intended to enter Soviet navy service during the 1990s. However, in the event only the Sukhoi Su-27K was procured for service.

Trials with the hooked **MiG-29KVP** proved that the MiG-29 could be operated safely from a ski-jump, and that arrested landings were possible at operationally useful weights. However, it was decided that the ideal carrierborne MiG-29 would require both additional wing area and additional thrust. Further, improved high-lift

devices might produce a useful reduction in approach speed, without unacceptably raising the angle of attack on touch-down.

Since a new variant of the MiG-29 would be required, Mikoyan adapted it from the new multi-role MiG-29M, with its lightweight airframe, multi-mode/multi-role radar and PGM capability.

Uprated engines

There was a degree of cross-fertilization between the MiG-29M and the MiG-29K, with the uprated RD-33K engines developed for the carrier aircraft eventually being adopted for the -29M, too. The

Wearing calibration markings enabling it to be accurately tracked during carrier trials work, the first MiG-29K is illustrated here in its standard MiG-29 camouflage finish.

new engine gave 92.17 kN (20,725 lb st) thrust for a limited period, useful on launch and in the event of a missed approach or go-around. It also had FADEC (full-authority digital engine control) and was made of advanced materials.

New wing

The quintessence of the MiG-29K lay in its new wing, designed with power-folding at roughly one-third span. The wing was fitted with broader-chord double-slotted trailing-edge

flaps, and it featured the extended-span ailerons of the MiG-29M, although they were modified to droop (as flaperons) at low speed. The tip was moved further outboard, and increased in chord and depth, housing new ECM systems. The leading edge was of reduced sweep-back, giving only slightly greater chord at the root. The leading-edge flaps were redesigned.

In addition to the new wing, the MiG-29K introduced a new, strengthened, long-stroke

The first MiG-29K, Bort '311', is seen during trials aboard Tbilisi. These included landing aboard with R-73 and R-77 missiles, the main air-to-air weapons of the type. The aircraft bore the brunt of the carrier trials, carrying photo-calibration marks on the nose. The extended and bulged wingtips housed electronic warfare equipment.

undercarriage, and it had a tailhook. The MiG-29K prototypes also introduced a neat, fully-retractable inflight-refuelling probe below the forward edge of the port side of the cockpit windscreen.

Production MiG-29Ks would have had a fully automatic carrier landing system, in addition to the Uzel beacon homing system. The prototypes used a system derived from that fitted to the Yak-38. This was sufficient to guarantee that the aircraft would touch down within a 6-m (20-ft) circle on the deck, within tight airspeed and vertical speed limits – not quite enough to guarantee getting a wire, and

also not quite enough to guarantee being on the deck centreline point.

Carrier trials

Commonality with the MiG-29M meant that only two prototypes of the MiG-29K would be required, to prove the carrier-specific items. The first prototype was flown on 23 June 1988, and was subsequently used for extensive trials aboard *Tbilisi* from 1 November 1989. The second prototype was used mainly for systems trials, and made only six carrier landings.

The end of the Cold War and the break-up of the Soviet Union led to the abandonment of *Tbilisi's* planned sister ships. *Tbilisi* itself became *Admiral Kuznetsov*, while procurement of two separate fighter aircraft

types for its air wing seemed unmanageably extravagant, and it became obvious that a competition was emerging between the Sukhoi Su-27K and the MiG-29K.

While the Su-27K emerged victorious from this competition, all was not lost for the MiG-29K. In 2000, India purchased the carrier *Admiral Gorshkov* from Russia. Requiring a multi-role fighter to equip the carrier, the country ordered 46 MiG-29Ks, for delivery after 2005.

While the first MiG-29K was finished in a standard light-grey scheme, the second aircraft, Bort '312', sported this slate-grey paint. Additional markings were MiG and MAPO (Moscow Aircraft Production Organization) badges, and the St Andrew's Cross ensign of the Russian navy. The aircraft was still active in 1998.

British Aerospace Sea Harrier FRS.Mk 1 STOVL naval fighter

The FRS designation reflected the Sea Harrier's triple capability as a fleet defence fighter, reconnaissance platform and strike/attack aircraft. This Sea Harrier FRS.Mk 1 carries the markings of the squadron commander of No. 801 Sqn, FAA. After the Falklands War, twin AIM-9 rails were added to the Sea Harrier's outer pylons.

The **BAe Sea Harrier** was developed from the RAF's Harrier close support and reconnaissance warplane, the world's first and, at that time, only operational short take-off and vertical landing (STOVL) aircraft. The Sea Harrier fortuitously filled the gap left by the phase-out of the Fleet Air Arm's Phantoms and the 1979 decommissioning of HMS *Ark Royal*, the last conventional aircraft carrier in service with the Royal Navy. The Sea Harrier's advent happily coincided with the introduction of a new generation of 20,000-ton light carriers intended primarily for the anti-submarine role. These three ships were intended to embark only helicopters, and the Sea Harrier was instrumental in retaining some fixed-wing strike capability when the FAA was otherwise destined to become an all-helicopter force. Concurrent with the RN's receipt of HMS *Invincible*, dubbed a 'through-deck cruiser' rather than an aircraft carrier to get it past UK

Treasury scrutiny, the Sea Harrier became one of the most important types ever procured by the FAA. The 1982 Falklands War proved the prudence of the decision to adopt the Sea Harrier.

Harrier at sea

Although a Harrier, in its original P.1127 form, had landed on *Ark Royal* as early as 8 February 1963, the Royal Navy initially had little interest in the programme. Naval interest gradually increased, however, spurred by the knowledge that no other fixed-wing aircraft could be ordered, and in May 1975 an initial order for 24 **Sea Harrier FRS.Mk 1** single-seat warplanes and one **Harrier T.Mk 4A** two-seat trainer was placed, followed by a further order for 10 more Sea Harrier FRS.Mk 1s in May 1978.

The main differences between the RAF's Harrier GR.Mk 3 and Sea Harrier FRS.Mk 1 were the latter's front fuselage contours, with a painted radome covering a Ferranti Blue Fox radar. The cockpit was raised by 0.25 m

(10 in) and the canopy was revised to give the pilot better fields of vision. An improved Pegasus Mk 104 turbofan was fitted. An autopilot, a revised nav/attack system and a new HUD were added. Magnesium was deleted from all airframe areas likely to be exposed to corrosion from salt water.

Into service, into war

Embarking aboard HMS *Hermes* in June 1981, No. 800 Sqn was joined by No. 801 Sqn. Both units were subsequently deployed as part of the RN's fixed-wing air assets during the Falklands

conflict, in which the Sea Harrier served with distinction. Scoring 22 confirmed victories, the Sea Harrier force lost six aircraft, all of them to causes other than aerial combat. Following the South Atlantic operation, 14 Sea Harrier FRS.Mk 1s were ordered as attrition replacements and, in 1984, nine more single-seaters as well as three **Harrier T.Mk 4(N)** trainers were added.

In 1979, the Indian navy, the only export operator, ordered the first of its 23 **Sea Harrier FRS.Mk 51** and six **Harrier T.Mk 60** machines. The survivors remained in service in late 2002.

SPECIFICATION	
BAe Sea Harrier FRS.Mk 1 **Type:** single-seat carrierborne STOVL fighter, reconnaissance and strike/attack warplane **Powerplant:** one Rolls-Royce Pegasus Mk 104 vectored-thrust turbofan engine rated at 96 kN (21,500 lb st) **Performance:** maximum speed more than 1185 km/h (736 mph) at low altitude; initial climb rate about 15,240 m (50,000 ft) per minute; service ceiling 15,545 m (51,000 ft);	radius 750 km (460 miles) on a hi-hi-hi interception mission **Weights:** empty 6374 kg (14,052 lb); maximum take-off 11,884 kg (26,200 lb) **Dimensions:** wing span 7.7 m (25 ft 3 in); length 14.5 m (47 ft 7 in); height 3.71 m (12 ft 2 in); wing area 18.68 m² (202.10 sq ft) **Armament:** up to a maximum of 3629 kg (8,000 lb) or normal 2268 kg (5,000 lb) of disposable stores for STO or VTO, respectively

British Aerospace Sea Harrier FA.Mk 2 Upgraded 'Shar'

In refining the Sea Harrier as a more capable interceptor while retaining its reconnaissance and strike/attack capability, BAe made some significant changes to the airframe. The company received a contract in January 1985 for the project definition phase of the programme, which included two conversions of the Sea Harrier FRS.Mk 1 to the standard that was known as the **Sea Harrier FRS.Mk 2** up to May 1994, when it was changed to **Sea Harrier**

F/A.Mk 2, then to **FA.Mk 2** in 1995. In 1984 it was reported that the Ministry of Defence planned to award a contract to BAe and Ferranti to cover a mid-life update of the entire Sea Harrier fleet, but these plans were substantially revised in 1985 to cover an upgrade of 30 airframes with Blue Vixen radar, improved RWR, JTIDS and provision for the AIM-120 AMRAAM. The first of two prototype conversions flew on 19 September 1988.

The FA.Mk 2 greatly improves the capabilities of the basic Sea Harrier, or 'Shar'. Nevertheless, the type is due for retirement.

A revised radome was needed to house the Blue Vixen radar, giving the Sea Harrier FA.Mk 2's nose a more elongated appearance than that of its predecessor. This aircraft carries the markings of No. 899 Sqn, FAA.

Despite the addition of an extra equipment bay and a recontoured nose to house the Blue Vixen radar, the Sea Harrier FA.Mk 2 is actually shorter overall due to elimination of the nose-mounted pitot tube of the earlier variant.

No increase in wing span was found to be necessary to carry additional stores, including a pair of 190-Imperial gallon (864-litre) drop tanks plus AIM-120s (or ALARM anti-radar missiles) on each of the outer pylons, though ferry tips are available to increase span to 9.04 m (29 ft 8 in). The Sea Harrier FA.Mk 2's cockpit introduced new multi-function CRT displays and HOTAS controls; the type is powered by the Pegasus Mk 106 turbofan, a navalized version of the Mk 105.

Building the numbers
On 7 December 1988 a contract was awarded for the conversion of 31 Sea Harrier FRS.Mk 1s to Mk 2 standard. On 6 March 1990 the MoD revealed its intent to order at least 10 new-build Sea Harrier FRS.Mk 2s. In January 1994 18 Sea Harrier FRS.Mk 2s and an additional eight conversions were ordered, for a total of 57 Sea Harrier FA.Mk 2s (taking account of attrition).

To enhance pilot conversion training, a new two-seat **Harrier T.Mk 8** trainer was created, the four such aircraft supplementing the three surviving Harrier T.Mk 4Ns from 1996. Essentially a reconfigured T.Mk 4N, the Harrier T.Mk 8 duplicates the Sea Harrier FA.Mk 2's systems except for the radar.

SPECIFICATION	
BAe Sea Harrier FA.Mk 2 **Type:** single-seat carrierborne STOVL fighter and attack warplane **Powerplant:** one Rolls-Royce Pegasus Mk 106 vectored-thrust turbofan engine rated at 96 kN (21,500 lb st) **Performance:** maximum level speed 1144 km/h (711 mph) at sea level; initial climb rate about 15,240 m (50,000 ft) per minute; service ceiling about 15,545 m (51,000 ft); radius 750 km	(460 miles) on a hi-hi-hi interception mission **Weights:** empty 6374 kg (14,052 lb); maximum take-off 11,884 kg (26,200 lb) **Dimensions:** wing span 7.7 m (25 ft 3 in); length 14.17 m (46 ft 6 in); height 3.71 m (12 ft 2 in); wing area 18.68 m² (202.10 sq ft) **Armament:** up to a maximum of 3629 kg (8,000 lb) or normal 2268 kg (5,000 lb) of disposable stores for STO or VTO, respectively

McDonnell Douglas/BAe Harrier II CAS aircraft

As fitted to the Harrier II Plus, the APG-65 radar uses an antenna cropped by 5 cm (2 in) to fit the AV-8B's fuselage cross-section.

With the AV-8A Harrier already in service, the USMC eventually backed the development of the advanced **AV-8B Harrier II**, intended to carry a larger warload and to provide better range/endurance characteristics. The design was based around a larger wing of supercritical section, and also had more carbon fibre in other airframe areas and a completely revised cockpit, with HOTAS controls and a higher seating position for the pilot. First flown on 9 November 1978, fitted to an AV-8A (which became the first of two **YAV-8B** service test aircraft), the new wing had six hardpoints.

Into production
The USMC took delivery of the first production aircraft in 1983, later aircraft introducing more powerful engines. A total of 286 was built, including six attrition replacements ordered after Desert Storm. Several two-seat **TAV-8B** aircraft were also built.

From the 167th airframe, all USMC AV-8Bs were provided with a night-attack capability with the installation of a FLIR, an improved HUD, an HDD and a colour moving map. The terms **Night Attack Harrier II** or **Night Attack AV-8B** are sometimes applied unofficially to these aircraft. The 205th AV-8B off the production line was the first fully equipped **AV-8B Harrier II Plus**. It first flew on 22 September 1992. Equipped with the APG-65 radar, the Harrier II Plus has a revised FLIR fairing, but is otherwise externally identical to late AV-8Bs. APG-65 gives compatibility with AIM-7 and AIM-120 AAMs. It also allows the use of the AGM-84 Harpoon AShM. The last 24 USMC aircraft were built as II Pluses; many more were converted.

Spain and Italy have also purchased the AV-8B. With the commissioning of the *Principe de Asturias* in 1989, the Spanish navy embarked 12 **EAV-8B** (**VA.2 Matador II**) aircraft. It also ordered 13 (later reduced to eight) Harrier II Pluses in 1992. A two-seat **TAV-8B** was ordered in March 1992. In 1989, Italy ordered two TAV-8Bs from the USMC. Its first batch of three ex-USMC Harrier II Plus aircraft was ordered in 1991, followed by 13 more in November 1992.

SPECIFICATION	
McDonnell Douglas/BAe AV-8B Harrier II Plus **Type:** single-seat STOVL multi-role warplane **Powerplant:** one Rolls-Royce F402-RR-408A (Pegasus 11-61) vectored-thrust turbofan rated at 106 kN (23,800-lb st) **Performance:** maximum level speed 'clean' at sea level 1065 km/h (662 mph); service ceiling over 15,240 m (50,000 ft); time on station for a CAP at a 185-km (115-mile) radius	2 hours 42 minutes **Weights:** empty operating 6740 kg (14,860 lb); maximum take-off 14,061 kg (31,000 lb) after short take-off **Dimensions:** wing span 9.25 m (30 ft 4 in); length 14.55 m (47 ft 9 in); height 3.55 m (11 ft 7¾ in); wing area 22.61 m² (243.40 sq ft) including LERXes **Armament:** up to 6003 kg (13,235 lb) of stores usually including two 25-mm GAU-12 cannon in underfuselage pods

AV-8B Harrier II Plus

This aircraft is shown as it appeared during the late 1990s on the strength of VMA-542 'Flying Tigers' of Marine Air Group 14 (MAG-14), 2d Marine Air Wing (2d MAW), at MCAS Cherry Point, North Carolina (the Fleet Marine Corps Atlantic uses '2d' rather than the more commonly accepted '2nd' terminology). VMA-542 traded its AV-8As and AV-8Cs for AV-8Bs in April 1986, after losing its last first-generation

Harrier late in 1985. VMA-542 was the second AV-8B squadron to deploy to the Persian Gulf in 1991, losing two aircraft in combat. It subsequently became the first squadron to operate the Harrier II Plus, with the first of these arriving on 8 July 1993. The squadron's full markings include a yellow triangular 'tiger skin' design on the rudders, and a tiger's head badge on the nose.

AGM-65E Maverick
In 1985 the USMC introduced into service a specialized version of the Maverick missile, the AGM-65E, which is a semi-active, laser-guided version of the original TV-/IR-guided Maverick. This version was developed specifically for the Marines, to be used as a precision weapon for close air support missions where friendly troops are in contact with enemy forces. The AGM-65E was based on development work done during the 1970s on the AGM-65C, which was intended for the US Navy and US Air Force, but never entered production. The AGM-65E introduced a new 136-kg (300-lb) blast penetrator warhead, as distinct from the previous 57-kg (125-lb) shaped-charge warhead, optimised for anti-armour missions. All 'E-model' Mavericks are painted grey.

AV-8B cockpit
When McDonnell Douglas and BAe were developing the Harrier II, substantial changes were made to the forward section of the aircraft. In addition to a completely revised airframe shape, the cockpit was totally rebuilt around the new navigation/attack suite and MFDs. The most obvious difference over earlier Harriers was the much improved field of vision for the pilot, courtesy of the single-piece wraparound bubble canopy. The pilot also sat much higher in the Harrier II, the new seat position providing much improved 'over-the-shoulder' vision.

Four Mk 82 dumb bombs (in this case inert), a pair of Sidewinder rails and the two underfuselage pods associated with the GAU-12/U 25-mm cannon system hint at the impressive capabilities of the Harrier II Plus. The aircraft has all the ground-attack capability and operational versatility of the AV-8B(AN), combined with the air-to-air capability of the F/A-18 Hornet.

Funding for the AV-8B Harrier II Plus programme was supplied by the United States, Italy and Spain. In the latter countries, Alenia and CASA, respectively, were chosen to join the programme. This demonstrator aircraft carries the flags of all three countries and also demonstrates the underfuselage strakes which are fitted in the absence of gun pods. At this stage, the aircraft had streamlined blanking plates covering the apertures that would house the AN/ALE-39 chaff/flare dispensers.

Avionics upgrade programme

In September 1997 the US Navy awarded a $14 million COTS (Commercial Off-the-Shelf) contract to Smiths Industries Aerospace, for an upgrade to the Weapons Management and Control System (WMCS) of the AV-8B. The upgrade was known as OSCAR (Open Systems Core Avionics Requirements) and was conducted in association with the Boeing Company – McDonnell Aircraft and Missile Systems. OSCAR was an important part of future advanced weapons integration for the Marine Corps' Harriers, as it allowed new air-to-air and air-to-ground systems to be more easily 'plugged in' to the WMCS. In addition, by late 2003, the entire USMC Harrier II fleet had been upgraded to II Plus standard.

Inflight-refuelling probe

Often described as 'bolt-on', the Harrier II's refuelling probe is a near-permanent feature. The retracted probe is housed in a streamlined fairing and, when in use, extends to a point slightly forward and to the left of the pilot's head. The probe is compatible with hose-type air refuelling equipment, as carried by USMC KC-130s, KC-10s, specially equipped KC-135s and all RAF tankers.

AN/ALE-39 chaff/flare launchers

The night-attack-capable AV-8B(NA) introduced additional chaff/flare countermeasures in the form of four AN/ALE-39 dispensers mounted on the upper rear fuselage. The dispensers are mounted as two pairs, with one pair to each side of the heat exchanger/ram air intake that is situated in the leading edge of the fin fairing.

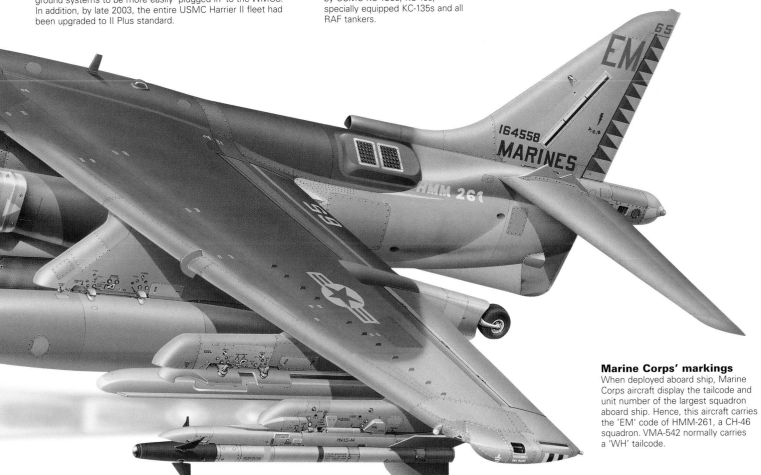

Marine Corps' markings

When deployed aboard ship, Marine Corps aircraft display the tailcode and unit number of the largest squadron aboard ship. Hence, this aircraft carries the 'EM' code of HMM-261, a CH-46 squadron. VMA-542 normally carries a 'WH' tailcode.

AN/APG-65 multi-mode radar for the Harrier II Plus

When the AN/APG-65 radar was introduced in the F/A-18, it revolutionized airborne radar technology. The new radar offered a combination of multi-mode, all-digital performance in the air-to-air and air-to-ground roles, coupled with an extremely compact size. As the Hornet fleet was re-equipped with the improved AN/APG-73, redundant AN/APG-65 units were cascaded down to the Harrier II fleet. The AN/APG-65 possesses a track-while-scan mode, which allows the Harrier II Plus to provide radar-guided BVR missiles, such as the AIM-7M and AIM-120, with mid-course guidance prior to their active-homing phase, while still searching for other targets. For air-to-ground missions the radar can provide terrain-avoidance information for low-level flight, locate moving targets on the ground, and provide precise range to targets, and also has a specific sea-surface mode to locate ships in all weather conditions.

Rolls-Royce Pegasus engine

When the AV-8B entered development, an uprated version of the Pegasus, the 11-21, was introduced (in 1984). In addition to providing a little extra power, with a standard rating of 96.75 kN (21,750 lb thrust), the new engine boasted much-improved reliability and reduced maintenance times. From 1986 onwards all Pegasus 11-21s were delivered with FADEC (Full-Authority Digital Engine Control) systems to further improve their performance. The US designation for this engine was F402-RR-406A. The 11-21 has now been further improved to Pegasus 11-61 standard, offering increased thrust (106 kN/23,800 lb thrust), even in hot and high conditions, and twice the overhaul life of the 11-21. In US service, the Pegasus 11-61 is designated as the F402-RR-408A.

European II Pluses

Both the Spanish and Italian navies fly the AV-8B Harrier II Plus. The United Kingdom never joined the programme, the RAF having no need for a radar-equipped Harrier, and the FAA buying the Sea Harrier FA.Mk 2.

MARINA MILITARE ITALIANA

Italy ordered 16 Harrier II Pluses (with options on eight more), and the first three of these aircraft were diverted from the USMC's allocation on 20 April 1994, being delivered to MCAS Cherry Point, North Carolina, for training. The Italian Harriers wear an unusual two-tone grey colour scheme, with the top surfaces very much darker than the undersides. Titles and codes are applied in the undersurface colour, and national insignia are of reduced size and have a lower proportion of white. An anchor insignia is carried on the forward zero-scarf nozzle fairing of the single-seaters, many of which also have markings on the rudder. The aircraft fly from *Giuseppe Garibaldi*.

ARMA AÉREA DE LA ARMADA

Under a Tripartite MoU of 1990, Spain ordered eight new-build Harrier II Pluses and a TAV-8B two-seater, and declared that 11 AV-8Bs would be upgraded to Harrier II Plus standard. The eight new-build II Plus aircraft were scheduled for final assembly by CASA. The aircraft are flown by 9ª Escuadrilla and deploy aboard the carrier *Principe de Asturias*. Standard AAM armament includes the AIM-9M Sidewinder and AIM-120 AMRAAM. 9ª was formed at Rota on 29 September 1987 to operate the Armada's EAV-8Bs, which were delivered between October 1987 and September 1988. Although McDonnell Douglas used the EAV-8B designation, to the Spanish the aircraft are known as the VA.2 Matador II. The squadron first deployed in 1989 with the standard VA.2 and, from late 1994, some 9ª Escuadrilla pilots were posted to the air force to gain experience with the F/A-18 Hornet and its APG-65 radar system, prior to the introduction of the APG-65-equipped Harrier II Plus.

Grumman F-14 Tomcat Swing-wing naval fighter

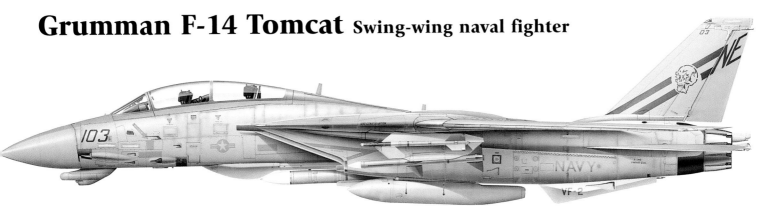

Designed as a successor to the F-4 Phantom II in the fleet air defence role for the US Navy, the **Grumman F-14 Tomcat** was originally conceived to engage and destroy targets at extreme range, before they could pose a threat to the carrier battle group. The **F-14A Tomcat** remains a formidable warplane, even though the original F-14A has been in service for many years.

Production of the F-14A for the US Navy eventually totalled 556 examples, while 80 broadly similar machines were purchased by Iran before the downfall of the Shah. Of the latter, only 79 were actually delivered (one being diverted to the US Navy). The F-14 continues to be the US Navy's primary air defence aircraft, although, with the introduction of the F/A-18E/F

Super Hornet into service from late 1999, the days of the F-14 have been increasingly numbered.

Weapons system

The key to the effectiveness of the F-14 lies in its advanced avionics suite, the Hughes AWG-9 fire control system representing the most capable long-range interceptor radar in service, with the ability to detect, track and engage targets at ranges in excess of 160 km (100 miles). Early aircraft also had an infrared search and track (IRST) system, which was replaced during production (and by retrofit) with a long-range video camera known as TCS. The armament options allow the F-14 to engage targets over a huge range from close up to extreme BVR (beyond visual range).

The AIM-54 Phoenix remained the longest-ranged air-to-air missile in Western service at the beginning of the twenty-first century and in tests it has demonstrated the ability to detect and kill targets at unparalleled distances. In the medium-range arena, the Tomcat employs the AIM-7 Sparrow, not having been upgraded for compatibility with the AIM-120 AMRAAM. For

From May 1995, VF-2 re-equipped with F-14D Tomcats. This aircraft is depicted with a typical air-to-air load of four underfuselage Phoenix long-range AAMs, and two each of the Sparrow and Sidewinder short-range missiles.

short-range, close-in engagements, the F-14 carries the well-proven AIM-9 Sidewinder. Finally, there is a single M61A1 Vulcan 20-mm Gatling-type rotary cannon in the lower port fuselage with 675 rounds of ammunition.

Tomcat development

Development of the Tomcat was initiated in the late 1960s, following the cancellation of the

Carrying a quartet of Mk 83 freefall bombs on its underfuselage stations, this F-14A is about to fly a practice strike. The aircraft hails from VF-211 'Checkmates', a US Navy unit which was based aboard USS John C. Stennis between January and July 2002 for the Tomcat's last cruise aboard the vessel.

SPECIFICATION

Grumman F-14A Tomcat
Type: two-seat carrierborne fleet air defence fighter and interceptor, with ground attack capability
Powerplant: two Pratt & Whitney TF30-P-412A/414A turbofans each rated at 92.97 kN (20,900 lb st) with afterburning
Performance: maximum level speed 'clean' at high altitude 2485 km/h (1,544 mph); maximum rate of climb at sea level more than 9145 m (30,000 ft) per minute; service ceiling more than 15,240 m (50,000 ft); radius on a combat air patrol with six AIM-7 Sparrows and four AIM-9 Sidewinders 1233 km (766 miles)
Weights: empty 18191 kg (40,104 lb) with -414A engines; maximum take-off 32,098 kg (70,764 lb) with six Phoenix
Dimensions: wing span 19.54 m

(64 ft 1½ in) spread, 11.65 m (38 ft 2½ in) swept and 10.15 m (33 ft 3½ in) overswept; length 19.1 m (62 ft 8 in); height 4.88 m (16 ft); wing area 52.49 m² (565 sq ft)
Armament: standard armament consists of an internal M61A1 Vulcan 20-mm six-barrelled cannon and an AIM-9M Sidewinder on the shoulder launch rail of each wing glove pylon. The main launch rail of each glove pylon can accommodate either an AIM-7M Sparrow or an AIM-54C Phoenix. Four further AIM-7M or AIM-54C missiles can be carried under the fuselage between the engine trunks. 1011-litre (267-US gal) fuel tanks can be carried under the intakes, while 454-kg (1,000-lb) Mk 83 or 907-kg (2,000-lb) Mk 84 GP bombs or other free-fall weaponry can also be carried

ill-fated F-111B naval fighter, which initially left the US Navy in the unenviable position of having no new fighter in prospect. Grumman had already invested a considerable amount of effort in the navalized F-111B, and the company used this experience in designing a new variable-geometry fighter (the **G-303**), which was duly selected by the US Navy in January 1969. Grumman's use of a variable-geometry wing allowed excellent high-speed performance to be combined with docile low-speed handling characteristics for operations around the carrier,

and a high degree of agility. A dozen **YF-14A** development aircraft were ordered, with the first making its maiden flight on 21 December 1970.

The programme made reasonably swift progress, culminating in deliveries to the navy from October 1972, with the first operational cruise in 1974. Production continued into the 1980s and a total of 26 frontline and four second-line squadrons was eventually equipped with the F-14A Tomcat.

Although it has been generally successful, the F-14 has suffered many difficulties

since entering fleet service. Many were engine-related, the TF30 turbofan proving something of an Achilles heel. Fan blade losses caused several crashes before improved quality control and steel containment cases alleviated the worst consequences of engine failure. In addition, the engine was prone to compressor stall, especially during air combat manoeuvring training, and the aircraft's vicious departure characteristics (especially with one engine out) resulted in many further losses. Many problems were solved when the revised TF30-P-414A version of the powerplant was adopted as standard.

Other missions

In addition to fleet air defence tasks, F-14As are utilized for reconnaissance missions, using the Tactical Air Reconnaissance Pod System (TARPS), and it is usual for three TARPS-capable aircraft to be assigned to each carrier air wing. New digital TARPS pods have replaced the original wet-film units. More recently, the F-14A has acquired a secondary air-to-ground role, capitalizing on a modest attack capability that was built in from the outset, but never utilized. The **F-14A 'Bombcat'** initially carried only conventional 'iron' bombs, but has now had the LANTIRN pod integrated for use with laser-guided bombs.

Continuing problems with the TF30 engine of the F-14A were

a key factor in the development of re-engined and upgraded variants of the Tomcat. One of the original prototype airframes was fitted with two F401-PW-400s and employed for an abbreviated test programme as the **F-14B** as early as 1973–74.

Technical problems and financial difficulties combined to the abandonment of the programme, and the aircraft was placed into storage, re-emerging as the **F-14B Super Tomcat** with F101DFE (Derivative Fighter Engine) turbofans. This engine was developed into the General Electric F110-GE-400 turbofan, which was selected to power improved production Tomcat variants. It was decided to produce two distinct new Tomcats, one which was designated **F-14A+** (primarily by conversion of existing F-14As) with the new engine, and another, designated **F-14D**, with the new engine and improved digital avionics. The F-14A+ was originally regarded as an interim type, all examples of which would eventually be converted to full F-14D Tomcat standard.

'Bs' and 'Ds'

Subsequently, the F-14A+ was formally redesignated as the **F-14B**, 38 new-build examples being joined by 32 F-14A rebuilds in equipping half a dozen deployable squadrons starting in 1988. These aircraft incorporated some avionics changes, including a modernized fire control system, new radios,

VX-9 'Vampires' is a test unit involved in developing all aspects of the F-14's air-to-air role. This F-14D has been finished in the black scheme traditionally worn by VX-4 aircraft and continued when VX-4 and VX-5 were combined into VX-9. The aircraft was photographed in 2002 during Operation Cope Snapper.

Engine problems have plagued the F-14 throughout its career. Later TF30 models solved the worst of these problems, but re-engining with the F110 has transformed the Tomcat's performance.

upgraded RWRs (radar warning receivers), and various cockpit changes. F-14Bs were the first re-engined Tomcats to enter fleet service.

Two modified F-14As flew as F-14D prototypes and the first F-14D to be built as such made its maiden flight on 9 February 1990. The F-14D also added digital avionics, with digital radar processing and displays (adding these to standard AWG-9 hardware under the redesignation of APG-71), and a side-by-side undernose TCS/IRST sensor pod. Other improvements introduced by the F-14D include OBOGS (on-board oxygen-generating system), NACES (Naval Aircrew Escape System) ejection seats, and AN/ALR-67 radar warning receiver equipment. Like the F-14A, the F-14D possesses a full ground-attack

capability. However, a subsequent US Department of Defense decision to cease funding the F-14D effectively halted the navy's drive to upgrade its force of Tomcats. In consequence, the service has received only 37 new-build F-14Ds, while plans to upgrade approximately 400 existing F-14As to a similar standard were cancelled.

F-14D deliveries to the navy began in 1990, when training squadron VF-124 accepted its first F-14D at Miramar. The type has been used in Operation Southern Watch over Iraq, including an unsuccessful Phoenix shot against a pair of MiG-23s. The F-14 performed well on attack missions during Operation Enduring Freedom. The F-14 is slowly being retired, with the last F-14D due to leave the fleet in 2008.

These F-14s were photographed late in 2001 preparing for the type's last departure from USS Enterprise. Note the over-sweep position of the wings.

F-14A+ Tomcat

This F-14A+ is depicted as it appeared with VF-103 'Sluggers', as part of CVW-17, aboard the USS *Saratoga* during Operation Desert Storm. *Saratoga* sailed in the Red Sea during the 1991 Gulf War, embarking another F-14A+ unit, VF-74, as its second Tomcat squadron. This aircraft wears the personal markings and '201' Modex of the 'Sluggers' Executive Officer, Lt Cdr Fitzpatrick, but was lost to an Iraqi SAM while being flown by Lt Devon Jones. A special

forces helicopter, working in concert with two A-10As, rescued Jones, while his luckless RIO, Lt Lawrence Randolph 'Rat' Slade, was taken prisoner. The crew had been engaged on a TARPS mission, with the callsign CLUBLEAF 212, when they were struck by an Iraqi-developed variant of the Soviet SA-2 'Guideline'. Post-war, VF-103 adopted the markings and traditions of the 'Jolly Rogers', while the F-14A+ became known as the F-14B.

Avionics

The F-14B retains the same basic analog avionics and systems as the F-14A, although a number of changes were incorporated in the 38 new-build aircraft and 32 conversions initially completed. A new AN/ALR-67 RWR was fitted, with its associated antennas positioned below the wing gloves. AN/ARC-182 V/UHF radios were installed and the modernized and modified radar fire-control system was redesignated AN/AWG-15F. None of the new-build aircraft is TARPS-capable. The F-14B standard was originally supposed to be an interim level of modification, pending the arrival of the F-14D and the modification of all F-14Bs to this later standard. Today, however, both B and D Tomcats remain in the inventory.

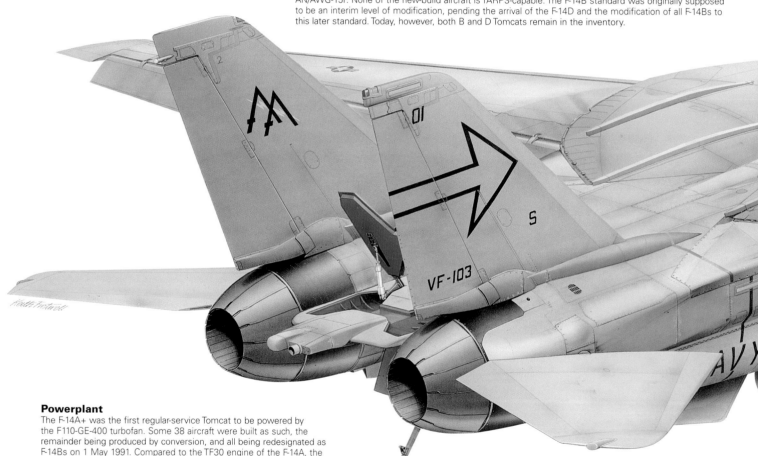

Powerplant

The F-14A+ was the first regular-service Tomcat to be powered by the F110-GE-400 turbofan. Some 38 aircraft were built as such, the remainder being produced by conversion, and all being redesignated as F-14Bs on 1 May 1991. Compared to the TF30 engine of the F-14A, the F110 provides greater power, while burning considerably less fuel. Thus, both outright performance and radius of action are radically improved. The new engine also offers benefits in commonality with the F110 turbofans fitted in some USAF F-16s. Fitting the F110 into the Tomcat airframe was surprisingly simple, with just a 1.27-m (4-ft 2-in) plug being required in the afterburner section of the engine due to its shorter length compared to the TF30, along with some changes to the secondary airframe structure.

Airbrakes

A pair of powerful hydraulically actuated speed brakes is located above and below the 'beaver' tail. These open to a maximum deflection angle of 60 degrees in just two seconds and are actuated at the push of a single button in the cockpit. The lower airbrake section has a deep cut-out in its centre, effectively separating it into two pieces, so that it does not snag the arrester hook when the latter is lowered. Indeed, deflection of the lower airbrake is limited to 18 degrees when the hook is lowered. Both upper and lower airbrakes are actuated by pairs of hydraulic rams, and the undersides of the airbrakes and the interiors of their bays are painted in a corrosion-resistant red paint.

An F-14D Tomcat assigned to VF-2 'Bounty Hunters' executes a hard landing on a carrier deck in the Arabian Gulf, after returning from a mission in support of Operation Iraqi Freedom in April 2003.

Desert Storm stores options

During the 1991 Gulf War, US Navy Tomcats flew both air-to-air and reconnaissance missions, the 'Bombcat' not seeing combat until operations over Bosnia in the mid-1990s. For air-to-air work, the F-14A+ employed the usual AIM-7/AIM-9/AIM-54 warload, but to the ignominy of the F-14 community, the only USN kills of the war came from F/A-18 Hornets (apart from one Mi-8 shot down by an F-14). TARPS pods were used in combat by both 'straight' F-14As and F-14A+ conversions such as the aircraft depicted. The pods employed wet-film and conventional cameras, although a digital system has subsequently been flown. The additional power of the F-14B compared to the F-14A meant that B-equipped squadrons were among the first to receive LANTIRN pods and Paveway LGBs for 'Bombcat' operations post-war.

Flaps and slats

Full-span, three-section, single-slotted flaps occupy the trailing edge of each wing. The innermost flap section can be used only when the wing is at minimum sweep, but the other two sections can be used at sweep angles of up to 55 degrees. When used as manoeuvre flaps, the surfaces are set at 10-degree deflection, but when used as landing flaps they are drooped at 35 degrees. A conventional constant-section, two-segment slat occupies the leading edge of each wing. The slats are deployed at 7 degrees for manoeuvring flight and 17 degrees for landing.

Undernose sensors

A number of sensors have been carried in this position, ranging from a simple ALQ-100 RWR antenna, to an IRST (infrared search and track) device, or an IRST with underslung RWR to the Northrop TCS (Television Camera Set) with underslung RWR as illustrated. The F-14D carries yet another variation on the theme, with TCS and IRST sensors mounted side-by-side and an RWR antenna mounted in the underslung position.

Two Naval Weapons Test Squadrons (NWTS) are maintained by the Naval Air Warfare Center. This F-14D belongs to the NWTS at Naval Air Weapons Station (NAWS) Point Mugu, California, the unit assuming responsibility for air-to-air weapons testing. NWTS Point Mugu also 'owns' a fleet of QF-4 drones for use as targets in live-missile shots.

F-14B/D: Expanded weapons capability

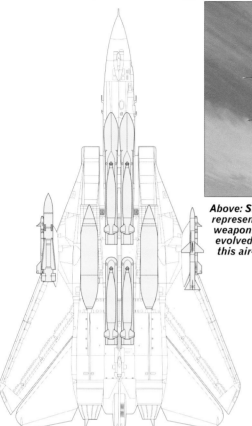

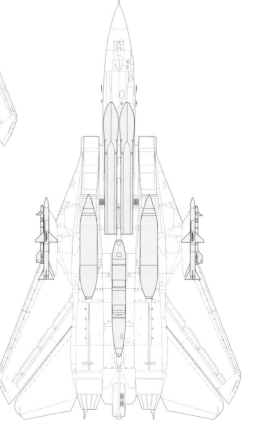

Above: Six Phoenix and two Sidewinder missiles represent an impressive if somewhat impractical weaponload. In F-14B and D forms, the Tomcat has evolved into a far more versatile fleet fighter than this air-intercept load would indicate.

1. Multi-role F-14D 'Bombcat'

Only the F-14D can carry AIM-54s without an active Phoenix pallet at station six. Therefore, the missiles may be carried on the glove pylons, while a full load of bombs, here Mk 83s (or a TARPS pod), are carried beneath the fuselage. In the configuration illustrated, the F-14D has the flexibility offered by short-range (AIM-9), medium-range (AIM-7) and long-range (AIM-54) air-to-air missiles, as well as a considerable bombload.

2. F-14D TARPS

With TARPS mounted at station five, empty AIM-54 pallets or inert AIM-7s must be carried forward in order to keep the aircraft's centre of gravity within acceptable limits. Only the F-14D can carry glove-mounted AIM-54s as well as a TARPS pod.

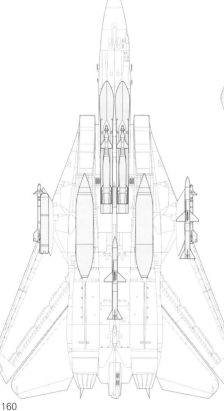

3. Paveway III LANTIRN 'Bombcat'

The 908-kg (2,000-lb) GBU-24 Paveway III gives the F-14 'Bombcat' greater stand-off range. A pair of GBU-24s, plus the full range of AAMs, are also carried by this F-14D. The LANTIRN targeting pod is carried on the starboard wing pylon.

4. LANTIRN 'Bombcat'

With a LANTIRN pod at station 8B, the F-14D is able to designate for its own LGBs, while still carrying AIM-9, AIM-7 and AIM-54 AAMs. The LGBs illustrated are 500-lb (227-kg) GBU-12s, but the GBU-10 and GBU-16 are also available.

5. F-14B TARPS

With TARPS denying the Tomcat the use of its No. 5 station, the F-14B and, for that matter, the F-14A, are prevented from carrying AIM-54s on their glove pylons, hence the Sparrows shown on this example.

Boeing F/A-18 A/B/C/D Hornet Carrier attack fighter

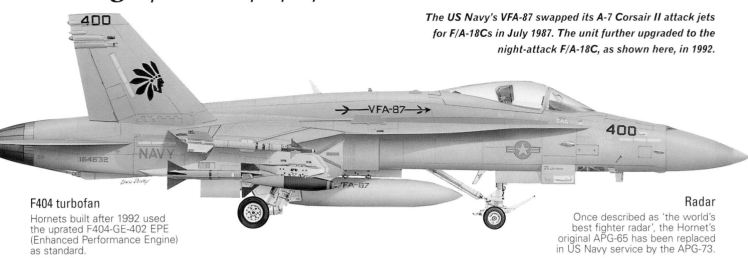

The US Navy's VFA-87 swapped its A-7 Corsair II attack jets for F/A-18Cs in July 1987. The unit further upgraded to the night-attack F/A-18C, as shown here, in 1992.

F404 turbofan

Hornets built after 1992 used the uprated F404-GE-402 EPE (Enhanced Performance Engine) as standard.

Radar

Once described as 'the world's best fighter radar', the Hornet's original APG-65 has been replaced in US Navy service by the APG-73.

The world's premier naval fighter originated as a derivative of the **Northrop YF-17** that was pitted successfully against the General Dynamics YF-16 in the US Navy's Air Combat Fighter programme of 1976. The first of 11 trials Hornets made its maiden flight on 18 November 1978.

Production of the initial **F/A-18A Hornet** single-seater eventually totalled 371 aircraft, the first US Navy squadron receiving its aircraft in 1983. Two examples of the **TF-18A**, later redesignated F/A-18B, featured in the original contract. Procurement of the **F/A-18B** for the USN and USMC ended with the fortieth example, and this version has never been employed by frontline forces.

The F/A-18 offers much greater weapons delivery accuracy than its predecessors, and is a genuinely multi-role aircraft, with remarkable dogfighting ability. The F/A-18 made its combat debut during the El Dorado Canyon action against Libya in April 1986 and was heavily committed to action during Operation Desert Storm in 1991. The F/A-18A was superseded by the **F/A-18C**, which remained the principal single-seat production model up to 1999, some 347 having been ordered for US service.

The first F/A-18C made its maiden flight on 3 September 1986. This introduced compatibility with the AIM-120

Mk 83 AIR (Air Inflatable Retard) bombs fall away from a US Marine Corps F/A-18D. The use of IR-decoy flares acts as a defence against IR-homing SAMs.

AMRAAM and the IIR version of the AGM-65 Maverick missile, as well as improved avionics – which from 1994 included the improved APG-73 variant of the Hornet's original APG-65 radar – and a new NACES ejection seat.

SPECIFICATION	
Boeing F/A-18C Hornet	fighter mission or 1065 km
Type: single-seat carrierborne and land-based fighter and strike/ attack warplane	(662 miles) for an attack mission
	Weights: empty 10,810 kg (23,832 lb); maximum take-off 15,234 kg (33,585 lb) for a fighter mission or 21,888 kg (48,753 lb) for an attack mission
Powerplant: two General Electric F404-GE-402 turbofan engines each rated at 78.73 kN (17,700 lb st) with afterburning	
Performance: maximum speed more than 1915 km/h (1,190 mph) or Mach 1.80 at high altitude; initial climb rate 13,715 m (45,000 ft) per minute, combat ceiling about 15,740 m (50,000 ft), radius more than 740 km (460 miles) on a	**Dimensions:** wing span 11.43 m (37 ft 6 in) without tip-mounted missiles; length 17.07 m (56 ft) height 4.66 m (15 ft 3½ in); wing area 37.16 m² (400 sq ft)
	Armament: one internal 20-mm M61A1 Vulcan six-barrel cannon; up to 7031 kg (15,500 lb) of ordnance

Canada's much-depleted CF-188 fleet is involved in anti-narcotics work, as well as the air defence of Canada.

Night attack

After 137 baseline F/A-18Cs had been delivered, production switched to a night-attack version with equipment including GEC Cat's Eye pilot's night-vision goggles compatibility, an AAR-50 TINS (Thermal Imaging Navigation System) pod, Kaiser AVQ-28 raster HUD, externally carried AAS-38 FLIR (Forward-Looking Infra-Red) targeting pod, and colour multi-function displays. The first 'night-attack' Hornet was delivered on 1 November 1989. In addition, some 31 baseline two-seat **F/A-18D** trainers were built before 109 examples of the F/A-18D counterpart to the night-attack F/A-18C were produced. The night-attack version of the F/A-18D replaced the Grumman A-6 Intruder with the USMC's all-weather attack squadrons. Originally dubbed **F/A-18D+**, the aircraft features 'uncoupled' cockpits, usually with no control column in the rear cockpit, but two sidestick weapons controllers. USMC F/A-18Ds served with distinction during combat operations including Desert Storm in 1991 and Allied Force in 1999.

Export sales

The Hornet's versatility has led to substantial export sales. Canada was the first foreign customer, taking delivery of 98 single-seat **CF-188A** and 40 two-seat **CF-188B** aircraft, while Australia followed with an order for 57 **AF-18A** and 18 **ATF-18A** trainers. Spain purchased 60 **EF-18A** and 12 **EF-18B** machines (local designation **C.15** and **CE.15**, respectively) and later acquired 24 former US Navy F/A-18As from late 1995. Kuwait received 32 **KAF-18C** warplanes and eight **KAF-18D** machines, while Switzerland took 26 F/A-18Cs and eight F/A-18Ds. Finland procured a fleet of 57 F/A-18Cs and seven F/A-18Ds, while Malaysia is unique in buying only the F/A-18D, of which eight were ordered.

Setting out on an Enduring Freedom mission, this F/A-18C carries a pair of JDAM (Joint Direct Attack Munition) weapons with Mk 84 warheads. Note the use of four drop tanks – the Hornet has always been plagued by lack of range and has relied heavily on RAF tanker support for Enduring Freedom strikes.

Multi-role 21st-century fleet fighter

Designed as a multi-role fighter to ultimately replace the A-4 Skyhawk, A-7 Corsair II and F-4 Phantom II in US Navy service, the F/A-18 is one of the world's most important – and most impressive – warplanes. Although always outshone by the F-16 in terms of sales won, the Hornet has also achieved considerable export success with air forces worldwide.

SPECIFICATION

F/A-18C Hornet

Dimensions

Length: 17.07 m (56 ft)
Height: 4.66 m (15 ft 3½ in)
Wing span: 11.43 m (37 ft 6 in)
Wing span with tip-mounted AAMs: 12.31 m (40 ft 4¾ in)
Wing span with wings folded: 8.38 m (27 ft 6 in)
Wing area: 37.16 m² (400 sq ft)
Wheel track: 3.11 m (10 ft 2½ in)
Wheelbase: 5.42 m (17ft 9½ in)

Powerplant

Two General Electric F404-GE-402 turbofans each rated at 78.73 kN (17,700 lb st) with afterburning

Weights

Empty: 10,455 kg (23,050 lb)
Take-off: 16,652 kg (36,710 lb) for a fighter mission or 23,541 kg (51,900 lb) on an attack mission
Maximum take-off: about 25,401 kg (56,000 lb)

Fuel and load

Internal fuel: 4926 kg (10,860 lb)
External fuel: up to 3053 kg (6,732 lb) in three 1250-litre (330-US gal) drop tanks
Maximum ordnance load: 7031 kg (15,500 lb) on nine external stores stations

Performance

Maximum level speed 'clean' at high altitude: more than 1915 km/h (1,190 mph)
Maximum rate of climb at sea level: 13,715 m (45,000 ft) per minute
Combat ceiling: about 15,240 m (50,000 ft)
Take-off run at maximum take-off weight: less than 427 m (1,400 ft)
Approach speed: 248 km/h (154 mph)
Acceleration from 850 km/h (530 mph) to 1705 km/h (1060 mph) at 10,670 m (35,000 ft): under two minutes

Range

Ferry range with drop tanks: more than 3336 km (2,073 miles)

Combat radius: more than 740 km (460 miles) on a fighter mission, or 1065 km (662 miles) on an attack mission, or 537 km (340 miles) on a hi-lo-hi interdiction mission

Armament

Gun: M61A1 Vulcan 20-mm cannon with 570 rounds
Air-to-air missiles: AIM-120 AMRAAM; AIM-7 Sparrow; AIM-9 Sidewinder
Precision-guided munitions: AGM-65 Maverick; AGM-84 Harpoon; AGM-84E SLAM; AGM-88 HARM; AGM-62 Walleye EO- (Electro-Optic) guided bomb; AGM-123 Skipper; AGM-154 JSOW; GBU-10/12/16 laser-guided bombs; GBU-30/31/32 JDAM
Unguided munitions: B57 and B61 tactical nuclear bombs; Mk 80 series general-purpose bombs; Mk 7 dispenser (including Mk 20 Rockeye II, CBU-59, CBU-72 FAE, CBU-78 Gator mine dispenser); LAU-97 Zuni FFAR pods

Radar

Hughes AN/APG-65 or AN/APG-73
Effective radar range: more than 185 km (115 miles)

F/A-18B/D Hornet

Type: two-seat, multi-role, attack fighter and trainer generally similar to the F/A-18A/C Hornet except

Weights

Normal take-off: 15,234 kg (33,585 lb) on a fighter mission
Maximum take-off for an attack mission: 21,319 kg (47,000 lb)

Fuel and load

Internal fuel reduced by less than six per cent to accommodate second seat

Range

Ferry range with internal and external fuel: 3520 km (2,187 miles)
Combat radius: 1020 km (634 miles)

Above: With one of the most coveted seats in US naval aviation, the F/A-18 had the most advanced cockpit in service when it appeared. Three monochrome CRTs (cathode ray tubes) and HOTAS (hands on throttle and stick) controls – the latter allowing head-up operation – were among its features. Subsequent developments have seen the introduction of colour displays and revised avionics.

In frontline US Navy service since 1985, with the introduction of the F/A-18E (illustrated) and two-seat F/A-18F Super Hornet, the type regains its position as the world's premier carrierborne warplane.

F/A-18A Hornet

This VMFA-314 F/A-18A was based aboard USS *Coral Sea* during attacks on Libyan SAM sites during Operations El Dorado Canyon and Prairie Fire in 1986. These operations marked the combat debut of both the Hornet and the AGM-88 HARM missile, one of which is seen being launched by this aircraft. For the duration of their cruise as part of CVW-13 aboard *Coral Sea*, VMFA-314's aircraft wore the 'AK' tailcodes of the Air Wing, rather than their own 'VW' codes.

VFA-115 was the US Navy's first frontline F/A-18E squadron. The Super Hornet will replace many of the older F/A-18C aircraft in service and will completely oust the F-14 Tomcat. Assuming that the EA-18G programme comes to fruition, it will also take over the Prowler's role and it also has a useful capability as an inflight refuelling tanker, allowing it to take over some of the missions of the Lockheed Viking.

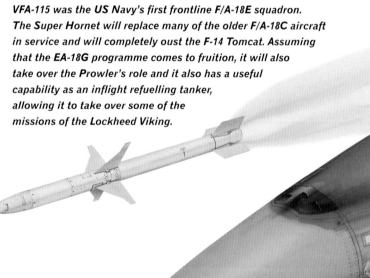

Radar and cannon
The F/A-18A, two-seat B and early-production C-model aircraft were fitted with a Hughes AN/APG-65 multi-mode radar set; later F/A-18C, D, E and F-model machines have the more capable APG-73, which boasts faster processing and a larger memory. Also mounted in the nose of the aircraft is a General Electric M61A1 Vulcan 20-mm rotary cannon with 570 rounds of ammunition. Another weapon that dates from the 1950s, the Vulcan has a 6000-round-per-minute rate of fire and has equipped numerous US combat types.

Work continues on the EA-18G Growler. This aircraft is based on the F/A-18F and adds podded and internal equipment suitable for the jamming missions currently undertaken by the hard-pressed US Navy/US Marine Corps EA-6B Prowler fleet.

Fly-by-wire controls

Digital fly-by-wire controls manipulate the outboard ailerons and differential tailerons for roll control (aided by drooping flaperons at low speed), twin rudders for yaw and tailerons for pitch. For take-off and landing, the rudders are automatically toed-in to provide a nose-up pitch moment. Trailing- and leading-edge flaps are automatically programmed for optimum performance for both low-speed lift and high-speed manoeuvring. Advanced materials are used extensively in the Hornet's structure. For example, the all-moving horizontal tailplanes are constructed from a carbon-graphite epoxy over a light alloy honeycomb core with titanium alloy root fittings.

Powerplant

For the initial versions of the F/A-18, General Electric developed the F404 afterburning low-bypass turbofan, rated at 71.2 or 78.3 kN (16,000 lb or 17,700 lb thrust), with afterburning, depending on the variant. Derived from the YJ101 engine in the YF-17, the powerplant has proved reliable and fuel-efficient. Fuel is fed from four main tanks in the aircraft's spine, which hold 5300 litres (1,400 US gal) in total. External fuel may be carried in 1249-litre (330-US gal) drop tanks on wing pylons. For the redesigned F/A-18E/F, a more powerful F404 derivative has been developed. The F414-GE-400, producing 97.9 kN (22,000 lb st) with a new afterburner, is closely related to the F412 turbofan intended for the ill-fated A-12 Avenger II.

Wingtip launch rail and FLIR pods

The wingtip launch rail is usually used to carry an AIM-9M Sidewinder heating-seeking air-to-air missile (AAM) as illustrated here. Like the AIM-7 Sparrow, the AIM-9 was developed, originally for the US Navy, in the early 1950s. The most widely used and most successful AAM in the world, this short-range missile is still in production. It will eventually be replaced on the F/A-18C/D and F/A-18E/F by the AIM-9X. The F/A-18's wingtip rails may also be used for AIM-120 AMRAAMs, although these are generally carried on the underwing or fuselage shoulder hardpoints. Although the AMRAAM is part of the Hornet's regular inventory, the older AIM-7M also remains in service. Another typical wingtip store is an ACMI (Air Combat Manoeuvring Instrumentation) pod, used when training on suitably equipped ranges. Useful night/all-weather capability is available with the AN/AAS-38 NITE Hawk forward-looking infrared (FLIR) pod, AAS-38A NITE Hawk FLIR-LTD/R (which adds a laser designating and ranging capability) or AAS-38B (with laser spot tracker). One of these occupies the port shoulder Sparrow/AMRAAM station when carried. The FLIR provides real-time thermal imagery on a TV-type display in the cockpit for target detection and tracking. Linked to the aircraft's computer, it can provide accurate line-of-sight angles and rates of angle change. The two-seat F/A-18D Night Attack Hornet, employed by USMC all-weather attack units, can also use an AN/AAR-50 navigation/FLIR pod for low-level night flying, on the starboard station.

Although the F/A-18E is now established in service and available for combat operations, the F/A-18C (illustrated) will remain an important frontline US Navy warplane for some time to come. Indeed, some units will relinquish their F/A-18Cs for Lockheed Martin F-35s. In USMC service, the F/A-18D is the primary combat type, assigned an all-weather attack role.

Boeing F/A-18E/F Super Hornet

VFA-122 'Fighting Eagles'
VFA-122 brought the Super Hornet into US Navy fleet service on 15 January 1999.

Weapons
This aircraft is equipped with a typical SEAD warload of AGM-88 HARMs, AGM-154 JSOWs (Joint Stand-Off Weapons dispensers) and AIM-9s.

The first of McDonnell Douglas's (Boeing from 1997) Hornet upgrade concepts to reach fruition is the **F/A-18E Super Hornet**. The first F/A-18E made its maiden flight in November 1995 and the first aircraft was formally accepted into service with the US Navy's VFA-122 on 15 January 1999.

New avionics

The avionics upgrade is centred on the Raytheon APG-73 radar as already fitted to late versions of the F/A-18C. The IDECM (integrated defensive electronic countermeasures) system has three major elements: an ALR-67(V)3 RWR, ALQ-214 radio-frequency counter-measures system and ALE-55 fibre-optic towed decoy system; the last two are still under development, so the F/A-18E is

initially being operated with the ALE-50 towed decoy system. The cockpit of the F/A-18E is similar to that of the F/A-18C, with the exception of a larger flat-panel display in place of the current three HDDs (head-down displays).

A bigger bug

The F/A-18E's enlarged airframe incorporates measures to reduce radar cross-section and includes a fuselage lengthened by 0.86 m (2 ft 10 in), an enlarged wing characterized by a thicker section and two more hardpoints, enlarged LERXes, and horizontal and vertical tail surfaces. The Super Hornet also has a structure extensively redesigned to reduce weight and cost without sacrifice of strength. The Super Hornet also features a new quadruplex

digital 'fly-by-wire' control system without the Hornet's mechanical back-up system.

The **F/A-18F Super Hornet** is the two-seat development of the F/A-18E, with the rear cockpit equipped with the same displays as the front cockpit and otherwise configured for alternative combat or training roles. The US Navy had originally planned to procure 1000 Super Hornets, but in 1997 the total was reduced to 548. Any delay in the service debut of the F-35 to a time later than 2008–2010,

Boeing is supplying the Super Hornet to replace the US Navy's F-14 Tomcats, many of its Hornets and, perhaps, the EA-6B.

however, will see the number of Super Hornets rise to 748.

An F/A-18F electronic combat variant has been proposed as a replacement for the Grumman EA-6B Prowler. This aircraft will be capable of active jamming, as well as lethal SEAD (suppression of enemy air defences), and is known in service as the **EA-18 Growler**.

*An **F/A-18F** (upper) and **F/A-18C** cavort during testing. The Super Hornet is most easily distinguished from the Hornet by means of its square intakes and enlarged **LERXes** (Leading Edge Root Extensions).*

SPECIFICATION

Boeing F/A-18E Super Hornet
Type: single-seat carrierborne and land-based multi-role fighter, attack and maritime air superiority warplane
Powerplant: two General Electric F414-GE-400 turbofan engines each rated at 97.86 kN (22,000 lb st) with afterburning
Performance: maximum speed more than 1915 km/h (1,190 mph) or Mach 1.80 at high altitude; service ceiling about 15,240 m (50,000 ft); radius 1095 km (681 miles) on a hi-hi-hi interdiction mission with four 454-kg (1,000-lb) bombs, two AIM-9 Sidewinder AAMs and two drop tanks; 1901 km (560 miles) on a hi-lo-hi interdiction mission with the same stores, or 278 km (173 miles) on a 135-minute maritime air superiority mission with six AAMs and three drop tanks
Weights: empty 13,864 kg (30,564 lb); maximum take-off

29,937 kg (66,000 lb)
Dimensions: wing span 13.62 m (44 ft 8½ in) including tip-mounted AAMs; length 18.31 m (60 ft 1¼ in); height 4.88 m (16 ft); wing area 46.45 m^2 (500 sq ft)
Armament: one 20-mm M61A2 Vulcan rotary six-barrel cannon with 570 rounds, plus up to 8051 kg (17,750 lb) of disposable stores, including the 10/20-kiloton B57 and 100/500-kiloton B61 freefall nuclear weapons, AIM-120 AMRAAM, AIM 7 Sparrow and AIM-9 Sidewinder AAMs, AGM-88 HARM, AGM-65 Maverick ASM, AGM-84 Harpoon anti-ship missile, AGM-62 Walleye optronically-guided glide bomb, Paveway LGBs, Mk 80 series bombs, Rockeye and CBU-series cluster bombs, BLU-series napalm bombs and LAU-series multiple launchers for 2.75-in (70-mm) air-to-surface unguided rockets

Northrop Grumman E-2 Hawkeye
Carrier- and land-based AEW&C aircraft

This E-2C Hawkeye is from the US Navy's VAW-126 'Seahawks', and is illustrated as it appeared when operating from USS John F. Kennedy *during the late 1990s.*

Since entering service in 1964, the **E-2 Hawkeye** has protected US Navy carrier battle groups and acted as an airborne controller for their aircraft. One of very few types designed specifically for the AEW role, it was first flown in prototype form as long ago as October 1960. As a consequence of its ability to operate from aircraft carriers, the basic **Hawkeye** is extremely compact. A total of 59 production **E-2A** machines was delivered from January 1964; 51 were updated to **E-2B** standard, before production switched to the improved **E-2C**.

E-2C Hawkeye

The first E-2C made its maiden flight on 23 September 1972.

Grumman had built 139 for the US Navy when the line closed in 1994; however, low-rate production began again in 2000.

External changes to the E-2 have been minor, but its systems have been progressively updated. The E-2C was initially equipped with APS-125 search radar, but this was replaced by the AN/APS-139 in **Group I** aircraft from 1988 and the AN/APS-145 in the latest **Group II E-2C**. The latter radar allows a low-flying, fighter-sized aircraft to be detected at up to 407 km (253 miles) away with the E-2C flying at its operational altitude. A passive detection system gives warning of hostile emitters at ranges up to twice the radar detection range.

The E-2C is still an evolving design after almost 30 years in service, and Northrop Grumman developed the even more capable **E-2C Group II Plus** or **Hawkeye 2000**; the first of 25 such new-build machines was delivered in October 2001. Subsequent to Hawkeye 2000, Northrop Grumman began developing the

Advanced Hawkeye, featuring all new systems. This should reach initial operational capability with the US Navy in 2011. The navy plans to buy 75 of these aircraft. E-2Cs have been exported to Egypt, France, Israel, Japan, Singapore and Taiwan. Many customers are upgrading their E-2s to Hawkeye 2000 standards.

Hawkeye 2000 (illustrated) represented a major increase in the E-2 design's capabilities. Advanced Hawkeye will look very similar.

SPECIFICATION	
Northrop Grumman E-2C Hawkeye (Group I configuration onwards) **Type:** carrierborne AEW aircraft **Powerplant:** two Allison T56-A-427 turboprops each rated at 3803 kW (5,100 ehp) **Performance:** maximum level speed 626 km/h (389 mph); maximum cruising speed at optimum altitude 602 km/h (374 mph); maximum rate of climb at sea level over 767 m (2,515 ft) per minute; service ceiling 11,275 m (37,000 ft);	unrefuelled time on station at 320 km (200 miles) from base 4 hours 24 minutes; endurance with maximum fuel 6 hours 15 minutes **Weights:** empty 18,363 kg (40,484 lb); maximum take-off 24,687 kg (54,426 lb) **Dimensions:** wing span 24.56 m (80 ft 7 in); folded width 8.94 m (29 ft 4 in); rotodome diameter 7.32 m (24 ft); length 17.54 m (57 ft 6¾ in); height 5.58 m (18 ft 3¾ in); wing area 65.03 m² (700 sq ft)

Lockheed Martin F-35B and F-35C Future tactical fighters

On 26 October 2001, the US government announced that Lockheed Martin had won the JSF (Joint Strike Fighter) competition in the face of stiff opposition from Boeing. The JSF requirement was set out to provide a largely common air frame to fulfil three distinct niches: a CTOL aircraft for the USAF, a carrier-capable aircraft for the US Navy and a STOVL machine for the USMC.

X-35 in detail

Lockheed Martin's **X-35** demonstrators will form the basis of the operational **F-35** fighters, with the first F-35 flight planned for 2005 and the **F-35C** due to enter US Navy service around 2012. F-35C will have a longer-span wing than the other initial variants, with provision for folding. The aircraft will also be fitted with an arrester hook and strengthened landing gear, these and other modifications making it heavier than the CTOL F-35A. All F-35s will primarily carry their armament internally, in bays along the fuselage sides. Stealth was a major design consideration and the aircraft has been carefully shaped to avoid producing large radar-reflecting surfaces. Doors,

apertures and other panels generally have serrated edges, similar to those on the F-117.

UK involvement

From an early stage, the United Kingdom has been a full partner in the JSF programme. Like the USMC, it has opted for the STOVL **F-35B**. All F-35 models will initially be powered by the Pratt & Whitney F135 turbofans, delivering around 178 kN (40,000 lb thrust) with after-

burning and exhausting through a vectoring nozzle. On the F-35B, a lift fan, developed by Rolls-Royce and mounted horizontally in the forward fuselage, is driven by the main engine via a gearbox to provide the major part of the thrust needed in vertical manoeuvres. The United Kingdom will base its F-35Bs on two new

Pictured in the hover, the X-35B demonstrates the large doors in its upper fuselage. These open to feed air to the lift fan.

BAE Systems/Thales aircraft carriers due to enter service in 2012 and 2015. Export orders for F-35C are unlikely, but F-35B may find a limited market.

The X-35C is immediately recognisable as a naval fighter demonstrator, thanks to the prominent arrester hook mounted beneath its rear fuselage.

Lockheed S-3 Viking Multi-role naval aircraft

The **S-3B Viking** carries out the US Navy's carrier-based sea control mission. The S-3 was originally designed in the early 1970s with a sophisticated ASW

sensor suite. The initial **S-3A** variant was replaced in the early 1990s by the S-3B. This incorporates anti-surface warfare upgrades such as the APS-137

inverse synthetic aperture radar and AGM-84 AShM capability. With the demise of the Soviet Union and increasing dominance of littoral warfare, there has

been decreased emphasis on the Viking's ASW role and more emphasis on anti-surface warfare and land-attack missions. Each carrier air wing includes one sea

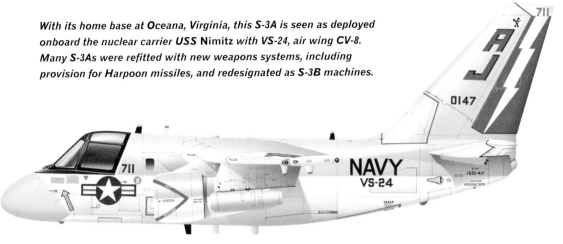

With its home base at Oceana, Virginia, this S-3A is seen as deployed onboard the nuclear carrier USS Nimitz with VS-24, air wing CV-8. Many S-3As were refitted with new weapons systems, including provision for Harpoon missiles, and redesignated as S-3B machines.

including the addition of GPS, Carrier Aircraft Inertial Navigation System II, new tactical displays, computer memory, SATCOM equipment and improved radios. Several S-3Bs have been involved in anti-drug trafficking duties, using camera systems, FLIR and hand-held sensors.

The S-3B is planned for replacement from 2015 by a variant of the Common Support Aircraft, but may be retired on an accelerated schedule.

Shadow

Sixteen S-3A airframes were converted to **ES-3A Shadow** standard during the early 1990s, with a variety of electronic surveillance and intercept equipment to locate and identify hostile emitters and communications stations. In mid-1998, the US Navy decided to withdraw the ES-3A from service without replacement, as upgrade was deemed too costly.

SPECIFICATION	
Lockheed S-3A Viking	(26,650 lb); maximum take-off
Type: four-crew carrierborne ASW warplane	23,832 kg (52,540 lb)
Powerplant: two General Electric TF34-GE-2 turbofan engines each rated at 41.26 kN (9,275 lb st)	**Dimensions:** wing span 20.93 m (68 ft 8 in); length 16.26 m (53 ft 4 in); height 6.63 m (22 ft 9 in); wing area 55.56 m² (598 sq ft)
Performance: maximum speed 814 km/h (506 mph) at sea level; initial climb rate more than 1280 m (4,200 ft) per minute; service ceiling more than 10,670 m (35,000 ft); radius 853 km (530 miles) with typical weapons load and a loiter of 4 hours 30 minutes	**Armament:** up to 3175 kg (7,000 lb) of disposable stores, including B57 or Mk 80-series bombs, Mk 53 mines, Mk 54 depth bombs, Mk 46 or Mk 53 Barracuda torpedoes, six Mk 20 Mod 2 Rockeye cluster bombs or LAU-10A/A, LAU-61/A, LAU-68/A or LAU-69/A rocket launchers
Weights: empty 12,088 kg	

control (VS) squadron equipped with S-3Bs. VS squadrons perform ASW, anti-shipping, mine-laying, surveillance and tanking missions for the carrier battle group. This latter mission is accomplished thanks to the D-704 'buddy-buddy' refuelling store, which incorporates a retractable hose for compatibility with the USN's probe-equipped combat aircraft. Several upgrades have been applied to the Viking,

Above: As a force multiplier, the S-3B Viking is a crucial US Navy asset. It is ultimately likely to lose its inflight-refuelling role to the F/A-18E/F.

Left: As a multi-role support type, the Viking continues to have an important frontline role. This Hornet is seen receiving fuel during an Iraqi Freedom mission.

Tupolev Tu-16 'Badger'
Maritime missile and recce variants

Many variants of the Tu-16 'Badger' were produced for the AV-MF either by new building or conversion. By far the majority of these were stand-off missile carriers tasked primarily with anti-shipping work, or various reconnaissance platforms.

Missile launchers

The first anti-shipping missile-carrying variant of the Tu-16, the **Tu-16KS**, was given the ASCC/NATO designation **'Badger-B'**. A minimum-change adaptation of the basic bomber, it was fitted with a radar altimeter and a missile-control radar in a retractable radome housed in the weapons bay. Its principal weapon was the large KS-1 Komet, known to NATO as the AS-1 'Kennel', one of which could be carried under each wing. The KS-1 became operational with the AV-MF in the late 1950s. Twenty-five 'Kennel'-armed 'Badger-Bs' were exported to Indonesia, the survivors being put into storage in the 1970s.

The **Tu-16K-10 'Badger-C'** was first seen at the 1961 Aviation Day display. Its major external difference from earlier Tu-16s was the addition of a large flat radome for a new radar system. 'Puff Ball' was an I-Band surface surveillance, target acquisition and designation radar with a range of about 250 km (155 miles). It was designed to operate with the K-10 (AS-2 'Kipper') supersonic AShM, which could carry a one-tonne warhead about 180 km (112 miles).

Next in line of the variants came the **Tu-16K-11-16 'Badger-G'**, which was a rebuilt 'Badger-B' equipped to carry two KSR-2 or KSR-11 (AS-5 'Kelt') missiles. The supersonic 'Kelt' weighed three tonnes and had a range of more than 300 km (186 miles). 'Badger-G' replaced the retractable radar of the 'B' with a new chin radar, leaving the bomb bay free for the carriage of conventional weaponry. 'Badger-Gs' have seen action with Egypt and Iraq.

Perhaps the most formidable of the anti-ship 'Badgers' were those which were equipped to fire the supersonic KSR-5 (AS-6 'Kingfish'). This Mach-3 weapon has a range in excess of 500 km (311 miles), and can carry a one-tonne conventional warhead or a nuclear warhead with a yield in the 350-kT range. Both the Tu-16K-10-based **Tu-16K-10-26 'Badger-C Mod'** and **Tu-16K-26 'Badger-G Mod'** were KSR-5 launchers, the latter having a new guidance radar in a large belly radome in front of the bomb bay.

The first of the dedicated reconnaissance Tu-16s identified by NATO was the **Tu-16Ye 'Badger-D'**. This was an Elint conversion most often based on redundant Tu-16KS airframes. It retained its predecessor's distinctive broad, flattened nose radome, although the chin radome was replaced by a slightly larger item. Three passive antenna blisters were added along the centreline and the crew complement was

*Mikoyan-Gurevich developed the impressive **KS-1 missile** which armed Tu-16KS aircraft in service from 1957. The weapon clearly owed much to the MiG-15 fighter.*

SPECIFICATION

Tupolev Tu-16KS 'Badger-B'
Type: twin-jet anti-shipping aircraft
Powerplant: two MNPK 'Soyuz' (Mikulin) AM-3A turbojets each rated at 85.22 kN (19,185 lb st)
Performance: maximum level speed 'clean' at 6000 m (19,685 ft) about 1050 km/h (652 mph); maximum rate of climb at sea level about 1250 m (4,101 ft) per minute; service ceiling 12,800 m (41,995 ft); radius 1800 km (1,128 miles) with two missiles
Weights: empty equipped about

37200 kg (82,012 lb); maximum take-off about 75800 kg (167,110 lb)
Dimensions: wing span 32.93 m (108 ft ½ in); length 36.25 m (118 ft 11¼ in); height 14 m (45 ft 11½ in); wing area 164.65 m² (1,772.34 sq ft)
Armament: two KS-1 Komet (AS-1 'Kennel') or KSR-2 or KSR-11 (AS-5 'Kelt') stand-off anti-shipping missiles, defensive armament of forward and rear ventral barbettes each containing two 23-mm NR-23 guns and two similar weapons in tail position

increased to eight or nine by equipment operators.

PR and EW 'Badgers'

The **Tu-16R 'Badger-E'** was a dedicated naval photo-reconnaissance aircraft in day/night versions. It had provision for a camera/sensor pallet inside the former bomb bay and could also perform EW missions, and carried two widely spaced passive receiver antennas under the fuselage. The **Tu-16P 'Badger-F'** was similar in appearance, but had large equipment pods on its underwing pylons and sometimes carried prominent blade antennas above and below the fuselage. The aircraft were modified Tu-16KS airframes, and their various antenna configurations also earned them the reporting names **'Badger-K'** and **'Badger-L'**.

Other EW variants included the **Tu-16PM 'Badger-L'** with a

thimble radome mounted in its transparent nosecone, and an unknown number of Tu-16A and Tu-16KS aircraft were converted to serve as **Tu-16PP 'Badger-H'** ECM escorts. 'Badger-Hs' were seen with a variety of antenna configurations, but most had a large hemispherical radome on the centreline, immediately aft of the former bomb bay. Passive receivers were used to detect hostile emissions, analyse threat priorities and cut strips of chaff to an appropriate length according to the frequency of the enemy signal. Carrying up to nine tonnes of chaff in special containers in the former bomb bay, together with a chaff cutter and dispenser, the 'Badger-H' released its anti-radar material through three slightly swept chutes along the centreline.

The **Tu-16RM 'Badger-J'** was a specific AV-MF active ECM jammer with a distinctive ventral canoe fairing, housing radomes for the noise, spot, click and barrage jammers and covering the A- to I-bands. Ram air inlets alongside the canoe provided cooling air for the black boxes in the ex-bomb bay. 'Badger-J' also had flat plate antennas on its wingtips.

By the middle of the 1990s, about 80 recce and ECM Tu-16s remained in AV-MF service, along with some 70 Tu-16N tankers and a few missile-carriers. At that time the Russian air force had reduced its 'Badger' force to a single squadron of Tu-16Rs. Belarus retained another squadron, and some 53 of these aircraft served in the Ukraine.

By mid-2003, the Tu-16 had been phased out of service in Belarus, Russia and the Ukraine. However, China's navy had a fleet of about 10 licence-built **H-6 III** attack aircraft and 20 H-6 tankers.

It is worth noting that the AV-MF also used Tu-16T 'Badger-A' torpedo bombers and, later, 65 Tu-16S 'Badger-A' SAR conversions of Tu-16Ts.

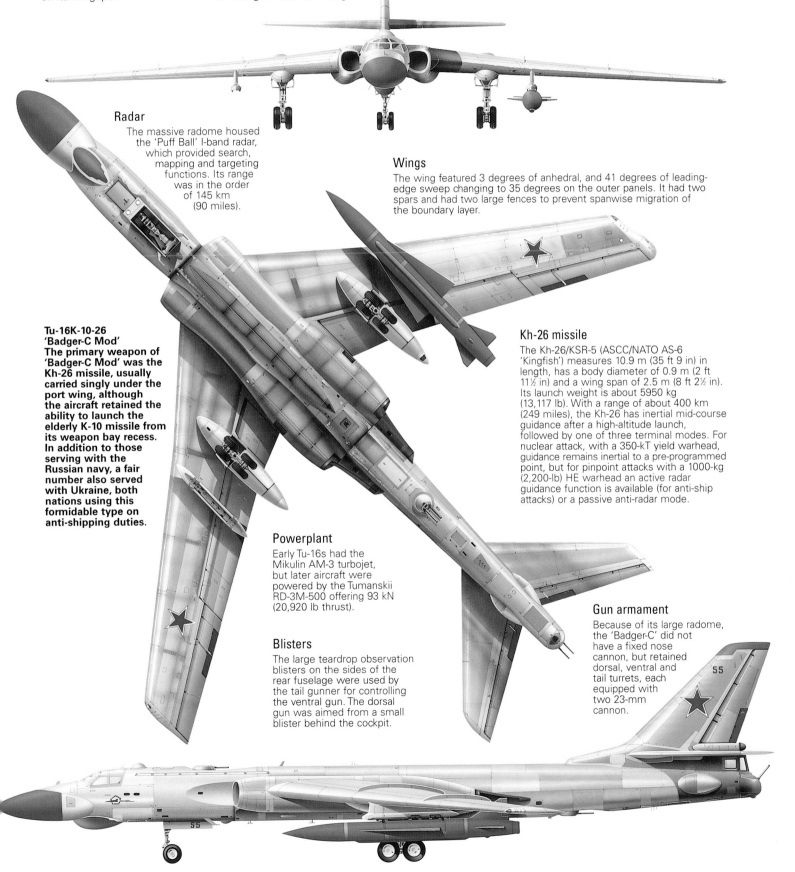

Radar
The massive radome housed the 'Puff Ball' I-band radar, which provided search, mapping and targeting functions. Its range was in the order of 145 km (90 miles).

Wings
The wing featured 3 degrees of anhedral, and 41 degrees of leading-edge sweep changing to 35 degrees on the outer panels. It had two spars and had two large fences to prevent spanwise migration of the boundary layer.

Tu-16K-10-26 'Badger-C Mod'
The primary weapon of 'Badger-C Mod' was the Kh-26 missile, usually carried singly under the port wing, although the aircraft retained the ability to launch the elderly K-10 missile from its weapon bay recess. In addition to those serving with the Russian navy, a fair number also served with Ukraine, both nations using this formidable type on anti-shipping duties.

Kh-26 missile
The Kh-26/KSR-5 (ASCC/NATO AS-6 'Kingfish') measures 10.9 m (35 ft 9 in) in length, has a body diameter of 0.9 m (2 ft 11½ in) and a wing span of 2.5 m (8 ft 2½ in). Its launch weight is about 5950 kg (13,117 lb). With a range of about 400 km (249 miles), the Kh-26 has inertial mid-course guidance after a high-altitude launch, followed by one of three terminal modes. For nuclear attack, with a 350-kT yield warhead, guidance remains inertial to a pre-programmed point, but for pinpoint attacks with a 1000-kg (2,200-lb) HE warhead an active radar guidance function is available (for anti-ship attacks) or a passive anti-radar mode.

Powerplant
Early Tu-16s had the Mikulin AM-3 turbojet, but later aircraft were powered by the Tumanskii RD-3M-500 offering 93 kN (20,920 lb thrust).

Blisters
The large teardrop observation blisters on the sides of the rear fuselage were used by the tail gunner for controlling the ventral gun. The dorsal gun was aimed from a small blister behind the cockpit.

Gun armament
Because of its large radome, the 'Badger-C' did not have a fixed nose cannon, but retained dorsal, ventral and tail turrets, each equipped with two 23-mm cannon.

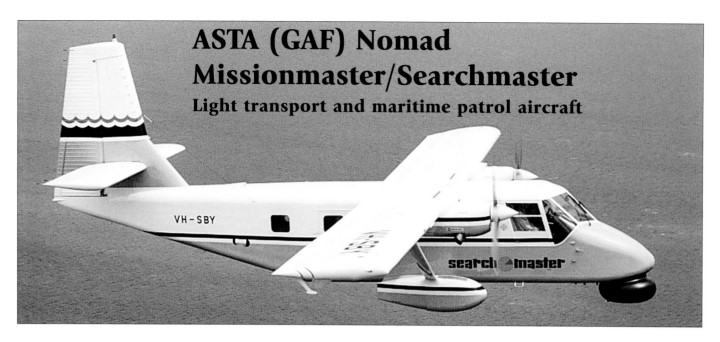

ASTA (GAF) Nomad Missionmaster/Searchmaster
Light transport and maritime patrol aircraft

The **ASTA** (**Aerospace Technologies of Australia** [PTY] Ltd, previously **Government Aircraft Factory** [GAF]) **Nomad** was the product of a mid-1960s effort to provide Australia with an indigenous twin-engined STOL utility aircraft with military and civil potential. The aircraft was built in **N22** and **N24** versions with different fuselage lengths. The basic N22 (and **N22B** with increased weights) seated 12, whereas the N24 could accommodate 17.

Military transport and maritime surveillance versions were marketed under the names **Missionmaster** and **Searchmaster**, respectively. The former has wing hardpoints for weapons and load-bearing drop-doors in the cabin floor; the latter carries search radar, either Bendix RDR-1400 in the nose (designated as the **Searchmaster B**) or Litton APS-504(V)2 in an undernose radome (as the **Searchmaster L**).

Nomad operators

Production of the Nomad series ended in 1984 with 170 built, including 40 **N24A** aircraft, the first of which made its maiden flight on 23 July 1971. Some 25 Missionmasters were delivered to the Australian military, and the survivors remained in service until 1995. At this time, the type was withdrawn as a result of its poor safety record and structural problems which prevented full flap deflection, therefore making STOL operations impossible. Twenty of these retired aircraft were subsequently sold to the Indonesian navy. The Philippine air force is another user of the transport Nomad, having acquired 12 Missionmasters for the 223rd Tactical Squadron in the 220th Heavy Airlift Wing. Around eight of these machines remained in service into 2003, all of the four Searchmasters that were acquired separately.

The Royal Thai air force took a total of 22 N22B Missionmasters

With its undernose radar antenna, the Searchmaster is able to provide 360-degree radar coverage. The aircraft has proven useful in the fisheries protection role.

for the counter-insurgency role. These were shared between Nos 461 and 462 Squadrons in 46 Wing at Phitsanulok and No. 605 Sqn in 6 Wing at Don Muang. Acquired in 1982/83, some were immediately pressed into service as gunships (possibly with cabin-mounted machine guns) to replace ageing AC-47s. About 19 remained in service early in 2003. Searchmasters are used by the Indonesian navy, as are transport-dedicated Missionmasters. The 2003 fleet of around 39 aircraft included some of those retired by Australia. With Australian aid, the Papua New Guinea defence force received up to seven assorted Nomad models and was operating three Missionmasters and a Searchmaster B in 2003. The latter is used on Economic Exclusion Zone (EEZ) patrols.

SPECIFICATION	
ASTA (GAF) N22B Searchmaster L **Type:** maritime patrol aircraft **Powerplant:** two Allison 250-B17C turboprops each rated at 313 kW (420 shp) **Performance:** normal cruising speed at optimum altitude 311 km/h (193 mph); maximum rate of climb at sea level 445 m (1,460 ft) per minute; service ceiling 6400 m (21,000 ft); range	1353 km (841 miles) **Weights:** manufacturer's empty 2092 kg (4,613 lb); maximum take-off 4127 kg (9,100 lb) **Dimensions:** wing span 16.52 m (54 ft 2¼ in); length 12.56 m (41 ft 2½ in); height 5.52 m (18 ft 1½ in); wing area 30.1 m² (324 sq ft) **Armament:** maximum ordnance 907 kg (2,000 lb)

Harbin SH-5 (PS-5) Multi-role flying boat

Developed in China on the basis of the wings and powerplant of the Y-8 (Chinese-built An-12 'Cub') combined with the empennage of the Be-12 'Mail' and a new fuselage/hull combination clearly owing much to that of Japan's US-1A, the **SH-5** (**Shuihong**, or **Shuishang Hongzhaji**, or

maritime bomber; **PS-5** in Westernized form) is a substantial flying boat of all-metal construction with a single-step hull and retractable tricycle beaching gear with single-wheel main units and a twin-wheel nose unit. The wing has a flat, constant-chord centre section

that includes the inner two engines, then increasing anhedral on the two tapered outer panels on each side.

Multi-role 'boat

The type first flew in April 1976, but entered service only in 1986 as the Chinese navy's dedicated

maritime reconnaissance/anti-submarine flying boat with a flight crew of five, a mission crew of three (expandable when required) or, in the 'boat's secondary transport role, passengers and/or freight. The SH-5 has two 23-mm Type-23-1 cannon, and is also able to carry

SPECIFICATION

Harbin SH-5

Type: eight-crew maritime reconnaissance flying-boat with anti-submarine, anti-ship, air/sea rescue and transport capabilities
Powerplant: four Dongan (DEMC) Wojiang-5A1 turboprop engines each rated at 2349 kW (3,150 hp)
Performance: maximum speed 555 km/h (345 mph) at optimum altitude; cruising speed 450 km/h (280 mph) at optimum altitude; patrol speed 230 km/h (143 mph) at optimum altitude; service ceiling 10,250 m (33,630 ft); range 4750 km (2,951 miles); endurance between 12 and 15 hours on two engines

Weights: empty less than 25,000 kg (55,115 lb) equipped for SAR and transport roles, or 26,500 kg (58,422 lb) for ASW role; maximum take-off 45,000 kg (99,206 lb)
Dimensions: wing span 36 m (118 ft 1¼ in); length 38.9 m (127 ft 7½ in); height 9.8 m (32 ft 2 in); wing area 144 m² (1,550.05 sq ft)
Armament: two 23-mm Type 23-1 trainable rearward-firing cannon in a power-operated dorsal turret, plus up to 6000 kg (13,228 lb) of disposable stores
Payload: passengers or 10,000 kg (22,046 lb) of freight

up to 6000 kg (13,228 lb) of disposable stores in a lower-fuselage weapons bay and on four underwing hardpoints.

Development was seriously delayed by the Cultural Revolution, explaining in part why a type that entered service comparatively recently has an elderly engine type and

Known to the West as the PS-5, the SH-5 was in service in the early part of 2003 to the extent of no more than four examples.

unpressurized accommodation. This last is no hindrance in the SH-5's low-altitude patrol regime, but means that transit flights between base and any distant operational area have to be flown at fairly low altitude and reduced speed. Perhaps only seven SH-5s were completed; the in-service fleet seems to be diminishing.

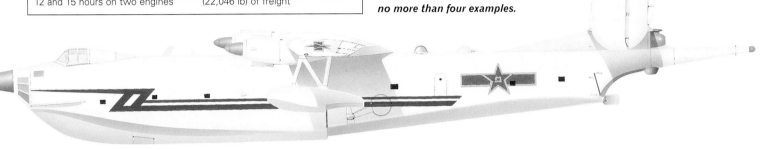

Breguet Atlantic 1 and Dassault Atlantique 2
Specialized maritime patrol aircraft

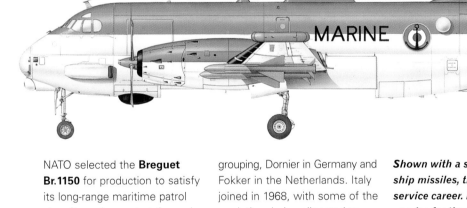

NATO selected the **Breguet Br.1150** for production to satisfy its long-range maritime patrol aircraft requirement at the end of 1958. The aircraft was called **Atlantic**, later altered to **Atlantic 1** after development of the **Atlantique 2**. The Atlantic was the first combat aircraft to be designed and built as a multinational project.

Responsibility for production was given to the specially created SECBAT (Société d'Etudes et de Construction du Breguet Atlantic). The original consortium members, led by Breguet, comprised Sud-Aviation, the Belgian ABAP

grouping, Dornier in Germany and Fokker in the Netherlands. Italy joined in 1968, with some of the work then being allocated to Aeritalia. A similar multinational organization was set up to build the Rolls-Royce Tyne engine.

The Atlantic incorporates a 'double-bubble' fuselage with a pressurized upper deck and a MAD boom extending rearward from the tail, a conventional tail unit with an ECM pod at the tip of the fin and two Tynes in wing-mounted nacelles.

Suitable for anti-ship, coastal recce, search and rescue, fleet escort, logistic support, freight

Shown with a somewhat unlikely external load of four Exocet anti-ship missiles, this Atlantique 2 is typical of the type early in its service career. France will retain the Atlantique 2 in front-line service for the foreseeable future.

and passenger transport and minelaying roles, the Atlantic was designed primarily for the ASW (anti-submarine) role. As such, it is equipped with sonobuoys and Thomson-CSF search radar.

For attack, the Atlantic carries bombs, depth charges and homing torpedoes in its weapons bay; additional capability is provided by the carriage of ASMs or rockets

on underwing attachments. The Atlantic's crew of 12 includes seven specialists to coordinate and direct the aircraft's operations.

Into service

The first prototype of the Atlantic made its maiden flight on 21 October 1961 and the first of 40 aircraft for the French navy was delivered in July 1965, followed by 20 aircraft for the

With its 'dustbin' radome in the retracted position, an 86° Gruppo Antisomergibili, 30° Stormo Atlantic returns to its base after a maritime patrol sortie.

German navy. A second production batch of Atlantics included nine aircraft for the Netherlands navy and 18 aircraft for the Italian air force. Three of those originally supplied to France were later transferred for service in Pakistan.

The Atlantic's sensors are primarily of Thomson-CSF manufacture, and are computer-integrated on display and control panels in the tactical compartment. Useful updating has been achieved within the limitations of the aircraft's 1950s-vintage electronics, but the Atlantic can now only be regarded as obsolescent; the French started to retire their aircraft as early as 1992.

Five of the German naval air arm's 15 survivors were extensively converted as Sigint aircraft, with E-Systems Peace Peek mission equipment installed by Vought and based on a Loral ESM suite with antennas in wingtip pods. The Italian aircraft were upgraded by Aeritalia with improved radar and navigation systems, as well as the Selenia ALR-730 ESM system.

New generation

Originally called the **ANG** (**Atlantic Nouvelle Génération**, or new-generation Atlantic), the **Dassault Atlantique 2** was planned as a multinational programme to replace the Atlantic 1. However, France has remained the sole customer, with a 30-aircraft order. After very prolonged studies, the Atlantique 2 was designed as a minimum-change type with totally new avionics, systems and equipment, packaged into an airframe differing from that of the original model only in ways to increase service life, reduce costs and minimize maintenance. The aircraft's sensors include

the Thomson-CSF Iguane frequency-agile radar, a SAT/TRT Tango FLIR in a chin turret, over 100 sonobuoys in the rear fuselage, a new Crouzet MAD receiver and the ARAR 13 ESM installation.

The Atlantique 2's main weapons bay can accommodate all NATO-standard bombs and depth charges, as well as other weapon types including two

ASMs or AShMs, up to eight Mk 46 torpedoes or seven Franco-Italian MU39 Impact advanced torpedoes. The Atlantique has a rarely used secondary transport function, and could also be used in a limited overland electronic reconnaissance role.

The first Atlantique 2 flew in May 1981 and production deliveries began in 1989.

SPECIFICATION

Dassault Atlantique 2
Type: 10-/12-crew long-range maritime patrol and ASW/anti-ship aircraft
Powerplant: two Rolls-Royce Tyne RTy.20 Mk 21 turboprop engines each rated at 4549 ekW (6,100 ehp)
Performance: maximum speed 648 km/h (402 mph) at optimum altitude; patrol speed 315 km/h (196 mph) between sea level and 1525 m (5,000 ft); initial climb rate 884 m (2,900 ft) per minute; service ceiling 9145 m (30,000 ft); operational radius 3333 km

(2,071 miles) for a 2-hour patrol in the anti-ship role with one AM39 Exocet missile; endurance 18 hours
Weights: empty 25,600 kg (56,437 lb); maximum take-off 46200 kg (101,852 lb)
Dimensions: wing span 37.42 m (122 ft 9¼ in) including wingtip ESM pods; length 31.62 m (103 ft 9 in); height 10.89 m (35 ft 8¾ in); wing area 120.34 m² (1,295.37 sq ft)
Armament: up to 6000 kg (13,228 lb) of disposable stores

Above: Of the 18 Atlantics remaining in German service, the 14 standard machines (illustrated) fly long-range recce for aerial patrols and ASW missions.

Left: Differences between the Atlantique 2 (seen here) and the Atlantic include the former's wingtip ECM pods, nose-mounted Tango FLIR turret, prominent cooling intakes below the cockpit and re-shaped fin top, housing an ECM aerial.

SEPECAT Jaguar IM Maritime strike aircraft

For anti-shipping duties with the Indian Air Force (IAF), BAe designed and Hindustan Aeronautics Ltd (HAL) built the **Jaguar IM**, with a Thomson-CSF/ESD Agave radar replacing the usual nose-mounted LRMTS installation. The aircraft are usually armed with the BAe Sea Eagle anti-ship missile, which is carried on the centreline pylon.

The IAF's first eight Jaguar IM dedicated maritime attack aircraft were included in Batch 3 Jaguar production by HAL. These Indian maritime Jaguars initially equipped 'A' Flight of No. 6 Squadron ('Dragons') based at Pune, operating alongside the unit's Canberras as part of the 2nd Wing of the South Western Air Command.

A total of 45 Jaguars, assembled by HAL, were to have been followed by the production

of 56 more examples, but instead India procured a further 31 aircraft (all single-seaters) which were again assembled largely from BAe-supplied kits.

An order for 15 extra aircraft was cancelled in 1989 (having been approved in January 1988), then resurrected in 1993. Four of these aircraft were delivered

as maritime Jaguar IMs, fitted with the ELTA EL/M-2032 radar, which is also due to be fitted to the Jaguar IMs already in service with No. 6 Squadron.

Above: The original batch of Jaguar IMs delivered to the IAF is planned to receive a radar upgrade, replacing the initial Agave unit (seen here) with the new ELTA EL/M-2032 radar. An additional four new-build aircraft were also delivered equipped to this standard.

Left: Had the French Jaguar M for the Aéronavale reached production, it might have looked very much like the Indian Jaguar IM (seen here), although the AM39 Exocet, rather than the Sea Eagle, would have been the primary anti-ship missile. In the event, France opted for the Super Etendard.

Canadair CL-215/CL-215T/Bombardier CL-415
Firefighting and multi-role amphibian

The **Canadair CL-215** was designed to meet a requirement for a firefighting amphibian which could replace the miscellany of types used in the 'water bombing' role during the 1960s. The Canadian Province of Quebec and the French Protection Civile

were the CL-215's first customers, although the robust and versatile amphibian was also available to military operators for use in the SAR and utility roles.

From the outset, simplicity of design was a primary requirement, with ease of

maintenance and reliability of equipment also receiving careful attention. Protection against saltwater corrosion was achieved through the use of corrosion-resistant materials and also by fully sealing appropriate components during assembly.

The CL-215 has a single-step hull, and fixed stabilizing floats are mounted just inboard of the wingtips. The tricycle landing gear comprises a nose unit with twin wheels and main units with single wheels, the former retracting into the hull and

*The Yugoslavian air force received four **CL-215** aircraft in 1981 for use in the firefighting role. Two **CL-215s** now serve with the Croatian air force, flying out of Zadar to tackle forest fires along the Adriatic coast.*

SPECIFICATION	
Bombardier CL-415	**Weights:** empty 12,861 kg
Type: two-/six-crew multi-role	(28,353 lb); maximum take-off
amphibian flying boat	19,890 kg (43,850 lb) from land or
Powerplant: two Pratt & Whitney	17,168 kg (37,850 lb) from water
Canada PW123AF turboprop	**Dimensions:** wing span 28.63 m
engines each rated at 1775 kW	(93 ft 11 in); length 19.82 m
(2,380 shp)	(65 ft ½ in); height 8.98 m (29 ft
Performance: maximum cruising	5½ in); wing area 100.33 m²
speed 376 km/h (234 mph) at	(1,080 sq ft)
3050 m (10,000 ft); initial climb	**Payload:** up to 30 passengers or
rate 419 m (1,375 ft) per minute;	3799 kg (8,375 lb) of freight in the
range 2426 km (1,507 miles) with	utility role, or 6123 kg (13,500 lb)
a 499-kg (1,100-lb) payload	of water in the firefighting role

the latter being raised to lie flat against the hull during operations from the water.

The high-mounted wing and tailplane are single-piece structures, with ailerons and flaps occupying the entire wing trailing edge. All fuel is carried in flexible wing cells, and the CL-215's engine nacelles are manufactured integral with the wing structure.

Firefighting mission

In its firefighting role the CL-215 is capable of lifting 5455 litres (1,200 Imperial gallons) of water or retardant fluid in two fuselage tanks. The water is scooped from a convenient sea, lake or river through two retractable inlets mounted under the hull, while the CL-215 taxis across the surface. The aircraft then takes off and flies to the area of the fire, where the load is jettisoned in less than a second. The operation is repeated until the fire is under

control. In most circumstances a load can be dropped at least every 10 minutes.

Configured for the SAR role, the CL-215 carries a crew of six. In addition to the pilot and co-pilot, a flight engineer is housed on the flight deck. The navigator's station is located farther back in the forward fuselage, and two observers are carried in the rear fuselage. The basic avionics are augmented by an AVQ-21 weather and search radar in the nose. The maximum endurance is 12 hours.

The maiden flight of the CL-215 took place on 23 October 1967, and deliveries to France began in May 1969. Production lasted until 1989 and included examples for the Canadian provinces of Quebec (15) and Manitoba (two), and for France (15), Greece (11), Spain (17 equipped for SAR but suitable also for firefighting and other roles), Royal Thai navy (two), CVG Ferrominera Orinoco CA

of Venezuela (two) and Yugoslavia (four).

A retrofit programme, resulting in the conversion of 17 aircraft up to August 1998 (15 aircraft for Spain and two for Quebec), resulted in the **CL-215T** version with features of the CL-415 turboprop-powered development. The major change is the revised turboprop powerplant, and an option adopted by several customers is that of powered flight controls.

In December 1986 Canadair Ltd was bought by Bombardier Inc., and in August 1988 merged with the parent group as the Canadair Group of Bombardier Inc. It was during this period that Canadair was considering

the development of a derivative of its CL-215 amphibian flying boat with a turboprop- rather than piston-engined powerplant for greater overall power, an improved power/weight ratio, and more ready availability of spares and fuel. In 1991 the improved type was designated as the **CL-415** to distinguish it from the CL-215T turboprop-powered conversion of the CL-215, and the official launch of the new model came in October 1991 with the receipt of an initial French order.

Turboprop production

The first CL-415 made its maiden flight on 6 December

In addition to its fuselage water tanks, the CL-415 also has foam concentrate tanks and a mixing system for the inflight production of foam/water retardant liquids.

changes include powered flight controls, a pressure refuelling system, a new electrical system, a revised 'glass' flightdeck with air-conditioning, structural changes and strengthening for greater operational efficiency despite the type's higher weights, and a four-tank firefighting system with the water capacity consequently increased to 6140 litres (1,351 Imp gallons).

The standard CL-415 designation is used for the water-bombing and utility version. This has eight inward-facing seats as standard, but with the above-floor water tanks removed can alternatively be operated with up to

1993, and the type received Canadian and US certifications in June and October 1994, respectively, allowing the delivery of the first machine to France in December 1994. An initial production batch of 50 aircraft was planned, and by 2001 orders stood at 56 aircraft, for France (12), Ontario (nine), Quebec (eight), Italy (14), Croatia (three) and Greece (10).

The CL-415 retains the proven airframe of the CL-215 in combination with a number of important changes. The most

obvious of these changes is the new turboprop powerplant, with the two Pratt & Whitney Canada PW123AF engines located in slender nacelles above the wing for a higher thrust line with the new Hamilton Standard four-bladed propellers. Other highly evident external changes are the addition of small winglets at the tips of the flat wing for improved lateral stability. For improved directional and longitudinal stability after the movement of the engines' thrust lines, the tail unit has been modified with a

'bullet' fairing on the leading edge of the tailplane/fin junction. There are also two swept finlets (their leading edges offset to port) on the tailplane between the inner edges of the engine nacelles and the outer edges of the centre section. Less evident

The CL-415 demonstrates its firefighting capabilities at Taipei during its Asia-Pacific tour of 2002. The aircraft covered 53,000 km (32,934 miles) in 90 days.

Bombardier's latest multi-role CL-415MP variant can carry mission sensors including surveillance radar, FLIR and SLAR, as well as communications and navigation equipment.

30 forward-facing seats. With the above-floor tanks retained, the CL-415 can also be outfitted for the combi role with freight and 11 passenger seats, respectively, forward and to the rear of the tanks. Bombardier has since developed a **CL-415MP** derivative for the maritime patrol, customs and immigration control, fisheries protection, special missions and SAR roles, with options such as radar, FLIR, precision navigation and other mission-specific equipment. Flight testing of the first of two SAR-configured CL-415MP aircraft began in February 2002.

ShinMaywa PS-1, US-1 and SS-2
Military seaplanes

The **ShinMaywa** (up to 1992 **Shin Meiwa**) **SS-2** family is one of the few modern flying-boat series in service anywhere in the world. The first family member to enter service with the Japan Maritime Self-Defense Force was the **PS-1**, a capable ASW machine. The SS-2's origins can be discovered in a JMSDF requirement issued in the early 1960s; the first of two prototypes made its maiden flight on 16 October 1967. Trials revealed excellent STOL performance, largely as a result of the wing's high-lift devices (outboard leading-edge slats and trailing-edge flaps) and a boundary layer control system on the flaps, rudder and elevators powered by a T58 gas turbine in the fuselage.

PS-1 described

Production was completed in 1979 with the 23rd machine,

and the type was withdrawn from first-line service in 1989. The PS-1 had accommodation for a flight crew of three and a mission crew of seven. The armament comprised up to 2000 kg (4,409 lb) of disposable stores carried in a lower fuselage weapons bay and on two underwing and two wingtip hardpoints. The weapons bay could carry four 150-kg (331-lb) depth bombs, the underwing hardpoints could each accommodate two Mk 46 torpedoes, and the wingtip hardpoints could each accept three 127-mm (5-in) rockets. The PS-1's electronics included APS-80N search radar, HQS-101C dunking sonar, HSQ-10A MAD, the 'Julie' active ranging system with 12 charges, AQA-3 'Jezebel' passive detection system with 20 sonobuoys and the HLR-1 ECM system.

The 71st Koku-tai at Iwakuni has operated the US-1 since 1976, and the original batch of 12 aircraft was augmented by at least five further aircraft. The US-1/1A was returned to production in 1992.

While on patrol the PS-1 was designed to make repeated landings and take-offs, dipping its sonar after alighting. This could be accomplished in seas with up to 3-m (10-ft) waves.

The **US-1** is a SAR variant of the PS-1 with retractable wheeled landing gear to turn the type into an amphibian. It has a crew of nine, and its cabin can accommodate three additional crew members, as well as 20 survivors, or 12 litters or, in the transport role, 69 passengers. The first example of the US-1 (company designation **SS-2A**) variant flew in October 1974, and production totalled six flying

boats before the line switched to the improved **US-1A** standard, to which the US-1s were later raised. The last 12 US-1 flying boats were delivered as US-1As, with an uprated powerplant of four 2605-kW (3,493-ehp) T64-IHI-10J engines supplied with fuel from an enlarged internal capacity.

The **US-1A KAI** is the updated version of the US-1A with the powerplant of four

SPECIFICATION	
ShinMaywa PS-1	(94,799 lb)
Type: ASW flying boat	**Dimensions:** wing span 33.14 m
Powerplant: four 2282-ekW (3,060-ehp) General Electric T64-IHI-10 turboprops (made under licence by IHI)	(108 ft 8¾ in); length 33.5 m (109 ft 11 in); height 9.71 m (31 ft 10¼ in); wing area 135.82 m² (1,462 sq ft)
Performance: maximum speed 547 km/h (340 mph); range at low altitude with maximum weapons 2168 km (1,347 miles)	**Armament:** internal weapons bay for four 149-kg (328-lb) AS bombs and extensive search gear, two underwing pods for four Mk 44 or Mk 46 homing AS torpedoes and triple launcher under each wing tip for 127-mm (5-in) rockets
Weights: empty 26,300 kg (57,982 lb); maximum 43,000 kg	

Withdrawal of the PS-1 did not mark the end of the ShinMaywa flying boat, as an amphibious SAR derivative had already been designed, under the designation US-1 (foreground).

3355-kW (4,400-shp) Rolls-Royce AE2100J turboprop engines driving six-bladed propellers, a fly-by-wire control system, improved cockpit avionics, and a pressurized fuselage to permit a higher cruising altitude within the context of a service ceiling increased to 7620 m (25,000 ft) and a range boosted to more than 5003 km (3,109 miles).

It is planned that all seven surviving US-1As will be upgraded to the US-1A KAI standard and supplemented by three flying boats built to this standard. The first US-1A KAI should fly in 2003 and enter service in 2005.

The original PS-1 was a dedicated ASW flying boat, optimized for very long-range patrol duties. The prototype and two pre-production aircraft were followed by 20 production aircraft. The type served from 1971–89, when it was replaced by land-based Lockheed P-3 Orions.

Fokker F27 Maritime and Maritime Enforcer/F50 Maritime Mk 2 and Maritime Enforcer Mk 2

ASW/maritime patrol aircraft

First flown in 1955, the F27 exceeded Fokker's expectations in terms of sales, becoming one of the world's most successful twin-turboprop airliners, and leading to the new-generation Fokker 50. Fokker also developed military transport and special missions versions of both the F27 and F50.

F27MPA Maritime

Fokker completed definition of a specialized maritime patrol version of the F27 as the **Fokker F27MPA Maritime** in 1975. Intended for all forms of coastal surveillance, SAR and environmental control missions, the Maritime has a crew of up to six and can mount 12-hour

The Maritime Enforcer Mk 2 was developed from the Fokker 50-100 for anti-submarine and anti-surface unit warfare, and would have been equipped with an impressive array of sophisticated avionics. Any future that this promising aircraft might have had was scuppered when Fokker was forced to declare a state of bankruptcy on 15 March 1996.

Spain bought three F27 Maritime aircraft fitted with APS-504 search radar in belly blisters. The aircraft's endurance of over 12 hours allows long-range SAR and patrol missions.

SPECIFICATION

Fokker 50 Maritime Enforcer Mk 2
Type: ASW and anti-ship aircraft
Powerplant: two Pratt & Whitney Canada PW125B turboprop engines each flat-rated at 1864 kW (2,500 shp)
Performance: normal cruising speed 298 mph (480 km/h) at optimum altitude; service ceiling 7620 m (25,000 ft); operational radius 2224 km (1,382 miles) with a 1814-kg (4,000-lb) mission payload

Weights: operating empty 13,314 kg (29,352 lb); maximum take-off 21,545 kg (47,500 lb)
Dimensions: wing span 29 m (95 ft 1¾ in); length 25.25 m (82 ft 10 in); height 8.32 m (27 ft 3½ in); wing area 70 m² (753.50 sq ft)
Armament: provision for up to 3930 kg (8,664 lb) of disposable stores including AShMs, depth charges and torpedoes

patrols. It is equipped with Litton APS-504 search radar in an underfuselage radome, nose-mounted Bendix weather radar and fully comprehensive navigation systems, as well as a fully equipped tactical compartment, crew rest areas and bulged observation windows to the flight deck and rear of the cabin. This **F27-200MPA** version was sold to Angola, the Netherlands and Peru (where it is no longer operated), and is currently in use with the air forces of Spain (three) and Thailand (three).

Maritime Enforcer

Thailand's aircraft are armed, but otherwise not to the **F27MPA Maritime Enforcer** standard.

This latter variant is tasked with armed surveillance, ASW, anti-ship attack and other combat roles, and is equipped with LAPADS (lightweight acoustic processing and display system) for active and passive sonobuoys, a magnetic anomaly detector (MAD), and comprehensive electronic support measures (ESM) equipment and infra-red (IR) detection systems, plus an optional underwing searchlight.

F50 Maritime Mk 2

The **F50 Maritime Mk 2** was to have been a considerably developed version of the Maritime, with a flightcrew of two or three, a mission crew of between two and four, and a mission suite that included

an IR detection system and the Texas Instruments APS-134 surveillance radar with its antenna in a ventral radome.

Enforcer Mk 2

The F50 Maritime Enforcer Mk 2 is a considerably developed version of the F27MPA Maritime Enforcer, based on the airframe and powerplant of the F50. It has basically the same airframe as the F27MPA Maritime Enforcer, but with aerodynamic refinements, flight deck improvements, and a powerplant of two PW125B turboprops. The avionics suite is basically an improved version of that which would have been carried by the F50 Maritime Mk 2. The weapons capability was increased to 3930 kg (8,664 lb) of disposable stores carried on eight hardpoints (two under the fuselage and six under the wings), allowing the carriage of up to eight torpedoes and/or

depth bombs, or two or four AGM-84 Harpoon or AM.39 Exocet anti-ship missiles, or a mixed load of torpedoes and missiles; more typical loads might be four torpedoes, or two anti-ship missiles. Singapore was the only customer for the type, buying five.

As well as the Maritime Mk 2 and Maritime Enforcer Mk 2, a range of special-purpose F50 variants was proposed, based for the most part on equipment fits originally proposed on the F27. These variants included the **Black Crow 2** Comint/Elint version with an ARCO Sigint system; the **Kingbird Mk 2** for airborne early warning (AEW) with phased array radar; and the **Sentinel Mk 2** with synthetic aperture radar, side-looking airborne radar (SLAR), and a podded electro-optical imaging system for surveillance and reconnaissance.

Thailand's Maritime aircraft carry a range of armament, including the depth charges and torpedoes illustrated here.

Ilyushin Il-38 'May' Maritime patrol and ASW aircraft

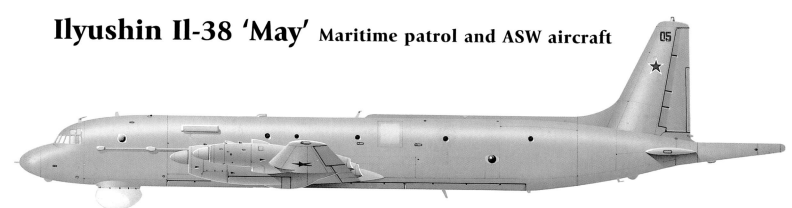

Above: The Il-38 is characterized by its prominent underfuselage radome and MAD 'tail sting'. The aircraft bears some similarity in configuration to the Lockheed P-3 Orion.

Right: Airframe modifications developed for the Il-18 airliner could easily be applied to Russian Il-38s and the related Il-20 command post.

The **Il-38**, which has the NATO reporting designation **'May'**, was derived from the Il-18 airliner. The Il-38 resulted from a 1959 AV-MF requirement for a long-range maritime patrol and ASW aircraft, and the prototype first flew on 27 September 1961. There followed a pre-production prototype and 57 production aircraft delivered from 1968 (although some sources quote a figure of about 100 aircraft delivered in 1965–68).

Il-38 changes

The changes involved in the evolution of the basic Il-18 into the Il-38 were the lengthening of the fuselage by about 4.00 m (13 ft 1½ in) and the forward movement of the wing by some 2.75 m (9 ft ¼ in), probably to compensate for the effect of the new role equipment on the type's centre of gravity. Most of the original cabin windows were removed; the remainder were mostly reduced in size. The Il-18's original passenger entry doors were all removed, to be replaced by a new door on the starboard side at the rear of the cabin in the location of the Il-18's service door. Other structural alterations included the provision of a MAD stinger projecting rearward from the tailcone, and a pair of internal weapons bays fore and aft of the wing carry-through structure.

SPECIFICATION

Ilyushin Il-38 'May-A'
Type: seven/eight-crew medium-/long-range maritime patrol and anti-submarine warplane
Powerplant: four ZMDB Progress (Ivchyenko) AI-20M turboprop engines each rated at 3169 ekW (4,250 ehp)
Performance: maximum speed 722 km/h (448 mph) at 6400 m (21,000 ft); patrol speed between 320 and 400 km/h (199 and 248 mph) between 100 and 1000 m (330 and 3,280 ft); service ceiling 11,000 m (36,090 ft); range 7500 km (4,660 miles) with maximum fuel

Weights: empty 35,500 kg (78,263 lb); maximum take-off 66,000 kg (145,503 lb)
Dimensions: wing span 37.42 m (122 ft 9¼ in); length 40.19 m (131 ft 10¼ in); height 10.17 m (33 ft 4½ in); wing area 140 m² (1,507 sq ft)
Armament: up to 8400 kg (18,520 lb) of disposable stores carried in two lower-fuselage weapons bays, and generally comprising 216 RGB-1 sonobuoys or 144 RGB-2 sonobuoys, as well as two AT-1 torpedoes, or 10 PLAB-250-120 depth charges, or eight AMD-2-500 mines, or one nuclear depth bomb

New engines may be fitted to the Il-38 and airframe, and avionics improvements are also being considered. With the demise of the Tu-95RTs in the 1990s, the Il-38 was increasingly tasked with surface reconnaissance missions in addition to its ASW tasking.

The standard **Il-38 'May-A'** has weather radar in the nose, with a large search radar ('Wet Eye') in a bulged radome below the forward fuselage, immediately to the rear of the nosewheel bay. The otherwise smooth skin is disrupted by a handful of antennas and heat exchanger outlets, and there are large heat exchanger pods and cable ducts ahead of the aircraft's wing.

'May' in service

Most of the former Soviet Il-38s remain in use with the AV-MF (naval air arm), but some were passed to the Ukraine. The only export customer was the Indian navy. Il-38s encountered over the Mediterranean in Egyptian markings during the early 1970s were Soviet aircraft operating from Egyptian bases and wearing 'flag of convenience' markings.

An upgrade programme, with the aim of keeping Russian Il-38s viable into the twenty-first century, was mooted around 2000 by the Leninets Holding Company. This upgrade, known as Sea Dragon, was initially to be applied to Indian Il-38s. However, India lost two of its four Il-38s in a collision at an air show in September 2002, and may not now upgrade its depleted fleet. The Russian aircraft are likely to have their airframes modified for at least a further 10 year's service, but the future of the Sea Dragon programme was still undecided late in 2002.

Tupolev Tu-142 'Bear-F' Long-range ASW/MP aircraft

'Bear-F Mod. 1' and 'Mod. 2' aircraft were without the fin-mounted MAD fairing. One of the former is illustrated.

Development of a Tu-95 variant optimized for ASW duties was officially initiated in 1963. Based on the airframe of the Tu-95RTs, the **Tu-142** introduced a search and track system and an ASW weapon system. The new aircraft carried a sophisticated and accurate navigation system that was also part of the weapons system targeting hardware. Tupolev's earlier attempts at an ASW platform based on the 'Bear' (the **Tu-95PLO** proposed in the early 1960s) had been rendered abortive by the lack of such a powerful sensor system.

The Tu-142 was also equipped for electronic reconnaissance, utilising Kvadrat-2 and Kub-3 EW systems. In accordance with Soviet military doctrine, the Tu-142 was required to be capable of operations from unprepared airstrips: as a result the aircraft incorporated a new undercarriage with six wheels on each main unit, accommodated in increased-size nacelles.

Further refinements included a larger-area wing housing new rigid metal fuel tanks, and a defensive ECM suite. From the second prototype onwards, the cabin was lengthened by 1.50 m (3 ft 5 in), providing space for new systems.

RTs commonality

The prototype Tu-142 first flew on 18 July 1968. Compared to the Tu-95RTs, with which it retained much commonality, the Tu-142 had the ventral and dorsal cannon turrets removed, and the large dielectric radome of the RTs was replaced by a smaller fairing for an IR system. New antennas were positioned in fairings on the horizontal stabilizer tips, replacing the Arfa system which was carried by the Tu-95RTs 'Bear-D'.

During May 1970 the first production Tu-142s were delivered for operational test and evaluation by Soviet navy ASW units. After the trials were successfully completed, and also the completion of testing of the Berkut-95 search radar, the Tu-142 was declared operational in December 1972.

Operational aircraft

Attaining initial operational capability for the Tu-142 was hampered by slow deliveries, and the 12 aircraft received (of 36 ordered) by the AV-MF in 1972 were fitted with the original 12-wheel main undercarriage units, as carried by the first prototype. In service, the Tu-142's rough-field capability was found to be of limited utility. Furthermore, the aircraft's performance was hampered by its weight, and these two factors were consequently dealt with by the introduction of a modification plan.

SPECIFICATION	
Tupolev Tu-142M ('Bear-F') **Type:** long-range ASW and maritime reconnaissance aircraft **Powerplant:** four 11033-kW (14,795-shp) Kuznetsov NK-12MV turboprops **Performance:** maximum speed 850 km/h (528 mph); service ceiling 10,700 m (35,100 ft); range with maximum load 12,000 km (7,460 miles)	**Weight:** maximum take-off 185,000 kg (407,850 lb) **Dimensions:** wing span 50 m (164 ft); length, overall 48.17 m (158 ft ½ in); height about 12.12 m (39 ft 9¼ in); wing area 289.90 m² (3,121 sq ft) **Armament:** two NR-23 23-mm self-defence cannon in tail turret, plus depth charges, bombs and torpedoes

The lengthened cabin of the Tu-142 series had no effect on fuselage length. Aircraft such as this 'Bear-F Mod. 3', which is illustrated as it would have appeared in the 1980s, were potentially formidable ASW assets.

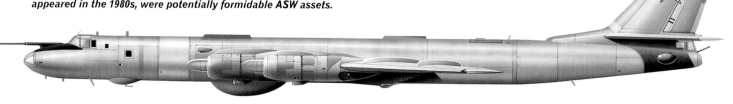

All maritime 'Bears' are equipped with IFR probes. A single inflight-refuelling typically increases range by some 2000 km (1,250 miles). This is a 'Mod. 3' aircraft.

The modified Tu-142 introduced a crew rest area for long-duration flights, and the main landing gear units were replaced by lighter examples, resulting in a 3630-kg (8,000-lb) weight reduction and improved flight characteristics. This modified aircraft received no new designation (only 18 Tu-142s were built before production was switched to the **Tu-142M**). but did receive the reporting name **'Bear-F Mod. 1'**. In 1972 the Kuibyshev facility produced its last Tu-142, and this became the standard configuration for production aircraft, which were now to be delivered as the **Tu-142M** ('Bear-F Mod. 2') from the Taganrog plant.

The Tu-142M was equipped with the extended cockpit and new undercarriage; however, other equipment remained unchanged compared to earlier aircraft. As a result of their similarity with the final Tu-142s delivered from Kuibyshev, the Taganrog-built aircraft were known by the AV-MF as Tu-142s, despite being given the Tu-142M factory designation.

New threats

Development of more 'stealthy' submarines, together with operational experience, indicated that conventional sonobuoys were becoming less effective. Instead, sonobuoys with explosive sound sources would have to be used. The **Tu-142MK** ('Bear-F Mod. 3') therefore combined improved sonobuoy equipment with a Korshun target acquisition system. The first example successfully completed its first flight on 4 November 1975. The new Korshun radar, avionics

Russia retains the 'Bear-F Mod. 3' (illustrated) in service alongside the Tu-142MZ.

suite and ASW equipment proved problematic, and it seemed likely that the Tu-124MK could become obsolete even before it entered service.

As a result, in July 1979, a year before the Korshun-equipped Tu-142MK entered service, it was declared that the aircraft needed substantial upgrading. Regardless, production of the Tu-142MK began during 1978, superseding that of the baseline Tu-142M, although the AV-MF elected to use its own designation system to identify the new model. Aircraft equipped with the new ASW system became known as Tu-142M machines, while older 'Bears' remained Tu-142s.

Improved capability

The first three Tu-142MKs entered service in November 1980, introducing a magnetic anomaly detector (MAD), a new navigation system, and improved ECM.

The Tu-142 continued to be updated and improved throughout the course of its long production run. The ultimate ASW 'Bear' variant is the **Tu-142MZ 'Bear-F Mod. 4'** with a more sophisticated ASW system, further improved ECM and new engines and APU.

Tu-142MZ's additional equipment effectively doubled its efficiency. After state acceptance trials beginning in 1987, the last Tu-142MZ 'Bear-F Mod. 4' was declared fully operational during 1993.

The only Tu-142 export customer was India, which received eight **Tu-142MK-A** aircraft. These aircraft have slightly downgraded avionics in

A pimple radome on the nose of this aircraft identifies it as the ultimate Tu-142MZ 'Bear-F Mod. 4'.

comparison to those of the Tu-142MK. Following the loss of two of its Il-38s, India may take ex-Russian 'Bears' to bolster its maritime aircraft fleet.

On the break-up of the Soviet Union, the Ukraine was left with a handful of Tu-142MZs.

Beriev Be-12 Chaika 'Mail' Multirole amphibian

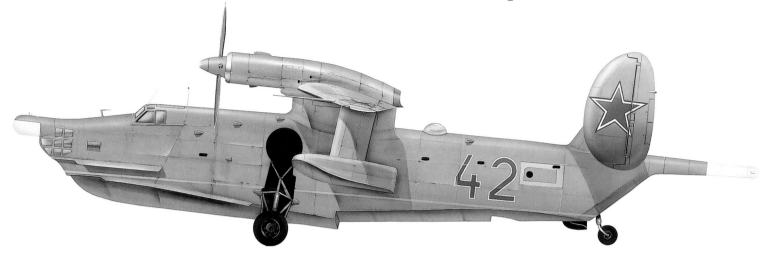

The lessons that had been learned in the design of the R-1 and Be-10 were incorporated into the design of a much improved flying boat, based loosely on the Be-6 and originally identified by NATO as a re-engined version of the older type. In fact the **Beriev Be-12 Chaika** (seagull) (given the NATO reporting name **'Mail'**) bears little more than a general resemblance to the Be-6, sharing as it does with its predecessor only the gull-wing layout and a tail unit with endplate vertical surfaces.

The greater power and lighter weight of a turboprop powerplant permitted a forward extension of the hull, with a new planing bottom similar to that of the Be-10. The prominent spray-suppressing strakes around the bow of the Be-10 were also utilized.

MAD 'thimble'

The most significant change, however, was the addition of massive and sturdy retractable tailwheel landing gear, which would sweep upwards into the hull recess, making the Be-12 amphibious and thus considerably more versatile than the earlier Beriev designs.

The turreted gun armament of the Be-6 was deleted, the tail turret being replaced by MAD (magnetic anomaly detection) gear in the tail above the aircraft's tailwheel well, while the antenna for the search radar

was installed in a long 'thimble' radome on the bow rather than in a retractable ventral dustbin radome, as on the Be-6. The electronics fit of the aircraft included an A321-A navigation radar, A-322Z doppler system, A-325Z navigation system, an IFF transponder and interrogator and an astonishing four radar altimeters of RV-UM, RV-3, RV-10 and RV-17 design. Other individual aircraft have tail-warning and passive radar warning recievers.

One of the drawbacks of the Be-12's high-wing layout, namely the great height of the engines above the water/ground, was mitigated by the design of engine cowling panels which dropped down to form strong working platforms for groundcrew. Special side hatches situated towards the aft of the hull allow weapons and other stores to be loaded onto the aircraft while it is floating on the water.

The first Be-12 flew in around October 1960 and the first of some 140 or more such aircraft entered service in 1964, with small numbers later transferred to the air forces of Syria and Vietnam. The considerable weight-lifting capability of the Be-12 was demonstrated in a series of class records for amphibians set in 1964, 1968 and 1970, suggesting a normal weapon load as high as 5000 kg (11,023 lb). The aircraft also had tubes positioned behind the

Designed for coastal anti-submarine missions around the coastline of the former Soviet Union, the Be-12 would also complement the Il-38 'May' maritime patrol aircraft together with naval helicopters.

SPECIFICATION	
Beriev Be-12 Chaika 'Mail' **Type:** six-crew maritime patrol, reconnaissance and ASW amphibian flying-boat **Powerplant:** two ZMDB Progress (Ivchyenko) AI-20D turboprop engines each rated at 3124 ekW (4,190 ehp) **Performance:** maximum speed 608 km/h (378 mph) at optimum altitude; patrol speed 320 km/h (199 mph) at optimum altitude; initial climb rate 912 m (2,990 ft) per minute; service ceiling 11,280 m (37,000 ft); range	7500 km (4,660 miles) **Weights:** empty 21,700 kg (47,840 lb); maximum take-off 31,000 kg (68,342 lb) **Dimensions:** wingspan 29.71 m (97 ft 5¾ in); length 30.17 m (99 ft); height 7 m (22 ft 11½ in) with landing gear extended; wing area 105 m² (1,130.25 sq ft) **Armament:** up to 5000 kg (11,023 lb) of disposable stores in the form of bombs, rockets or torpedoes on underwing pylons, and depth charges, mines and sonobuoys in fuselage bays

weapons bay for the ejection of sonobuoys, markers and flares.

The aircraft's wings have a minimum of one pylon on each side. There are also rocket rails mounted beneath the wings; both are mounted well away from the reach of the propellers.

The advent of 'Haze', 'Hormone' and 'Helix' helicopters and of the 'May' fixed-wing aircraft for the ASW role meant that there was a steadily diminishing ASW task for the Be-12, although the type was still in service in the late 1990s for the patrol, ASW and, in its **Be-12PS** form, high-speed search and rescue roles.

Chaika variants

The Be-12 has also been used for nuclear depth charge tests (**Be-12SK**), fire-fighting (**Be-12P**), as a flying laboratory (**Be-12LL**)

and as an experimental passenger transport (**Be-12Nkh**). Reports also circulated that an EW variant of the aircraft was also produced.

The crew of the Be-12 includes a captain, co-pilot/radio operator – both of whom have ejection seats – together with a navigator (in the glazed nose), an electronics operator and one or two ASW sensor operators, depending on the mission and configuration of the aircraft.

Although the aircraft was highly regarded by its crews, the noise from the engines could cause some discomfort for those inside. The interior of the aircraft was also unpressurized.

The aircraft was designed to operate in conjunction with surface shipping during anti-submarine operations. A vessel would localize the approximate

position of the enemy boat using its own sonar equipment. A Be-12 would then use its MAD detector, together with sonobuoys, to plot the exact location of the enemy boat and carry out an attack using its depth charges.

A Be-12 seen with the ensign of the Russian navy on the side of its hull. It is unknown how many, if any, Be-12s remain in service with the Russian navy, as its anti-submarine mission may now have been absorbed by helicopters and the Il-38 'May'.

Douglas C-47 Maritime light freighter

The capability revealed by the DC-2 convinced the US Army of the excellence of the basic transport's design and construction, and a study of the improved DC-3 enabled the US Army to outline the modifications required for a military DC-3. These changes included more powerful engines, strengthening of the rear fuselage and cabin floor, provision of large loading doors, replacement of the airline-type

The Dakota has found a new lease of life following a fuselage stretch and engine change. Those South African Air Force examples based at Cape Town are tasked with the important work of maritime patrol.

interior by utility seats lining the cabin walls, and adoption of a powerplant comprising two R-1830-92 radials. Ordered in large numbers in 1940, this type was designated the **C-47 Skytrain**, and was the forerunner of an enormous range which included the **C-53 Skytrooper** troop transport with 28 seats.

Glider tug

The C-47 was a notable glider tug serving over Sicily, Burma, Normandy, Arnhem and the Rhine crossing. In British service, the aircraft were named **Dakota**. C-47 aircraft also participated in the Berlin Airlift, and the Korean War, while **AC-47D** gunships were used in the Vietnam conflict.

The US Navy and US Marine Corps also used the aircraft under the designation **R4D**, although in 1962 they recieved C-47 designations. The US Navy

and US Marine Corps operated the R4D for personnel and cargo transport, and radar countermeasures, air-sea warfare training and, with ski-modified landing gear, Arctic and Antarctic operations.

Throughout the entire period of production there was little change in design, although the powerplants were improved with more powerful engines to provide enhanced performance. Manufacturer's lists show six variants of the Wright SGR-1820 Cyclone engine with ratings from 671 to 746 kW (900 to 1,000 hp), and six variants of the R-1830 Twin Wasp engine with ratings from 746 to 820 kW (1,000 to 1,100 hp).

Civil market

After World War II large numbers of the aircraft were sold onto the civil market, and so acute was the shortage of

civil aircraft that many were operated without any alteration to the military interior. The majority, however, were modified with internal furnishings and equipment, and some C-47s were even provided with VIP interior layouts.

Many efforts have been made to enhance the performance of the C-47 and prolong its service life. A number of turboprop installations have been made including that developed by Basler Turbo Conversions Inc. The **Basler Turbo-67** introduces two Pratt & Whitney Canada PT6A-67R turboprops each rated at 1061 kW (1,424 shp) and driving Hartzell five-bladed propellers, and a lengthening of the forward fuselage by 1.02 m (3 ft 4 in). The cabin layout increases the seating capacity

El Salvador appears to have recently phased its Basler Turbo-67 conversions out of service. The AC-47s have been re-engined in a similar manner.

to a maximum of 34 troops or five LD3 cargo containers. Deliveries of the Turbo-67 began in 1990, recipients including the air forces of Colombia, Bolivia, Guatemala and Salvador (with an AC-47 gunship and standard transport).

Early in 1992, the South African Air Force (SAAF) inducted the **C-47TP Super Dakota** conversion. This C-47 version is flown by 35 Squadron of SAAF in the transport role, and by the 80 Air Navigation School. In 1998 44 Squadron retired its C-47TPs upon recieving CASA 212s and CN-235s.

Mali makes use of a pair of Basler Turbo Dakotas, TZ-389 and TZ-390 (below). The original TZ-389 was written off before delivery and replaced by another with the same serial. TZ-390 was converted from a C-47, originally ordered by the USAAF in 1942.

SPECIFICATION	
Douglas C-47A Skytrain **Type:** two/three-crew short/medium-range transport **Powerplant:** two Pratt & Whitney R-1830-92 radial piston engines each rated at 865 kW (1,200 shp) **Performance:** maximum speed 370 km/h (230 mph) at 2680 m (8,800 ft); cruising speed 257 km/h (160 mph) at optimum altitude; climb to 3050 m (10,000 ft) in 9 minutes 36 seconds; service ceiling 7315 m (24,000 ft); range 6115 km (3,800 miles) with	maximum fuel and no payload, and 2575 km (1,600 miles) with standard fuel and payload **Weights:** empty 8103 kg (17,865 lb); maximum take-off 11793 kg (26,000 lb) **Dimensions:** wingspan 29.11 m (95 ft 6 in); length 19.43 m (63 ft 9 in); height 5.18 m (17 ft); wing area 91.69 m² (987 sq ft) **Payload:** up to 28 troops or paratroops, or 14 litters and three attendants, or 2722 kg (6,000 lb) of ssfreight

Dassault Gardian and HU-25 Guardian
Maritime Falcons

The Gardian variant of the Falcon 20 bizjet replaces the standard machine's forward port cabin window with an enlarged observation window.

SPECIFICATION	
Dassault HU-25A Guardian **Type:** medium-range maritime patrol and SAR aircraft **Powerplant:** two AlliedSignal ATF3-6-2 turbofan engines each rated at 24.19 kN (5,440 lb st) **Performance:** maximum cruising speed 855 km/h (531 mph) at 12,200 m (40,025 ft); economical cruising speed 764 km/h (475 mph)	at 12500 m (41,010 ft); initial cruising altitude 12,500 m (41,010 ft); range 4170 km (2,591 miles) with six crew **Weights:** empty 8620 kg (19,004 lb); maximum take-off 15200 kg (33,510 lb) **Dimensions:** wing span 16.3 m (53 ft 6 in); length 17.15 m (56 ft 3 in); height 5.32 m (17 ft 5 in); wing area 41.8 m² (450 sq ft)

In 1977 Dassault clinched the sale of 41 **Falcon 20G** aircraft, designated as the **HU-25A Guardian**, to the US Coast Guard. The fuselage was modified to incorporate two observation windows and a drop hatch for rescue supplies. The HU-25A was obtained for all-weather SAR, maritime surveillance and environmental protection duties with sophisticated communications, navigation and radar equipment. A number of these aircraft were modified as **HU-25B** machines with a SLAR fitted in a pod on the lower starboard side of the fuselage. These aircraft have the

responsibility for detecting maritime pollution. Further aircraft have been modified as **HU-25C Interceptors**, fitted with an AN/APG-66 search radar for pursuing and identifying suspicious sea and air traffic.

In the Pacific, the Aéronavale uses the **Falcon 20H** maritime surveillance version under the name **Gardian** (guardian). Two aircraft are tasked with patrol and SAR duties within French territorial economic zones. The Gardian has very comprehensive avionics including Thomson-CSF Varan radar and VLF Omega navigation, and is characterized by an extra-large observation

window in the port side of the fuselage. These aircraft will be joined in service by an MR-tasked **Falcon 50** derivative. In addition, a fleet of around 20

Falcon 20s is operated by the British company FR Aviation, to provide target-towing and anti-shipping threat simulation for the Royal Navy.

The HU-25 Guardian is used by the USCG for medium-range surveillance, up to 930 miles (1500 km) from the US coast. The Guardian can carry a variety of photographic and electronic sensors.

Lockheed C-130 Hercules Navy and maritime variants

Thanks to its long-endurance and load-carrying capabilities, the C-130 Hercules was adapted to the maritime patrol role by Lockheed. However, only two customers emerged for the resulting **C-130H-MP**, Indonesia, which bought one aircraft, and Malaysia, which bought three. Indonesia's aircraft was lost in 1985 and Malaysia's moved on to other roles from 1994.

US Marine Corps
During the mid-1950s, the US Marine Corps required a tactical transport which could double as

an inflight-refuelling tanker using the probe and drogue system. In August 1957 two USAF C-130As were borrowed and each fitted with two 1915-litre (506-US gallon) tanks in the fuselage and two underwing pods containing hose equipment. So successful were the trials that 46 Lockheed **KC-130F Hercules** were ordered for delivery from 1960. The KC-130F is based on the C-130B airframe, initially fitted with Allison T56-A-7 engines, but later re-engined with the T56-A-16. To cope with attrition, the USMC ordered

14 **KC-130R** tankers based on the C-130H. The last variant of the classic C-130 was the **KC-130T**, 22 of which were ordered for USMC service. More recently, the **KC-130J** is being procured for the USMC, which should have a fleet of about 30 aircraft in place by 2008.

Traditionally, each Marine Air Wing has had one Marine Aerial Refueller Transport Squadron which can also carry out on-the-ground refuelling of helicopters, tactical vehicles and ground support equipment. The Marine Corps Reserve also operates

the stretched **KC-130T-30**. A single **TC-130G**, named *Fat Albert*, provides air show logistic support and RATO (rocket-assisted take-off) demonstrations for the 'Blue Angels' US Navy flight demonstration team.

Navy ski-Hercules
The **Lockheed LC-130F**, **LC-130H**, **LC-130R Hercules** transports are winterized aircraft designed for support operations (as denoted by the 'L' prefix) on the Antarctic ice and Arctic DEW (distant early warning)

The EC-130V combines the capability of the E-2C Hawkeye with the endurance of the C-130. After the cancellation of USCG operations, the single EC-130V was handed over to the USAF on 1 October 1993, for use in an undisclosed 'black programme'.

line, and are equipped with skis. With slightly redesigned fuselages and intended for very long-range operations, LC-130F/H/Rs can be equipped with RATO (rocket-assisted take-off) gear for short-distance take-offs from ice fields. The LC-130F was the first US Navy variant for Antarctic operations; four joined VXE-6 'Puckered Penguins' in 1969. The LC-130R (six built) was the final ski-equipped Hercules, initially joining VXE-6, but later transferring to the USAF.

TACAMO

The US Navy acquired four C-130s through the USAF, which it modified to **EC-130G TACAMO (TAke Charge And Move Out)** configuration to provide a link between the National Command Authority and submerged fleet ballistic missile submarines. Messages

The USCG's HC-130 fleet is rapidly ageing, but deliveries of the HC-130J have already commenced. The USCG is in the throes of a major re-equipment programme.

The EC-130Q has been replaced by the Boeing E-6 Mercury in its task of communicating with US Navy ballistic missile submarines in time of war. Following removal of TACAMO equipment, the aircraft are operated as TC-130Q trainers and utility transports.

were received over the VLF to UHF range and transmitted via two trailing antennas on the tail and in the cargo door.

The EC-130Gs were later supplemented and eventually replaced by **EC-130Q** aircraft, which utilized the C-130H airframe and could be distinguished by their wingtip ESM pods.

Drone launcher

The US Navy's once sizeable fleet of Hercules has rapidly diminished in recent years, but the **C-130F** standard transport and LC-130F/R remained in service in 2003. Three **DC-130A Hercules** drone launcher aircraft also remained in use. In December 1998, the USAF transferred the **NC-130H** – the former EC-130V drug interdiction aircraft used briefly by the Coast Guard in the early 1990s – to the USN. The aircraft joined the

Naval Force Aircraft Test Squadron at Patuxent River, Maryland as a development platform for the Hawkeye 2000 radar system. The Naval Reserve operates **C-130T** aircraft for logistic support.

US Coast Guard

The US Coast Guard operates 30 **HC-130H Hercules** aircraft. While other air arms use the 'Herk' as a transport, to drop paratroops, or for utility missions, the Coast Guard also operates its **HC 130H-7** machines in the search and rescue, ice patrol and maritime surveillance roles. The potential replacement for the HC-130H-7 (of which the oldest was delivered in 1973) is the second-generation **HC-130J Hercules**, of which the US Coast Guard had received one from an order for six by March 2003.

The growing drugs problems in the United States led to an

intensification in the interdiction campaign against drug runners in the late 1980s. Following its use of borrowed E-2 Hawkeyes, the US Coast Guard decided to procure its own AEW platform by converting an HC-130H to **EC-130V** configuration. General Dynamics undertook conversion work to install the E-2's AN/APS-145 radar antenna above the

C-130's fuselage and three palletised operators' consoles inside the cabin. The aircraft went into service with the Coast Guard at Clearwater, Florida, in 1991. However, following extensive evaluations in interdiction patrols lasting up to 10 hours, the programme was considered to be too costly and so was subsequently cancelled.

Right: Three DC-130A aircraft fly special drone-support operations for the US Navy.

Below: These KC-130T tanker/transport aircraft were photographed while supporting USMC troops during ongoing work in Afghanistan as part of Operation Enduring Freedom.

EMBRAER EMB-110 Bandeirante and EMB-111 Patrulha Multi-role light transport and MP aircraft

The aircraft design which launched EMBRAER (Empresa Brasileira de Aeronáutica SA) as a significant force among aerospace manufacturers made its maiden flight on 19 August 1972, and resulted from a requirement for a light transport issued by the Força Aérea Brasileira (Brazilian air force) and the country's airlines. A nine-seat predecessor with the same basic features (low-wing cantilever monoplane configuration, retractable tricycle landing gear and powerplant of two PT6A turboprops) had been tested in prototype form as the **EMB-100** (military designation **YC-95**), but the **EMB-110 Bandeirante** (pioneer) featured a much larger cabin which found favour with

civil operators overseas, as well as with the Brazilian military.

The first three of 80 Bandeirantes ordered by the Brazilian air force were delivered in February 1973 and the type rapidly became the mainstay of the service's transport force. The 60 **C-95** models were 12-seat versions, and were supplemented by 20 **C-95A** (**EMB-110K1**) freighters.

These machines were followed by 31 examples of the **C-95B**, a military version of the improved EMB-110P civil model, two of which were also bought by Gabon.

The Uruguayan air force took delivery of five 15-seat **EMB-110C** aircraft in 1975, and the Chilean navy bought three

EMB-110CN navalised aircraft in the following year.

Four specialized versions also entered Brazilian military service. The first of these to join the Brazilian air force was the eight-seat **EC-95** for the checking and calibration of navigation aids. Four of these (designated **EMB-110A** by the manufacturer) entered service.

The EC-95 was followed by six examples of the seven-seat **R-95** (**EMB-110B**) photographic survey version. This model has apertures in the cabin floor to accommodate a Zeiss camera and associated equipment; Doppler and inertial navigation systems are also fitted. The R-95 serves with the Comando Costeiro (COMCOS, or coastal command) at Recife. One example of the EMB-110B was also acquired by Uruguay.

Two previously undelivered **EMB-110P1A** civilian transports were bought by the Colombian air force, along with three for the Peruvian government.

Dedicated MR version

COMCOS also operates the **P-95** maritime surveillance version which the company designates **EMB-111A**. An Eaton-AIL

The Chilean navy purchased six EMB-111ANs and three EMB-110CNs in 1976–77; these perform fixed-wing maritime reconnaissance and transport duties.

AN/APS-128 Sea Patrol search radar is housed in a large nose radome, and is fully integrated with the aircraft's INS. A high-power searchlight, signal cartridge launcher and an ESM system are also carried, and rockets can be launched from four underwing pylons. Wingtip fuel tanks increase the aircraft's endurance to nine hours.

The Brazilian P-95s are known locally by the name **Bandeirulha**, a contraction of **Bandeirante Patrulha** (patrol pioneer). Brazil later bought a second batch of improved **P-95B** aircraft with upgraded avionics and strengthened airframes, a standard to which the P-95 machines were upgraded. Six **EMB-111AN** aircraft were delivered to the Chilean navy, and a single example to the Gabonese air force. The Chilean navy's EMB-111ANs replaced four surplus Lockheed SP-2E Neptunes, the delivery of which was embargoed by the United

---

SPECIFICATION	
EMBRAER EMB-111 Bandeirante Patrulha (P-95A) **Type:** six/seven-seat coastal patrol and SAR aircraft **Powerplant:** two Pratt & Whitney Canada PT6A-34 turboprop engines each rated at 559 kW (750 shp) **Performance:** maximum cruising speed 360 km/h (223 mph) at 3050 m (10,000 ft); initial climb rate 362 m (1,190 ft) per minute; service ceiling 7770 m (25,500 ft); range 2945 km (1,830 miles) **Weights:** empty 3760 kg (8,289 lb);	maximum take-off 7000 kg (15,432 lb) **Dimensions:** wing span 15.95 m (52 ft 4 in) with tip tanks; length 14.91 m (48 ft 11 in); height 4.91 m (16 ft 1¼ in); wing area 29.1 m² (313.23 sq ft) **Armament:** up to 1000 kg (2,205 lb) of disposable stores carried on four underwing hardpoints and generally comprising eight 127-mm (5-in) air-to-surface unguided rockets or four multiple launchers each carrying seven 70-mm (2.75-in) air-to-surface unguided rockets

States. Two EMB-111As were also delivered to Angola.

SAR version

An SAR version is designated SC-95B, or **EMB-110P1(K)**. Deliveries began in late 1981 of eight to Brazil's COMCOS at Campo Grande; the type has a bubble window on each side of the fuselage, and can carry six litters in addition to observation and rescue personnel. A machine of the same basic type was also delivered to Senegambia.

Production of the Bandeirante for the civil as well as military markets lasted until 1990, and amounted to a total of some 500 aircraft.

Dornier Do 228 Maritime patrol and transport aircraft

This aircraft, marked as a Do-228, is one of the HAL-built Dornier Do 228MPA (Maritime Patrol Aircraft) machines for the Indian Coast Guard.

When Dornier adopted the designation 128-2 and 128-6 for the Skyservant variants previously known as the Do 28D-2 and Do 28D-6, two further derivatives of the basic twin-engined transport were in the project phase as the **Do 28E-1** and **Do 28E-2**. Given a go-ahead in November 1979, these then became the **Dornier Do 228-100** and **Do 228-200** respectively, differing essentially only in fuselage length and operational weights.

Using the same fuselage cross-section as the Skyservant, the Do 228-100 was sized to seat 15 passengers, while the longer 228-200 would seat 19. Prototypes flew, respectively, on 28 March and 9 May 1981, and first deliveries were made (for airline use) in 1982.

Indian orders

The majority of Do 228s were built for commercial use, the major exception being those of the Indian Air Force and the Indian Coast Guard. The latter began to operate the first of 36 **Do 228-201** aircraft in July 1986, these having MEL Marec II

radar, a Swedish IR/UV linescan sensor and other special features. By 2003, at least 15 Do 228-201s had been acquired by the Indian Air Force for transport, and the Indian Navy had 24 aircraft from a requirement for 27 on order. The Coast Guard had some 36 **Do 228MPA** machines on order, the naval and Coast Guard aircraft to be completed upon the assembly/licence-production line set up by HAL at Bangalore.

After Dornier had delivered three 228-201s to the Indian Coast Guard (as well as five for airline use), HAL flew the first Indian-assembled aircraft in January 1986.

One 228-201 was evaluated by both the Bundesmarine and the Luftwaffe, this later becoming a 'hack' for use by the latter, while the former acquired another fully equipped for

Finland's Air Patrol Squadron's two Dornier Do 228s are equipped with SLAR and other sensors for undertaking maritime patrol duties.

maritime pollution control. Other military users have included Finland (multi-sensor aircraft for the para-military Frontier Guard), Malawi (three 228-201s and a single **Do 228-202**), Niger (one -201 delivered in 1986), Nigeria (one -100 transport and two VIP -200s), the Royal Oman police air wing (two -100s), and the Royal Thai navy (three equipped for maritime recce with Bendix 1500 radar).

SPECIFICATION	
Dornier Do 228 Maritime Patrol Version A	minute; service ceiling 8535 m (28,000 ft); range 1740 km (1,982 miles) with standard fuel
Type: coastal and maritime patrol aircraft	**Weights:** standard empty 2960 kg (6,526 lb); maximum take-off 5980 kg (13,183 lb)
Powerplant: two Garrett TPE331-5-252D turboprops each rated at 533 kW (715 shp)	**Dimensions:** wing span 16.97 m (55 ft 6 in); length 15.04 m (49 ft 4 in); height 4.86 m (15 ft 11½ in); wing area 32 m² (344.46 sq ft)
Performance: average cruising speed at optimum altitude for maximum range 305 km/h (190 mph); maximum rate of climb at sea level 582 m (1,910 ft) per	**Payload:** maximum payload 2117 kg (4,667 lb)

Dassault Atlantique 2 ASW, ASV and maritime patrol aircraft

The **Dassault Atlantique 2** was originally named the **ANG** (**Atlantic Nouvelle Génération**, or new-generation Atlantic). It was intended as a multinational programme to replace the Atlantic (now known as the Atlantic 1) with the various air forces that use it. With a requirement for 30 aircraft, France remains the sole customer, making the project viable. Despite this, the rate of manufacture is too low for competitive costings.

After very prolonged studies, the Atlantique 2 was designed as a minimum-change type with totally new avionics, systems and equipment, packaged into an airframe differing from that of the original model only in ways to increase service life, reduce costs and minimize maintenance. In addition, an Astadyne gas-turbine auxiliary power unit is fitted, and production machines are fitted with Ratier/BAe propellers with larger composite blades.

Sensors and weapons

The Atlantique 2's sensors include the Thomson-CSF Iguane frequency-agile radar with a new interrogator and decoder, a SAT/TRT Tango FLIR in a chin turret, more than 100 sonobuoys in the rear fuselage, a new Crouzet MAD receiver in the boom, extending rearward from the tail, and the Thomson-CSF ARAR 13 ESM installation with frequency analysis at the top of the fin and D/F in the new wingtip nacelles. All processors, data buses and sensor links are of standard digital form, navaids include an inertial system and Navstar satellite receiver, and every part of the avionics and communications has been upgraded. The main weapons bay can accommodate all NATO standard bombs and depth charges, as well as other weapon types including two air-to-surface or anti-ship missiles, up to eight Mk 46 torpedoes or seven Franco-Italian MU39 Impact advanced torpedoes. The Atlantique has a rarely used

A key sensor of the 'Nouvelle Génération' Atlantique 2 is the Thomson-CSF Iguane radar, which is housed in a retractable 'dustbin' radome. Here it is seen deployed on the first production aircraft.

secondary transport function, and could also be used in a limited overland electronic reconnaissance role.

The first Atlantique 2 flew in May 1981 and production deliveries began in 1989.

Proposed variants of the Atlantique 2 have included a BAe Nimrod replacement for the RAF, with additional turbofan engines in pods under the wing and with either Allison T406 or General Electric T407 turboprop engines replacing the Tynes; an **Atlantique 3** with further improvements; and the **Europatrol**, a derivative aimed at replacing NATO's Lockheed P-3 Orions. A Tyne upgrade has also been proposed.

The most noticeable differences between the Atlantique 2 and the Atlantic are the former's wingtip ECM pods, nose-mounted Tango FLIR turret, the prominent cooling intakes below the cockpit and the reshaped fin top, housing an ECM aerial.

SPECIFICATION	
Dassault Atlantique 2 **Type:** 10-/12-crew long-range maritime patrol and ASW/ASV aircraft **Powerplant:** two Rolls-Royce Tyne RTy.20 Mk 21 turboprop engines each rated at 4549 ekW (6,100 ehp) **Performance:** maximum speed 648 km/h (402 mph) at optimum altitude; patrol speed 315 km/h (196 mph) between sea level and 1525 m (5,000 ft); initial climb rate 884 m (2,900 ft) per minute; service ceiling 9145 m (30,000 ft); operational radius 3333 km	(2,071 miles) for a 2-hour patrol in the ASV role with one AM39 Exocet missile **Weights:** empty 25600 kg (56,437 lb); maximum take-off 46200 kg (101,852 lb) **Dimensions:** wing span 37.42 m (122 ft 9¼ in) including wingtip ESM pods; length 31.62 m (103 ft 9 in); height 10.89 m (35 ft 8¾ in); wing area 120.34 m² (1,295.37 sq ft) **Armament:** up to 6000 kg (13,228 lb) of disposable stores carried as 2500 kg (5,511 lb) internally and 3500 kg (7,717 lb) externally

Airtech CN-235 Maritime variants

Following the success of their C.212 Aviocar, CASA of Spain and IPTN (Industri Pesawat Terbang Nusantara) of Indonesia joined forces on a 50/50 basis to create Airtech (Aircraft Technology Industries) specifically for the design and development of a larger and more efficient pressurized transport for both civil and military use.

Work on the resulting **CN-235** began in 1980, and prototypes were simultaneously constructed in the partner countries. The Spanish prototype made its maiden flight on 11 November 1983, the Indonesian prototype following it into the air on 30 December of the same year. Deliveries from the Indonesian and Spanish production lines began in December 1986 and February 1987, respectively.

In January 1990 a licence was signed with Tusas Aerospace Industries (TAI) for the assembly and then the construction of 50 aircraft in Turkey.

Variants

The main variants of the CN-235 series have been the **CN-235 Series 10** initial model with two 1268-kW (1,700-shp) CT7-7As; the Spanish-built **CN-235 Series 100** and Indonesian-built **CN.235 Series 110** improved model with CT7-9Cs; the **CN-235 Series 200** and **CN-235 Series 220** with structural strengthening and aerodynamic refinements; the Indonesian-developed **CN-235 Series 330 Phoenix** aimed at an RAAF requirement; the CN-235 M military transport; the Spanish-built **CN-235 MP Persuader** and the Indonesian-built **CN.235 MPA** maritime patrol types with advanced avionics and six underwing hardpoints; and the **CN-235 QC** quick-change

Irish Air Corps CN-235 MPs carry a mission fit comprising a Litton AN/APS-504(V)5 search radar, a FLIR Systems FLIR2000HP, and a two-man operator station with datalink and air-droppable stores (including life rafts).

Arguably Ireland's most important military aircraft is the CN-235, two of which are operated by the Maritime Squadron. They undertake coastal patrol work.

cargo/passenger transport. Military sales have been brisk, and air forces in at least 20 countries have taken various versions of the aircraft.

Maritime CN-295

In 1997, CASA announced its intention to produce the stretched **CN-295**, with a full EFIS cockpit and power provided by 1972-kW (2,645-hp) Pratt & Whitney Canada PW127G turboprops.

The first CN-295 flew on 28 November 1997 and the Spanish air force ordered nine in 1999. EADS CASA has since developed the **CN-295 Persuader** maritime patrol version, of which the UAE navy ordered four examples in 2001.

SPECIFICATION

Airtech CN-235 MPA
Type: maritime patrol/anti-ship aircraft
Powerplant: two General Electric CT7-9C turboprops each flat-rated at 1305 kW (1,750 shp) without automatic power reserve or 1395 kW (1,870 shp) with automatic power reserve
Performance: maximum speed 445 km/h (276 mph) at sea level; range about 4355 km (2,706 miles) with a payload of 3600 kg (7,936 lb)

Weights: operating empty 8800 kg (19,400 lb); maximum take-off 16,500 kg (36,376 lb)
Dimensions: wing span 25.81 m (84 ft 8 in); length 21.35 m (70 ft 2½ in); height 8.18 m (26 ft 10 in); wing area 59.10 m² (636.17 sq ft)
Armament: provision for three hardpoints under each wing, Indonesian navy aircraft can carry two AM39 Exocet AShMs

---

EADS CASA C.212 Aviocar Special mission versions

Since its introduction in 1979, three specialized variants of the **C.212 Series 200M Aviocar (Special Mission Variant)** have been developed: the **C.212-M Series 200M (ASW Version)**; **C.212 Series 200M (MP Version)**; and **C.212 Series 200M (DE Version)**, with a flight crew of two on the flightdeck and a mission crew generally of four personnel in the modified cabin.

The ASW Version is generally similar to the baseline Series 200M, except for its electronic suite and armament. In the anti-submarine role, the aircraft's primary sensors are search radar, sonobuoys, MAD, ESM and Stingray, Mk 46 and A 244/S lightweight torpedoes.

Maritime patrol

The MP Version is optimized for maritime patrol and anti-ship tasks, and has as its primary sensor the Eaton-AIL APS-128 search radar (with its antenna in a nose radome to scan through an arc of 270°), used in conjunction with Sea Skua or AS15TT lightweight anti-ship missiles. In other respects, the Maritime Patrol Version is basically similar to the ASW Version apart from its revised accommodation, lack of armament capability, modified avionics and carriage of a searchlight, smoke markers and a camera. Typical of the MP Version in its late-production form are the three such aircraft built under licence by IPTN for the Indonesian navy's air arm

with the Thomson-CSF AMASCOS (Airborne Maritime Situation Control System).

The DE Version of the special-mission Aviocar (such as the four aircraft built for the United Arab Emirates) is optimized for the Elint/ECM role with its automatic signals interception, classification and localization capability. Two similar aircraft delivered to Portugal also possess a jamming capability.

The **EADS CASA C-212 Patrullero** (patroller), which is otherwise known as the **EADS CASA C-212 Series 300M (Special Mission Version)**, is the special missions variant of the C-212 Series 300M and is available in the same three specialized variants as the C-212 Series 200M.

SPECIFICATION

CASA C.212 Patrullero (ASW Version)
Type: six-crew short/medium-range maritime and coastal-reconnaissance aircraft with ASW capability
Powerplant: two AlliedSignal TPE331-10R-513C turboprop engines each flat-rated at 671 kW (900 shp) without automatic power reserve and 690 kW (925 shp) with automatic power reserve
Performance: maximum cruising speed 354 km/h (220 mph) at 3050 m (10,000 ft); economical cruising speed 300 km/h (186 mph) at 3050 m (10,000 ft); initial climb rate 497 m (1,630 ft) per minute;

service ceiling 7925 m (26,000 ft)
Weights: empty 3780 kg (8,333 lb); maximum take-off 8000 kg (17,637 lb)
Dimensions: wing span 20.28 m (66 ft 6½ in); length dependent on the radar installed; height 6.30 m (20 ft 8 in); area 41 m² (441.33 sq ft)
Armament: up to 500 kg (1,102 lb) of disposable stores carried on one hardpoint on each side of the fuselage, and generally comprising two Stingray, Mk 46 or A 244/S lightweight torpedoes, or two AS15TT or Sea Skua lightweight anti-ship missiles

The Mexican navy operates 8 CASA 212-300s for a variety of roles, but primarily for littoral maritime patrol. This example belongs to the 3rd Naval Air Squadron based at Las Bajades, Vera Cruz.

Beriev A-40 and Be-42 Albatross 'Mermaid'

Multi-role military amphibian flying boat

Design of the **Beriev A-40 Albatross** (ASCC/NATO reporting name **'Mermaid'**) began during 1983 in an effort to create a successor to the Be-12 'Mail' and Ilyushin Il-38 'May' in the ASW, maritime patrol and minelaying roles, with search and rescue as a secondary capability. The prototype made its first flight during December 1986, and this new amphibian flying boat became known to the West during 1987. In 1988 the director of US naval intelligence revealed that the provisional reporting name, **'TAG-D'** (the fourth new experimental aircraft spotted at Taganrog), had been allocated to a new amphibian photographed by a US satellite. On 20 August 1989 the prototype made a flypast at the Aviation Day display at Tushino, and articles about the new flying boat began to appear in the Soviet press. The second prototype made the type's Western debut at the 1991 Paris air show.

The A-40 is the largest amphibian ever built, and is of completely modern design, with its turbofan engines nacelle-mounted on pylons above the wingroots. A turbojet take-off booster is fitted inside each pylon, with its nozzle usually covered by a vertically-split 'eyelid'. This powerplant location ensures that the inlets are protected from spray by the wing and small strakes on the sides of the bow.

The single-step hull is of revolutionary design, described by its creators as the world's first 'variable-rise bottom', with unique double chines. This sets new standards in stability and controllability in the water and gives smaller g forces on take-off and landing. 'Unsticking' from the water is aided by the incorporation of small wedge-shaped boxes aft of the step.

Powerful radar

The A-40 has a large surveillance, search and navigation radar with its antenna in a bow radome under the fixed inflight-refuelling probe, as well as a large stores bay in the hull aft of the step.

The large pods which form the wingroots accommodate

Neither of the two A-40 prototypes has yet flown with a full mission avionics fit. The precarious state of the entire Albatross project must place the future of this incredible aircraft in doubt.

avionics, as well as the aircraft's retracted four-wheel main landing gear bogies. Slim ESM pods are carried on the A-40's wingtips.

It has been suggested that the basic A-40 ASW and patrol amphibian was the subject of a 20-aircraft order by the Russian navy. The navy cannot afford the type, however, and the order has therefore lapsed.

In 2004, construction of the A-40 remains at just the two prototype aircraft, with one **Be-42** SAR version in a semi-complete state.

SPECIFICATION

Beriev A-40 Albatross 'Mermaid'
Type: eight-crew long-range ASW, maritime reconnaissance, minelaying and SAR amphibian flying boat
Powerplant: two Aviadvigatel (Soloviev) D-30KPV turbofan engines each rated at 117.68 kN (26,455 lb st) and two RKBM RD-60K turbojet engines each rated at 24.52 kN (5,511 lb st)
Performance: maximum speed 760 km/h (472 mph) at 6000 m (19,685 ft); cruising speed 720 km/h (447 mph) at 6000 m (19,685 ft);

initial climb rate 1800 m (5,906 ft) with one engine inoperative; service ceiling 9700 m (31,825 ft); range 5500 km (3,417 miles)
Weight: maximum take-off 86,000 kg (189,594 lb)
Dimensions: wing span 41.62 m (136 ft 6½ in); length 43.84 m (143 ft 10 in) including probe; height 11.07 m (36 ft 3¾ in); wing area 200 m² (2,152.85 sq ft)
Armament: up to 6500 kg (14,330 lb) of bombs, depth charges, mines and torpedoes

Beriev Be-200 Multi-role Russian amphibian

The **Beriev Be-200** is a multi-role amphibian flying boat which is designed primarily for civil tasks and is, in effect, a scaled-down and simplified version of the **A-40 Albatross**.

Among the differences from the A-40 are the omission of all military electronics and provision for them, the relocation of the

flying boats's stabilizing floats from the wingtips to points further inboard under the wing, the addition of winglets, the alteration of the main landing gear units to twin-wheel units, the omission of the booster turbojets and the introduction of a Western avionics suite created by AlliedSignal.

Fire-fighting role

The Be-200 is intended primarily as a forest fire-fighting machine with cabin provision for 30 fully equipped smoke jumpers, and tanks under the cabin floor for 12,000 kg (26,456 lb) of water that can be scooped up from any suitable water body. Other roles envisaged for the type include

passenger transport, with the cabin outfitted for 32 first-class or 68 tourist-class passengers, cargo-hauling with a range of 1200 km (684 miles) while carrying a 7000-kg (15,432-lb) payload, air ambulance and search and rescue. In 1998 it was reported that Beriev, now part of the Sukhoi industrial group, had suggested a militarized version to South Korea for use in the maritime reconnaissance role.

Troubled programme

The maiden flight of the first of four Be-200 prototype and pre-production aircraft was planned for November 1995; however, this machine was completed only in September 1996 and the first flight was not until October 1998, after development delays.

Orders for the Be-200 have been placed by three elements of the CIS's civil aviation organisation for an initial 109 aircraft, some of them for use in paramilitary roles.

Severe delays in the powerplant package's financing and in the Russians' integration of the AlliedSignal avionics into the Aria 200 integrated avionics suite have afflicted the Beriev Be-200.

SPECIFICATION	
Beriev Be-200 **Type:** two-crew multi-role amphibian flying boat **Powerplant:** two ZMKB Progress (Ivchyenko) D-436T turbofan engines each rated at 73.55 kN (16,534 lb st) **Performance:** (estimated) maximum speed 720 km/h (447 mph) at 7000 m (22,965 ft); cruising speed 700 km/h (435 mph) at 8000 m	(26,245 ft); initial climb rate 840 m (2,756 ft) per minute; service ceiling 11,000 m (36,090 ft); range 4000 km (2,486 miles) **Weight:** maximum take-off 36000 kg (79,365 lb) **Dimensions:** wing span 32.7 m (107 ft 3½ in); length 32.05 m (105 ft 1¾ in); height 8.9 m (29 ft 2½ in); wing area 117.44 m² (1,264.16 sq ft)

Hawker Siddeley/BAe/BAE Systems Nimrod
Turbofan-powered maritime patrol aircraft

The type now known as the **BAE Systems Nimrod** began life as the **Hawker Siddeley HS.801**, which was created on the basis of the de Havilland Comet's airframe as a maritime reconnaissance aircraft to replace the ageing, piston-engined Shackleton in service with the RAF's Coastal Command. Development began in 1964, and two unsold Comet 4Cs were converted as prototypes. A MAD 'stinger' was added to the tailcone, a search radar was added in the nose, a fin-tip radome ('football') was fitted to accommodate ESM equipment, and a new ventral weapons pannier was added beneath the cabin, giving a distinctive 'double-bubble' cross-section. These changes necessitated an increase in fin area.

The first prototype was powered by the production Nimrod's intended powerplant of four Spey turbofan engines and made its maiden flight on 23 May 1967, serving as an aerodynamic test bed and for airframe/engine integration. The second conversion retained the Comet's original Avon turbojets and recorded its first flight on 31 July, then serving as the avionics development aircraft.

Nimrod variants

The first of 46 examples of the production type, known as the **Nimrod MR.Mk 1**, flew on 28 June 1968, and the type entered service with No. 236 OCU in October 1969, eventually equipping five operational squadrons including one based overseas at RAF Luqa, Malta. The British withdrawal from Malta rendered the last batch of eight Nimrods surplus to requirements, although they could usefully have been used to spread hours more evenly across the fleet, extending the Nimrod's life. Five were delivered to the RAF, and the others were retained by BAe for trials, but their useful life was short, seven of them being

This Nimrod MR.Mk 2P is shown in the Hemp over Light Aircraft Grey scheme that had been replaced by an overall Camouflage Grey scheme as standard by 2003.

selected for conversion to **Nimrod AEW.Mk 3** standard, along with four earlier Nimrod MR.Mk 1s. All of these airframes were effectively wasted, as the Nimrod AEW.Mk 3 never entered productive service and all but one were scrapped, the survivor becoming an instructional airframe.

From 1975 the 35 remaining MR.Mk 1s were upgraded to Nimrod MR.Mk 2 standard, the first MR.Mk 2 being redelivered to the RAF in August 1979. The Nimrod MR.Mk 2 introduced a completely new avionics and equipment suite, in which all major sensors and equipment items were changed. The aircraft received a new GEC central tactical system, which was based on a new computer and three separate processors for

SPECIFICATION	
Hawker Siddeley (BAe) **Nimrod MR.Mk 2** **Type:** 12-crew maritime reconnaissance, anti-submarine and anti-ship aircraft **Powerplant:** four Rolls-Royce Spey RB.168-20 Mk 250 turbofan engines each rated at 54 kN (12,140 lb st) **Performance:** maximum speed 926 km/h (575 mph) at optimum altitude; cruising speed 880 km/h (547 mph) at optimum altitude; patrol speed 370 km/h (230 mph)	at low altitude; service ceiling 12,800 m (42,000 ft); range 9266 km (5,758 miles); endurance 19 hours with one inflight refuelling **Weights:** empty 39,010 kg (86,000 lb); maximum take-off 87,091 kg (192,000 lb) **Dimensions:** wing span 35 m (114 ft 10 in); length 38.63 m (126 ft 9 in); height 9.08 m (29 ft 8½ in); wing area 197.04 m² (2,121 sq ft) **Armament:** up to 6124 kg (13,500 lb) of disposable stores carried internally and externally

The Nimrod fulfils three primary roles in RAF service: anti-submarine warfare (ASW), anti-surface unit warfare (ASUW) and search and rescue (SAR). In addition to these roles the Nimrods also assist civil agencies such as HM Customs or the Department for Environment, Food and Rural Affairs when requested.

navigation systems, radar and acoustic sensors. The old ASV.Mk 21D radar was replaced by Thorn EMI Searchwater equipment with a colour display. The acoustics system was made compatible with modern sonobuoys, including the BARRA, SSQ-41 and SSQ-53, TANDEM and Ultra active and passive types.

Communications equipment was similarly upgraded.

Combat additions

The addition of an inflight-refuelling probe (initially to 16 aircraft for participation in Operation Corporate, the United Kingdom's campaign to regain the Falkland Islands in 1982)

created the **Nimrod MR.Mk 2P** – the 'P' was subsequently dropped in the late 1990s – and this change also necessitated the addition of tiny swept finlets on the horizontal tail surface. The Falklands War also resulted in the first operational use of the Nimrod's underwing hardpoints, giving the ability to carry AIM-9 Sidewinders for self-defence, or Harpoon anti-ship missiles, Stingray torpedoes, bombs or depth charges for offensive purposes. The planned wingtip Loral ARI.18240/1 ESM pods were added later, these requiring larger rectangular finlets. All the aircraft were then revised with both refuelling probes and ESM

pods. For operations from Seeb in Oman, during Operation Desert Storm, to drive the Iraqi occupying forces from Kuwait, a number of aircraft were drawn from Nos 120 (lead), 42 and 206 Sqns to form the Nimrod MR Detachment. Several of the aircraft were modified to what was unofficially known as **Nimrod MR.Mk 2P(GM)** standard, the **Gulf Modification** involving the addition of an underwing FLIR turret on the starboard wing, BOZ electronic countermeasures pods and a TRD (Towed Radar Decoy).

Nimrod MRA.Mk 4

During the mid-1990s, BAe was selected to create a radically updated and revitalised force of 21 Nimrods after winning the Ministry of Defence's Maritime

Patrol Aircraft competition. Due to re-enter service between 2002 and 2007, but now likely to be 2005 at the earliest, after virtually total reconstruction to the so-called **Nimrod 2000** standard, the **Nimrod MRA.Mk 4** retains only the pressure hull, keel, weapons bay, tailcone and fixed tail surfaces of its predecessor. The rest of the airframe is essentially new, and the powerplant is changed to a quartet of Rolls-Royce BR.710 turbofan engines each rated at 66.73 kN (15,000 lb st) to provide undiminished performance despite a 20 per cent increase in maximum take-off weight to 105,598 kg (232,800 lb), which also requires beefed-up landing gear units.

A new generation of mission avionics is also being provided by a Boeing-led team to maintain the MRA.Mk 4's maritime reconnaissance, anti-ship and anti-submarine capabilities at a very high level.

Left: The Nimrod MRA.Mk 4 has been beset by development problems and cost overruns, but should emerge as the world's most capable MR platform.

Below: Some Nimrods were given a limited self-defence capability during the Falklands campaign with the addition of AIM-9L Sidewinders under the wings; these were also to be used against Argentine Boeing 707s which were patrolling the same oceans. This aircraft is an MR.Mk 2P, with a retrofitted inflight-refuelling probe.

Lockheed P-3 Orion Maritime patrol aircraft

This P-3C Update III is shown as it appeared with VP-4 'Skinny Dragons' at Kaneohe Bay, Hawaii. All of the Orion units previously operating at MCAS Barber's Point transferred to this new location in July 1999. VP-4 was active during Desert Storm, flying from Masirah.

In August 1957 the US Navy issued Type Specification No. 146 calling for a new anti-submarine aircraft to replace the P-2 Neptune. The Lockheed proposal was based on the L-188 Electra airliner, and in May 1958 the company was awarded a contract for the new type. It modified the third Electra airframe as the prototype, with a tail-mounted MAD boom and a ventral bulge simulating a weapons bay. Following extensive adaptations (including a shortening of the fuselage), the aircraft made a successful maiden flight as the **YP3V-1** (later redesignated as the **YP-3A**) on 25 November 1959. The USN ordered an initial batch of seven in October 1960, and the first of these flew in April 1961. In 1962 the type was redesignated as the **P-3A Orion**.

The P-3A entered service in the summer of 1962 with 3355-kW (4,500-eshp) T56-A-10W turboprops and, from the 110th aircraft, the DELTIC (DELayed TIme Compression) acoustic data-processing system that doubled sonobuoy information-

VP-9 'Golden Eagles' was deployed with its P-3Cs to Misawa, Japan, when this photograph was taken in February 2003.

processing capability and also incorporated redesigned avionics. Within a short time most existing aircraft had also been retrofitted. In the summer of 1965, after the delivery of 157 P-3As, Lockheed began production of the **P-3B**. This was fitted with more powerful T56-A-14 engines and was heavier than its predecessor, mainly through having provision for the AGM-12 Bullpup ASM, but retained basically the same electronics fit. The P-3B secured the first export orders for the type, and became operational with New Zealand and Norway (five aircraft each) and also with Australia (10 aircraft). From 1977 the USN's P-3Bs were updated with improved navigation and acoustic-processing equipment, and with provision for the AGM-84 Harpoon missile. P-3B production ended in 1969 after

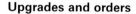

the completion of 144 aircraft (125 of them for the US Navy).

Surplus P-3As were later converted to **RP-3A** standard (three aircraft) for oceanographic reconnaissance, and to **WP-3A** standard (four aircraft) for weather reconnaissance. Six early aircraft were refitted as staff transports under the **VP-3A** designation, while a handful entered service as **TP-3A** aircrew trainers. Several early Orions were converted for utility transport duties as **UP-3A** and **UP-3B** machines.

Four P-3As were transferred to the US Customs Service under the **P-3A(CS)** designation with APG-63 nose radar to

complement four **P-3B AEW** aircraft with the APS-138 surveillance radar using an antenna in a rotodome above the rear fuselage.

Upgrades and orders

New Zealand's aircraft received an avionics upgrade (the first by Boeing and the other five by Air New Zealand) to become **P-3K** machines: the sixth of these aircraft was an ex-Australian P-3B. Norway acquired two P-3Bs in 1979 and one of these and one original aircraft were adapted to **P-3N** standard for pilot training and fishery protection. The other five were transferred to Spain to replace four P-3As leased from the USN and to augment the surviving two of three P-3As purchased by Spain. The six surviving Australian aircraft were upgraded to **P-3C** standard as **P-3P** machines and subsequently transferred to Portugal in 1986. Australia later purchased three surplus USN P-3Bs for use as trainers with the designation **TAP-3**. Later customers for ex-USN P-3As and P-3Bs include

Many JMSDF P-3Cs (a VP-2 aircraft is illustrated) carry a dorsal radome for SATCOMs.

Argentina (eight P-3Bs), Greece (six P-3Bs) and Thailand (two P-3As and one **UP-3T**).

Ultimate ASW Orion

The P-3C is now the USN's primary land-based ASW patrol aircraft. It retains the airframe/powerplant combination of the P-3B, and the first service-test **YP-3C** was a P-3B conversion that first flew on 18 September 1968. Since then, the P-3C has also been exported to Australia, the Netherlands, Norway, Japan, Pakistan and South Korea. The baseline P-3C has APS-115B search radar, ASQ-81 MAD and the AQA-7 DIFAR (Directional Acoustics-Frequency Analysis and Recording) system, as well as an integrated ASW and navigation system.

The P-3C entered service in 1969, and 118 baseline aircraft were followed by about 247 of various **Update** versions for the US Navy and export, of which the last was a machine delivered to South Korea in September 1995 from a newly established production line.

The **P-3C Update I** (31 built) introduced a seven-fold increase in computer memory and Omega navigation in place of the original LORAN. The **P-3C Update II** (37 built for delivery from August 1977) featured an advanced sonobuoy reference system, provision for the AGM-84 and the AAS-36 IRDS (Infra-Red Detection System). The

P-3C Update II.5 (24 aircraft) has a more reliable nav/comms suite, MAD compensation, standardised pylons and other improvements. The definitive P-3C Orion variant is the **P-3C Update III**, fitted with an entirely new IBM UYS-1 Proteus acoustic signal processor and a new sonobuoy communications link. These enable the aircraft to monitor concurrently twice the number of sonobuoys, as can the Update II.5 version. The Update III was the last production version and was first delivered in May 1984. Most baseline P-3C Orions were later modified to the **P-3C Update III Retrofit** standard.

Exports of the P-3C included 10 Update II aircraft for Australia with the Anglo-Australian Barra acoustic data processor and indigenously developed Barra

The RNZAF was the first export customer for the Orion, receiving five P-3B DELTIC aircraft for service with No. 5 Squadron at Whenuapai in 1966, to replace Sunderlands. In the 1980s the fleet was enhanced under the Rigel programme, resulting in the P-3K variant with APS-134 imaging radar and an infrared turret. Another upgrade programme, known as Sirius, was cancelled in 2000, but a new upgrade was implemented in 2003.

passive directional sonobuoys. Australia's second 10-aircraft batch comprised P-3C Update II.5 machines, but these are known locally by the designation **P-3W**. Ten Australian aircraft later received an Elta-developed ESM suite, and were then upgraded to **AP-3C** standard in a Raytheon-led programme including the Elta EL/M-2022 radar, Canadian UYS-503 acoustic processing system and improved nav/comm systems. The Netherlands and Japan also received Update II.5s. The P-3Cs operated by Norway and South Korea are Update IIIs. Japan received three aircraft, plus a

further five in component knocked-down kit form for assembly before Kawasaki switched to complete manufacture of the balance of the 110 aircraft required. Iran received six baseline P-3C aircraft to the **P-3F** standard with a receptacle for inflight refuelling. The **CP-140 Aurora**, which resembles the P-3C externally, was built to Canadian specification with different avionics, and the 18 such aircraft were complemented by three **CP-140A Arcturus** aircraft with no ASW equipment, which were therefore used for training and economic zone protection.

During operations against former Yugoslavia, US Navy P-3Cs operated from Sigonella, Sicily, where this aircraft is seen taxiing for a mission during Operation Allied Force. This VP-5 AIP Orion has AGM-65s under the wings for attacks against vessels which may have attempted to beat the NATO blockade. Although routinely carried, no Mavericks were fired in anger.

SPECIFICATION	
Lockheed P-3C Orion	10 in); height 10.27 m (33 ft 8½ in); wing area 120.77 m² (1,300 sq ft)
Type: 10-crew long-range maritime patrol and anti-submarine aircraft	
Powerplant: four Rolls-Royce T56-A-14 turboprop engines each rated at 3661 kW (4,910 ehp)	**Armament:** up to 9072 kg (20,000 lb) of disposable stores carried in a lower-fuselage weapons bay and on 10 underwing hardpoints; including 10/20-kiloton B57 nuclear weapons; 454-kg (1,000-lb) Mk 52 mines; 907-kg (2,000-lb) Mk 55 or Mk 56 mines; Mk 54 and Mk 101 depth bombs; Mk 82 and Mk 83 bombs; Mk 38 and Mk 40 destructors; Mk 46 and Mk 50 Barracuda torpedoes; AGM-84 Harpoon AShMs, AGM-65 Maverick ASMs; AIM-9L Sidewinder AAMs and rocket pods
Performance: maximum speed 761 km/h (473 mph) 'clean' at 4575 m (15,000 ft); maximum climb rate 594 m (1,950 ft) per minute; service ceiling 8625 m (28,300 ft); radius 2494 km (1,550 miles) with 3 hours on station	
Weights: empty 27,890 kg (61,491 lb); maximum take-off 64,410 kg (142,000 lb)	
Dimensions: wing span 30.37 m (99 ft 8 in); length 35.61 m (116 ft	

P-3 Orion
On patrol

With such a large number in service, Lockheed's P-3 Orion is the world's most important maritime aircraft. Constant updating has kept it at the forefront of patrol technology, even as its mission changed dramatically. The basic airframe is getting old, however, and a replacement is needed.

US Navy Orions regularly participate in joint exercises with other P-3 operators. Here 'Charlies' from VP-47 and the Japan Maritime Self-Defense Force fly past the joint US/Japanese fleet during exercise Rimpac 2000.

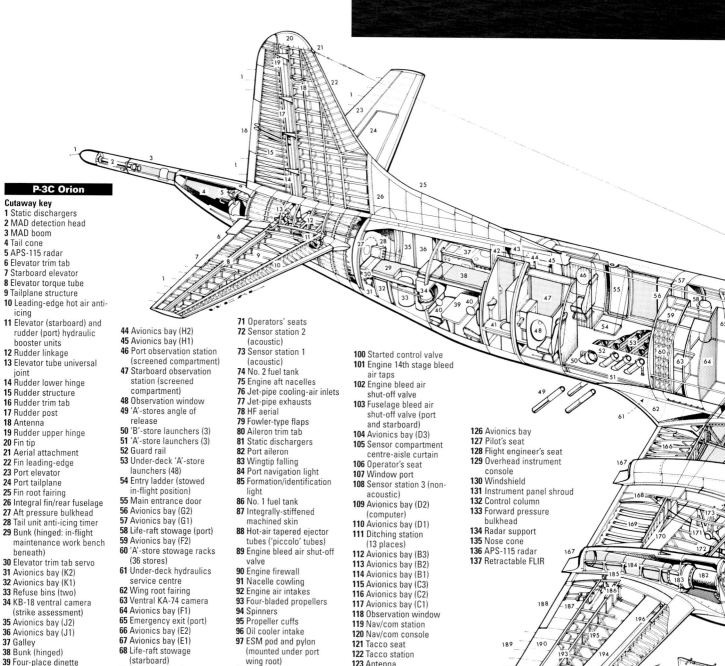

P-3C Orion

Cutaway key

1 Static dischargers
2 MAD detection head
3 MAD boom
4 Tail cone
5 APS-115 radar
6 Elevator trim tab
7 Starboard elevator
8 Elevator torque tube
9 Tailplane structure
10 Leading-edge hot air anti-icing
11 Elevator (starboard) and rudder (port) hydraulic booster units
12 Rudder linkage
13 Elevator tube universal joint
14 Rudder lower hinge
15 Rudder structure
16 Rudder trim tab
17 Rudder post
18 Antenna
19 Rudder upper hinge
20 Fin tip
21 Aerial attachment
22 Fin leading-edge
23 Port elevator
24 Port tailplane
25 Fin root fairing
26 Integral fin/rear fuselage
27 Aft pressure bulkhead
28 Tail unit anti-icing timer
29 Bunk (hinged: in-flight maintenance work bench beneath)
30 Elevator trim tab servo
31 Avionics bay (K2)
32 Avionics bay (K1)
33 Refuse bins (two)
34 KB-18 ventral camera (strike assessment)
35 Avionics bay (J2)
36 Avionics bay (J1)
37 Galley
38 Bunk (hinged)
39 Four-place dinette
40 Window ports
41 Lavatory
42 Avionics bay (H3)
43 Coat closet

44 Avionics bay (H2)
45 Avionics bay (H1)
46 Port observation station (screened compartment)
47 Starboard observation station (screened compartment)
48 Observation window
49 'A'-stores angle of release
50 'B'-store launchers (3)
51 'A'-store launchers (3)
52 Guard rail
53 Under-deck 'A'-store launchers (48)
54 Entry ladder (stowed in-flight position)
55 Main entrance door
56 Avionics bay (G2)
57 Avionics bay (G1)
58 Life-raft stowage (port)
59 Avionics bay (F2)
60 'A'-store stowage racks (36 stores)
61 Under-deck hydraulics service centre
62 Wing root fairing
63 Ventral KA-74 camera
64 Avionics bay (F1)
65 Emergency exit (port)
66 Avionics bay (E2)
67 Avionics bay (E1)
68 Life-raft stowage (starboard)
69 Emergency exit (starboard)
70 Main electrical load centre (starboard)

71 Operators' seats
72 Sensor station 2 (acoustic)
73 Sensor station 1 (acoustic)
74 No. 2 fuel tank
75 Engine aft nacelles
76 Jet-pipe cooling-air inlets
77 Jet-pipe exhausts
78 HF aerial
79 Fowler-type flaps
80 Aileron trim tab
81 Static dischargers
82 Port aileron
83 Wingtip falling
84 Port navigation light
85 Formation/identification light
86 No. 1 fuel tank
87 Integrally-stiffened machined skin
88 Hot-air tapered ejector tubes ('piccolo' tubes)
89 Engine bleed air shut-off valve
90 Engine firewall
91 Nacelle cowling
92 Engine air intakes
93 Four-bladed propellers
94 Spinners
95 Propeller cuffs
96 Oil cooler intake
97 ESM pod and pylon (mounted under port wing root)
98 Oil cooler system
99 Engine oil cooling augmentor (jet pump) control system

100 Started control valve
101 Engine 14th stage bleed air taps
102 Engine bleed air shut-off valve
103 Fuselage bleed air shut-off valve (port and starboard)
104 Avionics bay (D3)
105 Sensor compartment centre-aisle curtain
106 Operator's seat
107 Window port
108 Sensor station 3 (non-acoustic)
109 Avionics bay (D2) (computer)
110 Avionics bay (D1)
111 Ditching station (13 places)
112 Avionics bay (B3)
113 Avionics bay (B2)
114 Avionics bay (B1)
115 Avionics bay (C3)
116 Avionics bay (C2)
117 Avionics bay (C1)
118 Observation window
119 Nav/com station
120 Nav/com console
121 Tacco seat
122 Tacco station
123 Antenna
124 Curtains/doorway to flight deck
125 Flight crew emergency exit

126 Avionics bay
127 Pilot's seat
128 Flight engineer's seat
129 Overhead instrument console
130 Windshield
131 Instrument panel shroud
132 Control column
133 Forward pressure bulkhead
134 Radar support
135 Nose cone
136 APS-115 radar
137 Retractable FLIR

SPECIFICATION

Lockheed P-3C Orion

Powerplant

Four Rolls-Royce North America (Allison) T56-A-14 turboprops, each rated at 3661 ekW (4,910 ehp)

Performance

Maximum level speed: 761 km/h (473 mph) at 4575 m (15,000 ft)
Normal cruising speed : 608 km/h (378 mph) at 7620 m (25,000 ft)
Maximum rate of climb: 594 m (1,950 ft) per minute
Service ceiling: 8625 m (28,300 ft)
Normal mission radius: 2494 km (1,550 miles) with 3 hours on station at 457 m (1,500 ft)

Weights

Empty: 27,890 kg (61,491 lb)
Maximum normal take-off: 61,235 kg (135,000 lb)
Maximum permissible: 64,410 kg (142,000 lb)

Maximum landing: 47,119 kg (103,880 lb)

Dimensions

Length: 35.61 m (116 ft 10 in)
Height: 10.27 m (33 ft 8½ in)
Wing span: 30.37 m (99 ft 8 in)
Wing area: 120.77 m² (1,300 sq ft)

Fuel capacity

Maximum useable: 34,826 litres (9,200 US gal; 7,660 Imp gal)

Range

Normal: 765 km (475 miles)

Armament

Torpedoes, mines and bombs up to 3629 kg (8,000 lb) in internal weapons bay; 10 external hardpoints (four under centre section and six under outer wings) for carriage of further bombs, rockets and missiles (including AGM-65 Maverick, AGM-84 Harpoon/SLAM/ SLAM-ER; maximum expendable stores 9071 kg (20,000 lb)

Since 1973 a number of Orions have worn the orange and white colour scheme of NRL/Oceanographic Development Squadron Eight (VXN-8). Carrying various RP-3 designations, the aircraft have been involved in a variety of oceanographic and geomagnetic survey programmes, ostensibly fulfiling a scientific research programme. In reality, the research programmes provide a wealth of useful data for military studies, especially concerning anti-submarine warfare.

138 Pitot head
139 Nosewheel well beams
140 Rudder pedal
141 Nosewheel retraction jack
142 Nosewheel doors
143 Forward-retracting twin nosewheels
144 Nosewheel leg torque link
145 Nosewheel leg pivot
146 Co-pilot's seat
147 Forward electrical load
148 Under-deck APU computer

149 Under-deck weapons bay
150 Weapons bay doors
151 Bomb load (eight bombs)
152 Spinners

160 Fuselage fuel cell (No. 5 bag)
161 Water-alcohol tank
162 Wing centre-section front beam

173 Mainwheel leg pivot
174 Retraction jack
175 Mainwheel well forward doors
176 Engine air intake
177 Propeller reduction gear box
178 Oil cooler intake
179 Engine support struts
180 Drive shaft housing
181 Allison T56-A-10 turboprop engine compressor section
182 Combustion section
183 Turbine section
184 Jet pipe
185 Stainless-steel heat-resistant trough
186 Aileron control linkage
187 Twin (fail-safe) trim actuators

This view of one of the RNZAF's six P-3Bs, seen during an airshow display with 'everything down' and its starboard outer propeller feathered, shows well the position of the weapons bay in the forward fuselage. New Zealand purchased five P-3Bs in 1966, later adding a sixth ex-RAAF machine. All underwent a limited upgrade, to so-called P-3K standard, in the 1980s. A further upgrade programme occurred in 2003.

188 Aileron trim tab
189 Static dischargers
190 Starboard aileron
191 Starboard navigation light
192 Formation/identification light
193 Rear spar
194 Integrally stiffened wing planks
195 Wing rib construction
196 Front spar
197 Leading-edge structure
198 Underwing stores pylons (three outboard, two inboard)

153 Four-bladed propellers
154 Engine air intake
155 Intake trunking
156 Engine bearers ('V'-frame)
157 Oil tank
158 Inboard leading-edge section
159 Wing root fillet

163 Centre-section integral fuel tank (No. 5)
164 Centresection end rib
165 No. 3 fuel tank
166 Flap structure
167 Jet-pipe exhausts
168 Flap profile
169 Bonded double skin
170 No. 4 fuel tank
171 Mainwheel well aft doors
172 Twin mainwheels

Dassault Mirage IIIR Tactical reconnaissance aircraft

A Dassault Mirage IIIR of 33ᵉ Escadre, Armée de l'Air, based at Strasbourg. The unit later re-equipped with Mirage F1CRs.

Evolved from the definitive Mirage IIIE tactical strike fighter, the **Dassault Mirage IIIR** first flew in prototype form on 31 October 1961, with production aircraft beginning to replace the Republic RF-84F Thunderflash in Armée de l'Air service at Strasbourg during the course of 1963, all three escadrons of the parent wing eventually converting by the mid-1960s.

Right: The Mirage IIIR can be distinguished by its redesigned nose, which houses forward, downward and sideways-looking cameras.

Below: Switzerland retired its Mirage III fighters in 1999, but the Mirage IIIRS remains in service. A pre-canards aircraft is shown.

An initial batch of 50 aircraft was acquired by the French air force, and were subsequently joined by 20 examples of the **Mirage IIIRD**. This latter variant featured a number of detail changes over the original production model, such as an improved navigation radar. These aircraft were eventually replaced replaced by newer Mirage F1CRs.

Photo features

Like most photographic reconnaissance derivatives of fighter aircraft, the Mirage IIIR has a redesigned nose section, with the Cyrano II fire-control radar deleted to permit the installation of up to five cameras for day or night operation. To allow armed reconnaissance missions to be undertaken, the Mirage IIIR can be equipped with two 30-mm DEFA cannon, and it is also able to carry various types of ordnance underwing, the pilot being provided with a reflector gun sight and low-altitude bombing

*This was the development aircraft for the Mirage IIIR programme. It had its nose fire control radar (**Cyrano II**) removed and replaced this with cameras. The airframe was as the standard model, and weapons could be carried.*

Below: The last of the French Mirage IIIRs was not retired until 1994, although the type's replacement was begun as early as 1975.

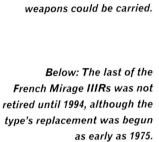

SPECIFICATION

Mirage IIIR
Type: single-seat tactical reconnaissance aircraft
Powerplant: one SNECMA Atar 9C turbojet rated at 60.78-kN (13,670-lb) afterburning thrust
Performance: maximum speed at sea level 1390 km/h (863 mph) or Mach 1.14; maximum speed at altitude 2350 km/h (1,460 mph) or Mach 2.2; range in clean condition about 1600 km (1,000 miles); ferry range with full external fuel 4000 km (2,485 miles)
Weights: empty 6600 kg (14,550 lb); maximum take-off 13,500 kg (29,760 lb)
Dimensions: wing span 8.22 m (27 ft); length 15.5 m (50 ft 10¼ in); height 4.25 m (13 ft 11½ in); wing area 35 m² (377 sq ft)

system equipment to assist in weapons delivery.

In addition to those aircraft acquired for service with the French air force, reconnaissance models of the Mirage III found favour overseas, close to 100 being built for the export market. These include variants of the Mirage IIIR for Pakistan (13 **Mirage IIIRP** aircraft), South Africa (eight **Mirage IIIRZ** aircraft) and Switzerland (18 **Mirage IIIRS** aircraft) plus numerous examples of reconnaissance-configured Mirage 5s, the latter being a simplified Mirage intended specifically for export. Customers for the Mirage 5R include Abu Dhabi, Belgium, Colombia, Egypt, Gabon and Libya, which between them took delivery of approximately 50 aircraft, and, with the exception of Gabon, retained the type into 2003.

Of the Mirage IIIRs, only Pakistan and Switzerland retained examples in frontline service during 2003. The 16 Swiss aircraft have been upgraded with canards and avionics improvements and are supported by a fleet of two Mirage IIIDS trainers. Switzerland plans to retire the type in 2006, while its future in Pakistan looks considerably brighter. Indeed, recognizing the Mirage III/5 as a relatively cheap but highly capable warplane, Pakistan has bought large numbers of used Mirages from around the world.

Dassault F1CR Tactical reconnaissance aircraft

*Dassault's Mirage F1CR provides l'Armée de l'Air with a most capable tactical reconnaissance platform. The aircraft are on strength with **ER 1/33** and **ER 2/33** (illustrated) and fly alongside two Mirage **F1CT** squadrons and a single **F1B/F1C**-equipped conversion unit.*

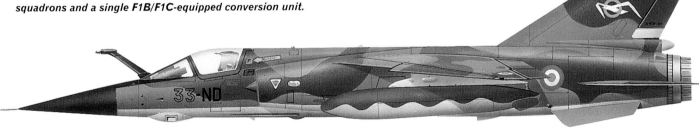

As soon as it became clear that the Mirage F1 would support a major production run, Dassault studied a dedicated reconnaissance version, the customer being the Armée de l'Air. Fully designated **Mirage F1CR-200**, the first example flew on 20 November 1981.

For its mission, the **Mirage F1CR** carries a wealth of reconnaissance equipment both internally and externally. An SAT SCM2400 Super Cyclope infrared linescan unit is installed in place of the cannon, and an undernose fairing houses either a 75-mm Thomson-TRT 40 panoramic camera or 150-mm Thomson-TRT 33 vertical camera. Other internal equipment includes a Cyrano IVMR radar with extra ground-mapping, blind let-down, ranging and contour-mapping modes, when compared to the fighter's radar, and provision of a navigation computer and ULISS 47 INS.

Pictured participating in a USAF Red Flag exercise at Nellis AFB, Nevada, this Mirage F1CR displays the bulged under-nose fairing housing the aircraft's panoramic camera. The F1CR is also able to carry the Raphaël SLAR 2000 pod on its centre fuselage pylon.

Above: In the late 1990s, the only Mirage F1s remaining in French service were F1CRs (illustrated), F1CTs, F1Bs and a few F1C fighters.

SPECIFICATION	
Mirage F.1CR	2335 km/h (1,450 mph) or Mach 2.2;
Type: single-seat tactical	ferry range 3300 km (2,050 miles)
reconnaissance aircraft	**Weights:** empty 7400 kg (16,314 lb);
Powerplant: one SNECMA Atar	maximum take-off 16,200 kg
9K-50 turbojet rated at 70.59-kN	(35,715 lb)
(15,873-lb) afterburning thrust	**Dimensions:** wing span 8.4 m (27 ft
Performance: maximum speed at sea	6¾ in); length 15 m (49 ft 2½ in);
level 1475 km/h (917 mph) or Mach	height 4.5 m (14 ft 9 in); wing area
1.2; maximum speed at altitude	25 m² (269.11 sq ft)

Additional sensors are carried in various centreline pods, these including Thomson-CSF Raphaël TH side-looking airborne radar, a HAROLD long-range oblique camera or Thomson-CSF ASTAC electronic intelligence pods. Various combinations of cameras can also be mounted in a pod. An inflight refuelling probe is fitted on the starboard side of the nose.

F1CR for ER 33

Sixty-four F1CRs were ordered, of which around 40 remained in

service early in 2003. The first production aircraft flew on 10 November 1982, and the first squadron, Escadron de Reconnaissance 2/33 'Savoie', became operational at BA124 Strasbourg/Entzheim in July 1983. ER 1/33 'Belfort' and ER 3/33 'Moselle' followed, conversion from Mirage IIIRs being completed in 1988. F1CRs were sent to Saudi Arabia for participation in operations Desert Shield and Desert Storm, where they were used for reconnaissance missions before

Above: Additional Mirage F1CR equipment can include the Thomson-CSF Raphaël side-looking airborne radar (SLAR), the Super Cyclope IR linescan, the ASTAC podded Elint system, the Thomson-TRT/Dassault Harold system and various other Dassault-designed optical systems.

being grounded to prevent confusion with Iraqi Mirage F1EQs. When allowed to resume flying, they displayed

their secondary ground-attack role, their radar making them more effective than the alternative SEPECAT Jaguars.

English Electric Canberra Photo-recce aircraft

Above: Wearing the Hemp uppersurfaces that became synonymous with the type, this Canberra PR.Mk 9 is shown as it appeared with 1 PRU in the 1980s. Note the camera aperture in the lower forward fuselage and the small windows for the navigator. The fighter-type canopy of the PR.Mk 9 is also evident.

Although the Canberra B.Mk 2 bomber replaced heavyweight Avro Lincolns and Boeing B-29 Washingtons with Bomber Command, the aircraft was perhaps better viewed as a 'Jet Mosquito' – an epithet widely applied at the time. The Canberra enjoyed unmatched performance, flying higher and faster than contemporary jet fighters, and able to out-turn many of them too. The aircraft clearly had great potential and versatility, and adaptation to new roles began almost immediately.

The most obvious new role for the Canberra was that of photographic reconnaissance, and a small number of **B.Mk 2**s was hastily adapted for top-secret reconnaissance missions over the Iron Curtain, some of them being fitted with long-focal length oblique cameras provided by the CIA. Even before the B.Mk 2 flew in production form, development of a dedicated reconnaissance version was well under way.

Canberra PR.Mk 3

The basic B.Mk 2 was the basis of a dedicated reconnaissance variant, the **Canberra PR.Mk 3**. This married the 'dry' wings and engines of the B.Mk 2 with a

modestly redesigned fuselage. The long bomb bay was replaced by an auxiliary fuel tank (forward) and a flare bay (aft). The fuselage was stretched by 36 cm (14 in) in front of the belly fuel tank to accommodate a new camera bay, which in turn could accommodate a variety of oblique cameras. Vertical cameras were carried aft of the flare bay, in what was the aft equipment bay on 'bomber' variants.

The prototype PR.Mk 3 made its maiden flight on 19 March 1950, with the first production aircraft following on 31 July 1952. In all, 35 PR.Mk 3s were built, entering service with the RAF's No. 540 Squadron in 1953, and subsequently with No. 82 Squadron at RAF Wyton, Cambridgeshire.

The PR.Mk 3, with its additional fuel tank, had the longest range of any of the first-generation Canberras, and was used for a number of record-

The first of the PR variants was the Mk 3. In many respects similar to the basic Canberra model, the PR.Mk 3 had part of its bomb bay replaced with additional fuel tanks, and the remainder was used to carry illumination flares. Seven cameras could be mounted in a section inserted in the fuselage forward of the wing.

SPECIFICATION	
English Electric Canberra PR.Mk 9 **Type:** high-altitude, long-range reconnaissance platform **Powerplant:** two 50.03-kN (11,250-lb) thrust Rolls-Royce Avon Mk 206 turbojets **Performance:** maximum speed 901 km/h (560 mph) at 12,192 m (40,000 ft); initial climb rate	3658 m (12,000 ft) per minute; service ceiling more than 18,288 m (60,000 ft); range 8159 km (5,070 miles) **Weights:** maximum loaded 26,082 kg (57,500 lb) **Dimensions:** wing span 22.3 m (69 ft 5 in); length 20.32 m (66 ft 8 in); height 4.75 m (15 ft 7 in); wing area 297.08 m² (1,045 sq ft)

breaking flights, including the England–New Zealand air race held in 1953.

Canberra PR.Mk 7

The second-generation Canberra bomber, the B.Mk 6, with integral fuel tanks in the wings and powered by more powerful Avon Mk 109s, formed the basis of the **Canberra PR.Mk 7**. The

PR.Mk 7 prototype actually beat the B.Mk 6 into the air, flying for the first time on 28 October 1953. The 74 PR.Mk 7s replaced the PR.Mk 3s, which were in turn relegated to No. 231 OCU for training, and to No. 69 Squadron (later re-numbered as No. 39 Squadron) in West Germany, and later on the island of Malta. No. 231 OCU's

reconnaissance element subsequently broke away as No. 237 OCU, although this was short-lived, and the last PR.Mk 3s remained in use with No. 231 OCU until 1969, when the PR.Mk 7 force began to disband. At the peak of Canberra reconnaissance operations, PR.Mk 7s had equipped reconnaissance squadrons in the Far East (No. 81), Near East (Nos 13 and 39) and in RAF Germany (Nos 17, 31 and 80). PR.Mk 7s saw active service in support of the Anglo-French Suez operation, and in Malaya, Kenya (the Mau Mau rebellion) and various other colonial 'hotspots'. The PR.Mk 7 remained in frontline service with No. 13 Sqn (latterly based at Wyton) until December 1981, but four

India was the largest export operator of the Canberra, with more than 100 aircraft being delivered. Out of this total, eight PR.Mk 57/67s were received in 1959, forming No. 106 Squadron. Early in 2003, the unit still remained, even retaining some of the original aircraft, though some attrition examples were obtained in 1963 and 1975.

survivors then began a long career as calibration and target facilities aircraft with No. 100 Squadron, later transferring to No. 39 Sqn, and finally being withdrawn from use in 1998.

The final reconnaissance Canberra was the **Canberra PR.Mk 9**, which was optimized for high-altitude use, with Avon Mk 206 engines, and greater wing area provided by increased span and increased chord inboard of the engines. The prototype, converted by Napier, retained a

The hinged nose of the PR.Mk 9 opens so as to accommodate the navigator, who sits in an enclosed compartment surrounded by equipment. Visual reference is provided by two small windows on each side of the nose.

PR.Mk 7 fuselage, and made its maiden flight on 8 July 1955. Production PR.Mk 9s were built by Shorts, and introduced a B(I).Mk 8 nose, with a higher cockpit behind the navigator's station, and had a fighter-type canopy offset to port. This B(I).Mk 8 nose was fitted only to the first PR.Mk 9, with

subsequent aircraft having their noses further refined, with an opening canopy for the pilot, and with the entire nose section hinging to allow the navigator access to his forward-facing ejection seat. The usual entrance door, side-facing chart table and prone bomb-aiming position of the B(I).Mk 8 were deleted.

Above: The PR.Mk 9 was intended for high-altitude photographic reconnaissance and was initially designated HA PR.Mk 9 to indicate this fact. In 2003, the Canberra was the oldest aircraft in RAF squadron service and operated with No. 39 Squadron.

High-altitude PR.Mk 9

The PR.Mk 9 was able to operate at heights in excess of 18,288 m (60,000 ft) and remained in frontline service until 1982. Its operational career went largely unreported, but is believed to have included sensitive missions 'looking over' the Iron Curtain, the 'Bamboo Curtain' and into Guatemala, using US-supplied LOROP cameras. There are persistent reports that the Canberra PR.Mk 9 provided photo imagery used in Operation Motorman in Northern Ireland, and that the

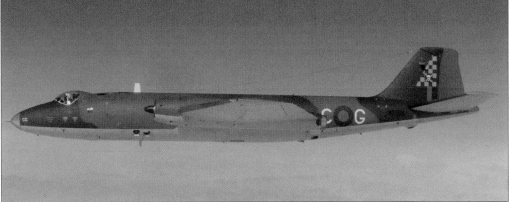

type saw active service over the Falklands, perhaps operating from Chilean airfields.

Since then, a flight-strength unit (in 2003 designated No. 39 (1 PRU) Squadron) has remained in use, principally in the survey role. The aircraft does retain a number of frontline capabilities, and was used during Operation Iraqi Freedom.

The full story of the PR.Mk 9 remains to be told, but the type

Based on the B.Mk 6, the PR.Mk 7's most significant advancement over the PR.Mk 3 was its increased range. This was achieved by the addition of extra fuel, located in integral tanks in the wing leading edges.

has undergone major sensor upgrades, adding state-of-the-art EO sensors including a high-performance LOROP fit, and will remain in service well into the twenty-first century.

Overseas customers to have utilized the Canberra in the

reconnaissance role include Argentina (where B.Mk 62s were flown in the photo-reconnaissance role), Chile (PR.Mk 9s), India (which originally received 10 **Canberra PR.Mk 57/ Mk 67** aircraft) and Venezuela (**Canberra PR.Mk 83**).

Mikoyan-Gurevich MiG-21R 'Fishbed-N'
Tactical fighter-reconnaissance aircraft

In common with other MiG-21 models, the Mikoyan-Gurevich MiG-21R was exported. This aircraft, of the Czechoslovakian air force, is carrying a centreline reconnaissance pod.

Without doubt the most widely used and prolific fighter aircraft of the post-World War II era, the Mikoyan-Gurevich MiG-21 'Fishbed' remains in widespread service in 2003. Since its debut during the mid-1950s, it has almost inevitably spawned a number of variants, including the specialized reconnaissance **MiG-21R** (known to ASCC/NATO as **'Fishbed-N'**).

Poland retained the MiG-21R in service late into the 1990s. All MiG-21Rs could carry a GP-9 gunpod in place of their standard reconnaissance equipment.

Based on the MiG-21PF fighter, the MiG-21R uses the wider-chord fin introduced on the MiG-21PFM. Although produced in only one basic form for both home use and export, MiG-21R relies on a centreline pod system for its reconnaissance mission. Various pods carry Elint, forward- and oblique-camera, IR linescan, night-photography or SLAR equipment.

SPECIFICATION	
Mikoyan-Gurevich MiG-21R 'Fishbed-N' **Type:** single-seat tactical reconnaissance aircraft **Powerplant:** one Tumanskii R-11F2-300 turbojet rated at 60-kN (13,492-lb) afterburning thrust **Performance:** maximum speed at sea level 1100 km/h (684 mph); maximum speed at 13,000 m (42,651 ft) 2230 km/h (1,385 mph) or Mach 2.1; service ceiling 15,100 m (49,540 ft); maximum	range 1600 km (994 miles) **Weight:** empty 5696 kg (12,557 lb); loaded 8100 kg (17,857 lb) **Dimensions:** wing span 7.15 m (23 ft 5½ in); length (excluding boom) 14.7 m (48 ft 2¾ in); wing area 23 m² (247.6 sq ft) **Armament:** provision for two R-3 (AA-2 'Atoll') missiles for self-defence, as well as bombs or rocket pods on inner underwing pylons

Alternatively, the MiG-21R can dispense with its recce pod for use as a standard tactical fighter, or can carry rockets or bombs on its inner underwing pylons. The latter would normally be carried at the expense of self-defence

AAMs, the outer underwing pylons generally being dedicated to hauling a pair of 490-litre (108-Imperial gallon) drop tanks. In summer 2003, the MiG-21R remained in service with Bulgaria, Croatia, Egypt and Yugoslavia.

Mikoyan-Gurevich MiG-25R 'Foxbat' High-speed recce MiG

The first prototype MiG-25 recce aircraft, the **Ye-155R-1**, actually made its maiden flight six months before the prototype fighter, on 6 March 1964. Changes introduced during flight trials of the three Ye-155Rs included the installation of R-15BD-300 engines in place of the earlier R-15B-300s. As the **MiG-25R 'Foxbat-B'**, the reconnaissance version passed

Above: The oblique camera provision of earlier RB variants was omitted from the MiG-25RBF. Instead, the nose was fitted with two pairs of dielectric panels for its Shar-25 Elint system.

Right: The Indian air force took delivery of six MiG-25RBs. One of the IAF's 'Foxbat-Bs' was written off in a crash, but only three were believed to remain operational in mid-2003.

its state acceptance tests in 1969, and series production began at Gorky in April 1969. The MiG-25R had five camera ports in the nose, one vertical and four oblique, with small square flush antennas further forward on the sides of the nose, probably serving a SLAR. Three cameras would usually be carried, one vertical and two oblique.

Trials unit

Even before the aircraft entered front-line service, a trials unit with four MiG-25Rs was deployed to Egypt for operational recce missions over Israel. These operated under the cover designation **X-500**, flying at speeds of up to Mach 2.83 (flight at this upper limit was officially limited to eight minutes), although one pilot took his aircraft to Mach 3 to avoid Israeli SAMs and the time

limit was frequently broken. The aircraft enjoyed a four-year immunity from interception, between their deployment in 1971 to their withdrawal in 1975, despite a lack of security which meant that the IDF/AF was warned of almost every mission.

The original MiG-25R was replaced on the production line by the **MiG-25RB 'Foxbat-B'** in 1970, this type remaining in production until 1982. The MiG-25RB was a dual-role reconnaissance bomber, with a new Peleng automatic bombing system, the Soviet Union's first operational inertial navigation system, and a Doppler to measure speed and drift. These allowed the aircraft to release its bombs from altitudes in excess

of 20,000 m (65,617 ft) at supersonic speeds. Four underwing hardpoints were provided for 500-kg (1,102-lb) bombs, with another two under the fuselage. Alternatively, a single nuclear weapon could be carried. The standard camera bay remained, but the SRS-4A Elint system was slightly

improved. All surviving Soviet MiG-25Rs were brought up to MiG-25RB standards.

Other variants

Further models which are understood to have retained their cameras included the **MiG-25RBS 'Foxbat-D'** with the new Sabla radio location

SPECIFICATION

Mikoyan-Gurevich MiG-25R 'Foxbat-B'
Type: single-seat all-weather tactical/strategic reconnaissance aircraft
Powerplant: two Tumanskii R-15BD-300 turbojets each rated at 11000-kg (24,250-lb) afterburning thrust
Performance: maximum level speed 'clean' at 13000 m (42,650 ft) 3000 km/h (1,864 mph); climb to 19,000 m (62,336 ft) in 6 minutes

10 seconds; service ceiling 21,000 m (68,900 ft); range with one external tank 2130 km (1,324 miles) at Mach 2.35
Weights: empty 20,755 kg (45,756 lb); maximum take-off 41,200 kg (90,829 lb)
Dimensions: wing span 13.42 m (44 ft ¼ in); length 23.2 m (76 ft 1½ in); wing area 61.4 m² (661 sq ft)

In MiG-25RBK form, the 'Foxbat' is equipped with SLAR and has no optical camera windows.

system. This variant entered service in 1972, and was produced until 1977. From 1981 many of these aircraft received new equipment and were designated **MiG-25RBSh**. The MiG-25RBS was replaced on the production line by the **MiG-25RBV 'Foxbat-B'**, with further improved equipment, and by the **MiG-25RBT 'Foxbat-B'** with SRS-9 Virazh Elint equipment.

The basic MiG-25RB also formed the basis of a model dedicated to Elint duties, with its optical sensors replaced by a variety of passive receivers and active SLAR systems. The first 'camera-less' 'Foxbat' was the **MiG-25RBK 'Foxbat-D'**, which has the usual flush antennas and cameras removed and replaced by much larger, longer dielectric panels on the sides of the cockpit stretching forward from a point immediately under the windscreen. These antennas reportedly serve the new Kub SLAR. The MiG-25RBK entered

service in 1972 and remained in production until 1980.

The final variant is the **MiG-25RBF 'Foxbat-D'**. These aircraft were upgraded MiG-25RBs, with new equipment including an inflight-refuelling probe and improved ECM/IRCM systems. The aircraft retained the basic camera window fit as the MiG-25RB, but in place of the oblique camera windows, the RBF had four small, symmetrically arranged, rectangular dielectric panels.

Unusually, the reconnaissance 'Foxbat' has its own dedicated

two-seat trainer, designated **MiG-25RU 'Foxbat-C'**. This has no operational equipment, but does seem to have a constant-sweep wing leading edge. By comparison with 'fighter' MiG-25s, all reconnaissance aircraft have slightly reduced wing span and a leading edge with constant sweep, instead of the fighter's 'cranked' leading edge.

In 2003, reconnaissance MiG-25 models were likely to remain in service with the air forces of Algeria, Azerbaijan, India, Libya, Russia and Syria.

McDonnell Douglas RF-4 Phantom II
Two-seat tactical reconnaissance aircraft

In late 1996, the SARA (Sistema Avanzado de Reconocimiento Aéreo) upgrade for Spain's RF-4Cs was announced to include Texas Instruments AN/APQ-172 terrain-following radar, ring laser-gyro INS and provision for an inflight-refuelling probe.

Consideration was given to the possibility of developing a reconnaissance-configured variant of the F-4 Phantom II at an early

stage in the type's operational career, but it was not until the USAF selected the basic fighter model to equip Tactical Air

Command units that this proposal began to move ahead rapidly. Known by the designation **RF-4C**, the resulting aircraft flew

in prototype form for the first time on 8 August 1963, this being the forerunner of over 500 similar machines, the last of which was formally handed over to the USAF over 10 years later, on 16 January 1974. The last of these machines was retired in 1995, the type having seen combat during Operation Desert Storm.

This RF-4EJ wears a typical camouflage scheme for the type. The aircraft belonged to the 501st Hiko-tai.

Greece paid $91 million for eight RF-4Es for delivery between June 1978 and April 1979. Five surviving aircraft served on until 1992, flying alongside a few veteran RF-84Fs before they were retired in 1991, when both types were replaced by 29 ex-Luftwaffe RF-4Es. One of the original RF-4E aircraft is illustrated to the left.

The RF-4E was produced to a German specification. From 1978 onwards, the Luftwaffe machines were given a ground-attack capability.

When that milestone was reached, overseas deployment followed quickly, aircraft being despatched to Southeast Asia for combat duty by the end of 1965, and the RF-4C remaining in use as the principal tactical reconnaissance tool for the remainder of the Vietnam War.

SPECIFICATION

McDonnell Douglas RF-4C Phantom II
Type: two-seat all-weather tactical reconnaissance aircraft
Powerplant: two General Electric J79-GE-15 turbojets each rated at 75.6-kN (17,000-lb) afterburning thrust
Performance: maximum speed at low level 1464 km/h (910 mph) or Mach 1.19; maximum speed at altitude 2414 km/h (1,500 mph) or Mach 2.27; ferry range 3700 km (2,300 miles)
Weights: empty 13,290 kg (29,300 lb); maximum take-off 26,309 kg (58,000 lb)
Dimensions: wing span 11.71 m (38 ft 5 in); length 19.2 m (63 ft); height 5.02 m (16 ft 5½ in); wing area 49.24 m² (530 sq ft)

Easily recognized by the modified nose section which contains cameras and other reconnaissance sensors, the RF-4C entered operational service at Shaw AFB, South Carolina, in September 1964, although nearly a year passed before the first unit could be considered as combat ready.

Marine Corps RF-4

The second reconnaissance model to appear, rather confusingly designated **RF-4B**, was intended specifically for service with the US Marine Corps and this made its maiden flight on 12 March 1965 with deliveries to El Toro, California, following just two months later. A total of 46 RF-4Bs was supplied to this service, and the survivors remained in frontline service to 1990, having been the subject of a modification and life-extension programme.

The revised radome of the RF-4C contained an AN/APQ-99 mapping and terrain collision avoidance radar. Cameras were housed in the nose.

211

Export RF-4s

In addition to producing reconnaissance Phantoms for the home market, McDonnell Douglas also developed the **RF-4E** variant, initially in response to a Luftwaffe requirement for 88 aircraft.

Flown for the first time on 15 September 1970, the RF-4E subsequently also joined the air arms of Greece, Iran, Israel and Turkey, just over 160 of the type being built before production ceased. In addition, Japan received an aircraft based on the RF-4C which was designated **RF-4EJ** in service, while Spain took a number of surplus USAF RF-4Cs.

Lockheed U-2 High-altitude spyplane

When the production line reopened for the TR-1 three aircraft were completed as two-seaters (two TR-1Bs and one 'strategic' U-2RT). Subsequent rationalisation saw the trainers redesignated TU-2R (1st RS, 9th RW example pictured) and TU-2S.

In July 1955 US President Eisenhower proposed an 'Open Skies' policy, under which both US and Soviet reconnaissance aircraft would be free to make unrestricted flights over each other's territory. This proposal was rejected by the Soviet Union; however, on 4 August 1955 Lockheed flew the first example of a remarkable new reconnaissance aircraft, the **U-2**, which had been designed and built under great secrecy in the company's 'Skunk Works'.

The aircraft's glider-like wing allowed range to be extended by shutting down the engine to flight idle and gliding over long distances. The aircraft was intended to operate at altitudes where detection and interception were unlikely.

SAM shoot-down

That the U-2 was detectable and vulnerable was demonstrated clearly on 1 May 1960 when, during an overflight of the Soviet Union, the **U-2B** flown by the CIA's Francis Gary Powers was knocked down by a SAM. However, the U-2's value was demonstrated in 1962 when

The huge pod above the fuselage of this U-2R contains the antenna for the Senior Span system, which transmits ASARS-2 data via satellite link.

these aircraft discovered attempts to install ballistic missile sites in Cuba.

Of the original U-2 series, the most important variants were the **U-2A** built for the CIA and USAF; the more-powerful, longer-range U-2B for the CIA; the further improved **U-2C**; and the research **U-2D**. As they were powered by Pratt & Whitney J57 turbojets, however, the first-generation U-2s were airframe-limited, so Lockheed began the development of an enlarged aircraft to provide the ability to carry far greater sensor loads on the same power. The result was the **U-2R**, which first flew from Edwards AFB, California, on 28 August 1967. At the same time as introducing fuel in a new 'wet wing', the new design also alleviated many of the aerodynamic flaws of the first generation.

U-2R into service

A first batch of 12 U-2Rs was built, and equally distributed between the USAF and the CIA. The former operated mostly in Southeast Asia, while the latter operated from Taiwan, over mainland China. In 1974 the CIA aircraft passed to the USAF.

In November 1979, the U-2 production line reopened to provide 37 new airframes. The initiative for this was the **TR-1A** programme, which used the U-2R as a platform for the ASARS-2 (Advanced Synthetic-Aperture Radar-2) battlefield surveillance radar. The TR-1A was also seen as a platform for the Precision Location Strike System (PLSS) radar location system, and for Sigint equipment as carried by the U-2R. The TR-1A force was progressively withdrawn, however, as the threat of the Cold War diminished, and the TR-1A designation finally reverted to U-2R.

The new-build batch of aircraft contained 25 TR-1As and seven U-2Rs that had been created from the outset of the programme as attrition replacements. Three two-seat trainers were included in the batch, these comprising two **TR-1B** and one **U-2RT** machines. The TR-1B designation eventually reverted to U-2RT.

The U-2's sensors are carried in the detachable nosecone, a large 'Q-bay' situated behind

SPECIFICATION

Lockheed U-2R
Type: single-seat high-altitude reconnaissance aircraft
Powerplant: one Pratt & Whitney J75-P-13B turbojet engine rated at 75.62 kN (17,000 lb st)
Performance: maximum cruising speed more than 692 km/h (430 mph) at 21335 m (70,000 ft); climb to 19,810 m (65,000 ft) in 35 minutes; operational ceiling

24,385 m (80,000 ft); maximum range about 10,060 km (6,250 miles); maximum endurance about 12 hours
Weights: empty about 7031 kg (15,500 lb); maximum take-off 18,733 kg (41,300 lb)
Dimensions: wing span 31.39 m (103 ft); length 19.13 m (62 ft 9 in); height 4.88 m (16 ft); wing area about 92.90 m² (1,000 sq ft)

Adding the large 'super pods' to the wings of the U-2R (illustrated) or U-2S significantly increases the airframe space available for the carriage of sensors.

the cockpit for cameras, and smaller bays along the lower fuselage and in two removable wing 'super pods'. At least six of the aircraft are equipped to carry the Senior Span satellite communications antenna in a huge teardrop radome mounted on a dorsal pylon.

In March 1989 Lockheed flew a TR-1A with a General Electric

F101-GE-F29 turbofan engine in place of the J75. Installed in operational aircraft from 1992, this engine confers a 16 per cent increase in endurance, restores the operational ceiling to a figure above 24,380 m (80,000 ft) and improves supportability across USAF bases.

Re-engining has brought a change of designation to **U-2S**.

*Just after the **Gary Powers** shoot-down in the **Soviet Union**, this early-model U-2 was given spurious **NASA** markings as part of a **CIA** disinformation effort.*

Transall C.160 Tactical turboprop transport aircraft

Originally conceived as a replacement for the Noratlas, which served France and West Germany, the **C.160** was one of the first successful joint European aerospace ventures, being produced by a consortium of companies collectively known as the Transport Allianz group. Indeed, the name and designation chosen for the resulting machine reflected the origins of the project, for the initial quantity to be acquired was set at 160 (50 **C.160F** aircraft for France and 110 **C.160D** aircraft for West Germany), while the name was merely a contraction of Transport Allianz. Members of the original production group included Nord, HFB and VFW, these companies joining forces in early 1959.

Prototype building

Three prototypes were built in all, one by each of the three major partners in the venture, and the first of these made a successful maiden flight on 25 February 1963. They were followed by six pre-production examples from May 1965, while production-configured C.160s began to emerge in the spring of 1967, deliveries getting under way soon afterwards; by the time manufacture ceased in 1972 a total of 169 had been built. In addition to the 160 supplied to the two principal partners, nine more of a variant known as the **C.160Z** were sold to South Africa, the only other air arm to operate the original type apart from Turkey, which took delivery of some 20 **C.160T** aircraft (former Luftwaffe C.160D aircraft) in the early 1970s.

Subsequently, at the end of the 1970s, it was decided to reopen the production line in France, l'Armée de l'Air ordering

As well as appearing in recent conflicts, the Gabriel pair has been active in areas such as the Baltic, where this aircraft was intercepted by a Swedish air force Viggen.

25 more aircraft under the designation **C.160NG** (**Nouvelle Génération**). These differed from their predecessors by virtue of additional fuel capacity and improved avionics. Early range limitations have been

Right: In 1970, the SAAF received the first of its French-built Transall C.160Zs, the Germans being politically unwilling to deal with the South African government. These were ordered largely because the United States had embargoed further deliveries of C-130s. They proved remarkably successful, however, and some were returned to service after being stored in 1993.

SPECIFICATION	
Transall C.160	ceiling 8500 m (27,885 ft); range
Type: twin-engined turboprop	4500 km (2,796 miles) with an
transport	8000 kg (17,637 lb) payload
Powerplant: two Rolls-Royce Tyne	**Weights:** empty equipped
RTy.20 Mk 22 turboprops each	28,758 kg (63,400 lb); maximum
rated at 4548 ekW (6,100 ehp)	take-off 49,100 kg (108,245 lb)
Performance: maximum cruising	**Dimensions:** wing span 40 m (131 ft
speed at 5500 m (18,045 ft)	3 in); length 32.4 m (106 ft 3½ in);
513 km/h (319 mph); maximum	height 11.65 m (38 ft 5 in)
rate of climb at sea level 440 m	**Payload:** maximum payload
(1,444 ft) per minute; service	160,00 kg (35,275 lb)

Right: This 'lizard'-type camouflage replaced the initial grey and green scheme applied to the Luftwaffe's C.160Ds. Around 83 Transalls remain in German service.

partly resolved by an extra centre-section fuel tank, but the later C.160s also feature an inflight-refuelling probe above the cockpit area.

Four more C.160NGs were added in 1982, and production ended in 1985. Ten aircraft were completed with a hose-drum unit in the port undercarriage sponson for refuelling tactical

aircraft, and five more have provision for the fitment of this feature so that they can be rapidly re-roled as tankers.

As replacements for eight Elint and jamming N.2501 Gabriel Noratlas variants, two Transalls were converted to **C.160 Gabriel (C.160G)** configuration and entered service in December 1988. Features

include wingtip pods with blade antennas, a group of five large blade antennas on top of the forward fuselage, a blister fairing on each side of the rear fuselage, and a retractable dome under the forward fuselage. Both have refuelling probes and tanker equipment. Prior to the 1991 Gulf War, Gabriel missions were flown against Iraq.

C.160H ASTARTE (Avion Station Relais de Transmissions Exceptionelles) is a Transall version adapted to carry Rockwell Collins TACAMO (Take Command and Move Out) VLF communications equipment, as used by the E-6A Hermes. This enables the aircraft to communicate with submarines without the need for surfacing.

Airbus Military A400M European tactical/strategic airlifter

In September 1997, seven European nations – Belgium, France, Germany, Luxembourg, Spain, Turkey and the United Kingdom – issued a joint Request for Proposals (RFP) to cover a new tactical/ strategic transport aircraft. The requirement for such a machine had been ongoing, with large numbers of C-130 and C.160 transports nearing retirement and a decided lack of strategic transport

capability being felt in western Europe as a whole.

In response to the RFP, aerospace companies from the seven countries combined within Airbus Military to propose the **A400M**, a project originally known as **FLA (Future Large Aircraft)**.

A400M described

As an adjunct of Airbus Industrie, Airbus Military plans to bring the practices that have been so

successful with its commercial airliner business to military procurement.

As such, A400M is seen as a cost-effective solution. A formal programme launch occurred in 2003. In December 2005, the Malaysian government signed an agreement to take four A400M military lifters, taking the total number of aircraft ordered to 194.

The A400M is schemed as a large aircraft of classic airlifter configuration. It features a moderately swept wing mounting four powerful next-generation turboprop engines.

These engines will turn advanced eight-blade propellers and the aircraft is designed to be suitable for both tactical, in-theatre operations, as well as strategic intra-theatre missions.

The first Ratier FH 386 propeller for the A400M was formally handed over to Airbus Military in December 2005.

Maximum payload has been set at 37,000 kg (81,570 lb), but some commentators have noted that a payload of 45,000 kg (99,206 lb) would be needed to lift medium armour as part of a rapid reaction force. The A400M will be ready for service in 2007.

SPECIFICATION	
Airbus Military A400M	**Weights:** for operation up to 2.25 g
Type: tactical/strategic transport	operating empty 66,500 kg
Powerplant: four turboprop engines	(146,605 lb); maximum take-off
each rated at 7457–9694 kW	130,000 kg (286,596 lb)
(10,000–13,000 shp)	**Dimensions:** wing span 42.4 m
Performance: maximum cruising	(139 ft 1¼ in); length 42.2 m
speed Mach 0.68–0.72; maximum	(138 ft 5½ in); height 14.7 m
operating altitude 11,278 m	(48 ft 2¾ in)
(37,000 ft); range 4540 km (2,821	**Payload:** up to 37,000 kg (81,570 lb)
miles) with maximum payload	of freight

This computer-generated impression shows an RAF aircraft engaged in a supply drop. Britain has committed to 25 A400Ms. Australia and Canada are also being courted as potential A400M customers and Airbus Military is suggesting tanker and special missions variants of the airframe.

Alenia G222/C-27/Lockheed Martin/Alenia C-27J Spartan Tactical airlifter and special mission aircraft

The first C-27J completed its maiden flight on 24 September 1999. The aircraft is a good performer which should be in full Italian service by 2005.

The **Fiat G222** proposal was drawn up to meet the outlines of NATO's Basic Military Requirement Four of 1962, which called for a V/STOL transport. None of the proposals was adopted, but the Aeronautica Militare Italiana (AMI) believed that Fiat's proposal could form the basis of a useful transport if finalized as a more conventional design. Therefore, in 1968, the AMI signed a contract for two **G222TCM** prototypes and a static test airframe.

Two total redesigns and Fiat's merger with IRI-Finmeccanica to form Aeritalia occurred before the first prototype made its first flight on 18 July 1970 as a twin-engined aircraft of typical modern airlifter configuration. Highly successful tests resulted in an initial contract for 44 production G222s and the type remained in production into early 1989, and was built in a number of subvariants, including the **G222R/M** (**Radio Misure**) radio/radar calibration aircraft; **G222SAA** (**Sistema Aeronautico Antincendio**) fire-fighter; Rolls-

Royce Tyne RTy.20 Mk 801-powered **G222T** for the Libyan air force and known locally as the **G222L** and the **G222VS** (**Versione Speciale**) or **G222GE** (**Guerra Elettronica**) electronic warfare aircraft.

C-27J Spartan

After the USAF selected the G222 for operations in Central America, production was restarted by Alenia (as Aeritalia had become in December 1990 after its merger with Selenia) for the provision of basic airframes

for completion in the United States by Chrysler as **C-27A Spartan** aircraft. Alenia has since worked with Lockheed Martin on the **C-27J Spartan**, a G222 version with two Rolls-Royce AE2100 turboprops and six-bladed propellers as fitted to the C-130J. The aircraft also shares some of the latter's systems and has been ordered by Italy and Greece.

Dubbed the 'mini Hercules', the Alenia G222 was Italy's response to a NATO requirement for a tactical airlifter. An AMI aircraft is shown.

SPECIFICATION

Alenia G222
Type: tactical medium transport
Powerplant: two Fiat (General Electric) T64-GEP4D turboprop engines each flat-rated at 2535 kW (3,400 shp)
Performance: maximum speed 540 km/h (336 mph) at 4575 m (15,010 ft); initial climb rate 520 m (1,706 ft) per minute; service ceiling 7620 m (25,000 ft); typical range 1371 km (852 miles) with maximum payload

Weights: empty 15,700 kg (34,612 lb); maximum take-off 28,000 kg (61,728 lb)
Dimensions: wing span 28.7 m (94 ft 2 in); length 22.7 m (74 ft 5½ in); height 9.8 m (32 ft 1¾ in); wing area 82 m² (882.67 sq ft)
Payload: up to 46 troops, or 40 paratroops, or 36 litters plus four attendants, or 9600 kg (21,164 lb) of freight

Airbus A310 Twin-engined transport

Belgium's two A310 transport aircraft fly in the VIP and general transport roles from Brussels.

The Royal Thai air force's sole A310, operating from Bangkok, is flown in the royal and VVIP transport role.

SPECIFICATION	
Airbus Industrie A310-300 **Type:** large-capacity short/medium-range transport **Powerplant:** two Pratt & Whitney PW4156A turbofans each rated at 249.1 kN (56,000 lb st) **Performance:** economical cruising speed 850 km/h (528 mph) between 9450 and 12,495 m (31,000 ft and 41,000 ft); range 8056 km (5,005 miles) with 220 passengers and 370-km (230-mile) diversion, or 8889 km (5,523 miles) with additional fuel and take-off weight of 157,000 kg	(346,125 lb), or 9630 km (5,984 miles) with additional fuel and take-off weight of 164,000 kg (361,560 lb) **Weights:** empty operating between 80,344 and 80,801 kg (177,130 and 178,135 lb); maximum take-off between 150,000 and 164,000 kg (330,675 and 361,560 lb) **Dimensions:** wing span 43.89 m (144 ft); length 46.66 m (153 ft 1 in); height 15.8 m (51 ft 10 in); wing area 219 m² (2,357.37 sq ft) **Payload:** maximum between 32,117 and 32,158 kg (70,805 and 70,896 lb)

Although established only in 1967 as a European collaborative organization, Airbus has rapidly matured to rival Boeing of the United States as the world's most important manufacturer of transports, most notably the twin-engined A300, **A310**, A320 and **A330**, the four-engined A340 and the forthcoming A380 double-deck ultra-large aircraft. The vast majority of these have been delivered to civil operators, but some Airbus types have started to enter military service in modest numbers, and the

A330 has been selected as the basis for the Royal Air Force's new tanker/transport type. Belgium is the latest military operator of the A310, having acquired two Series 225s for use by its main transport unit, 21 Smaldeel/Escadrille from Brussels-Melsbroek. The aircraft were delivered to the Belgian air force in September 1997 and April 1998.

Canada's five A310-304s were all ex-Wardair aircraft delivered to No. 437 Squadron at CFB Trenton between December 1992 and August 1993. They replaced Boeing Model 707 aircraft in the long-range transport role and

*Canada's five **CC-150 Polaris** transports are used to support long-range troop deployments on anti-terrorist and peacekeeping missions.*

The Luftwaffe has seven A310 transports, four of them which are to be adapted as tanker/transport machines.

Left: France's Armée de l'Air flies two A310 transport aircraft, largely in the VIP role, from Roissy on the outskirts of Paris.

Royal Jordanian A310-304s for service with ET 3/60 based at Creil/Senlis, but with the aircraft flying from Roissy (Paris-Charles de Gaulle).

The Luftwaffe acquired its first three A310-304s from former East German airline Interflug. Taken on charge in May 1991, these are used by 1. Staffel/FBS at Köln. Four more machines were then acquired for conversion to tanker/transports.

So far the only nation to buy a new A310 for military purposes, Thailand acquired a single A310-324 for the air force's Royal Flight, based at Bangkok-Don Muang and delivered in November 1991.

have been used on trooping flights in connection with UN peacekeeping missions. In Canadian service the A310 is known as the CC-150 Polaris.

In November 1993 the French air force took delivery of two ex-

NAMC YS-11 Twin-engined multi-role transport

The JASDF bases its YS-11E trainers with the Sotai Sireibu Hiko-tai's Densi-sen Sien-tai (ECM Support Unit) at Iruma air base. The unit began to equip with YS-11E aircraft on 29 January 1977 and uses its machines to provide ECM and EW training for ground-based radar sites. One of the YS-11E aircraft was modified to the YS-11EL Elint configuration in December 1983.

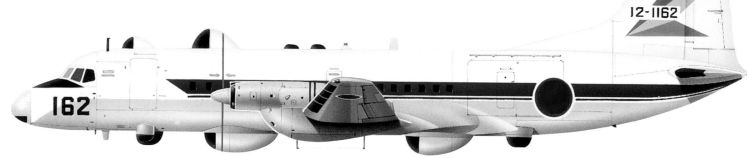

In 1956 six major Japanese aviation companies, namely Fuji, Kawasaki, Mitsubishi, Nippi, Shin Meiwa and Showa, set to work on the collaborative design of a medium-size airliner under the aegis of an umbrella organization they established as the Transport Aircraft Development Association (TADA). In 1957 the Japanese government agreed to contribute to the project's funding, and in recognition of this fact TADA was supplanted in 1959 by NAMC – the Nihon Aeroplane Manufacturing Company.

The first of NAMC's two YS-11 prototypes made its maiden

flight on 30 August 1962 with two Dart RDa.10 Mk 542 turboprop engines each driving a four-blade propeller. The type was to find a ready but limited market with Japanese and some export airlines, and production ended in 1974 after the delivery of 182 aircraft.

The **YS-11A-100** was the initial model, and the 48 such aircraft of this model included two **NAMC YS-11A-103/105** passenger transports delivered to the Japan Air Self-Defence Force in 1965–66 with the designation **YS-11P** for the VIP transport role, although the

SPECIFICATION	
NAMC YS-11A-300 **Type:** two-crew short/medium-range medium transport **Powerplant:** two Rolls-Royce Dart RDa.10/1 Mk 542-10K turboprop engines each rated at 2282 kW (3,060 ehp) **Performance:** maximum cruising speed 469 km/h (291 mph) at 4570 m (15,000 ft); economical cruising speed 452 km/h (281 mph) at 6095 m (20,000 ft); initial climb rate 372 m (1,220 ft) per minute;	service ceiling 6980 m (22,900 ft); range 1090 km (677 miles) with maximum payload **Weights:** empty 15,810 kg (34,854 lb); maximum take-off 24,500 kg (54,012 lb) **Dimensions:** wing span 32 m (104 ft 11¾ in); length 26.3 m (86 ft 3½ in); height 8.98 m (29 ft 5½ in); wing area 94.8 m² (1,020.45 sq ft) **Payload:** up to 60 passengers or 6170 kg (13,602 lb) of freight carried in the cabin

aircraft were later converted for the flight check role; and two **YS-11A-113** personnel/freight transports which were delivered to the Japan Maritime Self-

Defence Force in 1970 with the **YS-11M** designation.

The **YS-11A-200** was the second production model with a 1350-kg (2,970-lb) increase in payload to 6604 kg (14,559 lb). Production totalled 92 aircraft, and two were delivered as **YS-11A-218** troop transports to the Japan Air Self-Defence Force and six as **YS-11A-206** transports to the Japan Maritime Self-Defence Force. It later converted four of the aircraft (as well as two YS-11A-600 aircraft bought in 1970–74 after manufacture as a higher-weight version of the YS-11A-100) into **YS-11T-A** ASW trainers with surface-search radar, ESM and several other ASW systems. In 1971 the JASDF acquired a **YS-11A-213** surplus to airline requirement for conversion as the sole **YS-11FC** navaid calibration machine.

Other military operators of the NAMC YS-11A-200 were Greece and the Philippines, which took six and four such aircraft, respectively.

Freight versions

The **YS-11A-300** was the third production model, and was a mixed freight and passenger transport with accommodation for 48 passengers in the front of the fuselage and freight loaded into the rear of the fuselage via a large port-side door. Production totalled 16 aircraft, and two **YS-11A-305** aircraft were delivered to the JASDF in 1968 as personnel/freight transports with the **YS-11PC** designation.

The fourth production model was the **YS-11A-400** freighter with a maximum payload of 15,906 lb (7215 kg). Production totalled nine aircraft, and of these seven were **YS-11A-402** aircraft that entered JASDF service in 1969–70 with the **YS-11C** designation and two were **YS-11A-404** aircraft that entered JMSDF service in 1971-73 with the **YS-11M-A** designation. One of the YS-11C aircraft was converted into the sole **YS-11NT** navigation trainer in 1977. In 1971 the JASDF bought another three **YS-11A-402** aircraft for conversion to electronic warfare standards. The first two machines were adapted to **YS-11E**

standard as ECM trainers, with one machine further modified during 1976–77; the third became the sole **YS-11EL** in 1983 after conversion for Elint duties.

In the later 1980s the JASDF converted several of its existing YS-11A transports. One machine was fitted with the J/ALQ-7 jamming system and more powerful General Electric T64 turboprop engines to offset the weight of this electronic installation; two were adapted as navaid calibration aircraft with Litton avionics; two were converted as VIP transport aircraft; and three were adapted for the Elint role with the J/ALR-2 system.

Antonov An-28 'Cash' Twin-engined utility/STOL transport

The **Antonov An-28** (NATO reporting designation **'Cash'**) was designed in the Soviet Union (in what is now the Ukraine) as a turboprop-powered successor to the An-2 for short-range routes requiring semi-STOL capability and the ability to operate from indifferent airfields. The type was originally conceived in the early 1960s as the An-14A, an enlarged and turboprop-powered development of the An-14, but progress was very slow and the **An-14M** prototype flew only in September 1969 with retractable tricycle landing gear and two 634-kW (850-shp) Klimov (Isotov) TVD-850 turboprops.

Alteration

The An-14M completed its flight trials in 1972, but during 1973 its designation was altered to An-28 to reflect a major revision of the basic design to reduce cost and weight, and in 1975 it was decided to revise the type still further with two OMKB Mars (Glushenkov) TVD-10B turboprop engines.

As part of a Soviet/Polish agreement, it was decided in 1978 that the type would be built in Poland by WSK-PZL Mielec with a licensed version of the Soviet engine; the first Polish-built machine flew in July 1984.

Accessed by an upward/downward-opening double clamshell door arrangement below the upswept tail unit, the cabin of the An-28 can be configured for the all-passenger, the all-freight, and the mixed passenger/freight roles, and the handling of freight is facilitated by a 500-kg (1,102-lb) capacity hoist over the forward part of the cabin. Small numbers have entered service with the Polish air force as communications and liaison aircraft.

The **An-28RM Bryza 1RM** is a specialized SAR and medevac version with upgraded avionics (including a search radar with its antenna in a ventral radome, Doppler navigation and a GPS receiver), as well as provision for the release of a life raft and a cabin reconfigured for the

carriage of litters. Three of the type have been delivered to the Polish air force, which has a requirement for an eventual eight machines and may also take the **An-28TD Bryza 1TD** transport optimized for airdrop operations with the clamshell rear doors replaced by a single door arranged to slide forward under the fuselage. PZL Mielec

A single example of Antonov's An-28 provides light transport for the Djibouti air force.

has also flown an **M-28 Skytruck** Westernized model with US-sourced Bendix/King avionics and 820-kW (1,100-shp) Pratt & Whitney Canada PT6A-65B turboprops driving Hartzell five-blade propellers.

SPECIFICATION
Antonov An-28 'Cash' **Type:** two-crew short-range utility light transport **Powerplant:** two PZL Rzeszow (OMKB Mars [Glushenkov]) TWD-10B turboprop engines each rated at 716 kW (960 shp) **Performance:** maximum cruising speed 350 km/h (217 mph) at 3000 m (9,845 ft); initial climb rate 500 m (1,640 ft) per minute; service ceiling more than 6000 m (19,685 ft); range 1365 km	(848 miles) with a 1000-kg (2,205-lb) payload and maximum fuel, or 560 km (348 miles) with maximum payload **Weights:** empty 3900 kg (8,598 lb); maximum take-off 6500 kg (14,330 lb) **Dimensions:** wing span 22.06 m (72 ft 4½ in); length 13.1 m (42 ft 11¾ in); height 4.9 m (16 ft 1 in); wing area 39.72 m² (427.56 sq ft) **Payload:** up to 17 passengers, or 2000 kg (4,409 lb) of freight

Kawasaki C-1 Japanese short-range transport

This C-1 wears the markings of Japan's 402nd Hiko-tai of the 1st Koku-tai. Based at Iruma, the 402nd forms a vital component of the Yuso Koku-dan (Air Transport Wing). The second JASDF C-1 transport unit is the 403rd Hiko-tai, based at Miho. Between them the operators share the 27 remaining transport examples built exclusively for Japan.

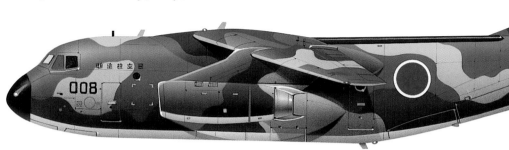

When the Japan Air Self-Defence Force decided to find a new type to succeed the C-46 Commando transport aircraft that it still had in service, it drew up its C-X specification for an indigenous medium-sized troop and freight transport in the early 1970s. The Nihon Aeroplane Manufacturing Company began the design of such a type in 1966, and even before the approval of a full-size mock-up the company had received a contract to build two **XC-1** prototypes for flight trials, as well as another airframe for static test. The first of the prototypes, assembled by Kawasaki, made its maiden flight on 12 November 1970, and the Japan Defence Agency completed its flight test programme of both prototypes during March 1973. Following construction of two pre-production aircraft, a first contract was placed for 11 full-production machines, which received the basic designation **Kawasaki C-1**.

C-1 design

The C-1 is of conventional design for a modern military transport with swept flying surfaces, and as such is based on a high-wing monoplane configuration to maximize cabin volume, a fuselage with a separate flight deck and cabin/cargo hold that are both pressurized and air-conditioned, and a ventral ramp/door arrangement that can be opened in flight for the paradrop of troops, equipment and stores. The tail unit is of the T-type with

a tall vertical surface, the landing gear is of the retractable tricycle type, and the type's two turbofan engines are installed in nacelles mounted on pylons below and ahead of the wing's leading edges. The C-1 is operated by a flight crew of five, and typical loads include 60 fully equipped troops, or 45 paratroops, or up to 36 litters plus attendants, or a variety of military equipment or various palletized cargo.

The result of a collaborative manufacturing process, the C-1 was built by Fuji (outer wing panels), Mitsubishi (centre/aft fuselage and tail surfaces), Nihon (control surfaces and engine nacelles) and Kawasaki (forward fuselage and wing centre section as well as final assembly and testing). Production of the C-1 totalled just 31 aircraft including the four prototype and pre-production aircraft, and the last of these machines was delivered on 21 October 1981. Although built to JASDF requirements, the C-1's maximum payload is decidedly on the small size and limits its

Although a handy and reliable aircraft, the JASDF's Kawasaki C-1 is very limited in payload and range, and is also relatively slow for a jet. The final five of 27 production C-1s have a long-range fuel tank, but they still seldom fly beyond Japan.

operational value. This is one of several reasons why plans for variants did not materialize.

ECM and testing

One C-1 was used as a flying test bed for the MITI/NAL FJR710 and Ishikawajima-Harima XF3 turbofan engines, the latter required for the Kawasaki T-4 trainer. More recently, Kawasaki modified one C-1 airframe as the sole **C-1KAI** electronic countermeasures trainer, the modification process giving the

aircraft a large, flat, bulbous nose and tail radomes, an indigenous ALQ-5 ECM system and antennas beneath the fuselage. Proposed C-1 variants for inflight refuelling, electronic warfare, weather reconnaissance and minelaying remained stillborn, as did a larger-capacity transport with a stretched fuselage. One aircraft served as the basis for the **NAL Asuka**, a dedicated quiet STOL test bed which flew with overwing engines and blown flaps.

SPECIFICATION	
Kawasaki C-1	range 3353 km (2,084 miles) with
Type: five-crew short-range	maximum fuel and a 2200-kg
transport aircraft	(4,850-lb) payload
Powerplant: two Mitsubishi (Pratt &	**Weights:** empty 24300 kg
Whitney) JT9D-M-9 turbofan	(53,571 lb); maximum take-off
engines each rated at 164.5 kN	45000 kg (199,206 lb)
(14,500 lb st)	**Dimensions:** wing span 30.6 m (100
Performance: maximum speed	ft 4¾ in); length 29 m (95 ft 1¾ in);
806 km/h (501 mph) at 7620 m	height 9.99 m (32 ft 9¼ in); wing
(25,000 ft); initial climb rate	area 120.5 m² (1,297.09 sq ft)
1065 m (3,495 ft) per minute;	**Payload:** maximum 11900 kg
service ceiling 11580 m (38,000 ft);	(26,235 lb)

Fokker F27, 50 and 60 Medium-range tactical transports

The Fokker 60U continues to provide useful service to the Dutch air force. The aircraft is able to carry a complete F100 turbofan engine.

Later Fokkers

At the time of its bankruptcy in March 1996, Fokker was producing the **Fokker 50** and **Fokker 60**. The F50 is a thoroughly modernized version of the F27, with Pratt & Whitney Canada PW125 turboprops driving high-technology six-bladed propellers. Stretching the F50's fuselage by means of a 1.62-m (5-ft 4-in) plug produced the F60, of which only four were sold, under the designation **F60 Utility** to the Dutch air force.

A small market was found for the F50, which was offered in basic transport and special missions variants. The basic machine entered service with the Netherlands (where it carries the designation **Troopship Mk 3**), Singapore, Taiwan, Tanzania and Thailand. Further F50 sales, from surplus airline stocks, are likely.

The Fairchild-built **F-27** and stretched **FH-227** also achieved military service, the former with countries including Mexico, Myanmar and the United States, and the latter with Angola, Mexico, Myanmar, Peru, the United States and Uruguay.

SPECIFICATION

Fokker F27 Friendship Mk 400M
Type: medium-range tactical transport aircraft
Powerplant: two 1596-kW (2,140-shp) Rolls-Royce Dart Mk 532-7R turboprops
Performance: cruising speed 480 km/h (298 mph) at medium altitude; range 2210 km

(1,373 miles) with maximum 6420-kg (14,153-lb) payload
Weights: empty 10,600 kg (23,369 lb); maximum take-off 20,410 kg (44,996 lb)
Dimensions: wing span 29 m (95 ft 2 in); length 23.56 m (77 ft 3½ in); height 8.5 m (27 ft 11 in); wing area 70 m² (753.5 sq ft)

In terms of numbers sold, the most successful post-war European airliner has been the **Fokker F27 Friendship**, and the type has also proved to be a popular medium military transport, variants of the type serving with close on 20 air arms throughout the world.

Small numbers of the early production **F27 Friendship Mk 100** and **Mk 200** models are still active with several air forces, but the most prolific derivative with regard to military contracts has been the **F27 Friendship Mk 400** which has sold in both its standard form and as the **F27 Friendship Mk 400M** built specifically for military customers such as Algeria, Argentina, Iran, Nigeria and

Sudan. Incorporating a freight door on the port side of the forward fuselage and flown for the first time during 1961, the F27 Mk 400M can carry up to 45 paratroops or 6025 kg (13,283 lb) of cargo. Other variants adapted for military transport duties are the **F27 Friendship Mk 500**, which features a 1.52-m (5-ft) fuselage

stretch, and the **F27 Friendship Mk 600**. Both of these also possessing a freight door.

In Dutch service, the military-specific **F27 Mk 300M** and Mk 400M were known by the name **Troopship**. Other members of the Friendship family were designed for more specific roles, but those that can be used for transport include the **F27MPA Maritime** with Litton search radar in a prominent ventral radome. Lacking the facility to carry armament, the Maritime derivative is mainly intended for peacetime duties such as fishery patrol, oil platform surveillance, SAR and environmental control, but Fokker also built the armed Maritime Enforcer.

Senegal used its F27-400M aircraft as replacements for C-47s. The Fokkers were delivered as basic 44-seat transports, with modification kits for the medevac and VIP roles.

CASA C.212/C-212 Aviocar Light tactical transport

CASA's **C.212 Aviocar** is a simple airlifter of modest performance which has proved attractive to a number of smaller

air arms, as well as civil operators. The aircraft has limited maintenance requirements, good STOL

performance and a rear ramp/door for easy loading. The freight capacity is often exchanged for accommodation

for 15 paratroops and an instructor/dispatcher, or 12 litters and three seated casualties plus attendants or 19 passengers.

Aviocar described

The Aviocar has an all-metal structure including a basically rectangular-section fuselage with an upswept tail unit, a high-set wing carrying the two engines and fixed tricycle landing gear. The type first flew on 26 March 1971 for a service debut in 1973, and Spanish production of the **C.212A** (later redesignated **C.212-5 Series 100**) and specifically military **C.212-5 Series 100M** (Spanish military designation **T.12B**, of which two were later converted to **D.3A** medevac standard) totalled 129 aircraft, while another 29 aircraft were made in Indonesia under the designation **IPTN (Nurtanio) NC.212-100 Aviocar**. Exports of the C.212-5 Series 100M military version were made to Chile and Portugal.

Aviocar variations

The **C.212AV** is the VIP version of the C.212A, and is known to the Spanish military as the **T.12C**. Under the designation **C.212B**, six pre-production C.212A machines were converted to photo-survey standard with Wild RC-10 cameras and a darkroom in the hold, and this variant is known to the Spanish military as the **TR.12A**.

The **C.212C** is the civil version of the C.212A Series 100, of which a few examples have

entered military or paramilitary service as well as operating with a modest number of airlines. The **C.212D** designation was applied to the last two of the eight pre-production aircraft after modification as navigation trainers for service with the Spanish air force under the service designation **TE.12B**. Some production aircraft followed to the same standard.

Series 200

Introduced in 1979, the **C.212 Series 200** is a stretched development of the C.212-5 Series 100 with the uprated powerplant of two TPE331-10-503C turboprops, each flat-rated at 671 kW (900 shp) and an increased-length hold. The Indonesian-built version is the **NC.212-200**.

This Chilean C-212 Series 300M is making full use of the C-212's ability to fly from semi-prepared strips. Note also the winglets that distinguish the 300- and 400-series aircraft.

The **C.212 Series 200M** has been widely exported to military operators, with Spain using **D.3B** SAR aircraft with APS-128 nose radar and **TR.12D** ECM trainers, and Swedish aircraft being designated **Tp 89**.

Series 300

Substituting the C.212-5 Series 100's powerplant of two TPE331-5-251C turboprop engines each flat-rated at 563 ekW (755 ehp) for TPE331-10R-513Cs produced the **C.212 Series 300**. First flown in September 1984, the **C.212-M Series 300** became the standard production version in 1987, and features Whitcomb winglets. The civil model is available in C.212 Series 300 Airliner and C.212 Series 30 Utility subvariants. The

specifically military version of the C.212 Series 300 is the **C.212 Series 300M** which has again been widely exported.

Series 400

The latest variant of the C.212 is the **C-212 Series 400**, or **C-212 Series 400M** for any military development. The C-212 Series 400 first flew in April 1997 and differs from the Series 300 mainly in its increased weight and modified flightdeck and cabin. The aircraft's powerplant comprises two 820-kW (1,100-shp) TPE331-12RJ turboprop engines and the flight deck has been revised with an EFIS.

By the middle of 1998, CASA and IPTN had sold some 570 examples of the C.212/C-212, including special-mission variants.

The Aviaciòn de la Marina Venezolana uses the C.212-200 in the ASW and SAR roles, while the C-212-400 aircraft illustrated are used as straight transports.

SPECIFICATION

CASA C.212-M Series 300 Aviocar
Type: two-crew STOL utility medium transport with capability for armed roles such as light attack
Powerplant: two AlliedSignal TPE331-10R-513C turboprop engines each flat-rated at 671 kW (900 shp) without automatic power reserve and 690 kW (925 shp) with automatic power reserve
Performance: maximum speed 370 km/h (230 mph) at optimum altitude; cruising speed 354 km/h (220 mph) at 3050 m (10,000 ft); initial climb rate 497 m (1,630 ft) per minute; service ceiling 7925 m (26,000 ft); range 1433 km (519 miles) with maximum payload
Weights: empty 4400 kg (9,700 lb);

maximum take-off 8000 kg (17,637 lb)
Dimensions: wing span 20.28 m (66 ft 6½ in); length 16.15 m (52 ft 11¾ in); height 6.6 m (21 ft 7¾ in); wing area 41 m² (441.33 sq ft)
Armament: provision for up to 500 kg (1,102 lb) of disposable stores carried on one hardpoint on each side of the fuselage, and generally comprising two machine-gun pods, or two multiple launchers for air-to-surface unguided rockets, or a combination of these weapons
Payload: up to 25 troops, or 24 paratroops, or 12 litters plus four attendants, or 2820 kg (6,217 lb) of freight

Ilyushin Il-76 'Candid' Long-range transport

First flown in prototype form on 25 March 1971, the **Il-76** was created as a successor to the An-12 in both the civil freighting and military transport roles. Design of the new type began in the late 1960s to meet a requirement for a freighter able to carry a 40,000-kg (88,183-lb) payload over a range of 5000 km (3,107 miles) in less than 6 hours, operate from short and unprepared airstrips and cope with the worst weather conditions likely to be experienced in Siberia and the Soviet Union's arctic regions. The configuration of the new Soviet transport was probably inspired by the smaller, lighter and less powerfully engined Lockheed C-141A StarLifter.

Above: Although carrying the markings of Aeroflot, these Il-76 variants were undoubtedly used for military purposes. The nearest aircraft is a standard Il-76T.

SPECIFICATION

Ilyushin Il-76M 'Candid-B'
Type: seven-crew long-range transport aircraft
Powerplant: four PNPP 'Aviadvigatel' (Soloviev) D-30KP turbofan engines each rated at 117.68 kN (26,455 lb st)
Performance: maximum speed 850 km/h (528 mph) at optimum altitude; cruising speed 800 km/h (497 mph) between 9000 and 12,000 m (29,530 and 39,370 ft); service ceiling about 14,500 m (47,570 ft); range 5000 km (3,107 miles) with maximum

payload
Weights: maximum take-off 170,000 kg (374,780 lb)
Dimensions: wing span 50.5 m (165 ft 8 in); length 46.59 m (152 ft 10¼ in); height 14.76 m (48 ft 5 in); wing area 300 m² (3,229.28 sq ft)
Armament: two 23-mm Gryazev-Shipunov GSh-23L trainable rearward-firing two-barrel cannon in the tail turret
Payload: up to 140 troops, or 125 paratroops, or litters plus attendants, or 40,000 kg (88,183 lb) of freight

The initial **Il-76 'Candid-A'** was built purely for military service. The aircraft's hold is accessed by a rear door arrangement including a powered lifting ramp, it is fully pressurized and fitted with freight-handling equipment including two winches and two overhead travelling cranes with a total of four cargo hoists.

'Candid-B'

The **Il-76M 'Candid-B'** is the military version of the Il-76T,

which is itself a civilian model with greater fuel capacity and higher weights. For military use, the Il-76M adds a rear turret, ECM blisters on the fuselage sides in line with the navigator's compartment as well as on the sides of the forward and rear fuselage sections, and provision for chaff/flare dispenser packs.

The **Il-76MD 'Candid-B'** is the military subvariant equivalent to the civilian Il-76TD. The Il-76MD differs from the Il-76M in its

Intended to compete with the Antonov An-70 for sales to CIS and foreign customers, the Il-76MF incorporates new engines, a front and rear fuselage stretch and modern avionics.

maximum payload of 48,000 kg (105,820 lb), D-30KP-2 engines and maximum take-off weight of 190,000 kg (418,871 lb).

Both the 'Candid-A' and 'Candid-B' variants are extremely capable as a result of their combination of advanced design, sturdy landing gear, excellent high-lift devices and powerful

engines, which bestow good field performance even under adverse conditions.

The Indian air force uses the type under the name **Gajaraj** (king elephant), and other military export customers have included Iran, Libya, North Korea, Syria and Yemen, as well as members of the CIS.

Ilyushin Il-78 'Midas' Tanker conversions

The **Il-78**, which has the NATO reporting designation **'Midas'**, is the inflight-refuelling tanker version of the Il-76MD. It has

three UPAZ-1A Sakhalin hose-and-drum units (HDUs) installed as one under each wing and one on the port side of the rear

fuselage, 28,000 kg (61,728 lb) of extra fuel in two tanks located in the erstwhile cargo hold in an arrangement linked to

the standard wing tankage, and a refuelling observation position replacing the rear turret. The two fuel tanks in the hold are

SPECIFICATION

Ilyushin Il-78 'Midas'
Type: seven-crew inflight-refuelling tanker and transport aircraft
Powerplant: four PNPP 'Aviadvigatel' (Soloviev) D-30KP-2 turbofan engines each rated at 117.68 kN (26,455 lb st)
Performance: nominal cruising speed 750 km/h (466 mph) at optimum altitude; refuelling speed between 430 and 590 km/h (267 and 366 mph) at between

2000 and 9000 m (6,560 and 29,525 ft); radius 1000 km (621 miles) with 143,298 kg (315,913 lb) of transfer fuel
Weights: empty 98000 kg (216,049 lb); maximum take-off 190000 kg (418,871 lb)
Dimensions: wing span 50.5 m (165 ft 8 in); length 46.59 m (152 ft 10¼ in); height 14.76 m (48 ft 5 in); wing area 300 m² (3,229.28 sq ft)
Payload: as Ilyushin Il-76M (p223)

Right: With the retirement of 'Bison-C' and 'Badger-A', 'Midas' has become the Russian forces' primary inflight-refuelling tanker.

Above: In the Il-78, the Russian air force has a highly capable tanker aircraft. The machine has considerable export potential and has already been sold to India.

able to be removed in order to allow the Il-78 to operate as a conventional transport.

The UPAZ unit is notably neat, and incorporates in its nose a partially retractable spike whose rearward movement opens the annular inlet through which free-stream air enters the unit before passing through the ram-air turbine and finally exiting via slotted exhaust ducts. The ram-air turbine drives the turbopump that allows fuel to be transferred at the rate of 2500 litres (550 Imperial gallons) per minute, which is a considerably higher rate than that achieved by any Western HDU. The Il-78 can also

be used for the refuelling of aircraft on the ground by means of conventional hoses, and it is thought that in Russian service the initial Il-78s operated in civil markings and the subsequent **Il-78M** machines were flown in military colours.

The Il-78 otherwise differs from the Il-76 in its Kupol navigation system and its RSBN short-range navigation system for the location of and approach to receiver aircraft from a distance of some 300 km (185 miles). The Il-78 entered service in 1987 as a replacement for the tanker version of the Myasishchyev M-4 bomber,

and the aircraft provides Soviet tactical and long-range warplanes with significantly improved refuelling capabilities. It is thought that Iraq has developed its own inflight-refuelling tanker version of the Il-76 with comparable capabilities.

The Il-78M is the pure inflight-refuelling counterpart of the Il-78 with three fixed rather than two removable tanks in the hold, the addition of the third tank increasing the fuel available for transfer by 10,000 kg (22,046 lb) at a maximum take-off weight of 210,000 kg (462,965 lb).

'Midas' service

The Il-78 and Il-78M are based on the Il-76MD standard, and it is believed that by the end of the twentieth century at least 31 Il-78 and 15 Il-78M aircraft had been produced, these serving both the Russian and Ukrainian air forces. In 2005, China and India signed a deal to take delivery of eight 'Midas' refuelling tankers.

Developments that have been proposed but are as yet unbuilt are the **Il-76V** with UPAZ-MK-32V HDUs, and the **Il-76MK** convertible tanker/transport.

Myasishchyev 3MS-2 'Bison-C' Tanker conversions

SPECIFICATION

Myasishchev 3MS-2 'Bison-B'
Type: inflight refuelling tanker
Powerplant: four MNPK 'Soyuz'
(Mikulin) RD-3M-500A turbojet
engines each rated at 93.2 kN
(20,944 lb st)
Performance: estimated maximum
level speed 'clean' at 11,000 m
(36,090 ft) 998 km/h (620 mph);
estimated service ceiling 13,700 m

(44,950 ft); range 12,400 km
(7,705 miles)
Weights: empty 75,740 kg
(166,975 lb); normal take-off
192,000 kg (423,280 lb)
Dimensions: wing span 53.14 m
(174 ft 4 in); length 51.7 m
(169 ft 7½ in); estimated height
14.1 m (46 ft 3 in); estimated wing
area 320 m² (3,444.56 sq ft)

The converted 'Bison' tankers bore the Russian designation **3MS-2** and were converted 3MS and 3MD bombers. They were given the **'Bison-C'** reporting name of the 3MD and it has been reported that they may have been re-engined with the 93.2-kN (20,944-lb st) RD-3M-500A turbojet. They were used to refuel probe-equipped receiver aircraft using a centreline hose-drogue unit mounted in the former bomb bay. Some sources suggested that the 'Bison' had been entirely withdrawn from Soviet/CIS service by the early 1990s, and there was a massive, heavily publicized scrapping of aircraft during the late 1980s. Certainly some 40 'Bison-B' and 'Bison-C' airframes were dismantled as part of the strategic arms reduction programme, but at least a handful of Russian tankers remained in use, notably with a regiment based at Engels, long after this.

As part of their conversion to tanker configuration, the 'Bison' bombers lost their distinctive nose probes and gained equipment for homing onto the receiver.

Tupolev Tu-16N 'Badger-A' Tanker conversions

Most Tu-16A bombers were rebuilt for other purposes after 1960, the **Tu-16N 'Badger-A'** conversion being developed as a tanker for other Tu-16s. It used a modernized version of the wingtip-to-wingtip refuelling system used on the Tu-4 'Bull'. The tankers could be recognized externally by a wingtip extension, outboard of a pipe-like tube which projected aft from the trailing edge. It had a total transferable fuel load of 19,000 kg (42,000 lb). A large white panel was often painted on the Tu-16N's rear fuselage to help the pilot of the receiver aircraft keep station.

Tanker conversion

In addition to the Tu-16N, further 'Badger-As' were converted as

tankers for the probe-equipped Tupolev Tu-22 'Blinder' bomber from 1963. These aircraft had a hose/drogue unit installed in the former bomb bay, but may not be converted from Tu-16Ns and may not retain the wingtip-to-

wingtip equipment needed to refuel other Tu-16s. The probe-and-drogue tankers had a total transferable fuel load of only 15,000 kg (33,000 lb) because the HDU took up room in the bomb bay usually occupied by

fuel tanks. About 20 tankers remained in air force service up until the mid-1990s, at which stage another 70 were believed to remain in use with the former AV-MF; however, by 2003 all had apparently been retired.

A Tu-16 'Badger-G' refuels from a Tu-16N 'Badger-A'. The Tu-16N was fitted with a modernized version of the refuelling system first tested by the Tu-2 'Bat' and Tu-4 'Bull'. IFR trials were first carried out by the Tu-16Z in 1955.

Antonov An-124 'Condor' and An-225 'Cossack'

Outsize cargo transports

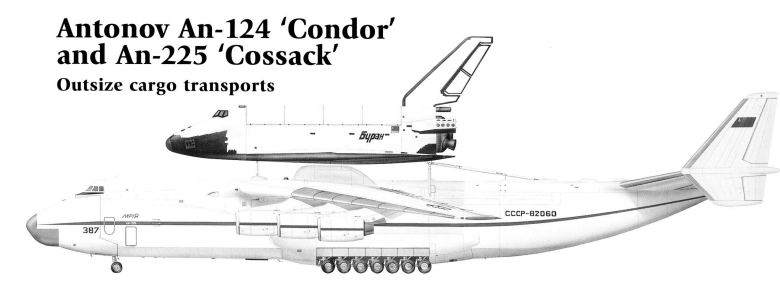

Only a relatively small number of the **Antonov An-124** aircraft built by 2003 have been assigned directly to the air transport arm of the Russian air forces, but there is provision for most civil-registered aircraft to be called into military service. Initially named **Ruslan** after Pushkin's legendary giant, the An-124 is in many respects comparable to the slightly smaller Lockheed C-5 Galaxy, which has a very similar configuration. The An-124 remains the world's largest production aircraft, although if plans to place the An-225 into production reach fruition, this latter machine will become the largest. Nevertheless, the An-124 has set a series of world records, most notably exceeding by 53 per cent the C-5's payload to an altitude of 2000 m (6,560 ft).

Soviet requirement

Allocated the ASCC/NATO code name **'Condor'**, the An-124 was designed to meet a requirement of Aeroflot and the Soviet air forces for a long-range heavy transport to replace the Antonov An-22 Antei. The An-124 first flew on 26 December 1982 and entered service with Aeroflot in January 1986 and with the Soviet air forces in 1987.

The aircraft has an upward-hinging 'visor-type' nose (with a folding nose ramp) and an enormous set of rear loading doors (with a three-part folding ramp), a combination which allows simultaneous loading or unloading from both ends, or allows vehicles to be 'driven through'.

The vast cargo hold has a titanium floor with roller gangs and retractable cargo tie-down points. It is only lightly pressurised, although there is a fully pressurized upper passenger deck for up to 88 people. For ease of loading the aircraft can be made to 'kneel' in a nose-down position by retracting the nosewheels and supporting the nose on retractable feet.

Equipped with fly-by-wire controls, the An-124 has a supercritical wing, and makes extensive use of composite materials for weight saving. It is capable of carrying virtually any load, including all Soviet main battle tanks, helicopters and other military cargo.

Derivatives of the baseline An-124 include the **An-124-100** commercial transport version with a maximum take-off weight of 392,000 kg (864,198 lb), the **An-124-100M** version of the An-124-100 with Western avionics, and the **An-124-102** version, which has an EFIS flight deck that allows the number of crew to be reduced to three personnel (two pilots and a flight engineer).

The **An-124-130** is a projected development of the basic type with four General Electric CF6-80 turbofans, and the type has also been considered in a convertible transport/firebombing version capable of lifting 200 tonnes.

An-225 'Cossack'

Despite making high-profile appearances at a number of international air shows and holding a headline-grabbing

One of the motivating factors behind production of the An-225 was the need for a transport aircraft able to carry the Buran orbiter. This capability was demonstrated graphically to the West at the Paris Air Show, when not only did the 'Cossack'/Buran combination perform in the 1989 flying display, but it was also taxied across the airfield's sodden grass.

In today's rationalized Russian air force, the An-124 remains an important asset for the Voyenno-Transportnaya Aviatsiya (VTA). Here, a 'Condor' in air force livery formates with four 'Flanker' interceptors during VE-Day 50th anniversary celebrations.

Rossiya (Russia), a division of Aeroflot, operates two An-124-100s on state missions. The An-124-100 designation is applied to commercial standard aircraft. The Russian air force itself has around 28 An-124s in service, most of which wear Aeroflot titles.

SPECIFICATION	
Antonov An-124 'Condor' **Type:** six-crew heavy freight transport **Powerplant:** four ZMKB Progress (Ivchenko) D-18T turbofan engines each rated at 229.47 kN (51,587 lb st) **Performance:** maximum cruising speed 865 km/h (537 mph) at optimum altitude; range 16,500 km (10,250 miles) with maximum fuel	or 4500 km (2,795 miles) with maximum payload **Weights:** empty 175,000 kg (385,802 lb); maximum take-off 405,000 kg (892,857 lb) **Dimensions:** wing span 73.3 m (240 ft 5¼ in); length 69.1 m (226 ft 8½ in); height 21.08 m (69 ft 2 in); wing area 628 m² (6,759.96 sq ft) **Payload:** up to 150,000 kg (330,688 lb)

series of 106 world records, the sole **Antonov An-225 Mriya** (dream) **'Cossack'** remained derelict until relatively recently, when the aircraft was restored to flight and initially used on relief flights into Afghanistan.

Maiden flight

The type made its maiden flight on 21 December 1988, and flew with the Buran space shuttle on its back on 13 May 1989, visiting the Paris air show in the same year. The first aircraft to fly with a gross weight in excess of 453,600 kg (1,000,000 lb), the An-225 is an ingenious derivative of the An-124 designed to offer a 50 per cent improvement in payload and maximum take-off weight. This goal was achieved by the provision of a stretched fuselage, the use of six engines, and a main landing gear with seven pairs of wheels on each side, together with redesign of the tail unit with a dihedralled horizontal surface and twin endplate vertical surfaces, deletion of the rear ramp/door arrangement, and enlargement of the wing's span and area.

A second aircraft began to take shape alongside standard An-124 transports in the early 1990s, and in 2003 it seemed likely that this machine would soon enter service, with the possibility of further developments being built in the future.

Antonov An-26 'Curl', An-30 'Clank' and An-32 'Cline' Turboprop transport family

Distinguished by its glazed nose, the An-30 is a specialized air survey aircraft, used for precision mapping and photogrammetric surveys. One of the few export operators of the type is the Romanian air force, which retained three in service early in 2003. The An-30 has found some favour with nations flying Open Skies missions in Europe.

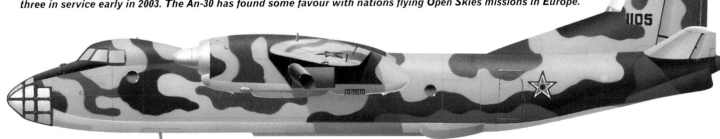

Evolved from the Antonov **An-24 'Coke'** airliner, the **An-26 'Curl-A'** first appeared in 1969, and soon became the Warsaw Pact's standard light tactical transport type, also achieving a quite significant degree of export success, examples being supplied to a number of nations such as Afghanistan, Congo, Cuba, Iraq, Libya, Mali, North Korea and Somalia.

Featuring a redesigned aft fuselage section with a rear ramp to facilitate loading and unloading, the An-26 also possesses a large bulged observation window on the port side of the forward fuselage to assist in paradropping missions. The aircraft's powerplant configuration is also unusual in that the An-26 has a small turbojet engine in its starboard nacelle, this being intended to enhance the aircraft's field performance when flying in 'hot-and-high' conditions.

The bulbous observation window on the An-26's starboard side is obvious in this view.

An-30 'Clank'

A derivative of the An-26 family which is only in fairly limited military service is the **An-30 'Clank'**, the existence of which became known during 1974. Optimized for photographic survey tasks, the aircraft is instantly recognizable by the extensive glazing in the vicinity of its nose section. This revised nose necessitated a redesign and relocation of the cockpit; the An-30 also possesses several ventral ports for cameras and associated survey apparatus, as well as onboard photographic processing facilities.

An-32 'Cline'

The third and final major variant in the An-26 family to appear was the **An-32 'Cline'**, which was revealed to the West in 1977. Intended to overcome the rather poor 'hot-and-high' field performance of earlier models, this has been re-engined with the substantially more powerful 3760-kW (5,042-ehp) AI-20D Series 5 engine. As it has also been necessary to fit larger-diameter propellers, the resulting aircraft rather unusually has the engines mounted on top of the wing, this being a most distinctive recognition feature. The maximum payload of the An-32 is 6700 kg (14,771 lb), and the type is in widespread military use. Many variants of the basic An-24/ 26/30/32 family have been produced, both as new-build aircraft and by conversion. They include Elint, calibration, weather modification and fire-fighting machines, as well as numerous others. The family remained in widespread service in 2005.

Instantly recognizable by the enlarged nacelles for its Ivchenko AI-40DM engines perched high above the fuselage, this An-32 belongs to the Indian air force (where it is named Sutlej). The good 'hot-and-high' performance of the 'Cline' was well appreciated by the Indians, who chose the aircraft over the G222, DHC-5 and Andover, and the IAF had around 110 of the type in service into 2003.

SPECIFICATION	
Antonov An-26B 'Curl-A' **Type:** tactical transport aircraft **Powerplant:** two ZMDB Progress (Ivchyenko) AI-24VT turboprops each rated at 2103 kW (2,820 ehp) and one Soyuz (Tumanskii) RU-19A-300 turbojet rated at 7.85 kN (1,765 lb st) **Performance:** maximum level speed at 5000 m (16,405 ft) 540 km/h (336 mph); range 1100 km (683	miles) with maximum payload **Weights:** empty 15,400 kg (33,957 lb); maximum take-off 24,400 kg (53,790 lb) **Dimensions:** wing span 29.2 m (95 ft 9½ in); length 23.8 m (78 ft 1 in); height 8.58 m (28 ft 1½ in); wing area 74.98 m² (807.1 sq ft) **Payload:** up to 5500 kg (12,125 lb) of cargo, or 40 passengers

Antonov An-70 Propfan airlifter

The **An-70** is the result of a programme initiated in 1975 to create a successor to the An-12. The An-70 has typical airlifter layout, but has the distinction of being the first aircraft to fly with an all-propfan powerplant. Each D-27 engine drives a contra-rotating assembly of 14 scimitar-type blades (eight and six in the front and rear propellers, respectively). Some 28 per cent of the airframe is made of composite materials, and other advanced features include a fly-by-wire control system.

Cargo capacity

The An-70's pressurized hold has an inbuilt cargo-handling system that can be outfitted with seats for 300 troops or racks for 206 litters as alternatives to freight and/or vehicles or paratroops. The An-70 can airdrop individual items up to a limit of 20,000 kg (44,092 lb). The hold's sill height can be varied to facilitate the loading and unloading of freight to and from vehicles of different truckbed heights.

The An-70 is slightly larger than the Airbus Military A400M (for which requirement the An-70 was recommended by Germany), but considerably smaller than the Boeing C-17 Globemaster III. The prototype An-70 first flew on 16 December 1994, but was lost on 10 February of the following year following an in-flight collision with its An-72 chaseplane. A

second An-70 prototype first flew on 24 April 1997 and was delivered for official trials in mid-1998, but this too suffered an accident, after double engine failure during take-off, on 27 January 2001.

With the second prototype flying again from 5 June 2001 after repair, the Russian military has a requirement for at least 200 and perhaps as many as 350 An-70s, but it seems unlikely that funding will be found.

SPECIFICATION

Antonov An-70
Type: four-crew STOL medium transport
Powerplant: four ZMKB Progress (Ivchenko) D-27 propfan engines each rated at 10290 kW (13,800 shp)
Performance: (estimated) cruising speed 750 km/h (466 mph) at between 9000 and 12,000 m (29,520 and 39,380 ft); range 1350 km (838 miles) with a 47,000-

kg (103,615-lb) payload after a conventional take-off, or 1450 km (901 miles) with a 25,000-kg (77,161-lb) payload after a short take-off
Weights: maximum take-off 130,000 kg (286,596 lb)
Dimensions: wing span 44.06 m (144 ft 6 in); length 40.73 m (133 ft 7 in); height 16.38 m (53 ft 9 in)
Payload: maximum payload 470,00 kg (103,615 lb)

Above: Antonov's second An-70 prototype demonstrates the type's extensive high-lift devices.

Each of the An-70's propfan blades is electrically de-iced and of composite construction. An export variant with a radical change to CFM56-5A1 turbofan engines has been proposed.

Antonov An-72 and An-74 'Coaler' Light transport

The Antonov **An-72 'Coaler'** was developed as a turbofan-powered STOL transport to replace the turboprop An-26. The first of the two prototypes made its maiden flight on 22 December 1977, and the prototypes and pre-production machines received the reporting designation **'Coaler-A'**.

In common with other transport types in military service with the Soviet Union and, later, Russia, this An-72 has Aeroflot markings.

Production was initiated of a slightly modified aircraft and this initial production version was designated **An-72A**, and received the reporting designation **'Coaler-C'** because it appeared after the West had seen the long-span wing and lengthened fuselage on the **An-74**, which was allocated the reporting designation **'Coaler-B'**.

The An-72's high-set wing gives an unobstructed freight hold and eases production, while the high-set engines allow upper-surface blowing, for high lift, and also minimize FOD ingestion problems. The landing gear is optimized for operation from semi-prepared strips with low-pressure tyres.

An-72 variants

The An-72 has been built in several versions for civil and military use. Variants for the latter including the **An-72P** dedicated maritime surveillance platform. Many operational An-72Ps wear three-tone camouflage, and are armed with a 23-mm GSh-23L cannon in the starboard main landing gear fairing as well as underwing rocket pods. A novel system of bombs carried on an internal hoist has been displayed, and the An-72P has been offered with a range of anti-ship missiles, torpedoes and depth charges. The An-72P retains the pressurized fuselage of the transport version and can accommodate up to 40 folding passenger seats.

An-74 'Coaler-B'

The original An-74 is a dedicated exploration support version optimized for operation in polar regions and designed to replace the ageing Il-14 aircraft then in use for supporting Arctic scientific stations, Antarctic expeditions, and for observing and monitoring ice floes and ice build-up.

The An-74 has no blister observation windows. It also has a larger radome, which gives a pronounced 'droop' to the nose. Fuel capacity is significantly increased and provision is made for a wheel/ski landing gear. It has spawned a family of variants, only some of which have the prominent radome, but most seem to have observation blisters. Antonov has also offered the **An-74-300**, with its engines in underslung wing nacelles.

An-71 'Madcap'

A further, more radical version of the An-72 is the **An-71 'Madcap'**, which was designed as a carrierborne AEW type. It was first observed by Western analysts in the mid-1980s, when its radically revised tail unit was seen in the background of a photograph of President Gorbachev visiting the Antonov design bureau's headquarters.

The An-71 features a revised rear fuselage and a completely different vertical tail surface, which is larger than that of the An-72 and swept forwards to carry the rotodome supporting the antenna for the radar of its integrated AEW system. The highly automated aircraft was designed for operations away from base for a period of up to 30 days without the need for special servicing or maintenance, but no orders were forthcoming.

SPECIFICATION	
Antonov An-72A 'Coaler-C' **Type:** three/four-crew STOL light transport **Powerplant:** two ZMKB Progress (Ivchenko) D-36 Series 2A turbofan engines each rated at 63.74 kN (14,330 lb st) **Performance:** maximum speed 705 km/h (438 mph) at 10,000 m (32,810 ft); service ceiling 10,700 m (35,100 ft); range 800 km (497 miles) with maximum payload	**Weights:** empty 19,050 kg (41,997 lb); maximum take-off 34,500 kg (76,058 lb) **Dimensions:** wing span 31.89 m (104 ft 7½ in); length 28.07 m (92 ft 1¼ in); height 8.75 m (28 ft 8½ in); wing area 98.53 m² (1,060.6 sq ft) **Payload:** 57 paratroops, or 24 litters and 12 seated casualties plus one attendant, or 10,000 kg (22,046 lb) of freight

Vickers VC10 Strategic transport and tanker

Modification of the **Vickers VC10** airliner into a transport gave the RAF useful passenger and cargo-carrying capacity at lower cost compared to the development of a new aircraft. Meeting specification C.239 of 1960 for a strategic long-range transport for what was then Transport Command, the first military VC10s were similar to the civil **Standard VC10**, but had uprated Rolls-Royce Conway engines and the additional fin fuel cell of the **Super VC10**. Rearward-facing seats were fitted, as was a side-loading freight door and a refuelling probe on the nose centreline forward of the cockpit windows. In addition, a Bristol Siddeley Artouste auxiliary power unit was located in the tailcone.

First RAF aircraft

The first RAF VC10 made its maiden flight on 26 November

1965, with initial deliveries to No. 10 Sqn at Fairford in July 1966. No. 10 Sqn was the sole operator of the transport version and undertook the first overseas training flight to Hong Kong in August 1966, regular route flights beginning on 4 April 1967. The latter squadron soon increased its VC10 flights, before relocating to the main RAF transport base at Brize Norton. Despite clipping 4 hours

This VC10 K.Mk 2 was photographed while refuelling a Strike/Attack Operational Evaluation Unit Harrier GR.Mk 7 in 1997.

30 minutes off the flight time of the Comet and 12 hours off that of the Britannia, the VC10's Far East destinations meant a long haul of just over 19 hours to Singapore and 22 hours to Hong Kong. Carrying less than half its full payload, the VC10 had a range exceeding 8047 km (5,000 miles).

VC10 tanker

Foreseeing retirement of the Victor K.Mk 2 tanker force, Air Staff Requirement 406 was made public in 1978, calling for a replacement type, to which a VC10 conversion was tendered. BAe secured the contract in May 1979, for 1982–83 delivery of nine aircraft. These comprised

Vickers VC10 C.Mk 1
Type: strategic transport
Powerplant: four Rolls-Royce Conway RCo.43 Mk 301 turbofans each rated at 96.97 kN (21,800 lb st)
Performance: maximum cruising speed at 9450 m (31,000 ft) 935 km/h (581 mph); service ceiling 12,800 m (42,000 ft); range 6273 km (3,898 miles) with

maximum payload
Weights: empty 66,224 kg (146,000 lb); maximum take-off 146,510 kg (323,000 lb)
Dimensions: wing span 44.55 m (146 ft 2 in); length (excluding probe) 48.38 m (158 ft 8 in); height 12.04 m (39 ft 6 in); wing area 272.38 m² (2,932 sq ft)
Payload: maximum 26,037 kg (57,400 lb)

The RAF's VC10 fleet is coming to the end of its useful service life. Its replacement is likely to be 767- or A330-based. The VC10 K.Mk 2 (illustrated) has already been retired.

five **VC10 K.Mk 2** machines produced from early-production ex-Gulf Air VC10s, and four **VC10 K.Mk 3** aircraft, the last of the type built, which were Super VC10s originating from East African Airways.

The first K.Mk 2 made its maiden flight on 22 June 1982, but not until 1 May 1984 was a specific operating unit formed when No. 101 Sqn was established at Brize Norton. The

type's missions included support of Phantom and Lightning (later Tornado F.Mk 3) interceptions of Soviet aircraft around the UK coast, and overseas flights with combat aircraft deployed for exercises and training. Refuelled by another VC10 and a TriStar, one K.Mk 3 established a non-stop flight record of 16 hours 1 minute 30 seconds between the United Kingdom (Brize) and Perth, Australia, on 2 April 1987.

British Airways flew its last scheduled Super VC10 service in 1981, and 14 of its Supers, plus extra Conways, were bought by the RAF for spare parts reclamation.

In March 1989, the Ministry of Defence requested tenders to meet two needs: Air Staff Requirement 415 for the conversion of five Super VC10s

to **VC10 K.Mk 4** standard and ASR416 to convert eight No. 101 Sqn aircraft to **VC10 C.Mk 1(K)** standard. The first of the K.Mk 4s entered service with No. 101 Sqn in 1993 and these aircraft, along with the K.Mk 3s and the last of the rapidly diminishing C.Mk 1(K) fleet, bore the brunt of the RAF's ever-increasing inflight-refuelling effort in 2003.

Shorts 330UTT and C-23 Sherpa Light transport

Developed from the Skyvan light transport, the **Shorts 330** was a regional airliner which could also be reconfigured for transport tasks. Its box-like fuselage offered exceptional load-carrying capacity for the aircraft's size, and the high-lift wing and powerful engines gave good STOL performance. Cargo versions were configured with a full-width rear loading ramp. In 2003, the Thai army continued to operate two aircraft of this type, designated **Shorts 330UTT**, in the transport role.

American Sherpas

The major military customer was the USAF, which bought 18 **C-23A Sherpa** machines for its EDSA (European Distribution System Aircraft) requirement, these being used to shuttle spare parts between the USAFE maintenance and distribution centres and the frontline bases. The C-23As served from November 1984 until 31 October 1990, when the EDSA programme came to an end.

Four C-23As remained in USAF hands at Edwards AFB, where they served the USAF Test Pilots' School. Eight were diverted to the US Forestry Service, and six were transferred to the Army National Guard, which also ordered 10 more new-build **C-23B** aircraft, which could be distinguished by their windows.

Seven C-23s remain in Army service, flying utility transport missions on behalf of the Army's maintenance organization. At least one Army C-23 is reputed to have had a special mission, perhaps involving electronic reconnaissance, and was seen on service during the Gulf War.

Under the designation **C-23B+**, modified **Shorts 360** commuter airliners were acquired by the US Army National Guard, a total of 43 remaining in service. These aircraft, bought back by Shorts, were converted to (twin-tailed) C-23 standard through addition of new tail sections, along with new avionics, in a programme undertaken in the United States.

In C-23B form, the Sherpa features a full complement of cabin windows, in contrast to the C-23A, which was almost devoid of cabin glazing.

Shorts C-23A Sherpa
Type: light transport
Powerplant: two Pratt & Whitney Canada T101-CP-100 (PT6A-45R) turboprops each rated at 893 kW (1,198 shp)
Performance: maximum cruising speed at 3050 m (10,000 ft) at 9526 kg (21,000 lb) 352 km/h (218 mph); service ceiling 6095 m (20,000 ft); range 1239 km

(770 miles) with a 7268-kg (5,000-lb) payload
Weights: empty equipped 6680 kg (14,727 lb), maximum take-off 11,566 kg (25,500 lb)
Dimensions: wing span 22.76 m (74 ft 8 in); length 17.69 m (58 ft ½ in); height 4.95 m (16 ft 3 in); wing area 42.08 m² (453 sq ft)
Payload: maximum payload 3221 kg (7,100 lb)

The Royal Thai Police took a pair of 330UTTs, one of which is seen here, in addition to those serving with the Royal Thai Army.

Saab 340/Tp 100A Multi-role passenger transport

Saab's original **1084** project was aimed at military and civil customers, whereas the Saab-Fairchild 340 was aimed simply at civil airline customers. Despite this, the aircraft attracted some military interest. The **Saab 340B Plus SAR-200** is a search-and-rescue version for the Japanese Maritime Safety Agency, with an underfuselage Telephonics AN/APS-143(V) 360-degree search radar, a turreted FSI

AN/AAQ-22 FLIR and a comprehensive navigation suite with GPS and VLF/Omega. The aircraft also has large 'search windows' and hatches to allow the dropping of life rafts and survival packs, and for the firing of flares and smoke floats. Two were delivered in 1997, although the agency reportedly still has a requirement for another eight aircraft of a similar type.

The first and main customer for the military Saab 340,

however, has been the Swedish air force. A single VIP-configured **Saab 340B** was delivered to the Royal Flight at Stockholm-Bromma in February 1990, using the local designation **Tp 100A**. In 2003, the Swedish air force's Tp 100A was used in the 'Open Skies' arms limitation verification role, with flights to be made over the former Soviet

Union. The aircraft is fitted with German camera equipment similar to that carried by the Luftwaffe's 'Open Skies' C.160 Transall and has adopted the designation **OS 100**. In 2006 the aircraft may be fitted with IR equipment.

The S 100B Argus AEW variant of the Saab 340 is discussed within a separate entry.

SPECIFICATION	
Saab Tp 100A	range 2427 km (1509 miles) with
Type: passenger transport	maximum payload
Powerplant: two General Electric	**Weights:** empty operating 8035 kg
CT7-9B turboprop engines each	(17,715 lb); maximum take-off
rated at 1305 kW (1,750 shp)	12,927 kg (28,500 lb)
Performance: maximum cruising	**Dimensions:** wing span 21.44 m
speed 522 km/h (325 mph) at	(70 ft 4 in); length 19.73 m (64 ft
6100 m (20,000 ft); maximum	8¾ in); height 6.86 m (22 ft 6 in);
climb rate 625 m (2,050 ft) per	wing area 41.81 m² (450 sq ft)
minute at sea level; service ceiling	**Payload:** up to 37 passengers
7620 m (25,000 ft); maximum	and baggage

The Flygvapnet's single Tp 100A was previously based at Stockholm-Bromma, from where it was operated on VIP transport duties by F16M 'Bravalla' Flygflottilj.

BAe 146 Troop/cargo and VIP transport

In August 1973 Hawker Siddeley announced government backing for design and development of a new short-range civil transport identified as the HS.146. This was to be powered by four turbofans and would have noise levels considerably below announced future legislation on noise emission.

Nationalization led to shelving of the scheme, but in 1978 the board of British Aerospace gave approval for a resumption of the programme. This involved not only BAe, but also Avco (now

Textron) Corporation in the United States and Saab-Scania in Sweden. Textron supplied the ALF 502R turbofan engines and through its Textron Aerostructures division manufactured the wing boxes. Saab was responsible for the tailplanes and movable control surfaces, while in the United Kingdom Short Brothers was subcontracted to fabricate pods for the engines.

The production of three basic passenger versions continued until 1992. The BAe 146-100 was designed

specifically to operate from semi-prepared airstrips. Following demands for versions with less rigorous STOL capabilities and increased accommodation/payload, subsequent variants featured progressively stretched fuselages and uprated engines, and were optimized for operations from paved surfaces.

Civilian revival

Relaunch of the BAe 146 was announced in June 1992, with new RJ (Regional Jet) designations followed by numbers denoting passenger capacities (for example RJ 85). The name Avro was revived to market the aircraft, the proposed joint UK/Taiwanese operation becoming known as Avro International Aerospace.

The RJ series featured more powerful engines, with structural strengthening permitting increased weights. Production was to take place in Taiwan, but the deal foundered in 1993.

In June 1983, two BAe 146-100s were leased as **BAe 146 CC.Mk 1** aircraft by the RAF. These were evaluated at Brize Norton for suitability as replacements for the ageing Andovers of the Queen's Flight. Designated **BAe 146 CC.Mk 2**, three aircraft were subsequently acquired for this unit. Two BAe 146-200s were delivered in mid-1986 and were followed by a further example in early 1991. All the aircraft have been fitted with Loral Matador infrared jamming systems. These aircraft are operated by the RAF's No. 32 Squadron.

Two BAe 146-100s were assessed during 800 hours of everyday cargo operations by the RAF. After this period, the original aircraft were returned to BAe, and three new BAe 146-200 machines were purchased to equip the Queen's Flight for VIP duties.

Four dedicated VIP/executive **Statesman** aircraft were also delivered to No. 1 Squadron (Royal Flight) of the Royal Saudi Air Force based at Riyadh.

Military transports

Military developments of the BAe 146 as a multi-role transport were announced in 1987. These included the **BAe 146STA** (Small Tactical Airlifter), **BAe 146MT** (Military Tanker), **BAe 146MRL** (Military Rear Loader) and **BAe 146MSL** (Military Side Loader). The BAe 146STA was based on the civilian BAe 146-QT Quiet Trader freighter and featured a 4.44-m (14-ft 7-in) wide rear fuselage cargo door in the port side. Loading flexibility was further enhanced by optional roller tracks which permitted the movement of pallets. A sliding door set within the main cargo hold permitted paradropping. This could include air-dropping of military pallets or up to 60 fully-equipped paratroops.

Variations included options for up to 24 stretchers in the casevac role. The variant could also be fitted with an optional refuelling probe.

The prototype BAe 146STA first flew in August 1988, and undertook a sales tour of Australasia and the Far East. However, the dedicated military versions received no orders.

No. 32 Squadron's small fleet of BAe 146 CC.Mk 2 VIP transport aircraft are operated out of Northolt by No. 32 (The Royal) Sqn on behalf of the Queen's Flight.

SPECIFICATION

BAe 146 Series 100 (BAe 146 CC.Mk 1)
Type: two-crew short-range commercial transport
Powerplant: four Avco Lycoming ALF 502R-3 or -5 turbofan engines each rated respectively at 29.8 kN (6,700 lb st) or 31 kN (6,970 lb st)
Performance: maximum cruising speed 767 km/h (477 mph) at 8840 m (29,000 ft); economical cruising speed 669 km/h (416 mph) at 8840 m (29,000 ft); range 1631 km (1,013 miles) with maximum payload or 3002 km (1,865 miles) with standard fuel
Weights: empty 23,336 kg (51,447 lb); maximum take-off 38,102 kg (84,000 lb)
Dimensions: wing span 26.21 m (86 ft); length 26.2 m (85 ft 11 in); height 8.61 m (28 ft 3 in); wing area 77.29 m² (832 sq ft)
Payload: maximum 7735 kg (17,053 lb)

Beech (Raytheon) C-12 Utility transport/communications aircraft

Widely used as a corporate business aircraft, a role for which it was specifically designed, the King Air 200 has also fulfilled a number of roles within the US armed forces and some overseas air arms.

Earlier versions of the Queen Air/King Air had been in military service for some years (mostly under the **U-21 Ute** designation) before the appearance of the King Air 200, a situation which smoothed the procurement path for the new variant.

Larger than its predecessors with a distinctive T-tail, the King Air 200 first flew on 27 October 1972. The first three military aircraft were electronic reconnaissance machines known as RU-21Js, which entered service in 1973. They were followed by a much larger batch of aircraft for the utility/VIP transport role, powered by PT6A-38 engines and ushering in a new designation: **C-12A**. The Army, which dubbed the new type the **Huron**, took 60 aircraft, while the USAF signed up for 30, with service entry commencing in July 1975. One aircraft was also supplied to the Greek army. In USAF service the C-12As were mainly used by Embassy Flights and overseas missions. Indeed, one C-12A assigned to the Embassy Flight at Pretoria was ordered out of South Africa for allegedly conducting spy flights with belly-mounted cameras.

In 1979 the US Navy and Marine Corps began to receive the **UC-12B** model, which had uprated PT6A-41 engines and a cargo door. Like those of the Army, the USN and Marine Corps UC-12Bs were dispersed around airfields to act as base 'hacks' and staff transports. Sixty-six were built.

Only 14 **C-12C** aircraft were built from new, this being an Army variant which was similar to the C-12A, but with the uprated Dash 41 engines. Many

The US Navy received two RC-12Fs (illustrated) and two RC-12Ms as RANSAC (Range Surveillance Aircraft), equipped with surface-search radar under the belly. The RC-12Fs fly from Barking Sands in Hawaii, while the RC-12Ms serve at Point Mugu, California.

SPECIFICATION

Beech King Air B200
Type: utility transport and communications aircraft
Powerplant: two Pratt & Whitney Canada PT6A-42 turboprops, each rated at 634 kW (850 shp)
Performance: maximum level speed 541 km/h (336 mph); service ceiling 10,670 m (35,000 ft); maximum range 3442 km (2,139 miles)

Weights: empty 3716 kg (8,192 lb); maximum ramp weight 5710 kg (12,590 lb)
Dimensions: wing span 16.61 m (54 ft 6 in); length 13.36 m (43 ft 10 in); height 4.52 m (14 ft 10 in); wing area 28.15 m² (303 sq ft)
Accommodation: flight deck crew of two, plus up to seven passengers in the cabin

Civilian-model King Air 200s serve in small numbers with a wide variety of nations, mostly employed as light transport/utility types, although a few undertake maritime patrol or training duties. No. 42 Squadron, RNZAF, at Ohakea, flies three leased aircraft on multi-engine training, general transport and VIP duties.

C-12As were subsequently brought up to this standard, however, including those of the USAF which also briefly carried a **C-12E** designation. The **C-12D** which followed had a cargo door, but around half of the 40 examples built for the Army were either built or converted to RC-12 standard for electronic reconnaissance duties. The USAF also took six aircraft of the C-12D variant.

Dash 42 engines

From 1984 the **C-12F** entered service with both the US Army and Air Force. This version had Dash 42 engines and a cargo door. The US Army took 20 from new, while the US Air Force acquired 46. Many of these were later declared surplus and handed over to the Army. The Army's own machines were destined for the National Guard, and were given the designations **C-12F-1** and **C-12F-2** to denote detail differences between the batches. When ex-USAF aircraft were received, they became **C-12F-3** machines. The US Navy also took a dozen under the designation **UC-12F**, although two were converted to serve as **RC-12F** radar-equipped range safety aircraft.

Chronologically, the next variant of the C-12 was the **C-12L**, a designation which covered three RU-21Js that were stripped of their Guardrail equipment and returned to service as transports. Next came the **UC-12M**, of which 12 were built for the Navy. Two of these aircraft

Six C-12Js were initially bought for ANG support. Four later served with active-duty USAF units and two with the US Army.

became **RC-12M** range safety machines, while earlier UC-12B/Fs were upgraded to the new standard, which had new cockpit instrumentation, lighting and voice comms, but was otherwise similar to the C-12F. Twenty-nine **C-12R** aircraft were bought for the Army, this being a version of the civilian B200C with EFIS cockpit. Two camera-equipped **C-12R/AP** aircraft were ordered for the Greek army.

The US Navy's UC-12s have mostly been retired to storage, while the bulk of the USAF's C-12C/D fleet has been transferred to the Army. The Embassy Flights remain, however.

The basic qualities of the King Air 200 which attracted the US services also led to significant overseas military sales, although for the most part these have been of the civilian models. A notable exception is that of Israel, which bought C-12Ds and RC-12D/Ks. Other overseas operators have included Algeria, Argentina, Bolivia, Cambodia, Chile, Colombia, Ecuador, Egypt, Guatemala, India, Ireland, Macedonia, Malaysia, Morocco, New Zealand, Peru, Saudi Arabia, South Africa, Sri Lanka, Sweden, Thailand, Togo, Turkey, the United Kingdom, Uruguay and Venezuela.

Maritime patrol

Malaysia's **B200T** aircraft have search radar and a FLIR under the belly, and have wing hardpoints for the carriage of long-range tanks or weapons. They patrol the seas around Malaysia on anti-piracy, fishery and other duties, supplanting costly PC-130Hs in the role.

Beech/Raytheon subsequently produced the King Air 350. This has increased-span wings with winglets, a lengthened fuselage and 783-kW (1,050-shp) PT6A-60 turboprops. The US Army has bought the type as the **C-12S**,

while a number of other air arms operate the aircraft. The most notable of these is Japan's army, which ordered 20 (as the **LR-2**) to replace the Mitsubishi MU-2 (LR-1) in the liaison and reconnaissance role, the LR-2 featuring a belly sensor radome.

Model 1900

Based on the King Air series, the Model 1900C was a new design intended for the commuterliner market. Although military interest was small, it did result in purchases by the USAF (on behalf of the Air National Guard) under the **C-12J** designation. Three other air arms also bought the type.

The Model 1900D was a development with stand-up headroom: only one example is in military service.

Lockheed C-130, C-130J and KC-130 Hercules

Tactical transport, inflight-refuelling tanker and special forces aircraft

The latest CC-130J for the USAF, based on the C-130J-30, is shown above during tests late in 2002. It is surprisingly similar to the first YC-130, shown at right.

The **C-130 Hercules** is the West's most popular and widely used military transport aircraft, and has been in production longer than any other aircraft type in history. Very large numbers remain in service on every continent, and many operators have replaced early variants with newer versions. The first of two **YC-130** (later **YC-130A**) prototypes made its maiden flight on 23 August 1954, in the process introducing the 2424-kW (3,250-eshp) Allison YT56A-1 turboprop engine, driving a three-bladed propeller.

Multiple variants

The basic soundness of the design has led to the creation of numerous variants optimized for specialized missions: AC-130 covers gunship models, **DC-130** covers drone control aircraft (**DC-130A**, **E** and **H**), EC-130 covers electronic warfare aircraft, **HC-130** covers long-range search-and-rescue aircraft (**HC-130B**, **H**, **N** and **P**), JC-130 covers temporary test aircraft (**JC-130A**, **B** and **F**), KC-130 covers inflight-refuelling tanker aircraft (**KC-130F**, **H**, **J**, **R**, **T** and **KC-130T-30**), LC-130 covers aircraft with Antarctic/Arctic capability (**LC-130F**, **H** and **R**), **MC-130** covers special forces support aircraft (**MC-130E** and **H**), **NC-130** covers permanent special test aircraft (**NC-130A**, **B**, **E** and **H**), **RC-130** covers reconnaissance aircraft (**RC-130A** and **S**), **VC-130** covers staff and VIP transport aircraft (**VC-130B** and **H**), and **WC-130** covers weather reconnaissance aircraft (**WC-130B**, **E**, **H** and **J**).

The design of the Hercules is based on a high-set wing, unobstructed cargo compartment, integral 'roll on/off' rear loading ramp, a fully pressurized cargo hold that can rapidly be reconfigured for the carriage of troops, stretchers or passengers, and a floor at truck-bed height above the ground. The Hercules can be employed for air drops of troops or equipment, for LAPES (low-altitude parachute extraction system) delivery of heavy cargoes, and the full range of cargo, troop transport and medical evacuation duties. The standard unstretched Hercules can carry 78 troops (92 in a high-density configuration), 64 paratroops or 74 litters.

Production history

While the two YC-130A prototypes came from the manufacturer's California Skunk Works, all the following 2156 first-generation aircraft were built at Marietta, Georgia. The

SPECIFICATION	
Lockheed Martin C-130J Hercules **Type:** two/three-crew tactical transport aircraft **Powerplant:** four Rolls-Royce AE2100D3 turboprop engines each rated at 3424 kW (4,591 shp) **Performance:** maximum cruising speed 644 km/h (400 mph) at optimum altitude; climb to 6095 m (20,000 ft) in 14 minutes; service ceiling 9315 m (30,560 ft); range 5250 km (3,262 miles) with a	18,144-kg (40,000-lb) payload **Weights:** empty 34,274 kg (75,562 lb); maximum take-off 79,380 kg (175,000 lb) **Dimensions:** wing span 40.41 m (132 ft 7 in); length 29.79 m (97 ft 9 in); height 11.84 m (38 ft 10 in); wing area 162.12 m² (1,745 sq ft) **Payload:** up to 92 troops, or 64 paratroops, or 74 litters plus two attendants, or 54 passengers, or 18,955 kg (41,790 lb) of freight

The RAF found itself with an urgent tanker requirement during the Falklands War. The first C.Mk 1K conversion (above left), seen here in trials with a C.Mk 1P, demonstrates how different the British solution to producing a Hercules tanker was to that of the production KC-130. A USMC KC-130R is illustrated below left.

Below: The USAF's MC-130H Combat Talon II is comprehensively equipped for the special forces support role, and can penetrate enemy airspace at ultra low level.

first of 231 production examples of the initial **C-130A** flew on 7 April 1955, and deliveries to the USAF began in December of that year. Surviving aircraft were later revised with four-bladed propellers, an extended tailcone housing a crash position indicator, and APN-59 radar in the reprofiled 'Pinnochio' nose, features which were originally associated with the later **C-130B** variant. The US Navy procured seven utility transport Hercules based on the C-130B for service with the designation **GV-1U** (later **C-130F**).

In 1961 production for the USAF and other operators changed to the **C-130E** (491 built) with the 3021-kW (4,050-eshp) T56-A-7 engine and increased maximum take-off weight. This required strengthened wing spars, thicker skins and beefed-up landing gear. The C-130E also introduced larger 5148-litre (1,360-US gallon) external underwing tanks mounted between the inner and outer engines, and most C-130Es have their forward cargo doors sealed. The US Navy's **C-130G** utility transport was based on the C-130E.

The definitive first-generation Hercules is the **C-130H**. It was developed for export customers and was delivered from March 1965. The first delivery to the USAF occurred in April 1975. The model displays many improvements, including 33,653-kW (4,900-eshp) T56-A-15 engines. The T56-A-15 engine and other features of the C-130H have been retrofitted to many earlier airframes.

C-130H served as the basis for a number of other variants, including the **C-130H(AEH)**,

airborne hospital for Saudi Arabia, and the **C-130H-MP** maritime patroller supplied to Malaysia and Indonesia. The United Kingdom's **C-130K** is essentially a C-130H with British avionics and equipment. The RAF's 66 C-130Ks were delivered to **Hercules C.Mk 1** standard, although subsequent modification led to new designations: the **Hercules C.Mk 1P** for aircraft with an inflight-refuelling probe; the **Hercules C.Mk 1K** for aircraft with additional fuel tankage and a hose-and-drum refuelling unit; the **Hercules W.Mk 2** for one meteorological research machine; and the **Hercules C.Mk 3** (later **C.Mk 3P**) for lengthened aircraft. The same type of 'stretched' machine was also built by Lockheed as the **C-130H-30**.

C-130J

The production variant from late in the twentieth century has been the **Lockheed Martin C-130J**. This variant is a much improved, high-technology development with AE2100 turboprops driving

Dowty propellers, each comprising six curved composite blades. Other major changes include a two-crew 'glass' cockpit, modern digital avionics, and a wing with no provision for pylons or external tanks. The type is offered in military C-130J standard-length and **C-130J-30** lengthened models.

The launch customer was the United Kingdom, with orders for the C-130J and C-130J-30 as the

Hercules C.Mk 5 and **C.Mk 4** respectively. Other customers include Australia, Italy and the United States.

Variants ordered by the USAF include the C-130J, **EC-130J Commando Solo** psychological warfare aircraft and **WC-130J** weather reconnaissance machine, while the USMC has ordered the **KC-130J** tanker. A number of the Italian aircraft will be configured as tankers.

Above: Special equipment for the LC-130 includes large ski attachments for the main and nose undercarriage. These allow operations from normal runways, as well as ice and compacted snow.

Below: At any time, part of the world's Hercules fleet will be involved in humanitarian operations. Here, a Hercules C.Mk 1P arrives with supplies.

C-130E Hercules

Transport versions of the Hercules utilized by the USAAF in the Vietnam War were the C-130A, C-130B and the C-130E. The C-130A was the original production variant with the radarless 'Roman nose' and three-bladed propellers. The C-130B had larger internal fuel capacity, a strengthened undercarriage and more powerful engines, driving four-bladed propellers. The C-130E was an extended-range version of the C-130B, with two 5148-litre (1,360-US gallon) underwing fuel tanks between the inboard and outboard engines, and the characteristic nose profile containing the AN/APN-59 radar. The USAF lost a total of 63 C-130s of all variants during the Vietnam War.

LAPES

For delivering bulky or heavy cargo in situations where landing the aircraft is not possible or desirable, the LAPES (Low-Altitude Parachute Extraction System) was devised. The aircraft flies at minimum altitude over the drop zone, while a parachute attached to the palletized cargo is released into the airstream behind it. The parachute deploys and pulls the pallet out of the C-130's hold, through its rear doors, allowing it to drop and skid along the ground to a halt in an undamaged state.

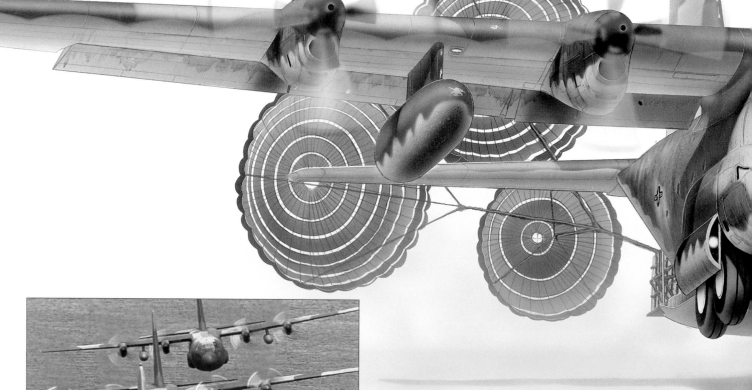

Cargo hold

Both the aircraft's flight deck and its cargo hold are pressurized and air-conditioned. In the transport role, the C-130E can carry a maximum of 92 troops, 64 paratroops or 70 stretchers with six attendants. The cavernous hold has a volume of 122 m³ (4,300 cu ft) and can accommodate a wide range of cargo, including the 155-mm Howitzer with its high-speed tractor, various types of small truck or helicopter, and up to six pre-loaded pallets of freight.

*Canada received 24 **C-130E**s between 1964 and 1967, known under the local designation **CC-130E**. The aircraft wore this dark-green and grey scheme for much of the 1980s and 1990s, but this has since been largely replaced by an overall grey finish with toned-down markings.*

In early 2003, South Africa had a fleet of 9 C-130Bs and 3 C-130Es. Originally, the country obtained 10 C-130Bs in 1963, C-130Es following in 1996. The Hercules shown here is wearing anniversary markings to celebrate 50 years of the SAAF.

Flight deck

USAF C-130s in Vietnam usually carried a flight deck crew of four, comprising pilot, co-pilot, navigator and systems manager. At least one, and more normally two, of three loadmasters were also carried. Today's C-130J requires a maximum crew of three.

Powerplant

The C-130E is powered by four 3020-kW (4,050-hp) Allison T56-A-7 turboprops, each driving a four-bladed Hamilton Standard propeller.

C-130Es for the USAF

Lockheed built a total of 490 C-130Es, comprising 122 for Military Air Transport Service, 255 for Tactical Air Command (of which all surviving aircraft were transferred to Military Airlift Command in 1974–75), four similar C-130Gs for the US Navy and 109 for export customers. Some 60 of the USAF's C-130Es were later modified to various configurations, receiving new designations. The first C-130E flew on 15 August 1961, deliveries to the 4442nd Combat Crew Training Group, TAC, at Stewart AFB, started in April 1962, and the first export C-130E went to the Royal Canadian Air Force in December 1964.

The C-130J has suffered a long, drawn-out gestation period, but is now beginning to show its full potential. The 100th aircraft is shown here, flying in the United States before its delivery to Italy.

This C-130H of 20 Sm is dropping World Food Programme packages while wearing EU colours. Training for humanitarian operations is an increasing part of the work of Belgium's C-130H fleet.

Lockheed C-5 Galaxy Strategic airlifter

Development of the **C-5 Galaxy** can be traced back to 1963 when the Military Air Transport Service (MATS) began to consider the acquisition of an extremely large strategic freighter aircraft. Initially, this was known as the CX-4 and early proposals called for a maximum take-off weight in the order of 272,160 kg (600,000 lb). Progressive refinement of the concept led to the CX-HLS (Cargo Experimental-Heavy Logistics System) specification which centred on the ability to carry a 113,400-kg (250,000-lb) payload some 4828 km (3,000 miles).

Proposals were invited from industry in May 1964, and of the three submissions from Boeing, Douglas and Lockheed deemed worthy of further study, the last company's entry was eventually adjudged most suitable in the autumn of 1965.

Building a giant

Work on assembly of the first Galaxy got under way in the following summer. It eventually made its maiden flight on 30 June 1968, deliveries to MAC (Military Airlift Command – which had replaced MATS) beginning just under 18 months later, on 17 December 1969. Originally, it had been intended to obtain 115 **C-5A** aircraft, but cost overruns (a problem which plagued the Galaxy viciously) resulted in procurement being limited to just 81, the last of which was delivered in May 1973. However, in the mid-1980s the production line was reopened for the construction of 50 improved **C-5B** aircraft. The first of these was delivered on 8 January 1986, and the last had been delivered by April 1989.

Galaxy in operation

In service, the Galaxy has had its fair share of problems, most of which centred on the wing structure, which has experienced a high degree of fatigue damage. This situation eventually led to Lockheed being awarded a contract in 1978 to manufacture new-design wings, and, following the successful evaluation of two sets, 77 examples of the C-5A Galaxy were rewinged between 1981 and 1987.

Able to carry virtually the entire range of US Army equipment and possessing the ability to operate from unpaved surfaces, the C-5 has made a vital contribution to MAC – and subsequently Air Mobility Command (AMC) – capability since it attained operational status in 1970, seeing extensive service in Southeast Asia during

In its C-5A form, the Galaxy was synonymous with the white and grey scheme of Military Airlift Command. The surviving C-5As and C-5Bs have been suffering from low serviceability levels, but the aircraft is being comprehensively upgraded for service well into the twenty-first century.

SPECIFICATION	
Lockheed C-5B Galaxy **Type:** strategic logistics transport aircraft **Powerplant:** four 191.27-kN (43,000-lb st) thrust General Electric TF39-GE-1C turbofans **Performance:** cruising speed between 888 and 908 km/h (552 and 564 mph) at 7620 m (25,000 ft); service ceiling 10,895 m (35,750 ft) at 278,960 kg (615,000 lb); range	5526 km (3,434 miles) with maximum payload **Weights:** empty 169,643 kg (374,000 lb); maximum take-off 379,657 kg (837,000 lb) **Dimensions:** wing span 67.88 m (222 ft 8½ in); length 75.54 m (247 ft 10 in); height 19.85 m (65 ft 1½ in); wing area 575.98 m² (6,200 sq ft) **Payload:** up to 118,387 kg (261,000 lb) of freight

Thanks to its visor nose, kneeling undercarriage and retractable ramps, the C-5 can offload large vehicles, such as this truck, with ease. This vehicle had been transported to Morocco from Dover Air Force Base, Delaware.

the last three years of the Vietnam conflict and also assisting in the resupply of Israel during the Yom Kippur War of October 1973 and every major US military action since.

Although most commonly used to move cargo, the C-5 can carry almost 350 fully-equipped troops should the need arise, while the provision of inflight-refuelling capability means that the Galaxy has virtually eliminated the United States' dependence on intermediate staging points.

Above: This C-5 was photographed as it prepared to depart Aviano Air Base in Italy during Operation Allied Force. The C-5 plays a vital role in overseas military and humanitarian missions.

Left: The key to successful resupply operations is the ability to carry vital large, heavy and bulky equipment, frequently over long distances. Air-to-air refuelling capability makes the C-5 possibly the best aircraft in the world at accomplishing these missions.

Lockheed C-141 StarLifter Strategic airlifter

The C-141B is some 7.11 m (23 ft 4 in) longer than the C-141A, a 4.06-m (13-ft 4-in) long fuselage plug being inserted ahead of the wing and a 3.05-m (10-ft) plug aft of the wing. Having served in grey/white and disruptive camouflage schemes, the C-141 now flies in an overall grey finish. The aircraft illustrated here sports a typical 1980s 'Lizard' scheme.

Although not the first jet-powered strategic cargo aircraft to join MATS, the **Lockheed C-141 StarLifter** was certainly the first such type to be developed from the outset specifically for this command, and in its current 'stretched' guise as the **C-141B** and upgraded **C-141C** it remained an important airlift asset, with around 200 machines in service.

Nevertheless, increasing numbers of C-17s are entering service and the StarLifter's days are distinctly numbered.

StarLifter origins

Conceived in the early 1960s, the C-141 was the winning entry in a design competition which also included contenders from Boeing, Douglas and

Like the USAF's other long-range transport assets, the StarLifter has been expected to perform its appointed roles in all conditions. This Compass Grey C-141B was photographed from a tanker over inhospitable territory during a training mission.

General Dynamics. Forming the airlift component of the integrated Logistics Support System the StarLifter first flew on 17 December 1963, subsequently entering service with the 1501st Air Transport Wing at Travis AFB, California, in the spring of 1965.

A total of 284 examples of the initial **C-141A** had been completed for MATS/MAC when production terminated in the late 1960s, with one further StarLifter being built by Lockheed to serve as a demonstrator for the unsuccessful **L-300** commercial freighter.

The advent of the C-141A more or less coincided with increased US involvement in Vietnam and the type was quickly introduced to the combat zone, being employed to move troops and equipment across the Pacific to Southeast Asia, as well as to ferry wounded personnel back to the United States for hospital treatment. However, operational experience revealed that airlift potential would benefit significantly from the provision of inflight-refuelling capability, while it also became apparent that the type was

The C-141 is increasingly becoming the mount of Air Force Reserve and Air National Guard units, as Air Military Command re-equips with C-17s.

often 'volume-limited' rather than 'weight-limited' with regard to payload.

Although the idea of 'stretching' the StarLifter first emerged during the 1960s, nothing was done about making this a reality until mid-1976, when Lockheed received a contract to develop the aircraft further, a process which basically consisted of inserting two new fuselage sections and installing an inflight-refuelling receptacle and associated plumbing.

A stretched StarLifter

The revised aircraft was first flown in prototype form as the **YC-141B** during March 1977. In addition to the aircraft's longer fuselage, a bulged fairing above the forward fuselage housed inflight-refuelling equipment. Lockheed then proceeded to

There was no StarLifter prototype as such, the first C-141A making its first flight at Marietta, Georgia, on 17 December 1963. Deliveries to the USAF began in October the following year. The last of 284 examples was handed over in February 1968. Note the lack of an inflight refuelling receptacle above the cockpit and the obviously short fuselage.

SPECIFICATION	
Lockheed C-141B StarLifter	miles) with maximum payload
Type: strategic logistical transport aircraft	**Weights:** empty 67,186 kg (148,120 lb); maximum take-off
Powerplant: four 93.41-kN (21,000-lb st) thrust Pratt & Whitney TF33-P-7 turbofans	155,580 kg (343,000 lb)
Performance: cruising speed 910 km/h (566 mph) at altitude; service ceiling 12,680 m (41,600 ft); range 4725 km (2,935	**Dimensions:** wing span 48.74 m (159 ft 11 in); length 51.29 m (168 ft 3½ in); height 11.96 m (39 ft 3 in); wing area 299.88 m² (3,228 sq ft)
	Payload: maximum 41,222 kg (90,880 lb)

modify all of the surviving C-141As and delivery of the resulting C-141B got under way in December 1979. By June 1982, when the project ended, MAC had gained the equivalent of 90 extra aircraft at no

increase in crew requirements. Subsequent conversions resulted in 13 **C-141B SOL II** low-level special operations aircraft and 64 **C-141C** aircraft with upgraded avionics and glass cockpits.

Boeing C-135 Stratolifter and KC-135 Stratotanker
Multi-role tanker/transports

In September 1955, Boeing received the USAF's first order for the **KC-135A Stratotanker** inflight-refuelling tanker, following successful trials with the 'Dash 80' prototype after it had been configured with a Boeing-designed flying boom under the rear fuselage. The USAF required that the cabin should have no windows and that the diameter of the fuselage should be increased slightly by comparison with that of the 'Dash 80'. The refuelling package was installed in the lower fuselage.

The first flight of a KC-135A came on 31 August 1956, for a service debut with the 93rd ARS on 28 June 1957. Production of the KC-135A totalled 732 aircraft in a long and efficient manufacturing programme. The first 582 aircraft were built with a short fin, but from the 583rd a taller fin (then retrofitted to earlier machines) was introduced in order to make the Stratotanker more stable during take-off. On top of this, an early modification saw the addition of strengthening straps around

the rear fuselage to dampen jet-induced resonance.

Internally, the KC-135A has 22 fuel tanks and the main cabin provides a considerable volume for freight, for which a side-loading door is fitted. The cabin can alternatively be fitted with seating for 80 troops. The refuelling boom operator works in a prone position in a fairing under the rear of the fuselage.

Stratolifter
The C-135A Stratolifter differed from the KC-135A in being equipped specifically for the long-range transport role. Its cabin was outfitted for the carriage of up to 126 troops, or 44 litters and 54 seated casualties, or freight. The first C-135A flew for the first time on 19 May 1961 and was delivered to MATS (Military Air Transport Service) from 8 June 1961, marking the move of the service into jet-powered transport capability. After the delivery of 18 C-135As, Boeing switched to the **C-135B**, of which 30 were completed with a tailplane of increased span and the revised powerplant

of four 80.05-kN (18,000-lb st) TF33-P-5 turbofans. The service life of the C-135 in this original role was short, however, and the C-135s were soon used as the basis of conversions to other roles. In addition, 17 **KC-135B** aircraft were also built, but were immediately adapted as EC-135C command posts.

'Qs' and exports
In the second half of 2002, the USAF had well over 500 KC-135s available and virtually none of these was still in its original KC-135A form, for the type has been steadily upgraded over the years in a number of programmes. Some 56 were converted to **KC-135Q** standard with additional navigation and communications equipment to support the SR-71. The KC-135Qs were also modified for the carriage and transfer of the JP-7 fuel used by the SR-71 in

Considerable numbers of KC-135Es remain in US service. Some crews prefer them over the KC-135R, in spite of their lower installed power. During operations into short fields, the extra stopping power provided by the KC-135E's thrust reversal facility, which is absent on the KC-135R, is much appreciated.

addition to the regular JP-4/5 used by the tanker.

Other early tanker variants were the **C-135F** (12 KC-135As supplied to France) and the **KC-135D**, of which four were converted from RC-135A survey aircraft. Between 1975 and 1988 Boeing replaced the lower wing skins of all surviving KC-135s to extend their useful lives to a time beyond 2020, and work also commenced on the re-engining of most surviving aircraft to replace their J57 turbojet engines with quieter, more fuel-economical and less maintenance-intensive turbofan engines.

Of the two re-engining programmes undertaken for the KC-135, the less ambitious was to upgrade ANG and AFRES KC-135As (together with 21 special-mission EC/RC/NKC-135 aircraft). The USAF bought large numbers of surplus Boeing

707s and stripped off their JT3D-3B (military designation TF33) engines for fitment to the tankers, which then received the designation **KC-135E**. At the same time the airliners' wider-span tailplanes were also fitted to the tankers to maintain stability with the greater thrust of the new engines. More than 160 KC-135As were modified, this total including the four KC-135Ds, which retain their original designation.

KC-135R

In 1980 Boeing announced a major upgrade programme for the KC-135, involving the installation of high-bypass-ratio turbofan engines. Under the company designation **KC-135RE**, the first conversion made its maiden flight on 4 August 1982. Designated in service as the **KC-135R**, the re-engined and upgraded tanker is now the mainstay of the USAF's tanker fleet, with conversions of various KC-135 variants continuing in 2003.

The engine selected for the KC-135R was the 97.84-kN (22,000-lb st) CFM International CFM56 (military designation F108-CF-100). The use of this engine gives the ability to offload 150 per cent more fuel than the KC-135A at a radius of 4633 km (2,879 miles). Other changes include fitment of an APU to provide for autonomous operations from austere locations, and many other systems were also upgraded during the conversion.

Delivery of the first KC-135R, to the SAC's 384th ARW, took place in July 1984. The 11

surviving C-135F tankers were also upgraded under this programme, in the process becoming **C-135FR** aircraft. The French machines were later fitted with Adèle RWR and underwing pods for probe-and-drogue work.

The **KC-135R(RT)** designation is applied to a few aircraft, most of them trials or ex-special mission machines, fitted with refuelling receptacles, and these have been joined by the surviving KC-135Qs. The latter were fitted with refuelling receptacles as they underwent re-engining, to emerge as **KC-135T** tankers with a primary role

of supporting the F-117 and other covert programmes. A feasibility study has also been undertaken to fit the KC-135R with underwing refuelling pods

for the refuelling of probe-equipped aircraft from other services. In addition, Turkey and Singapore operate small numbers of KC-135Rs.

SPECIFICATION

Boeing KC-135A Stratotanker
Type: four-crew inflight-refuelling tanker with secondary transport capability
Powerplant: four Pratt & Whitney J57-P-59W turbojet engines each rated at 61.15 kN (13,750 lb st)
Performance: maximum speed 982 km/h (610 mph) at optimum altitude; cruising speed 856 km/h (532 mph) at 10,668 m (35,000 ft); initial climb rate 393 m (1,290 ft) per minute; service ceiling 13,716 m (45,000 ft); range 14,806

km (9,200 miles); radius 5560 km (3,455 miles) to offload 10,886 kg (24,000 lb) of fuel or 1852 km (1,151 miles) to offload 54,432 kg (120,000 lb) of fuel
Weights: empty 48,220 kg (106,306 lb); maximum take-off 143,338 kg (316,000 lb)
Dimensions: wing span 39.88 m (130 ft 10 in); length 41.53 m (136 ft 3 in); height 12.7 m (41 ft 8 in); wing area 226.03 m² (2,433 sq ft)
Payload: up to 37,648 kg (83,000 lb) of freight

Lockheed TriStar RAF tanker and transport conversions

SPECIFICATION

Lockheed TriStar K.Mk 1
Type: inflight-refuelling tanker with secondary transport capability
Powerplant: three Rolls-Royce RB.211-524B4 turbofans each rated at 222.41 kN (50,000 lb st)
Performance: maximum cruising speed 964 km/h (599 mph) at 10,670 m (35,000 ft); maximum rate of climb at sea level 860 m (2,820 ft)
per minute; service ceiling 13,105 m (43,000 ft); range 7783 km (4,836 miles) with maximum payload
Weights: basic empty 110,163 kg (242,684 lb); maximum take-off 244,944 kg (540,000 lb)
Dimensions: wing span 50.09 m (164 ft 4 in); 50.05 m (164 ft 2½ in); height 16.87 m (55 ft 4 in); wing area 328.96 m² (3,541 sq ft)

A total of nine **Lockheed TriStar 500** airliners were acquired by the UK Ministry of Defence in 1982–84 (six ex-British Airways aircraft and three ex-Pan Am). In the first phase of a major programme, four of the British Airways aircraft were converted to **TriStar K.Mk 1** tanker/

transports. The conversion involved the installation of underfloor fuel tanks, providing an additional 45,360 kg (100,000 lb) of fuel and increasing the aircraft's total fuel capacity to more than 136,080 kg (300,000 lb), paired Flight Refuelling Ltd HDUs in

A typical TriStar mission might include supporting the long-range deployment of up to four tactical jets, while carrying supplies and personnel.

the lower rear fuselage and a closed-circuit TV camera to monitor refuelling. The first post-conversion flight was made on 9 July 1985.

Two of the four K.Mk 1s remain in service, with the remaining two aircraft and two newly acquired TriStars having been further modified as **TriStar KC.Mk 1** tanker/freighters. The KC.Mk 1 first flew in 1988 and introduced a large port side front fuselage cargo door and

freight handling system, to carry cargo and 35 passengers.

Two of the ex-Pan Am TriStars serve as **TriStar C.Mk 2** troop transports without probes. Planned modifications were abandoned to fit the third aircraft with underwing Mk 32B pods containing HDUs as the **TriStar K.Mk 2**. It was delivered as a **TriStar C.Mk 2A** instead, with military avionics, a new interior and the troublesome digital autopilot replaced by an analog autopilot as fitted to the K.Mk 1 and KC.Mk 1.

All RAF TriStars have been fitted with AN/ALR-66 radar warning receivers.

The TriStar's HDUs can transfer fuel at the rate of 1814 kg (4,000 lb) per minute. A refuelling probe is fitted above the forward fuselage and full passenger seating (all seats facing forwards) provided throughout the cabin. ZD950 is a TriStar KC.Mk 1.

Boeing C-17 Globemaster III
New-generation airlifter

This early test C-17A shows the type's upswept rear fuselage ramp and blunt nose to perfection. The C-17A offers three times the cargo capacity of the C-141B StarLifter and can handle some outsize loads.

On 29 August 1981 McDonnell Douglas (incorporated into Boeing since 1997) was selected to proceed with a design to fulfil the USAF's C-X requirement for a new heavy cargo transport. The new aircraft was designated **C-17A Globemaster III**. As well as a classic military transport aircraft configuration, the machine incorporates advanced-technology features such as winglets, a supercritical wing section and high-performance turbofans. An externally blown flap system aids short-field performance. The utility of these STOL features was negated to some extent when rough field capability was deleted as an economy measure; however, the C-17 can routinely operate from airfields previously denied to jet transports.

C-17A on duty
The C-17 has a flight crew of two, a loadmaster, and provision

The C-17A is able to operate from smaller strips previously denied to jet airlifters. Reverse thrust on the F117 engines, which are similar to those which power the Boeing 757 airliner, allows the aircraft to reverse up a shallow slope or to turn around on a narrow runway.

SPECIFICATION	
Boeing (McDonnell Douglas) C-17A Globemaster III **Type:** three-crew heavy transport **Powerplant:** four Pratt & Whitney F117-PW-100 turbofan engines each rated at 181.04 kN (40,700 lb st) **Performance:** normal cruising speed 816 km/h (507 mph) at 8535 m (28,000 ft); service ceiling 13,715 m (45,000 ft); range 8704 km (5,408 miles) on a ferry flight without inflight refuelling, or	4445 km (2,762 miles) with a 72,576-kg (160,000-lb) payload and no inflight refuelling **Weights:** empty 125,647 kg (277,000 lb); maximum take-off 265,356 kg (585,000 lb) **Dimensions:** wing span 51.76 m (169 ft 10 in) including winglets; length 53.04 m (174 ft); height 16.79 m (55 ft 1 in); wing area 353.02 m² (3,800 sq ft) **Payload:** up to a weight of 76,658 kg (169,000 lb)

for 102 troops/paratroops on stowable seats in the cabin. The hold is also capable of accommodating alternative loads such as 48 litters, three AH-64 Apaches, or air-droppable platforms up to a weight of 49,896 kg (110,000 lb). The cockpit of the C-17 has four multifunction displays, a fly-by-wire system is fitted, and the aircraft's pilots each have a control column rather than the conventional yoke.

The C-17A is able to take on the full spectrum of airlift operations. From the 71st aircraft built, additional tankage was provide in the wing centre section for a further 29,030 kg (64,000 lb) of fuel.

After an earlier full-scale development schedule had been abandoned, the single prototype of the C-17A made its maiden flight on 15 September 1991. Deliveries to the 17th Airlift Squadron began in June 1993 to replace the C-141B StarLifter. There was continued opposition to the C-17 for political and financial reasons, which had already resulted in the trimming of the C-17A procurement programme, but the controlling and radical reduction of production costs and the manifest capabilities of the new airlifter then resulted in an increase to a total of 120 again for delivery by 2005, with a further 15 later added for the use of the US Special Forces, and the prospect of another 45 standard airlifters under possible consideration. By late 2002, the USAF was calling for a fleet of at least 222 C-17As, with in excess of 180 almost certain to be built.

RAF lease

Seeking to reduce its reliance on the USAF for strategic airlift, Britain's RAF leased a total of four C-17A Globemaster IIIs from May 2001, the aircraft being based at RAF Brize Norton, Oxfordshire, with the reformed No. 99 Squadron.

With its typical military airlifter configuration, the C-17A is not the most visually distinctive aircraft, although the large winglets are a key recognition feature.

McDonnell Douglas KC-10A Extender Tanker/transport

The **KC-10A Extender** strategic tanker/transport is based on the DC-10 Series 30CF commercial freighter/airliner and was obtained off the shelf to satisfy the ATCA (Advanced Tanker Cargo Aircraft) requirement. The tanker/transport emerged victorious in a contest with the Boeing 747 in December 1977 when the USAF indicated its intention to procure 16 examples; however, the number on order rose substantially in December 1982 when the USAF placed a multi-year contract covering a further 44 aircraft.

The first example of the Extender made its maiden flight on 12 July 1980 and deliveries commenced in March 1981. Just over seven years later, the sixtieth and last KC-10A was formally handed over on 29 November 1988.

Great versatility is bestowed on the KC-10A by its integral hose unit. Here a Hornet is receiving fuel, but work with other probed receivers is common.

Operational Extender

Originally allocated solely to SAC, the KC-10A was not fitted with thermal blast screens, nor 'hardened' against electro-magnetic pulse effects. As a result, the type was neither designed nor intended to undertake Emergency War Order missions, being mainly concerned with supporting tactical rather than strategic forces.

Changes from commercial DC-10 standard include provision of an inflight-refuelling receptacle above the cockpit, the addition of an improved cargo handling system and the installation of some military avionics. The most visible evidence of modification for the ATCA role is the McDonnell Douglas Advanced Aerial Refueling Boom (AARB) sited beneath the aft fuselage. The KC-10's boom is fitted with digital FBW control and provides greater capability than the type fitted to the KC-135. The 'flying boom' is the preferred USAF method of transferring fuel in flight, but the Extender is also fitted with a hose and reel unit in the starboard aft fuselage and can thus refuel US Navy, Marine Corps and other probe-equipped aircraft during the same mission. This is a unique in-built capability for a USAF tanker.

Wing-mounted pods can be fitted to 20 KC-10s so as to allow three receiver aircraft to be simultaneously refuelled with the probe-and-drogue system. Seven bladder fuel cells have been installed primarily in the lower fuselage baggage compartments and are

interconnected with the aircraft's basic fuel system. Total onboard fuel is available either for transfer to other aircraft or for extended range. The KC-10 is able to transfer 90,718 kg (200,000 lb) of fuel to a receiver 3540 km (2,200 miles) from its home base and return to base.

Cargo too

One of the other notable aspects is the 2.59 m x 3.56 m (8 ft 6 in x 11 ft 8 in) cargo door on the port side of the fuselage, a feature that allows the KC-10A to undertake conventional strategic transport missions.

As the KC-10A is able to receive fuel in flight, it can effectively operate nonstop to any point on the globe, with the most important limiting factor likely to be crew duty restrictions. A modification to the aircraft introduced an onboard loading system to allow the KC-10 to operate from austere locations without the need for the prepositioning of ground loading equipment.

Finally, the aircraft may perform missions that call upon it to undertake aspects of both the tanker and the transport functions in a single mission. As an example, when accompanying deploying fighters, this is achieved during the transit by the provision of inflight-refuelling support. In addition, technicians, administrative staff and vital ground equipment can also be carried in the cabin, which is able to accommodate up to 75 personnel and 17 cargo pallets.

KDC-10 tankers

Two McDonnell Douglas DC-10s were procured by the Royal Netherlands Air Force, but were temporarily leased back to Martinair. These aircraft were later converted by McDonnell Douglas as **KDC-10** tankers.

SPECIFICATION	
McDonnell Douglas KC-10A Extender **Type:** strategic tanker and transport aircraft **Powerplant:** three General Electric CF6-50C2 turbofans each rated at 233.53 kN (52,500 lb st) **Performance:** maximum level speed 'clean' at 7620 m (25,000 ft) 982 km/h (610 mph); maximum cruising speed at 9145 m (30,000 ft) 908 km/h (564 mph); service ceiling 10,180 m (33,400 ft); maximum range with maximum	cargo 7032 km (4,370 miles) **Weights:** operating empty 108,891 kg (240,065 lb) as a tanker or 110,962 kg (244,630 lb) as a cargo transport; maximum take-off 267,620 kg (590,000 lb) **Dimensions:** wing span 47.34 m (155 ft 4 in); 55.35 m (181 ft 7 in); height 17.7 m (58 ft 1 in); wing area 358.69 m² (3,861 sq ft) **Fuel and payload:** total internal fuel 161,508 kg (356,065 lb); maximum payload 76,843 kg (169,409 lb)

The KC-10A is an invaluable asset, offering much greater capability than the KC-135. The KC-10/KC-135 fleet is likely to be bolstered by Boeing 767-derived tankers.

Above: Although they are not KC-10As, the Dutch KDC-10s share some of the capabilities of the USAF machine. They were produced by conversion of ex-civilian airliners.

Below: The KC-10A entered service in this distinctive livery, but has seen been through a number of schemes before arriving at the all-grey colour work in 2002/03.

Boeing 747, AL-1 and VC-25 Military 747 variants

One of the most prestigious roles assigned to the **Boeing 747** in military service is that of presidential transport. Operated by the USAF under the designation **VC-25A**, two specially equipped **Boeing 747-2G4B** aircraft are assigned to the 89th Airlift Wing at Andrews AFB, Maryland. The VC-25A can carry the US President and his staff, with 70 passengers and 23 crew members, a distance of 11,490 km (7,410 miles) without air refuelling. The crew includes 10 flight personnel for redundancy purposes, three communications specialists, and 10 flight attendants. The VC-25A can serve as an emergency war order aircraft to carry the President or others within the NCA during a nuclear conflict. For this role, the aircraft is equipped with 85 telephones, 19 television monitors, 11 video cassette players, secure voice and facsimile equipment, and other systems.

Stateroom

During flight operations, the President is accommodated within a stateroom equipped with twin beds, twin sinks, a dressing table, shower, and toilet. While the President is aboard the VC-25A during flight operations, the appropriate call sign AIR FORCE ONE is utilized. The first aircraft was delivered to the 89th Airlift Wing on 30 September 1990. The second VC-25A was delivered on 30 December 1990. The first operational mission took place on 6 September 1990, taking President George Bush to Topeka, Kansas, and Tallahassee, Florida. The following day, the Boeing VC-25A made its first overseas trip, taking President Bush to Helsinki, Finland.

747-400

The Boeing 747-400 has been selected as the platform for the USAF's new anti-missile laser system, known as the **Airborne Laser** system, which is now

under development. Using a modified 747-400F airframe, designated **YAL-1A** during testing, with the designation reverting to **AL-1A** for a service aircraft, the USAF plans to

Right: Two specially modified 747-400 aircraft service Japan's royal family and senior government officials. All -400 aircraft have winglets.

Below: Although any USAF aircraft carrying the US President becomes AIR FORCE ONE, the term is usually associated with the two VC-25A aircraft.

developing an airborne laser weapon capable of destroying ICBMs still in their boost phase. The AL-1A will carry a nose-mounted chemical oxygen iodine long-range laser and a sophisticated electro-optical targeting and fire control system. The laser will also be capable of engaging and destroying other airborne threats and targets on the ground. Modification of the first airframe began in 1998 and the YAL-1A completed a successful first flight on 18 July 2002, albeit without its laser and associated equipment.

SPECIFICATION	
Boeing 747-400 **Type:** long-range VIP transport (in JASDF service) **Powerplant:** four General Electric CF6-80C2B1F turbofans each rated at 252 kN (56,750 lb st) **Performance:** maximum level speed	984 km/h (612 mph); initial cruising altitude about 9998 m (32,800 ft) **Dimensions:** wing span 64.44 m (211 ft 5 in); length 70.67 m (231 ft 10¼ in); height 19.41 m (63 ft 8 in); wing area 541.16 m² (5,825 sq ft)

In early 2004 work to integrate the aircraft's systems was continuing, but America's Missile Defense Agency had decided to postpone the type's operational debut indefinitely pending the completion of a number of demanding tests.

With these completed, a move towards production might occur, with, at one time, as many as eight AL-1As expected to be built.

Other military users

Iran has traditionally been the largest military operator of

the 747, with around 11 **747F** aircraft in service, about seven of these as transports and the remainder as tankers.

While not strictly military variants of the 747-400, a pair of **747-47C** aircraft is operated by 701 Hiko-tai of the Tokubetsu Koku Yuso-tai (Special Air Transport Group), Japan Air Self-Defense Force, from Chitose Air Base. Equipped to fulfil a VIP role (principally for the Japanese royal family and the upper echelons of the Japanese government), these aircraft are equipped with an upper deck packed with additional communications equipment and are powered by General Electric CF6 engines.

As well as modifications to accommodate its unique weapon system, the YAL-1A prototype has been modified with an air-refuelling receptacle. Note the vast size of the 747-derivative compared to the NKC-135 tanker.

Boeing 757 and C-32 Military 757-based transports

Responsible for executive transport, the 89th AW at Andrews AFB has a large variety of aircraft types. The Boeing C-32A (seen here at Renton on a pre-delivery flight) has replaced the long-serving C-137s under the VC-X Large programme.

Four **Boeing 757-200** aircraft were ordered for the 89th Airlift Wing at Andrews Air Force Base in 1998, and these **C-32A** machines were delivered the same year for Special Air Missions (transporting senior cabinet members). The aircraft were procured to replace VC-9s and VC-137s, and to provide a smaller, shorter-range complement to the VC-25A, while carrying more passengers than the C-20 or C-37C. The aircraft serve with the 89th AW's 1st Airlift Squadron.

The last VC-137s were withdrawn in 1999, with the VC-9s soon following. The requirement which led to the order was tailored to ensure that the C-32As were as similar as possible to the standard Boeing 757 airliner configuration, to keep costs and timescales under the tightest possible control, although the aircraft are

This anonymously painted 757 is the mysterious '86006', the role of which has never been publicly announced. The aircraft is seen here departing Ramstein Air Base in Germany bound for Kuwait City. It is believed that the aircraft may be operated by the 486th Flight Test Squadron.

SPECIFICATION	
Boeing 757-200	**Weights:** operating empty 57,180 kg
Type: VIP transport (in Mexican	(126,060 lb); maximum take-off
service)	113,395 kg (250,000 lb)
Powerplant: four Rolls-Royce	**Dimensions:** wing span 38.05 m
RB.211-535E4 each rated at	(124 ft 10 in); length 47.32 m (155 ft
178.37 kN (40,100 lb)	3 in); height 13.56 m (44 ft 6 in);
Performance: initial cruise ceiling	wing area 185.24 m² (1,994 sq ft)
11,880 m (38,970 ft); range	**Payload:** maximum 26,096 kg
7070 km (4,399 miles)	(57,530 lb)

fitted with a decidedly non-standard VIP interior, usually accommodating only 45 passengers. The aircraft also have advanced secure communications equipment and a GPS-based navigation system, as well as TCAS (Traffic Collision Avoidance System). They wear a smart pale blue and white colour scheme, with 'United States of America' titles and thin gold cheatlines.

Situated as it is only about 13 km (eight miles) from Washington DC, Andrews AFB is ideally positioned for VIP operations.

Another US 757

At least one Boeing 757 is known to be used, or to have been used, by an unknown unit. Painted white overall, and bearing the serial 86006 (perhaps 98-6006) the aircraft has been seen visiting Rhein-Main in Germany – a destination for similarly painted Boeing C-137s and a C-22. These aircraft may be attached to the 486th Flight Test Squadron at Wright-Patterson AFB, which is believed to be a 'cover identity' for a unit whose role is to support the NSA, CIA or other special units.

The Boeing 757 has also been exported to the Argentine and Mexican air forces. Each air arm operates a single Boeing 757 in the VIP transport role, Argentina a **757-23A** delivered in 1992, and Mexico a **757-225** delivered in November 1987.

Quasi-military

A single Boeing 757-23A is owned by the Saudi government and since March 1995 has been used on VIP duties and possibly as a medical evacuation aircraft and flying hospital. Another 757-23A is owned by Akhal Aircompany of Turkmenistan, but used for government VIP flying with a 36-seat interior. The Kazakhstan Government had a **Boeing 757-2M6** assigned for VIP use, though this was operated by Kazakhstan Airlines.

Boeing KC-767 and E-10 Tanker/transport and MC²A aircraft

Although variations of the standard airliner **Boeing 767** have been used on military/governmental missions, including trials work with the US Army and VIP use with Kazakhstan, only very late in the aircraft's career has it been seriously considered for any special military role other than AWACS.

KC-767

With the Boeing 707 out of production, the 767 airframe became Boeing's favoured choice for future tanker contracts. As such, both Italy (four aircraft, for delivery from 2004) and Japan (four aircraft, for delivery by 2007) have ordered 767 tankers.

On 10 July 2003, the USAF presented Congress with a proposal to lease 100 KC-767 tankers to partially replace its ageing KC-135E fleet. The new aircraft would eventually be purchased and, in line with new Boeing policy, the aircraft would be powered by Pratt & Whitney PW4062 engines, previous military 767s having had General

Controversy surrounds the USAF's wish to lease a fleet of KC-767 tankers.

Electric engines. However, the US$20 billion programme has been mired in controversy and no firm decision on its future has been made.

E-10A

Another US-developed 767 variant, utilizing the 767-400, is the **E-10A**. Originally considered as a Multisensor Command and Control Aircraft (MC²A) programme to replace the E-3 and E-8, the E-10A is now most likely to be developed primarily with an anti-cruise missile role in mind. The five aircraft envisioned could cost in excess of US$5.3 billion to develop and, although a demonstrator has been funded, the programme has been called into doubt.

EMBRAER EMB-145 AEW&C
Airborne early warning and control aircraft

EMBRAER developed two special missions variants of its proven ERJ 145 regional airliner as part of the Brazilian government's SIVAM (Sistema de Vigilancia de Amazonia) programme. The aircraft retain the basic configuration of the civil machine, and its twin Rolls-Royce AE3007 turbofan powerplant. However, some structural modification has been carried out, as well as upgrades to the aircraft's electrical generating capacity. Internally the machines have full mission

Although EMB-145SA sales have been relatively slow, EMBRAER remains justifiably confident about the aircraft's future. There is a possibility that the type may be chosen to fulfil India's requirement for an AEW&C machine.

fits, with many new antennas being mounted externally.
The **EMB-145RS** is a remote-sensing aircraft designated **R-99B** in Brazilian air force service, while the **EMB-145SA AEW&C** (**R-99A**) is a dedicated airborne early warning and control systems aircraft.

The EMB-145SA carries its pulse-Doppler Ericsson PS-890 Erieye radar antenna in a 'plank'-like fairing mounted above the

fuselage. Operator stations for up to six personnel are provided, with provision for a relief crew if required. Additional fuel tankage allows for missions of up to eight hours' duration.

Service use
A total of five EMB-145SA aircraft has been ordered by Brazil. Only one of a hoped for order for three EMB-145SAs from the Mexican government

Additional ventral fins and finlets were required to ensure that the EMB-145SA retained the directional characteristics of the standard ERJ-145 airliner.

seems to have been confirmed, but a further machine – with additional sea-search radar – has been ordered by the Mexican government for anti-narcotics work. Lastly, the Greek air force will operate four EMB-145SAs.

Bombardier ASTOR Battlefield reconnaissance aircraft

Back in the 1980s, the British Army identified a requirement for what was termed the CASTOR (Corps Airborne Stand-Off Radar) system. Although some work was carried out on the requirement, including the flying of a prototype Britten-Norman Islander platform, the programme came to nothing.

CASTOR had been envisaged as a system allowing ground surveillance of eastern Europe from a safe stand-off range.

Gulf boost
With the thawing of the Cold War, there seemed little need for a CASTOR-type system, until the 1991 Gulf War and the debut

of the USAF's E-8 J-STARS aircraft. Prototype J-STARS airframes turned in star Desert Storm performances, leading to the joint British Army/ RAF **ASTOR** (**Airborne Stand-Off Radar**) requirement. In 1999, Raytheon was chosen to provide the ASTOR mission systems, while Bombardier has been

chosen to provide its **Global Express** bizjet as the platfrom for ASTOR.

The ASTOR radar system is based on the ASARS-2 (Advanced Synthetic Aperture Radar System) system, as used by the US Air Force's U-2S. Along with other mission systems it will allow ASTOR to reconnoitre the

A Global Express fitted with aerodynamic shapes representing the fairings for the ASTOR system was first flown on 3 August 2001. The main SAR antenna will be carried in a canoe fairing beneath the forward fuselage.

battlefield from a safe stand-off range and at altitudes of up to 15,240 m (50,000 ft). ASTOR will require a mission team of just three people, thanks to its high level of automation and the fact that, unlike J-STARS, it will not act as a control aircraft. Instead, its information will be downloaded to ground stations for immediate action. Britain hopes to have ASTOR fully in service by 2008, when the aircraft should also have been integrated into the United Kingdom's new ISATR (Intelligence, Surveillance, Target Acquisition and Reconnaissance) system.

IAI/Elta Phalcon Airborne Early Warning and Control system

Chile's Phalcon was specified with a 260-degree coverage system with only side fairings and the nose radome. Chile was the first confirmed customer for the system.

Israel Aircraft Industries is no stranger to the Boeing 707. Over the past 20 years the company has maintained the type for the IDF/AF, and also been involved in many conversions for special purposes. These have included tankers, signals intelligence platforms, command posts and other electronic specialists. Since 1990, IAI and its electronics subsidiary, Elta, have been developing an airborne early warning version, named **IAI/Elta Phalcon**.

The name Phalcon relates to the AEW system, rather than the carrier aircraft, which could be virtually any large aircraft such as a 747 or C-130. Efforts have even been made to integrate the system onto the Il-76 'Candid' for China, but these have stopped under pressure from the United States. Within the Phalcon system there are many options to suit customer requirements, including additional ESM, communications and reconnaissance equipment.

Elta radar

At the heart of the system is the Elta EL/2075 phased-array radar. For full coverage there are four antenna arrays – two each side of the forward fuselage housed in giant cheek fairings, one in the nose in a bulbous radome, and one under the rear fuselage. The radomes add considerable drag, eroding speed performance, but the main concern is for long endurance, which is not dramatically affected. The nose radome has a flattened underside for ground clearance, and its fitment on the 707 necessitates the re-siting of the pitot probes above the flight deck.

Each EL/2075 array consists of hundreds of fixed antennas, each with an individual transmit/

receive module in the forward fuselage. They are electronically steered and scanned, and mounted on a floating bed so that flexing in the aircraft's structure does not affect their alignment. Detection range is reported to be in the order of 400 km (250 miles) for fighter-sized targets, and around 100

such targets can be processed by Phalcon at any one time.

Fast scanning is possible, so that area coverage can be maintained while concentrating on an important target. To increase the detection range all power can be assigned in a specific direction. A sharp beam mode keeps track of a fast or

manoeuvring target, and scan area can be limited to just the battle area, thereby increasing the scan rate in this region. Track initiation is in the region of two to four seconds, roughly a tenth that of rotodome-equipped platforms. Augmenting the radar are IFF, ESM/Elint and Comint suites. Some 13 or so operator consoles

are provided in the main cabin. A command post option has a separate commander's cabin with a huge situation display.

Reports suggest that 1 IDF/AF operates two 707s in Phalcon configuration, and has plans to modify three or four Gulfstream V (G500) bizjets to accept the system.

Saab S100B Argus Airborne Early Warning and Control aircraft

The **Saab 340** regional transport was originally developed in partnership with Fairchild and first flew on 25 January 1983. It became a wholly Swedish programme in November 1985.

In early 1993, Sweden chose the **Saab 340B** as an airborne early warning platform, carrying an Ericsson Erieye side-looking radar in a 'plank' fairing above the fuselage. Erieye is a long-range,

S-band, pulse-Doppler radar which uses a phased array antenna housed in a 9-m (29-ft 6-in) long fairing and weighing some 900 kg (1,984 lb). The radar has a detection range of over 300 km (186 miles) against small airborne targets, from a cruising altitude of some 8000 m (26,000 ft).

S100 Argus

Saab dubbed the aircraft **Saab 340AEW&C**, as it also has a command and control role with one or more command consoles in the cabin, along with ESM capability, INS and GPS navigation systems and secure voice and

Saab pioneered the use of Ericsson's Erieye radar on its 340B airframe. With the 340 out of production there seems little future for the type.

datalinks. The prototype first flew, without the radar antenna, on 17 January 1994, and with the antenna on 1 July. It was delivered to the Flygvapen in early 1995. Named **S100B Argus** in service, six of the type were delivered to the Swedish air force. Two of these were later placed in storage and subsequently leased to Greece pending arrival of that country's EMB-145SAs.

Although only six S100Bs were built, their use in Sweden, especially in cooperation with Viggen and Gripen fighters, has shown them to be exceptional.

Beriev A-50 and Be-976 'Mainstay' AEW and control aircraft

Although it is uncomfortable and has some serious handling deficiencies, the A-50 will remain Russia's primary AEW asset for the foreseeable future.

The **'Mainstay'** was developed as a replacement for the Tu-126 'Moss'. Like many early Western AEW aircraft, the 'Moss' was virtually ineffective over land. Remarkably, development of what the Russians call SDRLO (Systyem Dalnovo Radiolocaciomnovo Obnarushenya, or Long-Range Radio Location and Detection System) was actually terminated during the 1960s as an economy measure, but was restarted in the face of Western development of the E-3 Sentry.

Based on the Il-76 transport, the **A-50 'Mainstay'** has a rotodome mounted above a modified fuselage.

'Mainstay' entered service during 1984, and after some

SPECIFICATION	
Beriev A-50 'Mainstay'	range 5,100 km (3,169 miles)
Type: airborne early warning aircraft	**Weights:** empty 119,000 kg
Powerplant: four 117. 70-kN	(262,350 lb); maximum take-off
(26,455-lb st) Aviadvigatel D-30KP-2	190,000 kg (418,875 lb)
turbofans	**Dimensions:** wing span 50.5 m
Performance: maximum level speed	(165 ft 8 in); length 46.6 m (152 ft
785 km/h (488 mph); service	10½ in); height 14.76 m (48 ft 5 in);
ceiling 10,500 m (34,440 ft);	wing area 300 m² (3,229.2 sq ft)

teething troubles has proved successful and popular. The system's designers admit inferior radar range and multiple target tracking capability in comparison to the E-3, but claim better discrimination of objects and targets on the ground or of low-flying targets against ground 'clutter'. A particular bugbear for crews (used to the luxuriously appointed 'Moss') is the inferior conditions in which they must work. Noise levels are high, and toilet and galley facilities barely adequate. Rest bunks are not provided at all. Morale problems have been worsened by the

move from the Baltic to Pechora in the polar region, where accommodation and facilities are poor even by Soviet standards. The move was made to allow the aircraft to meet threats from what one senior air force commander described as 'the most dangerous direction'.

Heavy avionics

As the Soviet electronics industry lagged behind that of the West and had no domestic market for home computers and computer games, its equipment tended to be bigger and heavier. Separate command and control systems

for the separate branches of the armed forces necessitates installation of duplicate systems for exchanging data, decoding IFF signals, etc. All decoding and interfacing is carried out onboard, whereas much of the latter is done on the ground for the E-3 Sentry.

The weight of the A-50's equipment is greater than had been anticipated, and landing-gear limitations prevent the aircraft from taking off with a full fuel load, reducing endurance by about half an hour. This problem is further exacerbated by the fact that disturbed airflow from the rotodome makes it extremely difficult to use the nose-mounted inflight-refuelling probe, and only the most experienced pilots are cleared for the practice.

Inside the cabin a single large screen is used for controlling fighters, with smaller screens monitoring the tactical situation on the ground and in the air. All the screens are fully digitized colour CRTs.

About 25 standard A-50s are available for regular service. Upgraded variants could include the A-50U with improved radar, A-50M with upgraded computers and A-50I, a machine developed by IAI and offered to China.

During missions, A-50s typically fly a figure-eight racetrack pattern at about 10000 m (33,000 ft) with 100 km (62 miles) between the centres of the two circles.

'Mainstay' operations

The A-50's mission computer allows automatic communication of data to and from fighters and ground stations directly, and via satellite using datalinks. When connected to the aircraft's autopilot the mission computer is also able to fly the aircraft through pre-programmed search patterns over programmed points on the ground.

During military exercises, the A-50s have been used to control MiG-31 interceptors, directing them onto incoming cruise missiles, while simultaneously supplying submarines with tactical information and also controlling Tu-22M-3 bombers and other fighters. During the 1991 Gulf War, two A-50s were deployed to a Black Sea airfield, where they maintained a single-aircraft, round-the-clock watch over the war zone. Further aircraft maintained a standing patrol over the Caspian Sea. The aircraft were supported by 3MS-2 (M-4 'Bison') tankers in this situation.

A second rotodome-equipped version of the Il-76 is the **Il-976**. A total of six of these range control and missile tracking platforms has been built. Esssentially the Il-976 differs from the A-50 in retaining the glazed nose of the Il-76, and the glazed tail turret, although its guns are replaced by a bulbous radome. The aircraft also lacks an inflight-refuelling probe and many of the A-50's minor antennas, but is fitted with fat cylindrical wing-tip pods.

Iraqi developments

Iraq has developed AEW versions of the Il-76. The first, **Baghdad 1**, mounted a Thomson-CSF Tigre radar in a large blister fairing over the position of the Il-76MD's rear loading doors. Baghdad 1 was followed by the **Adnan**, which mounts its radar in a conventional rotodome. One Adnan was destroyed in 1991, the other two fleeing to Iran.

Westland Sea King ASaC Shipborne AEW helicopter

Although the Fleet Air Arm remained the only operator of Westland Sea King AEWs in 2004, the Spanish navy had around three Sikorsky SH-3 Sea Kings modified to a similar configuration on strength.

The retirement of the Royal Navy's fixed-wing carriers left the fleet without organic airborne early warning cover. The threat of war in the South Atlantic posed by the Argentine invasion of the Falklands signposted the disadvantages of relying on the RAF's land-based Shackletons and radar picket ships, and after the loss of HMS *Sheffield* (acting as a radar picket) on 4 May 1982, a crash programme was instituted to provide the fleet with its own AEW platform. This was a tripartite effort by the Royal Navy, Westland and Thorn/EMI known as Project LAST (Low Altitude Surveillance Task), which resulted in flying hardware within only 11 weeks. At the heart of the programme lay the I-band Thorn EMI ARI 5980/3 Searchwater radar, a pulse-compression, frequency-agile search radar.

Conversions

The **Sea King AEW** was produced by conversion of Sea King HAS.Mk 1s and HAS.Mk 2s. The Searchwater radar fitted was the same as that used in the RAF's maritime reconnaissance Nimrods, and had a proven ability to detect low-flying targets in any sea state, and with severe weather clutter, although it had been optimized for the detection of surface targets (such as submarine periscopes) and not fast-moving airborne targets. At 3048 m (10,000 ft) the radar had a range of about 200 km (125 miles) against a fighter-sized target. Multiple Track-while-Scan capability allowed continuous target tracking without interrupting the radar's search pattern, although this capability was little used.

The result of an urgent requirement for a shipboard AEW platform, the Sea King AEW.Mk 2 has proved itself to be highly effective, able to detect hostile aircraft and missiles at distances well beyond the range of the fleet.

Although the original radar system was subsequently replaced, operational procedures remain similar. As soon as a contact is made, it is handed on to fighters or surface-to-air weapons controllers. Digital control of the radar gives very high performance while keeping operator workload low. The computer automatically controls pulse repetition frequency (PRF), beamwidth and antenna tilt once range has been selected, and if only a particular sector is of interest will automatically decide whether to rotate the antenna fully or to scan back and forth across a narrow arc. The radar is of modular construction, with comprehensive use of LRUs and built-in test equipment.

The antenna for the search radar is pitch and roll stabilised and offers a full 360-degree scan. It is housed in an unusual inflatable domed 'kettle drum' radome made of impregnated Kevlar fabric, which can be swung down to the vertical position in flight to project below the aircraft, and which can swing back to the horizontal to give sufficient ground/deck clearance to allow the aircraft to land. During early trials, a hole was dug in the airfield at Culdrose just large enough to accept a deployed Searchwater radome, in case an aircraft returned unable to retract its radar. This did not have to be used. The radome is 1.80 m (6 ft) in diameter. The installation was a masterpiece of improvisation, with the swivel being adapted from a standard Sea King undercarriage actuator, and with the swivel arm carrying the radar being made from 30-cm (12-in) diameter steel pipe bought directly from British Gas. The Nimrod's ram air cooling

system was not suitable for a slow-flying helicopter, and as a result a new system had to be designed for the Sea King Searchwater installation.

Into service

The radar antenna is bulky, and does cause some drag, and cruising speed with the radar deployed is limited to 90 kt (166 km/h; 103 mph). Weight is less of a problem, as the scanner is made of plastic, with carbon-fibre. The Sea King's original radar was retained for tactical and navigation purposes, but sonar was removed. The aircraft incorporated Racal MIR-2 'Orange Crop' ESM, which was standard on the HAS.Mk 5 then in frontline service. The **Sea King AEW.Mk 2A** also had a new Cossor IFF 3570 interrogator and a Ferranti FIN 1110 two-gimbal INS, but was otherwise similarly equipped to the ASW HAS.Mk 2.

The success of the project was such that neither of the initial two conversions appeared at the 1982 Farnborough SBAC show. Both were deployed to the South Atlantic in the immediate aftermath of the Falklands War, a period of some uncertainty in which further Argentine air attacks could not be discounted. In fact, the first of the AEW.Mk 2As made its maiden flight on 23 July 1982. The two prototypes undertook flying trials aboard HMS *Illustrious* as part of No. 824 Sqn, and from 27 August

provided AEW cover for ships operating within the Falklands total exclusion zone.

No. 849 Sqn reformed on 9 November 1984, and the two prototype conversions were joined by seven more AEW.Mk 2As. One of the aircraft was subsequently deconverted and returned to ASW configuration.

Crew

The AEW Sea King routinely operates with a crew of three, consisting of a single pilot and two observers. One of the observers occupies the co-pilot's seat during take-offs, landings and low-level operations, and would operate the manual throttles in the event of an emergency. The radar is located behind the observer's positions, in line with the radome swivel. The observers have two displays able to show a PPI (Plan Position Indicator) picture that is north-orientated and ground-stabilized by Doppler, or a selected enlargement, or an A-scope display showing the shape of the radar contact and its length. The fidelity of this type of display is often sufficient to allow accurate ship recognition.

A modest upgrade to the AEW.Mk 2A, with a new Mk XII IFF interrogator, Link 16 JTIDS, an extra secure voice Have Quick II radio and modernization of the Searchwater radar to incorporate a pulse-Doppler capability was carried out, as was the conversion of three Sea

King HAS.Mk 5 helicopters to a similar standard as attrition replacements, these becoming **Sea King AEW.Mk 5** machines. Some in the Royal Navy favoured replacement of the type altogether, arguing that the veteran Sea King airframes could and should have been replaced by up to nine AEW-configured Merlins. These aircraft, it was argued, could have been spared because of the diminished Soviet submarine threat, and would have boosted export prospects for the type.

Nevertheless, the Sea King AEW has remained in service, and the fleet has been extensively upgraded to **Sea King AEW.Mk 7** standard. This latter standard is based on the advanced Racal Searchwater 2000 radar and includes the Mk XII IFF and JTIDS of the upgraded AEW.Mk 2A and AEW.Mk 5.

By late 2003, the Fleet Air Arm had around 13 Sea King AEW.Mk 7 helicopters on strength, having lost a pair to a collision during Operation Iraqi Freedom. It was also officially referring to the type as **Sea King ASaC (Sea King Airborne Surveillance and Control)**. With the Royal Navy's planned acquisition of two new air carriers will come a requirement for a new ASaC type and, although this is most likely to be Merlin-based, the V-22 Osprey has also been mooted as a possible AEW platform.

Northrop Grumman E-2 Hawkeye Land-based aircraft

Although Japan's Hawkeye fleet was purchased amid animosity, it remains a key national asset.

No. 111 Sqn. The aircraft remained in the United States to allow crew training, and did not become operational at Tengah until March 1987. In 2004, Singapore was actively evaluating an upgrade programme or possible replacement of its Hawkeyes. It may opt for an Advanced Hawkeye-configured airframe.

Unsurprisingly, the first E-2 export customer was Israel. It purchased four Hawkeyes in 1977–78, all to Basic E-2C standard. These were flown by No. 192 Sqn at Hatzerim, and given the local name **Daya** (Kite). The aircraft saw some action, notably during the brief 1982 air war over the Beka'a Valley, in which they guided F-15s and F-16s to a claimed total of 85 kills over Syrian fighters. They also provided warning to strike aircraft, keeping Israeli losses to a minimum, and generally policed the flow of traffic into and out of the war zone. In the early 1990s the aircraft acquired inflight-refuelling probes, but by 1997 their operational status was unknown; it subsequently emerged that they had been put into storage, pending disposal. By early 2004, it had been announced that the aircraft were being upgraded by IAI, pending delivery to the Mexican navy.

Egypt

Egypt took delivery of five **E-2C Hawkeye** Group 0 aircraft in 1986 for service from Cairo West. They were joined by a sixth aircraft in 1993. The aircraft were later updated to a unique **Group 0/II** ('**Group I½**') status, employing the square, colour EMDU (Enhanced Main Display

Even during land-based operations, the E-2's folding wing feature is a useful storage device, as demonstrated by this Egyptian machine.

Unit) displays and new IFF system of the Group II, but retaining APS-138 radar, and have since been further upgraded with APS-145 radar.

Japan

Between 1982 and 1985 eight E-2Cs to Group 0 standard arrived at Misawa for service with the JASDF's 601 Hiko-tai. Five more aircraft were added in 1992–93, to bring the total to 13. The sale to Japan had been a long and, at times, bitter affair, but once in service the E-2s rapidly proved their value by extending coverage to the north. The choice of Misawa as the Hawkeye base was far from coincidental:

located in the north of the island of Honshu, it is conveniently located for providing radar coverage to Japan's north, close to Russia. Despite having procured four E-767s platforms, Japan is upgrading its E-2s to Group II standard with APS-145 radar, with the first due for completion in 2004.

Singapore

Not blessed with long borders along which to position ground radars, Singapore required an airborne radar platform as its only effective means of providing warning of attack. Accordingly, four E-2C Group 0 Hawkeyes were purchased for service with

Taiwan

Taiwan joined the Hawkeye club in 1995, when it received its four aircraft. In so doing, the RoCAF became the first customer to use refurbished US Navy aircraft (in this case E-2Bs). The rework programme, which resulted in the new designation **E-2T** (for Taiwan), raised the aircraft to full Group II standard, with APS-145 radar. The Hawkeyes achieved IOC with No. 78 Sqn at Pingtung in 1996, and provide a welcome extension of radar coverage across Formosa Strait. Two more E-2Ts were ordered in 1999.

Taiwan's six-aircraft E-2 fleet is now to E-2C Group II standard.

Boeing E-3 AWACS/Sentry Airborne Warning & Control aircraft

The USAF E-3A seen here was photographed as it landed at Incirlik AB, Turkey, after an Operation Northern Watch mission. The aircraft has the undernose and cheek installations associated with the AN/AYR-1 ESM system.

The requirement for an AWACS (Airborne Warning and Control System) aircraft was outlined by the USAF in 1963, when it was envisaged that a force of up to 64 aircraft would be required. Economic considerations meant that a much smaller number was eventually built, however.

The resulting **Boeing E-3A Sentry** is essentially a flexible, jamming-resistant, mobile and survivable radar station that also carries a command, communications and control centre. In addition to its long-range surveillance capability, AWACS can provide all-weather identification and tracking over all kinds of terrain, and the 22nd and subsequent aircraft added a maritime surveillance capability. While Boeing and the type's foreign customers refer to it as the Sentry, the E-3 is generally known as the AWACS in US service and the popular media.

Two main areas of use were planned by the USAF: first, the type would serve within TAC (Tactical Air Command) for airborne surveillance and as a command centre for the rapid deployment of TAC forces; secondly, the type would serve within ADC (Aerospace Defense Command) as a command and control post. Now flying under Air Combat Command, the two basic E-3 missions remain essentially largely unaltered.

Large-diameter engine nacelles, wing-tip ESM pods and aerials, plus a refuelling probe above the fuselage, identify this as an RAF Sentry AEW.Mk 1. The aircraft was flying as part of Operation Enduring Freedom over Afghanistan.

707 airframe

Boeing was the successful one of two contenders for the supply of an AWACS aircraft, being awarded a contract on 23 July 1970 to provide two prototypes under the designation **EC-137D**. The company's AWACS concept was based on the airframe of the Model 707-300B commercial transport, and the prototypes were modified in the first place to carry out comparative trials between the prototype surveillance radars designed by the Hughes Aircraft Company and by Westinghouse Electric Corporation. These tests continued into the autumn of 1972, and on 5 October 1972 the USAF announced that Westinghouse had been selected as the prime AWACS radar contractor.

Very little modification of the basic airframe was needed to make it suitable for the new role. Most important was the addition of a large rotodome assembly carried on two wide-chord streamlined struts. The remainder of the essential avionics antennas was housed within the wing, fuselage and tail unit. New engine pylon fairings were provided for the more powerful turbofan engines of the pre-production aircraft and of the production machines which were designated E-3A and given the name Sentry. Internal modifications included the provision of SDCs (Situation Display Consoles) and other equipment bays, and the addition of a crew rest area. Basic operations were schemed as requiring a flight crew of four plus 13 AWACS specialist officers,

but this number could be varied and other personnel could be carried for systems management and also for radar maintenance.

Radar details

Not surprisingly, the mass of avionics equipment required the installation of extensive cooling and wiring systems. There is also a large demand for electrical power, supplied by generators with a combined output of 600 kVA. The over-fuselage rotodome is 9.14 m (30 ft) in diameter and has a maximum depth of 1.83 m (6 ft). It originally carried the antennas for the APY-1 surveillance radar and IFF/TADIL C (Identification Friend or Foe/TActical Digital Intelligence Link – Command). When the radar is being used, the rotodome is driven hydraulically at 6 rpm,

but in non-operational flight the rotodome is rotated at one twenty-fourth of this speed to ensure that low temperatures do not cause the bearing lubricant to congeal.

The APY-2 radar installed in the 25th example of the Sentry (and representing the standard to which the radar of the first 24 machines was then upgraded) can function as a pulse and/or pulse-Doppler radar, and is operable in six different modes. The data-processing capability of the first 23 E-3As was provided by an IBM 4 Pi CC-1 high-speed computer, while the more powerful IBM CC-2 computer was introduced on the 24th Sentry. Also introduced was the newly developed JTIDS (Joint Tactical Information Distribution System), which provides a high-speed secure communications channel and is less vulnerable to jamming than earlier systems.

Sentry on duty

The first production E-3A was delivered on 24 March 1977 and a total of 34 aircraft (including

Its strut-supported distinctive rotodome makes the E-3 an easily recognized machine. The black sections of the radome are radar-transparent fairings.

SPECIFICATION	
Boeing E-3B Sentry	six-hour patrol
Type: 17-crew airborne early warning and command post aircraft	**Weights:** empty 77,996 kg (171,950 lb); maximum take-off 147,418 kg (325,000 lb)
Powerplant: four Pratt & Whitney TF33-PW-100/-100A turbofan engines each rated at 93.41 kN (21,000 lb st)	**Dimensions:** wing span 44.42 m (145 ft 9 in); length 46.61 m (152 ft 11 in); height 12.6 m (41 ft 4 in); wing area 283.35 m² (3,050 sq ft)
Performance: maximum speed 853 km/h (530 mph) at optimum altitude; service ceiling 8840 m (29,000 ft); operational radius 1612 km (1,002 miles) for a	**Armament:** up to four AIM-9 Sidewinder short-range AAMs can be carried under the wing

The only flying element of the Armée de l'Air's CASSIC (Commandement Air des Systèmes de Surveillance, or Air Signals and Ground Environment Command) is the four E-3Fs of the two squadrons of EDCA 36 (Escadrons 1/36 'Berry' and 2/36 'Nivernais'). The French originally required a total of six Sentries, but the options for the final two were dropped in 1988.

the two EC-137Ds upgraded to full production standard) had been delivered by June 1984. The first 24 were completed as E-3A 'core' machines, while the last 10 were completed as **E-3B** 'standard' machines for service from July 1984, with the APY-2 radar offering an improved over-water capability, ECM-resistant voice communications, CC-2 computer, more radio equipment, five more situation display consoles (making 14 in total), and provision for the 'Have Quick' secure communications system and self-defence AAMs. E-3As were then upgraded to E-3B standard, and in 1984 10 were further modified to **E-3C** standard, with five more situation display consoles, more radio equipment and the 'Have Quick A-Nets' communications system.

One E-3C has been used by Boeing as the **JE-3C** for the development and integration of the AYR-1 ESM system. The USAF has considered upgrading its E-3s with the installation of the 'glass' flightdeck of the Next Generation Model 737 and the Eagle system for the detection and tracking of theatre ballistic missiles with an IR search-and-track sensor and laser rangefinder. The service is also planning or considering major upgrades to the radar, computer and navigation systems, the last with the aid of GPS update. Indeed, by 2005, the USAF had 32 AWACS aircraft operational with Boeing's Radar Systems Improvement Program kit installed. The kit has also been fitted to French, NATO and RAF Sentries.

Export aircraft

Another 18 aircraft of the E-3A 'standard' configuration were delivered from December 1981 for the use of NATO forces based in Europe, while Saudi Arabia received five aircraft in addition to eight **KE-3A** inflight-refuelling tankers. The latter are based on the same airframe and were built alongside the E-3. A further two export customers have purchased E-3s with the revised powerplant of four 106.76-kN (24,000-lb st) CFM International CFM56-2A turbo-fans. France received four **E-3F** aircraft in 1991–92, while the United Kingdom received seven **E-3D** machines in the same period for service with the local designation **Sentry AEW.Mk 1**.

Boeing 737 AEW&C Project Wedgetail

This impression shows how Wedgetail is likely to appear in RAAF service. It is named after an indigenous eagle.

platform for Northrop Grumman's Multi-role Electronically Scanned Array (MESA) radar. MESA's antenna array, which is steerable through 360 degrees, does away with the conventional rotodome associated with AWACS and AEW&C aircraft such as Boeing's E-3 and Northrop Grumman's E-2. Instead, the antenna is housed in a long flat radome held above the aircraft's rear fuselage on a broad-chord pylon.

Wedgetail capabilities

Wedgetail's normal mission crew of 6–10 people will be able to track air and sea targets simultaneously using the MESA radar, while individual targets can be tracked while search modes also continue. The aircraft's integrated mission suite also includes IFF and ESM systems, open-system architecture to allow future incorporation of new or upgraded systems and a powerful self-defence capability. In addition, **737 AEW&C** is being designed to be fully interoperable with Boeing's own E-3 and 767 AWACS platforms.

MESA has been designed for a range in excess of 370 km (230 miles) in all weathers, with its IFF system having a range of 555 km (345 miles). As many as 3000 targets can be tracked and standard specialist communications systems include three HF radios, four VHF/UHF units, four UHF and Link 11 or Link 16 systems and 2 Have Quick radios.

Other contractors involved in the Wedgetail programme include Boeing Australia, which has been heavily involved throughout the design process, and BAE Systems Australia. The latter is producing the passive surveillance system, as well as the electronic-warfare self-protection equipment and other systems. Boeing and the RAAF expect to have the 737 AEW&C in service by late 2006,

In December 1997, Australia awarded an Initial Design Activity contract to Boeing against its Project Air 5077 **Wedgetail** requirement. Air 5077 sought to acquire a modern AEW&C capability for the Royal Australian Air Force. Following the announcement that Boeing's was the preferred proposal in 1999, on 20 December 2000 a System Acquisition contract was signed. Initially this covers four aircraft, but options exist which may expand this to seven.

Boeing's winning contender uses the 737-700-based Boeing Business Jet airframe as the

the entire Wedgetail programme involving not just the radar and its platform, but also an AEW&C Support Centre, Operational Mission Simulator, Operational Flight Trainer, Mission Support Segment and a building for ground-based systems, as well as continuing service support.

Although Australia is the lead

The first 737 airframe intended for conversion to Wedgetail configuration was rolled out at Boeing Renton in October 2002.

customer for the AEW&C 737, the basic type has also been ordered by Turkey, and Boeing has presented the aircraft to other potential customers.

SPECIFICATION	
Boeing 737 AEW&C **Type:** airborne early warning & control aircraft **Powerplant:** two 121-kN (27,300-lb st) CFM International CFM56-7B turbofans **Performance:** maximum speed 877 km/h (545 mph); nominal cruising speed range 760 km/h (472 mph); maximum operating	altitude 12,497 m (41,000 ft); nominal operating altitude 9144–12,192 m (30,000-40,000 ft); range 7042 km (4,376 miles) **Weights:** maximum take-off 77,566 kg (171,000 lb) **Dimensions:** wing span 34.31 m (112 ft 7 in); length 33.63 m (110 ft 4 in); height 12.55 m (41 ft 2 in)

Boeing 767 AWACS/E-767 (767-27C) New-generation AWACS

In December 1991 Boeing announced a project to create an AWACS version of the Boeing 767-200ER airliner, fitted with the Northrop Grumman AN/APY-2 radar.

Japanese interest

Japan expressed an immediate interest and in November 1993 two examples of the new machine were ordered for the JASDF. Two further examples were ordered the following year and in March 1998 the first two examples were delivered. They were followed by the final two machines in 1999 and, during 2000, all four were placed into operational service. The aircraft has a flight crew of two and up to 19 mission specialists, although this number can vary depending on the mission profile. Substantial structural modifications were needed, including two additional bulkheads

and reinforced floor beams, as well as the addition of a rotodome to hold the rotating radar antenna. The aircraft offers twice the floor space and three times the internal volume of the Boeing E-3.

Lack of orders

Known to Boeing as the **767 AWACS** or **767-27C** and to the JASDF as **E-767**, the new aircraft is fully interoperable with existing E-3 machines and will show similar compatibility with the 737 AEW&C. Although no further orders have been received for the 767 AWACS, Boeing remain confident of its potential. With the USAF embarking on a lease deal to cover an initial 100 KC-767 tankers, the 767 would seem to be well placed to receive future orders as a replacement for the USAF's E-3 and RC-135 AWACS and reconnaissance, respectively, aircraft.

E-767 retains the rotodome of the E-3. Thanks to its greater cabin volume, however, the 767-based AWACS has the potential to offer far greater utility than the 707-based E-3.

SPECIFICATION	
Boeing 767 AWACS (767-27C) **Type:** airborne early warning & control aircraft **Powerplant:** two 273.50-kN (61,500-lb st) General Electric CF6-80C2B6FA turbofans **Performance:** maximum speed more than 800 km/h (500 mph); service ceiling 10,360–12,222 m (34,000–40,100 ft); range	10,370 km (6,444 miles); endurance 9 hours 15 minutes on station at 1854 km (1,152 miles) radius, or 13 hours at 345-km (555-mile) radius **Weights:** maximum take-off 175,000 kg (385,000 lb) **Dimensions:** wing span 47.57 m (156 ft 1 in); length 48.51 m (159 ft 2 in); height 15.85 m (52 ft)

Boeing E-4 National Airborne Operations Center

The **Boeing E-4B** is the United States' **National Airborne Operations Center** (**NAOC**), a flying command post to be used by the country's leaders in time of war. Behind the familiar exterior of a Boeing 747-200B lies the United States' frightening potential to continue to wage war in the event that Washington is annihilated by a nuclear blast.

The E-4B was developed in the 1970s to ensure the survival of the national leadership in the event of an atomic exchange with the Soviet Union. It is kept in readiness to transport the President, or others in the chain of leadership known as the NCA (National Command Authority), during the initial hours or days of a general conflict. During an attack on US soil, some leaders would be taken to an underground command post in Virginia, while others would go aboard the E-4B to direct US air and ground forces.

When choosing the aircraft and planning its design, the USAF wanted speed, efficiency and a degree of comfort, but the primary need was for a very large aircraft that could remain airborne for a long time. The Pentagon wanted the E-4B to remain aloft at least during the first round of a nuclear exchange, when communication would be most difficult, and airfields would not be readily available. The wide-bodied Boeing 747 offered the size needed for redundant flight crew personnel, equipment and 'black boxes', and also lent itself to being modified for extreme endurance. The 747 was, in addition, an ideal candidate for the extra weight caused by 'hardening' the aircraft against EMP (electromagnetic pulse).

Delivered in late 1974, the first three aircraft were **E-4A** machines, with the initial example making its maiden

flight on 13 June 1973. Early equipment was that taken from the E-4's predecessor, the EC-135J. The fourth E-4, delivered in December 1979, was modified to such an extent that a new designation, **E-4B**, was adopted. A subsequent modification programme saw all the E-4 fleet being upgraded to the more capable E-4B standard.

Flying 'White House'

The E-4B accommodates the President (in his role as commander in chief of US forces) as well as key members of his battle staff on its 511 m² (5,500 sq ft) main deck. The area is divided into five operating compartments: the flight crew section, the NCA area (which roughly constitutes a flying equivalent of the White House Situation Room), a conference room, a battle staff area, and a C³I (command, control, communications and intelligence)

Based on the successful 747-200, the E-4 is a vital component in the US defence planning laid down to allow the country to retaliate in the event of a pre-emptive nuclear strike.

planning facility. A second deck on the aircraft provides a rest area for mission personnel.

As a 'war readiness aircraft', the E-4B is equipped with nuclear thermal shielding, LF/VLF (low frequency/very low frequency) radios and extensive satellite communications equipment. Among this vast array is equipment allowing the aircraft to tie into commercial telephone and radio networks to broadcast emergency messages to the general population.

The E-4B also carries an SHF (super high frequency) communications system, with antennas housed in a distinctive dorsal blister. Every component of the aircraft, including its

A dorsal blister above the E-4B's flightdeck contains a satellite/SHF communications antenna. This allows the aircraft to send and receive messages without risk of interception. Despite the ending of the Cold War, whenever the President is overseas, a single E-4B accompanies him.

SPECIFICATION	
Boeing E-4B	unrefuelled endurance 12 hours
Type: national airborne operations centre	**Weights:** maximum take-off 360,000 kg (800,000 lb)
Powerplant: four General Electric CF6-50E2 turbofan engines each rated at 233.47 kN (52,500 lb st)	**Dimensions:** wing span 59.7 m (195 ft 8 in); length 70.5 m (231 ft 5 in); height 19.3 m (63 ft 5 in)
Performance: service ceiling more than 9091 m (30,000 ft);	**Accommodation:** provision for a crew of up to 114

engines, avionics, and wiring, has been optimized for maximum flight endurance.

Mission plans call for the E-4B to cruise at a typical speed of 933 km/h (580 mph), to refuel in flight, and to remain airborne for 72 hours. In the event of a war situation, this duration could be extended to a full week. Like the Presidential VC-25A, the other Boeing 747 derivative in the USAF's inventory, the E-4B's airborne endurance is limited only by the quantity of oil carried for the lubrication of its engines.

The E-4B was originally known as the **AABNCP (Advanced Airborne National Command Post)**, and thereafter as the **NEACP (National Emergency Airborne Command Post)**, the latter acronym inevitably being pronounced **'kneecap'** by those who worked on the aircraft. Today's term for the E-4B, NAOC, was devised partly to reflect a changing world and additional duties.

Future role?

With the Cold War's thawing, the four E-4Bs have remained in USAF service with a basically similar but expanded mission. Air Combat Command maintains one aircraft at readiness at a convenient base anywhere in the world at all times, under US Strategic Command control.

Boeing E-6 Mercury Command and submarine comms aircraft

This aircraft is shown at Boeing's Cecil Field facility undergoing the most recent upgrade to the E-6B configuration.

The **E-6A Mercury** was designed as successor to the Lockheed EC-130Q Hercules and is operated by the US Navy in the TACAMO (Take Charge And Move Out) role.

In April 1983 Boeing was given the contract to develop the **TACAMO II** type and the company chose the airframe of its Model 707 as the platform for the new type. This offered commonality with the E-3, but with the revised powerplant of four CFM International F108-CF-100 turbofans, offering outstanding fuel efficiency and resulting in long endurance that can be extended through the use of inflight-refuelling. The first E-6A made its maiden flight on 19 February 1987. Flight trials revealed a flaw in the structure which caused part of the fin to be lost in a high-speed dive. With suitable remedies, the first pair of E-6As was delivered on 2 August 1989. The name *Hermes* was initially assigned but this was then changed to **Mercury**, and deliveries have totalled 16 aircraft.

The Mercury is packed with communications equipment, including UHF satellite communications, the antennas of which are housed in the wingtip pods along with the antennas for the ALR-66(V)4 ESM system. All communications equipment is secure against eavesdropping, and is hardened against the effects of EMP (electromagnetic pulse).

Unlike the USAF's E-8s, the E-6s were new-build aircraft, with production lasting from 1986–91. The aircraft operate with VQ-3 and VQ-4.

SPECIFICATION	
Boeing E-6A Mercury	ceiling 12,800 m (42,000 ft);
Type: airborne command,	mission range unrefuelled
submarine control and operations	11,760 km (7,307 miles)
centre	**Weights:** operating empty
Powerplant: four CFM International	78,378 kg (172,795 lb);
F108-CF-100 turbofan engines each	maximum take-off 155,128 kg
rated at 97.90 kN (22,000 lb st)	(342,000 lb)
Performance: maximum cruising	**Dimensions:** wing span 45.16 m
speed at 12,190 m (40,000 ft)	(148 ft 2 in); length 46.61 m (152 ft
842 km/h (523 mph); service	11 in); height 12.93 m (42 ft 5 in)

Mercury duties

The E-6A's principal task is the provision of a link between various national and military commands, including the E-4B presidential transport and command centre, and the US Navy's submarines. the E-6A uses two trailing-wire antennas to communicate with the submarines: one is 1219 m (4,000 ft) long and deploys from the tail cone; the other is 7925 m (26,000 ft) long and deploys from a position under the rear fuselage. With the E-6A flying a tight orbit, the antennas hang vertically, allowing VLF communications with submarines, which have a towed aerial array. In May 1997 Raytheon redelivered the first E-6A upgraded to the **E-6B** standard combining the original TACAMO role with the **Looking Glass** airborne command post task previously undertaken by the USAF's EC-135. By 2003, the rest of the fleet had been converted to this E-6B standard. Still, in May 2003 the first E-6B to be selected for a further upgrade was passed to Boeing.

Northrop Grumman E-8 J-STARS
Joint Surveillance Target Attack System

The **E-8 Joint Surveillance Target Attack System** (**J-STARS**) was developed by Grumman (now Northrop Grumman) for a debut in 1991 during Operation Desert Storm long before it was considered operational. The aircraft combines advanced mission systems based on the AN/APY-3 multi-mode side-looking radar with a remanufactured Boeing 707-300 airframe, with a ventral canoe fairing housing the radar's

Originally built for American Airlines, this aircraft became the second of two E-8A development aircraft built for the J-STARS programme.

antenna. It provides the kind of capability for monitoring and controlling the land battle that the E-3 provides for the air battle. The radar allows the onboard controllers to monitor the positions and movements of all ground vehicles, as well as serving other functions. It can also differentiate between wheeled and tracked vehicles.

Prototypes

The two **E-8A** prototypes flew in Desert Storm, but the USAF service variant is the **E-8C**, of which the 16 were delivered in 2004. The aircraft has already progressed through Block 10 and 20 upgrades and will be further upgraded through Blocks 30, 40 and ultimately 50 standards by the late 2000s, by which time AN/APY-X radar should be installed and additional capabilities should include automatic target recognition, Elint gathering, helicopter detection and tracking and maritime detection.

E-8 will ultimately be replaced by the **MC²A** (**Multi-Role Command and Control Aircraft**), which will go on to also replace the E-3 AWACS and RC-135. In 2003, Boeing received a contract for a 767-400-based MC²A technology demonstrator.

J-STARS has seen a great deal of operational service in recent years, being engaged over Bosnia, during Operation Allied Freedom, and during the recent operations Enduring Freedom and Iraqi Freedom.

SPECIFICATION	
Northrop Grumman E-8C J-STARS	**Weights:** empty 77,564 kg (171,000 lb); maximum take-off 150,139 kg (331,000 lb)
Type: ground surveillance and land battle management system aircraft	
Powerplant: four Pratt & Whitney TF33-P-102C turbofans each rated at 85.40 kN (19,200 lb st)	**Dimensions:** wing span 44.42 m (145 ft 9 in); length 46.61 m (152 ft 11 in); height 12.95 m (42 ft 6 in); wing area 283.35 m² (3,050 sq ft)
Performance: maximum operating speed Mach 0.84; service ceiling 12,800 m (42,000 ft); maximum endurance with one inflight refuelling 20 hours	**Accommodation:** flight crew of three, plus up to 18 systems operators

Sukhoi Su-24MR 'Fencer-E'/Su-24MP 'Fencer-F'
Reconnaissance and EW aircraft

By the mid-1970s it had become clear that existing reconnaissance aircraft in the Soviet air force were inadequate, as they suffered from limited range and outdated equipment. Sukhoi therefore modified two 'Fencer' airframes, the **T6M-26** and the **T6M-34**, to become **T6MR-26** and **T6MR-34** (R for *razvedchik*, reconnaissance), respectively. The resulting variant was known as the **Su-24MR** to the VVS, **T6MR** to Sukhoi and **'Fencer-E'** to the West. Its first flight took place in September 1980.

Most of the standard ground-attack equipment was removed from the Su-24MR, but the basic structure and layout remained unchanged. A smaller nose radome was complemented by a large SLAR (side-looking airborne radar) panel and two smaller dielectric panels. These covered reconnaissance equipment and were located on each side of

the nose. Three underfuselage hardpoints were removed and the built-in cannon omitted.

Reconnaissance suite

A comprehensive reconnaissance suite, known as BKR-1 Shtyk and claimed to be the best in the world, was developed by the Moscow Institute of Instrument Engineering. It affords both visual and electronic reconnaissance by day or by night, and can function efficiently in all weather conditions. Its constituent parts are a thermal imaging unit, a TV camera and a panoramic camera with an f/3.5 lens of 90.5-mm (3.6-in) diameter. It has a Shtyk MR-1 synthetic aperture side-looking radar, radiation monitor, radio-monitoring pod and a laser pod with 0.25-m (10-in) resolution from 400 m (1,315 ft) altitude. The laser scans an area four times the aircraft's height and provides almost photographic images.

Sukhoi Su-24MP

Design work on the **Su-24MP 'Fencer-F'** ECM aircraft began in 1976. Two Su-24M airframes were modified for this work, the **T6M-25** and the **T6M-35**, which were then redesignated **T6MP-25** and **T6MP-35**, respectively. The Su-24MP completed its first flight in December 1979. This variant is known to have a sophisticated network of systems for detecting, locating, analysing, identifying, classifying, storing and jamming all known electromagnetic emissions. Up to four R-60 or R-60M AAMs can be carried. The internal cannon is retained.

Su-24MRs based in Germany usually carried the Efir-1M radiation recce pod shown under the wing of this example.

Only 14 Su-24MPs were built and their mission is jamming, Elint-gathering and performing the invaluable service of escorting attack aircraft to their targets and neutralizing hostile radars.

The future

In Russian service, the attack 'Fencers' should be replaced by the Su-34 around 2010. It is likely that Su-24MP and MR aircraft will remain in service longer.

SPECIFICATION	
Sukhoi Su-24MR 'Fencer-E'	**Performance:** generally similar to Su-24M 'Fencer-D'
Type: two-seat variable geometry multi-sensor reconnaissance aircraft	**Weights:** generally similar to Su-24M 'Fencer-D'
Powerplant: two Perm/Soloviev (Lyul'ka) AL-21F-3A turbojets each rated at 109.83 kN (24,691 lb st) with afterburning	**Dimensions:** generally similar to Su-24M 'Fencer-D'
	Armament: provision for up to four R-60 AAMs

Antonov An-12 'Cub' EW and command post variants

Designated **'Cub'** by the ASCC (Air Standards Co-ordinating Committee), the An-12 transport aircraft has been produced in several versions. In addition, large numbers of military An-12s have been converted to perform other roles (and some production 'special duties' An-12s have also been manufactured). Not all have separate ASCC/NATO reporting names, but their various service designations are listed below.

Electronic 'Cubs'

The first 'special duties' An-12 to be developed was the **An-12B-I**.

These aircraft were produced by converting An-12B airframes, but little is known of their use. They were replaced by two types of **An-12BK-IS** aircraft based on the An-12BK. The Siren system fitted to the BK-IS, along with its associated antenna fairings, has probably led to this variant being included under NATO's **'Cub-D'** reporting name.

Further BK-based special-purpose machines include the **An-12PS 'Cub-B'**. The Soviets claimed this aircraft was a search-and-rescue type. Its Istok-Golub radio receiver equipment was

In 2005, 'Bear-D' remained the most important EW An-12 variant in Russian service. Note that equipment pods are carried on the forward fuselage sides and on the sides of the fin.

certainly able to detect signals sent out by emergency locator transmitters, but also had an

important Elint capacity. The deployment patterns of the An-12PS, as well as the fact that it

Egypt received at least 24 'Cubs' of different models, these including a few An-12PP 'Cub-Cs'. Note the bulbous tail cone and underfuselage antennas of this variant.

was often intercepted around Western naval groups, suggests that its primary role was Elint. A second **An-12 'Cub-B'** variant with a revised antenna fit was also reported, while an Elint-dedicated aircraft based on the An-12BK airframe and wearing full Aeroflot colours was frequently encountered by Western forces over the Mediterranean, the Persian Gulf and the Indian Ocean.

More extensive modification produced the **An-12PP 'Cub-C'**. Featuring a bulbous tail fairing and numerous underfuselage antennas, 'Cub-C' has special shielding to protect its crew from the EM radiation emitted by its powerful jamming system. The type was flown in Syrian markings by Soviet crews during the 1973 Yom Kippur War, where it was used to jam Israeli HAWK SAM radars. In later years, the

An-12PP has been seen with just its tail fairing in place, suggesting a change of role or equipment.

With the **An-12BK-PPS 'Cub-D'**, Antonov combined the capabilities and systems of the An-12BK-IS and An-12PP in a single airframe. An-12BK-PPS, in its basic form, is therefore little more than an An-12PP with the Siren system of the An-12BK-IS. Some aircraft, described in the Soviet press as **An-12BK-PPS**

Improved, do not have the bulbous tail fairing. Instead, they feature the gun turret of the standard transport, with a braced pipe structure beneath the rear fuselage which, it is believed, carries chaff dispensers. It seems likely that some BK-PPS aircraft were produced by conversion from BK-IS standard, while some may have used PP airframes.

Command posts
At least two An-12-based command post variants have been built. The **An-12B-VKP Zebra** was the first of these and was distinguished by streamlined fairings at its wing and fin tips. The An-12BK was subsequently used as the basis for the **An-12BK-VKP Zebra**, which may have been an interim type pending availability of the Il-22.

Ilyushin Il-18, Il-20 and Il-22 'Coot'
EW and command post aircraft

Both forward cabin windows are deleted on 'Coot-A' airframes, in order to provide accommodation for the bodies of the oblique cameras, the lenses of which protrude into the side fairings. 'Coot-As' are typically quite poorly finished in grey paint. The type is sometimes known as Il-20DSR.

Ilyushin's Il-18 airliner provided the basis for a number of electronic reconnaissance and command post aircraft for use by the Soviet Union.

The first of the true electronic reconnaissance machines was the Ilyushin **Il-20M 'Coot-A'** Elint platform. The most obvious features of the Il-20M are the large 'cigar' radome beneath its forward fuselage and a pair of 'canoe' fairings to either side of the forward fuselage. The former covers the antenna of the Igla-1 SLAR, while the latter

contain long-range oblique cameras in their forward portions, with Sigint sensors accounting for the remaining space. The starboard fairing also houses a cooling intake for the SLAR. In all, around 20 Il-20Ms were produced.

Intercepted by the Swedish air force over the Baltic, this Il-20M 'Coot-A' was on a typical, and ongoing, mission for the aircraft – collecting Elint on Western systems. The aircraft's crew includes eight 'crows'.

Command posts
With the exception of test-beds and the Il-38 'May', the remaining electronic Il-18s are all command or communications platforms.

The first of these was a pair of **Il-18V** command posts produced by conversion. These were joined by two aircraft

converted from **Il-18D** airframes. These featured a revised comms fit and retained their original designation. Three further Il-18Ds were modified, also retaining their original designation. These machines acted as communications relay aircraft, supporting HF

communications between the Kremlin and VIP aircraft.

Undoubtedly the most important of the Il-18 command posts is the **Il-22 'Coot-B'**. Known to Ilyushin as the **Il-18D-36 Bizon**, these aircraft have an extensive communications fit, which includes Satcom equipment and electronic support measures. A second variant, with the Ilyushin designation **Il-22M-11 Zebra**, has a shorter underfuselage fairing, but, like the earlier machine, it retains the fin tip fairing and 'Coot-B' reporting name. Such was the demand for Il-22s, that Ilyushin, having dismantled its Il-18 production line, converted four Il-18Ds 'confiscated' from Aeroflot to Il-22M-11 standard. The Il-22 and Il-22M, as well as the Il-20, will remain in service for some time.

This Il-22M-11 shows the type's Aeroflot colour scheme and the fact that all such airframes are marked as Il-18s.

Panavia Tornado GR.Mk 1A/4A and ECR
Recce and lethal SEAD warplanes

Unlike those of Germany and Italy, Britain's specialist recce Tornados have no SEAD tasking, this being assigned to specialist Tornado GR.Mk 1/4 units. Nos II (illustrated) and 13 Sqns fly the Tornado GR.Mk 1A (as here) and GR.Mk 4A.

The first example of the RAF's **Tornado GR.Mk 1A** tactical reconnaissance aircraft completed its maiden flight on 11 July 1985. Based on the Tornado GR.Mk 1, the GR.Mk 1A has no Mauser cannon, these being deleted to make space for the Tornado Infra-Red Reconnaissance System (TIRRS). This latter consists of an IR linescan and two side-looking IR systems which 'look' through gold-tinted windows on the sides of the forward fuselage. The system records its 'take' onto video tape, the first such system in the world to do so. TIRRS is primarily a low-level system, medium- and high-level work being carried out with the Vinten GP1 camera pod.

Some 14 Tornado GR.Mk 1As were produced by conversion and 16 were new-build aircraft. The type is being upgraded to **Tornado GR.Mk 4A** standard and retains the full attack capability of the standard Tornado IDS. Both Germany and Italy also have specialized reconnaissance variants of the Tornado IDS in service, although these aircraft also have an important lethal SEAD role.

Tornado ECR

The Luftwaffe received 35 aircraft to **Tornado ECR (Electronic Combat and Reconnaissance)** standard. These machines featured an IR linescan and FLIR, although the former proved troublesome and has been removed. An emitter location system for finding enemy air defence radars is also standard equipment for Tornado ECR and is used in combination with AGM-88 HARM. In service, lethal SEAD has become the primary role of the German ECRs, which have seen combat service over the Balkans. The aircraft will

Like their German counterparts, Italy's Tornado ITECRs employ AGM-88 HARM. Some Italian IDS machines have a recce tasking with podded systems.

SPECIFICATION
Panavia Tornado GR.Mk 4A **Type:** two-seat all-weather day and night tactical reconnaissance aircraft **Powerplant:** two Turbo-Union RB.199 Mk 103 turbofans each rated at 38.48 kN (8,650 lb st) dry and 71.50 kN (16,075 lb st) with afterburning **Performance:** maximum speed 2338 km/h (1,453 mph) or Mach 2.2 at 10,975 m (36,000 ft); climb to 9145 m (30,000 ft) in less than two minutes from brakes-off; service ceiling more than 15,240 m (50,000 ft) **Weights:** basic empty about 13,890 kg (30,620 lb); maximum take-off about 27,951 kg (61,620 lb) **Dimensions:** wing span 13.91 m (45 ft 7½ in) minimum sweep and 8.6 m (28 ft 2½ in) maximum sweep; length 16.72 m (54 ft 10¼ in); height 5.95 m (19 ft 6¼ in); wing area 26.6 m² (286.33 sq ft) **Armament:** usually none, but provision is made for a maximum ordnance load of 8165 kg (18,000 lb)

undergo a comprehensive midlife upgrade. Ironically, many Tornado IDS aircraft previously assigned to the Marineflieger – some of which had a limited AGM-88 capability – now serve with the Luftwaffe as reconnaissance aircraft. These employ a podded recce system, which includes the former ECR linescan.

ITECR

Italy converted 16 IDS aircraft to **Tornado ITECR (Italian ECR)** standard for the SEAD role. Although generally similar to the Luftwaffe's ECRs, some of the Italian aircraft feature an imaging IR system which records onto video tape, rather than the film used by the German machines.

British Aerospace Nimrod R.Mk 1 Sigint/Elint aircraft

In addition to the 46 Nimrod MR.Mk 1 aircraft ordered as Shackleton replacements for the RAF, three further aircraft were ordered (with a replacement for a crashed machine later created as a conversion) to replace the de Havilland Comet and English Electric Canberra aircraft specially modified for the signals intelligence (Sigint)-gathering role with No. 51 Sqn. This task has only just been formally admitted by the United Kingdom, and references to this publicity-shunning squadron have often described it as a calibration unit. The three aircraft were designated **Nimrod R.Mk 1**, and were delivered to RAF Wyton for fitting out in 1971. Security surrounding the aircraft was such that they were delivered as little more than empty shells, the RAF then fitting virtually all mission equipment. As a result, flight trials did not begin until late 1973, with the first operational flight taking place on 3 May 1974. On 10 May 1974 the type was formally commissioned, bringing the RAF's Comet era to a close.

Modified airframe

Initially the Nimrod R.Mk 1 differed from its maritime cousin in having no MAD tailboom and no searchlight, instead having dielectric radomes on the nose of each external wing tank and on the tail. The aircraft have been progressively modified since they were introduced, gaining more and more antennas above and below the fuselage and wing tanks, as well as Loral ARI.18240/1 wingtip ESM pods. When inflight-refuelling probes were fitted to the R.Mk 1s, their designation was changed to **Nimrod R.Mk 1P**. Subsequently, the 'P' appears to have been dropped from the designation. The addition of more equipment has led to the deletion of several cabin windows; in more recent years the aircraft have started carrying underwing chaff/flare dispensers.

The main Sigint/Elint receivers cover the widest possible range of frequencies, with DF (direction finding) and ranging, and are thus able to record and locate the source of hostile radar and radio emissions. The aircraft almost certainly have a computerized 'threat library', allowing a detailed 'map' of potential enemy radar stations, navaids and air defence systems to be built up. Emissions from hostile fighters can also be recorded and analysed. During Cold War operations, the aircraft often operated in international airspace around the peripheries of the USSR, or possibly flew feints toward Soviet airspace in the hope of provoking a response, necessitating extremely accurate navigation. One LORAN 'towel rail' antenna was thus removed, and the aircraft received a Delco AN/ASN-119 Carousel INS. The ASV-21 nose radar was replaced by an ECKO 290 weather radar during the early 1980s.

With long-range missions the norm during the Falklands War, the need for a Nimrod IFR capability soon became obvious. The R.Mk 1 fleet received its probes just after the MR Nimrod fleet.

The Nimrod R.Mk 1 flies with a very large crew (26–28 seems by no means extraordinary), the majority obviously being equipment operators. Most of the aircrew are extremely experienced, and are hand-picked for their skill and discretion.

R.Mk 1 at war

Such is its importance that the Nimrod R.Mk 1 has accompanied RAF operations around the world. During the 1982 Falklands War, a single aircraft operated out of Ascension Island, or possibly Chile. The Nimrod R.Mk 1 fleet was again active during Operation Granby, the British contribution to Operation Desert Storm in 1991. Subsequently, the R.Mk 1 has seen further operations in the Middle East and over the Balkans.

Further upgrades

The Nimrod R.Mk 1 continues to be updated and, as a result of project Starwindow, may now feature some systems in common with the USAF's Boeing RC-135V Rivet Joint aircraft. After some revision and cost-cutting, a further upgrade, known as Project Extract, was launched in 1998.

Joint Nimrod R.Mk 1/ RC-135 operations have been carried out, as have joint missions with the SR-71A. R.Mk 1 crews also fly with the RC-135 Rivet Joint and US Navy EP-3 Aries communities.

SPECIFICATION
BAe Nimrod R.Mk 1 **Type:** Sigint and Elint aircraft aircraft **Powerplant:** four Rolls-Royce Spey RB.168-20 Mk 250 turbofan engines each rated at 54 kN (12,140 lb st) **Performance:** maximum speed	around 926 km/h (575 mph) at optimum altitude; service ceiling about 12,800 m (42,000 ft) **Dimensions:** wing span 35 m (114 ft 10 in); length 36.19 m (118 ft 9 in); height 9.08 m (29 ft 8½ in), wing area 197.04 m² (2,121 sq ft)

The ill-fated Nimrod R.Mk 1 XW666 demonstrates the mark's revised tailboom when compared to that of the MR Nimrod. XW666 was ditched after a severe inflight fire and was scrapped.

McDonnell Douglas F-4G Phantom II Wild Weasel

At least 48, but perhaps as many as 70, Weasel Phantoms from George AFB, California, and Spangdahlem AB, Germany (illustrated), supported Operation Desert Storm with a total of 2800 missions.

Widespread use in Vietnam of Soviet-supplied SA-2 'Guideline' SAMs was only partly countered by the use of aircraft such as the Douglas EB-66 and Grumman EA-6A/EA-6B by the USAF and US Navy, respectively, and subsequent efforts were made to develop more potent anti-radar platforms. Greater success attended development of North American F-100s and Republic F-105s in the radar suppression role. This effort culminated in the adoption for a similar task of the McDonnell Douglas F-4 Phantom II, with its higher performance and greater strike capabilities. Thirty-six temporarily converted **F-4C Wild Weasel IV** aircraft were in service by 1972 (unofficially designated **EF-4C**), employing Westinghouse ECM pods in conjunction with AGM-45 Shrike ARMs, such aircraft often accompanying routine strike missions by standard F-4Cs.

Wild Weasel V

In due course much more extensive modification was undertaken, a total of 116 **F-4G** aircraft being produced (known initially as **Advanced Wild Weasel** or **Wild Weasel V**) by modifying F-4Es when they were returned for life-extension programmes. Changes included deletion of the internal M61A1 cannon and installation of an APR-38 radar homing and warning receiver (RHAWS), much of the component avionics for which were located in a long cylindrical fairing on top of the aircraft's fin. Associated with the APR-38 was a Texas Instruments computer, and the airframe sprouted no fewer than 52 other additional antennas.

Desert Storm was the high point of the F-4G's career; however, the aircraft soon fell foul of the 'peace dividend', leaving the United States without a truly effective lethal SEAD platform.

SPECIFICATION	
McDonnell Douglas F-4G Phantom II **Type:** two-seat SEAD aircraft **Powerplant:** two General Electric J79-GE-17A turbojets each rated at 52.53 kN (11,810 lb st) dry and 79.62 kN (17,900 lb st) with afterburning **Performance:** maximum level speed 'clean' at 12190 m (40,000 ft) 2300 km/h (1,485 mph); cruising speed at maximum take-off weight 919 km/h (571 mph); combat radius 964 km (599 miles) **Weights:** empty equipped	13,300 kg (29,231 lb); maximum take-off 28,300 kg (62,390 lb) **Dimensions:** wing span 11.71 m (38 ft 5 in); length 19.20 m (63 ft); height 5.02 m (16 ft 5½ in); wing area 49.24 m² (530 sq ft) **Armament:** AGM-45 Shrike, AGM-78 Standard ARM, or AGM-88 HARM as primary mission weapons; AIM-7 Sparrow and AIM-9 Sidewinder AAMs, AGM-65 Maverick AGMs and a selection of 'dumb' and cluster bombs up to maximum ordnance load of 16,000 lb (7258 kg)

The nearer of these two F-4Gs has a warload of AGM-65, AGM-88 and AIM-7 missiles. The lead aircraft has a rather more 'primitive' load of AGM-45, AIM-7 and M117 'dumb' bombs.

Self-defence weaponry was confined to a pair of Sparrow AAMs in the rear fuselage recesses (and perhaps a pair of AIM-9s if pylon stations were available), one of the forward Sparrow bays normally being occupied by an ECM pod. The APR-38 (and later, upgraded APR-47 system) was compatible with the AGM-45 Shrike, EO-guided AGM-65 Maverick and AGM-88 HARM, and featured automatic and blind weapon firing. Later aircraft were re-equipped with LORAN, and modified to carry an F-15-type centreline drop tank.

After highly successful operations in Desert Storm, the F-4G was finally retired from USAF service in June 1996.

Like all the F-4Gs, this aircraft, the F-4G prototype, was converted from an F-4E. Note the prominent undernose and fin tip fairings of the model.

Grumman EA-6B Prowler Primary US jammer

Production of the US Navy's standard carrierborne electronic warfare aircraft terminated in July 1991 with 170 aircraft built, but efforts at improving the already impressive potential of the **EA-6B Prowler** continued and led to **ICAP III (Improved Capability III)** aircraft entering operational use in 2004, for service at least into 2015.

Intruder origins

Fundamentally a four-seater variation on the well-proven A-6 Intruder, the EA-6B entered service during 1971 as a replacement for the EKA-3B Skywarrior. Key equipment includes the TJS (Tactical Jamming System), which is capable of operation in fully-automatic, semi-automatic and

manual modes and which employs 'noise' jamming originating from a maximum of five external transmitter pods.

Progressive update initiatives have resulted in the appearance of ever more capable versions. Excluding three prototype conversions of A-6As and five development airframes, the first 23 production Prowlers were to 'Basic' standard, using the ALQ-99 TJS and ALQ-92 communications jammer, with an EW potential that was limited to four specific frequency bands.

Improved variants

The first of 25 **EXCAP (Expanded Capability)** airframes with improved equipment and the ability to cover threats across eight bands using the ALQ-99A

TJS were to follow these 'Basic' aircraft in 1973.

The next version to appear was **ICAP** (retrospectively known as **ICAP I** when further upgrades were developed). This version made its debut in 1976 and incorporated new displays and reduced reaction times, along with AN/ALQ-126 multiple-band defensive breakers, updated radar deception gear and an automatic carrier landing system. In addition to the production of 45 new-build machines, 17 surviving 'Basic' and EXCAP airframes were brought to full ICAP standard.

Software and display improvements were among the changes made on the **ICAP II** version, which flew for the first time in June 1980, with all 55

surviving ICAPs being upgraded. ICAP II is the current service model, having been upgraded through various Block numbers, the most recent of which late in 2002, was **ICAP II Block 89A**). The external jammer pods were upgraded to be able to generate signals within seven bands (instead of one) and to jam in two bands simultaneously. ICAP II also acquired the ability to use more direct methods in countering the threat posed by enemy SAM sites, being able to function as a 'shooter' with the AGM-88.

Beyond ICAP II

Procurement of ICAP II followed a twin-track approach, the US Navy and Marine Corps receiving a mixture of rebuilt

This VMAQ-2 EA-6B is typical of the type in USMC service. Both Marine and Navy Prowlers have seen extensive combat action.

and new-build aircraft. These equip about 10 deployable USN squadrons, along with a training unit and five squadrons assigned to support USAF expeditionary wing operations.

An Avionics Improvement Program was started in the 1990s with the aim of producing remanufactured **Advanced Capability (ADVCAP)/Block 91** EA-6B aircraft with new displays, radar improvements, an improved tactical support jamming suite, AN/ALQ-149 communications jamming system and a digital auto-pilot. In addition, aerodynamic improvements were developed under the VEP (Vehicle Enhancement Program), the

VEP prototype first flying on 15 June 1992 and also featuring uprated powerplants and two additional dedicated HARM pylons. In the event, however, just three ADVCAP/Block 91 prototypes were built before the programme was abandoned, and effort is now focused on the ICAP III standard.

USMC usage of the Prowler is more limited, comprising four frontline squadrons at MCAS Cherry Point, North Carolina, which regularly deploy to sea.

When the Prowler entered service, it was finished in the old US Navy scheme of light grey over white. Note that this aircraft carries three jammer pods and a pair of tanks.

SPECIFICATION	
Grumman EA-6B Prowler	1769 km (1,099 miles) with
Type: two-seat carrierborne and	maximum external load
land-based all-weather SEAD	**Weights:** empty 14,588 kg
aircraft	(32,162 lb); maximum take-off
Powerplant: two Pratt & Whitney	29,483 kg (60,610 lb)
J52-P-408 turbojets each rated at	**Dimensions:** wing span 16.15 m
49.80 kN (11,200 lb st)	(53 ft); length 18.24 m (59 ft 10 in);
Performance: maximum level speed	height 4.95 m (16 ft 3 in); wing
'clean' at sea level 982 km/h	area 49.13 m² (528.90 sq ft)
(610 mph) with five jammer pods;	**Armament:** up to four AGM-88
cruising speed at optimum altitude	HARMs can be carried on four
774 km/h (481 mph); maximum	wing pylons, along with external
rate of climb 3057 m (10,030 ft)	AN/ALQ-99 emitter pods or
per minute with five jammer pods;	1136-litre (300-US gal) drop tanks;
service ceiling 11,580 m (38,000 ft)	a further AN/ALQ-99 pod can be
with five jammer pods; range	carried on the centreline pylon

With the premature demise of the USAF's EF-111A fleet, the Prowler is now the primary US jamming aircraft, supporting all US air operations.

Lockheed EC-130 Hercules Electronic Hercules

The EC-130E(RR) aircraft have a distinctive set of primary antennas. These include a massive blade antenna at the fin/fuselage junction, and prominent 'axe-head' blade antennas beneath the outer wings. Equipment pods are also often carried, mounted on pylons which are again beneath the outer wing.

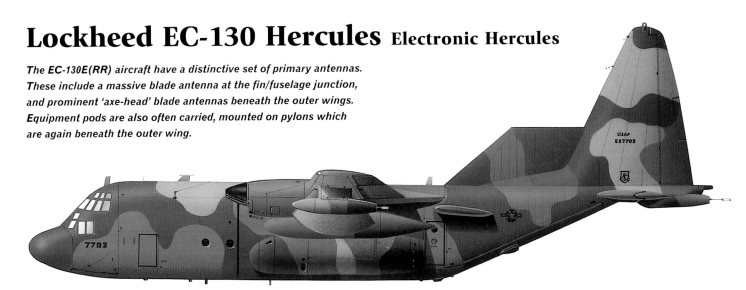

Based on what at the time was the definitive transport Hercules variant – the C-130E – the original 'electronic' Hercules aircraft were designated **EC-130E**. This has been the source of much confusion, however, resulting in completely unrelated variants receiving this designation as well.

The EC-130Es entered USAF service in the late 1950s and operated covertly within regular C-130 squadrons. Often wearing similar style markings to the transports, the EC-130s probed the borders of the Warsaw Pact. Nevertheless, it was in Vietnam that the full potential of the EC-130 was realized.

Serving in the **Airborne Battlefield Command and Control Center** (**ABCCC**) role, EC-130Es of the 314th TCW operated from Da Nang Air Base, South Vietnam, equipped with a module in the cargo bay that housed a comprehensive communications fit and accommodation for up to 16 operators. These aircraft were instrumental in coordinating SAR missions over North Vietnam. The same aircraft, but with updated avionics and now designated **ABCCC-III**, controlled nearly half of all air attack missions flown during Operation Desert Storm.

Rivet Rider

The EC-130s of the **Rivet Rider** programme are equipped with large blade antennas under the wings and forward of the tail fin, and wire aerials beneath the tail cone and outer wing panels. These **EC-130E(RR)** machines are regularly deployed to Europe and the Far and Middle East. Rivet Rider variants include the **Volant Solo** and **Comfy Levi**.

Each of these models has received progressively updated electronic equipment to undertake psychological warfare (Psywar) missions, broadcasting colour-TV propaganda. Rivet Riders were heavily committed to Psywar and psychological operations (Psyops) during Desert Storm.

Naval operations

The US Navy acquired four C-130s which it modified to **EC-130G TACAMO** (**TAke Charge And Move Out**) configuration to provide a link between the National Command Authority and submerged fleet ballistic missile submarines. The aircraft were eventually replaced by C-130H-based **EC-130Q** aircraft.

The USAF has continued to develop more sophisticated EC-130s. With fairings mounted on its rear fuselage and support struts for wire antenna arrays, the **EC-130H Compass Call** serves as a Command, Control and Communications Counter-measures (C³CM) platform.

Drug interdiction

As part of its campaign against drug runners, the US Coast Guard converted an HC-130H to **EC-130V** configuration with AN/APS-145 radar in a rotodome above the fuselage, but the programme was cancelled on cost grounds.

Future EC-130s will be based on the new C-130J airframe and a number of **Lockheed Martin EC-130J Coronet Solo** aircraft has already been ordered.

The tail-mounted antenna of the EC-130H consists of a huge number of suspended wires, forming a network around the aircraft's tail surfaces.

SPECIFICATION	
Lockheed EC-130E Hercules	ft); range 7560 km (4,698 miles)
Type: ABCCC or Elint/Comint/Sigint platform	**Weights:** empty 33,063 kg (72,892 lb); maximum payload
Powerplant: four 3021-kW (4,050 eshp) Allison T56-A-7 turboprops	20,412 kg (45,000 lb)
Performance: maximum speed 612 km/h (380 mph) at 9145 m (30,000	**Dimensions:** wing span 40.41 m (132 ft 7 in); length 29.79 m (97 ft 9 in); height 11.66 m (38 ft 3 in); wing area 161.12 m² (1,745 sq ft)

273

Boeing RC-135 Strategic Sigint and Elint collection platform

From an early date, the Boeing C-135 was recognized as an excellent airframe for various special missions. One of these was strategic reconnaissance, using the aircraft's capacious cabin to house large amounts of electronic equipment. Designated **RC-135**, several versions of reconnaissance Stratotankers remain in use in the early part of the twenty-first century.

All RC-135s serve with Air Combat Command's 55th Wing at Offutt AFB, Nebraska, previously the headquarters of Strategic Air Command, from where they are detached on a global basis to cover areas of the world where electronic intelligence-gathering is required. Regular detachments are made to RAF Mildenhall in England, Souda Bay on Crete, Kadena AB on Okinawa and Shemya AB on the Aleutian islands.

Many RC-135 variants have been produced since the type entered service in 1964, those still active being primarily dedicated to the collection of signals intelligence (Sigint) and Elint. All feature large amounts of electronic recording and analysing equipment on board, and have many aerials on the airframe. Of the most important recent variants, the RC-135U/V/W have slab-sided cheek fairings where many of the side-facing antennas are grouped. These serve the Automatic Elint Emitter Locator System, which gathers signals from across the frequency spectrum, sifts out those of particular interest and

relays data to operator stations in the cabin. Many other antennas, notably the farm of 'MUCELS' (pronounced mussels) under the fuselage, supply data for other systems.

RC-135U Combat Sent

Two **RC-135U** aircraft appeared to be no longer listed as part of the active USAF inventory early in 2003; these machines were characterized by cheek fairings and additional fairings in the chin, boomer, wingtip, tailcone and fin-top positions. Until 1991 they were fitted with 'towel rail' antennas above the cheek fairings. Known as **Combat Sent** aircraft, the pair of RC-135Us is believed to have had special purposes within the Sigint fleet, and may also have been used to trial new equipment.

RC-135V/W

Around eight aircraft are to **RC-135V Rivet Joint** standard, and six are of the essentially similar **RC-135W** variant. These are the workhorses of the Sigint fleet, and are distinguished by having extended 'thimble' noses and large plate aerials under their centre-sections. External differences between the two variants are restricted to a lengthened cheek fairing on the W model. A related variant is the **TC-135W**, which provides crew training for the RC-135 fleet. This has the 'thimble' nose and cheek fairing, but does not have mission equipment.

An altogether more specialized role was undertaken by two

RC-135S Cobra Ball aircraft which normally operated from Shemya. In addition to 'thimble' noses, electronic receivers mounted in cheek fairings and a teardrop-shaped fairing on the aft fuselage, these had large circular windows in the fuselage for the photography of foreign missile tests. The photographic equipment was known as the Real Time Optical System. The wings and engine nacelles on the starboard side were painted black to reduce glare for re-entry vehicle photography, while the aerials were used to gather telemetry data from the test launches and re-entries. Thus Telint (telemetry intelligence) was the role of the RC-135S, a mission in which, until February 1993, it was augmented by the sole **RC-135X Cobra Eye**. This had a single camera window behind a sliding door for missile photography, and fewer antennas. A single **TC-135S**, without mission equipment, provided aircrew training for the Telint fleet.

RC-135s in action

The RC-135 fleet has consistently proved of great value, both as a strategic reconnaissance tool during peacetime and as a more tactical asset during times of tension. The 55th Wing has been highly active in all the world's trouble spots, and played an instrumental part in Desert Storm and subsequent operations in the Gulf. The aircraft played crucial roles in the various conflicts surrounding the former Yugoslavia and were especially active during Operation Allied Force. The RC-135V/W was again called upon during Operation Enduring Freedom and will remain a critical element in any US action for the foreseeable future.

The RC-135 fleet is being upgraded with fuel-efficient CFM56 turbofans (military designation F108) and glass cockpits. It is interesting to note that, in the spring of 2003, the USAF listed its active RC-135 inventory as 14 V/W models, while independent sources quoted a 19-strong fleet.

SPECIFICATION	
Boeing RC-135V Rivet Joint	about 982 km/h (610 mph) at high
Type: Sigint/Elint platform	altitude
Powerplant: four Pratt & Whitney	**Weights:** Maximum gross (for taxi)
TF33-P-9 turbofans, each rated at	136803 kg (301,600 lb)
80.07 kN (18,000 lb st); re-engined	**Dimensions:** wing span 39.88 m
aircraft powered by four CFM	(130 ft 10 in); length 41.17 m (135 ft
International F108-CF-100	1 in); height 12.73 m (41 ft 9 in);
turbofans, each rated at 97.86 kN	wing area (less ailerons) 214.9 m²
(22,000 lb st)	(2,313.4 sq ft)
Performance: maximum level speed	

A crew as large as 27 might be employed aboard the RC-135V/W depending on the mission, and might include up to four maintenance specialists. An RC-135V is illustrated.

Lockheed EP-3 Aries Elint and Sigint aircraft

Two of the US Navy's original 12 EP-3Es have been lost: one in a crash and the other after a well-publicized collision with a Chinese J-8II fighter. Note the distinctive underfuselage radome.

Aries (Airborne Reconnaissance Integrated Electronic System) equipment, introduced on the **EP-3E Aries**, transformed the Elint Orions. Instead of relying on systems designed for shipborne use, the EP-3E Aries used new sensors which were linked together via a central processor. In addition, they were equipped with extensive electronic support measures and jamming equipment. Seven of the 10 EP-3Es were modified to this configuration from 1978, being further updated from 1985.

SPECIFICATION

Lockheed EP-3E Aries
Type: Elint and Sigint platform
Powerplant: four Allison T56-A-14 turboprops, each rated at 3661 ekW (4,910 ehp)
Performance: maximum level speed 703 km/h (437 mph) at 4575 m (15,000 ft); operational radius

4076 km (2,533 miles)
Weights: empty about 27,890 kg (61,491 lb); maximum take-off about 64,410 kg (142,000 lb)
Dimensions: wing span 30.37 m (99 ft 8 in); length 35.61 m (116 ft 10 in); height 10.27 m (33 ft 8½ in); wing area 120.77 m² (1,300 sq ft)

Perhaps the most successful P-3 Orion derivatives have been the EW/surveillance variants, known primarily as **EP-3** aircraft. The EP-3 developed out of 'black' operations flown by the CIA against Communist China during the mid-1960s. In 2003, the US Navy maintained 10 **EP-3E Aries II** aircraft, in two squadrons, VQ-1 at NAS Whidbey Island, Washington, and VQ-2 at NS Rota, Spain, providing real-time Elint and Sigint data.

MiG killing?

In 1963 the CIA began the modification of three P-3As for use in its 'black' operations. To enhance the 'black' Orion's survivability during these covert operations, several measures were undertaken to mask the aircraft's presence. The aircraft were painted black, while heat-dissipating exhaust shrouds were added, as were shortened propeller blades to reduce noise. Some flights even bore National Chinese markings in the event that the Orions were shot down over mainland China. A basic AIM-9 capability was added and, according to sources, was responsible for claiming one Chinese MiG.

The 'black' Orions operated nocturnal missions from bases in Taiwan until April 1967, after which reconnaissance operations were assumed by the new SR-71. In September of 1966, however, one of the CIA P-3s flew surveillance operations over Vietnam. The type was then selected to replace the Navy's EC-121 Elint aircraft. A test Orion was therefore modified with a large ventral radome in its bomb bay, and dorsal and ventral 'canoe' radomes containing a plethora of antennas; however, the **EP-3A** subsequently flew more test missions than it did operations.

The test EP-3A also served as proof-of-concept aircraft for the **EP-3B Bat Rack** electronic surveillance aircraft. Two full Bat Rack aircraft were produced, these serving in Vietnam and fully validating the Elint Orion concept.

Bat Rack to Aries

The successes of the Bat Rack aircraft led to the conversion of 10 additional P-3As to serve as a follow-on Elint aircraft, the **EP-3E Orion**. The two Bat Rack EP-3Bs were later upgraded to this standard, but retained the EP-3B designation as they were internally different than the EP-3Es.

CILOP Aries II

Due to their high rate of use, the EP-3E aircraft were starting to fatigue. As a result, in 1986 modification of 12 P-3Cs to EP-3E standard under a Conversion-in-Lieu-Of-Procurement (CILOP) programme began. Additional modifications under the **Aries II** programme improved connectivity between work stations and added SATCOM and GPS systems. Sparse funding soon began to complicate the situation, until the 1991 Gulf War proved the aircraft's worth; final deliveries were not made until 1997. Aries II updates have continued and include the Story series of communications upgrades, and the so-called J-Mod systems.

Although officially named 'World Watchers', VQ-1 has become known as 'Peter Rabbit' thanks to the 'PR' tailcodes worn by its aircraft. The surviving EP-3Es are severely overworked and small in number.

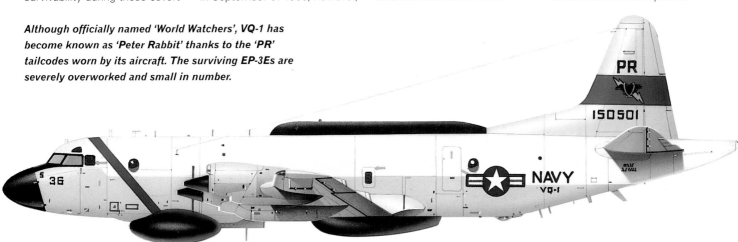

Beech RC-12 Battlefield Comint and Elint platforms

In the 1960s and 1970s, the US Army's battlefield electronic reconnaissance fleet was based on the Beech U-21, a Queen Air/King Air 90/100 hybrid. Under the generic **Guardrail** code name, a number of RU-21 variants was employed by MIBs (Military Intelligence Battalions), seeing service during the Vietnam War, and in support of US Army operations in Europe, Korea and Central America. Later the King Air 200's additional power and load-carrying ability led to it being adopted for the Elint mission. It gradually superseded the RU-21s, the last of which was retired in the mid-1990s. A succession of variants has been produced, all based on the King Air A200CT.

Early Guardrails

Despite their U-21 designation, three **RU-21J** aircraft were based on the King Air 200 airframe, becoming the first Super King Airs to be acquired by the US Army. They were modified for Comint duties with Guardrail equipment under the Cefly Lancer programme, and were active from 1973. They were 'de-modded' in 1979, but continued to serve on general transport duties. The designation **C-12L** was assigned in the mid-1980s.

Thirteen C-12Ds were converted to **RC-12D Improved Guardrail V** standard, the first being delivered in mid-1983. This was a Comint-gathering variant, and was allocated to the 1st and 2nd MIBs in West Germany. Five were also produced for Israel. Having been supplanted in Germany by the

Israel received at least five RC-12Ds and two RC-12Ks (as here) for battlefield recce.

RC-12K, the RC-12D fleet was dispersed, at least one being converted back to C-12D transport form. Others were retained by the 15th MIB for operations, and by various other units as trainers.

Crazy Horse

Under the codename **Crazy Horse**, three C-12Ds were converted in 1991 to a standard broadly equivalent to the RC-12D, but with additional equipment tailored to the LIC/OOTW (Low-Intensity Conflict/Operations Other than War) reconnaissance mission. Unlike other RC-12s, the Crazy Horse aircraft carry an operator in the cabin, to direct the aircraft's sensors towards the low-powered transmissions encountered in the task, or as a linguist. The trio was initially deployed with the MIB (Low Intensity) at Orlando, Florida, but subsequently moved to the 138th MICo. These **RC-12G** machines were used in the Caribbean/Central American theatre.

Common Sensor

Six aircraft were converted to **RC-12H Guardrail Common Sensor (System 3 Minus)** configuration, primarily for service with the 3rd MIB at Camp Humphreys in Korea. Outwardly similar to the RC-12D, the RC-12Hs carried additional Elint systems.

Known as **Guardrail Common Sensor (System 4)**, the **RC-12K** was the designated replacement for the RC-12D in Europe, and serves with the 1st MIB at Wiesbaden. A total of 11 was built, of which two went to Israel and one was retained for further conversion. The RC-12K added the Quick Look II Elint sensors (in miniaturized form) previously carried separately by the RV-1D Mohawk, allowing the aircraft to undertake both Comint and Elint missions. PT6A-67 engines rated at 820 kW (1,100 shp) allowed an increase in maximum take-off weight.

Known as **Guardrail Common Sensor (System 1)**, the **RC-12N** is based on the RC-12K (the first of 15 being a conversion of a K). The fleet was divided between the 224th MIB at Hunter AAF,

Georgia, and the 304th MIB at Fort Huachuca, Arizona.

The **RC-12P** designation covers nine **Guardrail Common Sensor (System 2)** aircraft converted from 1994 with generally similar systems to the RC-12N, but with smaller wing pods and other improvements, including improved datalink. The Ps were procured to replace the Hs in service with the 3rd MIB, Korea.

The latest variant is the **DASR (Direct Air Satellite Relay) RC-12Q**, of which three aircraft have been produced and fielded in the early 2000s. In addition to the standard Guardrail/Quick Look II antennas, the RC-12Q can act as a relay, cooperating with other RC-12s to extend their effective footprint.

SPECIFICATION	
Beech RC-12D	ceiling 9420 m (30,900 ft); range at
Type: battlefield Comint platform	maximum cruising speed 2935 km
Powerplant: two Pratt & Whitney	(1,1324 miles)
Canada PT6A-41 turboprops each	**Weights:** empty 3327 kg (7,334 lb)
rated at 634 kW (850 shp)	**Dimensions:** wing span 17.63 m
Performance: maximum level speed	(57 ft 10 in); length 13.34 m (43 ft
at 4265 m (14,000 ft) 481 km/h	9 in); height 4.57 m (15 ft)
(299 mph); maximum cruising	**Payload:** maximum more than
speed at 9145 m (30,000 ft)	1043 kg (2,300 lb)
438 km/h (272 mph); service	

The US Navy operates two RC-12Fs (illustrated) and two RC-12Ms. The aircraft were originally tasked with RANSAC (Range Surveillance Aircraft) duties, equipped with surface search radar under the belly. The RC-12Fs flew from Barking Sands in Hawaii, while the RC-12Ms served at Point Mugu, California; however, by late 2002 all four appeared to be flying on utility missions.

Gulfstream Aerospace Gulfstream Special missions versions

Gulfstream Aerospace, now owned by General Dynamics, produces a range of business jets, including the G400 (previously Gulfstream IV-SP) and G500 (previously Gulfstream V) long-range business jets. Both designs have sold well and attracted a number of military customers. The same is true of their immediate predecessors, the Gulfstream II and Gulfstream III – indeed, the latter has more military operators than all other aircraft in its class combined.

The most important military customer for Gulfstream has been the US government. There are currently 28 Gulfstreams in service with all five branches of the US armed forces – US Air Force Army, Navy, Marines and Coast Guard; the Gulfstream is the only fixed-wing aircraft to hold this distinction. The US has operated a mix of Gulfstream II, III, IV and V aircraft, chiefly on VIP and high-speed priority transport missions. The aircraft are grouped together under the **C-20** designation, although when the Gulfstream V was introduced into USAF service in 1998 it brought with it the **C-37A** designation.

Secret service

In US service, the most specialized and secretive Gulfstreams are the USAF's three **C-20C** aircraft which are understood to have a critical war readiness role, which has never been publicly revealed but which was a vital element of the United States' nuclear warfighting plans. In war, it would be the task of the C-20Cs to fly the heads of the US military chain of command – those with the authority to launch a nuclear counterstrike – to a place of safety, away from an enemy first strike. It is the C-20C's task to deliver these officials to one of the USAF's E-4B National Airborne Operations Center wartime command posts. Indeed, most government-owned Gulfstreams around the world are used for VIP and head-of-state transport tasks. However,

some aircraft have more specialized taskings. Denmark led the way in fielding a maritime patrol version of the Gulfstream III, when it acquired three modified GIII aircraft in 1982.

Special missions

Under its **SMA-3 (Special Missions Aircraft-3)** programme, Gulfstream developed the basic GIII, to be capable of carrying podded surveillance radar and air-droppable equipment. The GIIIs, operated by the Royal Danish Air Force, were able to perform long-range maritime patrol missions out as far as Greenland. They undertook fishery protection, medevac and remote-sensing missions in Arctic conditions, while still retaining a full VIP capability.

Along with the C-20Cs, the most secret Gulfstream IIIs were two examples delivered to the Indian air force, in 1986. Under a special 'black' programme, these aircraft were converted for border reconnaissance missions using a high-powered long-range camera system mounted inside the fuselage. The Indian GIIIs were fitted with large, optically-flat glass panels in their fuselages, covered by sliding doors, that allowed the cameras inside to 'see' up to 400 km (250 miles) into 'denied territory'. Few details are known about these aircraft.

Other publicity-shy Gulfstreams include the two highly modified Gulfstream IV-SPs operated by the Swedish air force, as Elint and reconnaissance platforms. The two GIVs, known by the local designation of **S.102B Korpen** (raven), replaced two Caravelles in this secretive role and are used by the Swedish authorities to gather radar and other electronic signals intelligence in the Baltic and Arctic regions.

Export operators

Gulfstream has over 30 years' experience in the special missions field (which began as far back as the TC-4 version of the Gulfstream I). With its latest

ultra-long range flagship design – the G550 (previously Gulfstream V-SP) – the capability of its aircraft has been increased to an unprecedented level. In 1998 Gulfstream, teamed with Lockheed Martin and Racal, was unsuccessful in winning the UK ASTOR requirement for a battle-field radar surveillance aircraft, based on the Gulfstream V airframe. However, Gulfstream's

expertise and experience mean that it has bounced back from this disappointment, with a radical new proposal based on the G550. Gulfstream's **RQ-37 BAMS (Broad Area Maritime Surveillance)** aircraft is a UAV based on the G550 airframe and designed to satisfy the US Navy's need for a new maritime surveillance platform to be in service by 2009.

Denmark's Esk 721 is retired the last of its three Gulfstream III Special Mission Aircraft (SMA) in 2003. The aircraft were used for maritime surveillance and VIP transport. The pod beneath the fuselage contains the EMISAR synthetic aperture radar, used chiefly for survey and earth science missions.

SPECIFICATION	
Gulfstream Aerospace Gulfstream SRA-4	1112 km (691 miles) for a 6-hour patrol with a 2811-kg (6,198-lb) mission payload
Type: multi-role special missions platform	**Weights:** manufacturer's empty 16,102 kg (35,500 lb); maximum take-off 33,203 kg (73,700 lb)
Powerplant: two Rolls-Royce Tay Mk 611-8 turbofans rated at 61.61 kN (13,850 lb st)	**Dimensions:** wing span 23.72 m (77 ft 10 in) over winglets; length 76.92 m (88 ft 4 in); height 7.57 m
Performance: maximum cruising speed at 9450 m (31,000 ft) 943 km/h (586 mph); maximum rate of climb at sea level 1219 m (4,000 ft) per minute, service ceiling 13,715 m (45,000 ft); operational radius typically	(24 ft 10 in); wing area 88.29 m² (950.39 sq ft)
	Payload: maximum payload 2811 kg (6,198 lb) including 272 kg (600 lb) of expendable stores

Sweden replaced its ageing SE.210 Caravelle (Tp 85) aircraft with two S.102B Korpens in the dedicated Sigint role. The first example, fitted with the removable ventral canoe fairing, is seen here during initial flight tests prior to delivery in 1995.

Civil Aircraft

From light private aircraft to the largest of airliners, the demand for civil aircraft continues to grow, despite high oil prices and other economic uncertainties. With Lockheed out of the civil airliner market and McDonnell Douglas absorbed by Boeing, the main sales battle of the last decade has been US-based Boeing versus Europe's Airbus. On annual sales figures, the two aerospace giants are now about even, but competition for new customers is fierce.

Meanwhile, Russian and Ukrainian aircraft manufacturers have been struggling to create products that either Eastern or Western airlines want in great numbers, and are facing increasing competition from the likes of Brazil's Embraer, who have slowly but steadily increased their range from small commuter turboprops to airliners to rival the 737 and the A320.

New civil markets include 'minijets' – small private jets for business and recreational use – but without the luxury and expense of the Learjet or the Gulfstream, and new forms of rotorcraft, such as tiltrotors. The supersonic business jet is still on the horizon, so those who once commuted by Concorde will have to wait before they again can have breakfast in London and lunch in New York.

A computer-generated image of the world's largest commercial airliner, the Airbus A380. The first model of the A380 carries 555 seats, with a mix of economy, business and first class passengers. Airlines can choose a single-class layout with as many as 800 seats.

Tupolev Tu-134 'Crusty' Tupolev's T-tail twin

Once the most important airliner in the Soviet Union, and to the airlines of its client states, Andrei N. Tupolev's Tu-134 remains in widespread service today. A distinctive shape, the 'Crusty' is identified by its pronounced T-tail, sharply swept wings, and main gear which folds back into wing fairings.

The lineage of the Tu-34 can be traced back to the Tu-124 'Cookpot', the first turbofan short-haul transport in the world when it entered service on 2 October 1962. The Tu-124 was itself, in turn, a scaled-down Tu-104 'Camel' and the original Tu-104 was simply a re-fuselaged derivative of the Tu-16 'Badger' bomber.

Although it was an excellent short-haul jet, the Tu-124 was not particularly efficient, with an outdated layout inherited from the Tu-104, dictating a high structure weight and reduced engine efficiency. The Tu-134 (initially designated Tu-124A) design aimed to iron out the deficiencies of the 'Cookpot'.

By adopting a T-tail configuration, the Tu-124A overcame most of the problems which afflicted its predecessor, and funding for OKB's 'Cookpot' derivative was cleared by the GVF (civil air fleet) as the Tu-124 was entering Aeroflot service in 1962.

The Tu-124A would be of modern design, in the same class as the Tu-104, but retaining nothing from the design of the original Tu-88/Tu-16 'Badger' medium bomber.

The prototype Tu-124A made its maiden flight on 29 July 1963. After the unveiling of the aircraft on its 100th test flight

In early Aeroflot service, the Tu-134 was principally employed on domestic routes, with limited international services to Europe and the Far East. Today's Aeroflot fleet includes 13 examples.

on 29 September 1964, the airliner's designation was changed to Tu-134. By this date, a number of other development aircraft had flown, although only slow progress was being made, and the airliner suffered the protracted development which was common to post-war Soviet transports. Too readily written off as a sign of mismanagement and technical shortfall, the prolonged development and pre-service regime typical of new Soviet aircraft was, in reality, a reflection of the rigorous nature of the aircraft development process under the centralized economy of the Soviet Union.

A large number of production-standard aircraft had been completed before the Tu-134 (which had by now received the uncomplimentary ASCC code name 'Crusty') began scheduled passenger flights with Aeroflot in September 1967, when the airliner began servicing the Moscow–Stockholm route. It was subsequently to become the most familiar airliner in the Eastern Bloc.

New look

Major parts of the fuselage and wing of the production Tu-134 appeared to be similar to those of the Tu-124. The engines of the

Left: Characteristic features of the Tu-134 (and a trademark of post-war Tupolev designs) are the main undercarriage bogies, 'somersaulting' to lie horizontal within the wing nacelles.

*Below: The Tu-134 was the first Soviet jetliner to be delivered to several foreign airlines, initially comprising **LOT**, Czechoslovak **CSA** (pictured), Interflug, Malev, Balkan and Aviogenex.*

Tu-124, which had been retained by the Tu-124A prototypes, had been replaced on the production Tu-134 with the new Soloviev D-30 and were now rear-fuselage mounted. The wing centresection was cleaned up in comparison to that of the Tu-124. The flaps' efficiency was also increased.

Wingspan was increased in comparison with that of the Tu-124, and the ailerons were divided into two parts. As on the Tu-124, all the undercarriage units retracted to the rear, the characteristic fairings aft of the wings being longer and more pointed. The addition of powerful anti-skid brakes rendered a tail parachute unnecessary.

Fuselage alterations

The change in engine installation required alteration to the rear fuselage, with a considerably larger tail, and the tailplane mounted on top of the fin with a pointed fairing over the junction. As in the Tu-124 'Cookpot', the tailplane was driven by an electric screwjack for trimming purposes. All flight controls were manual, with geared tabs. Spoilers for lift dumping and augmented roll control were increased in power, and the powered air-brake under the fuselage was retained from the Tu-124 in order to steepen the approach. De-icing remained

Following bankruptcy in 1996, Almaty-based Air Kazakhstan's fleet included eight Tu-134A/A-3s, alongside An-24s, Tu-154s, Il-76TDs, Il-86s and two Boeing 737-200s. Tupolev switched Tu-134 production to the 76-seat Tu-134A model in 1970.

unaltered, with electrothermal tailplane strips and engine-bled hot air for the wings, fin and engine inlets.

The fuselage length of the Tu-124A/Tu-134 was only 1.60 m (5 ft 3 in) longer than that of the Tu-124, but the capacity was increased by more than 50 per cent. A major improvement over the Tu-124 was that the main spar box no longer projected into the cabin, allowing a level floor with all seats and windows at the same level. From the start, the cabin was provided with capacity for 64 passengers: 16 first-class at the front of the cabin, 20 tourist-class in the main cabin and 28 tourist-class in the rear cabin. Cabin noise and vibration were significantly reduced compared to earlier jet airliners. The aircraft's crew comprised two pilots, a navigator in a glazed nose and

one steward. Baggage and cargo were stored behind the flight deck and at the extreme rear of the fuselage.

Service delays

A total of five pre-production aircraft flew, introducing the new D-30 powerplant. A take-off rating of 66.7 kN (14,990 lb thrust) allowed higher operating weights and production aircraft soon followed the Tu-124 from the production line. Most Aeroflot aircraft lacked first-class seating, and, as a result, the passenger seating was increased to 72 in total, with 44 seats in the front cabin and 28 in the unchanged rear cabin.

Despite flight testing being relatively problem-free, the Tu-134 did not actually enter service until 1967. By this time, various modifications had been incorporated into the production

Tu-134, including the introduction of inverters to supply most of the main electrical power loads as AC (alternating current). By 1969, the Tu-134 was carrying English Electric CSDs (constant-speed drives), giving unparalleled AC supplies. Another 1969 upgrade provided the Tu-134 with twin-clamshell thrust-reverser doors, dramatically reducing landing distances. A year later, a new rear fuselage APU system was installed, providing enhanced electric power for engine starting and cabin air-conditioning.

Following a 1999 International Civil Aviation Organization ruling, Russia grounded all aircraft not fitted with Kopsas-Sarsat emergency radio beacons on 1 July 2005. Most of the aircraft affected by this ruling are Tu-134s and Tu-154s. The status of the country's sizeable fleets of these particular aircraft was therefore difficult to assess at the time of writing.

Left: Formed in 1968 as Genex Airlines, Aviogenex was the air transport division of the Yugoslav General Export organisation, flying passenger charter flights around Europe and the Mediterranean. Four Tu-134A-3s served from 1971–90.

Right: Founded in Moscow in 1997, Skyfield Airlines Limited operated a fleet comprising a single Tu-134A-3 and one Tu-134B-3 (pictured), for executive charter flights.

Tu-134 evolution

The Tu-134 was widely used by East German agencies, and the national airline, Interflug, had 18 examples at its peak. The DDR's government was another major operator, with up to 14 Tu-134s on strength.

Above: This Tu-134A-3 was the personal aircraft of the Soviet commander of the Western Group of Forces in Germany, but was also used for other VIP flights.

Despite entering service 35 years ago, the Tu-134 remains at work with a number of airlines. The break-up of the Soviet Union means that this affordable aircraft assisted in the creation of dozens of new companies.

By 1970, production at Kharkov had switched to the Tu-134A. This had first flown prior to 1970, and it introduced a fuselage lengthened (mainly ahead of the wing) by 2.10 m (6 ft 10 in), overall length going up from 34.35 m (112 ft 6 in) to 37.10 m (122 ft). It retained the 28-seat rear cabin, but made possible various front cabins seating up to 80 in all or, exceptionally, up to 84. Seating throughout remained 2+2 so that, with 84 passengers,

21 rows were needed. The longer fuselage also increased cargo/baggage space by 2 m³ (71 cu ft). In addition, the D-30 Series III (or D-32 engine) had an extra zero-stage on the LP compressor, enabling existing ratings to be maintained with reduced turbine temperature, or under adverse (hot-and-high) conditions, and allowing maximum thrust to reach 70.24 kN (15,608 lb). The main wheels and brakes were also strengthened to handle the increased weights, maximum take-off weight having gone up from 98,104 lb (44500 kg) in the -134 to 103,600 lb (47000 kg) in the -134A. The most obvious external change was that the fin/tailplane bullet was extended

forwards as a long spike to form a VHF radio antenna.

Throughout the life of the Tu-134/-134A, the avionics fit was progressively increased, although it was always fairly basic. Arkhangelski once claimed that the type had the ability to make blind landings in ICAO Category III conditions, but this was certainly erroneous.

Customers

On the whole, the Tu-134 was certainly the best short-haul jet produced at that time in the Soviet Union. As early as 1968, export orders had been signed with Interflug of East Germany, Balkan Bulgarian, LOT of Poland, Malev of Hungary and Aviogenex of Yugoslavia. All these operators later also ordered the Tu-134A, Interflug

replacing the earlier type with 20 of the longer model. An additional customer for the -134A was CSA of Czechoslovakia, which bought 13.

Aeroflot might not have required any change, but in 1971 Aviogenex suggested that the retention of the glazed nose had become archaic, and that radar performance, and possibly aerodynamic drag, might be improved if the Tu-134A were to be redesigned in line with Western transports, with a scanner antenna of different shape looking ahead from the nose. The first two aircraft for this operator were already on the production line, but the changes were incorporated into the No. 3 aircraft. Subsequently, the more modern nose became an option on all aircraft, and it was adopted

This Tu-134A-3 was modified with underwing sensor pods as the Tu-134SKh (CX) for Agroprom (agriculture industry) use. It first flew in 1983 and could also be used for ice and pollution survey.

SPECIFICATION	
Tu-134A	**Service ceiling:** 12,000 m (39,400 ft)
Type: Short to medium-haul airliner	**Weights:** empty 29,000 kg
Powerplant: two 66.69-kN (15,000-lb-thrust) Soloviev D-30-II turbofans	(63,800 lb); maximum take-off 47,000 kg (103,400 lb)
Cruising speed: 900 km/h (558 mph)	**Dimensions:** span 29.00 m (95 ft 2 in); length 37.10 m (121 ft 8 in);
Climb rate: 888 m/min (2,914 fpm) at sea level	height 9.02 m (29 ft 7 in); wing area 127.30 m² (1,370 sq ft)
Range: 2000 km (1,240 miles) with 8215-kg (18,075-lb) payload or 3500 km (2,170 miles) with 4000-kg (8,800-lb) payload	**Accommodation:** 72 passengers, or 80 passengers with reduced baggage space

Several nations continue to use the Tu-134 for military purposes, the type being primarily operated in the transport and communications roles. The 'Crusty' pictured above was formerly operated by the East German air force.

Aeroflot still operates a small number of Tu-134s for short- and medium-haul routes around the Russian Federation. They are, however, slowly being replaced by more modern Western types.

immediately for CSA's complete fleet. Several other aircraft were retroactively modified. Even the last batch for Aeroflot was fitted with radar in the nose.

The last batches were of two sub-variants, incorporating further minor improvements. The Tu-134B had a revised flight deck, with no navigator, but retaining an engineer at the side panel. The spoilers were also modified, so that the pilot could use them for Direct Lift Control (DLC).

Production of the Tu-134 family ended in around 1984. The total was at least 300, around 200 seeing service on Aeroflot's shorter (up to about 1609 km/1,000 miles) trunk-route sectors for many years. Roughly 100 were exported, including 56 to major airlines in Europe.

Tu-134 today
Stringent noise and pollution controls mean that the ageing Tupolev aircraft are no longer allowed into major European airports such as Charles de Gaulle and Heathrow.

However, in East Europe and in the Russian Federation, the Tu-134 still plays a major part in the transport industry. The type was a popular choice for the many up-and-coming airlines that formed in the former Soviet states, and small companies such as Alania, Aviaekpress-kruiz, Perm Airlines, SAAK and Volga Aviaexpress ordered small numbers of the cheap, plentiful and relatively efficient Tu-134. Some of the bigger companies, such as Aeroflot, Russia State Transport Company and Tyumen Airlines, operated larger numbers, but began replacing the type with more modern aircraft.

Tu-134s also appeared in the livery of several other airlines outside the former Soviet Bloc, but in summer 2005 only Hemus Air of Bulgaria and Syrianair retained the type.

Tu-134A-3 'Crusty'

Formed in 1968, Aviogenex flew passenger charter flights in Europe and the Mediterranean, in association with Yugotours. The airline operated four Tu-134A-3s alongside a small fleet of American-built aircraft.

Avionics
The original -134 fit included R03-1 weather radar under the nose, the NAS-1A6 navigation system, based mainly on Doppler, and BSU-3P ILS steering when coupled via the AP-6EM-3P autopilot. The latter was replaced in the -134A by the Course MP-1 navigation and landing system, with several Sperry items, including the SP-50 autopilot, VOR and ILS (later duplicated). The radar was changed for the ROZ-1, and the Doppler for the DISS-013.

Seating
The Tu-134A-3 was fitted with lightweight seats of a less bulky shape, enabling 23 rows to be accommodated in an all-tourist layout, seating a total of 96. This gave a seat-mile cost which was 50 per cent lower than that of the original version.

Titles
Each of Aviogenex's Tu-134A-3s was named after a Yugoslavian town: this aircraft was *Titograd*, the others being *Beograd*, *Zagreb* and *Skopje*. They were replaced between 1986 and 1990 by Boeing 737-200s.

Specifications
The Tu-134 has a wingspan of 29 m (95 ft 1¾ in) and a length of of 37.05 m (121 ft 6½ in). Its maximum take-off weight is 47,000 kg (103,600 lb).

Radome
The third aircraft delivered to Aviogenex differed from previous Tu-134s in having the original glazed nose and undernose radome replaced by a more conical nose radome. This subsequently became optional on both the Tu-134 and the Tu-134A.

Performance
With its two Soloviev D-30 Srs II turbofans, each rated at 66.7 kN (14,990 lb thrust), the Tu-134 had a maximum speed of 885 km/h (550 mph) and a range of 3020 km (1,876 miles).

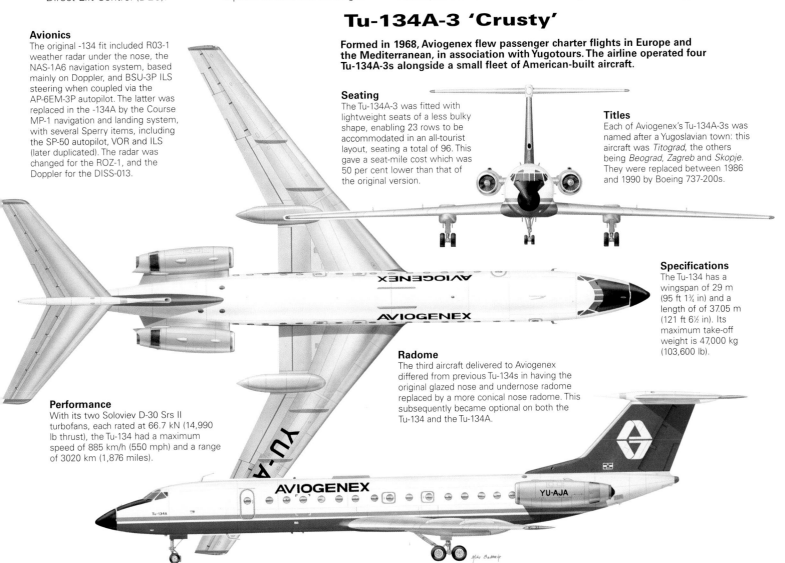

Tupolev Tu-154 'Careless' Second-generation Soviet jetliner

When Aeroflot came to replace its first-generation jets and turboprops on medium-range, medium-density routes, Tupolev was a natural choice, being the nation's most experienced builder of large jet aircraft. The resulting trijet design drew heavily on previous airliners, as well as introducing new features inherited from contemporary Western designs.

Tupolev's Tu-104, Tu-124 and Tu-134 provided the strong background of experience needed to tackle a challenging GVF (civil air fleet) requirement for a larger and much more powerful jetliner to replace the Tu-104 and turboprop-powered An-10 and Il-18. Passenger capacity had to exceed 120, and particularly difficult demands were that reduced payload sectors of up to 6000 km (3,725 miles) had to be flown, and that the new jets should be able to operate from airports with runways no longer than 2000 m (6,500 ft), with a surface of gravel or earth.

From the start there was never much doubt that the new aircraft would generally resemble an enlarged Tu-134, with three engines. The timing was perfect to adopt any good features from the British Trident and American Boeing 727. From the former it was decided to adopt triplexed (three independent) hydraulic systems. From the 727 came

two features never before attempted by the Tupolev bureau: leading-edge slats and triple-slotted flaps.

Like its predecessors, the Tu-154 was given a fuselage of circular cross-section. This was adequate for six-abreast seating and for the wing structure to be accommodated beneath the floor. It was eventually decided not to fit a rear airstairs door under the tail. Instead, two main doors were fitted on the port side, ahead of the wing, with service doors on the starboard side.

The sharply swept wing had a leading-edge sweep of 40 degrees outboard and an angle on the quarter-chord line of 35 degrees. Structurally, the wing had three spars, with the spaces between holding the integral tankage. The leading-edge slats were arranged in five sections and the hydraulically driven trailing-edge triple-slotted flaps in two sections, separated by the main landing gear. Also

Above: CCCP-85000 was the first Tu-154 prototype, which made its maiden flight on 4 October 1968.

Top: In total, 996 Tu-154s of all variants were delivered by Tupolev, many of which remain operational today. The aircraft remains the backbone of Aeroflot's fleet.

attached to the wing were airbrakes and spoilers for lower-speed control.

As in the Tu-134, a T-type tail was fitted, but with sweep increased to 45 degrees on the leading edges. Triplexed power units drove not only the elevators, but also the tailplane, which thus became the primary control surface. Hot high-pressure bled air was piped to de-ice the leading edges of the

wings and tail, and the centre engine inlet. The slats were electrically heated.

To meet the severe field-length requirement, considerable engine power was necessary, so that, although gross weight and seating capacity were lower than for the 727-200, the engine chosen was much bigger and more powerful than its US counterpart. The engine selected was the NK-8-2, a slightly less

In a bare metal finish, this Tu-154 was used for test and evaluation flights. The aircraft was one of the nine pre-production prototype Tu-154s.

SPECIFICATION

Tupolev Tu-154
Type: medium-range airliner
Powerplant: three 93.2kN (20,950lb thrust) Kuznetsov NK-82 turbofans
Cruising speed: 975 km/h (606 mph)
Range: 3460km (2150 miles) with maximum payload and reserves; 5280km (3280 miles) with maximum fuel and 13,650-kg (31,100-lb) payload
Service ceiling: 12,100 m (3688 ft)

Weights: operating empty 43,500 kg (95,900 lb), maximum take-off 90,000 kg (198,415 lb)
Dimensions: wing span 37.55 m (123 ft 3in); length 47.90 m (157 ft 2 in); height 11.40 m (37 ft 5 in); wing area 201.5m² (2168.4 sq ft)
Accommodation: flight crew of three or four; 158–164 passengers in a typical single-class layout, or 167 passengers in a high-density layout

In 1973 Egyptair became the third export customer when it received eight Tu-154As. The loss of one aircraft in a training accident, however, plus the unwillingness of Tupolev to install non-standard interiors, resulted in the aircraft being returned in 1975.

powerful version of the turbofan which had already been developed by Kuznetsov for the four-engined Il-62. The engines were grouped at the tail with the outer engines toed inwards and fitted with cascade-type thrust reversers.

To meet the severe demand for operations from unpaved runways, the main landing gears were designed as six-wheel bogies. Each unit was designed to retract hydraulically to the rear, the bogie somersaulting so that it could lie inverted in the fairing projecting aft of

the trailing edge. As in earlier Tupolev jetliners, the twin-wheel steerable nose gear retracted to the rear also.

The first of six development aircraft, CCCP-85000, was flown by test pilot N. Goryanov on 4 October 1968. CCCP-85006 was fully furnished and used for press flights in August 1970. Aeroflot (cargo-only) services began in late 1970. Irregular passenger services were flown to Tbilisi from July 1971, scheduled services began to Mineralnye Vody via Simferopol on 9 February 1972 and the first

international service was to Prague on 1 August 1972. Almost all early deliveries had 128 passenger seats, a few having a higher-density configuration for 146.

Later versions

From the outset strenuous efforts were made to clear the structure for a 30,000-hour crack-free life. Meanwhile, the designers had, by 1971, finished work on the Tu-154A, first delivered in April 1974 and in regular airline service from mid-1975. Almost indistinguishable from the Tu-154 externally, the -154A introduced the uprated

NK-8-2U engine, giving an improved maximum take-off weight. Oddly, most of this increase was taken up by an extra fuel tank in the centre section; the fuel in this tank could be transferred elsewhere only if the aircraft was on the ground. Thus, it was used merely to cut down purchases of fuel in foreign countries. Other improvements included uprated electrical systems, strengthened baggage holds with smoke detectors, passenger seats increased to 168 and an autolanding facility.

In 1977 production switched to the Tu-154B, which was quickly refined in 1980 to Tu-154B-2 standard. This variant again increased maximum take-off weight, and introduced two additional emergency exits in order to enable passenger accommodation to be raised to 180. The most important change in the B-2 was that the centre-section tank was made a normal part of the fuel system, usable in flight. Other changes included improved lateral-control spoilers and upgraded avionics, including French Thomson-CSF/SFIM autopilot and navigation equipment and a new weather radar. A curious feature was the addition of small actuators which, in cross-wind landings, can pivot the front axle of each main landing gear to reduce tyre wear.

The Tu-154B/B-2 was exported to many countries with friendly relations with the Soviet Union.

Of the total of 62 Tu-154A/Bs which were exported, Tarom of Romania operated 12. Tarom's aircraft, which were delivered in 1976, were the more refined Tu-154B-2.

By 1991, a total of 612 Tu-154s of all variants had been delivered to Aeroflot.

Tu-154M & current operations

In the mid-1980s a new version of the Tu-154 entered service, fitted with new, more efficient engines. Designated Tu-154M, the aircraft sold widely to Soviet client states before the Cold War's end made more advanced Western designs available.

In 1982 the Tu-154C freighter was announced – as far as is known, this version consists entirely of conversions of As and Bs. The main differences include the provision of a large door (measuring 2.80 m x 1.90 m/ 110 in x 73½ in) in the left-hand side of the forward fuselage, the stripping-out of the passenger accommodation to give a clear interior with a volume of 72 m³ (2,542 cu ft), and the fitting of special cargo flooring, with ball mats inboard of the door and

roller tracks along the main hold. The Tu-154C's maximum cargo load, above and below the floor, is 20 tonnes (44,090 lb).

Tu-154M

A new Tupolev airliner was announced in the early 1980s – the Tu-164 – but this designation was subsequently changed to Tu-154M. By this time, 600 of the earlier Tu-154 versions had been ordered, of which more than 500 had been delivered to Aeroflot. Thus it may seem to have been a little late to carry out a major update of the -154, especially as the Tupolev bureau was already thinking about a new airliner in this class, which materialized as the Tu-204.

Be that as it may, a total revision of the entire aircraft

Above: Nicaraguan airline Aeronica received its only Tu-154M in December 1989. It operated for three years before it was grounded due to financial problems and difficulties in obtaining spares.

Above top: China is the Tu-154M's most successful export market. In excess of 45 have been acquired by Chinese airlines, including this example seen in Civil Aviation Administration of China (CAAC) service before its transfer to China Xinjiang Airlines in 1991.

was requested, and, although there are obvious external similarities – apart from the bigger, forward-pointing fairing ahead of the tailplane – it is not possible to convert any earlier version to -154M standard.

The most important change is a switch to the Soloviev D-30KU-154-II engine, a newer and more efficient turbofan than the NK-8. Although its take-off rating of 105.21 kN (23,380 lb thrust) is only slightly greater,

Right: Between 1984 and 1989, Balkan received eight Tu-154Ms to supplement its fleet of Tu-154Bs and B-2s. The aircraft remained in service despite the airline's acquisition of more modern Western types such as the Boeing 737-500 and 767-200ER.

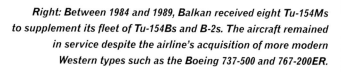

Left: Large numbers of Tu-154s served with the Soviet Union's national carrier Aeroflot throughout the 1980s and into the 1990s. This Tu-154B was delivered in 1977 and is seen in special markings celebrating the hosting of the Olympic Games in 1980.

Left: The German Democratic Republic ordered two Tu-154Ms for VIP duties with the state airline Interflug, which were delivered in 1989. With the re-unification of Germany in 1990, the aircraft were passed on to the Luftwaffe.

Below left: Military operators of the Tu-154 have included the Czech Republic, North Korea, Poland and Russia. The Czech air force has two Tu-154s in service, with a further machine in storage.

its mass flow is significantly increased, necessitating enlarged inlets. The centre engine has a plain, instead of a scalloped-shaped nozzle, and the side engines have totally new pods, arranged almost axially and fitted with clamshell reversers. The gas-turbine APU, previously above the centre engine, has been moved to the centre fuselage. The slats have been made smaller yet more efficient, and the outboard spoilers have been considerably enlarged, from three sections on each side to four. As noted, the only obvious change is that the spike fairing projecting ahead of the tailplane is slightly modified; what is less apparent is that the entire horizontal tail has been redesigned. The span remains unchanged at 13.40 m (43 ft 11½ in), but the surface has been cleaned up and increased in area from 40.55 m² (436.50 sq ft) to 42.20 m² (454.24 sq ft).

What is certainly remarkable is that, over the years, the basic operating weight (the weight of the equipped empty aircraft) has risen from 49,500 kg (109,127 lb) in the Tu-154 to 50,775 kg (111,938 lb) in the B and to 55,300 kg (121,914 lb) in the M version. This largely cancels out the payload/range improvements gained by the extra fuel and newer engines. The maximum

take-off weight of the M is 100 tonnes (220,459 lb) yet, while the original Tu-154 could carry a payload of 6700 kg (14,770 lb) with full reserves for a distance of 6900 km (4,287 miles), today's -154M can carry a payload of just 5450 kg (12,015 lb) for 6600 km (4,100 miles).

The Tu-154M was preceded by a Tu-154B-2, which was returned to Kuibyshyev and fitted with the D-30 engines. It began its flight test programme in 1982. Aeroflot took delivery of the first two production Tu-154Ms on 27 December 1984.

A single Tu-154 was modified to evaluate L/H$_2$ (liquid hydrogen)

as a fuel, with the designation Tu-155. The possibility of an eventual shortage of fossil petroleum could make L/H$_2$ very important, but it suffers from two major drawbacks. One is that its low density means that, for equivalent heat energy, the tankage has to be much bigger (though the fuel is lighter). The other disadvantage is that L/H$_2$ boils at –253°C (–423°F), so that it has to be stored at this intensely cold temperature, causing numerous problems. The test aircraft's centre engine was replaced by a modified type, designated NK-88. This was fed from a carefully lagged

tank, filling the rear of the cabin via a pipe in an insulated duct running along the right-hand side of the rear fuselage. Flight-testing began on 15 April 1988, and it was then expected that the test engine would later also be run on LNG (liquified natural gas).

Versions of the Tu-154M which appeared in the 1990s included the Tu-154-100 with new Aviacor interior furnishings, Tu-154M-LK-1 (two VIP aircraft for head-of-state use) and Tu-154M/OS with side-looking synthetic aperture radar for Open Skies Treaty observation flights. Production in 2005 has slowed to a trickle and some new-build aircraft have been placed into storage minus engines and other equipment. Various Tu-154 versions have been exported to the airlines of many countries aligned to the former Soviet Union, including Balkan, Cubana, Malev, Tarom, LOT, CSA, Syrianair, CAAC and Aeronica of Nicaragua. Among the latest operators were the Iranian carriers Iran Air Tours, Kish Air, and Bon Air. The 1 July 2005 implementation of the 1999 ICAO ruling concerning emergency radio beacons seriously affects older Tu-154s.

AJT Air International (above) and imair (right) were among the short-lived Tu-154 operators that emerged in the immediate aftermath of the demise of the Soviet Union.

Boeing 707 Introduction

Although it was not the first jetliner in commercial service, nor the best performing or most cost-effective, the Boeing 707 was, nevertheless, the first aircraft to introduce the concept of jet air travel for the masses. It was built in large numbers and in several different variants. Many remain in service.

Prior to the 1950s, the biggest contenders in the US airliner market were Douglas and Lockheed. Boeing, by contrast, remained largely a minor player, its Model 377 Stratocruiser, although technically advanced, selling only in modest numbers.

In 1954, the company rolled out a single prototype from its Renton assembly plant. Built as a private venture and at huge cost, this aircraft spawned two distinct families, the 717/C-135 military tankers/transports, and the commercial 707 airliner which became the jetliner of choice throughout the 1960s. During the development of the 707, Boeing had to fight arch rival Douglas, every step of the way; initially, it appeared that the DC-8 would find favour with the airlines.

Design flexibility

The fuselage of the prototype, known as the Model 367-80 (or Dash 80), had been criticized by the airlines as being too narrow. In order to outflank Douglas and satisfy the critics, Boeing completely redesigned the fuselage, making it both longer and wider, and able to seat as many as six passengers abreast, whereas the DC-8 could manage only four. This tactic worked, and demonstrated the enormous potential which existed in the basic 707 design. The aircraft entered service in 1958 and, at the time, caused quite a stir. The 707 was bigger, heavier and noisier than any airliner in service at the time and was able to carry many more passengers over greater distances than ever before. It had started a revolution in air travel and it was not long before other US manufacturers began developing their own jet airliners, eager to obtain a slice of the very lucrative market uncovered by the 707.

By 1965, Boeing had sold 430 707s, making it the most popular airliner since the pre-war Douglas DC-3, and still the orders for the aircraft kept coming in. As production continued apace, Boeing introduced improvements such as a taller tail and more powerful engines, plus an increasing number of sub-variants tailored to specific requirements. These included the intercontinental series 300 and 400, convertible/freighter variants, and the derivative 720, which was designed for high-capacity US domestic services.

Designed to introduce the world to the convenience of regular, high-speed, transcontinental jet travel, the 707 exhibited greater versatility than could ever have been expected. Aircraft were initially operated only by the major carriers, passing to smaller operators later in their careers. This Western Airlines 707 is typical; it was delivered on 13 May 1960, and later flew with Pan Am, Mandala Airlines and Egypt Air.

Far from perfect

Although it was proving tremendously popular with airlines, the 707 did have noticeable shortcomings. The Pratt & Whitney JT3 turbojets which powered early aircraft were noisy and required water injection for take-off, resulting in huge clouds of black smoke.

Early 707s were also not really capable of intercontinental flights, requiring pilots to fly the aircraft gingerly on long-distance services in order to conserve fuel. Furthermore, during the early days of 707 operations, stopovers on long-haul routes were mandatory and, compared to contemporary propliners, the

Boeing's privately funded Model 367-80 was built at huge risk to the company. This revolutionary aircraft spawned one of the greatest jetliner dynasties in the world.

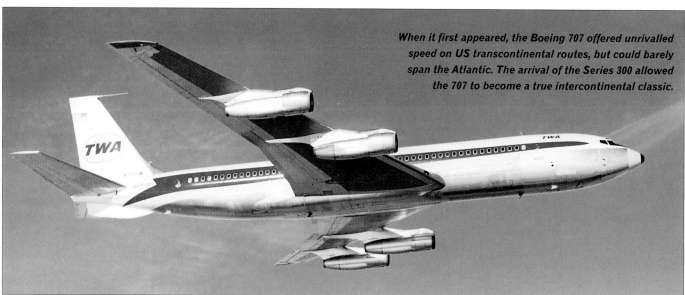

When it first appeared, the Boeing 707 offered unrivalled speed on US transcontinental routes, but could barely span the Atlantic. The arrival of the Series 300 allowed the 707 to become a true intercontinental classic.

SPECIFICATION	
Boeing 707-320C **Type:** four-engine long-range commercial transport **Powerplant:** four 84.52-kN (18,900-lb-thrust) Pratt & WHitney JT3D-7 turbofan engines **Cruising speed:** 885 km/h (549 mph) **Range:** 9262 km (5,742 miles) **Service ceiling:** 11,890 m (39,000 ft) **Weights:** operating empty 66,046 kg (146,093 lb); empty weight cargo version 64,002 kg (140,804 lb);	maximum take-off 151,318 kg (332,900 lb) **Dimensions:** wing span 44.42 m (145 ft 8 in); length 46.61 m (152 ft 10 in); height 12.93 m (42 ft 5 in); wing area 283.35 m² (3,049 sq ft) **Accommodation:** two pilots, flight engineer, flight attendants; seating for 147 (14 first-class, 133 coach) to 219 (high-density) passengers, plus 48.14 m³ (1,700 cu ft) of luggage; plus 2800 kg (6,160 lb of cargo)

Initially criticized for having too narrow a fuselage, the Boeing 707 was redesigned – Boeing took great trouble to ensure that the aircraft had the widest cabin available on the market. This early publicity shot shows a five-abreast layout, although a six-abreast arrangement was often specified.

aircraft was thirsty and required excessive runway lengths from which to operate. The 707 also proved to be less profitable than other jetliners and, initially, was expensive and difficult to maintain. In addition, the world's major airports had to embark on expensive projects to extend and strengthen their runways and improve facilities in order to accommodate the new Boeing jet. Although these drawbacks were quick to be exploited by traditionalists and propliner aficionados, the new airliner was welcomed with open arms by others, who foresaw a future of airline operations without government subsidies, and a proliferation of routes.

Boeing supreme

Despite the flood of orders from airlines eager to acquire Boeing's latest, the competition had not been standing still. Besides Douglas, Convair had begun developing its own four-engined jet, the 880, and, in the United Kingdom, Vickers introduced the technically advanced VC10.

Both the 880 and the VC10, however, failed to find sufficient orders, but sales of the DC-8 remained strong and, in an attempt to attract orders from overseas, Boeing launched the 707-320, which offered true intercontinental range. BOAC, which was under political pressure to 'buy British', displayed much interest in the 707 and managed to win approval for an order by specifying that its machines were to use Rolls-Royce Conway engines. Orders from Lufthansa and Sabena soon followed and, by 1965, it was clear that the 707 was proving more popular than the DC-8, despite the fact that Douglas was introducing stretched variants of the latter.

Furthermore, with the 707 selling so well, Boeing began developing a family of new models, using many components already proven on the 707. The first of these new aircraft became the 727, and so began the familiar pattern for Boeing civil designations which continues to this very day.

In addition to the acquisition of 707s by an increasing number of new airlines, original customers such as Pan Am and TWA remained faithful, and placed further orders for series 300 aircraft.

Not only was the 707 the first mainstream commercial jet, but it also introduced a number of features which are airline 'benchmarks'. For example, in the 1950s, new aircraft were often used to transport first-class passengers, while older and slower types were used to carry the tourist class. The 707 was the first aircraft to accommodate two or three different classes of passengers on the same aircraft. Moreover, the passenger entry/exit doors on the 707 were located fore and aft on the port side of the fuselage, with the cargo deck hatches located to starboard – a feature standardized on subsequent Boeing jetliners.

Record production

By the dawn of the 1970s, early 707s had begun to find their way on to the used airliner market, as larger and more efficient types became available. Used examples were quickly snapped up by smaller airlines and often employed on holiday charter flights. Still more were converted into dedicated freighters – as which the majority of 707 survivors continue to serve today. By 1982, when the last civilian model 707 was delivered to the government of Morocco, a grand total of 916 examples had been delivered.

*Above: American Airlines was typical of the big **US** carriers in adopting the Boeing 707 for its New York to Los Angeles route, on 25 March 1959. It bought the aircraft in large numbers, operating it until 1983 when the last of the type were retired.*

*Left: Air Mauritius received this 707-400 from **BEA** Airtours, to which it had been handed down by **BOAC**. The -400 was an anglicized variant of the intercontinental 707-300. The aircraft featured Rolls-Royce Conway engines as part of the offset package agreed by **BOAC** and Boeing when the aircraft were ordered.*

707 Development

Following the initial Pan Am order for 20 aircraft, the next US airline to choose the 707 was American Airlines, which placed an order for 30 series -123Bs. This was later followed by an order for the -300F freighter variant.

One of the most influential aircraft in history, Boeing's Model 367-80 prototype not only spawned the huge C-135 tanker family, but also gave rise to the 707/720 airliner dynasty. Its design was also the basis of subsequent Boeing airliners.

Boeing was convinced that both the airlines and the US Air Force would buy jet transports, and that the same design could basically be used for both tankers and civil liners. But Boeing had to do it the hard way. It had to tighten its belt and produce a prototype with its own money at an estimated cost of no less than $15 million.

One essential ingredient was Pratt & Whitney's JT3 engine, the lightweight commercial version of the fuel-efficient J57 used in the B-52. The transport would use four JT3s, hung in pods below and ahead of the 35-degree swept wing. Gross weight was at 86,184 kg (190,000 lb) and, although the military model would have an interior configured

for cargo and fuel, the commercial passenger aircraft could seat 130. Able to fly at 966 km/h (600 mph), the jetliner promised to do three times the work of the military KC-97 or contemporary propliners.

707 emerges

Boeing's model number for the prototype was 367-80, although it was more popularly known as the Dash-80. When the Model 367-80 finally became a flyable aircraft, it was given the new designation Model 707. Boeing deliberately capitalized on this memorable sequence by naming its subsequent jet transports Models 717, 727 and so on, through to the Model 787. There

N70700 lifted off from Renton Field, south of Seattle, Washington, on 15 July 1954, to inaugurate a worldwide era of jet transportation. After many years flying as a research platform for Boeing, this historic aircraft was rebuilt in its original form.

was still nothing certain about the 707's development when it was rolled out on 15 May 1954. During early taxi tests six days later, the left main gear smashed its way up through the wing and left the prototype crippled on its left outer engine pod. It was not, therefore, until 15 July of that year that the aircraft flew for the first time.

By now, the USAF had told Boeing that it wanted a new-build

jet tanker. In October 1954 the first tanker order came through, for 29 aircraft, launching a large programme for the Model 717 (military KC-135 and C-135).

However, Boeing failed to win any orders of a major nature, losing to its great rival Douglas with its DC-8. To compete with this aircraft, Boeing undertook one of the costliest modifications possible: it changed the body cross-section. The 707 retained its figure-of-eight fuselage with smoothly faired sides, but the upper lobe was increased in width to 3.56 m (140 in), beating Douglas by 5.08 cm (2 in) and

Above left: Aviation history was made on 26 October 1958 when a PanAm Boeing 707-121 opened the 'Big Jet' era with a scheduled service from New York to Paris.

Left: Boeing produced five 707-220s with JT4A-3 turbojets in response to a request from Braniff for its South American services. These engines improved take-off performance at high altitude.

Equipped with a longer wing, the -320B was powered by four JT3D-3 turbofans. Northwest Airlines received its first aircraft in 1963; the aircraft became the backbone of its intercontinental service for many years.

Special-purpose military developments

The USAF Military Air Transport Service was quick to introduce the 707 into military service. Illustrated above is a 707-153, one of the first of many military examples, which was delivered on 4 May 1959 to the service as a VC-137A. It was equipped with a convertible interior able either to seat 22 VIPs or to serve as an airborne command post.

enabling a triple seat unit to be installed on each side of the aisle for up to 150 passengers. In addition, fuel capacity was increased and the first models offered were the Model 707-120 series and the special Model 707-138 which was 3 m (10 ft) shorter. The standard launch engine was the JT3C-6 rated at 60.02 kN (13,500-lb thrust) with water injection, and fitted with a large noise-suppressing nozzle.

The first airline customer was Pan American, which bought 20 Model 707-112s; the airline also signed for 25 Douglas DC-8s on the same day, so souring any accomplishment that Boeing might have felt. Following this, Douglas announced its develop-ment of a longer-ranged DC-8 equipped with the JT4A engine. Boeing responded by developing a larger, long-ranged model, the Model 707-320 Intercontinental.

BOAC, like PanAm, was interested in Boeing's bigger and longer-range model. This

Boeing converted one 707 to serve as a tanker test-bed. This example was equipped with a fuselage HDU, a Beech 1800 refuelling pod under the starboard wing and a Sargent-Fletcher pod under the port.

had a new high-efficiency, longer-span wing, a longer fuselage seating up to 189 passengers and much greater fuel capacity. The launch engine was the JT4A at the increased rating of 74.68 kN (16,800 lb thrust), but Rolls-Royce's Conway bypass turbojet fitted perfectly and offered greater power, lower installed weight and much better fuel consumption, and was selected by a small minority of airlines. The Intercontinental's considerably greater capability quickly made this the standard Model 707, while the original aircraft was developed into the Model 720.

The first production Model 707 was flown at Renton on 20 December 1957, but was

actually numbered as the second of the initial batch of 20 Model 707-121s for PanAm. FAA certification was awarded on 23 September 1958.

PanAm opened services between New York and Paris on 26 October 1958. On these routes, the range of the Model 707-121 was marginal. It had not been designed for the North Atlantic, and the flight crews had to learn the correct take-off procedures and how to obtain the maximum number of air-miles per pound of fuel.

Spurred by competition from the DC-8 and CV-880, Boeing embarked on a programme to build an even better jetliner. Pratt & Whitney met the competition of the Conway with a startling modification to the JT3C, which replaced the first three stages of the compressor with two stages of enormous blades called a 'fan' – it dubbed this the 'turbofan'. The new engine, known as the JT3D, offered better fuel economy and a considerable reduction in noise levels over the JT3C.

Before this engine was available, the big Model 707-320 Intercontinental flew as the sixteenth off the Renton line on 16 January 1959. The introduction

of the -320 into service was not without problems, however, the most significant of which concerned the aircraft's handling in adverse weather. Eventually, to overcome this, a taller fin was retrofitted to the type and was later introduced on all civilian and military 707 models.

The first model to have the JT3D fan engine was the Model 707-120B. Based on the Model 720, it first flew on 23 November 1959, with a revised lightweight airframe, along with aerodynamic improvements to the wing which allowed for a higher cruising speed.

The last of the major variants was the Model 707-320C. Boeing had already fitted the fan engine to the 707-320B, and with it came a host of aerodynamic improvements including longer-span curved wingtips giving reduced drag. The 707-320B entered service in June 1962 with PanAm, which, a year later, pioneered the use of the Model 707-320C, a mixed-traffic version able to carry a total of 202 passengers or 43,603 kg (96,126 lb) of cargo. This variant soon became the standard 707 and the orders kept rolling in for the revolutionary airliner.

Operational history

The innovative Boeing 707 was eagerly snapped up by a host of airlines and, within a few years, was operating out of airports worldwide. Years later, even with the advent of more economical types, the 707 is still being operated by several airlines.

Many might be surprised to learn that Boeing built only 725 commercial 707s, plus 154 720s. The total number of aircraft built does not, however, reflect the type's enormous importance. The pace of aeronautical development in the late 1950s and early 1960s was such that no aircraft could expect to remain in production for long before being superseded by new and more advanced types. This contrasts with today, when a jetliner will remain in production for decades with minor 'tweaks' to produce new versions of the same basic design. And, in its time, the 707's lead was unassailable. The primitive Russian jet airliners of the time were good, as long as only minimal profits were

required, and the VC10 was unmatched from short runways or in hot-and-high conditions, but it was assumed (wrongly, as it now transpires) that operating costs would be higher than those of the 707. Convair's 880 and 990 were plagued by a host of technical and industrial problems. But the Boeing 707 did not succeed only by default, as it competed directly with the DC-8, which was an excellent aircraft in every respect.

The launch customer for the commercial Boeing 707 (originally known as the Jet Stratoliner) was Pan Am, an airline which then amounted to America's 'flag-carrier'. This was thus a useful and high-profile order for Boeing.

N709PA was the third 707 delivered to Pan Am, which was instrumental in the continued development of the aircraft.

Series 100s were also purchased by American, Continental, TWA and Western. QANTAS ordered a shortened version for long-range use, with provision for a streamlined engine ferry pod under the port wingroot. Some basic 707-100s were delivered with the turbofan engines associated with the Model 720, and with that aircraft's increased-span tail, and Krüger flaps on the leading edge and wingroot. These aircraft were operated by American and TWA; QANTAS had similarly modified 'short' 707s.

Boeing's willingness to provide modified, specialized variants for customers paid off with Braniff, which received five 707-227s in 1959. These aircraft had uprated JT4A-3 engines (equivalent to the military J75) to allow improved hot-and-high performance.

Boeing also developed a dedicated long-range, trans-oceanic version, the 707-300 Intercontinental, although many operators were already using the basic 707-100 on transatlantic services. The 707-300 had a lengthened fuselage, a wing of

Right: Trans World Airlines put its first jet airliner, the Boeing 707, into service on domestic routes in March 1959 and retired the last in 1982. This short-fuselage -131B was delivered in March 1962 and was operated by TWA until April 1982, when it was traded back to Boeing.

Below: During the mid-1960s, Flying Tiger leased four -300Cs from Aer Lingus, El Al and Caledonian for short periods, using them as cargo aircraft in North America.

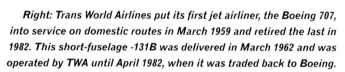

Continental Airlines was the third US domestic airline to order the -120 and some remained in service until 1976. Continental's -300Cs were ordered into MATS (Military Air Transport Services) service during the Vietnam War.

increased span and root-chord, an increased-span tail and JT4A-3 engines. The new variant had increased internal fuel capacity and could carry more passengers. Pan Am was the first customer for the 707-300, which became the most popular 707 model, although principally in the form of the improved -300B and -300C.

Further improvements and the fitting of JT3D turbofans resulted in the 707-300B, delivered to Aerolineas Argentinas, Air France, Air India, American, Avianca, El Al, Lufthansa, Malaysia, Northwest, Olympic, Pan Am, SAA, TAP and TWA.

The 707-300C was essentially a -300B with a cargo door in the port forward fuselage. Customers for the -300C included Aer Lingus, Air France, Air India, Airlift International, American, BOAC, Braniff, British Airways, British Caledonian, British Eagle,

Right: BOAC began to operate Conway-engined 707-400s from April 1960 and they initially flew the London to New York route. Later, they were used to develop new routes for the airline.

China Airlines, Continental, Egypt Air, El Al, Ethiopian, Executive Jet, Flying Tiger, Iranair, Iraqi, Kuwait, Lufthansa, MEA, Northwest, Olympic, Pan Am, PIA, QANTAS, SAA, Saudi, Seaboard World, TWA, Varig, Wardair and World Airways.

The final major service variant was the 707-400, with Conway turbofan engines. These were actually the first turbofan-engined 707s and proved very successful in service, although only 37 were built. The aircraft were delivered principally to BOAC, but others went to Cunard Eagle, Air India, Lufthansa, El Al and Varig.

When the original Model 367-80B prototype was finally retired to the National Air and

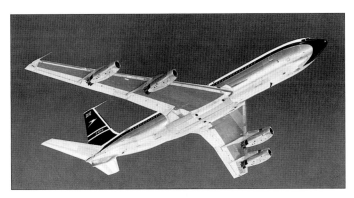

Space Museum in 1972, it was designated (by the Smithsonian) as one of the 12 most significant aircraft designs of all time. It was then still the jetliner produced in the largest numbers, and very large numbers remained in use as the flagships of some of the world's major airlines, although the age of the Jumbo was by then beginning to dawn. The 707's production total was finally overtaken (by the 727) in 1973.

The type remained in service with TWA and Pan Am until 1983, when a slow decline began. With tougher noise legislation coming into force in 1985, 707s operating in the United States had to be hush-kitted. Elsewhere, however, 707s retired by the major airlines were usually

eagerly snapped up by smaller operators. Large numbers of fan-engined passenger 707s were broken up in the 1980s, with engines and wide-span tailplanes being donated to the KC-135 re-engining programme.

End of the line

Boeing never modernized the 707 or 720 in the way that Douglas did with the DC-8 and, as a result, the aircraft is now a less common sight today than its old rival. The 707 is now used almost exclusively in the freight role, or as a corporate transport. There are around 80 707s still operational, mainly operated in ones and twos, many of them based in Africa and the Middle East. A handful in passenger/VIP configuration are in corporate or government use.

Some 707s were even hush-kitted as Comtran Q707s to meet Stage 2/Chapter 2 noise regulations. Time is now finally running out, however, for the 707, which fails to meet the most stringent Stage 3/Chapter 3 noise regulations, and which as a result of this is certain to disappear from service in the next few years.

With the downturn in airline fortunes following 9/11, and with large numbers of more modern and more economical airliners already sitting in desert 'boneyards' (available at bargain prices), the 707's survival so far looks little short of miraculous.

Originally a CIA 'front' organization, Southern Air Transport began operating 707s from 1985 and continued to do so until 1992, when the type was retired. This particular aircraft was later sold on to Air Afrique and crashed while landing in Mali in 1996.

Variants

The Boeing 707 established Boeing's dynasty as 'plane-maker to the world'. It shrugged off competition from Britain's Comet and the DC-8 to spawn a family of similar-looking but quite distinct variants over its 21-year production life.

Boeing Model 387-80 prototype ('Dash 80')

On 15 July 1954, the age of Boeing jetliners arrived when the Model 387-80 prototype first flew at Renton, Washington. Also known as the 'Dash 80', the Model 387-80 was aimed chiefly at the US Air Force's emerging requirement for a jet transport/air-to-air tanker. Structurally, it was very different to the civil Model 707, but it set the pattern for all that followed. Here it is illustrated flying engine test duties.

Boeing Model 707-100

The initial production version of the 707, the Pratt & Whitney JT3C turbojet-powered 707-100, was chiefly intended for the US domestic market and had only marginal transatlantic capability. It was wider and longer than the Model 387-80 and had a greater wingspan. The 707-100B introduced more fuel-efficient JT3D-1/3B turbofans, and some of the airframe refinements that were developed by Boeing for the Model 720. A total of 56 -100s and 78 -100Bs was delivered up to 1969, when production switched to the definitive 707-300.

Boeing Model 707-100 'Short Body'

Australia's QANTAS asked Boeing for a special version of the basic 707-100 to handle the extreme long-range requirements of its Sydney to London service. As a result, Boeing built seven short-fuselage 707-138s, which were 3.05 m (10 ft) shorter than the other 707-100s. The 707-138 was certified in June 1959. In 1961, the 707-138s built for QANTAS were replaced by six turbofan-powered 707-138Bs. The -138s all had the same maximum take-off weight as the standard -100s, but a reduced maximum landing weight.

Boeing Model 707-200

To provide improved take-off performance at high-altitude South American airports, Boeing produced just five examples of the JT4A-3 turbojet-powered 707 for Braniff Airways. 707-200s were dimensionally similar to the -100 series, but the new engines were rated at 70.28 kN (15,800 lb thrust).

Boeing Model 707-300

Designed for transoceanic flights, the 'Intercontinental' 707-300 was larger than its predecessors. The fuselage was stretched by 2.07 m (6 ft 8 in) to 44.37 m (145 ft 6 in), wingspan was increased by 3.53 m (11 ft 7 in) and fuel capacity was increased to 78,552 litres (21,200 US gallons). Basic -300s were powered by JT4A-11s and 69 were built.

Boeing Model 707-300C (all-freight)

When the -300C Combi version of the 707 was produced, a few customers, such as American Airlines, opted for a pure freighter ('707-300F') variant which had most of the cabin windows blanked out, all passenger seating facilities removed, and a large (231-cm x 340-cm/91-in x 134-in) cargo door inserted in the port fuselage side.

Boeing Model 707-300B

The 707-300B was based on the -300, but featured a longer wing, an increased maximum take-off weight (MTOW) and four 80.1-kN (18,000-lb-thrust) JT3D-3 turbofans. A total of 176 -300Bs was built, including a number of Advanced Series 300Bs (or -300BAs), which had three-segment leading-edge flaps. Some of these aircraft were built as 707-300BA-H ('Heavy') with a further increased MTOW.

Boeing Model 707-300C Combi

The 707-300C passenger/cargo convertible (Combi) variant of the -300B had a side-loading freight door in the forward fuselage with an associated Boeing-developed cargo loading system. A maximum of 215 passengers could be carried in the all-passenger configuration. A total of 337 -300Cs was built until 1979.

Boeing Model 707-700

This aircraft was used as a test-bed for the CFM56 turbofan developed by CFM International and SNECMA. The CFM56 was designed to have a much reduced fuel consumption and lower noise levels than any existing engine. It was planned that CFM56s would equip existing and new 707s, but the idea was later scrapped to avoid competing with the 757. However, CFM56s were used extensively on late-model military 707s, E-3s and E-6s and for the USAF's KC-135R programme.

Boeing Model 707-400

The 707-400 was very similar to the early 707-300 series, but was fitted with British Rolls-Royce Conway 508 turbojets, rated at 77.84 kN (17,500 lb thrust). Only 37 Conway-powered 707s were built, even though they proved to be more economical to operate than the rival US turbojets. By the time the 707-400 appeared in 1960, turbojets were being replaced by far more cost-effective turbofans. 707-400s were operated by BOAC, Air India, El Al, VARIG and Lufthansa.

Boeing 727 Seattle's trijet

This early Boeing 727-100 demonstrates the type's key features to good effect. The three rear-mounted engines are immediately obvious, but the aircraft also has its advanced leading-edge slats and flaps deflected.

Left: N7006U, a 727-122 (a designation often shortened to 727-22), was delivered to United Air Lines in November 1963. In a superb demonstration of the type's reliability and longevity, the aircraft remained with the airline until 1992, when it was sold and broken up for spares.

Taking significant components from its Model 707, Boeing combined them with a trijet layout and an advanced high-lift wing to produce a market-leading short-/medium-haul airliner.

Well before the introduction of its Model 720, Boeing was engaged in the preliminary design of a short-/medium-range and medium-capacity airliner to suit the growing needs of the US domestic and inter-city markets on routes unsuitable for the 720. The intention was to produce a high-performance utility jet transport with low approach speeds and short-field properties, combined with independence from ground support services. The market for such an aircraft was certainly there, but as always the go-ahead for production was dependent on securing orders.

In addition to the needs of the US domestic market, there was also an opening for high-performance, medium-range air transports abroad. And here, noted Boeing, the new de Havilland DH.121 Trident, with its unique trijet configuration, promised to be a keen and determined contender. By the late 1950s, the commercial aviation market was on the upsurge; the cry was for extra seating capacity on aircraft plying high-density routes in the United States and Europe. The old piston-engined DC-3, DC-6 and L-749, and the turboprop L-188 (although relatively new) were cheap to operate but too slow, while the Caravelle was too small.

Design of the Model 727, as the new type was designated,

started in February 1956, and the parameters laid before Boeing's preliminary design group were exacting. Other companies, notably de Havilland, were vying for high-cruise Mach numbers to reduce seat-air mile costs. Boeing wanted this factor on its Model 727, but combined with short-field characteristics that required a high power/weight ratio and a highly adaptable and efficient wing.

Wing technology

The 727 wing design broached new horizons, and its unique system of flaps and slats allied with spoilers also became the format for the 747. The basic 727 wing was actually of routine

design, but its high-lift and lift-dump devices most certainly were not. On the trailing edge of the wing, massive triple-slotted flaps were combined with four leading-edge slats on the outer two-thirds of the wing, and three Krüger leading-edge flaps on the inner portion. These were joined by seven spoilers on each upper wing surface which doubled as airbrakes and/or roll augmentation spoilers.

Taking shape

Allied to its excellent field performance, the 727 had lively performance and good fuel economy with the adoption of the 62.2-kN (14,000-lb st) Pratt

Air France's second 727-228 was delivered in 1968. In recent years, stringent noise regulations have forced the retirement of many 727s. However, hush-kitting extended the service lives of many, including this aircraft, which went on to fly with UPS.

Boeing's 727 test aircraft, including this 727-22, usually adopted house colours. Early on in the type's development this saw the application of the distinctive pale yellow (or cream) and brown scheme of the pioneering 'Dash-80'.

With the stretched 727-200, Boeing increased the 727's maximum passenger capacity to 189. Two fuselage plugs, each 3 m (10 ft) in length, were added to the 727-100 fuselage fore and aft of the wing to achieve the stretch.

& Whitney JT8D-1 turbofan in August 1960. The fuselage upper portion was identical to that of the Model 707/720 series. In addition, much stress was laid upon independence of operation: the Model 727 needed nothing on the ground if a stop-go transit were required, having a Garrett-AiResearch GTC85 APU, an airstair and a ventral staircase to the rear. With a very high maximum landing weight, as a result of wing stressing and landing gear strength, the 727 could take on fuel at the originating station, fly several transits, and gain quick turnarounds and the on-schedule departures that are so vitally important. All these facets were built in during the course of very thorough research and design.

Construction go-ahead was given in August 1960, with Boeing acting on the good faith of United Air Lines and Eastern Airlines. In fact, it was not until 5 December 1960 that these operators placed their orders: 20 aircraft for United, with

another 20 on option, and 40 aircraft for Eastern.

At 11.33 (local) on 9 February 1963 the first 727 flight was made from Renton, when Lew Wallick, Boeing's senior experimental test pilot, lifted N7001U off. N7001U weighed in at 58,968 kg (130,000 lb) and flew for 2 hours 1 minute, before Wallick put it down in 610 m (2,000 ft) on Paine Field's limited concrete. To the assembled press, Wallick said that, 'She behaved as expected, even better than expected in many respects.' Indeed, few problems cropped up during subsequent testing.

The second Model 727 (N72700) flew on 12 March, and by the end of the month four

SPECIFICATION	
Boeing 727-200	(99,370 lb); loaded 86,405 kg
Type: medium-range passenger or	(190,090 lb)
cargo airliner	**Dimensions:** wing span 32.92 m
Powerplant: three Pratt & Whitney	(108 ft); length 46.69 m (153 ft);
64.50-kN (14.500-lb-thrust) or	height 10.36 m (34 ft); wing area
77.38-kN (25,889-lb-thrust) JT8D-15	157.90 m² (1,699 sq ft)
turbofans	**Accommodation:** three crew plus
Cruising speed: 964 km/h (598 mph)	flight attendants; maximum
Range: 4400 km (2,278 miles)	189 single-class passengers;
Service ceiling: 10,000 m (33,000 ft)	typical load of 14 first-class and
Weights: emopty 45,168 kg	131 tourist-class

Model 727s were undergoing thorough flight trials from Paine, Seattle, Edwards AFB, Denver and Albuquerque. By mid-May N7001U had completed 430 hours on flutter and structural damping tests up to Mach 0.9; N72700 had completed 320 hours on systems and braking; 180 hours on 727 No. 3,

including handling high-*g* pull-ups, side-slipping and even barrel-rolls; while 313 hours had been completed in furnishing and air-conditioning on Model 727 No. 4. The order book was filling: 25 to American Air Lines, 40 to United, 10 to TWA, 12 to Lufthansa, and four to Australia's TAA and Ansett-ANA.

With increased capacity came the need to provide additional escape exits. The 727-200 (illustrated) therefore introduced a second emergency exit over each wing.

Success in service

Showing an economy of performance that exceeded the predictions of even Boeing's own engineers, the 727 dominated sales of medium-range airliners. Becoming the world's best-selling jet airliner (until overtaken by the Boeing 737), the 727 finally went out of production in 1984 after 1832 examples had been built.

When FAA certification for the production Model 727-100 was received in December 1963, Boeing had already launched an aggressive sales campaign to clinch export orders ahead of its main contemporary rival, the Hawker Siddeley Trident 1.

Production of the Boeing 727 was undertaken at Boeing's Renton facility near Seattle, Washington. Production peaked between 1967 and 1968, when 315 aircraft were delivered. After a lull in the early 1970s, deliveries again reached more than 100 per year during 1978–80.

Emphasizing the aircraft's excellent fuel consumption and superior performance from hot-and-high airfields, the 727 embarked on a world tour in September 1963. By the time the aircraft returned to the United States, domestic carrier Eastern Air Lines had placed a significant order, its services commencing in February 1964. Lufthansa's first 727-100 was rolled out in January 1964 and the first of its Europa-Jet

Most of Alaska Airlines' fleet of 23 Advanced Boeing 727-200s were delivered second-hand in 1980–89. The aircraft were replaced in service by the even more successful Boeing 737-400 in the early 1990s.

Inset: The initial sales success of the 727 in the early 1960s to domestic customers such as TWA (seen here), Eastern, United and American provided the platform for its outstanding sales performance over the following two decades.

scheduled services commenced on 16 April 1964.

The highly successful world tour began to bear fruit in 1964 with Japan Air Lines and

All Nippon's decision to order the aircraft for their domestic routes. Both airlines initially favoured the Trident, but required the higher-capacity

Right: Small numbers of 727s found their way into military and government service. The Royal New Zealand Air Force operated two 727-22QCs.

Below: Iberia was the last major European operator of the 727. Its fleet of Advanced 727-200s was replaced by the Airbus A319/320/321 and Boeing 757.

Trident 1F, which was not scheduled for certification until 1966. With both airlines intending to start services in April of that year, the alternative of ordering the 727, which would be ready for delivery in October 1965, became increasingly attractive. The balance was tipped in the 727's favour by its performance from Osaka's short runway. In temperatures exceeding 95°F (35°C), the Trident was unable to operate with an economic load, while the 727 was able to carry a full complement of passengers. In July 1964 JAL signed a deal for six Model 727-100s, and All Nippon soon followed suit.

By mid-1964, 727 orders were increasing, but were still 100 short of the aircraft's break-even mark. Therefore, to capitalize on an expanding air cargo market, Boeing introduced the 727-100C convertible cargo/passenger derivative in July 1964, able to carry 13,608-kg (30,000-lb) loads over a distance of 3058 km (1,900 miles). The aircraft was able to fly passengers by day

Although now rarely seen at European or Asian airports, the 727 remains in limited use with smaller operators in the United States. Champion Air currently operates the Model 727-200 Advanced on domestic routes.

and freight by night, something that was particularly attractive to US domestic customers. Northwest Orient signed as the first customer for the 727-100C, and 727 orders quickly surged past the 300 mark.

Many European and Far East airlines had now placed orders for the aircraft, and by April 1967 the 727 was the most widely used jet airliner in service. Later 727-100 versions included the 727-100QC with palletized passenger seats and galleys, and advanced cargo-loading technology, and the 727-100 Business Jet.

New variant

In November 1967 certification was granted to a stretched 727. Capable of carrying up to 189 passengers, the 727-200 became the standard model for the remainder of the production run, with more than 1000 being produced. Featuring JT8D-9s or uprated JT8D-11s or -15s, the 727-200 featured a 3.05-m (10-ft) fuselage extension and localized structural strengthening to cope with its higher weights.

Boeing's grip on the medium-haul market was strengthened

in the early 1970s with the introduction of the 727-200 Advanced which, with increased fuel capacity and weight, and extended range, continued the outstanding sales success into the early 1980s. In the late 1970s the availability of a new generation of efficient turbofans prompted Boeing to start designing a 727 replacement. By this time the aircraft had become the best-selling jet airliner of all time, establishing Boeing's position as the world's premier airliner manufacturer.

The last of 1832 Model 727s, a 727-200F freighter, was delivered to Federal Express in August 1984.

Boeing 737 Introduction

The 737 capitalized on design work done on the 707/727, retaining the same cabin cross-section. As shown here by the prototype, the original 737-100 model featured a short fuselage.

Boeing's superlative 737 is by far the world's best-selling airliner. Indeed, it seems unlikely ever to lose this title, as the most recent incarnations of the 1960s-vintage basic design utilize the very latest in airframe, avionics and engine design, to propel the 737 into the next century.

On Friday 19 February 1965, Boeing's international sales manager was biting his fingernails as he sat in an outer office at the headquarters of Lufthansa. He was hoping that the carrier would place an order that would launch a brand-new jetliner, the Model 737. Boeing was not yet committed to building it, but was already losing out to its competitors in the important short-/medium-range airliner market, and knew that it must go ahead with the programme if its own airliner business was to survive.

Many of the major airlines had already bought small twinjets, although Eastern, United and Lufthansa had yet to choose their aircraft. Boeing needed all three airlines to order 737s before it could invest in the type. It was therefore the worst possible news when Boeing's chief executive announced that Eastern was buying the McDonnell Douglas DC-9.

Pressing on regardless

In spite of Eastern Airlines' decision, Boeing decided to continue with development of the 737. It was launching the aircraft with an order for just 21 machines from a foreign airline!

However, despite its verbal promise to Lufthansa, Boeing did not commit itself to the 737 on the strength of that single order. Instead, it strove to present the best possible case to United, trying to overcome the late arrival of the first 737s by offering large numbers of 727s on almost giveaway lease terms to bridge the gap.

Boeing went through a second nail-biting day on 5 April 1965. United held a board meeting, after which the airline gave a press conference. It was going along with Boeing's big 727 deal and, on top of that, was buying 40 of the new 737s, as well as signing options for another 30 aircraft.

The 737 was to be in the 100-seat class, which saved weight compared to its rivals – the rear-engined DC-9, Caravelle and BAC One-Eleven – by putting the engines under the wings. Boeing saved money and attempted to keep the unit cost down by using the same cabin cross-section as on the 707 and 727. From that instant, Boeing worked flat out on the small twinjet. Even coming from behind, Boeing hoped that the aircraft's qualities would

eventually bring about enough orders for the programme to show a profit. Certainly, nobody ever expected the 737 to become the best-selling airliner in history, with total sales exceeding 5750 examples and continuing to rise.

As far as possible, Boeing made use of parts and experience from previous programmes, especially that of the 727. The fuselage, including the nose and cockpit, was almost identical, although it was much shorter and had a totally different tail section.

United, in fact, had ordered a slightly longer aircraft than Lufthansa, and Boeing designated this as the 737-200. The 737-200's cabin was normally configured to seat 115 passengers in triple seats on each side of the cabin's central aisle. Lufthansa's Dash-100 seated 103.

Inauspicious start

Although the new product obviously had many good features, its early history was not auspicious. From the first flight, on 9 April 1967, measured drag was significantly higher

As the 737's popularity grew, it found purchasers all over the world. Sales were initially slow, but the brilliance of the design inevitably won through.

SPECIFICATION	
Boeing 737-400	**Weights:** empty 33,434 kg
Type: short-/medium-range	(73,709 lb); loaded 62,822 kg
transport	(138,499 lb)
Powerplant: two 97.86-kN (22,000-lb-thrust) CFM International	**Dimensions:** wing span 28,88 m (28 ft 7 in); length 36.45 m (119 ft
CFM56-3C turbofan engines	7 in); height 11.13 m (36 ft 6 in);
Cruising speed: 900 km/h (559 mph)	wing area 105.40 m² (1,135 sq ft)
Range: 5000 km (3,107 miles)	**Accommodation:** typically,
Service ceiling: 6890 m (22,600 ft)	146 passengers in two classes

All three members of the 737-300/-400/-500 family fly in formation. The -400 (top) is the largest of the three, while the -300 (lower) and -500 (leading) have smaller capacities.

than predicted. This was the opposite of what had happened with the 727, and it hurt both Boeing's pride and the 737's image. The cures, which took months, included a new nacelle/wing fairing and vortex generators on the rear fuselage. It was also found that the engine thrust reversers were not very effective, and the solution here was to extend the jetpipes well aft of the wing, and use target buckets hinged straight up and down.

Not least of the problems was the Air Line Pilots' Association's (ALPA) totally negative ruling that the 737 must have a three-man crew, adding 50 per cent to crew costs by comparison with the rival McDonnell Douglas DC-9. Eventually, ALPA let sense prevail, but not until it had lost Boeing several potential sales.

Advanced 737

United's 737-200 immediately became the standard aircraft. Apart from those ordered by Lufthansa, only seven more 737-100s were sold. The 737-200 gradually began to pick up a number of small orders, although the process was a slow one, and five years had elapsed before the superiority of the Boeing product had been realized and had allowed Boeing to start matching the DC-9 on equal terms. This gradual penetration into the marketplace was aided by the introduction of 737-200C convertible passenger/cargo and 737-200QC quick-change convertible models. In addition, a 'gravel kit' was offered, allowing operations from semi-prepared runways.

The major change, however, came with the 737-200 Advanced. The new machine featured a remarkable 81 per cent increase in fuel capacity, largely thanks to the higher take-off weights made possible by the increased power of its uprated JT8D turbofans.

Weight-saving graphite composite control surfaces were also installed, along with a new interior, offering seating for 130 passengers, while improved flaps and brakes meant that the aircraft was able to use smaller airports. With the arrival of the Advanced 737, Boeing began to win almost every competition with the DC-9.

The 737 was beginning to suffer, however, from having outdated engines. This became particularly apparent when Boeing produced an even longer-ranged High Gross Weight version. It was clear that major changes had to be made.

CFM56 power

Boeing looked to the next-generation CFM International CFM56 turbofan, mounted in a new nacelle held ahead of the wing. The new engine offered not only increased thrust, but also improved fuel economy, enabling Boeing to produce the even more successful 737-300/-400/-500 family. Responsible for 1,936 737 sales, this series has now made way for the next-generation 737-600/-700/-800/-900, which seem set to extend the stunning and sustained success of the Boeing 737 well into the twenty-first century.

A key feature of the Next Generation 737 is its all-glass cockpit. Modern avionics improve economy and safety.

Below: With the first-generation 737 Higher Gross Weight version and the 737-400 (illustrated), Boeing moved its short-ranged 737 into the medium-haul sector.

737 Development Building the 'baby'

Boeing was a late-comer to the small medium-range jet airliner market and the success of its first design, the 737, was once far from assured. Despite its initial troubles, however, the 737 went on to be a huge success.

Studies of what would today be termed a 'regional airliner' had begun at Boeing in 1962, but it was not until November 1964 that the 737 emerged as a firm project. At that time, Boeing designers had conceived an aircraft approximately 25.90 m (85 ft) in length, with a wingspan of 22.86 m (75 ft). Versions of the JT8D engine were slated to power the new aircraft, which would have a maximum take-of weight of 35,834 kg (79,000 lb). Adopting a low-winged design with underwing engines allowed the airframe to be lighter, but crucially also permitted many common parts and structures to be incorporated from the Model 727 production line.

The 737 had its engines fitted snugly against the wings, not in pods on pylons as on the 707 and the 747. This allowed the aircraft to be even lighter and also kept the cabin floor as close to the ground as possible.

Lufthansa was the launch customer for the 737, initially ordering 21 Series 100 aircraft. The airline added a further 737-100, and later signed up for a batch of the definitive early-generation Series 200.

The 737 had a wider cabin than the DC-9 or One-Eleven. The design was undergoing constant revision and, under pressure from the market, began to grow in size. On 19 February 1965 the 737 received its formal go-ahead with a launch order from Germany's Lufthansa for 21 aircraft. This marked the first time that a Boeing programme had gone ahead without a firm commitment from a US airline. Lufthansa, already a 727 operator, had told Boeing that, if it did not offer the 737 as a firm project, then the airline would buy the DC-9 instead.

Fuselage stretches

The aircraft that was delivered to Lufthansa became known as the 737 Series 100 (737-100) and was larger than originally planned. It was 28.65 m (94 ft) long and had a maximum take-off weight of 43,999 kg (97,000 lb). This growth, however, was not enough and to win the 737's next critical order, from United Airlines, the design had to change again. United demanded a longer version of the 737, with a 2.01-m (6-ft 6-in) fuselage stretch. This allowed the 737 to accommodate two extra rows of seats; with these changes in place United ordered 40 aircraft in 1965, with options on another 30 machines.

This revised design was the 737-200 and it would prove to

Indonesia continues to operate three 737-2X9 Surveillor maritime patrollers. They carry side-looking radar above their rear fuselages.

be the definitive 737 for the next 20 years. But before this aircraft could write itself into the history books, the 737 encountered some serious teething troubles. The prototype 737 made its first flight on 9 April 1967 with first deliveries set for just nine months later. The aircraft proved to be much more 'draggy' in the air than its designers anticipated, and the engine nacelle fairings had to be completely redesigned. A problem also arose with the thrust reversers, which were too close to the wing trailing edge,

Rough-field operation

Boeing also developed a rough-field kit for the 737, allowing the aircraft to operate from unpaved runways. On these aircraft, the underfuselage surface was given a protective coating to reduce gravel damage and the antennas were all strengthened to avoid being broken off. The landing gear and flap sections were also given reinforced protection and the main landing gear tyres were increased in size. A deflector plate was fitted to the nose gear, which did not retract into the wheel well, but remained outside, flush with the fuselage. An air blower was fixed to the front of each engine inlet, to bleed off engine pressure and reduce the chances of debris being sucked into the (low-slung) engines. This kit was fitted by several 737 operators, particularly in Africa and Alaska.

Left: An option offered on the 737 was a kit for gravel strip operations. To prevent damage from debris thrown up by the nosewheel a retractable guard was added.

Above: Boeing's rough-field demonstrator is seen operating from a dirt strip high in the Andes.

Right: An important part of the rough-field modification kit was the addition of an air blower below the intake lip to reduce the amount of debris sucked up by the low-slung engine intake.

weights which stretched from 45,360 kg (100,000 lb) to 58,106 kg (128,100 lb).

After the first 280 aircraft had been delivered, Boeing introduced the 737-200 Advanced, which became the main production version from May 1971 onwards. It had an aerodynamically refined wing with changes made to the engine nacelle fairings, leading-edge, trailing-edge, slats and flaps. The first 737-200 Advanced first flew on 15 April 1971 and it was this version which took the lion's share of 737-200 sales.

Boeing built a military version of the 737-200 Advanced, the T-43A, which served with the USAF primarily as a navigation trainer. These distinctive aircraft had only nine cabin windows and two cabin doors. They had a strengthened floor to carry the required avionics consoles and view ports in the cabin roof for sextant alignment/astro navigation training. A total of 19 aircraft was delivered between 1973 and 1974; several were later adapted as VIP and staff transports.

Another military development of the 737-200 was a maritime patrol/surveillance version fitted with a Motorola SLAMMR (side-looking airborne multi-mission radar), which was announced in 1981. Three of these aircraft were delivered to Indonesia in 1982/83.

Cargo versions of the 737-200 were also developed by Boeing, allowing it to operate in all-freight or Combi (with passengers and freight on the same deck) layouts. A cargo door was fitted to the front forward fuselage and the aircraft was given a reinforced floor, with cargo-handling equipment, restraint netting, etc. Two versions were offered, the 737-220C which used conventional non-palletized seats, and the 737-200QC with palletized seating.

so the rear of the engine nacelles had to be extended by 102 cm (40 in). These problems seriously affected the 737-100's sales and only 30 of this version were built. However, the 737's troubles had been cured by the time the 737-200 was ready for airline service.

The 737-200 was a far more economical version to operate –

chiefly because of its improved passenger capacity, but also because of its higher fuel load and improved Pratt & Whitney JT8D-7 engines. The 737-200 could be powered by the JT8D-7/9As, JT8D-9/-15/-15As or JT8D-17/-17A. This array of engines was required to cope with the 737's range of take-off

Canada's Pacific Western flew this aircraft, a 737-275 Advanced delivered in 1982, as part of its large domestic fleet. The aircraft is now with Air Canada.

Operational history

The 737 became an airline workhorse during the 1970s and 1980s. The basic aircraft changed little over its service life and a large fleet of 737-200s is still in everyday use around the world.

Lufthansa launched the 737 programme on 19 February 1965, acquiring the largest fleet of 737-100s. Lufthansa placed a follow-on order for three aircraft in August 1967, but only one of these was ever delivered. Further 737-100 customers included Colombia's Avianca (two ordered in January 1967) and Malaysia-Singapore Airlines (five ordered in May 1967). An order for two aircraft from Mexicana was cancelled. The last 737-100 (of 30 built) was delivered to MSA on 31 October 1969. Most of these aircraft soldiered on, if not with their original owners, into the 1990s – though the bulk of them have now been retired.

The very first prototype 737 was acquired by NASA in 1973 and remained in service with NASA until September 1997, when it was donated to the Seattle Museum of Flight.

Soon after the 737's launch, Boeing had gathered 86 orders – chiefly for the much-improved 737-200. The first 737-200, a 737-222 destined for United Airlines, flew on 8 August 1967. FAA type certification was awarded on 21 December 1967, only a week after the 737-100, and the first 737-200 entered service on 24 April 1968. This aircraft remained in daily use with United until withdrawn in 1996. The first European customer for the 737-200 was Braathens SAFE, which took delivery of its first 737-205 on 31 December 1968, followed closely by Aer Lingus in March 1969.

Three-person crew

The Boeing 737 was initially hit by a US pilot's union ruling that dictated the aircraft had to be

Aer Lingus received its first Boeing 737 on 28 March 1969. The airline slowly acquired a sizeable fleet, finding the type ideal for its major Dublin–London route.

flown by a crew of three – even though the DC-9 had already been accepted as a two-crew aircraft. This badly affected sales in the US market and Boeing was also beaten to several important European orders by Douglas and the DC-9. By the early 1970s Boeing was on the verge of a major crisis, as the massive investment it had made in the 747 had yet to be repaid. Nor were its other aircraft doing as well as expected – in 1972 just 14 737s were sold. In later years the aircraft became a consistent seller, but only in moderate numbers – approximately 40 aircraft per year were sold until the late 1970s. In 1978, however, the potential of the US market was unleashed when the laws governing the US airline scene were changed and the market

was 'deregulated'. This made it much easier for smaller airlines to expand and for new airlines to be established.

The 737 was ideal for this market. A total of 145 Boeing 737 orders was won that year, from airlines such as USAir, Southwest and Frontier, and from British Airways and Lufthansa which began to replace their existing medium-haul fleets with the 737-200. From then on, the 737, 'Boeing's baby', became a consistent and established seller.

A total of 249 basic model 737-200s was built before the 737-200 Advanced was introduced (a 737-281 for ANA), in May 1971. The 737-200 remained largely unchanged from then until early 1984 when Boeing began to integrate composite materials into its structure to save weight. The last 737-200 was ordered by the (then) Chinese state airline CAAC, in December 1987 and was delivered on 2 August. In all, a total of 865 Advanced 737-200s was built, bringing the

Apart from Lufthansa, only Avianca and MSA bought short-body Series 100s from new. Both Avianca aircraft were delivered in November 1968, but served only briefly before being sold to the Luftwaffe in 1971.

Norwegian operator Braathens SAFE was the first 737-200 customer in Europe. The type later became a common sight on the continent, as large numbers were adopted by British Airways, Air France, Lufthansa and numerous smaller airlines.

total of JT8D-powered 737s built to 1125. By that time the next generation of CFM56-powered 737s had been introduced; as a result, the 737 exceeded the Boeing 727's record sales figure of 1832 aircraft in June 1987.

Today, a large number of 737-200s remains in service, the type's low acquisition price and affordable operating costs, coupled with a generally excellent track record, make it a desirable aircraft, but the biggest obstacles to 737-200 operations are its noisy JT8D engines. Most existing 737-200s were built with the 'quiet' nacelle, but none meets current noise requirements without the addition of hushkits.

Several firms offer JT8D hushkits for the 737-200 and hush-kitted aircraft are in service with several operators. The availability of second-hand 737-300s and 737-400s made -200 re-engining effort unlikely. In 1991 and 1994 two unexplained crashes shook the Boeing 737 community's confidence and concerns were expressed about the possibility of uncommanded rudder movements which may have fatally destabilised the aircraft. In March 1997 the FAA issued a directive ordering modifications to be made to the rudder power-control units of all in-service 737-200s. Boeing was given just two years to make the changes, a schedule which it announced it would meet. The estimated cost of repairs was $126 million, or about $50,000 per aircraft.

Despite the major first order from United, US domestic sales of the 737 were slow in getting started. N310AU was the first 737-2B7 of a large order for USAir which began delivery in November 1982.

Boeing 737-200

Based in Texas at Dallas and Houston, SWAL has built up a huge fleet of Boeing 737s which it operates on low-cost economy operations across the southern United States. The airline operates only 737s, now with just Series 300s, 500s and 700s on strength.

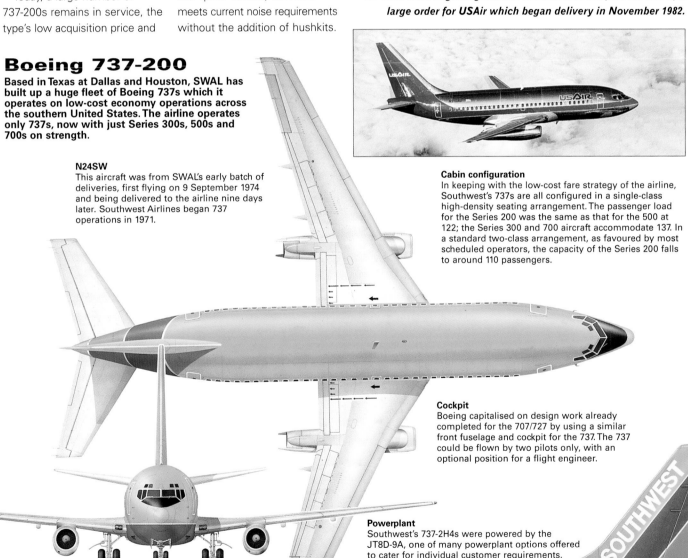

N24SW
This aircraft was from SWAL's early batch of deliveries, first flying on 9 September 1974 and being delivered to the airline nine days later. Southwest Airlines began 737 operations in 1971.

Cabin configuration
In keeping with the low-cost fare strategy of the airline, Southwest's 737s are all configured in a single-class high-density seating arrangement. The passenger load for the Series 200 was the same as that for the 500 at 122; the Series 300 and 700 aircraft accommodate 137. In a standard two-class arrangement, as favoured by most scheduled operators, the capacity of the Series 200 falls to around 110 passengers.

Cockpit
Boeing capitalised on design work already completed for the 707/727 by using a similar front fuselage and cockpit for the 737. The 737 could be flown by two pilots only, with an optional position for a flight engineer.

Powerplant
Southwest's 737-2H4s were powered by the JT8D-9A, one of many powerplant options offered to cater for individual customer requirements.

Nacelles
Boeing mounted the engine nacelles directly under the wings, rather than on pylons. This reduced the required length of the landing gear, with a considerable saving in weight.

Boeing 747 Introduction

One of the most familiar sights in modern civil aviation, the 'Jumbo Jet' helped to create a new era of mass-market long-distance air travel.

No sooner had the first long-range jets entered service in the early 1960s than a boom in traffic and forecasts for continuing growth indicated a need for larger aircraft. The fact that airports and airspace were already congested suggested that increased flight frequency and better aircraft utilization were no longer enough to meet future demand. While Douglas was able to stretch its DC-8 series, Boeing's 707 did not lend itself to a similar exercise.

At the same time, both US manufacturers were competing with Lockheed to fulfil a USAF requirement for a large logistic transport, made possible by the availability of new high bypass-ratio turbofan engines.

In the event, both lost out to Lockheed's C-5A Galaxy in September 1965, and immediately switched to the commercial market in order to salvage something from the considerable design effort. While Douglas eventually produced the medium-capacity DC-10, Boeing decided to make a great leap into the unknown, taking its biggest step to date in the airliner

Above: Pan Am and Boeing had already caused a stir by their bold decision to go ahead with the revolutionary 707, and the pair teamed up again to launch the 747. The airline received its first aircraft in 1969 and the 'Jumbo' was soon creating an impressive spectacle at airports around the world.

Top: With its eye-catching colour scheme, the CP Air-owned Empress of India (C-FCRA) stands out against the white of the Rockies. The aircraft is typical of the early 747s in that it displayed remarkable longevity and remained in service into the late 1990s.

Boeing never created a prototype 747. Instead, the original aircraft, a demonstrator, was rolled out on 30 September 1968 at Paine Field, Everett. The aircraft first flew the following February and has since remained Boeing-owned. The logo of each airline to have shown an interest in the 747 is displayed on the forward fuselage – a hint at the global success that was to come.

market. It did, however, have the support of Pan Am, which had always been bolder than its contemporaries in setting the pace of airliner development. But early designs for a double-deck aircraft not much wider than the 707 found little favour; neither did a mid-wing, wide-body design with upper and lower cabin areas. The airlines felt that such an aircraft would pose serious problems for emergency evacuation, and was virtually impossible to use as a convertible passenger/freighter.

*Below: This ANA 747-400D, with its unique paint scheme, is called **Marine Jumbo**. The scheme was designed by a 12-year-old Japanese girl who won a contest to commemorate ANA's carriage of its 500 millionth passenger. The -400D was developed to replace the high density 747SRs used on Japanese domestic routes.*

Above: British Airways operates a large fleet of 747-400s, its 100 and 200B (illustrated) series aircraft having been retired. The 747 has proved immensely successful on the carrier's long-haul routes, which it now works alongside the airline's twin-engined Boeing 777s.

The final design

After experimenting with some 50 double-deck design concepts, Boeing ceded to the airlines' concerns and came up with a new low-wing design with four wing-mounted engines, and based on a single deck. It had seating (nine to 10 abreast) for up to 380 passengers. Below the cabin floor, there was plenty of room for cargo, and the main cabin could be converted to an all-freighter configuration, with a hinged nose option for ease of loading. Boeing, however, kept an upper storey for the cockpit, and a lounge reached via a spiral staircase. This parabolic frontal section was faired down gradually to the circular cross-section, streamlining appearance. Pratt & Whitney was tasked to produce a powerplant for the 747, capable of generating more than 178 kN (40,000 lb thrust). The result was the JTD9 high bypass-ratio turbofan, then the most powerful jet engine in the world.

The latest production version of the Boeing 747, the -400, is a greatly improved development of the -300, with reduced operating costs, increased range and significant weight reductions. The Series 400 also introduces an all-glass, two-crew cockpit.

Armed with this new design, Boeing went back to the airlines in January 1966. This time, the reception was far more favourable and, on 13 April 1966, Pan Am placed an order for 25 aircraft, including two all-cargo machines. Although Boeing pointed out to Pan Am that it would need further orders from other airlines before firmly committing itself to the programme, its confidence in the market potential of the 'Jumbo Jet', as it was soon dubbed, grew by the minute. It immediately began construction of an entirely new factory at Everett, and production proceeded at a breakneck pace. Boeing's commitment was soon translated into more orders and, within a year, around 20 major airlines had signed for more than 100 747s.

The modern 747

Since then, the 747 has gone from strength to strength. It now flies with airlines all over the world and carries thousands of passengers every day. The aircraft comes in many different civil versions, varying from the Combi to the extra long-range LR series, used by Japan Air Lines. The 747 has also attracted the attention of the military; there are several further variants, such as the E-4 series, which operate in the communications, transport and refuelling roles. A 747-400 armed with an anti-missile laser and designated YAL-1A is also being developed in the United States. An even more radical use for the 747 is NASA's ferry aircraft which carries the Space Shuttle Orbiter.

SPECIFICATION	
Boeing 747-200B **Type:** high-capacity commercial transport **Powerplant:** four 243.55-kN (54,800-lb-thrust) Pratt & Whitney JT9D turbofans **Cruising speed:** 940 km/h (584 mph) at 6096 m (20,000 ft) **Range:** 10,500 km (6,524 miles) (normal payload) **Cruising ceiling:** 13,725 m (45,000 ft) **Weights:** empty173,272 kg	(382,000 lb); loaded 356,100 kg (785,066 lb); maxium take-off 377,800 kg (832,906 lb) **Dimensions:** wing span 59.64 m (195 ft 8 in); length 70.66 m (231 ft 10 in); height 19,33 m (63 ft 5 in); wing area 510.95 m² (5,500 sq ft) **Accommodation:** 490 seats maximum; typically 394 seats including first-class, 70 business-class and 290 standard-class passengers

'Jumbo' shapes up

Showing great courage and foresight, Boeing forged ahead with probably the most radical jetliner in history, creating the first of the wide-bodies and revolutionizing air transport in the process. Boeing finalized its 747 design with a flight deck placed above the ceiling of the passenger deck, forming a slight blister above the nose and extended to the rear in an upper deck for, typically, 32 passengers. The main deck could seat up to 500 passengers in high-density, 10-abreast seating (3+4+3), but 350 was judged a more likely number, with an ultra-luxurious first-class section (seating passengers in pairs along the sides of the nose) extending right up to the radar filling the tip of the nose.

Boeing went for a high cruising speed, with the Model 747 adopting an advanced design of wing with the exceptional sweepback angle of 37 degrees at 25 per cent chord. The leading edge was given an ambitious high-lift system, with three sections of Krüger flap hinged down from the undersurface of the wing inboard of the inner engines, five sections of novel variable-camber flap between the engines, and five more sections between the outer engines and the tip on each side. The variable-camber flaps resembled traditional slats, but comprised flexible skins carried on pivoted links in such a way that, as they were hydraulically extended ahead of and below the leading edge, they arched into a curve to give maximum control of the airflow at high angles. On the trailing edge were placed enormous triple-slotted flaps, with each section running on steel tracks with prominent fairings projecting behind the trailing edge.

Above the wing on each side were added six sections of aluminium honeycomb spoiler, four outboard for control in flight (augmenting the roll power of the conventional trailing-edge low-speed ailerons) and two ground spoilers inboard to destroy lift after landing and thus increase braking power. High-speed ailerons were added at the trailing edge behind the inboard engines where flaps could not be used.

Unprecedented scale

Although the engine installation looked conventional, being arranged on four widely separated wing pylons, it was on a scale never before seen except on the military C-5A. In fact, Boeing picked the losing engine supplier in the C-5A engine competition, Pratt & Whitney, whose JT9D was offered as a robust and reliable turbofan of the new high-bypass-ratio type with 182 kN (41,000 lb thrust). Extremely difficult engineering problems

Both the JT9D and CF6 (illustrated) turbofans were tested beneath the wing of a B-52. The problems later encountered when the JT9D was installed on the 747 failed to show up, however.

Boeing's 747 manufacturing facility was built at Everett, just north of Seattle. Building work on the forested site began in spring 1966 and the first 747 was rolled out in September 1968.

had to be solved in hanging the engines, in arranging a fan-duct reverse and hot-stream spoiler, and in reducing drag.

Another tough engineering problem was the landing gear, eventually solved by using four four-wheel main-gear bogies, two of them on tall inward-retracting legs pivoted to the wings and the other pair on forward-retracting units pivoted to the fuselage, the

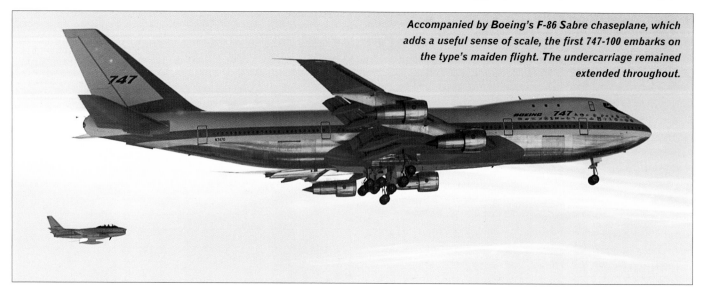

Accompanied by Boeing's F-86 Sabre chaseplane, which adds a useful sense of scale, the first 747-100 embarks on the type's maiden flight. The undercarriage remained extended throughout.

four retracted bogies lying together in a large bay amidships under the floor. All flight controls were hydraulically powered, the rudder and elevators being divided into equal-size halves, no tabs being used anywhere. The APU (auxiliary power unit) for ground air-conditioning and electric power was placed in the extreme tail of the fuselage.

Not only did Boeing have to build the 747, it also had to build a factory for this purpose, and the new plant at Everett, swiftly created in a 316-ha (780-acre) clearing in a forest, is the largest building (in cubic capacity) in the world. Boeing's commitments were awesome, and employment in 1968 peaked at 105,000, compared with 60,000 in World War II. The risk on the Model 747 easily topped one billion dollars but, thankfully, orders kept rolling in, and, when the first aircraft off the production line (Ship RA001) emerged from the new plant on 30 September 1968, a total of 158 orders had been gained from 26 airlines.

Engine snags

With so new and complex an aircraft it would have been surprising if there had been no snags, but in fact the difficulties, mainly centred on the engines, were prolonged. In crosswinds, the engines were difficult to start and ran roughly, and distortion (so-called ovalization) of the casings caused blades to rub in a way that had not been apparent in more than two years of ground testing and flight development

using a B-52 Stratofortress. Pratt & Whitney had to devise a Y-shaped frame to hang the engine differently, and eventually produced a new version of the JT9D that avoided the problem, although the first flight was delayed until 9 February 1969. This aircraft was retained by Boeing for many development purposes. The first to be delivered was handed over to Pan Am on 12 December 1969. It was this airline that finally entered the Model 747 into service on the New York–London route on 22 January 1970.

Popularly called the 'Jumbo Jet', the Model 747 hit the headlines as well as the pockets of its customers and the world's airport authorities. For a while it appeared almost to be premature because traffic did not grow as expected and the proportion of seats filled was often low. With great courage, Boeing continued production at maximum rate, and both the orders and the variants continued to grow. From the outset, Boeing had organized a vast manufacturing programme with major sections of airframe made by subcontractors: Northrop made the main fuselage sections, for example, and Fairchild Republic built the flaps, ailerons, slats and spoilers. With such large structures, exceptional precision was vital if there were not to be problems when the parts all came together at Everett. One unusual assembly technique was to mount aircraft on air-cushion pads so that they could be easily moved in any direction across a smooth concrete floor.

Multiple variants

The initial model was the 747-100, which had achieved a total of 167 orders before Boeing introduced the much improved 747-200. The new variant offered greater fuel capacity and increased weights, with a succession of improved and more powerful variants of the JT9D, along with General Electric CF6 and Rolls-Royce RB.211-524 turbofans being

offered as customer options. Several models of the basic 747-200 were made available, including the 747-200B passenger aircraft, the -200B Combi with provision for the carriage of passengers and main deck cargo simultaneously, the -200C Convertible, designed for use in either the passenger or cargo role, and the -200F pure freighter.

Subsequently, in addition to further subvariants of the -200, Boeing produced the 747-300 with an extended upper passenger deck, and the short-fuselage, ultra-long range 747SP, before taking the 747 into the 1990s and beyond with the high-technology 747-400, which remains in production.

Inside the Everett assembly hall during the early 1980s, three 747-200s and a single SP are visible. As seen from their rudder colours, two of the -200s are destined for Alitalia and Air France, while the SP is for Qantas.

Boeing 747 Operational history

Remarkably, it was not until the mid-1990s that any challenge was offered to the 747's monopoly. Even then, Boeing responded with new winning designs. The beginning of the spacious age – this is how launch customer Pan American Airways described the Boeing 747 on 22 January 1970. It was truly a momentous day in the annals of commercial air transport.

Although minor engine problems had delayed service introduction by several weeks, and overheating had caused a further hold-up when the aircraft was readied for take-off, the 747-100, christened *Clipper Young America* by President Nixon's

wife, Pat, left New York at 1.52 am and arrived at London's Heathrow Airport later that day. Pan Am took delivery of all its 25 aircraft (later orders brought the fleet to 60) during that year, introducing the type on other transatlantic routes, as well as on trans-Pacific services. American Airlines followed suit in March 1970, and the first foreign operator was Lufthansa, putting the type on the Frankfurt–New York run in April. By the end of the year, 747s were also flying with Air France, Alitalia, Continental, Delta, Japan Air Lines, National, Northwest Airlines and United.

The 747 quickly established itself on the world's long-haul

routes, but the early years were anything but trouble-free, two aircraft being destroyed. The first accident with loss of life occurred on 20 November 1974, when a Lufthansa 747 crashed at Nairobi. Worse was to come on 27 March 1977, when 583 people died as 747s belonging to KLM and Pan Am collided on the ground at Tenerife in the Canary Islands.

Another problem was that the bottom had fallen out of the air transport market as a result of the oil crisis in 1973, forcing many airlines to cut back services and put some 747s into storage. These misfortunes proved to be only a temporary hiccup, however, and had no lasting effect on the career of the 747.

Lufthansa was the earliest European operator of the 747, acquiring the first of its airliners and freighters in 1970. With the purchase of 747-400s, its fleet has now been considerably upgraded, with none of the original aircraft left in service.

747 upgrades

As early as June 1968, Boeing had announced the availability of a heavier model with improved payload and range which, as the 747-200B, entered passenger service with KLM in February 1971. More powerful Pratt & Whitney engines brought higher take-off weights, and CF6-50 and RB.211 engines also became available. KLM took delivery of the first GE-powered 747 Combi in October 1975, while British Airways ordered the Rolls-Royce powerplant for its 747-200Bs.

Pan Am also persuaded Boeing to produce a variant which could carry a full payload nonstop on its longest route between New York and Tokyo, as the 747SP. Boeing continued

Left: Northwest Airlines was the first airline to receive the 747-400 series. The airline was a natural recipient of the new aircraft, as much of its business is conducted across the Pacific, where the additional range of the -400 is useful.

Below: Pan Am and Boeing collaborated on a number of projects and the 747 represents their greatest success. Pan Am was the first airline to order the 747 and, even by that stage, had been intrinsically involved in the design.

KLM has retired its earlier 747s, like the -200 seen here, but still owns over twenty 747-400s.

The future

With Airbus penetrating the high-capacity market with the A340-600 and A380, Boeing began considering new 747 derivatives. Through various proposals which included fuselage stretches and producing a 747-400LRX with the wing and strengthened undercarriage of the -400 freighter for extra range, these matured as the extended-range 747-400ER and 747-400ERF.

In summer 2005, however, it was becoming increasingly likely that Boeing would launch a stretched 747-400 Advanced. This new machine would offer increased range and also feature the engines of the all-new 787 Dreamliner.

to look towards increasing the 747's passenger load and, in June 1980, revealed the 747SUD (stretched upper deck). This was essentially a Model 200 with the upper deck extended by 7 m (23 ft), providing economy seating for up to 69 passengers. It was redesignated 747-300 by the time of its maiden flight on 5 October 1982, and entered

service with launch customer, Swissair. Later, the latest materials and technology made the 747-400 a much more advanced aircraft, with a new wing, a two-crew glass cockpit and considerably enhanced performance. Externally, it is similar to the -300, apart from its large winglets. Even before the first roll-out on 26 January

1988, 18 operators had placed orders for 118 aircraft.

Northwest Airlines was the launch customer with an order for 10 aircraft placed on 22 October 1985. Japan Airlines operates the 747-400D (Domestic), fitted out for 546 passengers in a two-class arrangement. From May 1990, 747-400 derivatives became the only 747s on offer.

BOEING 747-200B

Among the most gaudy and brightly coloured of the 747s to have flown so far were the two aircraft operated by Braniff on the 'Big Orange' service between Dallas and London-Gatwick, until the airline went bankrupt in 1982. A new Braniff emerged as a domestic operator and the 747s (including one 747SP) were sold. This aircraft was a Series 200, powered by Pratt & Whitney JT9D-3 engines.

Accommodation

The 747-200B has a cabin length of 57 m (187 ft) and a width of 6.13 m (20 ft 1½ in). The basic layout of the aircraft provides seating for 48 first-class and 337 economy-class passengers (including a 16-passenger upper deck lounge). Alternatively, 447 passengers can sit nine-abreast in single-class conditions, or 500 passengers can sit ten abreast, with 32 on the upper deck. The aircraft is flown by a flight crew of three.

Records

On 12 November 1970, a test 747-200B set a new heavyweight record by taking off at a gross weight of 372,261 kg (820,700 lb). An even more remarkable fact is that the cabin of the 747 is longer than the distance covered by the first flight of the Wright brothers, a sign of how far aviation progressed in the twentieth century.

747-200 variants

The 747-200 was produced in a number of variants. These included the -200B, a Combi version, and the -200C, a factory-built, fully convertible variant that can be configured for all-passenger, all-freight or a combination load. A special freighter version of the 747 was the -200F, with straight-in loading of bulk cargo through a hinged nose (called a visor by Boeing). The -200M designation is applied to -200Bs that have been modified to incorporate side cargo doors.

Powerplant

Depending on customer choice, the 747-200 was delivered with Pratt & Whitney JT9D-7R4G2 turbofans rated at 243.5 kN (54,750 lb thrust), General Electric CF6-50E2 turbofans rated at 233.5 kN (52,500 lb thrust) or Rolls Royce RB.211-524D4-B turbofans rated at 236.2 kN (53,110 lb thrust).

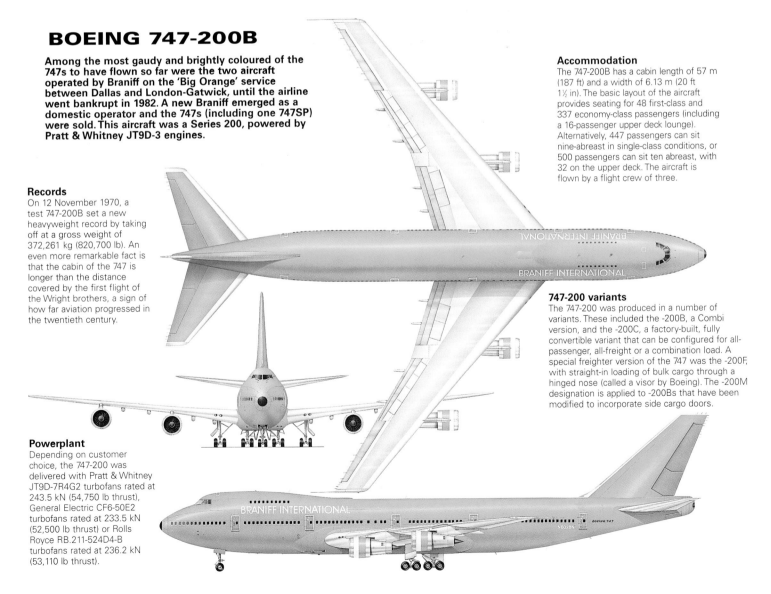

A 747 operator since 1970 (as BOAC), British Airways ordered 57 examples, the last of which was delivered in 1999. The airline's controversial 'World Images' colour scheme, with themed tailfin designs, was applied to a number of 747s, including 747-436 G-BNLR which displays the Far Eastern-inspired 'Rendezvous' design.

Fuselage and accommodation

The Series 400 has the same extended upper deck as introduced in the 747-300. Not only does this provide extra seating, but it also improves aerodynamic flow around the forward fuselage, reducing drag and allowing a slight increase in normal cruise Mach number. BA's aircraft are operated in a number of seating configurations, providing accommodation for up to 351 passengers, the exact configuration used depending upon the route on which the aircraft is expected to operate. The most capacious 747-400s are the 747-400Ds used by Japanese airlines on domestic routes. These can carry as many as 566 passengers in a high-density, two-class layout.

Wing structure

While retaining the same wing structure as earlier models, the 747-400 employs new materials (advanced alloys in the main) in its construction to achieve a considerable weight saving. The Series 400's wing, despite a 5.18-m (17-ft) span increase, to 64.44 m (211 ft 5 in) overall, is actually lighter than that of the 747-300. With its fuel tanks full the aircraft's wing bends downward slightly, causing the tips of the winglets to swing out and increase span to 64.92 m (213 ft) overall.

Boeing 747-400 variants

Apart from the basic 747-400 passenger variant, three other versions based on the standard -400 have entered service:

747-400 Combi: mixed passenger/freight version. Identical to the all-passenger version, but with a 305-cm x 340-cm (120-in x 134-in) side cargo door (SCD) in the port rear fuselage, aft of the wing. Two end zones of the cabin have a strengthened floor with cargo handling gear (including a roller floor)

747-400F: All-cargo, full freighter version. This version is structurally identical to the 747-400, but has the original short upper deck of the 747-100/200, to save weight. Uses the same SCD as the Combi aircraft, but also features a 345-cm x 249-cm (136 in x 98-in) nose door. The -400F has a maximum take-off weight of 394,632 kg870,000 lb) and can carry a typical 9958-kg (44,000-lb) payload over 5,000 nm (9253 km; 5,750 miles).

747-400D (Domestic): This special version, announced in October 1989, is intended for high-density domestic routes in Japan (where airlines such as JAL and ANA already operated the 747-200SR). The 747-400D is configured for 5a maximum 66 passengers in a two-class layout. As the 747-400D fleet can expect to accrue a much higher number of cycles compared to the rest of the worldwide 747 population these aircraft have a strengthened structure, no horizontal fin fuel tank and use de-rated engines.

747-400ER (Extended Range): Increased maximum take-off weight of 412,770 kg (910,000 lb) for a range of 7,670 nm (14,205 km; 8,827 miles). Boeing Signature cabin, using 777 interior design.

747-400ERF: Freighter version of 747-400ER.

Boeing 747-436

G-BNLE *City of Newcastle* **was the fifth 747-436 delivered to British Airways (and the 753rd 747 completed by the Boeing Airplane Company) and was delivered in late 1989. Most of the airline's 747-400 fleet was named after British cities, though the aircraft later lost their names as they were repainted in the 'World Images' and current 'Union Flag' colour schemes.**

Powerplant

The 747-400 is offered with Pratt & Whitney PW4056, General Electric CF6-80C2 or Rolls-Royce RB.211-524G/-524H engines generally rated at between 249.2 and 258 kN (56,000 and 58,000 lb st), though variants of both the P&W and GE engines are available for the 747-400 rated at up to 276 kN (62,000 lb st). Most Series 400 operators have chosen the GE engine, but British Airways followed Cathay Pacific Airways' lead in specifying RB.211s for its aircraft and was later joined by Air New Zealand, Cargolux, QANTAS and South African Airways in choosing the Rolls-Royce engine for some or all of their 747-400s. A feature of the RB.211 is the use of wide-chord fan blades at the front of the engine, these being lighter and less vulnerable to bird strike damage.

Compared to the 747-200F, the 747-400 Freighter can carry 20 per cent more payload over ranges more than 1,000 nm (1853 km; 1,152 miles) longer. HL7419 is operated by South Korea's Asiana Airlines which also flies Series 400 airliners.

Winglets
The main identifying features of the 747-400, compared to the otherwise similar 747-300, are the former's 1.83-m (6-ft) high graphite composite winglets, fitted to reduce drag caused by spanwise migration of boundary layer air. The drag-inducing vortices which would otherwise result are caused by the difference in air pressure between the upper and lower surfaces of the wing.

Fuel
The bulk of the 747's fuel is housed between the spars of the wing, in four huge internal tanks. In addition there is a centre-wing tank and reserve tanks in the outer wings. The 747-400 also has an optional tailplane fuel tank, with a capacity of 12,492 litres (2,748 Imp gal), feeding directly into the centre-wing tank and giving the aircraft another 340 nautical miles (650 km; 404 miles) of range at normal cruise altitude. Total useable fuel capacity with the tailplane tank installed is increased to 216,846 litres (47,700 Imp gal), weighing over 175086 kg (386,000 lb), or about 45 per cent of the maximum take-off weight of a 747-400. Design range with 420 passengers aboard an aircraft operating at the highest optional take-off weight is 7,135 nautical miles (13214 km; 8,211 miles) with fuel reserves; ferry range is around 15,570 km (9,675 miles).

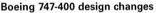

G-BNLE

Boeing 747-400 design changes
The basic 747-400 fuselage length is no different to all the other 747s that have gone before it. Boeing has never stretched the 747, though plans for such a move are now being considered as part of Boeing's answer to the challenge from the A380. Several other aspects of the 747's design were changed on the -400, however, and these include:
- wingspan extended by 1.83 m (6 ft), with additional composite wingtips measuring a further 1.83 m (6 ft) in length
- additional fuel tank installed inside the tail fin, adding 12,492 litres (3,300 US gal)
- carbon fibre brakes, saving 816 kg (1,800 lb) in weight
- PW901A auxiliary power unit, reduces APU fuel-burn by 40 per cent
- increased maximum take-off weight, up to 394,632 kg (870,000 lb)
- higher thrust General Electric CF6-80C2, Pratt & Whitney PW4056 or Rolls-Royce RB.211-524G/H turbofans
- six-screen EFIS cockpit fit for two crew operation
- re-styled cabin, with typical three-class seating for 412 passengers
- up to 7,200-nm (13325-km; 8,280-mile) range, with 400 passengers and baggage

Among the world's first all-jet airlines, Air India sold its last propeller-driven aircraft (a Constellation) in June 1962 and has been operating 747s since March 1971. Its first 747-400 (pictured) was delivered in 1993 and is one of 11 in the Indian flag-carrier's fleet.

Boeing 747SP Mini 'Jumbo'

Delivered in March 1976, this aircraft (ZS-SPA) was the first of six Boeing 747SPs delivered to South African Airways. On its delivery flight the aircraft set a new world nonstop distance record, emphasizing the type's long-range capabilities.

As the original ultra-long range airliner, the Boeing 747SP was not the prettiest aircraft ever built, nor did it break any sales records – but breaking performance records was another matter. Seattle's 'special performer' flew higher, further and faster than any of its contemporaries and set many speed and distance records during its career.

Soon after the launch of the 747-100, it became clear that many customers needed a similar aircraft capable of covering great distances. Douglas and Lockheed were eating into this market with the DC-10 and the TriStar, but Boeing felt it had the edge with its existing four-engined design. Boeing took the basic 747-100 and chopped out 14.60 m (48 ft) of fuselage, losing about 100 seats. Everything else was left untouched, so the new smaller, lighter aircraft would have the same engines – and all the power – of a 747-100 with reduced fuel consumption and increased range. The uninspiring in-house design name of 747SB (short body) was dropped in favour of the attention-getting 747SP (Special Performance); the project received its official go-ahead on 23 August 1973.

This new version boasted increased rate of climb, cruising altitude and cruising speed and

a range in excess of 11,112 km (6,904 miles). The aircraft's centresection was redesigned to retain the 747's trademark upper deck, along with the rear fuselage that was radically 'pinched in' to fit the tail unit. The reduction in length necessitated an extension of the fin by 1.52 m (5 ft). The fin chord was also extended and a distinctive double-hinged rudder was fitted. The tailplanes were lengthened by 3 m (10 ft). The standard engine was the 209-kN

Right: The first 747SP made its maiden flight on 4 July. The SP's shorter fuselage and larger tail fin were highlighted when parked adjacent to a standard Model 747.

Below: Braniff International's distinctive orange colour scheme adorned three 747SPs in the early 1980s. This example was returned to Boeing in 1981, before being sold to the Omani government in July 1984.

(46,950-lb-thrust) JT9D-7A. Alternatively, 229.6-kN (51,600-lb-thrust) RB.211-524 turbofans were available. JT9Ds powered 39 of the 45 SPs built.

The launch order came from Pan American, which ordered 10 in September 1973, with 15 options. Boeing sales executives predicted a 20-year production run and planned at least six distinct versions (such as an SP Combi). The first SP, the 265th production 747, was rolled out

on 19 May 1975 and the maiden flight took place on 4 July. Described as one of the most ambitious first flights in Boeing's history, it included a full stall and speeds up to Mach 0.92. On 4 February 1976 the 747SP received FAA type certification.

Pan Am accepted its first aircraft on 5 March 1976 and the type entered service on the Los Angeles–Tokyo route on 25 April. On 3 November 1975 the fourth SP undertook a month-long

CAAC ordered the 747SP in 1980. When the organization was dismantled in 1988, the aircraft were transferred to Air China.

CAAC, China Airlines, Iran Air, Korean Air Lines, Pan Am, QANTAS, SAA, Syrian Arab Airlines and TWA, with the last delivery coming in 1989. This was, in fact, a specially ordered VIP aircraft, and the last true airline delivery occurred in 1982. The largest operators were Pan Am and United, the latter obtaining Pan Am's 10 aircraft when it took over its Pacific routes during the late 1980s. United began to retire its fleet from 1995 onwards. One ex-United aircraft was been modified to serve as NASA's Stratospheric Observatory for Infrared Astronomy. Today, a little over half the SPs built are still in service.

international sales trip. A South African Airways (SAA) aircraft later set a new nonstop distance record of 16,560 km (10,290 miles) from Everett to Cape Town on its delivery flight during 23/24 March 1976 and still had two hours and 27 minutes of fuel on board. Over 1–3 May 1976 Pan Am's *Clipper Liberty Bell* set a new round-the-world record of 46 hours 26 minutes over a distance of 37,234 km (23,137 miles). On 2 August 1977 Pan Am's *Clipper New Horizons* (*Liberty Bell* renamed) set a round-the-world record via the poles of 54 hours and 7 minutes for a distance of 42,212 km (26,230 miles), plus six additional FAI records. Finally, United Airlines' *Friendship One* set a new round-the-world record of 35 hours 54 minutes over a distance of 37,215 km (23,125 miles) on 29/30 January 1988.

In the end, the 747SP failed for several reasons. It was too expensive. Its market was limited – although Boeing made serious proposals to 40 other potential customers, not one signed up. Finally, the 747-200's performance largely caught up with that of the SP, while still retaining its original passenger and cargo capacities.

A total of 45 747SPs was built for customers such as Braniff,

SPECIFICATION

Boeing 747-400
Type: high-capacity long-haul airliner
Powerplant: four high-bypass-ratio turbofans rated at 258 kN (58,040 lb thrust) (engines available Pratt & Whitney PW4056, General Electric CF6-80C2 or Rolls-Royce RB-211 425G)
Maximum speed: 980 km/h (608 mph)
Range: 13,398 km (8,307 miles)
Service ceiling: 13,716 m (45,000 ft)
Weights: empty 182,754 kg (402,059 lb); loaded 394,625 kg (868,175 lb)
Dimensions: wing span 64.44 m (211 ft 4 in); length 70.66 m (231 ft 9 in); height 19.41 m (63 ft 8 in); wing area 511 m^2 (5.498 sq ft)
Accommodation: two (flight deck), 390 passengers in standard configuration

VIP flagship

The 747SP has proved to be a popular VIP aircraft. Boeing attempted to sell it to the US government as a replacement for the then AIR FORCE ONE, a VC-137. Attempts were also made to sell an SP to the Shah of Iran. The first VIP sale was made to King Khaled of Saudia Arabia. This aircraft (HZ-HM1, later re-registered as HZ-HM1B when replaced by a 747-300) was outfitted with a fully equipped hospital and a luxuriously appointed interior. Other VIP SPs with government/royal owners have included three in the UAE (Abu Dhabi and Dubai); two in Qatar, Saudi Arabia and Bahrain; and one in Oman. The Omanii aircraft (A40-SP) and one UAE aircraft (A6-ZSN, seen immediately below) were fitted with a satellite communications dome behind the main 'hump'. Another of the UAE aircraft (A6-SMR) was fitted with a 'glass' EFIS cockpit and is thus unique among SPs. A VIP 747SP (YI-ALM) was also delivered to the government of Iraq, although it wore basic Iraqi Airways colours.

Above: Pan Am was the launch customer for the 747SP, having ordered 10 examples in September 1973. N533PA Clipper Freedom was the third built and the first to be delivered in March 1976.

Below: The longest continuous operator of the type is Syrian Arab Airlines. Its two Boeing 747SP-94s were delivered in May and July 1976, and remain in service three decades later.

Above: One of the more recent operators of the 747SP in Asia was Mandarin Airlines of Taiwan. The airline has leased this example from China Airlines since August 1992.

Douglas DC-9 Series 10, 15 and 30

If the capacity for development is the mark of a great design, the DC-9/MD-80/MD-90 family deserves a place in that small and exclusive category. Over a 15-year period, Douglas had based an entire line of transports on the DC-4, before it moved into the jet age with the DC-8, which entered service in 1959.

The first jets to appear on long-distance services contrasted sharply with the older aircraft used on shorter flights, particularly in the United States, but there was no basic agreement on the best way to replace the latter. Some argued that fast turboprop aircraft would not be much slower than the jets on the shorter routes, and would be more economical. Others felt that the travelling public would regard the jet as standard, and would identify any propeller-driven aircraft as old-fashioned. The correct size for such a new aircraft was also a matter of controversy and, as a result, the market for new short-haul aircraft became a fierce and confusing battlefield. Lockheed and Vickers were pushing advanced turboprop aircraft. France already had the Caravelle short-haul jet in production.

Neither Boeing nor Douglas had any firm programme to offer, but each believed that jets were the solution. Both started out by looking at scaled-down versions of their big jets, and by

1959 Douglas had made serious presentation of the first DC-9, with four Pratt & Whitney JT10 turbojets, to United Airlines and other major carriers. But at the end of 1960, United and Eastern (the two biggest US domestic carriers) placed orders for the advanced Boeing 727.

Douglas immediately saw that there was room for a smaller aircraft. Of its two US rivals, Boeing was preoccupied with the 727 and Lockheed was still salvaging the Electra programme. The competition would most probably from the Caravelle. United had ordered 20 Caravelles in 1959, and the US airframers were worried that lower European labour rates would give the type a competitive edge.

Following the 727's launch, Douglas, Sud-Aviation and General Electric began to hold serious discussions about joint development of an improved and Americanized Caravelle, powered by General Electric's CJ805-23 aft-fan engine. But the Caravelle was already eight years old and, from the systems viewpoint, it was a first-generation turbine

Above: Rolled out from Douglas's production line at Long Beach, California in February 1965, the DC-9 Series 10 was the shortest variant developed. The T-tail and rear-mounted engines can clearly be seen in this view.

Top: Regional American airline Republic operated a fleet of DC-9-50s throughout the early 1980s. The airline was later taken over by Piedmont which, in turn, was later absorbed by US Air.

Below: Wearing the colours of launch customer Delta Air Lines, this DC-9-14 illustrates the original short fuselage, which offered a maximum passenger capacity of 90.

Wearing the colours of the now defunct US regional airline Best, this DC-9-15 operated throughout the late 1970s and early 1980s.

Right: SAS inspired the production of the DC-9 Series 20 and Series 40. The carrier also flew -30s, as here.

airliner. With General Electric engines, it would also be close in capacity to the 727. Then, in May 1961, British Aircraft Corporation announced the go-ahead for its BAC One-Eleven.

In 1962, Douglas salesman began to show airlines a totally new design, the D-2086. Like the Caravelle, One-Eleven and 727, it had rear-mounted engines, a clean wing and a short landing gear. The last was particularly important because the new jet was designed to operate in the absence of complex ground-handling facilities, as airport development in the United States had lagged behind the expansion of the airlines.

The wing design philosophy, however, was closer to that of the Caravelle than the advanced wing of the 727; Douglas chose a relatively large and moderately swept wing, with double-slotted trailing-edge flaps. The powerplant was to be a pair of Pratt & Whitney JT8Ds. The JT8D was a little more powerful than needed, but provided room for

growth and would be common to the airlines' 727 fleets.

This was the DC-9, launched with a 15-aircraft order from Delta Air Lines in April 1963, with an option for a further 15 examples. By this time, the One-Eleven was only a month away from its first flight, and had secured major US orders from American and Mohawk Airlines; speed would be vital if the DC-9 was to catch up. The flight-test programme was intensive. The first aircraft flew on 25 February 1965, and five were flying by June. The initial production version, the DC-9-10, was certified in November.

Modified version

By the time Delta was operating with the new type, Douglas was well advanced with development of a new, considerably modified version, designed primarily for

McDonnell Douglas DC-9 Series 30
Type: short- to medium-range airliner
Powerplant: two 62.3-kN (14,018-lb-thrust) Pratt & Whitney JT8D-7 turbofan engines
Cruising speed: 821 km/h (510 mph)
Range: 2775 km (1,724 miles) at long-range cruising speed of 821 km/h (510 mph)
Service ceiling: 10,180 m (33,400 ft)

Weights: empty 24,011 kg (52,935 lb); maximum take-off 44,450 kg (97,995 lb)
Dimensions: wing span 28.47 m (93 ft 5 in); length 36.37 m (119 ft 4 in); height (8.38 m (27 ft 6 in); wing area 92.97 m^2 (1,000 sq ft)
Accommodation: two pilots, flight engineer and 105 passengers; 115 passengers may be carried with limited facilities

operations on the US east coast and in Europe, where runways in the 3050-m (10,000-ft) bracket were generally available and the 727's near-transcontinental range was not needed. The new version was to be stretched by 4.57 m (15 ft), raising passenger capacity from 80 to 105, and the JT8Ds were used at their full design rating. The first order for this new version, the DC-9-30, came from Eastern Airlines in February 1965. The higher-rated

engines were also made available on the basic aircraft, as the DC-9 Series 15 or DC-9-15.

The DC-9-30 was substantially bigger than any One-Eleven, and was more economical, but it faced competition from the new Boeing 737, launched just two months later. Douglas held one decisive advantage: the DC-9-30 would enter service in early 1967, before the first 737 flew. The airline industry was growing so rapidly that airlines were racing to be the first to bring jets into competitive markets. To take advantage of its lead, Douglas decided to build up production as fast as possible, so that the maximum number of airlines could receive DC-9s before Boeing could start delivering 737s.

The DC-9F (Series 30) was fitted with an upward-hinging door on the port fuselage, forward of the wing. This example was operated by Alitalia, which received its first aircraft on 13 May 1968.

Right: Through the 1970s, the majority of DC-9s sold were -30s. Toa Domestic Airways (TDA) was the only customer for the DC-9-40, apart from SAS. TDA had an extensive fleet, including 22 DC-9s.

DC-9 Series 20, 40 and 50

The DC-9 Series 30's success enabled Douglas to develop new versions, tailored to meet customers' needs. However, spiralling costs and increased competition led to the company's demise and subsequent takeover by the McDonnell organization.

With Boeing preparing to launch its 737 competitor to the DC-9, Douglas responded in the mid-1960s by offering to meet any configurations the customer might express. It even developed two versions of the DC-9 specifically for Scandinavian Airlines System. These were the DC-9-40, stretched by two seat rows compared with the -30 to match the seating capacity of the 737-200, and the DC-9-20, a 'hotrod' version with the original short fuselage, the high-lift wing of the -30 and the same high-thrust engines as the -40. Douglas offered customers a huge variety of other options: different fuel capacities, different engine models and different weights, as well as a wide choice of finishes and internal fits.

The sales strategy was phenomenally successful. The DC-9 sold as no airliner had sold before, and Douglas had orders

Designed specifically for SAS for operations from shorter regional airport runways, only ten DC-9-20s were built.

for more than 400 aircraft by the end of 1966. Douglas was also going broke, and doing so very quickly. It was still spending money on DC-9 development, in all its versions, and new versions of the DC-8 were also on the point of certification. Moreover, Douglas was losing money on every DC-9 that it delivered; the company had sold many aircraft at low 'introductory' prices, but they were proving more expensive to build than predicted. Production had been built up so fast that a great many DC-9s were being produced 'off the top of the learning curve';

assembly procedures were still being refined, and the workers were still learning their jobs, so that each aircraft was taking more man-hours to build than would be the case later in the programme. This problem was compounded because Vietnam War production had already used up all of southern California's pool of trained aerospace workers and because there were some 20 different airline configurations on the production line within a few months of the first deliveries. War production was also causing delays in supply of components. The

crisis came to a head when deliveries began to slip behind schedule, and some of the airline customers launched massive lawsuits to recover estimated losses. Facing bankruptcy, Douglas was taken over by the McDonnell company at the end of April 1967.

The new management brought DC-9 deliveries back on schedule, and the aircraft retained its hard-won status as the world's best-selling twinjet airliner through the early 1970s. The type was selected by a number of large European carriers, outselling the 727 and

*Left: The prototype DC-9 Series 40 (seen here overflying **Queen Mary**) first flew in November 1967. The 71 production aircraft were delivered to **SAS** and **TDA**.*

Delivered to Hawaiian Airlines in July 1978, this DC-9-51 was one of a total of 96 Series 50s built between 1974 and 1981. The majority of these remains in service today.

Essentially a Series 30 with a 1.87-m (6-ft 4-in) fuselage stretch, the DC-9-40 was ordered by TDA for its high-capacity short-range domestic routes.

737 in that market. The aircraft also went on to equip affiliated charter airlines. Delta and Eastern were major US operators; outside the trunk airlines, too, the DC-9 proved popular with US regional airlines.

Nearly all the DC-9s sold in this period were DC-9-30s; TDA was the only customer for the DC-9-40 apart from SAS, and demand for the short-runway performance of the DC-9-10 diminished as airport worldwide improved. The DC-9-20 remained an SAS special. An all-cargo version, the DC-9-30F, was delivered to Alitalia in 1968; a main-deck cargo door was also fitted to the DC-9-30CF (convertible) and DC-9-30RC (rapid-change convertible) variants. In the course of the 1970s, the -30 was made available with more powerful JT8Ds, higher weights and auxiliary fuel tanks in the lower fuselage, the latter option proving attractive to European

charter airlines, which needed an aircraft to fly nonstop from northern Europe to the Canaries.

Competition in the twin-jet market grew more intense in the early 1970s, as Boeing introduced its new Advanced 737 series. The DC-9, though, was an inherently easier aircraft to stretch than the Model 737; McDonnell Douglas took advantage of this attribute of the design in mid-1973 by launching the 139-seat DC-9-50. The second major stretch of the DC-9, the -50 compared with the -30 as the latter had compared with the -10. The fuselage of the new version was 4.34 m (14 ft 3 in) longer than that of the basic DC-

9-30; higher-thrust engines, also to be offered on the -30, were standard, but the wing was externally unchanged and the maximum take-off weights were only slightly increased. The -50 was not intended to replace the DC-9-30, but to complement it. It had better economics, but was less flexible in terms of range and runway performance.

Quiet powerplant
Swissair was the first customer for the -50, and began operations in August 1975. The aircraft performed as advertised, but was, inevitably, noisier than the -30s to which the people around Swissair's base airports were accustomed. The community reaction caused Swissair to cut back its planned purchases of DC-9-50s, and the airline, a loyal Douglas customer, started to press for a new and quieter large-capacity DC-9.

In the early 1970s, the US government had launched a number of programmes aimed at reducing aircraft noise. One

of these was development of a modified JT8D with a larger-diameter fan and other changes, specifically intended to make future versions of the 727, 737 and DC-9 significantly quieter.

Meanwhile, McDonnell Douglas was engaged in a long drawn-out sales effort in Japan. In early 1975, McDonnell Douglas proposed a DC-9-QSF (quiet, short-field) to the Japanese airlines, a -40-sized version with refanned engines and a highly modified wing. While the Japanese market never opened up, the new wing and engines formed the basis for a new DC-9 variant to supersede the -50. With a new wing, much increased weights and refanned engines, the revised aircraft would have better economics than the DC-9-50, the operating flexibility of the -30, and lower noise. First discussed in 1976, the type was initially known as the DC-9-RSS (refan, super-stretch), then as the DC-9-55. It was later designated as the DC-9 Super 80.

Above: BWIA began DC-9-51 operations in 1977. A 'new look' interior gave the cabin a more spacious and modern appearance, appealing to passengers accustomed to widebody comforts.

Right: Europe proved to be an excellent market for the DC-9. The DC-9-50 was popular with airlines such as Inex-Adria, which used the aircraft on holiday routes, as well as on scheduled flights connecting European cities.

Left: In 1981 Finnair received the last DC-9 Series 50 to be built. The type was used on regional scheduled services.

DC-9 variants

A major competitor to Boeing's 737 throughout its production life, the DC-9 was sold in a number of major variants culminating in the Series 50. The aircraft also formed the basis of the MD-80 family.

Ozark Airlines was one of the initial DC-9 operators, ordering six Series 10s, the first of which was delivered in May 1966. This example is one of 13 DC-9-31s ordered two years later.

DC-9 Series 10

The initial DC-9 production version was the DC-9 Series 11. The DC-9-11 did not have its centre fuel tank activated, keeping the maximum take-off weight below 36,287 kg (80,000 lb), allowing two-crew operations in line with US regulations. For export customers the tank was activated and the DC-9 was offered in the form of the DC-9-12 with Pratt & Whitney JT8D-1 or JT8D-7 engines and the DC-9-14 with JT8D-1s, -5s or -7s. In the event, the US regulations were relaxed in 1965 to a 40,823-kg (90,000-lb) limit, allowing the Series 14 to be offered to US airlines as well. Bonanza Air Lines was the only carrier to adopt the initial Series 11 in service, taking delivery of three examples (above right). No customers were found for the Series 12 and production centred on the Model 14, of which Texas International, Delta Air Lines, Air Canada, TWA, Eastern Air Lines, West Coast Airlines, Continental (right) and AVENSA of Venezuela all purchased examples. Maximum take-off weight for the Series 14 was 41,141 kg (90,700 lb), which included the allowance of 318 kg (700 lb) for start-up and taxiing. The extra fuel carried by the Series 14 increased the aircraft's range to more than 1609 km (1,000 miles) with a standard payload. A total of three Series 11s and 54 Series 14s was produced.

DC-9 Series 15

The ultimate version of the initial variants was the Series 15, which featured 63-kN (14,000-lb st) JT8D-1 or JT8D-7 engines. This version carried the standard passenger load of 79. Major operators of the DC-9-15 included KLM (above) and TWA, and a total of 55 entered airline service around the world. Two convertible passenger/cargo versions of the Series 15, designated DC-9-15MC (multiple change) and DC-9-15RC (rapid change), were produced for Trans-Texas Airways (five) and Continental Airlines (19), respectively. These aircraft featured reinforced cabin floors and and an upward-hinged cargo door on the port side.

DC-9 Series 20

The DC-9 Series 20 was developed specifically for operations from short runways. The driving force for the variant was SAS's requirement for a Convair CV-440 replacement. To meet performance criteria, Douglas married the Series 10 fuselage to the longer-span Series 30 wing and integrated upgraded JT8D-11 engines, each producing 67.50 kN (15,000 lb thrust). This allowed the aircraft to operate from 1372-m (4,500-ft) runways at 84°F (29°C) ambient temperature, permitting operations on all but one of SAS's domestic routes. The first of 10 DC-9-21s, for the sole operator SAS, entered service in January 1969.

DC-9 Series 30

The breakthrough in DC-9 sales was triggered by the decision of the FAA in April 1965 to abolish a weight limit for airliners with two-man crews. Douglas moved quickly to offer a new model with an increased maximum take-off weight. The basic model was stretched by 4.57 m (15 ft), allowing an extra five rows of seats and increasing maximum capacity to 119. However, a more typical all-coach arrangement consisted of 105 seats at a 86-cm (34-in) seat pitch. The first of the Series 30s was the DC-9-31 (left) which was priced at $3.4 million and was powered by 68-kN (14,000-lb st) JT8D-1 or -7 engines and had a maximum take-off weight of 44,444 kg

(98,000 lb). The fuselage extension was achieved by adding a 290-cm (114-in) plug forward of the wing and a 65-in (165-cm) plug aft. The baggage and cargo volume was also increased by some 50 per cent. To prevent an inhibitory take-off run, the wingspan was increased by 1.22 m (4 ft) at the tips and full-span leading-edge slats were fitted. Unofficially known as the 'king-size' DC-9, the first sale of the DC-9-31 was announced on 28 April 1965 when Allegheny Airlines ordered four examples. The DC-9-32 (above right) again increased the power, with JT8D-9/-11 or -15 engines and its maximum take-off weight increased to 48,988 kg (108,000 lb). The final variant of the Series 30 was the DC-9-34 which featured 72-kN (16,000-lb st) JT8D-17 engines and had a maximum take-off

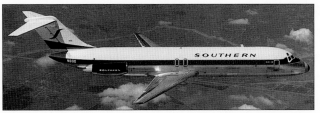

weight of 54,885 kg (121,000 lb). The three standard Series 30 versions, along with the DC-9-33 (powered by JT8D-9 engines), were offered in rapid-change, convertible freighter or all-freighter versions. The all-freight versions were allocated the 'F' suffix (above left; DC-9-33F). The other variants followed the suffix system established for the Series 15, with convertible freighters receiving the suffix 'CF' (above; DC-9-32CF and below left; DC-9-34CF), and the rapid-change versions receiving the suffix 'RC'. In all, 589 standard Series 30s were produced, with the largest customers being Allegheny Airlines (61), Delta Airlines (63) and Eastern Airlines (72). The biggest export order came from Air Canada, which received a total of 44. In addition, 27 DC-9-30CF/RC combis were delivered along with five DC-9-30Fs. The sole military customer for the Series 30 Combi was the Kuwaiti air force, which received two DC-9-32CFs.

DC-9 Series 40

The Series 40 was created by lengthening the existing plugs ahead and aft of the wing on the standard Series 30 by 96.5 cm (38 in) each, allowing two extra seat rows to be added and passenger capacity to rise to 115, with a standard 86-cm (34-in) seat pitch. The aircraft proceeded, like the Series 20, to meet the needs of SAS which required a high-capacity short-range aircraft. The DC-9-40's limited range was not appealing to most carriers and the only other customer was TOA Domestic of Japan which received 22 examples. SAS, however, did place a significant order for 49 examples (right).

DC-9 Series 50

The DC-9 Series 50 introduced yet another stretch to the airframe, increasing the overall length to 40.71 m (133 ft 7 in), allowing a maximum of 139 passengers to be carried. The wing was identical to that fitted to the Series 30, but installed thrust was increased to 144 kN (32,000 lb thrust) by incorporating the JT8D-17 engine. After the first flight in December 1974 the production versions were designated DC-9-51 and a total of 96 was delivered. Major customers included Republic (28), Finnair (left; 12), Swissair (12) and Hawaiian (10).

C-9 variants

Experience gained during the early stages of the Vietnam War highlighted the need for a dedicated aeromedical transport aircraft. Already in production, the DC-9-30 was seen as the ideal basis for such an aircraft and an order was rapidly placed. Modifications included the provision of a special-care compartment, galleys, and toilets fore and aft, and the addition of a third access door, 3.45 m (11 ft 4 in) wide, in the front fuselage with an inbuilt hydraulic ramp to facilitate the loading of litters. Accommodation was provided for up to 40 litters or more than

40 ambulatory patients, two nurses and three aeromedical attendants. This version was designated C-9A Nightingale (left) and entered service in 1968. A total of 21 C-9As was delivered to the USA. In addition, three C-9C executive transports were delivered and operated with the 89th Airlift Wing. A subsequent version of the DC-9 was developed as the C-9B Skytrain II (above), ordered by the US Navy as a fleet logistic transport. Combining features of both the Series 30 and 40, a total of 19 aircraft was manufactured for use by US Navy logistic support squadrons in the United States, while two were delivered to the US Marine Corps' Station Operations and Engineering Squadron. The US Navy subsequently purchased 10 similar DC-9-30s.

Lockheed L-1011 TriStar Development

Lockheed's entry into the widebody airliner market was one of the most advanced aircraft of its day, yet it never achieved sufficient sales to recoup its huge development costs. At one point the type almost sank Lockheed and Rolls-Royce – two of the most famous names in aviation – into oblivion.

Lockheed began studies into a widebody airliner in early 1966, based on a far-reaching requirement laid down by American Airlines for a 250-seat airliner to fly on US domestic routes. In the event, American went on to buy the rival DC-10, but Lockheed's design attracted the interests of Eastern, TWA and Air Holdings Ltd, the latter a financial consortium handling overseas sales. A combined total of 144 orders was sufficient to launch the L-1011 programme on 1 April 1968. The date proved prophetic, for the L-1011 became a major loss-maker for Lockheed, with just 250 aircraft being built.

Initially designed with two engines, the L-1011 became a three-engined aircraft (giving rise to the popular name TriStar) as a result of a scaling-up of the

N1011, the prototype TriStar, remained with Lockheed throughout its working life. In March 1968 Lockheed chose the British RB.211 engine to power the L-1011. The S-duct intake of the centrally mounted engine precluded the fitment of optional engines without incurring huge extra cost, a problem which did not affect the rival DC-10.

original requirements. Work on the first prototype began in early 1969 in a newly built facility at Palmdale, California, from where the aircraft undertook its first flight on 16 November 1970.

Financial struggle

By this time Lockheed was in deep financial trouble, largely through cost overruns incurred by the C-5 Galaxy contract, and by Lockheed's huge investment in the TriStar. Government money propped up the L-1011 programme, while thousands of workers were laid off and the production effort slowed to a trickle. Worse was to follow: on 4 February 1971 Rolls-Royce, supplier of the L-1011's RB.211 engines, collapsed. This was

again due to cost overruns on a fixed-price agreement. After much wrangling between governments, airlines and the two manufacturers, the UK government nationalized the engine company, which became Rolls-Royce (1971) Ltd, and new contracts were forged. The TriStar programme could continue, but the delays had dealt a blow to the long-term prospects of the type from which it would not recover.

Into service

Eastern received its first TriStar on 5 April 1972 and, following award of FAA Type Certification on 14 April, flew the first scheduled service on 26 April. TWA acquired its first aircraft on 9 May. Deliveries got into their stride over the next two or three years, with important customers such as Air Canada, Delta, All Nippon and British Airways acquiring the type. Indeed, the initial TriStar 1 version, tailored

Ten TriStars are seen at Palmdale during trials in 1972, the furthest aircraft being the prototype. Orders began to pick up during the year, following the bleak prospects and financial crises of 1971, when only two firm orders were placed.

to the medium-haul US domestic market, outsold the rival DC-10-10. However, McDonnell Douglas had followed up its medium-haul DC-10 version with the long-haul Series 30 almost immediately, while Lockheed had no competition to offer. The effects of the 1970–71 financial crisis had caused any development of a long-range TriStar or more powerful RB.211 engines to be put on hold. Such studies had been made in the late 1960s, under the L-1011-2 and L-1011-8 programmes, but it was to be the mid-1970s before any attempts were made to provide a meaningful rival to the DC-10-30.

The TriStar was measurably quieter than the 747 and DC-10, a fact which was plugged by Lockheed's marketing department. To reinforce the message, Eastern Air Lines rechristened its aircraft as 'Whisperliners'. This is the second TriStar to be built, used for flight trials before being delivered to the airline in 1973.

Increased weight

The first TriStar 1 derivative was the 100, which had an increased maximum take-off weight allowing greater fuel loads. A considerable degradation in field performance, particularly in hot-and-high conditions, was the esult. The increased-thrust RB.211-524' advent allowed this situation to be redressed in the L-1011-200, and subsequent conversions to L-1011-50, -150 and -250 variants further increased weights and ranges.

More important was the TriStar 500, which emerged as a true long-haul variant with a shortened fuselage and extended wingspan. These aircraft offered true intercontinental performance at economic operating costs; however only 50 were built, as most potential customers were already flying the DC-10-30. Further development studies were aimed at creating a family of TriStars offering several fuselage lengths and range/payload options. Some, like the Series 400, were aimed at breaking into the Airbus A310/Boeing 767 market. None of these was built.

Throughout its career the TriStar remained at the forefront of technological advance. It introduced a below-deck galley, although later variants returned to a traditional main-deck unit.

The No. 1 aircraft tested many new features, the most important being active control which was incorporated into the L-1011-500. Late in its life, it flew as the 'Advanced TriStar' with automatic brakes, automatic take-off thrust, cockpit CRTs and an all-moving tailplane.

Global recession in the early 1980s forced the inevitable demise of the TriStar. With outstanding orders for 21 aircraft, Lockheed announced the termination of TriStar production in December 1981.

The 250th and final aircraft, a TriStar 500 for the Algerian government, made its first flight on 3 October 1983.

SPECIFICATION

Lockheed L-1101-500 TriStar
Type: long-range commercial transport
Powerplant: three 222.42-kN (49,900-lb-thrust) Rolls-Royce RB.211-524B turbofans
Cruising speed: maximum 973 km/h (603 mph) at 9000 m (29,000 ft); economy cruise 890 km/h (552 mph) at 10,500 m (34,000 ft)
Range: 11,286 km (7,000 miles) with maximum fuel; 9905 km (6,140 miles) with maximum passenger

and baggage load
Service ceiling: 13,200 m (43,300 ft)
Weights: empty 111,311 kg (244,884 lb); maximum 228,615 kg (502,942 lb)
Dimensions: wing span 50.09 m (164 ft); length 50.05 m (164 ft); height 16.87 m (55 ft); wing area 329 m² (3,540 sq ft)
Accommodation: three flight crew; typically 24 first-class passengers and 222 economy-class passengers

Active Control

The ACS (Active Control System) was developed with the aim of improving cruise fuel efficiency. It employed a system which detected aerodynamic loads on the wings and automatically moved the ailerons up or down to counteract the load. This allowed the wings to be extended in span without the need for a structural redesign, increasing wing aspect ratio and improving cruise economics. The result was a significant reduction in fuel flow and greater comfort. Tested on the prototype, ACS was applied to production 500s shortly after the first deliveries.

Below: Three big US airlines accounted for 110 of the 161 L-1011-1s built, Eastern buying 37, Delta 35 and TWA 38. TWA's aircraft performed sterling work on high-density US domestic services from the airline's main hub at St Louis, Missouri.

Above: The first aircraft was fitted with a variety of new features, several of which found their way on to production aircraft. Although it retained the original-length fuselage, it effectively served as the prototype for the TriStar 500. Its final guise was as the Advanced TriStar. It was eventually withdrawn from use in August 1986.

McDonnell Douglas DC-10 Development

Dogged by an undeserved bad press after several serious accidents, the DC-10 nevertheless sold in considerable numbers and was, for some time, the best-selling US widebody after Boeing's 747.

The 'Big Ten' can trace its origins back to Douglas's proposals for a 650-seat aircraft to fill the USAF's 1965 CX-HLS requirement for a very large logistic transport, a contract won by Lockheed with a design that became the C-5 Galaxy.

Undeterred, Douglas set about salvaging something from the project, and from the 650-seater derived a new design aimed squarely at the 250-seat widebody market. This market had already been spotted by Lockheed (US domestic carrier, American Airlines, was the potential launch customer), which intended to exploit it with its new L-1011 TriStar.

Meanwhile Douglas, unable to fund its continued existence as a separate entity, merged with McDonnell Aircraft to form McDonnell Douglas. The 'Douglas

Commercial 10' thus became a McDonnell Douglas product and was officially launched in February 1968, having gained 50 orders, with promises of more.

First flight

The first DC-10 Series 10 took to the air on 29 August 1970. The distinctive trijet design had capacity for up to 380 passengers and was powered by three General Electric CF6 turbofans. The initial deliveries were made simultaneously in July 1971 to US carriers, American Airlines and United Airlines, with domestic services beginning the following month. In all, 122 DC-10-10s were built, including Series 10CF combi freighters with side cargo doors.

Series 40

In early 1972, the first DC-10-40 (originally known as the Series 20) was completed and flown. This variant was powered by Pratt & Whitney JT9D engines at the request of Northwest Orient. With a longer range, the 42 examples completed were

Above: The only DC-10s to be built with engines other than General Electric CF6s were the 42 DC-10-40s purchased by Northwest Orient and Japan Airlines. Initially, the long-range Series 40 was known as the Series 20, hence the titles on this aircraft, N141US, the first of Northwest Orient's fleet.

Above: With much pomp and ceremony, officials representing the two launch customers for the DC-10, United Airlines and American Airlines, take delivery of their first aircraft on 29 July 1971. United retained two 'Big Tens' as freighters in 2005.

delivered to airlines Northwest Orient and JAL.

Within four months of the first flight of the Series 40, the first Series 30 was ready. This variant was developed alongside the Series 40 with transatlantic routes in mind and, upon its

launch in 1969, had been ordered by airlines in the European KSSU group, namely KLM, Swissair, SAS and UTA. As it operated at higher weights than previous versions, the DC-10-30 sported an extra undercarriage leg beneath its centresection,

The long-range Series 30 was the best-selling DC-10 variant. I-DYNA Galileo Galilei was the first of Alitalia's eight examples and was delivered in early 1973. After nine years with the Italian carrier, the aircraft was sold back to McDonnell Douglas and leased to Aeromexico.

The DC-10's potential as a freighter was exploited towards the end of its production life, principally by FedEx which amassed a fleet of more than 30 Series 30CF combi freighters and Series 30AF all-freight aircraft. The DC-10-30CF formed the basis of the USAF's KC-10A.

a greater wingspan and more powerful CF6 engines. Swissair was to put the Series 30 into service across the Atlantic on 15 December 1972.

Engine failures plagued the first few months of DC-10 operation, while problems with an underfloor cargo door culminated in the crash of a Turkish THY Series 10 near Paris in March 1974, in which all 346 on board were killed. In June 1979, an American Airlines DC-10-10 crashed on take-off at Chicago's O'Hare airport. The FAA grounded the type and, in an unusual move, withdrew the DC-10's type certificate. By year's end, operations had resumed, but the DC-10 was again in the news in November, when an Air New Zealand Series 30 on a sightseeing flight over Antarctica crashed in white-out conditions, with the loss of all 257 passengers aboard. Although none of these

tragedies could be attributed to any major inherent flaw in the airliner's design, the DC-10's reputation never fully recovered.

The final DC-10 variant was the Series 15, which was certified in 1981. Based on the lightweight DC-10-10, the Dash-15 was tailored for 'hot and high' operations. Only seven were built, for Mexicana and Aeromexico, for operations from Mexico City.

Top-selling model

The Series 30 was to be the best-selling of the DC-10s – 266 of the 446 aircraft completed were of this variant. Between 1982 and 1988, a small number of DC-10-30ERs, with extra fuel and improved CF6 engines, was built, along with 28 Dash-30CF combi freighters and nine DC-10-30AF pure freighters. Most examples of the latter variants were delivered to Federal Express. The last commercial DC-10 off the production line

SPECIFICATION	
McDonnell Douglas DC-10 Series 30 **Type:** long-range airliner and freighter **Powerplant:** three 227.52-kN (48,100-lb-thrust) General Electric CF6-50C high-bypass turbofans **Cruising speed:** 920 km/h (570 mph) **Range:** 7500 km (4,270 miles) with maximum payload **Service ceiling:** 10,810 m (35,465 ft) **Weights:** operating empty	121,200 kg (267,200 lb); maximum loaded 263,000 kg (559,000 lb) **Dimensions:** wing span 50.40 m (161 ft 4 in); length 55.50 m (181 ft 5 in); height 17.70 m (58 ft); wing area 367.70 m² (3,921 sq ft) **Accommodation:** up to 405 passengers maximum; 323 passengers in typical two-class configuration; 293 passengers in three classes

was a Series 30 delivered to Nigerian Airlines in 1989.

Meanwhile, the Series 30CF freighter served as the basis for McDonnell Douglas's contender to satisfy the USAF's off-the-shelf ATCA (advanced tanker/cargo aircraft) requirement, a contract awarded to McDonnell Douglas in 1977. Sixty aircraft, known as KC-10A Extenders, were built, allowing the DC-10 production line to be kept open into the late 1980s, pending the development of a next-generation design.

A number of variants were proposed, but most failed to leave the drawing board, including a downsized 'DC-10 Twin' to compete with the Airbus A300. However, a stretched version – first sketched by designers in the 1970s, when it was known as the DC-10-60, but shelved during the recession of the early 1980s – showed promise and was revived in 1982. The new design was designated MD-100, then MD-XXX and it ultimately entered production in the 1990s as the MD-11.

Left: Within the proposed DC-10-60 series were the -61, -62 and -63 models, each having varying degrees of 'stretch'.

Below: In 1981, this Continental Airlines Series 10 became the first widebodied airliner to be fitted with winglets. A NASA/McDonnell Douglas test programme studied their drag-reducing effects and this led to the planned fitting of similar devices on the proposed Series 60 and its successor, the MD-11.

DC-10 variants

The DC-10 began life as a Douglas project and was one of a generation of US airliners (including the Boeing 747) that owed its existence to the US Air Force's 1965 CX-HLS airlifter programme. The DC-10 airliner that emerged in 1968 was a McDonnell Douglas product, after those two companies merged in 1967. Production continued from 1968 to 1989. In 1997 McDonnell Douglas merged with the Boeing Company, and was effectively taken over. Thus the DC-10, like all the other great Douglas airliners, has been subsumed into Boeing corporate history and, in places, is shamelessly referred to as the 'Boeing DC-10'.

DC-10 Series 10

The basic model DC-10 Series 10 (or DC-10-10) was built as a wide-bodied high-capacity airliner for domestic US trunk routes. It was similar in role and concept to Lockheed's TriStar 1 – and both were intentionally smaller than Boeing's 747, the future success of which was anything but assured at that time. The DC-10-10 was 55.56 m (182 ft 3 in) long with a wingspan of 47.36 m (155 ft 4 in) – almost identical figures to those of the TriStar. The Series 10 could accommodate up to 380 passengers in a 10-abreast configuration, but a load of 250-300 was more usual. The DC-10-10 was powered by three General Electric CF6D/-6D1 turbofans, each rated at 178 kN (40,000 lb thrust) and 182.5 kN (41,000 lb thrust), respectively. The Series 10 was built as a relatively short-range aircraft for the United States, but some aircraft were fitted with additional fuel tanks giving them transatlantic endurance. The type was certified by the FAA on 29 July 1971 and the first deliveries were made to American Airlines and United Airlines simultaneously. The DC-10-10 entered service with American on 5 August 1971, on the Los Angeles-Chicago route. Over 90 per cent of all DC-10-10 production was sold to five airlines in the United States, with American and United between them accounting for 76 per cent. A total of 122 was built before production ceased in 1982.

DC-10 Series 10CF

Nine convertible cargo/freight models of the DC-10-10 were built from new, followed by two additional conversions from existing aircraft. The CF was identical to the basic Series 10 but was fitted with a large (2.59-m x 3.56-m/102-in x 104-in) cargo door to port and a cargo handling system, including a roller floor, restraint nets, etc. The Series 10CF offered over 453 m³ (16,000 cu ft) of cargo space – enough for 30 standard 2.22-m x 2.22-m (88-in x 88-in) pallets. The first aircraft was delivered to Continental Airlines in 1974.

The bulk of the DC-10-30's much higher take-off weight was fuel. At its maximum load of 36,300 US gallons (137,410 litres; 30,226 Imperial gallons) this represented 70 per cent more fuel than the load carried by the DC-10-10.

DC-10 Series 15

The Series 15 was a development of the Series 10, intended for 'hot and high' operations and was produced specifically to meet a requirement from the Mexican airlines Aeromexico and Mexicana. Only seven were produced, between 1981 and 1982, and the final two examples served with the Minneapolis-based holiday carrier Sun Country Airlines. The DC-10-15 was powered by uprated 207-kN (46,500-lb-thrust) CF6-50C2F turbofans. These new engines allowed the DC-10-15 to operate from an 11,000-ft (3353-m) runway at 2438 m (8,000 ft) AMSL (above mean sea level) and carry 275 passengers and baggage over 3,750 nm (6940 km; 4,312 miles).

DC-10 Series 20

The Series 20 became the Series 40 (q.v.), but the prototype of this re-engined DC-10 model flew with 'DC-10 Series 20' titles before it was renamed in 1972.

DC-10 Series 30

The Series 30 was the most successful of all DC-10 variants. It was developed as a long-range version of the DC-10-10, with more powerful engines and increased operating weights. The new engines were General Electric CF6-50C/C1/C2s which were rated at between 51,000 lb and 52,500 lb (227 kN and 233.6 kN) of thrust. Maximum take-off weight could be as high as 580,000 lb (263088 kg), some 40 per cent higher than that of the DC-10-10. To cope with the weight of the airframe a distinctive two-wheel undercarriage bogie was added, under the wing centre section, between the existing main gear assemblies. This spread the DC-10-30's weight, allowing it to stay within airfield load limitations. The DC-10-30 also had an extended wing with a span of 165 ft 4 in (50.4 m). The DC-10-30 typically operates with between 220 and 260 seats, though Germany's holiday charter airline Condor did have aircraft configured for 370 passengers. The launch order for the DC-10-30 came from the KSSU group of KLM, SAS, Swissair and UTA, which ordered a total of 36 aircraft on 7 June 1969. The DC-10-30 first flew on 21 June 1972 (the third major variant, following the DC-10-10 and -20) and deliveries began to KLM and Swissair in November 1972. On 15 December 1972 the type entered service with Swissair, on its transatlantic routes. The DC-10-30 sold consistently, to numerous operators, but only in small numbers to each. The largest operator of passenger aircraft, Swissair, only acquired 13 examples from the production line. A total of 156 basic model DC-10-30s was built, not including the DC-10-30ER, DC-10-30AF/CF and KC-10A variants (described separately). The last of the 446 DC-10s to be built was a DC-10-30 (the 266th DC-10-30 if all sub-types are included). It was built for Nigeria Airways, and was delivered in 1989.

DC-10 Series 30CF and AF

Like the DC-10-10CF before it, the DC-10-30CF was a convertible passenger/freight version of the DC-10-30. It added the same cargo door and cargo system to the Series 30 airframe. A total of 28 DC-10-30CFs was built at Long Beach and several conversions of existing airframes have since been undertaken. The first DC-10-30CF was delivered to Trans International Airlines (TIA) in March 1974. Most of the -30CFs had several owners, but the bulk of the fleet saw out its time in service with FedEx Express (formerly Federal Express). It was Federal Express which was behind the development of the all-freight DC-10-30AF in the mid-1980s. This was a pure freighter version, also referred to as the DC-10-30F. Nine DC-10-30AFs were built and the first was delivered in May 1986. Distinctively, the DC-10-30AF has no cabin windows. Between November 1991 and November 1992 Sabena converted three of FedEx's DC-10-30CFs to -30AF standard.

DC-10-40

At the insistence of Northwest Orient Airlines, McDonnell Douglas developed a DC-10-30 fitted with Pratt & Whitney engines. This was the JT9D-powered DC-10-40, which began life as the DC-10-20. Northwest Orient was an early customer for the DC-10, but specified Pratt & Whitney engines for commonality with its Boeing 747s. The prototype DC-10-20 flew on 28 February 1972. The JT9D is a less powerful engine than the DC-10's baseline CF6 – rated at 203 kN (45,700 lb thrust) in its JT9D-20 version and 210 kN (47,200 lb thrust) in the -59A version. A total of 42 DC-10-40s was built for just two customers, Northwest Orient (JT9D-20) and Japan Airlines (JT9D-59A). The first delivery was made to Northwest Orient on 10 November 1972 and the type entered service on 13 December. The JAL order came much later, in 1973, when more powerful versions of the JT9D became available. The first DC-10-40 was delivered to JAL in March 1976 and subsequent orders ensured the last did not arrive until 1981.

DC-10 Advanced Freighter Conversion/MD-10

In September 1996 FedEx and McDonnell Douglas announced the DC-10 Advanced Freighter Conversion, to convert passenger DC-10s to freighters and to modify FedEx's existing DC-10 freighters to a common standard by fitting them with the Advanced Common Flightdeck (ACF). The Honeywell-developed ACF is a 'glass' EFIS cockpit (based on that of the MD-11), which allows the DC-10s to be operated by a two-person crew. The ACF was added to the newly converted freighters, and all of the modified aircraft are known as Boeing MD-10s. FedEx Express acquired a substantial number of early-model DC-10s (chiefly from United Airlines and American Airlines) and fitted them with the standard 2.59-m x 3.56-m (102-in x 104-in) cargo door of earlier freighter versions, removing all passenger equipment and fitting them out for total freight operations. A total of 70 FedEx DC-10s was covered by the contract, with a further 50 options. In August 2005, FedEx Express had 41 MD-10 conversions in service, the modification work having been undertaken at Aeronavali, in Italy, the Boeing Air Support Center/BASC (formerly Kelly AFB), Texas, Dimension Aviation, Arizona, and Mobile Aerospace, Alabama.

DC-10-30ER

Five CF6-50C2B-powered DC-10-30s were built with additional fuel tanks in the rear cargo hold for extended range (ER) operations. Seven were later modified to the same standard. These tanks could hold either 1,530 US gal (5791 litres; 1,274 Imp gal) or 3,200 US gal (12,113 litres; 2,665 Imp gal) of fuel. First deliveries were made in 1982 to Swissair and Finnair.

DC-10 cargo conversions

In 1990 Italy's Aeronavali was certified to undertake cargo conversions to existing DC-10-10s, DC-10-30s and DC-10-40s using all of Douglas's original drawings, parts and standards. Since then Aeronavali has rebuilt DC-10 freighters for various customers, including DAS Air Cargo, Gemini Air Cargo, ILFC, Aeroflot and FedEx. Aeronavali was an important modification centre for the MD-10 programme.

KDC-10

The Royal Netherlands Air Force acquired two DC-10-30CFs from Dutch cargo charter airline Martinair and converted them, in 1994/95, to act as tanker/transports – in a similar fashion to the KC-10A. The two Dutch aircraft were fitted with a refuelling boom and the unique RARO (Remote Aerial Refuelling Operation) system. The palletized RARO system allows an operator in the cabin to control the refuelling using a TV monitor, and does away with the need for a boom operator's station. The KDC-10s can also be fitted with wing-mounted hose drum units (HDUs). The first modified KDC-10 (T-264, formerly PH-MBT) flew in July 1995 and was delivered to No. 334 Squadron in August. The second followed in February 1995.

KC-10A Extender

From its original roots as a military design, the DC-10 came full circle when the USAF selected a version of the DC-10-30CF to fulfil its ATCA (Advanced Tanker Cargo Aircraft) competition, in December 1977. The airframe was fitted with an air-to-air refuelling boom, and a boom operator's station, at the rear of the fuselage. An air-to-air refuelling receptacle was also added above the cockpit. The underfloor cargo doors and all but two cabin windows were deleted. The resulting aircraft was designated KC-10A Extender. The USAF acquired a total of 60 KC-10As, which were delivered from March 1981 to November 1988. One aircraft was destroyed in a fire in 1987, but the other 59 remain in everyday service.

Airbus A300 The European challenge

Today, Airbus Industrie and Boeing fight as equals for almost every jet airliner contract. This remarkable situation come about in the three decades since the A300 made its first flight.

In the early 1960s, when the concept of a new European wide-bodied aircraft was first mooted, there were many who expressed serious doubts about the venture, especially those across the Atlantic. Yet today Airbus Industrie is on course to achieving parity with the mighty Boeing Airplane Company. The decision to develop a pan-European aircraft by Britain, France and Germany to challenge the domination of US manufacturers – a leap of faith both politically and economically – has proved right.

The emerging mass-travel era, made possible by powerful new jet engines and plummeting air fares, directed attention to high-capacity short-range aircraft, and manufacturers on both sides of the Atlantic began to develop a variety of wide-bodied concepts.

After discarding many imaginative and fanciful design concepts, which included jet flaps, canards, tandem wings, and horizontal and vertical double-deck layouts, the Airbus partners eventually settled on a fairly conventional 200-250 seat aircraft designed by a Hawker/Breguet/Nord team.

Designated the HBN 100, it proposed a circular fuselage and two Rolls-Royce high-bypass-ratio turbofan engines mounted under the low wing. When Britain pulled out on 10 April 1969 and, with Rolls-Royce concentrating on the RB.211 turbofan for the Lockheed TriStar, Airbus decided to go with the General Electric CF6-50, under development for the DC-10. The aircraft, then referred to as the A250, was renamed the A300B, alluding to the maximum seating capacity.

Design definition

By the beginning of 1969, the overall definition was complete. The length of the aircraft had

been fixed at 50.95 m (167 ft 2 in), with a 5.64-m (18-ft 6-in) fuselage diameter. The cabin would accommodate 250 passengers in comfortable eight-abreast seating, with standard freight containers in the lower cargo hold. Economic considerations dictated a cruising speed of Mach 0.84 and a typical range of 2200 km (1,367 miles).

The Hawker Siddeley-designed high-speed 28-degree swept wing was notable for the application of the rear-loading principle. This technique was designed to increase lift over the rear portion of the aerofoil before the onset of flow separation and buffet.

Plans were being drawn up to build four development aircraft, designated A300B1, around the General Electric CF6-50 turbofan, although the smaller

F-WUAB, the first A300B1 prototype, flew initially on 28 October 1972. The excellence of the design was soon revealed, but for a while it seemed as though the Airbus would never sell in numbers. Eventually, European cooperation, on an unprecedented scale, drove the programme on to success.

Rolls-Royce RB.211 engine remained an option, primarily to win orders from British customers. Across the Channel, Air France was pressing for the inclusion of 24 more passengers, and this was achieved by inserting two extra fuselage frames ahead and three aft of the wings, providing space for three more rows of eight seats each. It was decided that the last two development

Building an Airbus

Hawker Siddeley worked on the A300 wing design for almost nine years. The wings of all subsequent Airbus aircraft have been designed and produced in Britain, latterly at British Aerospace's Filton and Chester works. Main components are also constructed in France and Germany, with various subcontractors responsible for more minor systems, and components spread throughout Europe. Final assembly of the A300, as with all Airbus types except the A319/A321, is carried out at Airbus's Toulouse headquarters.

SPECIFICATION	
Airbus A300B4	**Weights:** empty 79,831 kg
Type: medium-haul twin-engined	(175,628 lb); loaded 165,000 kg
airliner	(363,000 lb)
Powerplant: two 233.45-kN	**Dimensions:** wing span 44.84 m
(52,390-lb-thrust) General Electric	(147 ft); length 53.62 m (175 ft
CF6-CI advanced technology	10 in); height (16.53 m (54 ft 3 in);
turbofan engines	wing area 260 m² (279 sq ft)
Maximum cruising speed: 911 km/h	**Accommodation:** flight deck crew
(565 mph) at 7620 m (25,000 ft)	of two; 8 to 12 flight attendants;
Service ceiling: with passengers	seating layouts for 220 to
13,000 m (42,460 ft); empty	336 passengers; maximum
15,000 m (49,200 ft)	capacity 375

A triple-slotted trailing-edge flap arrangement had become accepted as the normal system for large airliners. In its quest for reliability and maintainability, Airbus ruled out this traditional flap installation in favour of tabbed Fowler flaps, an option which offered greater mechanical simplicity.

line. The completed A300B was introduced to the public at a roll-out ceremony at Toulouse on 28 September 1972. Exactly one month later, on 28 October, A300B1 F-WUAB took off on its maiden flight, returning one hour and 23 minutes later.

Service debut

In 1973, the prototype, joined by the second A300B1, fitted in an ambitious demonstration programme, including an extensive world tour, to stimulate interest in Europe's new airliner. The final certification flight was made on 31 January 1974, with French and German certification granted on 15 March 1974, two months ahead of schedule. Launch customer Air France took delivery of its first A300B2 on 10 May 1974, and the airline introduced the type into service on its Paris–London route 13 days later.

aircraft were to be built to this A300B2 configuration.

The long-expected first order for the Airbus was finally signed on 9 November 1971, with Air France contracting to buy just six A300B2s and taking options on 10 more. That same month, Airbus Industrie decided to offer an increased-range model, the A300B4, to widen its market appeal, and it was this which

became the standard model. The B4 differed in having an additional centre wing tank, and a changed fuel-management system which increased the range to more than 3700 km (2,300 miles). Iberia was the first to place a contract for the A300B4 in January 1972. Lufthansa signed a contract for three A300B2s on 7 May 1973. The Airbus work was shared

among the partners roughly in proportion to their financial holdings. From the aircraft's inception, it had been planned that each partner would contribute complete sub-assemblies in a 'ready-to-fly' condition, with all cables, pipe runs and equipment installed and checked. The result was that just 4 per cent of the man-hours were spent on the final assembly

First customers

Air France and Lufthansa were obvious first customers for the all-European airliner. With the UK government having withdrawn at an early stage, leaving Hawker Siddeley to make Britain's contribution privately, it was unlikely that an order would hail from British Airways. Boeing was already the dominant manufacturer represented in BA's fleet, while Lufthansa had to be persuaded to break its 'all-Boeing' policy. Air France flew its first A300B2 service on 23 May 1974; Lufthansa its first on 1 April 1976.

A300 variants Family planning

Above: The extended-range A300-600R first flew on 9 December 1987 and features the tailplane trim tank developed for the A310. This example is seen prior to delivery to Thai Airways and is one of 10 -600Rs currently operated by the airline.

Left: With two extra rows of seats, the A300-600 can carry more passengers than the standard A300B4 (361 in all-tourist class). Saudi Arabian Airlines currently operates 11 examples.

The short/medium-range A300 was the first wide-bodied twin-engined aircraft to enter airline service. It evolved through the design stage to meet different and changing airline requirements, and later benefited from the application of new technologies as they became available.

Only the first two aircraft were built to the original A300B1 configuration before a demand for more seats produced the A300B2, which became the first model to go into service. South African Airways specified Krüger flaps on its A300B2s to improve hot-and-high airfield performance, as the A300B2K. Increased range was provided in the A300B4 through the addition of a new centre wing fuel tank.

The A300B4 made its first flight on 26 December 1974 and received its type certificate on 26 March 1975, entering service with Germanair in May. To bring some semblance of order to the growing number of variants and permutations of weights and engine combinations, Airbus devised a new designation system, which took effect from 1978. Standard A300B2 and B4 models were given the -100 suffix, while aircraft with higher gross weights took on the -200 suffix. A special heavier model for Scandinavian Airlines System (SAS), the first to introduce the Pratt & Whitney JT9D turbofan, was designated A300B2-300.

As sales of the A300 boomed, Airbus introduced the A300C4 convertible freighter. Hapag-Lloyd of Germany was the first customer and introduced the type into service in 1980.

The two engine types also had their own groupings, so that aircraft which were numbered from -100 to 119 and -200 to -219 had CF6-50 engines, and those numbered from -120/220 to 139/239 were powered by the JT9D-59A.

As a means of extending the market appeal of the aircraft, Airbus also offered convertible and all-freighter versions of the B4, both fitted with a 7.07-m x 2.54-m (23-ft 2-in x 8-ft 4-in) upward-opening cargo door on the port side and

Built originally as an A300B2-320, which was a specially developed heavier version for SAS with Pratt & Whitney JT9D turbofans, LN-RCA was converted to an A300B4-120 in 1983. At this time the aircraft was leased to Scanair, SAS's charter and inclusive tour subsidiary, *and operated on summer flights to the Mediterranean. The aircraft operated with Scanair until bought by Conair of Denmark in 1987.*

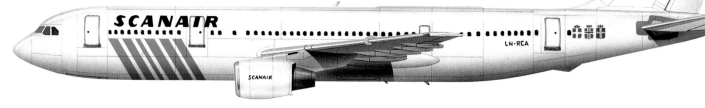

Right: The needs of South African Airways prompted the development of the A300B2K, which featured Krüger flaps to improve hot-and-high take-off performance. SAA introduced the variant into service in 1976.

Left: Delivered in 1980, A300B4-203 SX-BEE typifies the durability of the A300, having racked up almost 20 years' service with Olympic.

SPECIFICATION

Airbus A300-600
Type: medium-range wide-body airliner
Powerplant: wo 262.4-kN (59,000-lb-thrust) General Electric CF6-80C2A1s, or two 273.6-kN (61,500-lb-thrust) CF6-80C2A5s, or two 249-kN (56,000-lb-thrust) Pratt & Whitney PW-4156s or two 258-kN (58,000-lb-thrust) PW-4158 turbofans
Cruising speed: 875 km/h (544 mph)
Range: typical weight with 267 passengers with 370 km

(230 miles) of reserves and standard fuel 6670 km (4145 miles)
Weights: empty with CF6s 90,115 kg (198,665 lb), with PW-4000s 90,065 kg (198,565 lb); maximum take-off 165,900 kg (365,745 lb)
Dimensions: wing span 44.84 m (147 ft 1 in); length 54.08 m (177 ft 5in); height 16.62 m (54 ft 6.5 in); wing area 260.0 m² (2798.7 sq ft.
Accommodation: flight crew of two; typical two-class arrangement of 2366 passengers (26 first-class and 240 economy-class)

capable of carrying a 40-tonne payload a distance of 1850 km (1,150 miles). Only three and two, respectively, were later built on the production line, although there were some subsequent conversions.

Hapag-Lloyd took delivery of the first convertible A300C4-200 in January 1980, while Korean Air Lines followed in August 1986 with the A300F4-200 all-cargo variant.

New variant

In parallel with the development of the advanced shortened A310, Airbus produced what it called the 'world's largest twin-aisle aircraft'. Designated the A300B4-600, generally simplified to A300-600, this model was launched on 16 December 1980 with an order from Saudia.

The A300-600 incorporated many new design features, headed by a new two-crew cockpit with digital avionics and flight management systems and a unique electronic centralised aircraft monitor (ECAM) providing extensive aircraft systems information. Other key improvements were a substantially modified wing, electrical signalling for flaps, slats and spoilers, wingtip fences for drag reduction, carbon brakes, and a saving of 1.5 tonnes in weight through the use of composite materials. The new aircraft provided typical two-class seating for 266 passengers in a slightly longer fuselage, or up to 361 in an all-tourist layout. The A300-600 made its first flight on 8 July 1983 and received its type approval on 9 March 1984.

Next to fly, on 12 April 1984, was the convertible A300C4-600. Equipped with a large forward port-side cargo door and capable of being operated in all-passenger or all-freight modes with a maximum structural payload of 46.8 tonnes, the first 'C' variant was delivered to the Kuwait Airways on 30 May 1984. The A300-600 replaced previous models after the last deliveries of the A300B4 were made in early 1985, but the process of product improvement was far from complete.

Extended range

On 2 March 1987, American Airlines launched the extended-range A300B4-600ER, but soon shortened to A300-600R. The -600R differed in its installation of a 6,150-litre (1,620-US gallon) fuel tank in the horizontal stabilizer, with a computerized fuel transfer system for active centre-of-gravity control, and the required equipment fit for 180-minute ETOPS (extended range twin-engine operations) approval. The A300-600R first flew on 9 December 1987 and entered service with American Airlines the following May.

Apart from a handful of orders, cargo versions of the A300 had attracted little interest from airlines until the giant US package operator Federal Express signed a huge order for the all-cargo A300-600F. This definitive freighter version can accommodate a single or double row of standard pallets, plus four pallets and 10 LD3 containers, or 22 LD3s, on the lower deck. Main structural changes from the passenger aircraft include the addition of a large maindeck cargo door on the port side (as fitted to the convertible 'C' models), a reinforced main deck floor, and the deletion of cabin windows. The A300-600F took to the skies on 2 December 1993, with the first delivery to Federal Express taking place on 27 April 1994.

The introduction of the vastly improved A300-600/-600R models created a buoyant market for freighter conversion programmes, carried out on older passenger service models. Both ChryslerBenz Aerospace Airbus (Dasa) and British Aerospace Aviation Services developed conversion kits, which include the same large port-side cargo door, reinforcement of the main deck floor and other features from the production freighter.

With the widest fuselage in its class the A300-600F is an ideal aircraft for cargo-carriers such as Federal Express. The aircraft features a large maindeck cargo door and a reinforced floor.

Airbus A310 Shortening the A300

Developed initially as the Airbus A300B10, one of the many proposed versions of the original A300, the A310 was launched in 1978 after interest was shown in the project by Lufthansa and Swissair.

Recognized at the time as one of the most fuel-efficient, medium-haul transports in the world, despite keen competition from Boeing's 767, Airbus Industries' A310 was originally planned as a huge airliner, with a fuselage diameter of 6.4 m (20.9 ft). Airlines thought this too big, however, and it was subsequently cut back to a diameter of 5.64 m (18.50 ft). The number of seats (typical mixed-class) was reduced from 300 to around 250.

Originally called the A300B10, it eventually matured into the A310. Lufthansa and Swissair, were the main backers for the new smaller aircraft.

In late 1977 the brilliant aerodynamics team of British Aerospace at Hatfield – which a decade earlier had designed the wing of the larger A300B – began scheming a totally new wing for the proposed 'all-new' A300B10. But BAe was not a member of the consortium, so other new wing designs were started by German partners MBB, VFW-Fokker, and French partner, Aérospatiale.

Above: Along with Lufthansa, Swissair was the A310's launch customer, the aircraft illustrated here being the first pre-production example painted in Swiss colours. With deliveries commencing in 1985, six A310s served with the airline, operating on high-density, short-/medium-haul services, until the last example was withdrawn in 1999.

Has anything changed?

The public first saw the A310 in the form of a model at the Hanover air show in April 1978. It looked very much like the A300B, but the wing was smaller and the fuselage was 12 frames shorter. The engines were expected to be lower-thrust versions of those used on the A300B. The only real argument still concerned the wing, but a solution was in sight when, in January 1979, British Aerospace returned to Airbus as a full partner. BAe accordingly

As with all early-generation Airbus aircraft, the final assembly of the A310 took place at Aérospatiale's factory in Toulouse-Blagnac in southern France.

handled the main responsibility for the wing.

The final wing configuration, however, differed significantly from that of the A300B. From the front it looked very thin, apart from the portion inboard of the engines – where the wing grew thicker rapidly – and its undersurface curving sharply down towards the very bottom of the fuselage. Fowler flaps were fitted outboard, while inboard the flaps were of the double-slotted variety.

The A310 fuselage had a redesigned rear end, with the rear pressure bulkhead nearer the tail. So while the fuselage was reduced in length, by 13 frames, compared to that of the A300B the cabin is only 11 frames shorter. Other changes included a smaller horizontal tail

The A310 first flew in April 1982 and, by September that year, the order book stood at 102 due to the aircraft's excellent performance and fuel economy which had become evident in test flights.

Left: Operating with the Dutch airline, KLM, and supplementing its Boeing 737s were six A310-200s. The aircraft served on KLM's short-haul routes throughout Europe. They were later sold to Fed Ex in summer 1996, and converted to an all-freight configuration.

Below: British Caledonian was absorbed by British Airways in 1988. The remaining A310s were sold by BA a short time later.

and revised engine pylons that were able to accept either General Electric or Pratt & Whitney engines without modification. Regarded as the main pioneering breakthrough was the adoption of Airbus Industrie's FFCC (forward-facing crew cockpit), with multi-function cathode-ray tube displays and digital avionics.

Workshare changes

In organizing the A310 manufacturing programme, there were a few changes compared to that of the A300B. Aérospatiale constructed the nose, including the cockpit, the lower centre section, including the wing box under the floor, the engine pylons and airbrakes. This took place, along with the assembly of the aircraft and flight testing, at Toulouse-Blagnac. MBB constructed almost all of the entire fuselage, as well as the vertical tail, flaps, spoilers and final assembly of the wings. When completed they were dispatched to Toulouse. British Aerospace at Chester made the wing inter-spar boxes, which are by far the strongest and heaviest parts of the whole aircraft. CASA's plants in Spain constructed the horizontal tail, forward passenger

Lufthansa demonstrated its fleet renewal policy with the purchase of nine A310s in 1982, receiving the -200 model (illustrated). This was later replaced by the -300 variant.

doors and landing-gear doors. In the Netherlands, Fokker made the all-speed ailerons between the flaps, wingtips, main-leg doors and flap-track fairings. A specially formed Belgian consortium, Belairbus, supplied full-span slats and forward wing/body fairings.

Production begins

Aérospatiale did not set up any separate assembly line for the A310, but slotted the smaller aircraft in among the A300Bs and A300-600s. There was no prototype, though the first four differed from production aircraft in various ways. The first two had an emergency crew escape route

through the nose-gear bay and another had provision for explosive bolts on one of the main cargo doors, to comply with FAA regulations.

Airbus had planned a short-haul A310-100, but this was never built and the first aircraft

SPECIFICATION	
Airbus A310-300 **Type:** twin-engined medium- to long-range passenger airliner **Powerplant:** two 262-kN (59,000-lb-thrust) General Electric CF6-80C2AB or 249-kN (56,000-lb-thrust) Pratt & Whitney PW4156A turbofans **Maximum speed:** 804 km/h (498 mph) at 9450 m (31,000 ft) **Range:** 8056 km with P&W engines	**Service ceiling:** 12,912 m (40,000 ft) **Weights:** empty 71,480 kg (158,048 lb); maximum take-off 150,900 kg (331,980 lb) **Dimensions:** wing span 43.89 m (144 ft); length 46.666 m (153 ft); height 15.80 m (51 ft 10 in); wing area 219 m² (2,356 sq ft) **Accommodation:** standard seating for 250 passengers; maximum 280

were A310-200s, which became the basic passenger version, with internal fuel capacity of 55,000 litres (12,098 Imperial gallons).

The first flight took place on 3 April 1982, and from the very beginning it was clear that the new Airbus was a winner.

Airbus A310 Further development

Proving its critics wrong with a series of publicity-staged long-distance flights, Airbus Industrie's A310 was ordered by a host of airlines to fulfil the niche for a twin-engined, long-distance airliner. Even though now overshadowed in production by later Airbus models it remains in service around the world.

The A310's performance during its first flight directly contributed to the design of the new wing, which was absolutely 'clean' in having no flaws (such as gaps in the slats at the inboard end or above the engine pylon), an outstanding aerofoil profile with a flat-top section, and an average thickness/chord ratio of almost 12 per cent. Perhaps the greatest surprise was the buffet boundary (the combination of speed and altitude at which aerodynamic buffet will be encountered even in level flight) which exceeded expectation by almost 10 per cent, which meant that the A310 could either cruise 900 m (2952 ft) higher for any given weight, or carry 10.8 tons more payload at a typical cruise altitude.

Confounding the critics
The no. 2 aircraft (F-WZLI) flew on 13 May 1982, and soon made a route-proving trip to the Far East. Up to this time, an army of rivals, led by America's Boeing Company, had poured scorn on the European A310, pointing out how poor its high-altitude performance would be, being penalized by so small a wing. On this trip, the aircraft silenced such critics for ever.

It carried a full load, equivalent to 218 passengers and baggage, a distance of 4818 km (2,994 miles) from Toulouse to Kuwait. It then fought against headwinds of 53 mph (85 km/h) all the way to Singapore – a distance of 7415 km (4,607 miles), once more with a full load. But it was the sector from Kuala Lumpur to Bangkok that surprised the critics. Again with a full payload, F-WZLI took off and climbed straight up to a height of 13,100 m (42,979 ft). Throughout the 26000-km (16,155-mile) trip, the Mach 0.8 cruise returned an average fuel burn of 6.67 litres/km (2.7 Imp gal/ nautical mile) – 6.5 per cent below the prediction of the Airbus engineers.

Powerplant choices
The first two aircraft were powered by Pratt & Whitney JT9D-7R4D1 engines, each rated at 213.5 kN (48,000 lb thrust).

Before Pan Am's demise, the airline was one of the major US airlines to embrace Airbus products – ordering significant batches of A300s and A310s. At one stage its A310 fleet stood at 19, made up of seven -200s and 12 -300s. Several served on Pan Am's European network.

An alternative launch engine was the JT9D-7R4E1, or the lighter General Electric CF6-80C2A2, both rated at 222.4 kN (50,000 lb thrust). In 1980, widespread interest in the aircraft from the Middle East appeared to offer an opening to Rolls-Royce which, by this time, was beginning to realize that it had been mistaken in not becoming involved in the development of the A310.

Above: The first prototype of the A310-300 wore this striking colour scheme during its publicity sales tour. The aircraft was displayed at both the Farnborough and Paris airshows.

Below: Two A310-300s, delivered in 1991, were operated by the former Czechoslovakia's national airline, CSA. Following partition of the country, the aircraft continued to serve with the airline, although in a slightly revised colour scheme.

Below: FedEx currently operates the largest fleet of A310s. All their A310-200F aircraft have undergone conversion to a freighter configuration, which involved introducing a large cargo door on the front port side of the fuselage.

Above: Air India still operates a fleet of 20 A310-300s (12 of which are leased) on its medium- and long-haul routes. This example is seen wearing a trials colour scheme that was ultimately not adopted by the airline fleet.

In the course of production of the A310-200, various improvements were introduced, the most visible being the addition of winglets. Airbus Industrie called these 'wingtip fences', and they are larger than those of the A300-600, and of a quite different shape. The first example to receive these additional winglets was a Thai Airways aircraft, delivered on 7 May 1986. The winglets were subsequently retrofitted to a few A310-200s in service. Another version, first delivered to Martinair of the Netherlands in November 1984, was the A310-200C convertible. This had an upper-deck cargo door with a width of 3.58 m (11.7 ft), and a convertible interior which can accept 16 cargo pallets or any combination of cargo and passengers. Martinair's two examples were later sold to freight operator FedEx. In response to a request, Airbus developed the -200F, a dedicated all-cargo version, with a weight-limited payload of 38.7 tons.

Cargo conversions of the aircraft have firmly established the A310 within the United States. FedEx operates the aircraft on freight routes around the world, the aircraft having proved themselves to be extremely versatile and economical to operate.

In 1982, Airbus announced a third version, the A310-300, aimed at even longer routes. The programme was announced during the handover of Swissair's first A310, and that same airline again became the launch customer. Visually, the A310-300 is almost identical to the -200, although it does carry the distinctive winglets as standard. Again, there was a choice of powerplants; the first Swissair A310-300 example took to the air on 8 July 1985, powered initially by JT9D-7R4E1 engines, although Pratt & Whitney PW4000-series engines were intended for the final aircraft. The first A310-300 powered by CF6-80C2 engines flew on 6 September 1985.

Perhaps the most important development for the new longer-range version was the tailplane trim tank. Most conventional aircraft have a natural tendency to go into a dive. It is prevented by the tailplane or elevators continuously being angled to push the tail down. This fights against the lift of the wing and increases drag. In the A310-300, the tailplane is full of fuel, and this exerts the required download with no drag.

Optional 7,200-litre (1,853 Imperial-gallon) tanks can be carried in the hold but, without these, the A310-300 still has remarkable range – 8300 km (5,157 miles) with a full payload. This ability has allowed many airlines to qualify the A310 for ETOPS overwater routes.

Military service

Although aimed purely at the commercial market, the A310 has adopted a limited military role within some armed forces. The first military delivery was in September 1991, comprising one aircraft for the Royal Thai air force for governmental transportation tasks. In the following year, the German Luftwaffe took delivery of three A310s originally operated by the East German airline Interflug. Similarly, the Canadian Forces adopted five A310s as replacements for its five elderly Boeing 707s (CC-137s) used by No. 437 Sqn, designating the type CC-150 Polaris.

At present, the only other European military operators are Belgium and France's Armée de l'Air, which operates three A310s, replacing DC-8s operated by ET 3/60.

Thailand was the first to put the A310 into military service, one being employed on VIP transport duties. France, Germany and Canada later followed.

Airbus A320 The first FBW airliner

The first A320 was ceremonially rolled out at Toulouse on 14 February 1987 and flew on 22 February. Certification was achieved on 26 February 1988, and scheduled services began with Air France and British Airways in April 1988.

The A320 is a true multinational project, with sections built by Aérospatiale, BAe, CASA and Deutsche Airbus (MBB and VFW). The various components are then assembled in Toulouse.

After successes with the A300 and A310, Airbus turned to the A320, hoping that it would emulate the successes of its relatives. A delay in development allowed the A320 to become the world's most advanced airliner on its introduction into service.

Airbus Industrie has, from the start, been identified in the minds of the public and of its customers with fat wide-body, or twin-aisle, aircraft. But for commercial success a manufacturer (of almost anything) needs to be able to offer a broad spectrum of products. From as early as 1970 the Airbus management studied possible single-aisle (SA) aircraft, much smaller than the A300B and A310 and more in the class of the 737 or DC-9.

Dassault was building the Mercure (and losing all its investment, with a production run of 10). BAC wanted to build the One-Eleven 700 or 800, as well as wide-body 3-11s. BAC was also a partner in the rival Europlane consortium. Hawker Siddeley wanted to build a QTOL (quiet take-off and landing) aircraft in partnership with Dornier and

VFW-Fokker. Later came a spate of national or international projects, including the European JET family and the Dutch Fokker F29. But in 1979 British Aerospace became a member of Airbus Industrie, and the JET family became the Airbus SA-1 and SA-2, single-aisle projects with different body lengths to seat from 130 to 180.

In 1980 it looked as if such aircraft could be designed for propfan propulsion, offering reduced fuel consumption, without any significant loss in cruising speed. Airbus carried out a prolonged study of propfans, in partnership with Hamilton Standard and Pratt & Whitney. The outcome was a decision to stick to advanced turbofans. The resulting A320 was announced in February 1981 and given the go-ahead at the Paris air show four months later. The go-ahead was more in spirit than practice, however. For one thing, no decision had been made between a number of candidate engines in the thrust range 90–122 kN (20,006–27,000 lb), some of which existed only on paper. But

Below: When it entered service, the A320 completely outclassed the market in terms of high technology, both in its aerodynamics and onboard equipment. The A320 set a standard that is only today being challenged by other manufacturers.

Subsequently, IAE (International Aero Engines, a powerful five-nation consortium including Rolls-Royce and Pratt & Whitney) offered a newer and even more advanced engine, the V2500. It was soon clear that the V2500 was a superb engine, clearly the toughest and also the quietest in its class, and from 1989 it offered the very keenest of propulsion competition.

Range extension

Except for the 100 series, all aircraft have a large centresection fuel tank, which increased fuel capacity from 15,588 litres (3,429 Imperial gallons) for the -100 to 23,430 litres (5,154 Imperial gallons), giving the aircraft a range with 150 passengers and baggage of around 3,000 nm (5550 km; 3,450 miles). And, except for the early Dash-100s, all A320s have winglets, or as Airbus calls them, 'wingtip fences', which further enhance aerodynamic efficiency and correspondingly save a significant amount of fuel.

SPECIFICATION	
Airbus A320-200 **Type:** twin-engine short- and medium-haul airliner **Powerplant:** two 111.21-kn (20,000-lb-thrust) IAE V2525 or two 117-kN (26,500-lb-thrust) CFM56 turbofans **Cruising speed:** 960 km/h (600 mph) **Range:** 5460 km (3,400 miles) (V2525); 5615 km (3,500 miles) (CFM56) with optional long-range tanks	**Weights:** empty 41,500 kg (91,500 lb); loaded 73,000 kg (161,000 lb) **Dimensions:** wing span 33.91 m (111 ft 3 in); length 37.57 m (123 ft 3 in); height 11.80 m (38 ft 8 in); wing area 122.40 m² (1,318 sq ft) **Accomodation:** two flight deck crew; four cabin attendants; maximum 179 passengers (single class) or 150 passengers (two classes)

far more serious was the fact that the British government had failed to reach any agreement with British Aerospace regarding support and launch costs. Not until 1 March 1984 could BAe at last announce an agreement, in which the early part of the programme was to be assisted by a loan of £250 million, repayable by BAe, to help the company with massive tooling costs in building the wings.

Design refinement

The three 'lost' years were not wasted because throughout this period both the design of the A320 and its exceedingly advanced systems were refined and improved. The main externally obvious development was to make all aircraft the same length and, though this was fixed at only 37.70 m (123 ft 3 in), not much longer than the 'short' Dash-100, the internal cabin length was almost the same as that of the previous 'long' -200.

The wing passed through several evolutionary stages with six different spans, finally settling at 33.91 m (111 ft 3 in). It was long and slender, with an aspect ratio of over nine, making for an aerodynamic efficiency significantly greater than that of

the wings of the 737 or MD-80. Another advantage over those older-technology rivals was that the fuselage diameter was greater: the internal cabin width is 3.70 m (12 ft 1 in), compared with 3.25 m (10 ft 8 in) for the 737 and 757, and 3.07 m (10 ft 1 in) for the MD-80 series.

Looking at an A320, an aerodynamicist might comment on the almost perfect external

form, and on the unique way in which the wings have only two sections of slotted flaps on each side, running aft and down on tracks to form an unbroken lifting surface from root to aileron. Whenever an A320 flies through turbulence, accelerometers in the fuselage sense vertical accelerations and, via the universal electrical fly-by-wire signalling, power the ailerons and spoilers to damp out and virtually eliminate disturbance.

In the end, CFM International came up with an engine specially tailored to the new airliner, and Airbus went ahead with this. The CFM56-5-A1 has active clearance control and full authority digital control, with a take-off thrust of 112.5 kN (25,000 lb).

When the A320 was launched, this was the only engine available.

State-of-the-art equipment

Probably the most visible aspect of the avionics is the flight deck. At first sight there seems to be no way to fly the aircraft because the traditional control yoke is missing! In its place is a small SSC (sidestick controller), as in the F-16, which responds electronically to the force exerted upon it by the pilot (complex laws have been followed to enable two pilots to transfer control, and to allow one pilot to override another, should this ever become necessary). Absence of the yoke makes room for a pull-out table in front of each pilot, and also gives a perfect view of the instruments. But again there is a surprise, because there seem to be no instruments. Instead, there are just six multi-function colour displays, two facing each pilot and two on the centreline. These displays are bigger than any seen previously, at 18.4 cm (7¼ in) square. They comprise a PFD (primary flight display) and an ND (navigation display) for each pilot, while the two in the middle serve the ECAM (electronic centralised aircraft monitor). Each display can be made to tell the pilot almost anything, driven

by three management computers. When one counts all the displays and instruments, the total comes to 12, compared with 42 in the 737-300 and 43 in the MD-80, yet the A320 pilot can call up a far greater amount of information.

On the central console are the usual throttles (which are not connected to the engines but to the FADECs (full-authority digital engine controls)) and other controls. There are also new systems, such as a compact and totally integrated RMP (radio management panel) on each side of the engine controls, giving instant and faultless control of every radio and navaid in the aircraft, and two NICD1Js. The latter, the multi-function controller display units, are the human interfaces with another piece of equipment possessed by older aircraft, a CFDS (centralized fault display system). Previous BITE (built-in test equipment) developed haphazardly, but in the 320 the CFDS is a perfect system from nose to tail and from wingtip to wingtip. It records every error or fault, or even a fault about to happen.

Airbus A320/A321 Stretching the family

Left: British Midland became an Airbus customer when it ordered 11 A320s and nine A321s in July 1997. Deliveries began in spring 1998. At the time the largest single Airbus order by a UK customer, the acquisition allowed Europe-wide operations.

Below: Northwest Airlines, one of the world's largest Airbus operators, maintains a fleet which includes 70 A320s, alongside examples of the same manufacturer's A319 and A330.

Moving from strength to strength, the A320 and higher-capacity A321 have now, together with the A319, created a family of mid-sized airliners that compete directly for orders with Boeing's 737 family.

From the third quarter of 1988, the standard A320 version became the Dash-200, with the manufacturer placing emphasis on this model's greater capability compared to the initial A320-100 series. In early 1989, A320s started rolling off the Airbus production line with the new IAE V2500 engine. This powerplant was first flown on a Boeing 720 in Canada, and first powered an Airbus Industrie test A320 in July 1988. Visually, the V2500 engine pod is differentiated from the CFM56 by its smooth unbroken curve from the inlet to the single nozzle at the rear. The CFM56 pod, by contrast, has a large forward section which discharges fan air, followed by a slim aft fairing over the core.

First V2500 sales
The first customer for the V2500-powered A320 was Cyprus Airways, which began receiving a batch of eight of the type in 1989. These allowed the airline to replace its ageing BAC One-Elevens and Boeing 707s, to become an all-Airbus operator. Shortly afterwards, V2500-engined A320s were delivered to Indian Airlines, fulfilling an initial order for 19 of the type. Indian Airlines' A320s were the first examples to be fitted with new four-wheel bogie main landing gears.

Originally, it had been intended that A320 customers would have been offered the option of a two-wheel main landing gear with enlarged tyres inflated to reduced pressure, giving a bigger footprint area, and thus enabling the A320 to operate from unimproved surfaces; however, it was found that a four-wheel main gear bogie would complete this task more effectively.

Future developments
From 1985 onwards, Airbus Industrie began to study a range of A320 developments, the first – which was launched in 1989 – being the A321-100. The A321 had begun life as the projected 'A320 Stretch' or 'Stretched A320', a longer-fuselage higher-capacity version of the A320. In June 1989 it formally became the A321, with accommodation for 185 passengers within a lengthened fuselage.

Fuselage stretch
Remaining a minimum-change version of the A320, the A321 incorporates a 6.93-m (273-in) fuselage stretch, with a reinforced centre fuselage and undercarriage, and redesigned trailing-edge flaps. The fuselage stretch comprises two plugs forward and aft of the wing. This length increase dictated the repositioning of the four

Above: The A320 was the first commercial aircraft to be equipped with fly-by-wire (FBW) control throughout the flight regime. Bahrain-based Gulf Air operates a fleet of 12 A320s.

Left: British Airways' A320s were ordered by British Caledonian. The airline currently operates a mixed fleet of A320-100 and -200 models, the latter now being the standard production variant.

A subsidiary of Cyprus Airways, Eurocypria Airlines operated a fleet of three Airbus A320s in the 1990s. The airline replaced its A320s with new-generation Boeing 737-800s in 2003.

emergency exits, which are now positioned to either side of the wing leading and trailing edges.

The first A321 prototype (F-WWIA) made its maiden flight with V2530 engines, on 11 March 1993, while the second, CFM56-5B-powered, prototype first flew in May 1993. The A321-100 is offered with a choice of CFM International CFM56-5B or IAE V2530-A5 turbofans.

It was initially planned to assemble the A321 alongside the A320 on Airbus Industrie's Toulouse production lines. However, the A321 became the first Airbus to be assembled in Germany, with the airframes being constructed at DASA's facility in Hamburg.

Launch customers for the A321 were Lufthansa, choosing the higher-powered V2530 for its 20 aircraft, and Alitalia, which ordered 40 examples. Lufthansa took delivery of the first production A321 on 27 January 1994, followed by Alitalia, whose first CFM56-5B-powered A321 arrived on 22 March.

Launched in April 1995, the A321-200, meanwhile, was developed as an extended-range version, incorporating greater fuel capacity and a maximum take-off weight increased from 182,980 lb (83,000 kg) to 196,200 lb (88,996 kg).

The A321-200 was introduced in 1997, after making its four-and-a-half-hour maiden flight from Hamburg, Germany, on 12 December 1996. The A321-200 has an increased range of 2,700 nm (5000 km; 3,107 miles), an increase of approximately 350 nautical miles (404 miles; 650 km) over the baseline A321-100.

Sales success

With the introduction of the A320/A321, Airbus Industrie has succeeded in conquering a share of the North American market, where the family (including the A319) has accumulated in excess of 1600 orders. United Airlines became the largest A320 operator, and in April 1999 took delivery of the 1001st A320 family airliner. United Airlines ordered 50 A320s in July 1992, followed by options on a further 50, and received its first V2500-engined example in November 1993. Today, United has received a total of 153 A320 family examples with a further 42 on order.

Another North American Airbus operator, US Airways, introduced the A320 on its Washington D.C. (Reagan National) to New York (La Guardia) shuttle service in October 1999. Replacing the Boeing 727 on this heavily travelled East Coast route, the US Airways' A320s have inevitably proved themselves quieter, more fuel-efficient and more comfortable for passengers (each seat also provides a laptop computer port and there is a telephone in every row).

In March 1998 three South American airlines (Chilean flag carrier LanChile, Brazilian TAM and the Central American TACA group) signed a contract for the joint purchase of 179 Airbus aircraft, comprising A320s and A319s, the then largest-ever order for Airbus Industrie.

The year 1998 saw the first Airbus operator within the former Soviet Union, as Kyrgyzstan Airlines flew its first A320 service between Frankfurt, Gemany, and Bishkek on 3 July. Furthermore, on 24 September, Chengdu-based Sichuan Airlines received its first A321, marking the A321's entry into the Chinese market.

Impressive figures

It is more than 17 years now since the first A320 entered commercial operations, and to date the A320 family has carried well over a billion passengers. Some 2500 examples of the A320 family have been delivered, with another 1000 on order. Some 240 customers have selected the A320 family, which comprises the 124-seat A319, 150-seat A320 and the 185-seat A321. From just 16 deliveries in the first year of production, Airbus Industrie now delivers in excess of 16 A320 family airliners every three weeks.

Right: A stretched version of the A320, the Airbus A321, was launched in November 1989. The extra fuselage length offers 24 per cent more passenger seating and 40 per cent more hold area than its A320 brethren.

Left: Launch customer for the A321 was Lufthansa, introducing the type on its European routes in March 1994. Lufthansa chose the more powerful IAE V2530 turbofans for its 182-seat airliners.

Airbus A319/A318

Having stretched the A320, Airbus then addressed the possibility of 'shrinking' the aircraft to produce a 124-seat version. The result was the A319, which not only kept the Airbus consortium intact, but also became a best-seller and an essential element of the Airbus single-aisle family. Airbus followed this with the introduction of the 'baby' A318.

The roots of what became the A319 can be traced back to the original 130- to 140-seat SA1 designs of the early 1980s. By 1990 Airbus had revived these plans as the A320M-7 (minus seven rows of seats), or the A319. However, several of the Airbus group members already had plans for similar small airliners on their own drawing boards, such as British Aerospace's 146NRA and the Aérospatiale/DASA Regioliner projects. It took some time to get a unified Airbus design back on track, then disagreement broke out between France and Germany over where the final assembly site should be. A formal launch, once scheduled for March 1992, was delayed

until a decision was reached to allocate A319 assembly to DASA, while the A320 stayed at Toulouse. This paved the way for the marketing launch of the A319 on 22 May 1992.

Both Northwest Airlines and Air France were touted as major early customers, but in December 1992 Northwest cancelled most of its Airbus commitments and ceased to be a near-term prospect. In June 1993 Airbus finally announced the formal launch of the A319 with just six orders from ILFC. Only in January 1994 did Air France's long-awaited interest emerge when a letter of intent for nine aircraft and nine options was signed. Swissair next became the first airline to place a firm order, for three aircraft, and in June 1994 the Air France interest was elevated to the status of a firm order.

Short fuselage

Some 3.77 m (12 ft 4 in) shorter than the A320, the stubby A319 was the smallest Airbus available, until the A318 arrived. The A319 is aimed at sectors of approximately 2,000 nm

Above: The A319 has been a tremendous sales success for Airbus. A total of 1053 had been ordered by June 2005. Many customers, such as TAM Brasil, were already A320 operators and commonality of maintenance made the A319 an obvious choice.

The first two A319s were retained by Airbus and completed the 650-hour flight test programme which resulted in certification of the aircraft with both CFM56-5A/-5B and IAE V2500-A5 turbofans. The aircraft has subsequently been certified to operate with IAE V2524 engines.

(3700 km; 2,300 miles) with a load of 124 passengers. It is an integral member of the Airbus single-aisle family and shares many common features with the A320 and A321. The A319's wing is identical to that of the A320, although minor software

Above: Air Canada was one of the first airlines to order the A319, receiving the first of 35 CFM International CFM56-5A5-powered A319-114s on 12 December 1996. The airline has progressively increased its fleet and currently operates 48 examples

Left: German airline Eurowings operated five A319-112s on both charter and scheduled flights to European destinations. To maximize profit the aircraft had a single-class layout accommodating up to 142 passengers – the largest number carried by any A319 operator.

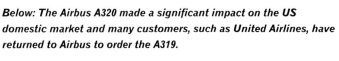

Below: The Airbus A320 made a significant impact on the US domestic market and many customers, such as United Airlines, have returned to Airbus to order the A319.

Above: After a troubled start the Airbus A318 managed to garner 61 orders, although this number pales in comparison with other members of the A320 family. Pictured is an early Air France model flying above Paris.

Below: Pictured is a representation of a TWA A318 powered by two PW6122 turbofans. TWA became the second US airline customer for the aircraft when it ordered 25 examples in December 1999.

SPECIFICATION	
Airbus A319	**Cruising altitude:** 9500 m (31,170 ft)
Type: short- to medium-range airliner	**Weights:** operating empty 40,149 kg (88,238 lb); maximum take-off 64,000 kg (140,800 lb)
Powerplant: two 97.9-kN (22,025-lb-thrust) CFM56-5A4 turbofans, or two 104,5-kN (23,510-lb-thrust) IAE V2524-A5 turbofans	**Dimensions:** wing span 33.91 m (111 ft 3in); length 33.80 m (110 ft 10 in); height 11.80 m (38 ft 8 in); wing area 122.4 m² (1,317 sq ft)
Cruising speed: 903 km/h (560 mph) at high altitude	**Accommodation:** 124 passengers in two classes
Range: 4907 km (3,040 miles)	

changes have been made in the flight control system to account for different handling characteristics.

The use of composite materials in the A319 is even more extensive than in the A320 and includes the wing leading edges, landing-gear doors, the fuselage belly fairing, spoilers, fin leading edge, elevators, rudder and tailplanes.

Maiden flight

On 23 March 1995 the first A319 entered final assembly at Hamburg; it was rolled out on 24 August and made its maiden flight on 25 August 1995. This first of two prototypes flew with CFM56-5B6/2 engines. The second prototype A319 also took to the air powered by CFM56s, on 31 October 1995, and this allowed the first aircraft to be re-engined with IAE V2524-A5 engines.

The first A319 to enter airline service was delivered to Swissair on 25 April 1996, followed by deliveries to Air Inter, Air Canada and Lufthansa. Slow initial sales were compensated by subsequent substantial deals with customers such as United Airlines and British Airways.

In April 1999 an A319 delivered to Air France became the 1000th single-aisle Airbus. The A319 has now outsold the A321 by a factor of nearly 2:1 and, in just four years, it has secured almost half as many orders as the A320.

Airbus 'Baby'

In April 1999 Airbus Industrie formally launched the A318, adding the latest and the smallest member of the single-aisle A320 family. After a relatively short development period, the A318 made a successful 3-hour 44-minute first flight from the company airfield at Finkenwerder near Hamburg, Germany, on 15 January 2002. The A318 is able to carry 107 passengers in a standard two-class layout up to 3700 km (2,300 miles) in its baseline version.

Airbus Corporate Jetliner (ACJ)

In 1996, to compete with the Boeing Business Jet (BBJ), Airbus launched a derivative of the basic A319 airframe, the A319CJ (Corporate Jet). Available from 1999, the A319CJ is designed to accommodate between eight and 50 passengers in relative luxury, with a maximum range of 11,667 km (7,250 miles) – representing nonstop flights from Frankfurt to Los Angeles, Los Angeles to Tokyo and Tokyo to Frankfurt. Most significantly, the A319CJ features minimal changes to the standard A319, so that it retains a high residual value to customers, as it is readily capable of conversion back to standard airline configuration. On 13 June 1999 an Airbus Corporate Jetliner (ACJ) flew nonstop from Toulouse to Buenos Aires, in a 14-hour 50-minute flight covering an air-distance of 6,553 nm (12,140 km; 7,543 miles), setting a new record for its class. On 16 August 1999 the ACJ received its basic certification from the European JAA prior to the first two aircraft being delivered for interior outfitting. The type certificate for the ACJ is not a new one, but is an amendment of the existing A319 type certificate required by the additional modifications implemented in the ACJ. These include the installation of up to six auxiliary fuel tanks which permit the maximum 11,667-km (7,250-mile) range. The first A319CJ was delivered to a Kuwaiti corporation in 1999 and the type has also entered Italian air force service, where it replaced VIP-configured DC-9s. Further orders by private companies and VIP-specialist carriers has seen the ACJ firmly established within the VIP market.

Airbus A330 The A330/A340 concept

French carrier Air Inter was the first airline to begin A330-200 operations. European support for the A330/A340 programme was predictably strong, with Lufthansa and Air France taking the A340 into service.

Airbus Industrie was a latecomer to the commercial airliner market and initially struggled to win orders away from well-established US giants Boeing and McDonnell Douglas. Part of Airbus's strategy for success was to offer distinct families of aircraft that could be tailored to meet a wide range of performance and capacity demands. Key to this strategy was establishing a place within the important long-range, high-capacity market with the A330 and A340.

Airbus's first designs, the A300 and A310, were both high-capacity aircraft that ultimately evolved into long-range airliners. Their development gave Airbus valuable experience in designing and developing true long-range airliners. Airbus perfected the

family concept with the A320, which has led to the A318, A319 and A321. Each of these types is essentially the same, but they offer different fuselage lengths (and thus seating capacities), with a range of engines to suit different markets and airline requirements. Furthermore, there is commonality between engines, systems and, most importantly, cockpits, which allows airlines to maintain and operate the aircraft with the same personnel and flight crews. This is where the family concept starts to make serious economic sense. The concept of cross-

In August 1994, Airbus received cross-crew qualification for pilots transitioning from the A320 to the A330/A340. This allows crew to fly all three types and represents a major cost-saving for airlines.

qualification of crews, pioneered by Airbus (whereby a crew could step out of one type of aircraft and go fly another without extensive re-qualifications), was

one of the most valuable 'family' benefits and became essential to A330 and A340 operations.

While the A300, A310 and A320 family were able to take

Family members: Airbus Industrie's A330 and A340 long-range, high-capacity airliners fly together with an A321, a member of the smaller A319/A320/A321 family.

SPECIFICATION	
Airbus A330-300 **Type:** twin-engined wide-body airliner **Powerplant:** (typical) two 300-kN (67,500-lb-thrust) General Electric CF6-80E1A2 turbofans **Maximum speed:** Mach 0.86 **Range:** (longer-range variant with CF6 engines) 8982 km (5,140 miles) with 335 passengers and baggage, and fuel for 370-km (230-mile) diversion	**Weights:** operating empty 120,170 kg (264,374 lb); maximum take-off 230,000kg (506,000 lb) **Dimensions:** wing span 60.30 m (197 ft 9 in); length (63.65 m (208 ft 9 in); height 16.74 m (54 ft 11 in); wing area 363.10 m² (3,907 sq ft) **Accommodation:** two flight crew plus cabin crew and (typically) 295 (three-class) or 335 (two-class) passengers; maximum 440 passengers

In a dramatic demonstration of its long-range ability, an A340 departed the Paris Air Show on 17 June 1993 for a one-stop around-the-world flight. It returned a record-breaking 48 hours 22 minutes later.

two versions. The shorter-fuselage A330-200 can carry 256 passengers over 6,400 nm (11,824 km/7,347 miles). The longer A330-300 (the first version developed) can carry 335 passengers over 4,650 nm (8590 km/5,338 miles). The A340 is the same basic aircraft, but with four engines and a much-increased fuel load for extra range. The A340 was rolled out first, appearing in October 1991. The first production aircraft was delivered to Lufthansa in February 1993. The A330 followed in November 1992, entering service, with Air Inter, in January 1994.

Tough competition

Upon its introduction, the A330 became the largest twin-jet in service. The Boeing 777-200 has greater range, a larger cabin and more payload, but the A330 had

the advantage of being first and is better suited to operations on routes 4,000 to 5,000 nm long (7390 to 9237 km; 4,592 to 5,740 miles). The A330 and A340 have been targeted towards so-called 'long thin routes', which demand long range but not very high capacity.

While the A340 cannot rival the 747-400's ultra-long range credentials, it has successfully challenged the total dominance of Boeing at this 'top end' of the market. Boeing's response was the 777, but it was a long time coming. Still, Boeing has now adopted the family concept with the highly advanced 777.

Airbus had its problems with the A330/340, and sales were sluggish to start. This trend was reversed after initial A330 engine faults were rectified. As of June 2005 total A330 orders stood at 524, with 348 delivered. A340 orders stood at 381, with 301 delivered. New competition for Boeing's 777 comes from the introduction of the 'stretched' A340-600 and the ultra long-range A340-500, capable of flying sectors in excess of 18 hours.

The A330 (illustrated) and A340 exhibit a high degree of commonality of major components.

on and beat the best competition on offer in their market, Airbus still had to develop an aircraft that could compete with the long-haul 'kings' – chiefly the Boeing 747 and, to a lesser extent, the McDonnell Douglas MD-11 (now the Boeing MD-11). Airbus also realized that there was a sizeable number of older, wide-bodied aircraft, such as the DC-10, L-1011 TriStar and 767-200, that would need replacing. Drawing on its experience, and in close consultation with the airlines, Airbus proposed two designs (with two and four engines) that would seat about 326 to 410 passengers. These emerged in 1986 as the twin-engined A330 and four-engined A340.

The A330-300 is the high-capacity, medium-range version of the A330. Airbus has faced strong competition from Boeing's 777 as the two manufacturers continue to struggle for dominance of this important market.

Two-aircraft programme

The A330 and A340 are essentially the same aircraft, with a different number of engines and some important but not obvious structural changes. Each type is built around the same wing, uses the same advanced (two-pilot) cockpit and uses the same fuselage cross-section. Airbus treats the two types as one programme.

The A330 is a medium-range, twin-aisle aircraft, offered in

A330: Developing the twin

The A330 is the 'junior' member of the long-range, high-capacity Airbus family. It shares a common fuselage and wing design with the A340, but has only two engines for more economical operation over shorter routes.

By the early 1970s Airbus was looking at launching a larger family of airliners, based on the A300 design. Two concepts took shape, the A300B9 – which was bigger than the original A300 – and the smaller A300B10. The B10 design went on to become the Airbus A310, but the 330-seat A300B9 was joined by another new design, the B11, a 200-seat, four-engined aircraft which was based on the B10. Driven by market demand, however, Airbus proceeded with the A310.

By 1980, it had the confidence and the financial security to return to the B9 and the B11. The two designs were redesignated TA9 and TA11 (TA for twin aisle) and partially revealed at the 1982 Farnborough Air Show. TA9 would have an A300-like fuselage stretched to 62 m (203 ft 6 in). Seating capacity would be about 326 to 410. Two variants were sketched out, the TA9-100 and the TA9-200. The -100 was optimized for 1,500-nm (2771-km/1,722-mile) routes, while the -200 would be aimed at sectors of 3,300 nm (3,788 miles/ 6096 km). The final designs were smaller, but far surpassed this performance.

By the 1983 Paris Air Show, Airbus was treating the TA9 and the TA11 as a common design, using as many components from the A300/A310 as possible. By 1985, a variable-camber wing had been introduced and the size and shape of the two aircraft were becoming virtually identical – only the number of engines remained different. The variable-camber wing idea was abandoned, however, as being too expensive to develop, and then, in 1986, TA9 received its designation.

A330 christened

In January 1986, the TA9 was officially christened as the A330, while the TA11 became the A340. The two aircraft shared a common fuselage length of 59.16 m (194 ft 10 in), with a cockpit design based on that of the A320. The A330 would be powered by two General Electric CF6-80C2 or Pratt & Whitney PW4000 turbofans, allowing it to carry 308 passengers over 5,800 nm (10,715 km/6,658 miles). Development of the A340 proceeded first as competition in its intended market was more immediate (the McDonnell Douglas MD-11).

As the A340 progressed, changes were made to the basic A330, lengthening its fuselage to allow 24 more seats to be

Composites account for some 13 per cent of the structural weight of the A330/A340 wing, while the principal structures are of aluminium alloy. BAE Systems manufactures the wings in the UK.

accommodated, while cutting back its range slightly.

Just before the 1987 Paris Air Show, the A330 and A340 received their official launch. The A330 had been sized to fit between the two planned versions of the A340 – the longer A340-300 and the shorter A340-200. During 1987/88, the

A340 underwent several changes which influenced the A330. The A330 was stretched again to match the fuselage length of the A340-300, and became the A330-300. The A330-200 then became equivalent in size to the A340-200. Up to that time, the -200 designation had been applied universally to the A330.

Below: In August 1997, Airbus flew the first example of the shorter A330-200. With the CF6 and PW4000 engines already test-flown, operations with Trents began in the summer of 1998.

Above: An A330 test airframe undergoes vibration testing. Simultaneous European and US certification for the A330 with CF6 engines was achieved in October 1993, and 120-minute ETOPS approval was granted in November 1994. Aer Lingus flew the first transatlantic ETOPS service with a CF6-powered aircraft in May 1994.

In 1987, British Aerospace completed design of the new wing. The wing is swept to 30 degrees and has distinctive 2.74-m (9-ft) tall winglets. The wing is identical to that of the A340 and only small structural changes are needed to adapt it to carry the A340's extra engines. In 1987, the flight-deck configuration was also finalized. The A330 has a six-screen EFIS cockpit fitted with a sidestick controller. The only difference between it and that of the A340 is in the number of throttles.

The A330 was the first of the Airbus designs to be offered with powerplants from all three major engine manufacturers, General Electric, Pratt & Whitney and Rolls-Royce.

A330-300

The A330-300 is capable of seating up to 440 passengers; however, a typical seating arrangement is 335 in a two-class layout. With 335 passengers and baggage, the aircraft has a maximum take-off weight of 212,013 kg (467,400 lb) and

Pratt & Whitney delivered the first PW4168 turbofans for the A330 to Toulouse in the second half of 1993.

a typical range of 4,500 nm (8313 km/5,166 miles).

The twelfth airframe from the A340/A330 production line became the first A330 – though it was actually the seventh to take to the air. The A330-300 prototype made its maiden flight on 14 October 1992. The CF6-powered A330 was certified jointly by the US FAA and the European JAA on 23 October 1993. The A330 entered revenue service with Air Inter on 17 January 1994. The PW4168-powered version was certified on 2 June 1994, but deliveries were delayed after problems were found with the engine's thrust-reversers. The first PW4168-powered aircraft entered service with Thai International on 19 December 1994. Rolls-Royce Trent-powered A330s were the last to enter service. This version was certified on 22 December 1994 and deliveries were made to the

launch customer, Cathay Pacific, on 27 February 1995.

On 30 June 1994, tragedy struck the programme when one of the test aircraft crashed during trial flights at Toulouse, killing all eight on board. The accident was blamed on pilot error and this led to a revision of the cockpit operating procedures. Further difficulties struck the A330 in 1996 when Cathay Pacific and Dragonair temporarily grounded their aircraft after three in-flight shut-downs of their Trent engines. Following the incidents, each aircraft continued to fly on its remaining engine and landed safely. The problem was traced to a fault in the gearbox – although it was not experienced by Garuda which also operates Trent-powered A330s.

A330-200

In 1995 Airbus announced a major development of the basic A330, the short-fuselage, increased-range A330-200. A 256-seat aircraft with a 6,400-nm (11,824-km/7,347-mile) range, the A330-200 is fitted with an additional centre wing fuel tank, a revised tail fin and has a maximum take-off weight of 507,055-lb (230000 kg). Leasing company ILFC placed the first order, for 13, in March 1996. The -200 made its first flight on 13 August 1997, received its FAA/JAA and Transport Canada certification on 31 March 1998, and the first aircraft was handed over to Canada 3000 (via ILFC) on 30 April 1998.

Above: Sparks fly from the protected underside of an A330's rear fuselage during trials to determine the aircraft's minimum unstick speed. An intensive period of test-flying followed the 1992 first flight.

Right: On 25 April 1995, just two years after the A340 entered commercial service, the hundredth airframe was rolled off the A330/A340 line. The historic machine was an A330-300.

A330: In service

In its early days, the A330 struggled with a sluggish order book and bad publicity. It is a measure of the soundness of the basic design, and Airbus's high-powered sales technique, that the A330 became the best-selling aircraft in its class, beating off stiff competition from the Boeing 777 and all other comers.

On 31 March 1987, Airbus announced that it had signed a letter of intent with Northwest Airlines for 20 A340s, with options on 10 A330s. This was a major order from an important US carrier, just the kind of deal needed by Airbus to launch its new twin-jet. The trail was soon to grow cold on the Northwest order, however. Instead, the real launch orders for the A330 were gained, also in March 1987, from Air Inter (five aircraft and 15 options), and Thai International (eight aircraft). The next significant order was to come from Cathay Pacific, in 1989, which signed a contract for nine A330s (later increased to 11) for delivery from 1995 to 1998.

The first delivery of a CF6-powered A330 was made to Air Inter on 30 December 1993, the aircraft entering service on 17 January 1994. First deliveries of PW4168-engined aircraft to Malaysian Airline System (MAS) and Thai International were delayed by delamination faults in the composite materials of the engine thrust-reversers. MAS should have received its aircraft in August 1994 and Thai in September, but the timetable was further delayed by the tragic crash of one aircraft involved in PW4168 certification.

The first A330-321 for Thai International was introduced into service on 19 December 1994, on routes from Bangkok to Seoul and Taipei. Airbus paid compensation to Thai for the late delivery of its A330s. Initial

Right: Cathay Pacific currently operates 23 A330-300s. All of Cathay's A330s are powered by Rolls-Royce Trent 700 engines.

A330 operations were then further affected by 'wing weeping' – leakage from the wing fuel tanks – which postponed delivery of Thai's third aircraft until the problem was corrected by British Aerospace. The first MAS A330-322 was delivered on 1 February 1995, but the airline then rescheduled the deliveries of the 10 aircraft it had on order.

The launch customer for the Trent/A330 combination was Cathay Pacific, which took delivery of its first A330-342 on 27 February 1995. Cathay discovered that it could operate profitable night-time pure freighter operations with its A330s (and A340s), using the lower cargo hold only. Operating charters for express package delivery firms, the Airbus could carry loads of 1 to 25 tons, but still be profitable. Cathay Pacific also became the first airline to

LTU International Airways of Germany operates four A330-300s, all of them leased.

have pilots triple-rated on the A320, A330 and A340.

During the early 1990s, A330 orders dropped off and Airbus

Above: The A330 has been particularly successful in the Asian market, where almost every major airline has placed orders for aircraft from the family.

entered an alarming period when orders for the A330 and A340 came in at no more than a trickle. One important new

Left: An Airbus A330 powered by Pratt & Whitney PW4168s made a successful first flight (of 3 hours 28 minutes) from Toulouse on 14 October 1993. This flight was part of a 500-hour programme which was aimed at certifying the PW4168 engine in the A330.

Below: Air Inter received its first A330 in December 1993 and so became the first airline to operate the type.

operator of the type was Aer Lingus, which took delivery of its first aircraft, via International Lease Finance Company (ILFC), in May 1994. Aer Lingus was the first airline to operate the A330 on ETOPS (Extended-range Twin-engined OPerationS) routes across the North Atlantic. It was instrumental in gaining full 180-minute ETOPS qualification for the (CF6-80E1-powered) A330-300, which was awarded on 6 February 1995. Like Cathay, Aer Lingus, too, discovered that its A330s made good freighters; by mid-1995, the four aircraft initially in service were soon carrying half of the airline's yearly cargo business (approximately 15,000 tons).

Full ETOPS clearance for the PW4168-powered A330 was awarded in July 1995, although this model received its 90-minute clearance on 10 November 1994 – before it entered service. The A330-300 was the first airliner to achieve this distinction. Full ETOPS clearance for the Trent 700 was gained in May 1996.

A330 deliveries in the early 1990s continued largely via ILFC. Between 1990 and 1995, however, hardly any new A330 orders were won; several operators announced their intention to acquire aircraft, but deliveries never materialized.

By 1 January 1992, Airbus had 143 firm orders for the A330. In 1995, the situation began to

Dragonair, an associate of Cathay Pacific, currently operates a fleet of 11 Airbus A330-300s on its mainland China to Hong Kong routes.

change as orders were won from Gulf Air (six A330-300s) and Philippine Airlines (eight A330-300s) in the face of stiff competition from Boeing.

The year 1996 started well when ILFC ordered 13 A330-200s, one A330-300 and a mix of five A330/A340 options. Korean Air added two extended-range A330-200s to its existing fleet, when it signed an order in May 1996, for delivery in August and September 1998. Korean already held seven A330-300 orders with 10 options, and deliveries of these aircraft commenced on 6 March 1997. In November 1996, Emirates signed for 16 A330-200s with seven options. On 18 December 1996, Garuda took delivery of the first of a total of nine Trent 700-powered A330-300s it had on order.

The upward trend continued in 1997, as Dragonair ordered its sixth A330-300, Cathay Pacific (then Dragonair's parent company) increased its A330 tally by ordering its thirteenth A330-300, Sabena and Swissair became the first European customers for the A330-200, Thai ordered four additional A330-300s, Asiana became

another new customer for the A330 and Air Canada became the first major North American airline to order the A330.

In 1998, Air Lanka signed for six A330-200s; US Airways announced seven firm A330-300 orders, seven options and 16 future reserved delivery positions for the A330, making the airline the first A330 operator in the United States; Canada 3000 became the first airline to introduce the A330-200 into service, with Austrian Airlines following on 21 August 1998 and Korean Air on 1 September.

The list of current operators and future customers of the A330 continues to grow. After a promising start, the A330 suffered a period of sales drought which placed the future of the type in doubt. However, the correction of initial problems and growing consumer confidence has rejuvenated the A330 order book and by 3 August 2005, A330 orders stood at 524, with 356 delivered and the aircraft serving as the basis for Airbus' new A350 which is being developed to rival the all-new Boeing 787 Dreamliner.

Airbus A340 Development

Initial development of the A340 was led by the TA9 or, as it later became, the A330. However, market forces ensured that it was the four-engined A340 offered first to customers. This aircraft would become the first true European competitor in the prized, and US-dominated, long-range airliner market.

Like the A330, the A340 began life in the mid-1970s as a development of the A300B2. In the A340's case, this was the 200-seat four-engined A300B11 design, redesignated TA11 in 1980. By 1982 the TA11 had become a CFM56-powered airliner with a design range of 6,830 nm (7,860 miles; 12650 km). Airbus flirted briefly with making the TA11 a tri-jet, but abandoned these plans in favour of the original four 133.4-kN (30,000-lb-thrust) class engines. The TA11 was given form at the 1982 Farnborough Air Show and, although still A300-based, the new aircraft would be stretched to accommodate around 326 mixed-class passengers, or up

to 410 in a single-class layout. The TA11 (and TA9) were envisaged as L-1011 and DC-10 replacements and would also provide a challenge to the 'new' Boeing 767's intended market.

Parallel development

By the Paris Air Show of 1983 Airbus had refined both the TA11 and TA9 concepts to the extent that it began to treat the two as one common project, built around a similar wing and fuselage design. Airbus also introduced several technical innovations in the shape of a variable-camber wing (which was later deleted from the design) and the revolutionary EFIS cockpit of the A320. January 1986 saw the TA11 officially join the Airbus

On 26 February 1993, Air France became the first airline to receive the A340-300 variant. A340-311, F-WWCA, first flew in July 1992 and underwent a year of trial and test flying before being delivered to Air France in August 1993.

product line as the A340. The A340 was defined as a very long-range 261-seat aircraft aimed at routes of 6,700 nm (12,378 km; 7,692 miles). While the developed CFM56-5S1 was still earmarked as the primary A340 powerplant, Airbus was also considering the V2500 (then under development by the International Aero Engine

consortium), and even all-new ultra-high bypass designs of both engines, dubbed 'SuperFans'.

Airbus had concerns about the performance of the A340's intended engines, which were not helped by the emergence of the three-engined McDonnell Douglas MD-11 as a direct competitor. The SuperFan

Right: Airbus unveiled the first A340 in a spectacular ceremony held at Toulouse on 4 October 1991, attended by more than 5500 people. The first flight was made on the 25th of that month.

Below: The A340's landing gear differs from that of the A330 in having an additional twin-wheel auxiliary undercarriage unit fitted to the underside of the centre-section.

Right: Named **Nuernberg,** *A340-211* **D-AIBA** *was the first A340 to enter commercial service. It was delivered in February 1993 – only 10 months after the first flight of the A340-200 variant.*

concept, driven by IAE and the V2500, offered the required thrust with much reduced fuel consumption. It would give the A340 a huge payload/range advantage and Airbus began to offer a 262-seat SuperFan-powered A340-200 and the stretched A340-300. Based on projected performance, on 15 January 1987 Lufthansa announced that it would buy 15 SuperFan-powered A340s, with 15 options. Lufthansa was soon joined by Northwest Orient, in March, with an order for 20 A340s. Then, a week after the Northwest order, IAE announced that it would not proceed with SuperFan development due to the technical risks involved.

The SuperFan's disappearance meant that Airbus had to match its performance guarantees with existing technology. The solution came in the shape of an uprated version of the CFM56, the 139-kN (31,200-lb-thrust) CFM56-5C2. Airbus also increased the A340's wing span and added winglets. By 1995, the 151-kN (34,000-lb-thrust) CFM56-5C4 was available. With these changes the A340 was within reach of its intended performance and orders began to build slowly again.

Two A340 versions evolved after a June 1987 formal go-ahead: the 375-seat A340-300 and the short-fuselage, extended-range A340-200, normally seating 263 passengers. The first A340 to fly was an A340-300 on

Right: In the summer of 1991, a complete A340 airframe underwent extensive ground-based static-strength trials at the Centre d'Essais Aeronautique de Toulouse (CEAT). The front fuselage is seen here being unloaded from a Super Guppy in October 1990.

25 October 1991. During the test programme, Airbus and CFM International had to adapt airframe aerodynamics and engine parameters. Despite this, the new aircraft proved to be lighter, and to have a higher fuel load, than expected.

European JAA certification was awarded on 22 December 1992 and the first A340-200 was delivered to Lufthansa on 2 February 1993. The first A340-300 was delivered to Air France on 26 February.

Higher capacity

The standard aircraft was followed by an increased maximum take-off weight (MTOW) version. This extra available weight could be traded for fuel or payload. A growth version of the A340-300, the A340-300X (now A340-300E), with a further increased MTOW and a range of 7,304 nm (13,519 km; 8,400 miles) was ordered by Singapore Airlines.

SPECIFICATION	
Airbus A340-300	295 passengers and reserves for a
Type: long-range wide-bodied	370-km (230-mile) diversion
airliner	**Service ceiling:** 12,495 m (41,000 ft)
Powerplant: four CFM International	**Weights:** between 257,000 kg and
CFM56-5C2 turbofans each rated	260,000 kg (566,575 lb and
at 138.78 kN (31,200 lb) or four	573,200 lb) maximum take-off
CFM-5C3 turbofans each rated at	**Dimensions:** wing span 60.30 m
144.57 kN (32,500 lb st) or four	(197 ft 10 in); length 63.65 m (208 ft
CFM56-5C4 turbofans each rated	10in); height 16.74 m (54 ft 11 in);
at 151.24 kN (34,000 lb st)	363.1 m² (3908.4 sq ft)
Cruising speed: 915 km/h (569 mph)	**Accommodation:** (in typical mixed
Range: 12,416 km (7710 miles) with	class) 295 passengers

The first example flew on 25 August 1995 and deliveries followed on 17 April 1996. Since then, all A340s have been built to the same structural standard allowing for extended-range operations. A follow-on extended-range A340-400 development was dropped in favour of the

stretched 313-seat A340-500 and 380-seat A340-600, which were launched in December 1997. The Trent 556-powered A340-600 has Virgin Atlantic its launch customer and deliveries began in July 2002. In August 2005 orders for the A340 stood at 384, with 239 delivered.

Above: Intended for the lucrative Boeing 747 replacement market, the A340-600 will be able to carry up to 380 three-class or 419 two-class passengers up to 7,932 nm (9,134 miles; 14700 km).

Left: Air Canada became the first North American airline to receive the ultra long-range A340-500 (foreground). The type entered Air Canada service in mid-2004.

A340: Operational history

Above: The A340-200 and A340-300 were marketed simultaneously by Airbus. Egyptair ordered the -200 version in 1995 and currently operates them on the Egypt–United Kingdom–United States route.

Top: Air Mauritius operates five Airbus A340-312s which were delivered in 1994–99. This aircraft was the first delivered, and is named **Paille-en-Queue.**

The A340 was launched on the understanding that the SuperFan engine option would give the aircraft outstanding payload/range capability, putting it far ahead of similar sized aircraft such as the MD-11, and within reach of the larger and more expensive Boeing 747. While the SuperFan option failed, the A340 emerged with its reputation intact.

The first expressions of interest in the A340 came from TAP Air Portugal, in 1987 and ILFC in 1988, both of which 'ordered' two aircraft. On 15 January 1987 Lufthansa announced that it had committed to 15 A340s and 15 options – although this did not become a 'real' order until April 1989 (when the firm order became four A340-200s and 11 A340-300s, followed by seven additional A340-200s in May of the same year).

Just as it had done with the A330, Northwest Orient placed a significant 'order' for 20 A340s, but again these aircraft were never delivered. Many other 'customers' signed up for aircraft that were never delivered, but confirmed customers did come in the shape of Air Lanka, TAP, Kuwait Airlines and Austrian Airlines.

By March 1991, Airbus figures recorded 94 orders for the A340. The failure of the SuperFan concept had caused Airbus, and its customers, major concern and no doubt this accounts for the vagueness surrounding the early order book.

Into service
The A340 flight test programme involved six aircraft – four -300s and two A340-200s. The first short-fuselage -200 flew on

1 April 1992 and with European JAA certification awarded, the rapidly expanding Asian and Far Eastern markets were targeted by Airbus. In 1992 important orders from Gulf Air, China Eastern, Philippine Airlines and Singapore Airlines was thus won. The first A340 entered Lufthansa service on the Frankfurt–New York (Newark)

route on 15 March 1993. Air France took delivery of the first A340-300 on 26 February 1993, and Lufthansa accepted its first A340-300 on 7 December 1993. US FAA type certification was awarded on 27 May 1993.

Airbus took great delight in promoting the A340's economical long-range credentials and organized a series of high-profile flights, culminating in a world record attempt. In July, during the 1993 Paris Air Show, an A340 dubbed *The World Ranger*

Below: Virgin Atlantic has been one of the most important customers of the type and currently has 18 in service and 15 on order, all the outstanding aircraft being A340-600s.

Above: To emphasize the A340's impressive range performance Airbus Industrie adorned one of its fleet with the name **The World Ranger** *in 1993 – it conducted a number of record-breaking flights.*

VIP A340s

Airbus does not reveal the identities of its VIP and government customers and such sales are recorded as being made to an 'undisclosed customer'. Despite its size, complexity and price, the A340 has proved to be a popular choice for those who demand a special personal aircraft. The first VIP sale for the A340 came early, in 1993, when the Government of Qatar (Qatar Amiri Flight) took delivery of a single A340-211 in April. In 1994 the Bahrain government also acquired an A340, but this aircraft has since been passed on to the Sultan of Brunei. The Sultan's personal fleet now comprises two A340s – along with a Gulfstream V, Boeing 767 and Boeing 747-400. Brunei has operated the sole A340-8000 – a special, ultra-extended range version with three additional fuel tanks giving it a range of at least 8500 nm (15742 km; 9,775 miles). Egypt bought an A340-212 for government use which was delivered in February 1995. The example below, operated by the Saudi Arabian government, is painted in an anonymous colour scheme and carries a number of additional aerials and antennas on the top side of the fuselage.

flew around the world with only one stop, breaking many records previously set by a Boeing 747SP.

Later, in November 1996, the A340 set a new nonstop distance record of 7,800 nm (14,410 km; 8,954 miles)

flying from Zhuhai, in China, in a flight time of 15 hours and 20 minutes.

After Lufthansa and Air France, deliveries were made to Sabena (March 1993), THY Turkish Airlines (commencing in July) and, most crucially, Virgin

Atlantic, which had previously operated an all-Boeing 747 fleet. The first A340 for Virgin, an A340-311 named *Lady in Red*, was handed over to the airline on 26 November 1993.

Into North America

In 1994 major orders were received from Cathay Pacific, Singapore Airlines and Air Canada – the A340's first break in the North American market. In 1994 deliveries were made to Air Mauritius, Gulf Air, Air Lanka, Cathay and TAP. In February 1995 Austrian Airlines took delivery of its first A340-200, while Kuwait Airlines received its first A340-300 in May 1995 and the first for Air Canada followed in June 1995. That year, sales of the aircraft were sluggish and, although deals were signed with Egyptair, Lufthansa and Austrian, only seven A340s were sold – while orders were cancelled by PAL and a deal with BWIA fell through.

In 1991 a vital sale had been initiated with Singapore Airlines when, in August, that company had announced that it was abandoning its plans to acquire the MD-11 and would instead

opt for up to 20 extended-range, higher-gross-weight versions of the A340, then designated A340-300X. The first of these aircraft, now redesignated the A340-300E, flew on 25 August 1995 and was delivered on 17 April 1996. New sales continued to be achieved in 1996 and in May China Eastern Airlines became the first A340 operator in China. In November of that year Egyptair also took delivery of its first aircraft.

In 1997 Airbus won A340 orders from Cathay Pacific, Virgin, Olympic, Lufthansa, Air Canada and Air France. The following year, 1998, proved to be a very successful one, with the newly launched A340-500 and A340-600 winning the bulk of new business. This trend continued, although affected by the post-9/11 slowdown, but the A340 has continued to sell strongly. Indeed, while the A340-600 continues to impress in service after early teething troubles, the A340-500 is used by Singapore Airlines on the world's longest scheduled nonstop route, direct from Singapore to New York, in a flight time of around 18 hours.

Above: The first A340-311 for Turkish Hava Yollari is seen here during test-flying from Airbus's factory at Toulouse. The airline has a current fleet of seven A340s.

Right: Air France has been a staunch Airbus customer since the A300 was launched in the 1970s and has operated the -200, -300 and -300E versions of the A340.

Airbus A380 Europe's new Super Jumbo

With the A380, Airbus heralds a new era in commercial operations. The aircraft is the largest and heaviest airliner ever conceived and many see it as the answer to increasing airport congestion. It is also proving attractive to cargo-only operators, competing and winning against the Boeing's 747 freighters.

On 27 April 2005 a new era in commercial aviation began with the first flight of the largest passenger transport aircraft in the world – the Airbus A380. This event marked a major milestone following a decade of study, design and development work, and raised the stakes in the ever-escalating battle between Airbus and Boeing for the crown of premier commercial airliner manufacturer worldwide.

A380 genesis

In the early 1990s almost every major civil aircraft manufacturer in the world was developing plans to produce a next-generation high-capacity long-range airliner to challenge the mighty Boeing 747's dominance. As industry consolidation and the enormous cost of developing such an aircraft hit home in the 1990s, the end of the decade saw only Boeing and Airbus harbouring hopes to dominate this most prestigious of markets. In the mid-1990s the future animosity between

Airbus aims to offer as much commonality as possible between the cockpits of the A380 (shown here as a computer-generated impression) and the in-service A330/340 airliners.

Airbus and Boeing had yet to emerge, as the pair cooperated on the joint VLCA (Very Large Commercial Aircraft) programme. As the study progressed, Airbus, sensing Boeing's lack of commitment, began its own independent project and, when the VLCA teaming disintegrated in 1996, Airbus integrated the work into its own efforts. Boeing, heavily committed to funding its Model 777, decided to withdraw from the race – expecting that improved versions of its 747 would suffice for what it perceived to be a shrinking market. Airbus, however, as the flagship of European industry and cooperation, was determined to press ahead.

A380 design

The mid-1990s saw Airbus consider a range of novel and occasionally outrageous configurations before, in 1998, settling on a twin-passenger deck, four-engined design, known as the A3XX. It was a true monster, able to carry some 550 passengers in standard and more than 800 in all-economy configurations.

Two full-length passenger decks, complemented by a lower cargo deck, ensured the aircraft's take-off weight would exceed a mammoth 550 tonnes (1,200,000 lb) and its colossal length of 72.75 m (238 ft 8 in) and wing span of 79.80 m (261 ft 9¾ in) dwarfed anything the company had previously built. A multitude of strict performance, economic and operating criteria would have to be met, however, before Airbus could consider putting the aircraft into production.

To keep the aircraft's weight within realistic limits, reduce fatigue and corrosion problems and reinforce the company's reputation for innovation, Airbus proposed unprecedented levels of composite materials in the aircraft's structure. Some 25 per cent of the aircraft is of composites, of which 22 per cent is carbon fibre reinforced plastic and three per cent GLARE fibre-metal laminate

(used for the first time on a civilian airliner). The use of these materials not only saves weight, but also leads to decreased fuel burn, fewer emissions and lower operating costs. The aircraft's powerful hydraulic system also provides a weight saving by allowing smaller pipes and components to be incorporated. Back-up electric systems provide the aircraft with the ability to land in the event of total hydraulic failure and this, combined with the triple redundancy fly-by-wire flight control system, provides the level of safety so vital on any airliner.

The A380's 'glass' two-crew cockpit builds on the successful format developed for Airbus's other products, incorporating integrated modular avionics datalinks, pull-out keyboards for the pilots and the latest in electronic flight aids, with all vital information displayed on large multi-function flat-panel

April 2005 saw the first flight of the giant twin-decked A380. The aircraft has continued to be used intensively on test duties, having made the type's public debut at the Paris Air Show in June 2005.

Left: Various exotic cabin configurations have been suggested for the A380, but it is likely that customers will opt for less ambitious configurations, choosing passenger capacity above luxury.

Below: In an unusual move, the A380 flight-test crew cycled the aircraft's undercarriage (retracted and extended it) during the type's maiden flight, an indication of Airbus' confidence in its systems.

displays. The commonality of the A380's cockpit layout with that of the A330/ A340 series also reduces the amount of training needed for pilots transitioning to the type.

The range of advanced technologies is not restricted to the cockpit. The passenger cabin is equipped with an advanced fibre-optic distribution network, the first on a commercial airliner, offering an unprecedented choice of inflight entertainment. With 49 per cent more floor space in its A380 than in the rival 747-400, Airbus has also proposed a wide range of interior designs for the aircraft, including casinos, bars, sleeping areas and even onboard spa baths and massage suites.

New-generation engines

With the environmental movement making increasing demands on air travel, and customer airlines looking for unparalleled operating efficiency, the A380 could not succeed

without new, efficient, quiet and lower-emission engines. After exhaustive development work two options are available for potential A380 customers – Rolls-Royce's Trent 900 and Engine Alliance's GP7200 (a joint venture between Pratt & Whitney and General Electric). Rated in the 311 to 356 kN (70,000 to 80,000 lb thrust) range, these engines not only produce a significantly lower noise footprint than those of the older 747, but also offer the fuel efficiency to allow Airbus to claim a seat-per-mile cost 17 per cent better than that of its rival.

Into the air

In December 2000, with sufficient interest from potential customers garnered, the aircraft was officially launched under its new name – A380 (the out-of-sequence '8' designation chosen to represent the shape of the aircraft's twin passenger decks). At the same time Airbus offered a dedicated freighter

version as the A380F. Setting new standards in air cargo, the A380F will be able to carry in the region of 150 tonnes of payload over intercontinental distances. The launch customer for this cargo-hauling giant is Federal Express, with deliveries due to commence in 2008.

Construction of the first A380 continued apace at Airbus facilities around Europe until a triumphant first flight from Airbus's Toulouse Flight Test

Centre. A further four A380s will join the test and certification programme, before the aircraft's entry into commercial service with Singapore Airlines in 2006.

With 159 A380 orders and commitments received by July 2005, Airbus is confident it will exceed its 250-order break-even point, and the company is already planning new variants, including the stretched 656-seat A380-900 and the ultra long-range 'shrunk' A380-700.

SPECIFICATION	
Airbus A380-800 **Type:** high-capacity long-range twin-deck wide-body airliner **Powerplant:** four 311-kN (70,000-lb-thrust), initially derated to 302kN (68,000lb thrust), later growing to 374-kN (84,000lb thrust) Rolls-Royce Trent 900 or 363-kN (81,500lb thrust) Engine Alliance (General Electric-Pratt & Whitney) GP-7200 turbofans **Cruising speed:** Mach 0.85	**Range:** 14,800 km (9,196 miles) **Service ceiling:** 13,100 m (43,000 ft) **Weights:** operating empty 277,000 kg (610,700 lb); maximum take-off 560,000 kg (1,234,600 lb) **Dimensions:** wing span 79.8 m (261 ft 10 in); length 72.75 m (238 ft 8 in); height 24.08 m (79 ft) **Accommodation:** flight crew of two; standard seating for 555 passengers on two decks in a three-class arrangement

With the A380 Airbus can offer a complete range of airliner capacities, a situation that is forcing Boeing to reconsider its options for a 747 Advanced development of the 747-400.

A380 Customers

Customer	Variant	Orders
Air France	A380-800	10
China Southern Airlines	A380-800	5
Emirates	A380-800	41
Emirates	A380F	2
Etihad Airways	A380-800	4
Federal Express	A380F	10
ILFC	A380-800	5
ILFC	A380F	5
Kingfisher Airlines	A380	5
Korean Air Lines	A380-800	5
Lufthansa	A380-800	15
Malaysian Airlines	A380-800	6
QANTAS	A380-800	12
Qatar Airways	A380-800	2
Singapore Airlines	A380-800	10
Thai Airways	A380-800	6
UPS	A380F	10
Virgin Atlantic	A380-800	6
Total		**154**

Ilyushin Il-86 'Camber'/Il-96 Russia's airbus

Above: A fleet of 11 Il-86s is maintained by Aeroflot. The aircraft are configured to carry 20 first-class and 296 tourist-class passengers and have retained their thirsty NK-86 engines despite negotiations to re-engine them with CFM56s.

The Il-86 was the Soviet Union's first attempt at a modern wide-bodied airliner, but it was not a success. The aircraft failed dismally in meeting the expected performance levels, and just over 100 were built. Its successor, the modernized Il-96, promised to be a far better and more versatile aircraft, but a lack of funding halted its development.

The driving force behind Ilyushin's Il-86 was the 1980 Moscow Olympic Games. The Soviet authorities wanted to have a new prestige airliner in service to take passengers to the games, and the Ilyushin Design Bureau was awarded the task. Ilyushin was the natural choice as the manufacturer had produced the Il-62 – the backbone of Aeroflot's long-range fleet, and the aircraft which the Il-86 was intended to

replace. The first plans for a Soviet wide-body were revealed as early as the 1971 Paris Air Show, but little progress was made, due largely to the lack of a suitable turbofan engine. Ilyushin's early designs resembled a fattened-up Il-62, with the same four-jet configuration and T-tailed layout as its predecessor. However, the structural limitations of the rear-engined layout, when combined with new, larger engines, were unacceptable, and the Il-86 that finally emerged had a conventional podded underwing engine design.

Double-decker
The Il-86 (ASCC code name 'Camber') was designed to accommodate up to 350 seats, with an unusual two-deck design. Passengers could carry

Initial discussions for a new wide-bodied airliner began between Ilyushin and the Soviet Ministry of Civil Aviation following the launch of Boeing's 747 in 1966. After a long design gestation, the prototype made its maiden flight on 22 December 1976.

on their own luggage and coats, stowing them on the lower deck, before climbing upstairs to be seated. This system was intended to allow the Il-86 to operate from the Soviet Union's under-developed airports, which lacked modern baggage- or passenger-handling facilities.

The Il-86's timetable was dictated by the availability of its new Kuznetsov NK-86 high-bypass turbofans – the first such engines to be built in Russia. The first prototype entered assembly during 1974, but did not make its maiden flight until

22 December 1976. The first Il-86 underwent its flight test trials at Moscow's Zhukhovskii airfield, where it was eventually joined by the first production Il-86. This aircraft was rolled out in 1977 and made its maiden flight on 24 October.

By this time, the Il-86 was running well behind schedule and it was clear that it would not be in quantity service for its 1980 target. Aeroflot took delivery of its first aircraft on 24 September 1979 and the Il-86 entered service on 26 December 1980 – well after the Olympics.

Above: AJT Air International operated five Il-86s (including three ex-Aeroflot examples) from Moscow-Sheremetyevo. With a 350-seat layout, the aircraft were used on both scheduled and charter services.

Below: Transeuropean Airlines was one of a number of Russian charter airlines established since the deregulation of the airline industry. This Il-86 was leased by the airline for high-density routes.

With a cargo door forward of the wing on the port side, the Il-96T is capable of carrying standard international freight containers and pallets.

Above: The Il-96-300 was designed to resolve the performance difficulties of the Il-86. The aircraft has distinctive winglets, a shorter fuselage and more efficient Aviadvigatel PS-90A turbofans.

Heavy emphasis has been placed on the Il-96M's Western engines, avionics and systems and low unit cost of US$75 million in the so-far unsuccessful attempts to attract Western airlines.

The Il-86 was designed to handle Aeroflot's high-density 'tourist' routes, such as Moscow–Leningrad or Moscow–Kiev. It was also intended to fly prestige international routes, including transatlantic services, on which it would replace the ageing Il-62M – but this soon proved to be problematic. When the new airliner was launched, Ilyushin claimed that it had a maximum range of 5000 km (3,420 miles); however, these figures were later scaled back to 3600 km (2,235 miles) with a 40,000-kg (88,185-lb) payload. Most evidence pointed to a failure to achieve even that level of performance. Indeed, the East German state airline refused to take delivery of the Il-86s it was offered, and quoted its maximum range as just 2500 km (1,550 miles) – Interflug went on to order three Airbus A310-300s to augment its Il-62 fleet. The Il-86 flew its first international service from Moscow to East Berlin on 3 July 1981. On their routes from Moscow to east coast destinations in the United States, Aeroflot Il-86s had to make two regular fuel stops at Shannon Airport, Ireland, and again in Gander, Newfoundland. Headwinds sometimes even forced an intermediate stop in Luxembourg.

In the early 1980s, the general designer at Ilyushin, G. V. Novozhilov, spoke of at least 200 Il-86s being built; however, production ceased in 1994, at a total of just 104 aircraft. About 70 remain in service today. They are spread among airlines in Russia and the former CIS republics.

Il-96 family

Although it is outwardly similar to the Il-86, the Il-96 is a new aircraft in every respect. The Il-96 introduced Aviadvigatel (formerly Perm) PS-90A turbofan engines, a new supercritical wing of greater span and slightly reduced sweep, and improved structure and materials to give lower weight and longer life.

New avionics and systems are provided, including a triplex fly-by-wire control system. Internal fuel capacity is doubled by comparison with the Il-86, while reduced drag also contributes to the new aircraft's dramatically increased range. The lower deck of the Il-96 is designed purely for cargo and luggage, and passengers enter only at cabin level.

The basic production version seats up to 300 passengers and is designated Il-96-300, but the mixed-class layout that is normally used seats 235. The prototype made its maiden flight on 28 September 1988. Russian state certification was achieved on 29 December 1992. Deliveries began to Aeroflot in 1995 and proceeded at a very slow rate. By August 2005 Aeroflot had 12 aircraft. Another three were in service with Domodedovo Airlines, along with two operated by the Russian government.

Ilyushin also developing the stretched Il-96M (originally the I-96-350). This version had Pratt & Whitney PW2337 turbofans, a smaller tailfin and a cabin that could accommodate up to 375 passengers. The prototype Il-96M was converted from the first Il-96-300 and flew on 6 April 1993. The first production aircraft was rolled out in April 1997. The first deliveries (of 17 on order) were due to Aeroflot in 1998 and a further six were on order for TransAero, but a severe shortage of funds held back the programme.

The all-freight Il-96T was also developed, with a 4.85- x 2.87-m (15-ft 11-in x 9-ft 5-in) cargo door fitted on the port side. Its maiden flight was on 16 May 1997. The first customer to take up the Il-96T was to be Aeroflot, with three on order, followed by Volga Dnepr. However, the US-engined Il-96M/T aircraft eventually came to nothing.

Instead, Ilyushin reworked the aircraft with Russian avionics and PS-90 engines as the Il-96-400 airliner and Il-96-400T freighter. Aeroflot now expects to take four Il-96-400Ts in 2006 to replace DC-10 freighters, while Atlant-Soyuz and Volga-Dnepr will receive four Il-96-400s by 2007.

Aeroflot has also taken a further six Il-96-300s and on 26 July 2005 Ilyushin, trading as the Voronezh Joint-stock Aircraft Manufacturing Company, unveiled the first of two Il-96-300VIP aircraft for Cubana.

SPECIFICATION	
Ilyushin Il-96-300 'Camber' **Type:** wide-bodied airliner **Powerplant:** four 156.9-kN (35,300-lb-thrust Aviadvigatel PS090A turbofan engines **Cruising speed:** 850–900 km/h (525–558 mph) **Range:** 9000 km (5,570 miles) with 30,000-kg (66,000-lb) payload **Service ceiling:** 12,000 m (39,360 ft)	**Weights:** empty 117,000 kg (257,400 lb); maximum take-off 216,000 kg (475,200 lb) **Dimensions:** wing span 60.11 m (197 ft 2 in); length 55.35 m (181 ft 6 in); height 17.57 m (57 ft 7 in); wing area 391.6 m² (4,214 sq ft) **Accommodation:** 235 passengers in three classes or a maximum of 300 passengers

Tupolev Tu-204/214 Russia's new hope

Designed to replace the Tu-154 in Aeroflot service, Tupolev's Tu-204 suffered during the period of the break-up of the Soviet Union. Unfortunately, even with the integration of Western avionics and engines, the aircraft has struggled to gain vital export orders.

When the Tu-204 first emerged, it resulted in a widespread feeling of déjà vu, but the Tu-20 – while it looked uncannily like a Boeing 757 – was not merely an unlicensed copy of the Boeing twinjet. Intended to replace the Tu-154, the new aircraft was designed to match the latest Western airliners, while still satisfying Soviet requirements. It was drawn up around a pair of Perm-Soloviev PS-90A high-bypass turbofans, and was planned from the start to incorporate a modern glass cockpit and the most sophisticated navigation and flight management systems.

The aircraft was optimized for two-crew operation; the Tu-204's designers included a flight engineer's station only to meet Aeroflot requirements, and anticipated selling many two-pilot aircraft to export customers. The aircraft was modern from nose to tail, making use of advanced aluminium-lithium alloys, and composites in its construction, and had a highly advanced supercritical wing.

Tupolev envisaged using varying proportions of Western equipment for different customers, with a Rockwell Collins EFIS cockpit virtually standard across the range, except for Aeroflot.

By the time the prototype first flew on 2 January 1989, Tupolev had received firm orders for 80 and provisional orders for 350 aircraft from Aeroflot (of a stated requirement for 500 of the type), but these later lapsed when the Soviet Union disintegrated, and Aeroflot split into fragments. Some of the fragments of the old Aeroflot within Russia itself placed new orders for small numbers of Tu-204s, but, generally, the new Russian and former Soviet civil operators turned westward for their equipment. Without massive support from Aeroflot, the Tu-204 programme has struggled to turn a profit ever since, despite brave efforts by the company to offer a range of variants tailored to different requirements.

Tu-204 variants

The original 214-passenger Tu-204 used PS-90 engines and Russian avionics, as did the original Tu-204C cargo aircraft and the extended-range Tu-204-100. The Tu-204-120 introduced RB.211-535E4 engines (actually with slightly higher fuel burn, but with much greater

Russia State Transport Company operated two PS-90A-powered Tu-204s on VIP flights for the Russian government. By August 2005 it had three PS-90 powered Tu-214s on charge.

reliability, and thus lower operating costs), while the -122 was similar, but with Rockwell-Collins avionics. Production Tu-204-120s for Kato of Egypt used Honeywell avionics.

The Tu-204-200 introduced further increases in fuel and maximum take-off weight, with a strengthened undercarriage. A combi freighter version of the -200 is designated Tu-214, and this became the first 200-series Tu-204 to obtain an order, and to fly. The Tu-204-220 is offered with RB.211-535E4, -535F5 or Pratt & Whitney PW2240 engines, or as the -222 also with Rockwell Collins avionics. The Tu-204-230, with Samara propfan engines remained at the project stage, while shortened, short-range,

99-166-seat trunkliner derivatives have also been offered. These consist of the Tu-224 with RB.211-535E4 engines and the Tu-234 with PS-90As. The latter aircraft was also known as the Tu-204-300, and a prototype was produced by shortening the fuselage of the very first Tu-204 prototype. Production -300s have been delivered to Vladivostok Avia and KMV is also looking at the type. Further advanced projects include the dual fuel (mixed kerosene/liquid natural gas) Tu-206 and the wholly cryogenically fuelled Tu-216.

Financial failure?

One should not judge the Tu-204 too harshly, however. The collapse of the old Soviet Union

The similarity between Tupolev's Tu-204 and the Boeing 757 is clear in this view of one of the four flying prototypes. The most notable feature distinguishing the aircraft from the 757 is the incorporation of drag-reducing winglets.

Moscow-based Vnukovo Airlines included four Tu-204s in its large fleet, which also included a large number of Tu-154s. Three of the aircraft, including that illustrated, were flown as airliners, while a fourth had been converted to Tu-204-100C freighter configuration.

took place almost 15 years ago, and the memory of what its society and economy were like, and how they operated, is fading fast. It is too easy to judge the Tu-204 by normal Western 'capitalist' standards, giving no thought to the unique demands of the system it was designed to serve. For most of the Soviet era, Aeroflot operated a gigantic, heavily subsidized rural 'bus service', taking peasants to market across the vast distances of the Soviet Union, and using austere airfields without the usual 'razzmatazz' of luggage conveyors and sophisticated passenger/freight-handling facilities. Carry-on luggage bins were the norm in Aeroflot aircraft, and hand baggage was as likely to consist of a live chicken or a small pig as anything else. Shaving the last percentile point off fuel burn

figures was not the most important criterion in Soviet airliner design, whereas rugged dependability and ease of maintenance were highly prized.

A Western commercial aircraft manufacturer would pat itself on the back if a particular maintenance procedure could be undertaken by a single, college-educated and expensively trained technician in minutes. Russian practice would prefer a procedure which could be undertaken reliably and without error by half a dozen barely trained mechanics, even if it took them an hour!

Manpower was cheap, but skilled man-power was in very short supply.

New generation

Despite the environment in which it was created, the Tupolev Tu-204 did mark a tenuous first step

towards modern Western design practice and operating concepts in what was still a Soviet Aeroflot airliner, and in that alone, it was a remarkable, significant and historic aircraft. The type deserved to find a market among Third World airlines, and the carriers of developing nations, where its easy, flexible pricing, operating characteristics, tolerance of austere airfields and

undemanding maintenance procedures should have been sought after. Unfortunately for Tupolev, the same nations whose air forces demand the latest supersonic fighters rather than easier-to-fly, easier-to-operate and more useful armed trainers also have airlines which want the dubious prestige of operating the latest Boeing or Airbus design. Accordingly, Tu-204 sales have continued to be disappointing, although by the second half of 2005 there were some signs of a resurgence in the Russian market. Many Russian carriers are reporting a scarcity of older airframes and new Tu-204/-214 orders are coming in. There is also renewed interest in the type from China.

SPECIFICATION

Tupolev Tu-204-100
Type: medium-range airliner
Powerplant: two 157-kN (35,320-lb-thrust) Aviadvigatel PS-90A turbofan engines
Maximum cruising speed: 850 km/h (527 mph)
Range: 4000 km (2,480 miles)
Maximum fuel capacity: 40,730 litres (10,760 gal)
Weights: empty 59,000 kg (129,800 lb); loaded 103,000 kg

(226,600 lb)
Dimensions: wing span 42.00 m (137 ft 9 in); length 46.22 m (151 ft 7 in); height 13.88 m (45 ft 6 in); wing area 182.40 m² (1,963 sq ft)
Accommodation: standard accommodation for two crew and 184 passengers, although a third crew member is often carried and passenger seating can be increased to 214

The extended-range Tu-204-100 is offered in all-passenger and Tu-204-100C freighter versions. Marketed from 1994, the -100C offers increased payload at the expense of reduced range.

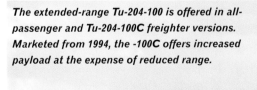

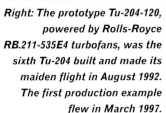

Right: The prototype Tu-204-120, powered by Rolls-Royce RB.211-535E4 turbofans, was the sixth Tu-204 built and made its maiden flight in August 1992. The first production example flew in March 1997.

Boeing 737 Series 300/400/500 Building on the 'baby'

The best-selling airliner of all time, the 737, was rejuvenated in the 1980s and fitted with the revolutionary and highly efficient CFM56 engine. Produced in three variants, the aircraft was a hit around the world.

The arrival of a new Boeing 737 variant allowed the 737-200 production line to close in the summer of 1988. This new aircraft was the Series 300, which itself spawned variants to cover the short-/medium-range, low- to medium-density requirements of customers.

By the late 1970s, it had become obvious to Boeing that tackling the increasing problems of fuel economy and noise pollution would require the use of high-bypass-ratio turbofans. However, at the time, the smallest new-technology engines were far too powerful for an airliner in the 737 class.

The answer to Boeing's conundrum lay in the CFM56 engine, the first of a new breed of small fans in the 89-kN (20,000-lb-thrust) class.

Engine experiments

The CFM56 was first used in 1979, when the CFM56-2 was picked to re-engine the DC-8-60 and this gave Boeing the confidence to begin work on the new 737 in early 1980. The resulting 737-300 retained about 70 per cent commonality with the Series 200, with minor wing improvements such as extended wingtips. The most radical feature was the lengthening of the fuselage by the addition of two plugs forward and aft of the wing. This allowed the new model to take advantage of the increase in power to provide additional passenger and baggage capacity. To cater for longitudinal stability problems, a dorsal fin fillet was added.

The first CFM56-3 engines caused something of a problem when installed on the prototype 737-300. There was insufficient ground clearance for the engines to be attached without modification. The problem was solved by moving all the engine accessories from underneath the

Above: The first Series 737-300, appropriately registered N73700, made its maiden flight in February 1984. After 14 months of test and evaluation flights, the aircraft was delivered to USAir.

Top: An early export customer for the 737 Series 300 was Australian Airlines, which eventually acquired 16 737-376s. In October 1993 the airline became part of QANTAS.

engine to the sides, so that the nacelle need to be only as deep as the compressor blade. This solution gives a characteristic squashed shape to the nacelle.

On 24 February 1984, the first 737-300 flew. Certification was achieved on 14 November and, by the 28th of the month, the first delivery was being made to USAir. Southwest Airlines flew the type's first revenue-earning service on 7 December. By 31 March 1990 orders covered 948 aircraft, of which 602 had been delivered. Many 737-200

operators, and not a few new ones, came to Boeing for the new aircraft. Douglas could only offer updated versions of the JT8D-powered MD-80 until the new-technology fan-powered MD-90 became available. Many of the US majors bought the 737-300 in huge quantities, while across the globe influential majors, charter carriers and small national airlines alike adopted the type.

Modern cockpit

The two-person crew had the latest in avionics and systems to aid them. INS and Omega navigation was optional, and newer aircraft had a full electronic flight instrumentation system (EFIS). Another

The Series 500 is of similar length to the original Series 200. The aircraft is particularly suited to lower-density, longer-distance services.

Left: Piedmont Airlines took delivery of the first 737-400 in September 1988. The airline's aircraft were configured to carry 146 passengers.

Below left: The 737 has competed for sales with Airbus' A320 series. The Series 400 has the largest capacity and was a direct rival of the lengthened version of the A320, the A321.

welcome option was Boeing's windshear detection and guidance system. Digital autothrottle was fitted as standard. With regulatory permission, the 737-300 can undertake extended-range operations over water or undeveloped land, being able to travel further than the statutory one-hour's flying time to the nearest airport.

With the 737-300 proving to be a great success, Boeing produced a family of variants offering different range/load capabilities. The first variant to be developed was the 737-400, a lengthened version offering greater capacity, but with negligible reduction in range. The first details of this type were announced in June 1986; the first aircraft made its maiden flight on 19 February 1988.

The 737-400 is considerably longer than the Series 300, having a 1.83-m (6-ft) plug forward of the wing and a 1.22-m (4-ft) plug aft. To maintain performance, uprated CFM56-3B-2 (97.86 kN/ 22,000 lb thrust) or CFM56-3C (104.5 kN/23,500 lb thrust) engines are fitted. To cope with a raised maximum take-off weight the undercarriage and outer wings were beefed up and a tail bumper was fitted as standard. Internally, the 737-400 offers a typical mixed-class accommodation for 146 passengers, although high-density charter operators regularly carry up to 170 passengers. The FAA

certification awarded on 2 September 1988 covers the aircraft for up to 188 passengers.

Piedmont Airlines was the launch customer, and it received its first aircraft on 15 September 1988. Subsequently the airline was absorbed into the huge USAir concern, itself an early customer for the 737-400 and now part of US Airways. Sales were brisk, particularly among charter operators, which found the increased capacity ideal for their type of work.

By 31 March 1990, orders for the 737-400 stood at 224, but doubts were cast over the new aircraft and its engines after a CFM56-3C-engined 737-400 of British Midland crashed while attempting an emergency landing at East Midlands Airport in England, but despite a brief grounding, the aircraft were soon plying their trade again.

Further development of the Series 400 resulted in an increased-weight version, with revised avionics, increased fuel capacity and local strengthening. Power came from further uprated CFM56-3C-1 engines of 111.2-kN (25,000 lb thrust).

In order to complete its new-technology family of 737s, Boeing needed an aircraft of the same capacity as the original Series 200. Originally known as the 737-1000, this was

announced on 20 May 1987 as the 737-500. Combining the features of the 737-300 and -400, the -500 has a reduced length of 31 m (101 ft 9 in), comparing with that of the 737-200 of 30.53 m (100 ft 2 in). Accommodation is for 108 to 132 passengers.

Power comes from the CFM56-3B-1 of 88.97 kN (20,000 lb thrust), or the same engine derated to 82.29 kN (18,500 lb thrust), depending on customer preference. With auxiliary fuel tanks, a 737-500 with 108 passengers has a still-air range of 5552 km (3,450 miles), making it easily the longest-legged of the family.

With the development of its Next Generation 737s, Boeing closed what now became 737 Classic production in 2000.

Right: Formed in the late 1980s, South Korea's Asiana Airlines chose the Series 300 and 400 versions of the Boeing 737 to operate its domestic and regional short/medium-haul services.

SPECIFICATION	
Boeing 747-400	**Service ceiling:** 13,716 m (45,000 ft)
Type: high-capacity long-haul airliner	**Weights:** empty 182,754 kg
Powerplant: four high-bypass-ratio	(402,059 lb); loaded 394,625 kg
turbofans rated at 258 km	(868,175 lb)
(58,040 lb thrust) (engines available	**Dimensions:** win span 64.44 m
Pratt & Whitney PW4056, General	(211 ft 4 in); length 70.66 m (231 ft
Electric CF6-80C2 or Rolls-Royce	9 in); height 19.41 m (63 ft 8 in);
RB-211 425G)	wing area 511 m² (5,498 sq ft)
MAximum speed: 980 km/h	**Accommodation:** two (flight deck),
(608 mph)	390 passengers in standard
Range: 13,398 km (8,307 miles)	configuration

Second generation today

VARIG of Brazil has a large fleet of Boeing 737s, including 25 Series 300s. The reliability and economy of the second-generation 737 persuaded the airline to purchase Next-Generation Series 800s.

The only replacement for the Boeing 737 turned out to be another 737. The trio of 737-300, 737-400 and 737-500 dominated the airliner market throughout the 1980s and well into the 1990s. As their place has been taken by the Next-Generation 737s, so Boeing has come to call the -300, -400 and -500 the '737 Classics'.

In an era of airline deregulation in the United States, Boeing was faced with rising customer demand for an improved small airliner to take the place of older 737s and the 727. Both types were becoming less economical to operate and faced tougher international noise and environmental regulations. There was also the threat of Europe's Airbus A320, which promised a quantum leap in technology. Thus a new generation of 737 was developed. The 737-300 programme was launched in March 1981, with orders for 10 each from Southwest Airlines and USAir. The 737-300 also borrowed the 757-200's interior design, which included large

The Series 400 has the largest 737 Classic capacity. The Polish operator LOT has six examples, which are configured to carry 147 passengers in a two-class layout.

enclosed overhead bins, galleys and toilets located fore and aft, and a wider cabin.

First deliveries of the new 737 went to USAir, followed by aircraft for Southwest Airlines. Southwest was the first to put its new 737-300s into revenue service, on services from Dallas and Houston. The UK CAA awarded type certification on 29 January 1985, the same day that Orion Airways became the first non-US operator. During 1981 and 1982 orders for the 737-300 were almost nonexistent, but they accelerated rapidly in 1983 and 1984. A total of 1061 737-300s was delivered from 1981 to 1999, the last delivery being made in December 1999.

Boeing 737-400

In December 1985 Boeing decided to offer a 737 with a fuselage stretch that would add

Virgin launched its Express subsidiary to link its North American passengers with European destinations. It operated 737-300s for a number of years in the 1990s before relaunching its short-haul routes as holiday airline Virgin Sun.

three more seat rows. The 737-400 was formally launched in June 1986, with an order for 25 (with 30 options) from Piedmont Airlines. A total of 486 737-400s was ordered over the type's 12-year production period from 1986 to 1998. The last of the 737-400s was delivered in February 2000.

Boeing 737-500

The Boeing 737-500 was launched on 20 May 1987 with

an order for 38 aircraft from Southwest Airlines. The 737-500 was designed as a replacement for the 737-200, one which incorporated the newer technologies of the 737-300 and 737-400. The resulting aircraft seats between 108 and 138 passengers depending on seating layout.

Significant technology that had been developed for the 757 and 767 was incorporated into

The second-generation Model 737s have proved popular with leasing companies. One such organization, Sailplane Leasing, provided the Russian carrier Aeroflot with 10 Bermudan-registered 737-4MOs, which were used on European routes.

British Airways has long been a staunch supporter of Boeing designs and has operated -200, -300, -400 and -500 (illustrated) versions of the 737.

the 737-500. This included the wing leading-edge design for aerodynamic efficiency; lightweight advanced composites on flight control surfaces, aerodynamic fairings and engine cowlings; and weight-saving aluminium alloy wing skins. A fully integrated flight management system (FMS) provides automatic control and guidance of the aircraft. With optional equipment, the FMS makes Category IIIA automatic landings possible. The same EFIS cockpit is fitted to the -500 as is

found on the -300 and -400, allowing a common crew type rating across all three versions.

The 737-500 also introduced Boeing's windshear detection system. Windshear is caused by a violent downburst of air that changes speed and direction as it strikes the ground. The system alerts flight crews to windshear and provides flight-path guidance.

The first 737-500 rolled out of the Renton plant on 3 June 1989; the maiden flight came on 30 June 1989. The 737-500 received its FAA certification on 12 February 1990 and the first delivery was made to Southwest on 2 March 1990. On 15 February 1991 a 737-500 for Lufthansa became the 2000th 737 to be delivered and it was also

Lufthansa's 100th 737. By June 1999 all 389 of the 737-500s ordered had been delivered.

A successful partnering

The largest operator by far of the 737-300 is Southwest Airlines – a company that has built its phenomenal success entirely around the Boeing 737. Southwest currently has a fleet of 194 737-300s, plus 25 737-500s (and 210 737-700s). Indeed, Southwest was the launch customer for the Next-Generation 737.

USAir (which, renamed as US Airways after it absorbed Piedmont, became the 737-300 launch customer alongside Southwest) is another substantial 737 operator, with a fleet of 67 737-300s and 45 737-400s. United Airlines is yet another important customer, with a mix of 35 737-500s and 76 737-300s. Delta also has a small fleet of 737-300s (although it still has a sizeable fleet of active 737-200s).

Boeing's Classic 737 family fitted admirably into the US hub-and-spoke concept of airline operations. The range of

different aircraft sizes, all with a common crew type rating and essentially the same technical specification, allowed operators to mix and match aircraft to routes, depending on load and frequency.

European Classics

The Classic 737s also sold well to existing 737 operators in Europe, with airlines such as Lufthansa, Aer Lingus, Air France and British Airways placing the family into service. The 737-400, in particular, found a valuable niche market in Europe, as its mix of long range and high capacity appealed to IT holiday charter airlines. Europe was also an important market for the 'baby' 737-500.

The launch customer for the 737-500 was Norway's Braathens SAFE, even though the first actual deliveries went to Southwest. In 1990, when it took delivery of its first 737-500, Ireland's Aer Lingus was the first airline in the world to have all three variants in service at the same time.

Europe also saw the end of the Classics when, on 28 February 2000, the last two 737-400s were delivered to CSA Czech Airlines. These aircraft were the last of the Classic 737s to roll off the Renton production line. In all, a grand total of 1936 examples of the Classic 737-300, -400 and -500 aircraft were built.

Left: Configured to carry 121 passengers, Luxair's two 737-5C9s are named after famous chateaux in Luxembourg. This model of 737 allows the airline to operate to destinations which would be inaccessible to the Series 400 without refuelling.

Boeing 737-600/700/800/900 New generation

Boeing's new generation of 737s has continued the unprecedented success of the world's favourite airliner. This example is a 737-600, originally known as the 737-500X, which is the smallest of the family.

Faced with increasing competition from Europe's A320 family, Boeing took a long, hard look at its Classic 737. Instead of launching a whole new type, Boeing overhauled the basic design, making it more efficient and 'operator friendly'. The result was the Next-Generation 737, which looks a lot like its predecessors, but conceals many changes inside.

Keeping the basic fuselage sizes the same, in 1993 Boeing launched the 737-X programme. Three versions were initially on offer: the 737-500X, the 737-300X and the 737-400X (a stretched version of the 146-seat 737-400). To further emphasize the difference between the Classic and Next-Generation 737s, or 737NGs, the new aircraft were all soon redesignated. The 737-500X became the 737-600,

the 737-300X was the 737-700 and the 737-400X the 737-800. In 1997 a fourth model, the 737-900, was added. This version is a further-stretched 737-800. The 737-600 – slightly larger than the 737-500 – is the smallest member of the family and can carry 110 to 132 passengers. The 737-700 can accommodate between 126 and 149 seats. The 737-800 can carry between 162 and 189 passengers. Finally, the 737-900 is capable of carrying 177 to 189 passengers. Though the 737-900 is longer than the -800, its seating capacity is limited by the number of emergency exits.

Boeing had several key aims for its 737NGs. The new aircraft had to have greater range, higher cruise speed, a (12,496 m/41,000 ft) cruise capability, lower fuel burn,

Equivalent to the Classic 737-300, the Boeing 737-700 was the first of the new generation to be launched, and it had attracted 1,030 orders by August 2005.

decreased emissions and noise, and reduced maintenance costs. In addition, the new models would offer flight-deck commonality with earlier 737s and allow flight crews to maintain the same type ratings.

To achieve this, the 737NGs called for improved engines, with a new wing and several other aerodynamic refinements. They also needed a redesigned cabin and a modernized flight deck. They are powered by derivatives of the FADEC-

equipped CFM56-7 turbofan. The CFM56-7 has a 10 per cent higher thrust capability than the CFM56-3C and, to take additional advantage of the engine's increased thrust, the 737NG's vertical fin and horizontal stabilizer are larger.

The 737NGs incorporate a new, advanced-technology wing design with increased chord and span. This boosts fuel capacity and efficiency, which in turn extends range. Overall, the range of the Next-Generation

Tunisair is unusual in currently operating all three generations of Boeing's 'Babyjet'. The airline has already seven 737-600s (illustrated) and one 737-700 in service.

SPECIFICATION	
Boeing 737-800	**Weights:** operating empty
Type: twin-turbofan short- to	41,554 kg (91,419 lb); maximum
medium-range airliner	take-off 70,535 kg (155,177 lb)
Powerplant: two 116.5-kN	**Dimensions:** wing span 34.31 m
(26,200-lb-thrust) CFM International	(112 ft 6 in); length (39.47 m (129 ft
CFM56-7B turbofan engines	6 in); height 12.55 m (41 ft 2 in);
Maximum operating speed: Mach 0.82	wing area 125 m² (1,345 sq ft)
Range: 5426 km (3,364 miles) with	**Accommodation:** alternative cabin
maximum passenger load	layouts for 162 to 189 passengers;
Cruising altitude: 10,730 m	overhead baggage capacity of
(35,200 ft)	9.3 m³ (329 cu ft)

Above: Transavia Airlines is a low-cost Dutch operator, offering scheduled and charter services to leisure destinations. The airline currently has 18 737-800s in service.

Below: A staunch supporter of Boeing designs, Air China selected the 737-800 thanks to its ability to carry almost 200 passengers combined with the economy of the CFM56-7B engine.

737s is approximately 3,300 nm (6111 km; 3,795 miles), giving a 737NG true US transcontinental reach. The design of the new 737s also incorporates important interior improvements which were pioneered on the 777.

Baseline version

The 737-700 is the baseline 737NG and was the first of the family to be launched, on 19 January 1994, when Southwest Airlines signed an order for 63 aircraft. The first 737-700 was rolled out on 8 December 1996 and flew on 9 February 1997. FAA type approval was awarded on 7 November 1997. However, JAA approval was delayed until 19 February 1998.

Southwest is the leading customer for the 737-700, with a total of 249 ordered. Other important 737-700 customers include Alaska Airlines, Continental Airlines, easyJet and Germania, alongside lessors ILFC, GE Capital and Bouillioun Aviation Services. A special version of the 737-700 (the 737-700IGW QC) has been developed for the US Navy as the C-40A Clipper. Fitted with a side cargo door and a combi interior, the C-40 is replacing the C-9 fleet. Eight have been delivered, with a ninth on order, and the USN has a requirement for up to 30 aircraft.

On 5 September 1994 the 737-800 was launched. The first 737-800 customer to identify itself was Hapag-Lloyd, which ordered an initial batch of 16. The first 737-800 made its maiden flight on 31 July 1997 and received its FAA type certification on 13 March 1998. JAA certification followed on 9 April. To date, the largest order for 737-800s has been placed by Ryanair, which has signed for 230. Other important customers include Air Algerie, Air Berlin, American Airlines, Continental Airlines, Delta, KLM, Olympic Airways, Transavia, THY plus GE Capital and ILFC. In addition, the 737-800 is the basis for the US Navy's 108 P-8A Multi-Mission Maritime Aircraft for service from 2013.

Scandinavian Airlines became the launch customer for the 737-600 on 15 March 1995, when it ordered 35 aircraft. The first 737-600 made its maiden flight on 22 January 1998 and SAS took delivery of its first example on 18 September. On 10 November 1997, Alaska Airlines became the launch customer for the Next-Generation 737-900, with an order for 10.

Boeing has been toying with the launch of a higher-capacity 737-900X for some time and a 30 June 2005 Lion Air order for 30 such aircraft, plus 30 options, will probably see the model developed.

Sales figures

Since programme launch, Boeing claims that the 737NG family has outsold all other aircraft in its market segment. The 737NGs have proved popular, but not universally so. Sales of the 737-600 have been disappointing, but discontinuation of the Boeing 717 may ease the problem. Current 737-600 orders stand at 73 aircraft. The 737-900 has also been slow to win orders, with just 55 on order. By August 2005 total 737NG orders stood at 2726.

Deliveries of the 737-900 began to launch customer Alaska Airlines in May 2001. The lengthened and strengthened fuselage can accommodate 177 passengers in a two-class layout.

Boeing Business Jet (BBJ)

The BBJ is an innovative offshoot of the 737NG with which Boeing has developed a new market niche. Together with engine supplier General Electric, Boeing launched the BBJ in July 1997 as a dedicated, large-capacity business jet with a 6,000-nm (11,104-km; 6,900-mile) range. The 737-700BBJ (illustrated) combines the fuselage of the 737-700 with the strengthened wing and landing gear of the larger, heavier 737-800. Large blended winglets to further boost performance are available as a customer option. The BBJ can carry up to 68 passengers and is available in a wide range of interior fittings to suit the needs of all customers. The first aircraft was rolled out in September 1998, with GE as the launch customer. Boeing has also added a larger 737-800BBJ to its line up. Announced BBJ orders currently stand at 95 aircraft.

Boeing 757 New-generation narrowbody

Designed to replace the prolific Boeing 727 on the production line, the Model 757 had little in common with its predecessor. New, efficient engines and a modern cockpit made the 757 a cost-efficient option for a number of the world's larger carriers.

Until the 727, no airliner had notched up 1000 sales. The 727 sold 1832, the last thousand being gained despite the existence of the Airbus A300B, which offered greater comfort, far better fuel efficiency and much less noise. Even though no airlines in the early 1970s seemed to want to buy the quiet wide-body, Boeing could see that it would have to improve the 727; its first idea was the stretched 727-300 with fuel-efficient engines. By 1976 this had become the 7N7, with just two engines hung under a wing more like that of the A300B.

Increasingly, attention focused on the biggest 7N7 versions, and Rolls-Royce came into the picture with the new RB.211-535 engine of an initial 144 kN (32,000-lb thrust). It was obvious that, instead of trying to sell engines for European A300B and A310 aircraft, Rolls-Royce was eager

to get aboard the new Boeing, and it was backed to the hilt by British Airways. Indeed, in 1976–78, great efforts were made by Boeing, British Airways and Rolls-Royce to get the British aircraft industry to build 757 wings instead of joining Airbus Industrie.

In 1979 it was decided to drop the T-tail and mount the horizontal tail on the fuselage. A little later, the old 727 'cab' – giving commonality with the 707, 727 and 737 – was discarded in favour of the 767's wider nose and flight deck. By now Boeing was already in full development, the go-ahead being announced in early 1978 and British Airways and Eastern placing launch orders on 31 August 1978.

Slow sales

Initially, sales of the 757 were very disappointing. Thanks to its narrow body, it had been planned

to offer the lowest fuel burn per passenger-kilometre of any jetliner, yet no new customers appeared until, in April 1980, three were signed for by Transbrasil and three by Aloha. Both selected the CF6-32 engine, in which General Electric proposed to collaborate with Volvo Flygmotor of Sweden. Still there were no sales until at last, in November 1980, came the breakthrough Boeing had been waiting for – 60 for Delta. The giant US line deferred its choice of engine, and when its decision was announced in December 1980, it was for yet a third engine, the Pratt & Whitney PW2037. Pratt & Whitney marketed the engine as the most efficient in the world. The attraction of this proposed performance encouraged American Airlines, at the end of 1980, to announce selection of the PW2037 for its

Despite a strong home lobby canvassing for the national airline to buy Airbus, British Airways signed up as the launch customer for the 757, its first aircraft entering service in February 1983.

757s, before it had even announced it would buy the Boeing aircraft! In January 1981 GE announced that it would no longer compete in this market, and ended CF6-32 development. Aloha and Transbrasil picked the PW2037, although this meant delayed delivery.

The first 757 was rolled out at Renton on 13 January 1982, to make its first flight on 19 February. It was the first time that a major US airliner had been launched with a foreign engine, but development of the 535C had progressed so much more efficiently than predicted

Left: The Boeing Model 757 and 767 projects were launched in a blaze of publicity in the late 1970s. It would, however, be a number of years before the 757 order book began to fill.

Below: Delta was the first operator to select the Pratt & Whitney PW2037 engine. It operated its 757s alongside Boeing 767s and Lockheed TriStars on US domestic routes.

Air Europe, owned by the International Leisure Group, was one of a number of European operators which found the aircraft an economical choice for charter flights.

Above: Eastern was the first airline to place the Model 757 into service, this occurring on 1 January 1983. The airline eventually received 25 examples, delivered from 1983 to 1986.

that everyone (except P&W) was delighted. Scheduled services began with Eastern on 1 January 1983, and with British Airways on 9 February. By this time, Boeing had thought better of its original plan to offer various sub-types of 757, and early sales were of the 757-200 type, with a fuselage length of 46.96 m (154 ft 10 in), customers merely having two choices of engine and a choice of regular or long-range fuel capacity.

Although the nose and cockpit section are similar to those of the appreciably wider 767, the main tube section of the fuselage is almost identical to that of the 707, 727 and 737. Boeing offered nine interior arrangements for 178 to 239 passengers, seated basically in a 3 + 3 arrangement with a central aisle. Customers could have three doors each side plus four overwing emergency exits or four doors each side. In most configurations there is a galley at the front on the right and

another at the rear on the left, and toilets at the front on the left and two or three either amidships or at the rear.

Technically, the 757 is very conventional. The wing has a quarterchord sweep of 25 degrees. The leading edge is fitted with full-span powered slats, though these have a gap at the engine pylon, there being a single large slat inboard and four sections outboard. On the trailing edge are inboard and outboard flaps mounted on faired tracks. All are double-slotted, except the outer portion of each inboard flap which is single-slotted to avoid interference with the jet wake. Outboard are powered all-speed ailerons of quite long span. Ahead of the flaps are two inboard and four outboard spoilers on each wing, the innermost being a ground lift-dumper only. The other 10 spoilers are opened together as speed brakes or differentially for roll, augmenting the ailerons. The horizontal tail is pivoted to

serve as the longitudinal trim control, carrying the graphite-composite elevators. Likewise, the fixed vertical tail carries a graphite rudder.

New systems
In its systems the 757 did break some new ground, notably in the use of laser-light gyros in the navigation IRS (inertial reference system). It was also one of the new breed of all-digital aircraft. There was simply no way that Boeing could have launched a jetliner in the late 1970s with the analogue-type avionics of the 707, 727 and Classic 737s and 747s. The flight deck, very like that of the 767, is a mix of old and new, new parts including basic EFIS displays and an EICAS (engine indication and crew-alerting system). The overall flight management was a generation earlier than that of the A320, but it did offer automatic trajectory guidance, terminal navigation, thrust management and an optional feature offering some protection against windshear. A Garrett APU is mounted in the tailcone, the ECS (environmental control system) packs are under the floor in the centre section, and there are two ram-air turbines to provide emergency electrical

and hydraulic power in flight. Each main gear is a four-wheel bogie retracting inward, with Dunlop wheels, tyres and carbon brakes. The steerable twin-wheel nose gear retracts forwards, all gear doors being of Kevlar.

From the start of service the 757 did all that was asked of it, and the 535C did more. It was soon clear that this was the most trouble-free engine in history, almost never suffering an inflight shutdown. Over the first four years of service the engine-caused removal rate was only 0.051 per thousand flight hours, described as 'many times better than the previously claimed industry best'.

In October 1984 the advanced E4 entered service, and quickly established not only a reputation for reliability which is, if anything, even greater, but also a reduction in fuel burn of over 10 per cent. The rival PW2037 followed it into service on 1 December 1984, and the unequalled combination of economy, reliability and low cost of ownership resulted in the British engine being selected by each of the next 11 customers for the 757. Many airlines, including several UK charter operators, began operating E4-powered 757s on services to North America.

An important customer to have picked the Pratt & Whitney engine (in the uprated PW2040 version) was United Parcel Service, which ordered the 757-200PF (Package Freighter). This is a dedicated freighter, with a windowless fuselage and a large cargo door in the port side. It can carry 15 standard containers on its main deck.

SPECIFICATION	
Boeing 757-200	miles) at maximum economy
Type: twin-engine medium-range transport	**Service ceiling:** 13,932 m (45,700 ft)
Powerplant: two 166.37-kN (37,230-lb-thrust) Rolls-Royce RB211-53C, or 169.93-kN (38,119-lb-thrust) Pratt & Whitney PW2037, or 178,38-kN (40,015-lb-thrust) RB211-535E4, or 185.50-kN (41,613-lb-thrust) Pratt & Whitney PW2040 high-bypass turbofans	**Weights:** empty 57,180 kg (125,796 lb); loaded 113,400 kg (249,480 lb) **Dimensions:** wing span 38.05 m (124 ft 9 in); length 47.35 m (155 ft 9 in); height 13.60 m (44 ft 7 in); wing area 181.25 m² (1,950 sq ft) **Accommodation:** two pilots, six attendants; typically 194 passengers in mixed-class service; 239 passengers on charter; up to 39,690 kg (87,318 lb) of cargo and pallets in freighter version
Maximum speed: 981 km/h (608 mph) **Range:** 5150 km (3,193 miles) with maximum load; 7400 km (4,588	

757 today

The 757 is the backbone of many major airline fleets, particularly in the United States. Adept at handling both transcontinental and short-range shuttle routes, the 757 has matured into an efficient specialized freighter, a head-of-state transport and the high-capacity, stretched 757-300.

Europe and America are the centres of 757 operations, though significant sales have been won in the Far East. Furthermore, European airlines were behind the development of the final member of the 757 family, the stretched 757-300, which was designed to appeal to IT (inclusive tour) charter airlines.

The United States remains the 757's stronghold. Many airlines there chose the bigger, twin-engined Boeing to replace their 727s. Leading that pack was Delta Airlines, which ordered a total of 116 757-200s between 1980 and 1999. American Airlines was also a major US customer, signing up for 103 aircraft between 1988 and 1996. Other

North American 757 operators include United Airlines, Northwest Airlines, Continental Airlines, US Airways, TWA and American TransAir. Away from the regular airline world, UPS is the primary operator of the 757-200PF freighter version – indeed, the Package Freighter variant was developed specifically to a 1985 UPS order; the first example was delivered on 16 September 1987.

In Europe the 757 is popular among holiday charter airlines, where operators have included Air 2000, Air Europe, Airtours International, Condor, JMC, LTU, Monarch Airlines, Thomas Cook and Transavia. China has proved to be an important market since Boeing sold its first 757 to CAAC in 1987. Operators have included China Southern, China Southwest, China Xinjing Airlines, Shanghai Airlines and Xiamen Airlines. Among the most significant 757 customers have been the international aircraft leasing companies, which were early adopters of the type. Several

*Above: **US** domestic airlines were always the 757's principal market, with operators such as **American Airlines** operating large fleets. **America West** is one of many smaller carriers, operating 13 examples on shuttle services between **West Coast** towns and cities.*

*Above: **T**ypical of the many **European** charter airlines which operate the 757, **Monarch Airlines** has a fleet of seven examples, which fly the popular **Mediterranean, United States** and **Caribbean** holiday routes.*

lessors have 757s on their books, the most important of which include ILFC, Ansett Worldwide Aviation and GPA Ltd.

Boeing took the 757 into a new realm in August 1996 when it won an order for four aircraft from the US Air Force. Designated C-32A, these 757-200s are used for VVIP transport tasks in the hands of the 89th AW, where they

replaced VC-137s. Other air arms have also acquired the 757, and the type has also attracted orders from civil VIP and business jet operators.

Increasing appeal

Boeing sold a total of 1049 757s, with the majority remaining in service. It is difficult to place the 757 into a particular market slot, however, as airlines use it to fly both transatlantic services and high-frequency shuttle routes. One concern that operators did have, particularly in Europe, was that the 757 did not have enough seating capacity to benefit fully from its long legs. This was the driving force behind the

*The **US Air Force's** four **C-32As** are powered by **Pratt & Whitney PW2040** turbofans and were delivered between **May** and **November 1998.***

Above: Flying Colours began operations in 1997, and in March 2000 it was integrated with Caledonian, forming JMC Airlines, which was later renamed as Thomas Cook Airlines.

Above: Royal Brunei Airlines operated two smartly painted 757-2M6s, powered by Rolls-Royce RB.211-535E4 turbofans. The aircraft were delivered in 1986 and served into 2004.

development of the 757-300, Boeing revived earlier plans for a scaled-up 757, considering two versions, the higher gross weight 757-200X and a larger aircraft altogether, the 757-300X. It chose the second option and launched the 757-300 at the 1996 Farnborough Air Show. The new 757 could carry 20 per cent more passengers, and increased the available cargo volume by nearly 50 per cent. Designed to carry 243 passengers in a typical mixed-class configuration, the 757-300 can accommodate up to 289 in charter service, putting its capacity between that of the 757-200 and the 767-300.

Maximum take-off weight has increased to 123,600 kg (272,500 lb) to preserve the passenger/cargo load capability. The wing, landing gear and portions of the fuselage were strengthened and new wheels, tyres and brakes added to handle the extra weight. Because the 757-300 is longer, Boeing made several modifications to protect against possible damage from tail strikes during take-off and landing. A retractable tail skid, similar to that on the 777-300, was added.

The two-crew flight deck of the 757-300 is similar to that of the 757-200, and the two are cross-crew qualified. Latterly, flight deck improvements were made to the 757. These included the addition of the Pegasus flight management computer (FMC) and an enhanced engine indication and crew alerting system (EICAS). With the Pegasus FMC, operators could choose optional software providing the ability to use the global positioning system and satellite communications.

The EICAS upgrade replaces existing computers with enhanced devices that are software-driven. The new EICAS has improved built-in test equipment functions that allow for improved self-diagnosis of faults in a more readable format. Other improvements to the 757 have included an enhanced ground proximity warning system (EGPWS), a new software-loadable flight control computer (FCC) and an enhanced windshear warning system. The 757-300 also incorporated the latest technology air data/inertial reference system (ADIRS).

Launching the 757-300

Although parts of the 757-300 were manufactured at Boeing facilities in Wichita, Kansas, and by external suppliers at many locations (including major sub-contractor Northrop Grumman), major assembly was undertaken in Renton. The 757-300 was launched with an order for 12 aircraft from Germany's Condor Flugdienst on 2 September 1996. The next customer was Icelandair, which announced an order for two at the 1997 Paris Air Show. The first aircraft was rolled out on 31 May 1998 and made its maiden flight on 2 August. By that time, additional orders had been received from Condor and Arkia Israeli. FAA certification was awarded on 22 January 1999, with JAA approval following on 25 January.

The first 757-300 was handed over to Condor on 10 March 1999 and entered service nine days later. Arkia Israeli Airlines took delivery of its two 757-300s in January/February 2000. The first of an eventual four 757-300s ordered by Icelandair was delivered in March 2002. Despite Boeing's high hopes, sales of the 757-300 remained slow. When 757 production ended late in 2004, just 55 orders had been placed for the -300.

Launched in 1996, the 757-300 entered service in 1999 with Condor Flugdienst. Seat-mile costs have been reduced by around 10 per cent compared to the airline's 757-200s.

The 757-300 was the longest single-aisle twinjet ever produced. The aircraft's cabin interior is the same as that used in the company's next-generation 737 family, giving a more open, spacious feel.

Boeing 767 Twin-jet wide-body

In the late 1970s, Boeing launched the wide-bodied Model 767 airliner project in response to Airbus's success with its A300. Offering excellent range performance, the aircraft was soon ordered by major airlines around the world.

Boeing eventually dominated the jet airliner club with the Model 707, an epoch-making airliner that successfully married swept-wing technology with lightweight, powerful turbojets. At this juncture, Lockheed dropped from the competition, leaving Douglas as the only rival to Boeing's meteoric rise in the market. The 707 initiated a memorable sequence of aircraft designations, each of which proved to be as successful and as revolutionary in its own way. The 717 designation was used by the KC-135 tanker series, built in huge numbers for the USAF, and was later reapplied to the MD-95 when Boeing inherited the twinjet from McDonnell Douglas. The 727 was a revolutionary trijet that brought jet power to the smaller fields and short-haul routes, a tradition

continued with the twinjet 737. Then came the 747, ushering in a new era of wide-body transports powered by high-bypass-ratio turbofans.

European competition
Flying nearly three years after the 747 had first been delivered, Europe's Airbus A300 offered a different kind of competition to Boeing's dominance. It entered an area where rival products were nothing more than paper projects, and consequently established itself rapidly as a world leader. Technological excellence was at the heart of the Airbus's success, which was continued with the A310. Both Boeing and McDonnell Douglas were caught out, neither having an aircraft with which to compete in this twin-engine, medium-haul, high-density market.

Boeing's answer lay in the 7X7 programme. This project was under discussion and study for 10 years, and during a long gestation had several different configurations, including the use of a T-tail, overwing engines and many other features. In July

Above: Following its roll-out, the prototype 767 was towed across the highway from assembly plant to active apron in preparation for its maiden flight from Everett, Washington, in September 1981.

Above top: The first European 767 operator was Britannia Airways, which received eight examples, mainly for its Mediterranean destinations. This example operated with the airline from 1984 to 1995 and was named the **Lord Mountbatten of Burma.**

1978, the company eventually announced the launch of the aircraft as the 767, in the same month as Airbus announced the go-ahead of its A310. Also proceeding roughly in parallel with the 7X7 was the 7N7, a narrow-body airliner intended to replace the 727, but sharing many of its larger brother's features. Despite its redesignation as the 757, this aircraft actually followed the 767 into service.

Boeing eventually settled on a conventional configuration for the 767, and, although this mirrored that of the much smaller 737, it also looked remarkably like the Airbus with which it was in direct competition. Critics, especially in Europe, were quick to point out this fact, but to be fair Boeing had pioneered the configuration nearly 20 years earlier. Also, it must be remembered that there is every chance that two superb design teams will arrive at the

United Airlines was the launch customer for the Model 767. Built as a 767-222, N605UA was the sixth example to be delivered to United and was later converted to ER standard.

Boeing relied on the loyalty of US carriers such as Delta to home-produced designs for initial 767 orders. The sixth aircraft built, N101DA, was used for proving flights before entering service in March 1983.

same answer if it happens to be the right one.

Where the Boeing design differed was that it had a smaller fuselage and bigger wing. The latter was designed to provide higher-altitude cruise performance, and also, not surprisingly, higher gross weights for future enlarged versions. What was surprising was the fuselage, for although the narrow diameter of the 767 (compared to the A300 and A310) produced less drag and consequently greater range, it could not accept standard cargo/baggage containers, and the standard eight-abreast seating was rather cramped. In broad terms, the Airbus products were better in load-carrying performance, but inferior in terms of range and altitude.

Despite the shortcomings of the design, the 767 was virtually assured of a large market at home, where the giant domestic carriers were crying out for a suitable type to transfer large numbers of passengers between US cities at economic rates. Nevertheless, this market provided the 767 with fewer sales than might once have been expected, for the Airbus products had made small yet notable in-roads into the US domestic market. Eastern and Pan Am were important Airbus customers, and these have been joined in recent years by many more, particularly since the smaller A320 family has been available.

Notwithstanding this European competition, the 767 at once began to pile up the orders. An order of 30 from United Airlines

had sparked the final go-ahead for the airliner on 14 July 1978. Other giants such as American Airlines, Delta Air Lines, Trans World Airlines and USAir also acquired the type, although the latter's aircraft were picked up when it absorbed Piedmont.

Powerplant variety

Construction of the prototype began on 6 July 1979. From the outset, the 767 was designed with two different engines in mind, according to customer preference. These were the Pratt & Whitney JT9D and General Electric CF6. The first aircraft (N767BA) flew on 26 September 1981, with Pratt & Whitney power. The next three aircraft from the line also featured this powerplant. General Electric engines powered the fifth aircraft, and this flew for the first time on 19 February 1982.

After an intensive flight trial period, FAA certification for the 213.5-kN (48,000-lb-thrust) Pratt & Whitney JT9D-7R4D-powered aircraft was received on 30 July 1982, allowing the first delivery to be made to United Airlines on 19 August. The General Electric-powered aircraft, with CF6-80A engines of the same power, received its certification on 30 September, 22 days after United had begun revenue-earning services. Delta received the first CF6-powered 767 on 25 October, with services beginning on 15 December.

These 767-200s, with the others that rapidly followed, were soon showing excellent economy over medium-haul routes, Delta's aircraft being configured with 18 passengers

Piedmont Airlines was an early operator of the 767-200ER, using the aircraft on ETOPS services across the North Atlantic. The airline was absorbed by USAir in 1989 and the aircraft were repainted in their new owner's colours.

SPECIFICATION	
Boeing 767-300ER **Type:** twin-engined long-range wide-bodied airliner **Powerplant:** two 252.4-kN (80,925-lb-thrust) Pratt & Whitney PW4056 or 266.9-kN (60,042-lb-thrust) General Electric CF6-80C2B4 or Rolls-Royce RB2311-542H turbofans **Cruising speed:** Mach 0.80 **Range:** (with reserves) 11,230 km (6,965 miles) **Service ceiling:** 12,192 m (40,000 ft)	**Weights:** empty 81,374 kg (179,023 lb); maximum take-off 181,437 kg (399,161 lb) **Dimensions:** wing span 47.57 m (156 ft); length 54.94 m (180 ft 3 in); height 15.85 m (52 ft); wing area 283.30 m² (3,048 sq ft) **Accommodation:** basic 269 passengers (24 first-class and 245 tourist-class); maximum capacity 350 passengers **Cargo hold:** 147.0 m³ (5,191 cu ft)

in first-class and 186 in economy, while United opted for a 24/180 split. Both operators would join the ranks of 757 operators, flying the smaller aircraft alongside the 767 from major hub centres.

As recounted earlier, the large wing of the Boeing 767 made the basic Series 200 a natural step for sizeable development. Aimed particularly at overseas customers, the 767-200ER was introduced, offering a higher gross weight (156,490 kg; 345,000 lb) and increased fuel capacity for a considerable range increase. Two further increases in weight and fuel capacity were also developed under the 767ER designation, the heaviest weighing in at 175,540 kg

(387,000 lb). Design range was extended from under 6000 km (3,730 miles) for the basic versions, to 12,611 km (7,836 miles) in the heaviest ER variant.

The -200ER version proved popular overseas, especially with small operators seeking new jet equipment, but not needing the capacity of a Boeing 747. Those in geographic isolation have found the incredible range performance of the 767ER perfect for covering the longest sectors, Air Mauritius and QANTAS being good examples.

Indeed, during a delivery flight on 17 April 1988, one of the Air Mauritius machines covered the 14,044 km (8,727 miles) between Halifax, Nova Scotia, and its new home nonstop, in a flight lasting 16 hours and 27 minutes. This set a world distance record for a twin-engined commercial aircraft.

Although United and Delta were the initial customers for the 767, other US majors followed them in adopting the type. American Airlines currently operates a total of 86 Model 200s, 200ERs and 300ERs.

Beyond the 200

The range of Boeing's original 767-200 was increased in the 767-200ER; however, to answer calls for yet more capacity and increased range, Boeing developed the 767-300 and the 767-300ER. These workhorses have now been joined by the radically redesigned 767-400, which raises the overall capabilities of the 767 family to an entirely new level.

The 767 was Boeing's first wide-bodied twin and one of the pioneers of transatlantic and trans-Pacific ETOPS.

When the 767-200 entered service, with United Airlines in September 1982, it faced competition from the Airbus A300 and A310 families, in particular the long-range A300-600R and the A310-300. Boeing developed the 767-200ER to offer more range, but to provide more seats the 767 had to be stretched. Boeing announced the 767-300 stretch in February 1983 and hoped that the new aircraft would be ready

for delivery in early 1986. It was not until September 1983, however, that the first firm order, from JAL, was placed.

The first 767-300 flew on 30 January 1986 and was certified in September. The first customer delivery was made to JAL on 25 September. The -300 incorporated a 6.42-m (253-in) fuselage extension, in the form of two plugs, forward and aft of the wing. In a typical two-class seating layout, the 767-300 can accommodate 261 passengers (about 20 per cent more than the -200), or 210 in a three-class layout. Maximum seating capacity is dictated largely by emergency exit capacity, however, and since 1989 the -300 has been permitted to operate with up to 360 passengers.

The 767-300 boasted a maximum take-off weight of 158,760 kg (350,000 lb) and a range, with 261 passengers aboard, of 4,150 nm (7680 km; 4,772 miles). The initial engine options for the 767-300 were

the 222.5-kN (50,000-lb-thrust) General Electric CF6-80A2 or the Pratt & Whitney JT9D-7R4D.

In the years that followed, a wide range of variations was developed, tailored almost to the needs of individual customers. Pratt & Whitney later introduced its 252-kN (56,750-lb-thrust) to 267-kN60,000-lb-thrust) PW4000 family, while Rolls Royce introduced its 270-kN (60,600-lb-thrust) RB.211-524H.

Launch customer Japanese Airlines chose the basic CF6 engines, while the JT9D made its debut on a Delta Air Lines aircraft, in November 1986.

Longer reach

The decision to launch the extended-range 767-300ER, in 1984, came soon after the launch of the basic -300. The development aircraft first flew on 9 November 1986, but Boeing had no orders for the ER until American Airlines ordered 15, in March 1987. The -300ER

incorporated more fuel and thus had a much increased maximum take-off weight. When Boeing first unveiled the -300ER it set the maximum take-off weight at 172,368 kg (380,000 lb), but, by 1986, the design had been revised several times to allow an maximum take-off weight of up to 184615 kg (407,000 lb). By 1993 this had grown to some 186,883 kg (412,000 lb). Engine choices included the CF6-80C2B2 and the PW4000. Austria's Lauda Air became the launch customer for the Pratt & Whitney engine in April 1987. More powerful Rolls-Royce RB.211-524G/H engines were certified in December 1989 and British Airways was the launch customer for this combination.

The 767-300/-300ER not only proved popular with existing 767 customers, but also helped to fill the gap in Boeing's product range below the 747, before the arrival of the 777. A total of seven airlines opted for the -300, while another 36 placed the -300ER into service. By 10 August 2005, orders (and

Left: Asiana Airlines has operated 767-300, -300ER and -300F aircraft. This 767-38E was the first to be delivered to the airline and began services in October 1990.

Above: Seen over Mount St Helens, which erupted in 1981, the first test 767-300 flies in Boeing's house colours. After trials, the aircraft was delivered to JAL in December 1986.

deliveries) for the 767-300 stood at 104 (104), along with 520 (505) for the 767-300ER.

Next generation

By the late 1990s, the 767 was facing increasingly stiff competition from the Airbus A330 and even the A340. In answer to this, Boeing took the 767-300 airframe and stretched it yet again to hold more fuel and more passengers. The new aircraft became the Boeing 767-400ER and it was formally launched in January 1997. Soon afterwards, Delta became the launch customer with an order for 21, in March 1997. In October a second order, for 26 aircraft, was placed by Continental (although later reduced to 16). The -400ER is intended to fit between the 767-300ER and the 777-200 in Boeing's line-up. It is aimed at replacing ageing TriStars, DC-10s and A300s, and is targeted at potential A330-200 customers.

The 767-400ER adds another 6.42-m (253-in) fuselage stretch, again in a plug on either side of the wing. Passenger capacity is raised to 303 in a standard two-class layout, or 245 in a three-class layout. Maximum take-off weight is increased to 204,000 kg (449,735 lb) and the -400ER has a design range of 10,460 km (6,500 miles).

More power

Higher-thrust versions of the standard engines, the CF6-80C2 and PW4060, have been developed, all rated in the 267-kN to 276-kN (60,000-lb-st to 62,000-lb-st) class. Boeing initially included winglets in the 767-400ER design, but these have been replaced by a pair of swept-back wingtip extensions. These raked wingtips are a less complex aerodynamic feature than conventional winglets, but offer similar improvements in wing performance. The new wing has an overall span of 51.82 m (170 ft 4 in), compared to the 47.45-m (156-ft) wingspan of the 767-300. The 767-400ER features the advanced six-screen EFIS cockpit of the 777 (which is also cross-compatible with the 737NG family and the 747-400) and a 777-style passenger cabin interior. The first 767-400ER made its maiden flight in August 1999, and the type entered service in 2000. Orders currently stand at 38, from a total of three customers.

All Nippon Airways has been one of the 767's most important export customers. The airline's 58 examples are a mixture of 767-200, -300, -300ER and -300F variants and are all powered by CF6-80 engines.

Freighter versions

In January 1993 UPS placed an order for the dedicated 767-300F freighter (inset above). A mock-up was completed in early 1994 and the first example flew on 20 June 1995. UPS has ordered a total of 32 -300Fs. South Korea's Asiana became the launch customer for a freighter version of the 767-300ER (above), in 1993. The aircraft is also known as the 767-300 General Market Freighter and differs from the UPS version in having mechanical freight-handling on the main and lower decks, air conditioning for animals and perishables on the main and forward lower decks, and more elaborate crew facilities. The first aircraft flew in June 1996 and was delivered to Asiana on 23 August of the same year.

The 767-400 is marketed as the 767-400ER and features sharply swept-back wing extensions which reduce take-off distance, increase climb rate and improve fuel consumption. The two major customers, as of August 2005, are Continental Airlines with 16 and Delta Air Lines with 21.

Boeing 777 Introduction

New design and manufacturing initiatives to support Boeing's commitment to deliver a 'service ready' product have propelled aircraft manufacture into the computer age.

Back in the winter of 1986, Boeing discarded plans to build a larger 767 in favour of an entirely new twin-turbofan airliner to fit between the 767-300 and 747-400. In doing so, it accepted that to meet the increasing competition from Airbus it had to harness new technology and take a pioneering leap in the development process. This decision was spurred on by the knowledge that by the time the new aircraft would enter service in 1995, the market would already be occupied by three competing types, the three-engined McDonnell Douglas MD-11 and, more significantly, the four-engined Airbus A340 and its twin-engined A330 stablemate.

Then, still referred to as the 767-X, Boeing's new aircraft was presented to airlines on 8 December 1989, and launched into production, as the 777, on 29 October 1990, following a launch order for 34 firm aircraft plus 34 options from the US operator United Airlines.

Digital design

Making full use of new digital design and definition techniques, the 777 took shape with virtually no paper drawings. It became the first airliner to be 100 per cent digitally defined and pre-assembled, using the Dassault/IBM-developed CATIA CAD/CAM (computer-aided design/computer-aided manufacturing) software system. This powerful tool allows parts and systems to be viewed in three dimensions, with misalignments and errors easily corrected on a computer screen, ensuring enhanced accuracy and consequently fewer production changes. The software also eliminated the need for costly full-scale mock-ups to be built.

Boeing also tackled the 777 programme from a multi-disciplinary perspective, establishing 238 design/build teams which, via access to a common database, were able to work concurrently from concept to completion. Boeing took this process a step further, however, by making suppliers and airline customers an integral part of the design teams, giving both unprecedented access to the design process from an early stage. This 'working together' concept considerably reduced post-engineering changes and provided fewer 'in-service' surprises and enhanced reliability. Following this method also ensured that customer airlines were receiving exactly the aircraft they required.

British Airways has remained faithful to Boeing, by purchasing the 777 in the face of stiff competition from Airbus. The American manufacturer has produced one of the most capable airliners on the market, allowing it to compete head on with both the twin-engined Airbus A330 and the four-engined A340.

Below: Boeing's T-38 Talon chase-plane lends some scale to the first 777 prototype (N7771). The unique nature of the 777 programme extended to flight testing, which utilized nine airframes, each assigned to a different aspect of the test schedule. Such an intensive and rapid test period gave airlines confidence in the new aircraft, and Boeing received several advance orders from carriers which were convinced that they would suffer a minimum number of teething problems with the aircraft.

Left: United Airlines began revenue-earning services with the 777 on 7 June 1995, having received its first aircraft on 15 May 1995. United was a crucial partner during 777 development, keeping Boeing design teams in touch with the real world of day-to-day airline flying. With United's guidance, Boeing was able to optimize such features as overhead baggage bins, cabin entertainment systems and even interior decor. Here, one of the airline's 777s poses with a Boeing airliner of a much earlier period, the Model 247. The 247 is often described as the first airliner of truly modern design.

Cathay Pacific was the first airline to choose the Rolls-Royce Trent 800 turbofan for its 777s. The British engine had been flown on a Boeing 747-100 test-bed in March 1995, before its first flight on a Boeing-owned 777 on 26 May 1995. Two Cathay aircraft were subsequently used in certification and service readiness trials.

Testing and validation of aircraft systems installation was carried out in a purpose-built Flight Controls Test Rig and Systems Integration Laboratory (SIL), identifying any potentially expensive problems.

The 777 stands out through not only its innovative design and manufacturing concepts, but also its incorporation of leading-edge technologies, which keeps Boeing in the vanguard alongside Airbus.

The 777 features a new aerodynamically efficient, large-area swept wing, with increased thickness and long span. These features optimize the wing for improved payload/range characteristics, enhanced climb performance, and a Mach 0.83 cruise, at higher altitudes than previous airliners. A folding wingtip option was made available, allowing operations from gates and taxiways used by other wide-bodied aircraft, but has not been taken up.

Undercarriage advances
Another area where the 777 differs from other heavy aircraft is its use of a two-leg main undercarriage, with six-wheel bogies, and the use of 'clever' brakes, which reduce wear through alternate application of brakes during taxiing. The 777 was Boeing's first fly-by-wire airliner and the world's first to achieve 180-minute ETOPS (extended-range twin operations) clearance from the outset.

The first 'Triple Seven' was unveiled to the world during a roll-out celebration at Everett on 9 April 1994 and took off on its three-hour 48-minute maiden flight on 12 June.

'Triple Seven' testing
Nine aircraft were used in the flight test programme; five powered by Pratt & Whitney PW4000 engines, two by General Electric GE90s and two by Rolls-Royce Trent turbofans. Simultaneous Federal Aviation Administration and Joint Airworthiness Authorities certification was awarded on 19 April 1995 and service entry with United Airlines on the Chicago–London route occurred on 7 June 1995. The initial model was the 777-200, with a higher gross weight and longer range

SPECIFICATION	
Boeing 777-200 **Type:** long- and ultra long-range wide-bodied airliner **Powerplant:** two 329.1-kN (74,000-lb-thrust) Pratt & Whitney PW4074 or 342.5-kN (77,000-lb-thrust Pratt & Whitney PW4077 or 333.3-kN (75,000-lb-thrust) General Electric GE90-75B or 338.0-kN (76,000-lb-thrust) General Electric GE90-76B or 333.6-kN (75,000-lb-thrust) Rolls-Royce Trent 875 or 342.5-kN (77,000-lb-thrust) Rolls-Royce Trent 877 turbofan engines	**Maximum speed:** 946km/h (588mph) **Range:** 7785 km (4840 miles) with 363 passengers **Service ceiling:** between 11,795 m and 13,135 m (38,697 and 43,100 ft) **Weight:** 233,604 kg (515,000 lb) maximum take-off weight **Dimensions:** wing span 60.93 m (199 ft 11 in); length 63.73 m (209 ft 1 in); height 18.51 m (60 ft 9 in) **Accommodation:** up to 440 passengers

777-200IGW (Increased Gross Weight) variant entering service with British Airways on 9 February 1997. Boeing planned several future variants and these have matured into the 777-200F, 777-200LR, 777-300 and 777-300ER. The 777-200IGW is now designated as the 777-200ER.

At the time of the 777's first flight, Boeing had firm orders for 147 aircraft but, by June 1997, the order book had grown to 323 from 25 customers, including re-orders from impressed customers. Although late on the market, the early success of this 'paperless' aircraft would appear to vindicate Boeing's leap of faith and, by August 2005, total 777 orders stood at 702, with 525 aircraft delivered.

Despite the continued growth of its 777 fleet, All Nippon Airways operated A340s for a time. ANA received its first 777 in December 1996, initial construction work on this, Boeing's 50th 777, having been started in the preceding May. By early 1996, the rate of 777 production had risen from three and a half per month to five.

Technical details

Subcontracting component manufacture to other companies is a common practice in the airliner business. Boeing went one stage further, however, with the manufacture of its 777.

Aerospace manufacturing companies in Japan have been associated with Boeing products since the 1970s. This was particularly true of the 767, with Mitsubishi, Kawasaki and Fuji taking a 15 per cent workshare in the 767-200/-300. These three companies, represented by the Japan Aircraft Development Corporation (JADC), were therefore an obvious choice when it came to the 777.

A final agreement between Boeing and JADC, signed on 21 May 1991, made the Japanese companies risk-sharing partners for 20 per cent of the entire 777 programme. This unprecedented move, along with sizeable subcontracts which were issued to companies around the world, allowed Boeing to utilize the very best manufacturers.

Representatives of JADC's constituent companies and two important Japanese subcontractors, Japan Aircraft Manufacturing Co. Limited and ShinMaywa, were soon based in Seattle, Washington.

Other subcontractors play a less major but nonetheless important role in manufacture of the 777.

Boeing carries out all 777 final assembly and flight testing. The barrel sections of the airliner's mid- and rear fuselage are built by JADC in Japan. A hoist holds the Boeing-built wings, which are united with the Japanese-built centre section.

Structural breakdown

Boeing sources 777 structural components from companies in the United States and abroad. US subcontractors include Kaman, Northrop Grumman and Rockwell, while international suppliers include Aerospace Technologies, Alenia, EMBRAER, Boeing Australia, Korean Air, Shorts and Singapore Aerospace.

- Boeing
- International subcontractors
- US subcontractors
- JADC

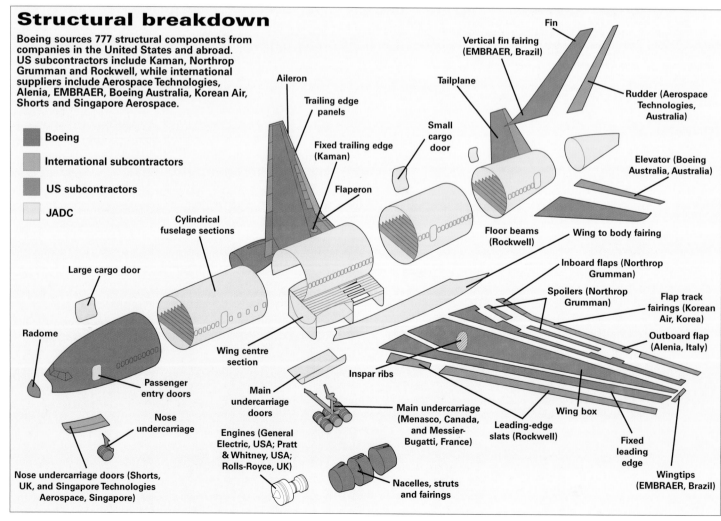

Fin

Vertical fin fairing (EMBRAER, Brazil)

Aileron

Tailplane

Rudder (Aerospace Technologies, Australia)

Trailing edge panels

Small cargo door

Fixed trailing edge (Kaman)

Elevator (Boeing Australia, Australia)

Flaperon

Cylindrical fuselage sections

Floor beams (Rockwell)

Wing to body fairing

Inboard flaps (Northrop Grumman)

Spoilers (Northrop Grumman)

Flap track fairings (Korean Air, Korea)

Large cargo door

Outboard flap (Alenia, Italy)

Radome

Inspar ribs

Passenger entry doors

Wing centre section

Main undercarriage (Menasco, Canada, and Messier-Bugatti, France)

Wing box

Leading-edge slats (Rockwell)

Fixed leading edge

Main undercarriage doors

Nose undercarriage

Engines (General Electric, USA; Pratt & Whitney, USA; Rolls-Royce, UK)

Wingtips (EMBRAER, Brazil)

Nose undercarriage doors (Shorts, UK, and Singapore Technologies Aerospace, Singapore)

Nacelles, struts and fairings

777-200

As lead customer for the 777-200, United Airlines flew its first revenue-earning service with the type between London and Washington, DC, on 7 June 1995. United was initially unhappy with its 777s, leading to much public animosity between the airline and Boeing. These problems were resolved, however, and United ordered a total of 60 777-200 and -200ER aircraft.

Fuel capacity

A single integral tank in each wing, combined with a centre-section tank, gives the 777-200 a fuel capacity of 63,216 litres (13,905 Imp gal). Both the 777-200ER and -300ER extended-range models have a second centre-section tank, allowing an extra 28,163 litres (6,195 Imp gal) of fuel to be carried, for a total capacity of 91,379 litres (20,100 Imp gal).

Australian input

Australian aerospace companies provide many of the components for the tail section of the 777. The all-composite rudder is made by Aerospace Technologies, while the elevators are fabricated by Boeing Australia.

Fly-by-wire

Airbus had flown its first fly-by-wire airliner, the A320, as early as 1987, giving it a considerable lead over Boeing. The 777 emerged with a highly advanced system, however, with Britain's GEC-Marconi Avionics taking responsibility for the primary flight control computers.

Fuselage cross-section

During the early to mid-1980s, Boeing perceived a need for an aircraft with a capacity between that of the 767-300 and 747-400. In order to provide such a machine, the company opted for a fuselage cross-section of 6.20 m (20 ft 4 in), which compares with 5.03 m (16 ft 6 in) for the 767 and 6.49 m (21 ft 3½ in) for the 747. According to customer requirements, seats may be arranged in the 777 up to a maximum of 10 abreast.

Folding wingtips

A reduction in span to 47.32 m (155 ft 3 in) is possible with the provision of optional folding wingtips. This would allow the 777 to use airport facilities designed for older wide-bodied airliners such as the A300. No airline has taken the wing-fold option.

Cabin layout

Boeing achieved maximum flexibility with the 777 cabin. The 777-200 offers maximum seating for 440 passengers. Internal fittings such as galleys and toilets are easily re-positioned throughout the cabin thanks to plumbing and electrical connections being available across wide areas.

Unique undercarriage

Menasco/Messier-Bugatti designed the six-wheeled main undercarriage units. Using a multi-bogie arrangement allowed weight to be distributed more evenly onto the runway surface, avoiding the need for a third, auxiliary main unit, mounted on the fuselage centreline.

Cockpit systems

In keeping with modern airline practice, the 777 is flown by a crew of two. Cockpit instrumentation is based around an advanced five-screen electronic flight instrumentation system, which uses Honeywell colour liquid crystal display screens in place of conventional analogue instruments.

A family of airliners

As lead customer, United began operations with the basic 777-200. Like British Airways, United has since opted for the 777-200ER which allows a maximum range of 13,584 km (8,441 miles) with 305 passengers. Having flown late in 1997, the stretched 777-300 provides a 10,556-km (5,700-mile) range with 368 passengers.

777 Powerplant

General Electric's 409.30-kN (92,000-lb-st) GE90-92B entered service on the 777-200IGW with British Airways in November 1995.

The high-technology 777 is propelled by the most powerful engines yet developed for application to a commercial aircraft. Further developments of these engines have seen thrust ratings up to 513 kN (115,300 lb st) being achieved in order to power heavier versions of Boeing's twin jet.

Customers have a choice of three big high-bypass-ratio turbofan engines, specifically aimed at the 777. The only all-new engine is the General Electric GE90 which, at a diameter of 3.12 m (10 ft 2½ in) has the biggest fan among the competing engines. It uses solid composite wide-chord fan blades, single-crystal blades in the high-pressure turbine to withstand high temperatures, and a double-annular combustor to reduce noxious emissions. The GE90 has been certificated up to 513 kN (115,300 lb st) in its most powerful GE90-115B form for the 777-300ER.

Pratt & Whitney's derivative PW4000 was the launch engine for the 777, entering service with United in June 1995. It has a 2.84-m (9-ft 3¾-in) diameter fan with shroudless hollow titanium blades, single-crystal

A technician lends scale to the fan and nacelle of a Trent 800 on a Singapore Airlines 777. Note the distinctive shape of the fan blades and the exceptionally broad nacelle.

Boeing and Rolls-Royce have tested this unusual nacelle and exhaust nozzle configuration on a Trent 800. The test aircraft is a 777-200ER and take-off noise levels have been reduced by some 4 dB.

high-pressure turbine blades and an advanced combustor to reduce emissions. Certification has been received for thrusts up to 436 kN (98,000 lb st) in the PW4098 version. The Rolls-Royce Trent 800 is derived from the highly successful RB.211 family of three-shaft engines and entered 777 service with Thai International in April 1996. It has a diffusion bonded/superplastically-formed wide-chord fan with a diameter of 2.79 m (9 ft 1¾ in) and also uses single-crystal high-pressure turbine blades. The Trent's maximum certificated thrust is 415 kN (93,400 lb st) in the Trent 895 on the 777-200ER, but it is capable of producing up to 422 kN (95,000 lb st).

ETOPS and undercarriage

Keen to avoid the extra weight and structural compromise represented by an underbelly main undercarriage leg, Boeing opted to fit the 777 with six-wheel main undercarriage bogies. The aircraft has also been certified to the highest possible degree for ETOPS operations.

The 777 was the first commercial aircraft to achieve 180-minute ETOPS certification at the time of its service entry. To achieve this industry first, the reliability of each engine type was evaluated in 3000-cycle accelerated stress and endurance tests, and one aircraft with each different engine combination was dedicated to a 1000-cycle flight test programme to simulate airline service. In addition, the Honeywell GTCP331-500 APU, now a flight-critical part of the aircraft's operation, also had to undergo a 3000-cycle test series to validate satisfactory operation in extreme hot and cold weather conditions. The P&W-powered 777 obtained ETOPS clearance on 30 May 1995.

Undercarriage

The retractable tricycle landing gear was the largest on any commercial aircraft. It differs from that of other heavy aircraft in having six-wheel bogies on each leg, eliminating the need for a third, centreline main leg and simplifying the braking system. Steering rear axles are automatically engaged by the nose gear steering angle. The Bendix Carbenix 4000 carbon brake system is programmed to apply brakes to alternate sets of three wheels only, when initial

The 777's ETOPS qualifications are founded on the proven reliability of its engines and systems, as well as its comprehensive avionics fit.

toe-pedal pressure is used during taxiing. Full toe-pedal pressure activates all six brakes on landing or during an aborted take-off.

Above: In order to spread its weight over the maximum possible area on the ground, the 777 uses unusual triple pairs of mainwheels. It has no centreline main gear leg.

Left: Twin wheels are used on the nose gear, with all wheels having Honeywell Carbenix 4000 carbon brakes. The main gear retracts inward, while the nose gear retracts forwards.

Boeing 777 variants

N7771 was the second 777 to fly, making its maiden flight on 12 June 1994. The aircraft has remained with Boeing and has been used extensively on flight test and promotional duties.

Boeing has successfully used the 777-200 airframe as the basis for incremental important improvements and the larger 777-300 has moved the big Boeing twin-jet firmly into 747 territory. On 15 February 2005, Boeing unveiled its super long-range 777-200LR Worldliner, following this in May with the derived 777F freighter.

The 777 was designed to fill the gap between the 767 and 747, but Boeing initially drew up plans for a range of variants based solely on the -200 airframe. The first 'A-Market' aircraft was aimed at US domestic operators, and had an outline gross weight of between 229,068 kg and 233,604 kg (505,000 lb and 515,000 lb).

This later rose to a maximum take-off weight of 247,210 kg (545,000 lb), which is now standard for the 777-200. Carrying a load of 349 passengers, the 'A-Market' 777-200 could cover about 7773 km (4,830 miles).

The increased-range 'B-Market' 777 that followed had a similar passenger capacity, but with transatlantic range. This version introduced a substantially higher gross weight of between 263,088 kg and 267,624 kg (580,000 lb and 590,000 lb). Plans were also drawn up, but later dropped, for a trans-Pacific 'C-Market' 777.

Boeing simplified the designations by referring to the variants as the 777-200A and 777-200B, respectively, but this

approach was later changed – ostensibly to fall in line with Boeing's established practice of not differentiating between similar aircraft with different operating weights. The 777-200A then became simply the 777-200 and the 777-200B became the 777-200(IGW) – Increased Gross Weight.

The IGW variant offered an impressive maximum range of

up to 12,215 km (7,590 miles), but in 1992 Boeing began to study ways in which even more performance could be squeezed out of the existing 777-200 airframe. By accommodating yet more fuel, and upping the maximum take-off weight to 286,902 kg (632,500 lb), Boeing was able to extend the 777's range to around 13,695 km (8,510 miles). The resulting

Above: British Airways operates both -200 and -200ER variants. In a marked change of policy the airline initially opted for US-built engines in the shape of the GE90; however, the last batch of 16 aircraft was ordered with Rolls-Royce Trent 800s.

Below: Many of the early purchasers of the 777-200 (seen here) later opted to acquire the improved and extended range -200ER. United Airlines has some 53 777s in service.

Above: Two of Cathay Pacific's four 777-200s were used for certification and service readiness trials for the Trent-powered version before certification was granted in April 1996.

version was initially known as the 777-200B+, but later (briefly) became the 777-200HGW (Higher Gross Weight). The weight was increased yet again, to 297,824 kg (656,000 lb) for the definitive production-standard variant, which boasted a maximum range of 14,260 km (8,861 miles).

This is now the standard production version and, in yet another name change, the model is now known as the 777-200ER (Extended Range).

777-300

The 777-300 is stretched by 10 m (33 ft) from the 777-200. As a result, capacity is increased to between 368 and 386 passengers in a typical three-class configuration. In an all-economy layout, the 777-300 can accommodate as many as 550 seats. The 777-300 can serve routes up to 10,805 km

(6,710 miles) with almost the same passenger capacity and range capability as the 747-100/-200 models, but burning one-third less fuel and with 40 per cent lower maintenance costs. Baseline maximum take-off weight is now 299,375 kg (660,000 lb).

Formal authorisation for the programme followed announcements at the 1995 Paris Air Show that ANA, Cathay Pacific, Korean Airlines and Thai Airways intended to order 31 aircraft, and the first 777-300 was delivered to Cathay Pacific in June 1998.

Since 1997 Boeing had been studying improved performance versions of both the 777-200 and 777-300, as the 777X (777-200X and 777-300X). A 'shrink' version, the 777-100X, was under consideration in the mid-1990s, but was eventually shelved. The importance of the

777X programme increased as Boeing's rival, Airbus, pressed ahead with the A340-500 and A340-600. Despite their four-engined configuration, the new A340s are aimed squarely at the 777 market, while also seeking to take sales from the 747-400.

Throughout the late 1990s a 777X launch was expected 'imminently', but never materialized, as Boeing fought a tough behind-the-scenes battle to convince airlines that it could meet its projected performance levels. In February 2000 the 777X was formally launched, as the awkwardly named 777 Longer-Ranged Derivative (LRD).

In July 2000 the first commitments were received from lessors GECAS, during the Farnborough air show. The deal for 10 777 LRDs, with another 10 options, was confirmed in October 2000. Also that month, Air France announced its

intention to acquire 777 LRDs as part of a larger 777 order.

LRD to ER and LR

Both the 777-200 LRD and 777-300 LRD were to use the same basic airframe as their predecessors, mated with new engines and increased fuel loads, for their new 'long-range' capability. The 777-200 LRD was intended to achieve a range of 8,860 nm (16,405 km; 10,194 miles) – making it (according to Boeing) the longest-ranged airliner in the world.

The 777-300 LRD would offer 747-class passenger capacity over 747-400 ranges, with 777 operating costs. Power would be supplied by the General Electric GE90-115B and a derated version, the GE90-110B1, would power the 777-200 Longer-Range Derivative. In the event, the 777-300 LRD evolved into the 777-300ER with a 351,534 kg (775,000 lb) maximum weight and 513-kN (115,300-lb-st) -115B engines for a range of 7,880 nm (14,594 km; 9,069 miles).

The -200 LRD emerged as the 777-200LR Worldliner (Longer Range), with a 347,452 kg (766,000 lb) maximum weight, 489 kN (110,100-lb-st) thrust GE90-110B1 engines and a maximum range of 9,420 nm (17,446 km; 10,841 miles). The -300ER is already in service, while the -200LR was scheduled for service entry with Pakistan International Airlines in January 2006. An all-freight 777F derivative of the -200LR should enter service late in 2008.

The 777-300 is able to provide a similar seating layout to the 747, combined with the economy of a twin-engined layout.

Right: Emirates is unusual in operating 777-200, -200ER, -300 and -300ER variants. This 777-300 was the first of four to be leased by the airline and was delivered in November 1999. All of Emirates 777s are Trent-powered.

Boeing/McDonnell Douglas 717/MD-90
Last of the MD line

The MD-90 series was an ultimately unsuccessful attempt by McDonnell Douglas to further extend the life of the DC-9/MD-80 family. The smaller MD-95, however, survived the takeover by Boeing to be marketed as the Boeing 717.

Intended as an advanced-technology follow-on to the MD-80 series, the MD-90 was distinguished by the use of IAE V2500 turbofans, in place of the Pratt & Whitney JT8Ds that have been used to power every DC-9 and MD-80. The programme was launched in November 1989, with an order for 50 from Delta Air Lines plus 115 options (numbers that were soon revised downwards). McDonnell Douglas decreed that the aircraft should be referred to as the MD-90, but when dealing with specific sub-types the hyphen was omitted.

The baseline MD90-30 has an MD-80-type fuselage stretched by 1.45 m (4 ft 9 in), combined with the enlarged tail of the MD-87. It is capable of carrying a maximum of 172 passengers and is powered by V2525-D5 turbofan engines. A developed version of this aircraft, the MD90-30ER, was subsequently introduced with an order for two aircraft from Egypt's AMC Aviation. The first of these MD90-30ERs was delivered on 24 September 1997.

Unbuilt variants

McDonnell Douglas also planned, but did not build, the MD90-50, an extended-range version of the -30 carrying fewer passengers, but powered by more powerful V2528-D5 engines and the MD90-55, identical to the previous model, but with additional exits fitted for up to 187 passengers.

The first MD-90 flew on 22 February 1993 and two aircraft were engaged in the flight test programme that led to certification on 16 November 1994. Assembly of the first production example began at Long Beach in February 1994, and the first aircraft was handed

Saudi Arabian operates the largest fleet of MD-90s, having received the last of its 29 examples in the spring of 2000. The aircraft are configured with 18 first-class and 103 economy seats.

over to Delta on 24 February 1995. It entered service on 1 April of the same year. The first European MD-90 operator was SAS, which placed its first aircraft into service on 11 November 1996.

From April 1986 the Shanghai Aircraft Manufacturing Factory (SAMF) assembled MD-82s and MD-83s for the Chinese airline market, and in 1992 SAMF and McDonnell Douglas announced the Trunkliner agreement, to develop the MD90-30T Trunkliner with dual main landing gear for operations from rough Chinese airfields. The terms

of the deal were re-negotiated several times, and finally called for the delivery of 20 MD-90s from the United States (beginning in 1996), along with 20 aircraft built in China. Construction of Chinese-built MD-90s began in 1995, but no deliveries were ever made.

Following the August 1997 acquisition of McDonnell Douglas by Boeing, Boeing announced in June 1998 that MD-90 production would cease in 2000. By early April 2000 MD-90 orders totalled 114. Current operators include China Eastern Airlines (9), China

Left: Delta Air Lines was the launch customer for the MD-90 and currently operates 16 of the baseline -30 variant. The aircraft were delivered between February 1995 and December 1996.

Below: This Japan Air System MD-90 wears one of seven colourful paint schemes designed for the airline's fleet by the famous Japanese motion picture director Akira Kurosawa.

When it took over the MD-95 programme, Boeing predicted a 2600-aircraft market for the 80- to 120- seat short-range airliner market over the next 20 years. Hopes that the 717 would capture a significant percentage of these sales proved unfounded.

Southern Airlines (13), Delta Air Lines (16), Japan Airlines Domestic (16), Saudia (29), SAS (8) and Uni Air (13).

Boeing 717

What we know today as the Boeing 717 actually began life at Long Beach as the McDonnell Douglas MD-95. The aircraft was announced by McAir in June 1994 after a long series of design studies for new 100 to 130-seat aircraft. The MD-95 was conceived as an MD-80 'shrink' (dubbed MD-87-105), powered by the MD-80's JT8D-200 engines, or perhaps Rolls-Royce Tays. The aircraft that emerged owed far more to the DC-9, using the wing and empennage of the DC-9-34, the enlarged fin of the MD-87 and new-technology BMW Rolls-Royce BR700 turbofans. It was intended to assemble the MD-95 in China as part of McDonnell Douglas's MD90-30 Trunkliner programme, but this deal was never signed and, after several changes of mind, production reverted to the line at Long Beach, California.

After the August 1997 takeover, the historic family of Douglas airliners was rechristened as Boeing's and, in January 1998, the MD-95 became the Model 717. This decision was greeted with

surprise, as Boeing had already devoted the Model 717 designation to the huge C-135 family. The production version became the 717-200, with Boeing reserving the 717-100 designation for a possible future 85-seat version.

The 717 was aimed at the 100-seat 'regional' market, over routes of 2414 km (1,500 miles). Two versions were planned – the basic gross weight (BGW) and high gross weight (HGW) 717. McDonnell Douglas struggled to find a launch customer, but finally announced an order for 50, with 50 options, from Florida's ValuJet (now AirTran Airways), on 19 October 1995. By summer 2005 Boeing had accumulated just 169 orders for the aircraft. Against this background of sluggish demand, suggestions grew that Boeing would terminate the programme even from its earliest days. In fact, Boeing remained committed to the 717, reportedly studying closely the 85-seat 717-100X and 130-seat 717-300X concepts.

The first 717-200 was rolled out on 10 June 1998, and it made its maiden flight on 2 September. Four aircraft were dedicated to the nine-month

flight test programme. After joint US and European FAA/JAA certification AirTran took delivery of its first aircraft on 23 September 1999. The first European customer was Bavaria International Aircraft Company, a leasing firm. Bavaria took delivery of its first four aircraft on 29 December 1999.

Its first client was Greek start-up carrier Olympic Aviation, which received two aircraft on 7 January 2000. Bavaria's next customer was new Australian regional operator Impulse Airlines, which took delivery of two aircraft at the end of April 2000 amid plans to acquire three 717s from Bavaria and two from Irish-based Pembroke

Capital. Pembroke also announced lease deals with Bangkok Airways (two aircraft) and accepted its first aircraft from Boeing in August 2000. TWA took delivery of its first Model 717 on 18 February 2000.

The hoped for increase in demand for the 717 never materialized, however, in spite of the quality of the airframe. Added to this, the type offered a passenger capacity uncomfortably close to Boeing's own Next-Generation 737 and as such, in 2004 the company announced is decision to cease 717 production in 2005. Aircraft were being delivered as late as June 2005, but with the deletion of 14 orders, the line has closed.

SPECIFICATION	
McDonnell Douglas MD-90-30 **Type:** twin-engine, medium-range airliner **Powerplant:** two 111.21-kN (25,020-lb-thrust) IAE V2525-D5 turbofan engines **Maximum speed:** 844 km/h (523 mph) at 6960 m (23,000 ft) **Maximum cruising speed:** 809 km/h (502 mph) at 10,670 m (35,000 ft) **Initial clim b rate:** 885 m/min (2,900 fpm) at sea level **Range:** 4200 km (2,604 miles) with	153 passengers and fuel reserve **Service ceiling:** 12,100 m (39,700 ft) **Weights:** empty 40,007 kg (88,015 lb); maximum take-off 70,760 kg (155,672 lb) **Dimensions:** wing span 32.87 m (1,017 ft 10 in); length 46.41 m (152 ft 7 in); height 9.33 m (30 ft 7 in); wing area 112 m² (1,205 sq ft) **Accommodation:** two pilots (flight deck); maximum of 172 passengers (standard 153), plus flight attendants

Below: Low-cost airline AirTran was typical of the operators at which the 717 was aimed. In the summer of 1999 the 717 undertook a major tour of Europe, seen as a key market for the type.

Above: The 717's economy over short sectors influenced Hawaiian Air's decision to purchase 13 Series 200s for operating its inter-island services in the Hawaiian Islands.

McDonnell Douglas MD-80 family DC-9 successor

By the end of the 1970s the DC-9 had been flying for 15 years and McAir decided to open a new chapter in its story. The stretched MD-80 family maintained its forerunner's sales records and spawned a new family, the MD-90/Boeing 717.

In 1973 the Douglas Aircraft Company division of the McDonnell Douglas Corporation, which was then finalizing design of the DC-9 Series 50, began looking to the next major development of its versatile airliner. A number of proposals was considered, all based on quieter, more fuel-efficient, re-fanned versions of the JT8D engine which had powered all DC-9s to date.

Several options were discussed with potential customers and eventually evolved into the DC-9 Super 80, which was launched in October 1977 when an order for 15 aircraft was received from Swissair. While bearing a clear resemblance to its DC-9

forerunners, the Super 80 was to all intents and purposes an entirely new aircraft. McDonnell Douglas recognized this fact by dropping the DC-9 title in favour of the designation MD-80, a generic term for the entire series of contemporary twinjets.

Compared with the DC-9 Series 50 which it succeeded, the Super 80/MD-80 had a fuselage lengthened to 45 m (147 ft 10 in) by means plugs forward of the wing and in the rear fuselage. The cabin provides accommodation for 137 passengers in typical mixed-class configuration and up to 172 in high-density layout. Underfloor cargo volume was increased. The MD-80 series wing incorporated a new centre-section and an extension at each wingtip.

The engine selected for the MD-80 was the 83.25-kN (18,500-lb-st) JT8D-209 high-bypass-ratio turbofan, with a further 3.38-kN (750-lb-st)

automatic power reserve (APR) available in engine-out situations. Enlarged, acoustically treated nacelles were designed to accommodate the engines, enabling the aircraft to meet FAA Federal Air Regulation Part 36 noise emission standards, as well as the more stringent ICAO standards.

A key feature of the MD-80's advanced two-crew flight deck was its Sundstrand digital electronic integrated flight-guidance and control system, incorporating speed command with digital full-time autothrottles and Sperry CAT IIIA autoland.

The clean lines of the Super 80's significantly stretched fuselage quickly set it apart from the earlier DC-9 models.

A Honeywell Electronic EFIS with CRT screens was available optionally in place of electro-mechanical flight instrument displays. An electronic Performance Management System (PMS), similar to that previously developed for the DC-10, was introduced as standard from 1983, coupling through the autopilot and autothrottle systems to control automatically the aircraft's pitch

Above: The prototype Super 80 was equipped with a stall recovery parachute. It would have been deployed in the event of the aircraft entering an unrecoverable deep stall.

Above: The MD-83 was an extended-range variant of the family. This example served with the now-defunct Minneapolis-based Republic Airlines.

Below: By far the biggest operator of the MD-80 has been American Airlines, which, at its peak, had 350 examples in its fleet. Today, it retains a huge fleet of MD-82s and MD-83s.

The final member of the MD-80 family was the MD-88. Equipped with a 'glass' cockpit and constructed of composite materials, this variant was sold in the greatest numbers to Delta Air Lines, which retained a large fleet in 2005.

SPECIFICATION

McDonnell Douglas MD-87
Type: short- to medium-haul airliner
Powerplant: two 88.78-kN (19,950-lb-thrust) Pratt & Whitney JT8D-217C turbofan engines
Maximum speed: 922 km/h (573 mph)
Long-range cruising speed: 811 km/h (5504 mph)
Range: 4385 km (2,725 miles)
Weights: empty 33,112 kg

(73,000 lb); loaded 63,370 kg (139,706 lb)
Dimensions: wing span 32.92 m (108 ft); length 36.27 m (119 ft); height 9.14 m (30 ft); wing area 117.00 m² (1,270 ft)
Passengers: flight crew of two; maximum of 139 passengers (single-class seating); 109 in typical two-class configuration (12 first-class and 97 economy)

attitude and engine thrust to provide optimum speed and fuel efficiency in climb, cruise and descent.

First in line
The first aircraft in the Super 80/MD-80 series, an MD-81, made its maiden flight on 18 October 1979. The first of launch customer Swissair's aircraft was delivered on 12 September 1980, flying its inaugural revenue service from Zurich to Frankfurt on 5 October.

On 16 April 1979 McDonnell Douglas announced development of the MD-82. Powered by 90-kN (20,000-lb-st) JT8D-217 turbofans with 3.83-kN (850-lb-st) APR, the model is generally similar to the MD-81, but was optimized for operation from 'hot-and-high' airports and has a higher maximum take-off weight of 66,679 kg (147,000 lb).

On 12 April 1985 McDonnell Douglas signed an agreement with the China Aero-Technology Import/Export Corporation (CATIC) and the Shanghai Aviation Industrial Corporation of the People's Republic of China for the sale of 26 MD-82s for use by the Civil Aviation Administration

of China. Five aircraft had already been supplied for use by China Eastern Airlines and China Northern Airlines. This agreement provided for licence assembly of all but one of the 26 aircraft by the Shanghai Aircraft Manufacturing Factory (SAMF), using components and sub-assemblies shipped from Long Beach, California. A further 20 aircraft were added to the agreement in April 1990.

Announced on 31 January 1983, the MD-83 is a long-range development of the MD-80 series, externally similar to the MD-81/2, but powered by 94.5-kN (21,000-lb-st) JT8D-219 engines. It has an additional 4391 litres (1,160 US gallons) of fuel in two cargo bay tanks, and a maximum take-off weight of 72,576 kg (160,000 lb). It was first flown on 17 December 1984 and entered service early in 1986 with launch customers Alaska Airlines and Finnair. Finnair's first MD-83 made the longest nonstop flight ever recorded by an MD-80 series aircraft during its delivery flight on 14 November 1985, flying the 6308 km (3,920 miles) from Montreal, Canada, to Finnair's

base at Helsinki, Finland, in 7 hours 26 minutes.

The only version of the basic MD-80 series to display a major airframe change was the MD-87, announced on 3 January 1985. This had a fuselage shortened by 5 m (16 ft 5 in), seating 109 passengers in mixed-class or 139 in single-class accommodation. The MD-87 was first flown on 4 December 1986; deliveries to launch customers Austrian Airlines and Finnair began in October 1987.

The fifth member of the MD-80 family, designated MD-88, was announced on 23 January 1986, following receipt of a launch order for 80 aircraft (subsequently increased to 110) from Delta Air Lines. Similar to the MD-82, this version is powered by 94.50-kN (21,000-lb-st) JT8D-219 engines and featured an EFIS flight deck, flight management system (FMS), inertial reference system

(IRS), and windshear detection system as standard. Increased use was made of composite materials in the airframe, and its 142-passenger, five-abreast seating cabin interior was extensively redesigned with a wider aisle and new overhead storage bins.

The MD-88 first flew on 15 August 1987, received FAA certification on 9 December and entered service with Delta on 5 January 1988.

In addition to airliner variants of the MD-80 series, McDonnell Douglas also built MD-83 and MD-87 Executive Jets. Designed to individual customer specifications, these are typically configured to carry 20–30 passengers and have maximum ranges of 4,100–4,500 nm (7593–8334 km; 4,718–5,179 miles).

A total of 1191 aircraft of the MD-80 series was ordered by operators ranging from Adria Airways through Continental to Venus Air. Late in 1999, however, Boeing, which by then controlled McDonnell Douglas, brought production of the family to a close.

Powered by two 90-kN (20,000-lb-st) JT8D-217C turbofans, the MD-87 was the first aircraft in the series to offer an EFIS, an attitude and heading reference system (AHRS) and a head-up display as standard in its avionics/flight deck configuration.

The -80s today

The book has now been closed on the MD-80 story, following the delivery of the last aircraft by Boeing in 1999. The production life of Long Beach's 'Super 80' lasted 20 years and spanned two continents. It is a tribute to the quality of the basic design that most MD-80s were acquired by airlines that already had many happy years of DC-9 experience.

The 'Super 80' title did not follow on from the earlier DC-9 designations, reflecting the fact that these latest developments would be a family of new aircraft for the 1980s. There was never an actual type designated DC-9-80. Instead, the first production variant was the DC-9-81 (this was the form that appeared on all aircraft construction plates until the end of MD-80 production).

Initial sales were slow, with just 100 orders logged in the five years after the programme was announced in 1977. This situation improved remarkably during the early 1980s, when sales rose to an average of 125 a year. The DC-9-80 was launched on the back of 36 orders and options from Swissair, Austrian Airlines and Southern Airways (though the latter never actually proceeded). The first customer for the type was Swissair, with an order for 15 aircraft. The Swiss national carrier took delivery of its first DC-9-81 on 13 September 1980, placing it into service on 10 October, on the Zurich–London–Heathrow route.

Swissair's first two aircraft were used by McDonnell Douglas for the DC-9-80's flight test programme and, during this process, both were rendered undeliverable. The very first DC-9-81 was damaged and retained by the manufacturer until 1990, when it was finally sold on. The second aircraft was actually damaged beyond repair in an incident at Yuma on 19 June 1980. Both were replaced further down the delivery schedule and different DC-9-81s were handed over to Swissair in December 1981 and March 1982.

After Swissair, DC-9-81 deliveries continued to Austrian Airlines, Austral Lineas Aereas, Muse Air, AirCal, TOA Domestic Airlines (later Japan Air System), Pacific Southwest Airlines/PSA (later merged with USAir, now US Airways), Hawaiian Airlines and Inex Adria Airlines. Other operators included Aeromexico, Avioimpex, Continental Airlines, Harlequin Air, Midwest Express, SAS, Spirit Airlines and Sun Air.

First Super 80 variant

In 1979 McDonnell Douglas announced the first variant in the Super 80 family, the DC-9-82.

This version was almost identical to the DC-9-81, but was fitted with more powerful engines for 'hot-and-high' operations. The launch customer was officially Aeromexico, but Inex Adria later swapped two of its existing Super 80 series orders to become DC-9-82s. The first delivery was made to the United States' Republic Airlines (later merged with Northwest Orient, now Northwest Airlines) on 5 August 1981, and the first Inex Adria aircraft followed on 11 August. Aeromexico received its first DC-9-82 on 14 December 1981. Other operators included AirCal, Jet

While the MD-87 will remain an important type in Iberia's fleet for a few years, the type is set to be ousted following a major Airbus purchase by the Spanish national carrier.

America Airlines (later merged with Alaska Airlines), Frontier Airlines, VIASA, ALM Antillean Airlines, New York Air (later merged with Continental Airlines), Martinair Holland, American Airlines, Trans World Airways/TWA, Alitalia, Austrian Airlines, Ozark Airlines (later merged with TWA), Alisarda, Continental Airlines, Finnair, Far Eastern Air Transport, Nouvelair

Below: Continental's huge fleet includes dwindling numbers of MD-80 series aircraft, including MD-81s, -82s (illustrated) and -83s. The airline has retired its DC-9-31 and -32 aircraft.

Bottom: In either 164-seat high-density, or 131-seat layouts, the MD-82 remains the backbone of Alitalia's fleet. Note the 'Super 80' titles on the engine nacelles of this aircraft.

***SAS** remains a major **McDonnell Douglas** twinjet operator. This **MD-81** is typical of the earliest examples of the **MD-80** series to enter service.*

Tunisie, Sun Air, Air Philippines, Beiya Airlines, Pacific Airlines, U-Land Airlines, Meridiana, SAS, Spanair, Midwest Express and Spirit Airlines.

MD-82s built under licence in China remained in service with China Eastern Airlines, China Northern Airlines and China Northern Swan Airlines into the twenty-first century.

In January 1983, McDonnell Douglas launched the next version in the family, the DC-9-83. This extended-range, higher gross weight aircraft was aimed at holiday charter airlines and other specialist operators flying long, thin routes. In June 1983 McDonnell Douglas finally dropped the illustrious 'Douglas Commercial' (DC) prefix in favour of 'MD'.

First of the 'MDs'
The Super 80 series thus became the MD-80 family, the DC-9-81 became the MD-81 and the DC-9-82 the MD-82. Launch customer for the MD-83 was Alaska Airlines, which took delivery of its first aircraft in February 1985. Other MD-83 operators included American Airlines, Finnair, Korean Airlines, Nouvelair Tunisie, Far Eastern Air Transport, British Island Airways, Aero Lloyd, Air Liberté, AOM French Airlines, Austrian Airlines, Eurofly, Meridiana, SAS, Spanair, Aerolineas Argentinas, Aeromexico, Air Jamaica, Allegro Air, Austral, Avianca, BWIA, Continental Airlines and Midwest Express.

***Finnair** has a reduced fleet of **MD-82** and **-83** (illustrated) aircraft remaining in service.*

Shrinking the -80
Introduced in 1985, the MD-87 featured the first significant change in the basic MD-80 design. The short-fuselage MD-87 was an MD-80 'shrink', designed to replace ageing short DC-9s. The first orders were won from Finnair and Austrian Airlines in December 1984 and the first aircraft were handed over on 1 November 1987 and 27 November 1987, respectively. A total of 75 MD-87s had been delivered to 10 customers when production ceased in 1992. Other current operators include Austrian (one, for sale), Iberia, Japan Airlines Domestic, SAS and Aeromexico.

The final member of the MD-80 family was the MD-88.

Developed specifically for Delta Air Lines, the MD-88 added an advanced technology EFIS cockpit to the basic airframe of an MD-82 or MD-83. Delta itself chose the new designation, and launched the programme with orders and options for 80 aircraft. The first MD-88 was delivered on 19 December 1987 and entered service on 5 January 1988. Delta later increased its total by converting earlier deliveries to MD-88 standard. Other MD-88s currently serve with Onur Air, Aerolineas Argentinas, Aeromexico and Midwest Airlines.

The 1000th MD-80, MD-83 N960AS, was delivered to Alaska Airlines on 23 March 1992. An MD-83 (N596AA) handed over to American Airlines on 11 June 1992 became the 2000th twinjet to be delivered by McDonnell Douglas.

The final countdown
Following the August 1997 acquisition of McDonnell Douglas by Boeing, a shadow was cast over the future of the entire MD airliner series. Uncertainty reigned for nearly a year until May 1998, when Boeing announced that it would phase out production of the MD-80 (and the MD-90, which shared the same final assembly line). In a ceremony held at Long Beach, California – home of the Douglas airliners – Boeing handed over the last MD-80 to TWA on 21 December 1999. The aircraft was an MD-83 and the 26th MD-80 delivered to TWA that year. It brought the number of MD-80s operated by TWA to 102, and the aircraft was christened *Spirit of Long Beach*.

In 1933 TWA had taken delivery of the very first twin-engined airliner built by the Douglas Aircraft Company, the (one and only) DC-1. Douglas Aircraft, McDonnell Douglas and Boeing delivered 1191 MD-80s from 1979 to 1999. In 2005 remaining MD-80 operators included American Airlines, Delta Air Lines, Alitalia, SAS, Continental Airlines, Iberia, Alaska Airlines, Aeromexico, Finnair, Japan Airlines Domestic, Spanair, Meridiana, China Southern Airlines, Austrian Airlines and Avianca.

***Alaska Airlines** was launch customer for the **MD-83**, its first being delivered in 1985.*

McDonnell Douglas MD-11 DC-10 successor

McDonnell Douglas spent a lot of time examining the aircraft that would succeed its popular DC-10, but, through a combination of poor timing and bad luck, it failed to quite hit the mark. The MD-11 was not a substantial improvement over the DC-10, although it did boast new technology and design features.

In tried-and-trusted form, McDonnell Douglas used one of its existing aircraft – the DC-10 – as the basis for the MD-11. The new, larger aircraft would be an advanced technology trijet, with extended range, modern engines and digital avionics. Work had begun on such an aircraft as early as 1978, when McAir began to examine its options for a DC-10 'stretch'. The plan was to introduce an aircraft in the early 1980s to compete with the Boeing 747 and to pre-empt the efforts of Airbus. A proposed DC-10 Series 60 was drawn up in three different versions: the DC-10-61, aimed at the US domestic market, using the wing of the DC-10-30 with a larger, heavier fuselage; the transatlantic DC-10-62, with a shorter fuselage and extended wing with winglets; and the DC-10-63 that coupled the Series 62 wing with the Series 61 fuselage. Each of these aircraft would have been larger than the MD-11 of today, though their maximum take-off

weights would have been roughly equivalent. Despite early optimism, however, customer interest in the Series 60 proved to be illusive and, as time passed, the aircraft began to look increasingly dated. As fuel prices climbed, McAir shelved its DC-10 developments and began to look at an all-new design as the next way forward.

New proposals

In 1982 the resultant MD-100 proposal was unveiled. This aircraft retained the trijet configuration and was roughly the same size as a DC-10. Differences included its two-crew flight deck and Pratt & Whitney PW2037 or Rolls-Royce RB.211-535 engines (both as found on the Boeing 757). Like the Series 60, the MD-100 failed to gain much interest and, remarkably, McDonnell Douglas began to reconsider a 'quick and easy' DC-10 derivative once more. This led to the MD-XXX of 1984, an aircraft that was little more than a DC-10-30 with General Electric CF6-80C2 or Pratt & Whitney PW4000 engines. A fuselage stretch was proposed and, by the end of the year, MDC had adopted the MD-11 title for its new project.

With the MD-11 came a whole family of proposed aircraft – the MD-11X-10ER, the MD-11X-20

The third MD-11 to fly, N311MD was part of the three-aircraft test programme which resulted in the aircraft's certification with PW4460 engines in November 1990.

and the MD-11X-MR. The -10ER would have a DC-10-sized fuselage, while the other two would both be stretched. In July 1985 the McDonnell Douglas board of directors gave the go-ahead for the MD-11 to be offered to the airlines and a launch date was suggested for early 1986. A market for 1400 aircraft in the class of the MD-11 was foreseen, with McAir hoping to make at least 300 sales. First deliveries were scheduled for 1989.

By October 1985 several changes had been made to the MD-11 design and the family options had been chopped, as little interest had been shown in

Below: VASP was an early operator of the MD-11 airliner, leasing two examples in the spring of 1992. Success in service subsequently led to VASP leasing a further six.

the short-range MD-11X-MR or the short-fuselage MD-11X-10ER. The MD-11's overall fuselage stretch was also reduced. The two-crew cockpit and CF6-80C2/PW4000 engines were retained.

Initial orders

The MD-11 received its formal go-ahead on 30 December 1986, when McDonnell Douglas announced commitments for 82 aircraft from 12 customers. Few of these, however, were firm orders and, of those that

Below: The first MD-11 to enter service with Finnair is seen at the official roll-out in 1990. The type entered service at the end of the year on Finnair's Helsinki–Tenerife route.

Left: The DC-10 ancestry is readily evident in the MD-11's layout. Although a number of loyal Douglas/McDonnell Douglas customers ordered the type, performance figures never reached the initial predictions and production was halted.

Right: The first MD-11 to fly was N111MD, which took to the air on 10 January 1990. After participating in the flight test programme the aircraft was delivered to Federal Express as an MD-11F in June 1991.

were, events conspired to block several of them. By 1987's end the official figures comprised 30 firm orders and 47 commitments. Such low figures quickly attracted criticism, as did the fact that no major orders from a US carrier had been won. Along with the passenger version came two cargo versions, and it was as a freighter that the MD-11 would eventually find its most successful niche.

The baseline MD-11 was built around a DC-10-30 fuselage with two plugs inserted fore and aft of the wing section. The MD-11 has an overall length of 61 m (200 ft 11 in) when fitted with PW engines, or 61.30 m (201 ft 4 in) when fitted with GE turbofans. One difference from the DC-10 comes with the addition of the MD-11's aluminium and carbon-fibre winglets. These are credited with reducing overall drag by 4 per cent. The MD-11's fin and tailplanes are revised, with reduced sweep and area, again to reduce drag.

Engine options came in the form of the 273.6-kN (61,500-lb st CF6-80C2D1F or 270-kN) (60,000-lb st) PW4460. Rolls-Royce proposed a Trent 665 option for the MD-11, but the one customer for this solution, Air Europe, collapsed in 1991 before deliveries could begin. The Trent was quietly dropped from the MD-11 programme.

On the flight deck the MD-11 is configured with a six-screen EFIS cockpit and an advanced flight management system. In the cabin, it can be fitted with up to 405 seats in a single-class configuration, although a more typical layout is 293 seats in three classes.

Hand-in-hand with the all-passenger MD-11 (sometimes referred to as the MD-11P) came three other variants: the MD-11C Combi, MD-11F Freighter and MD-11CF Convertible Freighter. The Combi is fitted with a side

SPECIFICATION	
McDonnell Douglas MD-11	**Weights:** empty 131,035 kg
Type: long-range airliner	(277,500 lb); maximum take-off
Powerplant: three 266.9-kN (60,042-lb-thrust) Pratt & Whitney PW4460 or 273.57-kN (61,542-lb-thrust) General Electric CF6-80C2D1F turbofans	273,289 kg (602,500 lb)
	Dimensions: wing span 51.77 m (169 ft 6 in); length 61.24 m (200 ft 10 in); height 17.60 m (57 ft 7 in); wing area 338.90 m² (3,648 sq ft)
Maximum speed: 945 km/h (586 mph) at 9450 m (31,000 ft)	**Accommodation:** up to 410 passengers maximum; 323 in typical two-class configuration; 293 in three-class configuration
Range: 12,569 km (7,793 miles) with 323 passengers	

cargo door, on the port side of the fuselage. The side cargo door was developed by Alenia, at its Aeronavali facility – one with great experience in developing cargo conversions for aircraft such as the DC-8 and DC-10. The Combi configuration allowed up to 214 passengers and six standard cargo pallets to be carried in the main cabin. Structurally, the aircraft can handle up to 10 pallets and 120 passengers. The MD-11F has a slightly smaller side cargo door

when compared to the MD-11C. This improves the structural integrity of the aircraft and gives it a higher maximum landing weight. The MD-11F's lack of cabin windows and absence of all passenger access doors make it unmistakable.

The MD-11CF offers a user the ability to switch the aircraft from all-passenger to all-freight configurations, giving maximum flexibility with one airframe. The CF has the same side cargo door as the MD-11F, and this variant can be converted from all-passenger to all-cargo configuration in 35 hours.

Delta Air Lines placed an order for 15 MD-11s in 1988, seven of which remain in service with the airline today. They are powered by PW4460 turbofans and were delivered between 1992 and 1994.

MD-11 in service

Typical of many operators, Eva Air of Taiwan found the MD-11 more suitable as a freighter than as a passenger-carrying type. The airline currently operates 12 MD-11Fs.

The MD-11 was never a 'best seller' and its very public difficulties hurt its order book severely. Although the freighter versions are seen as invaluable by those lucky enough to have them, this was not enough to save the production line, which closed in 2000.

The MD-11 was launched on 30 December 1986, with 82 announced 'commitments', of which many were never firmed up. In fact, only 11 firm orders were placed in 1986. The next tranche of orders came in March/April 1987 as deals were struck with Finnair (two), Swissair (six, plus four in December) and Alitalia (one). Alitalia also became the launch customer for the MD-11C Combi, with an order for five, while FedEx launched the MD-11F Freighter, with an order for two.

As the first MD-11 entered the assembly phase in March 1988, the order book stood at just 31 aircraft. At the same time, it was announced that the slow delivery of components from suppliers would delay the first completion by a month, to February 1989, with the maiden flight now rescheduled to April. During 1988 McDonnell Douglas received orders from Thai International (four), FedEx (two),

China Airlines (four), Delta Air Lines (nine), China Eastern (four, plus one MD-11F), Finnair (two), Garuda (six), ILFC (three, plus two MD-11Fs), LTU (three) and VARIG (four). The Delta order was, at the time, the most significant. Its full terms included nine firm orders and 31 options, but it also marked the first MD-11 purchase by a major US airline.

In 1989 the slow pace of orders continued, with signings by FedEx (two MD-11Fs), Swissair (two), American Airlines (15), LTU (one) and EVA Air (two, plus three MD-11Fs). The order from American was the first of two that would see it become the largest operator of

MD-11s in passenger service. Also in 1989 Air Europe announced its order, but the airline went out of business before these aircraft were ever built. Air Zaïre also announced orders that were never fulfilled.

The first MD-11 took to the air on 10 January 1990 – eight months behind schedule. This CF6-powered aircraft launched the flight-test programme and to speed up the process, McDonnell Douglas had the MD-11 certified as a derivative of the DC-10, rather than a completely new type. FAA type certification was awarded on 30 November 1990, with certification of the PW4460-powered MD-11

following on 19 December. The first customer delivery of an MD-11 was made to Finnair on 29 November 1990. Finnair placed the aircraft into revenue service on 20 December 1990. The first PW4460-powered MD-11 was delivered to Korean Airlines on 25 January 1991.

The year 1990 was a good one for the MD-11 as several (comparatively) large orders rolled in from important customers. These included deals with American Airlines (11), KLM (10), Japan Airlines (10), Korean Airlines (one), FedEx (two MD-11Fs), Delta Air Lines (two) and GATX Capital (one). The next year, business dropped sharply, with

LTU International Airways operated four PW4462-powered MD-11s – first ordered in 1988 – until the aircraft were sold to Swissair in the late 1990s.

After acquiring the four ex-LTU examples, Swissair had a total fleet of 19 MD-11s by 1999. However, the fleet was sold to FedEx, which converted them into MD-11F freighters.

orders placed by Delta Air Lines (two), FedEx (five MD-11Fs) and Martinair Holland (three MD-11Fs).

Improving performance

The reason for the decline in interest soon became clear. Although it was only in the earliest days of its service life, the MD-11 was already suffering serious problems. The aircraft was falling well short of its promised payload/range performance, through a combination of aerodynamic flaws and poor engine operating economy. The brochure figures for the MD-11 quoted a maximum range of 7,000 nm (12,955 km; 8,050 miles) with 293 passengers and a 27,670-kg (61,000-lb) payload, but even before the flight test programme was complete McDonnell Douglas knew that the aircraft would not perform as advertised.

Much of the problem could be traced to higher than expected fuel consumption by both engine types – which was falling between 4 and 9 per cent outside the contract specification. The MD-11 was also overweight and suffered from excess drag. To

try to solve the problem, McAir implemented a multi-phase performance improvement package (PIP) that reduced drag, reconfigured the wing and other external surfaces and boosted take-off weight, allowing more fuel to be carried, and reduced overall empty weight.

As the various phases of the PIP were introduced, the MD-11's range began to creep upwards. Both engine manufacturers developed their own powerplant PIPs and Delta Air Lines introduced a novel auxiliary fuel tank arrangement which could be fitted in the cargo hold, replacing two LD3 containers. By 1996 McDonnell

Douglas believed that it had reached the limit of what was possible without profound airframe changes and that performance had been boosted by some 8 per cent. This put the MD-11 back into the 7,000-nm bracket, but the damage had been done. For example, a vital order from Singapore Airlines for 20 aircraft was lost, as the MD-11 could not meet SIA's range requirements.

Cargo versions

In the specialist cargo market the MD-11F was beginning to shine. The first MD-11F was delivered on 29 May 1991, to FedEx, while Alitalia took delivery of its first MD-11C Combi on 27 November 1991. Martinair Holland became the launch customer for the MD-11CF, on 26 August 1991, with an order for three aircraft (with two options). The first Convertible Freighter was delivered in December 1994.

During the mid-1990s McDonnell Douglas announced several dramatic developments of the MD-11, including twin-engined derivatives and extended-range versions. The MD-11ER was announced in 1994 as an aircraft that would be 'the longest-range 300-seat airliner in revenue service'.

Capable of carrying 298 passengers over 13,350 km (8,295 miles), the MD-11ER was developed to be in direct competition to the Boeing 777 and Airbus A340. However, as sales of the basic aircraft declined, plans for the ER died some time before McDonnell Douglas was taken over by Boeing in August 1997.

After the takeover, despite some hopes that the MD-11F would be saved, after a small flurry of late orders, Boeing announced – in June 1998 – that all MD-11 production would cease during 2000. Some 200 MD-11s were built.

The MD-11F received a welcome boost in 1996 when Lufthansa Cargo ordered five aircraft, with options on a further seven, in an order worth more than $550 million. A total of 19 is now in service, all powered by General Electric CF6-80C2D1F turbofans.

VARIG of Brazil leases 15 MD-11s which are utilized on a number of the airline's long-haul routes. They are configured to carry either 12 first-, 49 business- and 180 economy-class passengers, or six, 49 and 230, respectively.

EMBRAER EMB-120 Brasilia Brazilian commuter

When introduced by EMBRAER, the Brasilia twin-turboprop feederliner was viewed as another progressive design from the company that had built the successful EMB-110 Bandeirante. The EMB-120 went on to become a popular small airliner throughout the Americas, and inspired EMBRAER to launch a new family of regional jets that have helped to revolutionize the world airline market.

The EMB-120 Brasilia grew out of a number of studies made by the Brazilian manufacturer, based on a pressurized Bandeirante development and driven by an increasing need for a larger, 30-plus seat aircraft. EMBRAER officially launched the new aircraft in September 1979, even though it was another 10 years before Bandeirante production ended.

EMBRAER began by drawing up its EMB-12X proposal around a twin-engined, T-tailed turboprop with a circular (pressurized) fuselage cross-section. This initial design work gave birth to

the EMB-121 Xingu, a smaller high-speed twin aimed at the executive market. For the airlines, EMBRAER had proposed the 20-seat EMB-120 Araguaia and the even more compact EMB-123 Tapajos. However, the airlines universally wanted a larger aircraft, as demand was outstripping the capacity of the current crop of 19-seat aircraft. The initial concepts were put to one side in favour of a 30-seat aircraft that was to become the EMB-120 Brasilia.

EMBRAER's new airliner had a low-mounted unswept wing and a swept fin. It employed a conventional semi-monocoque/stressed-skin structure, with some composites found in the wing, tailplane leading edges, flaps, ventral fins, nose and tailcone. Power was provided by two 1118-kW (1,500-shp) Pratt & Whitney PW115 turboprops, each driving a four-bladed Hamilton Standard 14RF propeller. The two-crew cockpit was built around Collins ProLine II digital

Above: The prototype Brasilia made its first flight in July 1983 and is seen here undergoing wet runway trials. A large nose-mounted instrumentation probe was fitted during flight tests.

Top: The first European customer for the EMB-120 was Deutsche Luftverkehrsgesellschaft (DLT), receiving its first example in January 1986. The airline was renamed Lufthansa Cityline in 1992.

avionics, to which the improved EFIS-86 and MFD-85 display systems were later added. The cabin was fitted out for 30 passengers (plus an attendant), in three-abreast seating.

First flight

The prototype EMB-120 made its initial flight on 27 July 1983. In all, three flying prototypes,

two static test aircraft and one pre-series production Brasilia were dedicated to the development programme. With the basic PW115 engines, the EMB-120 received its Brazilian certification on 10 May 1985, followed by FAA type approval on 9 July 1985. The first customer, Atlantic Southeast Airlines of the USA (a member

United Express/WestAir operated a fleet of 20 EMB-120RTs, each of which was configured to carry 30 passengers on US commuter routes. United Express was split into its constituent parts in 1998 and a number of the Brasilias were absorbed into Great Lakes Airlines.

Wearing both its pre- and post-delivery registrations, this aircraft is seen prior to becoming the first EMB-120 to be delivered to Australian carrier Flight West Airlines in May 1990. The airline later received seven more examples for operations in Queensland.

By June 1999, EMBRAER had delivered a total of 350 Brasilias and the type was in service with 32 operators in 13 countries. On busy commuter routes, each aircraft spends an average of 6.87 hours in the air each day, the fleet leader (the 10th production aircraft) had amassed some 33,711 flying hours, and the worldwide Brasilia fleet had spent over 4,000,000 hours in the air. When, in the early 1990s, EMBRAER made the daring decision to make a regional jet its next project, it used the EMB-120 as a starting point.

of the Delta Connection feeder network), put the Brasilia into service in October 1985, having taken ceremonial delivery of the second prototype at the Paris Air Show in June 1985.

Improved performance

Initial production EMB-120s had a maximum take-off weight of 23,810 kg (10,800 lb). The EMB-120RT (Reduced Take-off) introduced more powerful 1342-kW (1,800-hp) PW118 engines, in early 1986, to improve performance at a higher gross weight of 25,353 kg (11,500 lb). Maximum cruising speed was also increased, and most aircraft have now been brought up to this standard. An 18-seat corporate model was handed over to the United States' United Technologies in the same year. Late in 1987, a 'hot-and-high' version became available. This had improved PW118A engines which maintained maximum output up to a temperature of ISA+15°C at sea level. Empty weight was also reduced by 390 kg (858 lb) through increased use of composites. The first customer was Skywest Airlines,

another member of the Delta Connection and based in Utah.

EMBRAER investigated improved-performance versions of the Brasilia under the designations EMB-120X and Improved Brasilia. These studies led to the increased-weight, extended-range EMB-120ER Brasilia Advanced, which was announced in 1992. The Advanced did not incorporate any major structural changes, but range was extended after an increase in allowable take-off weight – now 11,990 kg (26,433 lb). This also permits increased passenger baggage limits, a very popular move in the US market. The Advanced features interchangeable leading edges on its flying surfaces, improved flaps, new seals to cut interior noise, a redesigned flight deck, increased cargo capacity and a number of cabin improvements. Cabin lighting, ventilation and baggage space were all improved, while EMBRAER also developed a passive noise and vibration reduction system.

The Brasilia Advanced became available in May 1993, when the

first deliveries were made to Skywest, and it is now the standard production variant. Earlier models can be brought up to ER standard with a simple retrofit. The first customers for such an upgrade were Belgium's DAT and Luxair. Alongside the improved passenger version, three cargo versions are still available. These include the all-freight EMB-120C, based on the ER with an 4000-kg (8,818-lb) payload; EMB-120 Combi, a mixed-configuration version capable of carrying 19 passengers and 1100 kg (2,425 lb) of cargo; and the EMB-120QC (Quick-Change), convertible in 40 minutes to an all-freight or all-seating configuration.

The first jet to emerge, the hugely successful EMB-145 (now the ERJ-145) uses a stretched Brasilia fuselage, combined with a new wing and a revised tail section. The smaller ERJ-135 is again based on a similar structure. Several other essential components are also common between the jets and the EMB-120. EMBRAER has become one of the very few manufacturers in the regional airliner business to translate its success with turboprops into success with jets. For this, it can thank the EMB-120.

SPECIFICATION	
EMBRAER EMB-120-ER **Brasilia Advanced** **Type:** pressurized twin-turboprop transport **Powerplant:** two 1342-kW (1,800-hp) Pratt & Whitney PW118 or PW118A turboprops **Maximum level speed:** 606 km/h (376 mph) **Range:** 1575 km (975 miles) at 9150 m (30,000 ft) with maximum fuel, payload and reserves	**Service ceiling:** 9755 m (32,000 ft) **Weights:** empty equipped 7150 kg (15,730 lb); maximum take-off 11,990 kg (23,353 lb) **Dimensions:** wing span 19.78 m (64 ft 11 in); length 20.07 m (65 ft 10 in); height 6.35 m (20 ft 10 in); wing area 39.43 m² (424 sq ft) **Accommodation:** three crew and up to 30 passengers or 3500 kg (7,700 lb) of cargo

The Brasilia's biggest market was the United States, due to its massive commuter and feederliner demand. The type's sales success with airlines such as Skywest allowed the development of today's ERJ series of aircraft, which continue to score major sales in this sector.

EMBRAER ERJ 145/135 Basic appeal

EMBRAER has established a firm foothold at the high-power end of the regional jet market. With its ERJ 145, 140 and 135, it has produced three innovative airliners, sold under the twin slogans of 'Back to Basics' and 'Everything you need. Nothing you don't'.

EMBRAER studied a number of follow-on projects to the Bandeirante and Brasilia to maintain a foothold in the regional aircraft market. The most advanced of these was the pusher turboprop CBA-123, but the trend towards jet aircraft persuaded EMBRAER to change direction. Its first twin-jet design was a low-risk development of the Brasilia, with a stretched fuselage for 45 passengers, wing-mounted Allison GMA 3007 turbofans, and the same straight wing. However, wind tunnel tests revealed significant performance shortcomings, leading to the adoption of a supercritical swept wing. The

33-kN (7,246-lb-thrust) engines were also moved to the rear of the fuselage and capacity increased to 50 seats at the behest of potential customers.

The estimated US$300 million development costs were beyond EMBRAER's means, however, and it took on board a number of risk-sharing partners, which took a one-third share, plus some 70 risk-share suppliers for another 10 per cent of the cost. EMBRAER itself contributed one third, with Brazilian institutions providing the remainder.

Assembly of the first prototype (PT-ZJA) began in October 1994, and this made its maiden flight on 11 August 1995. Three further pre-production aircraft were flown on 17 November 1995 (PT-ZJB), 14 February 1995 (PT-ZJC) and 16 April 1996 (PT-ZJD). FAA and Brazilian CTA certification was obtained on 16 December 1996, with European JAA certification following on 15 May 1997. On

To minimize risk, development costs for the EMB145 were split between a number of companies. The ensuing savings ensured that the aircraft's US$15 million price tag was competitive compared to rivals such as Canadair's Regional Jet.

10 March, the FAA had approved the EMB-145 to operate safely in a cold-weather environment.

The first North American carrier to fly the EMB-145 jetliner, Continental Express, began regular revenue flights on 6 April 1997, initially linking its Cleveland, Ohio, hub to destinations in six US states. During the year, several new models were developed to meet requests from customers, and the designation was changed to

ERJ-145 to reflect the regional jet (RJ) terminology now widely used by the industry, while a further revision to ERJ 145 occurred latterly.

The new models differ primarily in take-off weight and improved payload/range performance. These include: the ERJ 145EU, increasing take-off weight from the 19,200 kg (42,330 lb) of the standard model to 19,990 kg (44,070 lb); the ERJ 145ER, with a further increase to 20,600 kg (45,415 lb); and the ERJ 145EP, heavier still at 20,990 kg (46,275 lb). The ERJ 145MR introduced the AE3007A1 engine with increased thermodynamic thrust and a take-off weight of 22,000 kg (48,500lb). At the Paris Air Show in June 1997, EMBRAER also announced a new long-range ERJ 145LR

The first two European operators of the ERJ 145, launch customer Regional Airlines of France (as here) and Portugalia, took delivery of their first aircraft on 16 May 1997.

The fourth ERJ-145 appeared at Farnborough in 1998 alongside the first ERJ-135 prototype which was making its European debut – the two aircraft put on a scintillating display, which included opposition passes.

Left: Seen here, pre-delivery, over Brazil, is City Airline's first ERJ 145. The aircraft now flies with Sweden's Skyways Express. EMBRAER based its construction programme on total sales of 400 ERJ 145s.

Right: PT-ZJA was the prototype ERJ 135 – the shortened version of the 145. During flight testing, the aircraft reached a ceiling of 11,278 m (37,000 ft) and a maximum operating speed of Mach 0.78.

version, which differs from the MR in having an additional 810 kg (1,786 lb) of fuel, giving a range of 1,600 nm (2963 km; 1,840 miles). Ultimately, EMBRAER has bowed to the demand for even greater range with the ERJ 145XR, able to fly 50 passengers some 2,000 nm (3706 km; 2,303 miles).

Protecting the Amazon

Border invasions, illegal mineral exploration, deforestation and drug smuggling in the vast and sparsely populated Amazon region of Brazil prompted the Brazilian government in 1990 to create the Amazon Surveillance System (SIVAM) as part of the Amazon Protection System (SIPAM). In March 1997 a SIVAM contract was given to EMBRAER to develop and build eight surveillance and remote-sensing systems, based on the ERJ 145. Five EMB 145SA (incorporating the Ericsson Erieye AEW&C system) surveillance versions were produced, along with three EMB 145RS aircraft for remote-sensing operations.

As the EMB 145 AEW&C, the EMB 145SA is also being targeted at other potential customers in Latin America,

Europe and the Far East, with orders from customers including Greece and Mexico. Likewise, the EMB 145RS has been developed for export as the EMB 145RS/AGS electronic reconnaissance and intelligence gatherer. Other military developments include the EMB 145MP/P-99 multi-role maritime aircraft.

Smaller still

On 16 September 1997, EMBRAER announced the development of a new regional jet for 37 passengers, designated ERJ 135. The new jet was based heavily on the EMB-145 design, sharing its Rolls-Royce Allison AE3007A3 engines and main systems, cockpit, wing and tail assembly, and having the same cross-section fuselage, albeit 3.5 m (11 ft 6 in) shorter. EMBRAER targeted a market forecast of 500 units over 10 years for the aircraft. It converted one of the four EMB-145 prototypes to the ERJ 135 configuration by replacing two of the central fuselage sections with a shorter single section. The first aircraft was rolled out on 12 May 1998 and made its maiden flight, ahead of schedule, on 4 July.

After two flights and a total of five hours in the air, the full operational envelope had been explored, including all gear and flap configurations, longitudinal and directional stability at the extremes of the centre of gravity, and full stalls at clean and full-flap configurations. A second prototype took to the air on 24 September 1998 and Brazilian certification was granted in June 1999, FAA in July 1999 and JAA in October 1999. The first aircraft was delivered, to Continental Express, in July 1999. The ERJ 135 has a take-off

weight of 19,000 kg (41,895 lb) and a typical range, with 37 passengers and baggage, of 1,190 nm (2200 km; 1,369 miles). The ERJ 135 also formed the basis of a successful business jet, the EMBRAER Legacy, which continues to sell strongly.

Interestingly, the ERJ 135 was joined by another downsized ERJ 145 variant when EMBRAER responded to calls for a capacity midway between the ERJ 135 and ERJ 145, to produce the ERJ 140. By summer 2005, almost 900 ERJ 145-family aircraft were in service.

EMBRAER 170 series

Looking to expand its regional airliner business, EMBRAER realized that the next step was to develop a higher-capacity aircraft with the potential for future 'stretches' built in. Abandoning the winning formula established with the ERJ 145, the company decided on a very high technology design based on a conventional-looking airframe. The resulting EMBRAER 170 suffered a number of delays relating to its advanced cockpit systems and other equipment, but eventually completed a successful first flight on 19 February 2002. The first customer machine was delivered to US Airways in February 2004, with LOT Polish airlines receiving its first machine soon after. Seating 70 to 78 passengers, the 170 has been joined by the 78- to 86-seat 175, which was certified in December 2004, the 98- to 106-seat 190 which was due for certification in August 2005 and the 118-seat 195, which is due to gain certification around mid-2006. In June 2005, total orders for the series stood at 187 (EMBRAER 170, with 66 delivered), 19 (175), 177 (190) and 29 (195).

SPECIFICATION

EMBRAER ERJ 145ER
Type: regional jet airliner
Powerplant: two 31.32-kN (7040-lb-st) Rolls-Royce Allison AE3007-A1 turbofan engines
Cruising speed: 823 km/h (511 mph)
Range: 1569 km (975 miles) with maximum payload
Service ceiling: 11,280 m (37,000 ft)

Weight: operating empty 11,667 kg (25,722 lb); 19,200 kg (42,328 lb) maximum take-off weight
Dimensions: wing span 20.04 m (65 ft 9 in); length 29.87 m (98 ft); height 6.75 m (22 ft 1.75 in); wing area 51.2 m² (550.9 sq ft)
Accommodation: up to 50 passengers

De Havilland Canada DHC-6 Twin Otter
Canada's STOL liner

Excellent STOL performance, good load-carrying capability and the ability to land on virtually any surface made the Twin Otter the world's standard 'go anywhere' light transport. De Havilland Canada, with a long history of manufacturing successful utility and bush aircraft behind it, began detail design work in November 1963 on a twin-engined development of the DHC-3 Otter. An experimental Otter powered by two Pratt & Whitney Canada PT6 turboprops had earlier shown great promise, and this engine was selected for the new design, which was designated DHC-6.

DHC's design philosophy was to create an aircraft which could operate unsupported in the most inhospitable environment, from land, water, ice or snow. It was to offer good short take-off and landing characteristics, have low operating costs and simple maintenance requirements, and employ as many components and as much of the production tooling of its single-engined forebear as possible.

The Twin Otter retained the Otter's wing section (with increased span), its fuselage cross-section and many other components. The resulting design was a conventional strut-braced high-wing monoplane of all-metal construction with double-slotted trailing-edge flaps and drooping ailerons to enhance STOL performance, cruciform tail surfaces with a slightly swept fin and fixed tricycle undercarriage with float or ski options.

Work began on the prototype in July 1964 and the first flight occurred on 20 May 1965. In July 1966 the first production-standard Series 100 went into service with launch customer Trans-Australia Airlines, followed shortly by the Ontario Department of Lakes and Forests.

Commuter liner

Although designed primarily with the needs of bush operators in mind, the Twin Otter quickly attracted great interest from airlines operating feeder and commuter services.

After 115 Series 100s had been completed, production was switched to the Series 200 introduced in April 1968. This featured an extended nose housing a larger baggage compartment, and an expanded rear baggage area.

From the spring of 1969 DHC began delivering the definitive production Twin Otter – the Series 300. Improvements included a large two-part passenger/cargo door on the port side, an additional passenger door to starboard, separate crew doors, increased fuel capacity, optional wingtip tanks, an increase in maximum take-off weight and the powerplant upgraded to the PT6A-27s. The floatplane version of the Series 300 differed in having the shorter nose of the Series 100 fitted.

Special versions of the Series 300 have included the 300S,

Below: Developed as a bushplane, the Twin Otter is very rugged, with exceptional performance. Series 100s (seen here) are identified by their shorter, more rounded nose.

Above: Between 1979 and 1985 the Civil Aviation Administration of China purchased 11 Twin Otter Series 300s for operations in less accessible areas of the country.

Below: The Twin Otter had global appeal, operating on every continent, and sold to both civil and military customers. This example is one of two purchased by Air Mali in 1973.

with upper wing spoilers, high-capacity brakes and an 11-seat cabin. This was developed for operations on the STOLport service, run by Air Canada subsidiary Air Transit Canada, between Ottawa and Montreal. In 1977 a maritime patrol variant was developed for Greenlandair Charter to operate on ice patrol and surveillance duties. It had a Litton LASR-2 search radar in a chin radome, Omega navigation system, four observers' stations with bubble windows, additional fuel capacity, and 'finlets' on the tailplane similar to those installed on floatplane variants.

Optional equipment developed for the Twin Otter included a ventral baggage pannier, a cabin-mounted chemical retardant tank for firefighting missions and oversize low-pressure 'tundra' tyres for soft field operations.

Survey version

Among the most extensively modified examples were two Series 300s delivered to China and Kenya for geophysical survey work. These were equipped with a Scintrex Tridem airborne electromagnetic system housed in two wingtip pods. They also carried a long noseboom housing a proton magnetometer, a VLF electromagnetic system, a radiometric spectrometer sensor in the rear cabin and a strip camera and sophisticated Doppler navigation system for accurate positioning during survey runs.

The Twin Otter's ruggedness and reliability has also resulted in the aircraft being chosen for a number of particularly demanding roles. One Series 300 was flown in support of the British Trans-globe Expedition operating from remote strips. Other Series 300s have been used for many years by the British Antarctic Survey. Able to operate in the harshest of climates, the aircraft supports the British survey team throughout the Antarctic summer and is one of the few aircraft types to have been based on this continent. In the winter the aircraft returns to the United Kingdom for much-needed maintenance.

Throughout the 1970s and 1980s the Twin Otter was in widespread service around the world with both commuter airlines and specialist operators. Since the last of the 844 Twin Otters left DHC's Downsview factory in 1988, the numbers in service (particularly in airline use due to the advent of more efficient types) have steadily declined; however, the Twin Otter's great ability to operate from any terrain in remote areas has ensured its popularity with smaller operators and it is likely to continue its important but little-recognized work well into the twenty-first century.

SPECIFICATION	
de Havilland DHC-6-300 Twin Otter **Type:** utility STOL (short take-off and landing transport) **Powerplant:** two 486-kW (650-hp) Pratt & Whitney Canada PT6A-27 turboprop engines **Maximum speed:** 338 km/h (210 mph) at 3050 m (10,000 ft) **Range:** 1297 km (804 miles) **Service ceiling:** 8140 m (26,700 ft) **Weights:** operating empty 3363 kg	(7,400 lb); maximum take-off 5670 kg (12,474 lb) **Dimensions:** wing span 19.81 m (65 ft); seaplane length 15.09 m (49 ft 5 in); landplane length 15.77 m (51 ft 9 in); height 6.05 m (19 ft 10 in); wing area 39.02 m² (420 sq ft) **Accommodation:** two pilots; 13 to 18 passengers (early aircraft); 20 passengers (later aircraft)

High-lift wing
Along with a high power/weight ratio, the Twin Otter's high-lift wing gives the aircraft its excellent STOL performance. Rectangular in form, the high-mounted mainplanes have a single bracing strut and very effective NACA-type double-slotted flaps along the entire length of their trailing edges. The outer halves act differentially as ailerons for roll control. Wing loading is moderate, allowing good manoeuvrability and a low stalling speed.

Powerplant
Series 200 Twin Otters are powered by two Pratt & Whitney PT6A-20 engines developing 432 kW (579 shp). The Series 300 is fitted with the 462-kW (620-shp) PT6A-27. The three-bladed Hartzell propellers are fully feathering.

Twin Otter Series 300

In the 1980s, a fleet of Twin Otters and DHC-8 Dash 8s was operated on behalf of NorOntair (based at North Bay, Ontario) by other airlines such as Labrador Airways, Air Dale and Bearskin Lake. This Series 300 is painted in the company's standard bright colour scheme which also served as a conspicuity aid during the winter, where aircraft might have had to force-land in the snow. The bird motif represents the loon, a well-known bird of eastern Canada.

Flight crew
The Twin Otter is usually operated by a crew of two, although single-pilot operation is possible. The control column, located on the aircraft's centreline, has 'Y' arms at the top, carrying the pilot's and co-pilot's control wheels.

Reshaped nose
The popularity of the Twin Otter with commuter airlines prompted DHC to fit the Series 200 and 300 with a lengthened nose, containing an additional baggage hold.

De Havilland Canada DHC-7 Dash 7 Civilian STOL

Renowned for its family of rugged 'bush' aircraft and STOL freighters, de Havilland Canada made a bold step into the 'third level' airline market with its outstanding DHC-7 Dash 7.

Many of the 'third level' airlines emerging in the 1960s had a requirement for an aircraft seating 15–20 passengers. DHC's solution was the DHC-6 Twin Otter, a high-wing STOL machine, powered by two PT6A-20 turboprops. As airlines matured and looked for larger aircraft, they had little choice but to consider machines such as Fokker's F27, and DHC realized that there was a strong market opportunity for a new 48-seat aircraft with good field performance that would appeal especially to existing Twin Otter users. The new DHC-7 was conceived and given the obvious but effective name Dash 7.

Design work began in 1972, and the first prototype made its maiden flight on 27 March 1975.

US certification

DHC pressed on urgently with the test flying and soon brought a second prototype into the programme to speed up the certification process.

The Canadian Department of Transport awarded a Canadian-type approval certificate on 19 April 1977, which was followed immediately by FAA type certification. By now, the basic model in standard passenger configuration had been given the designation Dash 7 Series 100 and DHC was ready to begin deliveries.

Sound design concept

The DHC-7 was designed specifically for short-haul routes of around one hour's duration. DHC gave special consideration to environmental factors because of the need for many operators to fly from smaller airports, which were often located close to city centres. As

Above: The high wing of the Dash 7 is an integral part of its STOL design. An additional benefit of such a configuration is ease of passenger access, as the cabin doors are close to the ground.

Top: The first prototype de Havilland Canada Dash 7 is seen flying over Toronto. With its impressive STOL capabilities, the Dash 7 was a worthy successor to the DHC-6 Twin Otter.

a result, the Dash-7 has demonstrated particularly low noise levels and, in testing of the aircraft for approval under the American FAR Part 36 noise regulations, the Dash 7 was

flown into Chicago's Meigs Field Airport at noise levels which were virtually inaudible against a background of normal Chicago road traffic.

DHC aimed to give the Dash 7 excellent short-field performance and it has a FAR Part 25 take-off field length of 689 m (2,260 ft) and a landing distance of 594 m (1,950 ft) at maximum take-off gross weight, at sea level under standard

Both of Inex-Adria Aviopromet's Dash-7 Series 102s are seen outside DHC's factory in October 1982.

Operated by Transport Canada, C-GCFR is a Series 150 modified to Dash 7IR (Ice Reconnaissance) standard. Equipment includes a SLAR in a port fuselage fairing, and an observation cupola.

conditions. The high-aspect ratio wing is fitted with double-slotted large-chord flaps which extend across 80 per cent of the wing span. In addition, the four turboprops are positioned well apart, augmenting the airflow across the wings and flaps with maximum propeller thrust. As a consequence, considerable safety advantages accrue to the Dash 7 in critical 'go-around' situations arising from an aborted landing.

Short-field landings are particularly effective with the combined use of spoilers, propeller pitch control and

standard wheel braking. Normal practice is to move the propellers into ground fine pitch control as soon as the main wheels touch the ground. This neutralizes up to 90 per cent of the wing lift immediately. At the same time, the inboard spoilers are deployed. When the aircraft's nosewheels touch down, the pilot deploys the outboard spoilers and completes the landing run with the anti-skid mainwheel braking system. This ability, along with

the DHC-7's low level of noise emissions, helped to promote fledgling airline services to city

airports, including London's now extremely successful Docklands airport.

SPECIFICATION

de Havilland Canada Dash 7
Type: STOL regional airliner
Powerplant: four 835-kW (1,120-hp) Pratt & Whitney Canada PT6A-50 turboprop engines
Maximum cruising speed: 426 km/h (265 mph)
Range: 1270 km (790 miles)
Initial climb rate: 372 m/min (1,220 fpm)

Service ceiling: 7315 m (24,000 ft)
Weights: empty 12,534 kg (27,633 lb); maximum take-off 21,274 kg (46,902 lb)
Dimensions: wing span 28.35 m (93 ft); length 24.54 m (80 ft 6 in); height 7.96 m (26 ft 2 in); wing area 82.31 m² (886 sq ft)
Accommodation: 50 passengers (standard)

Powerplant
All versions of the Dash 7 were powered by four 835-kW (1,120-shp) Pratt & Whitney Canada PT6A-50 turboprops fitted with four-bladed Hamilton Standard 24 PF constant-speed propellers.

Dash 7 variants
Two basic main variants were developed: the Series 100 (and its Series 101 all-cargo sub-variant); and the Series 150 (and its Series 151 all-cargo sub-variant) with increased weights and extra fuel capacity.

Passenger load
Standard seating is provided for 50 passengers in a four-abreast arrangement with a centre aisle. Alternatively, 56 passengers may be accommodated in a high-density layout.

DHC-7 Dash 7 Series 110

Dash 7 Series 110 G-BRYA, the 62nd aircraft produced, was delivered to Brymon Airways in October 1981 and named *Ville de Paris*. The name was appropriate because it was, at times, operated on behalf of Air France. When Brymon became a subsidiary of British Airways in 1993, the name was changed to *Aberdeenshire/Siorrachd Obar Dheathain*.

High-set tailplane
The high-mounted tailplane of the Dash 7 is kept well clear of the considerable wash from the aircraft's four propellers. Such a configuration must be carefully designed, however, as the tailplane must be mounted high enough to avoid it being aerodynamically blanked by the wing at high angles of attack. Such blanking can result in a deep stall and catastrophic loss of control.

Turnaround
With its ability to use short runway lengths and to make steep landing approaches, the Dash 7 is able to fit into otherwise crowded airport traffic patterns. This effectively increases airport capacity, while the DHC-7's ability to disembark and re-embark passengers quickly increases the cost-effectiveness of the aircraft.

Fuel capacity
Each wing contains two integral fuel tanks giving the Series 100 a total capacity of 5652 litres (1,243 Imp gal). Refuelling is accomplished via a single pressure refuelling point on the underside of the rear fuselage.

Bombardier Dash 8 Q Series Canadian commuter

By the late 1980s the Dash 8 had established itself, along with the ATR 42, as a market leader for the 40-passenger commuter aircraft market. Domestic operators in this role included Canadian Airlines (seen here) and Air Canada.

Previously renowned for its rugged bushplanes, de Havilland Canada placed its faith in a new market – commuterliners. The Dash 8 introduced a new level of sophistication and remains in production by Bombardier in a number of distinct variants today.

During the 1970s de Havilland Canada began studying the prospects for an aircraft to fill the gap between the DHC-6 Twin Otter, typically seating 20, and the Dash 7 seating around 50. By 1979 these studies had crystallised into the Dash-X project, disclosed at that year's Paris Air Show. On 2 April 1980 it accepted an order from NorOntair for two, designated as DHC-8s, or Dash 8s, showing that the design was going ahead. The first of four flight prototypes made its maiden flight on 20 June 1983. Orders came in a healthy stream, reaching 137 by mid-1987 and topping 150 by 1988.

In planning the Dash 8, careful note was taken of changing requirements. There was never any doubt that the aircraft should have a high wing, two turboprops, a pressurized cabin and good STOL qualities. At the same time, it was clear that almost all sectors would be flown from reasonable airports, and the field length was pitched at the 1000-m (3,280-ft) level, appreciably longer than for all previous DHC aircraft. This fitted in well with the modest size of wing needed for cruising faster than the Dash 7, in order to get close to jet schedules on short sectors within the United States.

At an early date, 36 seats was decided upon as the optimum size, and this has continued to be a popular size, although – like almost all its rivals – the Dash 8 has since been developed into a number of stretched versions. With the wholly conventional wing design more or less decided, attention was turned to powerplant choice. After carefully looking at the General Electric CT7, de Havilland Canada's choice of engine predictably fell on the home product, the Pratt & Whitney Canada PW120A turboprop, rated at 1432 kW (1,800 shp). The aircraft's original 3.96-m (13-ft) diameter propellers were Hamilton Standard, each with four glass-fibre blades.

The fuselage is of almost circular section, with a maximum diameter of 2.69 m (8 ft 10 in). Again, the structure is conventional, with adhesively bonded stringers and cut-out reinforcement. Almost the only striking feature is the nose, which is a long pointed cone angled downwards so that its upper line almost follows the angle of the pilots' windscreens. The latter are flat, while the large side windows are curved and bear structural loads in flight. There is a passenger/crew door forward on the port side, with integral airstairs, and a baggage/cargo door on the same side behind the wing. The 9.20-m (30-ft) long passenger cabin of the original aircraft normally has nine rows of 2+2 seats, each row being opposite a window. The rear compartment area is 8.5 m³ (300 cu ft) and can accept a spare engine or 907 kg (2,000 lb) of cargo (depending on the amount of baggage).

Dutch airline Schreiner Airways operated Dash 8 Series 300s on behalf of SABENA of Belgium. The aircraft had a single-class configuration for 48 passengers.

Austrian carrier Tyrolean has been a staunch supporter of the type since receiving its first Series 100 aircraft in May 1985. The airline has since acquired the Series 300 and Series 400.

Left: The increased capacity of the Series 300 appealed to airlines such as Lufthansa CityLine, helping to decrease the seat cost/mile ratio.

Below: Great China Airlines (now Uni Air) was the launch customer for the Series 400 (illustrated), ordering six with six options. It now operates Q200s, Dash 8-300s and Q300s.

There is normally a toilet and small buffet. A movable rear bulkhead enables mixed passenger/cargo operations to be flown, and the Dash 8 can be operated in the all-cargo mode, in which case the payload is 4268 kg (9,409 lb). Normal fuel capacity is some 3160 litres (695 Imperial gallons), in integral tanks outboard of the engines. Auxiliary long-range tanks can be provided. The Dash 8 can fly four 185-km (115-mile) sectors with full payload on internal fuel, or a single sector of 1650 km (1,025 miles).

New versions

Early in the 1980s de Havilland Canada (DHC) planned a Dash 8 Series 200, with 1614-kW (2,200-shp) PW122 engines, and displayed a model of a proposed 200M in anti-submarine warfare configuration. This subsequently gave way to the more developed Triton maritime patrol version of the Series 300. The latter was announced in 1985 and first flown (by stretching the first prototype Dash 8) on 15 May 1987. It had 1775-kW (2,380-shp) PW123 engines and fuselage plugs ahead of and behind the wings, extending the fuselage by 3.43 m (11 ft 3 in) to provide standard seating for 50 passengers.

Wingtip extensions increased the span from 25.91 m (85 ft) to 27.43 m (90 ft). Other changes include dual ECS air-conditioning packs, a Turbomach T-40 APU, a rear service door on the starboard side and more space for toilets and coat-hanging. Maximum weight is increased from 14,968 kg (32,402 lb) to 18,642 kg (41,000 lb). Cruising speed is increased to a maximum of (526 km/h (326 mph), but there is little change in other aspects of performance. Deliveries began in February 1989, immediately following certification.

In June 1987 DHC, by now a subsidiary of Boeing, disclosed its interest in a further stretched version – the Series 400. This had additional plugs added to the front and rear fuselage, extending the length by a further 6.83 m (22 ft 5 in) to 32.84 m (107 ft 9 in), allowing the aircraft to seat up to 78 passengers.

In 1990 the improved Series 100A was introduced, with a restyled interior and PW120A engines. However, at this time Boeing announced its intention to sell DHC and in January 1992 the company was absorbed by Bombardier Inc. of Canada.

Bombardier's stewardship has seen the progressive introduction of new models, including the Series 100B with PW121 engines allowing enhanced airfield and climb performance, the Series 200A which is an increased payload/ performance version of the 100A with PW123C engines, the 200B with PW123D engines for full power at high ambient temperatures, the Series 300A/B/C which have, respectively, increased payload/ range, airfield performance and hot-and-high performance and the Series 400.

Q Series

Bombardier redesignated the production versions Dash 8 Q100, Q200, Q300 and Q400 in 1996, in recognition of a redesigned interior and noise and vibration suppression system (NVS), which reduced cabin noise levels by 12 dB. It uses the slogan 'The Quiet One' to promote the series.

Today, all four variants of the Dash 8 remain in production, with the first Q400s having been delivered in 1999. Total orders for the Dash 8 series have exceeded 780 and, although the introduction of the new generation of regional jets has undoubtedly affected sales, Bombardier is confident that the aircraft will remain in production for many more years. Indeed, the company currently has an order backlog of two Q200s, 23 Q300s and 50 Q400s.

SPECIFICATION	
de Havilland Canada Dash 8 Series 300A **Type:** twin-turboprop regional transport **Powerplant:** two 1175-kW (2,380-hp) Pratt & Whitney Canada PW 123A turboprop engines **Maximum cruising speed:** 532 km/h (330 mph) **Take-off field length:** 1085 m (3,360 ft) **Maximum climb rate:** 549 m/min (1,800 fpm)	**Range:** 1527 km (950 miles) **Service ceiling:** 7620 m (25,000 ft) **Weights:** operating empty 11,666 kg (25,655 lb); maximum take-off 18,642 kg (41,012 lb) **Dimensions:** wing span 27.43 m (90 ft); length 25.68 m (84 ft 3 in); height 7.49 m (24 ft 7 in); wing area 56.21 m² (605 sq ft) **Accommodation:** maximum 56 passengers

Military operators

The only non-standard aircraft of the original Series 100s were six for the Canadian Department of National Defence. Two of these were CC-142 transports and were fitted with rough-field landing gear, strong cargo floors, long-range tanks and special avionics. The other four were CT-142 navigation trainers, distinguished by their extended noses. Even more remarkable aircraft are the two E-9As (left) completed by Sierra Research of Buffalo for the USAF. These are flying datalinks operating up to 370 km (230 miles) off the Florida coast, performing radar surveillance and sending back voice and telemetry data during test, training and drone operations. Equipment includes a large, electronically-steerable, phased-array radar in a fairing on the right side of the fuselage, an APS-128D sea surveillance radar in a ventral radome and extensive internal avionics. The only other military operator is Kenya, which operates three Series 103s in the transport role.

Bombardier CRJ Canada's commuter

The Bombardier CRJ is a ground-breaking aircraft. It was the first of the new breed of regional jet airliners that were to sweep the airline marketplace during the 1990s. Based on the proven Challenger business jet family, the CRJ has given birth to a whole new family of its own, with a range of versions in production.

Canadair was already a well-established firm when it was acquired by Bombardier in 1986. Canadair's main product was the wide-bodied Challenger business jet and this twin-engined, T-tailed design was to become the basis for a whole new class of aircraft – backed by substantial funding from Bombardier.

Using a stretched Challenger airframe, Canadair launched its Regional Jet – a type of aircraft which conventional wisdom had always decreed could not exist. The argument, until then, had always been that only turboprops could operate on routes of less than 500 miles (805 km), with relatively small passenger loads (40/50 seats). The counter argument ran that the latest developments in small turbofan engines could make the figures for the institution of

jets work and that passengers would always choose jet-powered aircraft in any case – once one airline introduced jets on its regional routes, the others would be forced to follow.

Design finalization

By June 1988 Canadair had decided on the fundamental design features of its Regional Jet. The aircraft was, indeed, a scaled-up Challenger 601, stretched to accommodate 50 passengers and powered by two General Electric CF34-3A turbofan engines. The Regional Jet was launched on 31 March 1989 with 56 commitments, but only one identified firm customer – Lufthansa subsidiary DLT, which had signed for six firm aircraft, and six options.

In June 1989 Bombardier bought the Northern Ireland-based firm Short Brothers, which became the chief provider of sub-assemblies for the Regional Jet programme. This also had the useful side effect of eliminating Short's competing FJX design. At the same time, however, the Brazilian company EMBRAER announced its own EMB-145 proposal for a regional jet airliner, and one which would

Capable of nonstop services over 2,265 miles (3646 km), the Bombardier CRJ100LR was the longest-range version of the original 100 Series. Lauda Air was the launch customer and received eight examples between 1994 and 1996.

become the Canadair Regional Jet's main rival.

During 1989 the Regional Jet's order book expanded to 126 commitments from nine customers. On 15 May 1990 DLT signed the first firm contract for a Regional Jet, ordering 13 aircraft and securing 12 options. Final assembly of the first aircraft began in late 1990 and, at that year's Farnborough Air Show (in September), Canadair announced a growth version of the original Regional Jet 100, the Regional

Jet 100ER. This version had a higher maximum take-off weight, with an additional centre fuel tank to extend range.

The first Regional Jet was rolled out on 6 May 1991 and made its maiden flight on 10 May. Following a 1400-hour, 14-month test programme, the RJ was awarded its Canadian Type Approval on 31 July 1992, although US and European certification was delayed by several months.

The aircraft's name has changed several times over the

Above: The CRJ200 cockpit display includes an integrated all-digital suite with dual primary flight displays and dual multi-function displays. A ground-proximity warning system (GPWS) and a windshear detection system are fitted as standard.

Left: Lufthansa CityLine remains one of the most significant CRJ operator outside the United States. The airline has 43 CRJ100LR/200LRs and 20 of the larger CRJ700 in service.

Left: Skywest is one of a number of airlines which operate the CRJ200 and CRJ700 on connection flights for the major carriers. Skywest's 134 CRJ200s are flown in Delta Connection (left) and United Express colours.

Below: Air Nostrum operates under a franchise agreement with Iberia of Spain, its aircraft flying in Iberia Regional colours. The airline has, so far, received 32 of 56 CRJ200ERs ordered.

intervening years, abbreviated first to RJ and then expanded to CRJ, in the late 1990s, in order to differentiate it from the competing 'RJs' that have sprung up. The first RJ100 was delivered to Lufthansa CityLine (into which DLT had been merged) on 19 October 1992. Full JAA certification was awarded on 14 January 1993, by which time CityLine had three aircraft in service. The US RJ launch operator, Comair, took delivery of its first aircraft on 29 April 1993, and put the type into service on 1 June.

The Xerox Corporation placed a new development of the RJ into service in January 1994,

when it took delivery of the first Corporate Regional Jet. An extended-range corporate version, the Special Edition, was launched in 1995. In February 1994 Canadair announced the introduction of the RJ100LR (Long Range), along with a series of improvements to the both the RJ100 and the RJ100ER.

The RJ100 was replaced by the CRJ200 as the standard production version in 1996 and the first delivery was made to Tyrolean Airways on 15 January. The CRJ200 is powered by improved CF34-3B1 engines and so can cruise higher, further and faster than the RJ100, with a

50-passenger load. CRJ200ER and CRJ200LR versions, with higher operating weights and increased range, are also available. The latter version has a maximum range of 3713 km (2,307 miles). Three equivalent hot-and-high versions – the CRJ200B, CRJ200BER and CRJ200BLR – have modified CF34-3B1 engines.

Fuselage stretch

On 27 May 1999 the prototype of the 70-seat CRJ700 made its maiden flight. The CRJ700 (previously known as the CRJ-X) was launched in 1997, and Brit Air received the first aircraft in February 2001. The stretched CRJ700 is powered by the CF34-8. The standard CRJ700 Series 701 seats between

64 and 70 passengers, while the Series 705 seats 75.

In October 1999 Bombardier announced the 90-seat CRJ900, which is based on the CRJ700 with two additional fuselage plugs, taking the aircraft's overall length to 36.19 m (118 ft 9 in). The basic aircraft has an 86- to 90-passenger interior with two-by-two seating at a pitch of 78.70 cm (31 in). Other new features include 5 per cent higher-thrust CF34-8C5 engines, strengthened landing gear, increased underfloor baggage capacity with an additional underfloor baggage door and two additional overwing emergency exits. Like the CRJ700, the CRJ900 is available in ER (extended-range) and LR (long-range) versions.

Above: The CRJ100/200 has been purchased in small numbers by major corporations attracted by the aircraft's economy and low noise signature, as well as by commuter and regional airlines.

Below: First flying in May 1999, the CRJ700 is a 70-seat derivative of the CRJ200. Orders currently stand at 295, with entry into service, with Brit Air, occurring in February 2001.

SPECIFICATION	
Bombardier CRJ100	(47,450 lb) maximum
Type: regional jet airliner	take-off weight
Powerplant: two 41-kN (9220-lb-thrust) GE CFE34-3A1 turbofans	**Dimensions:** wing span 21.21 m (69 ft 7in); length 26.77 m
Maximum cruising speed: 851 km/h (529 mph)	(87 ft 10 in); height 6.22 m (20 ft 5 in); wing area 54.5 m²
Range: 1818 km (1128 miles)	(587.1 sq ft)
Service ceiling: 12,500 m (41,000 ft)	**Accommodation:** flight crew of two;
Weights: operating empty 13,653 kg (30,100 lb); 21,523 kg	up to 52 passengers typical layout; 52 passengers maximum

Fokker F27 Friendship/50 Dutch twin

First flown in 1955, the F27 exceeded Fokker's expectations in terms of sales, becoming one of the world's most successful twin-turboprop airliners, and leading to the new-generation Fokker 50.

Following World War II, Fokker was keen to develop a design to target the DC-3 replacement market. Hampered by a lack of funding for its new project, in 1948 Fokker sent designers to Boeing and Canadair to validate the concept. In contrast to the North American companies, Fokker intended to adopt a turboprop powerplant, giving advantages in terms of weight, smoothness and reliability.

Initial response

Building on its pre-war civil aviation experience, in August 1950 Fokker introduced its P.275 design. This incorporated a high-aspect-ratio wing and 32 seats, and offered optimum efficiency in cruising flight. The Armstrong Siddeley Mamba engine was considered, before Fokker opted

for the Rolls-Royce Dart. In 1952, the P.275 – now redesignated F27 – went ahead, with advanced features such as the extensive use of fibreglass for unstressed parts and pressurization.

In 1953, following Dutch government approval and funding, the go-ahead was given for two prototypes, plus static and fatigue test airframes. Concurrently, Handley Page was tailoring its similar four-engined Herald in response to global operators' requirements. The piston-engined competitor appeared in 1955, as Fokker began talks with Fairchild in the United States with a view to a licence agreement in Maryland. Resisting the US firm's desire for piston engines, Fokker persuaded Fairchild to sign its deal on 26 April 1956.

The first prototype F27 began trial flights on 24 November 1955, helping to clinch the Fairchild deal.

In Australia, Trans Australia Airlines (TAA) persuaded Fokker to strengthen the F27's wing

Above: The first prototype Fokker F27 (PH-NIV) had 1044-kW (1,400-hp) Dart 507 turboprops and a 73-ft (22.25-m) long fuselage, features that were revised on the second prototype.

Top: NLM Cityhopper, later absorbed by the Dutch national carrier KLM, flew the Friendship in its Mk 200, 400 and 500 guises, the example illustrated being an F27 Mk 500.

and add a modernized interior with four more seats. TAA ordered six aircraft on 9 March 1956, following orders by Aer Lingus and Braathens.

Fairchild, marketing the aircraft as the F-27 in the United States, received orders from West Coast, Bonanza and Piedmont. Sales over the next two years continued apace, but 1958 saw only eight Fokker and 16 Fairchild

orders. With costly tooling now complete the first production F27 flew on 23 March 1958, followed by the first F27 on 14 April. West Coast flew the first commercial service on 28 September 1958.

The fifth F27 Friendship off the production line was delivered to Aer Lingus on 19 November 1958. A Mk 100 airliner with Dart 511 turboprops, the aircraft went on to serve for over 25 years, with operators which included NZ National Airways Corporation and Air New Zealand.

Orders for the F27 picked up in 1959, keeping the Amsterdam production line busy. Later developments saw major sub-components being built across Europe, while the US production line closed in July 1973, after producing 173 aircraft, despite the introduction of the FH-227 (with stretched 52-seat fuselage) after the merger of Fairchild and Hiller in 1964.

The American-built FH-227 (illustrated), which first flew on 27 January 1966, featured a 1.83-m (6-ft) fuselage stretch. In total, 79 of the variant were produced. Fokker also built a stretched F27 variant, the Mk 500, which flew in November 1967.

Increased range

Requiring increased range, several customers prompted Fokker to develop the standard Friendship 200 model (Dart 528 engines) with increased fuel capacity. Subsequently, this aircraft was re-engined with the 1700-ekW (2,280-ehp) Dart 532-7 (and later 536-7R) and, from the early 1980s, hush kits were supplied, significantly reducing noise, in particular that of the notoriously loud first-stage compressor. By now the Dart was becoming aged, with poor fuel economy by modern standards. However, Rolls-Royce decided not to proceed with a replacement, leaving the F27 apparently stranded with uncompetitive engines in a marketplace that was, by the 1980s, dominated by newer turboprop designs. As a stop-gap measure, Rolls-Royce had introduced its upgraded Dart 551 engine and this became available as a retro-kit for earlier airframes.

Fokker watched the situation with disquiet, as the F27 approached the early 1980s with diminishing sales. With the company focusing on its F28 jetliner, it appeared likely that the Friendship would disappear. However, with a new interest in local-service turboprop airliners emerging, the stage was now set for the appearance of an F27 successor, which began life as the P.335, before appearing in 1985 as the Fokker 50.

Fokker 50

In 1983 on the F27's 25th anniversary in service, Fokker announced the Fokker 50 (F50). Similar in size and configuration to the F27, the F50 (so-called because of its seating configuration) featured new Pratt & Whitney PW120 series engines with six-bladed propellers, substantial use of composite materials and a totally redesigned Honeywell EFIS cockpit. The wing was also much improved and featured small 'Fokklets' (or winglets). From a passenger's point of view, a less satisfactory change was the removal of the F27's large windows in favour of an increased number of smaller ones.

The first two prototypes were modified from F27s, and Fokker's official documentation and some registration certificates referred to the F50 as the F27-050.

Ansett Transport Industries placed the launch order for 15 aircraft. The first flight took place on 28 December 1985, followed by the first production F50 on 13 February 1987. Deliveries commenced to Lufthansa CityLine on 7 August 1987, although the first revenue service was made by DLT.

The baseline model was the Fokker 50 Series 100 powered by PW125B engines. Depending on the seating configuration, which can range from 46 to 68, the Series 100 was further divided into the Fokker 50-100 (with four doors) and Fokker 50-120 (three doors).

By early 1993, Fokker was delivering the F50 Series 300. This PW127B-powered, hot-and-high version was first ordered by Avianca, and was available in F50-300 and F50-320 models. Fokker also considered a stretched version as the Fokker 50 Series 400.

In 1993 DASA acquired 51 per cent of the Fokker company, which by this time was suffering from financial difficulties. In January 1996, however, DASA withdrew its financial investment and the company was declared bankrupt in March. Fokker was unable to find a saviour and once outstanding orders had been fulfilled all manufacture of the F50 ceased.

Production totalled 205 Fokker 50s and four military Fokker 60s, but had the company remained liquid the aircraft would undoubtedly have gained many additional customers.

Major purchasers of the Fokker 50 included Air UK (nine), Ansett (12), Austrian Airlines (8), Avianca (10), DLT/Lufthansa CityLine (34), KLM Cityhopper (10), Maersk Air (8), Malaysia Airlines (11), Philippine Airlines (10) and SAS Commuter (22).

SPECIFICATION	
Fokker F27 Mk 300 Friendship	**Service ceiling:** 9020 m (29,600 ft)
Type: passenger transport	**Weights:** empty 10,257 kg
Powerplant: two 1424-kW	(22,612 lb); maximum take-off
(1,910-hp) Royce Dart Mk 528-7E	17,710 kg (39,044 lb)
turboprop engines, eaching	**Dimensions:** wing span 29.00 m
pvoiding an addition 2.25 kN	(95 ft 2 in); length 23.50 m (77 ft
(506 lb) of auxiliary thrust	1 in); height 8.40 m (27 ft 7 in);
Cruising speed: 428 km/h (266 mph)	wing area 70.00 m² (754 sq ft)
at 6100 m (20,000 ft)	**Accommodation:** two pilots, flight
Range: 2010 km (1,249 miles) with	attendant and 40 passengers
3050-kg 6,724-lb) payload and	(standard), or 52 passengers in
maximum fuel	a high-density layout

Sudan Airways received its first two Fokker 50s in August 1989, and has four of the type in service today. PW125B engines combined with the Dowty six-bladed composite propellers endow the F50 with a 12 per cent greater cruising speed than that of the F27.

Fokker F70/F100 A new fellowship

Fokker's 70 was fighting for orders in a fiercely competitive marketplace when the company went bankrupt. Competition from rival types such as the 146/RJ family and CRJ contributed to Fokker's downfall.

AirUK received 17 Fokker 100s. The carrier has since become part of the KLM group and 15 F100s continue to fly under the KLM 'cityhopper uk' banner.

The Fokker 100 and 70 – the JetLine as they became known – were logical follow-ons from the successful F28 series. These next-generation aircraft proved popular, particularly with established Fokker customers, but the Dutch manufacturer found itself hamstrung by high production costs and a difficult market, factors that eventually drove it to bankruptcy.

By the late 1970s Fokker was already searching for a new design to replace its F28 Fellowship. The obvious first step was a stretched 100- to 130-seat 'Super F28', and plans were drawn up to offer such an aircraft by 1984. Airlines were then still wary of 'small' jets, however, and Fokker felt that there were better sales prospects for a larger aircraft. The 'Super F28' design became the 150-seat F29, although exactly what this aircraft would be remained

unclear. At one stage, Fokker was believed to be discussing the use of Boeing 737 fuselage sections. Fokker then joined forces with McDonnell Douglas on the MDF 100 design, but this was quietly abandoned in the late 1980s. Fokker was left to come up with the design and funding for a new aircraft of its own, returning to the proven formula of the F28 for its inspiration.

In November 1983 Fokker announced that it was working on a 100-seat F28 development. It was launched as the Fokker 100 (F100), alongside the turboprop

Fokker 50 (a developed F27 Friendship). The $14.9-million F100 would be available for delivery in early 1987 and Fokker predicted a market for 750 aircraft.

The new aircraft used an F28 airframe, stretched by 5.51 m (18 ft 10 in) compared to that of the F28-2000. It would carry up to 107 passengers. The F100 also had a new, longer wing, a 'glass' cockpit and Rolls-Royce Tay turbofans. Early versions were powered by the 61.6-kN (13,850-lb-st) Tay 650-15 engine, but these were later replaced by uprated Tay 650-15s, offering 67.19 kN (15,100 lb st).

Fokker went into partnership with several other European manufacturers and a few US

companies, all of which supplied F100 components.

The launch customer was Swissair, which ordered eight aircraft to replace early-model DC-9s, in July 1984. Fokker then endured a wait of almost a year before another airline signed for the F100. This was KLM, which ordered 10 aircraft in May 1985. The up-engined version was launched with an important order from American Airlines in August 1985. American initially ordered just 10 aircraft, but this total was later revised upwards to an astonishing 75.

Production line changes

Fokker was forced to make several changes to the F100 on the production line as a result of customer demands, including the addition of a full six-screen Collins EFIS cockpit (with a Honeywell FMS) and increasing the operating weights. Fokker also suffered manufacturing delays caused by launching two major new aircraft projects in parallel. As a result of this, the predicted first flight was delayed from mid-1986, and certification was pushed back to autumn 1987. The prototype F100 finally made its maiden flight on 30 November 1986.

American Airlines' final four F100s out of a once-sizeable fleet are for sale. The excellence of the Dutch product allowed it to make considerable headway into the US market, where airlines have a reputation for choosing 'home-grown' aircraft.

KLM's mainline fleet briefly included a handful of F100s (illustrated).

and Dutch type approval was awarded on 14 October 1994. The first production aircraft was delivered to the Ford Motor Company, as a corporate shuttle, on 25 October 1994. The first delivery to an airline was made to Sempati Air on 9 March 1995.

On 9 June 1994 Fokker delivered its 250th jet to an American airline – the 75th for American Airlines – but things had been increasingly difficult since the DASA takeover. A crowded marketplace and cut-throat competition were hitting its well-built but expensive aircraft. By 1996 the workforce had been cut in half. Then, in January 1996, Daimler-Benz (as DASA had become) withdrew its investment. When no other buyers came forward, Fokker was forced to declare bankruptcy on 15 March.

Limited production continued under the liquidators, mostly finishing off uncompleted aircraft, but the end of Fokker brought an end to the Fokker Jetliners. The last F100 was delivered to TAM Brasil on 21 March 1996 and the last F70 went to KLM cityhopper on 18 April 1997. In all, 280 F100s and 45 F70s were built.

SPECIFICATION

Fokker F100
Type: twin-engined regional airliner
Powerplant: two 44-kN (9,900-lb-thrust) Rolls-Royce Tay Mk 620-15 turbofans
Maximum speed: 861 km/h (534 mph) at operating altitude
Range: 1380 km (856 miles) with maximum load
Service ceiling: 10,670 m (35,000 ft)

Weights: empty 23,250 kg (51,150 lb); maximum take-off 41,500 kg (91,300 lb)
Dimensions: wing span 28.08 m (92 ft 1 in); length 35.31 m (115 ft 10 in); height 8.50 m (27 ft 10 in); wing area 93.50 m² (1,006 sq ft)
Accommodation: four crew (two flight deck and two cabin attendants) and 107 passengers

The F100 was finally certified by the Dutch authorities on 20 November 1987. Swissair took delivery of its first aircraft on 9 February 1988 and placed the type into service on 3 April. The first F100 to fly with the uprated engines took to the skies on 8 July 1988; its arrival triggered American Airlines' 75-aircraft order in February 1989. The more powerful F100 was certified on 30 May 1989 and the first delivery was made to USAir on 1 July. USAir (now US Airways) went on to acquire 40 F100s.

Fokker 70

Several developments of the F100 – most notably the 80-seat Fokker 80 and the larger Fokker 130 – were examined before the 70-seat Fokker 70 was settled on in 1992. Equivalent in size to the F28-4000, powered by the Tay 620 engine, it would launch the development of the Fokker JetLine family of regional jets. However, Fokker became mired in discussions with its new owner, DASA, which took over in 1993. As a result, F70 development and marketing

were hampered and the programme went ahead without any firm orders. The second F100 prototype was cut down to produce the first F70, which made its first flight on 2 April 1993. The F70 programme was formally launched at the 1983 Paris Air Show, where Sempati Air and Pelita Air Services announced combined orders for 15, with five options. British Midland became the European launch customer on 16 November 1993 when it signed a long-term lease for five F70s and four F100s. In the United States, Mesa Air became the first customer, on 10 December 1993, when it signed for two (with options on six more).

Into liquidation

During 1994, the F70 had a very successful flight-test programme, the aircraft proving to be faster and quieter than expected. FAA

Right: In addition to its noticeably shorter fuselage, the Fokker 70 omits a pair of overwing emergency exits when compared to the F100.

Left: The main light-alloy structure of the F100 has a 45,000-cycle crack-free life, while the control surfaces, fairings and the cabin floor are of composites. Externally, however, the aircraft is similar to the F28 Mk 4000. Like Fokker, Air Inter has ceased trading.

ATR 42/ATR 72 Franco-Italian success

The Avions de Transport Régional family of twin-engined airliners was the result of successful collaboration between France's Aérospatiale and Italy's Alenia, both newcomers to the regional airline market. Despite this, the ATR 42 and 72 have been a tremendous success, notching up healthy worldwide sales.

Nord (which was later absorbed by Aérospatiale) had enjoyed a brief foray into the design of turboprop commuter aircraft with the Nord 262, and had played a major part in the development of the highly successful military Transall. In Italy, Alenia's experience of turboprop aircraft had been limited to the G222 military tactical transport. During the late 1970s, however, it became increasingly clear that there would be a healthy market for 30- to 50-seat turboprop regional

aircraft during the next decade, and the two companies teamed up (as Avions de Transport Régional, or ATR), to develop a new-technology regional airliner. During much the same period, de Havilland Canada began work on the broadly similar DHC-8, Saab-Fairchild on their 340, Aero on the L-610, Fokker on the F50, and BAe on the ATP.

The ATR 42 was formally launched in October 1981, after selection of the Pratt & Whitney PW120 turboprop as the powerplant of choice, and following finalization of the T-tail and high-wing configuration.

The first of two prototype ATR 42s made its maiden flight on 16 August 1984, and the first production aircraft followed on 30 April 1985. The aircraft carried a flight crew of two on the modern flight deck, and was able to seat up to a maximum of 50 passengers. The aircraft has

Being built by Aérospatiale and Alenia, which have both been involved in high-tech ventures, the basic ATR 42 is available with a number of advanced features. Overcomplexity has been avoided, however, as the aircraft was aimed at a market that required a 'workhorse rather than a racehorse'.

dynamic sound absorbers in its fuselage adjacent to the plane of the propellers, with skin damping fore and aft of the wing. Active noise control is offered as a customer option. Composites are used on the leading edges (Kevlar/Nomex sandwich) and on control surface skins, nose and tailcone, landing gear doors and wing/fuselage fairings.

The initial production variant was the PW120-powered ATR-42-300, which gave way to the ATR 42-400 and ATR 42-500 in 1996. (The ATR 42-320 was similar to the -300, but with PW121 engines).

The ATR 42-400 introduced PW121A engines and six-bladed

propellers, and made its maiden flight on 12 July 1995. The ATR 42-500 remains the primary ATR 42 variant, with more powerful PW127E engines and many features borrowed from the newer ATR 72. The prototype ATR 42-500 made its maiden flight on 16 September 1994.

Other ATR 42 variants ito be produced included the ATR 42 Cargo, with a 'quick-change' interior, and the similar ATR 42L with a lateral cargo door. The ATR 42F was a military freighter, of which one was delivered to Gabon in 1989.

Stretched ATR

The increased-capacity ATR 72 was announced in 1985, and the first of three development aircraft made its maiden flight on 27 October 1988. The new

As a subsidiary of American Airlines, American Eagle provides feeder services across the United States. American Eagle has been the largest operator of the ATR 42/72 series, its subsidiaries still retaining an ATR 42 and some 42 ATR 72s.

Left: RFG Regional was a German commuter airline which possessed 12 ATR 42-300s, purchased from 1989 onwards. In 1993, the airline was merged with Eurowings, which went on to purchase further ATR 42s and ATR 72s and now has a fleet of 24 ATR 42/72s.

Below: Prior to its bankruptcy, Pan Am operated six ATR 42s on regional and short-range flights. This example was photographed over Toulouse prior to delivery and, although it wears Pan Am colours, it carries a French test registration.

type had its fuselage stretched by 4.5 m (4 ft 9 in), and it was also given new, increased-span mainly composite outer wing panels, and greater fuel capacity.

The baseline ATR 72-200 was powered by PW124B engines. The hot-and-high ATR 72-210 possessed the same, more powerful PW127 engines as the ATR 42-500. There was a further improved hot-and-high version, the ATR 72-210A, with more powerful PW127F engines driving six-bladed propellers and these engines remain standard on the current ATR 72-500 production variant.

The ATR 42 intially formed the basis of the ATR 42MP maritime patroller and latterly the multi-role Surveyor. Other specialized versions of the aircraft are available, including the ATR 42 In-flight Inspection designed for airfield and en-route navigation and landing aid calibration

duties, and Corporate versions of both the ATR 42 and 72.

ATR 72-only developments include the ATR 72 ASW which combines the mission systems of the ATR 42MP with a rotary sonobuoy launcher, MAD (magnetic anomaly detector), provision for torpedoes and other equipment to provide a multi-role capability against submarines and surface vessels, as well as advanced patrol and search-and-rescue abilities.

ATR merger and beyond

In January 1997, ATR became part of the larger Aero International (Regional) or AI(R) Consortium, which included the Jetstream and BAe 146 (Avro RJ) business of BAe. Under this arrangement, AI(R) marketed, sold and supported the aircraft within the consortium. The company has reportedly held discussions with the Chinese

Xian factory and there were reports that ATR might team up with Fairchild-Dornier, but in the end no alliance was formed and the AI(R) group was dissolved.

Today ATR continues to successfully market and develop its turboprop range and, with some signs of an increase in interest in turboprop commuter aircraft, the future looks bright for this successful design.

SPECIFICATION	
ATR-42-300	**Service ceiling:** 3140 m (10,302 ft)
Type: short-haul twin-turboprop regional airliner and cargo aircraft	**Weights:** empty 10,285 kg (22,674 lb); loaded 16,700 kg (36,817 lb)
Powerplant: two 1342-kW (1,800-hp) Pratt & Whitney Canada PW 120 turboprops	**Dimensions:** wing span 24.57 m (80 ft 7 in); length 22.67 m (74 ft 4 in); height 7.58 m (24 ft 10 in); wing area 54.50 m2 (543 sq ft)
Maximum speed: 463 km/h (305 mph)	
Initial climb rate: 640 m/min (2,100 fpm)	**Accommodation:** up to 50 at maximum density in four-abreast layout
Range: 1946 km (1,209 miles) with 45 passengers	

Above: The principal production ATR 42 since 1996, the -500 has more powerful PW 127E engines, reinforced wings and improved electrical systems.

Left: By July 2005 348 ATR 72s had been ordered, in addition to more than 390 examples of the shorter ATR 42.

CASA CN-235 Multi-role airlifter

Left: In military guise the CN-235 can carry up to 46 troops or 48 paratroops. Simultaneous deployment of paratroops on either side of the fuselage allows more rapid egress over the drop zone.

Below: The Royal Saudi Air Force purchased four CASA-built CN-235M-10s, which are operated by No. 1 Squadron (Royal Flight). The aircraft are used for VIP/governmental transport duties.

The CASA, previously Airtech, CN-235 has won a substantial portion of the international market for light tactical military transports. The joint Spanish–Indonesian design never won the airline orders it once sought, but instead its military versions have been steadily expanded and improved, and joined by the CASA-only stretched C-295.

During the 1970s the state aircraft manufacturers in Spain and Indonesia – CASA and IPTN – established a long-distance working relationship that saw CASA's Aviocar light transport built under licence on the other side of the world. After a few short years of partnership the two unveiled an ambitious plan to build a new and much larger transport. In 1980 the Airtech consortium was established to handle design and production of the new 35-seat aircraft aimed at both civil and military markets.

Dubbed CN-235, the project received its formal launch at the 1981 Paris Air Show and was hailed as a promising design. In its early stages the CN-235 was positioned chiefly as a civil aircraft, but could not have been more different to contemporaries such as the Dash 8, EMB-120 or the SF-340. First and foremost, it was optimized for operations from unprepared airstrips. Its high wing, prominent undercarriage sponsors, upswept rear fuselage and rear ramp gave made it look like a 'mini Hercules'. The aircraft had several military features, such as a main undercarriage housing with no doors that allowed the wheels to protrude slightly and protect the aircraft in the event of a forced landing. The air-operable rear ramp used a two-section door and two rear cabin doors were provided for paradropping.

Power was supplied by a pair of 1311-kW (1,760-shp) General Electric CT7-7 turboprop engines. Production of structural components was shared between CASA (forward and centre fuselage, wing centre section, inboard flaps, engine nacelles) and IPTN (rear fuselage, tail unit, outer wings, outboard flaps), with separate production lines in each country. Later, a subcontract for elements of the tail unit was awarded to Chile's ENAER, by CASA.

CASA and IPTN staged a dual roll-out ceremony of the first prototypes, held at the same (local) time on 10 September 1983. The first Spanish-built aircraft made its maiden flight on 11 November 1983, followed by Indonesia's example on 30 December 1983. As the flight-test programme proceeded, several design changes had to be made before joint national type certification was awarded on 19 August 1986; approval from the FAA came on 3 December.

Above: One of the few civilian operators was Spanish carrier Binter Canarias, which received the first of four examples in December 1988. The airline withdrew the type from service a decade later.

Right: Construction of a single prototype by both manufacturers began in May 1981. CASA's example (ECT-100) is seen here at the roll-out ceremony on 10 September 1983.

SPECIFICATION

CASA CN-235-100
Type: utility transport and regional airliner
Powerplant: two 1395-kW (1870-shp) General Electric CT79C turboprops, driving four blade constant speed Hamilton Standard propellers
Maximum cruising speed: 454 km/h (282 mph)
Initial climb rate: 543 m/min (1780 fpm) at sea level
Range: 796 km (495 miles) at

5486 m (18,000 ft) with maximum payload and reserves
Weights: operating empty 9800 kg (21,605 lb), maximum take-off 15,100 kg (33,290 lb)
Dimensions: wing span 25.81 m (84 ft 8 in); length 21.40 m (70 ft 3in); height 8.18 m (26 ft 10 in); wing area 59.1 m² (636.17 sq ft)
Accommodation: flight crew of two; 45 passengers in four-abreast seating; 4 or 5 LD3s or 5 LD2s or palletized freight in cargo version

Above: The French air force has acquired a total of 18 CN-235s which are used for light military transport duties. The aircraft can be configured to carry 24 stretchers in the casevac role.

The CN.235MPA Persuader is a maritime patroller that has search radar, FLIR surveillance sensors, and six wing pylons for armament.

Early promise

Great expectations accompanied the CN-235 in its early years. The Indonesian government announced its intention to acquire 100 aircraft, but at the time of the Paris launch Airtech had just 54 orders and 18 options, all from civil customers. By 1985 Airtech was in serious discussions with Turkey to supply up to 50 tactical transports and other, smaller, military orders were won – but civil orders faded away. The CN-235 was never truly suited to the civil market; it was too heavy, lacked range and had a

rugged appearance that tended to scare off the airlines. Any commercial operators that needed the CN-235's rough field capabilities probably did not need an aircraft of its size, or cost, but gradually the military order book began to fill out.

In December 1986 the first CN-235 was delivered to Indonesia's Merpati Nusantara Airlines and that same month the Royal Saudi Air Force took delivery of the first military CN-235M. The first 30 aircraft became known as Series 10 machines (CN-235-10, CN-235M-10). The Series 100

that followed was powered by uprated CT7-9C turboprops, which remain the standard powerplant. A distinction was also drawn between CASA-built aircraft (-100) and those built by IPTN (-110). In 1990 Airtech introduced the CN-235-200/-220 which has a vastly improved range when compared to the earlier versions. The first CASA-built aircraft was certified in March 1992, but an IPTN prototype did not fly until 1996. The 200 Series and 300 Series, the latter with improved hot-and-high performance, are the current basic transport variants.

Growing family

From the earliest days Airtech planned to build a family of CN-235 variants for specialist missions such as maritime patrol and Elint. Both IPTN and CASA developed different maritime patrol versions, but only CASA has placed the type

in service. The Irish Air Corps was the first operator of the CN-235MPA Persuader (it took delivery of two in December 1994). IPTN developed a similar aircraft, dubbed the CN-235MPA Sky Guardian. This is a reflection of the slow pace of the overall IPTN CN-235 programme, which won few sales outside its domestic market and was troubled with reports of poor quality control. IPTN development eventually ceased and the CN-235 is now considered an active product only of EADS CASA.

According to CASA in summer 2005, almost 250 aircraft were in service, although the only airline to buy new aircraft were Spain's Binter Mediterraneo and Indonesia's Mandala Airlines and Nusantara. Only the Merpati aircraft remain in service.

C-295

At the 1997 Paris Air Show CASA announced a completely independent development of the CN-235, the 'stretched' C-295. At an overall length of 24.45 m (80 ft 3 in), the C-295 is 3.05 m (10 ft ½ in) longer than the CN-235. Maximum payload has been increased by more than 50 per cent to 9700 kg (21,385 lb), allowing the C-295 to carry 78 fully equipped troops or five standard pallets. The C-295 is powered by two 1972-kW (2,645-hp) Pratt & Whitney Canada PW127G turboprops, driving six-bladed Hamilton Standard HS0568F-5 propellers. It is fitted with the Sextant Topdeck EFIS cockpit which includes a flight management system, attitude and heading reference system, autopilot and three colour LCD screens, with associated TCAS (traffic collision avoidance system) and GPWS (ground-proximity warning system). A technology demonstrator made its maiden flight on 28 November 1997 and the first production-standard C-295 flew on 22 December 1998. FAA type certification was awarded in December 1999. In February 2000 the Spanish air force confirmed its launch order for nine aircraft, announced in April 1999. The first of these was received in 2001.

Morocco established an additional transport squadron in 1990 to operate seven CN-235Ms from their base at Kenitra. One of the aircraft is configured for the VIP transport role.

BAe/Avro146/RJ Development

Having run the gauntlet of protracted development, cancellation and initially poor sales, the 146/RJ matured into a British success story.

In a world that has become increasingly conscious of noise pollution, aircraft such as the BAe 146 and Avro RJ have played an important part in commercial aviation. With four fuel-efficient and very quiet engines, the 146 can slip virtually unnoticed into any regional airfield.

After what was a protracted development period which initially involved Hawker Siddeley and

*Below: As the first of the 146 family, **G-SSSH** wore a highly appropriate registration. The aircraft was used during the flight test programme, which resulted in type certification being awarded in February 1983.*

almost brought the nationalized British Aerospace (BAe) to its knees, the 146 eventually sold well around the world, paving the way for the improved Avro RJ.

A series of design proposals was considered over a 20-year period before the HS.146 layout was frozen and the programme launched. Four Lycoming (later AlliedSignal and now Honeywell) ALF502 engines were chosen to power the machine and, although some critics said it was ridiculous to use four engines, the economy and performance offered in service have easily justified their use. The capital cost, fuel burn and installed weight of the ALF502s were in every case better than the traditional short-haul airliner layout of two larger engines. Most importantly, the ALF502 offered extremely low noise levels.

With its low noise signature, the 146 is able to operate from many airports with night-time curfews on jet operations. Based on the 146-200, the 146QT is optimized for overnight freight transport.

Bearing in mind the required field performance, the wing was fitted with powerful high-lift flaps. Contrary to all the previous proposals which had featured low-set wings, this wing was set on top of the fuselage. The new configuration allowed the engines to be mounted in undisturbed air,

while the wing could provide maximum lift as it was unaffected by the wide fuselage below. Coincidentally, it also allowed the fuselage to be positioned close to the ground so that passengers could embark via short airstairs. This facility opened up the possibility of operations from less-developed regional airports.

The high wing also dictated that the main landing gear be fuselage-mounted.

Below: Air UK was an important 146 operator, with its fleet centred around the 146-300 variant. The airline was typical of those employing the 146 intensively on regional and short-haul routes.

Right: Taiwan's Makung Airlines, UNI Airways Corp. from May 1996 and now Uni Air, operated a fleet of 146s, including five 146-300s as seen here. Several Asian airlines purchased the 146, many buying used aircraft from BAe's Asset Management Organisation (AMO).

Three 146-100s were assessed during 800 hours of everyday cargo operations by the RAF. After this period, the original aircraft were returned to BAe, and two new machines were purchased to equip the Queen's Flight for VIP duties.

Comfort a priority

Hawker Siddeley was determined to make the 146 as comfortable as possible. From the outset, a design objective was to provide five-abreast seating with a general level of comfort not less than that of the Boeing 747. The 146 mock-up was initially furnished with actual 747 seats, and the internal cabin width was greater than that of the 146's principal competitors, the Fokker F28 and F100, and McDonnell Douglas' DC-9 and MD-80. The aircraft's cabin height was also generous. In service, the 146 has proved easily adapted to any desired seating or cargo configuration.

Programme delays

A combination of a worldwide recession and major changes in

Many airports which were previously the preserve of turboprop types, such as the DHC-7, benefited from the introduction of the 146. Operations from London City Airport were revolutionized, as jet services could now be offered from the city centre.

the UK aerospace industry almost destroyed the 146 before its first flight. In August 1973, the British government announced that the project would go ahead and had plans for a new nationalized aircraft company, known as British Aerospace, which would take over Hawker Siddeley.

As it became apparent that the 146 was heading for a loss, potential shareholders in BAe grew concerned. Thus, in October 1974, the government cancelled

the 146, making Hawker Siddeley and BAe a much more attractive option to investors.

A vigorous reaction from Hawker Siddeley workers led to work continuing at a much diminished rate. BAe was duly formed in 1977. One of the first tasks undertaken was to review the 146 and reassess the potential market. During the delay of almost four years, much work had been done to refine the design. Market analysis yielded positive responses, and the BAe board recommended a relaunch. This time there were no delays, and in 1987 output had to be stepped up from 28 to 40 aircraft per year, and a second assembly line was set up at Woodford.

The 146-100 prototype was flown on 3 September 1981 and Dan-Air began scheduled services on 27 May 1983. It was typical of the 146 that one of the first Dan-Air destinations should be Innsbruck, never previously served by scheduled jetliners. While production of the 146-100 continued, it became increasingly obvious that some operators would gladly trade the 146-100's amazing field capabilities for increased payload. Accordingly, the stretched 146-200 was flown on 1 August 1982 and soon became the baseline standard aircraft, only to be surpassed in turn by the 146-300 and the much-revised RJ series.

SPECIFICATION	
BAe/Avro RJ 100 **Type:** short-range commercial transport **Powerplant:** four 31.4-kN (6,985-hp) Textron Lycoming LF 507 turbofans **Cruising speed:** 670 km/h (415 mph) at 8800 m (29,00 ft) **Range:** 2909 km (1,800 miles) **Weights:** operating empty 22,453 kg (49,397 lb) (146-100), 23,269 kg (51,192 lb) (146-200);	maximum take-off 38,102 kg (83,824 lb) (146-100), 42,184 kg (92,805 lb) (146-200) **Dimensions:** wing span 26.21 m (86 ft); length 30.99 m (101 ft 8 in); height 8.50 m (28 ft 2 in); wing area 77.29 m² (832 sq ft) **Accommodation:** two pilots plus 100 passengers in a standard airline layout; maximum of 128 passengers in high-density layout

Technical details

Ignoring conventional wisdom, Hawker Siddeley dispensed with leading-edge lift-enhancing mechanisms, thrust reversal and the twin-jet layout, achieving the fine STOL performance of the quietest jet airliner.

Hawker Siddeley designed a comparatively simple, thick wing for the 146, featuring hardly any sweepback. This fits in well with the planned short field length and Mach 0.7 maximum operating speed, and enables the required high lift performance to be achieved with a plain leading edge. In addition, the trailing-edge flaps are very powerful.

The 146's superb field performance is mainly due to its well-designed wing. The lift coefficent is greatly increased during landing by huge trailing-edge flaps. The petal airbrake can be snapped shut to provide instant lift in the event of an emergency.

Flying controls

To keep the horizontal tail out of the wing wake, it was put on top of the vertical tail. This T-tail arrangement also made it easy to fit powerful airbrakes, which form the tailcone at the extreme end of the fuselage. These, together with lift dumpers above the wing and powerful wheel brakes, made it possible to achieve the required landing field length without using engine thrust reversers. The aircraft is cleared for ILS-coupled approaches down to Cat II minima (runway visibility down to 400 m (1,312 ft) and decision height down to 30 m (1,312 ft). Its stall protection system, which operates with a stick shaker, takes into account the rate at which the boundary of safe flight is approached. It is doubtful that any previous large aircraft had had such safe handling qualities combined with such outstanding performance.

Key performance features

Now out of production, the 146 and RJ still offer unbeatable noise, fuel economy and field performance. In the improved RJ form, the machine is equipped for service well into the twenty-first century.

1 Quiet operations: A new chapter in jet airliner operations was opened by the 146. Many airports never before visited by a jet could now be served on a regular, scheduled basis by the new machine. The accompanying diagram illustrates the ground area exposed to a 90 Perceived Noise Decibel (PNdB) sound level around the approach and take-off routes of selected types.

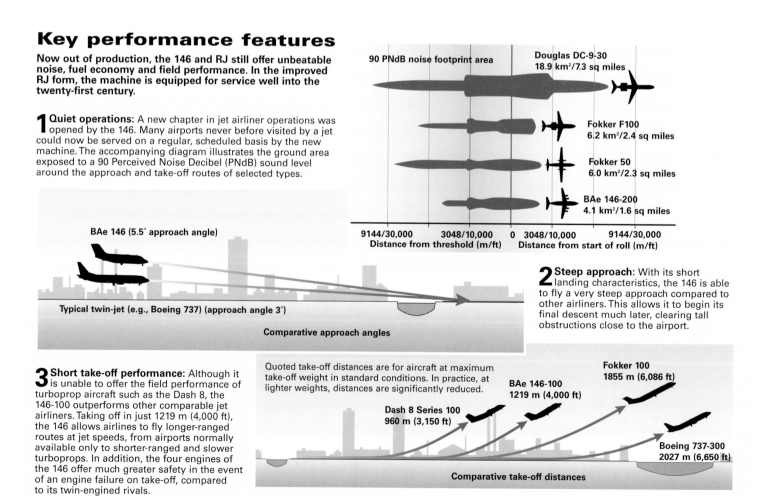

2 Steep approach: With its short landing characteristics, the 146 is able to fly a very steep approach compared to other airliners. This allows it to begin its final descent much later, clearing tall obstructions close to the airport.

3 Short take-off performance: Although it is unable to offer the field performance of turboprop aircraft such as the Dash 8, the 146-100 outperforms other comparable jet airliners. Taking off in just 1219 m (4,000 ft), the 146 allows airlines to fly longer-ranged routes at jet speeds, from airports normally available only to shorter-ranged and slower turboprops. In addition, the four engines of the 146 offer much greater safety in the event of an engine failure on take-off, compared to its twin-engined rivals.

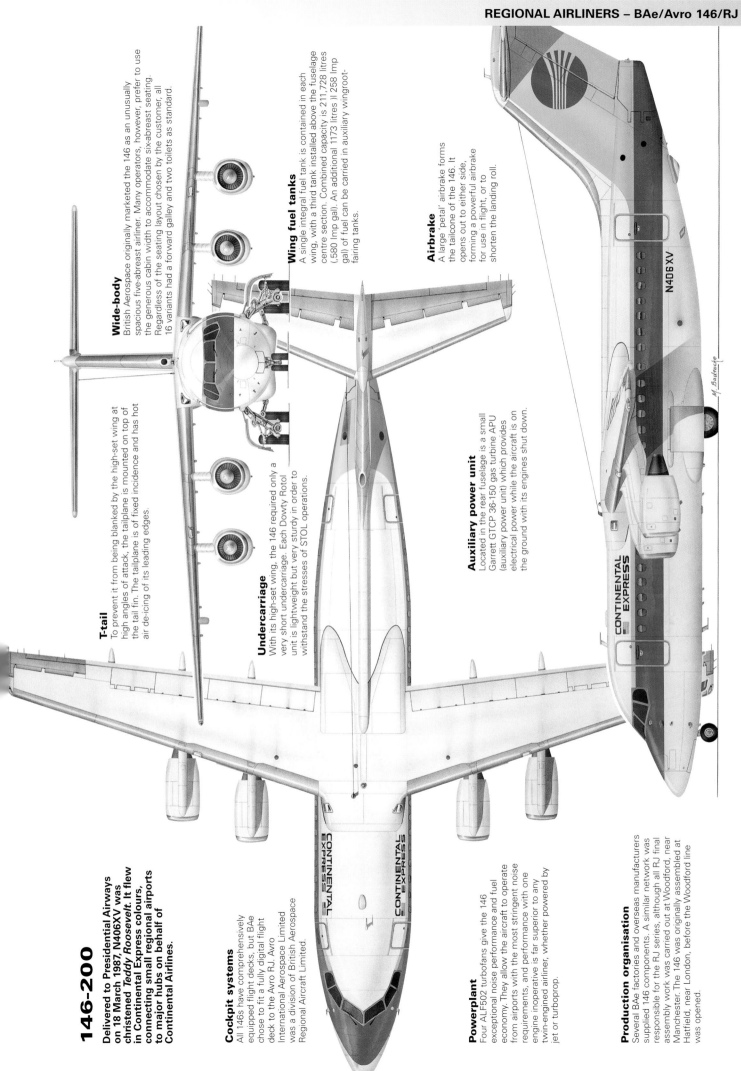

146-200

Delivered to Presidential Airways on 18 March 1987, N406XV was christened *Teddy Roosevelt*. It flew in Continental Express colours, connecting small regional airports to major hubs on behalf of Continental Airlines.

Cockpit systems
All 146s have comprehensively equipped flight decks, but BAe chose to fit a fully digital flight deck to the Avro RJ. Avro International Aerospace Limited was a division of British Aerospace Regional Aircraft Limited.

Powerplant
Four ALF502 turbofans give the 146 exceptional noise performance and fuel economy. They allow the aircraft to operate from airports with the most stringent noise requirements, and performance with one engine inoperative is far superior to any twin-engined airliner, whether powered by jet or turboprop.

Production organisation
Several BAe factories and overseas manufacturers supplied 146 components. A similar network was responsible for the RJ series, although all RJ final assembly work was carried out at Woodford, near Manchester. The 146 was originally assembled at Hatfield, near London, before the Woodford line was opened.

T-tail
To prevent it from being blanked by the high-set wing at high angles of attack, the tailplane is mounted on top of the tail fin. The tailplane is of fixed incidence and has hot air de-icing of its leading edges.

Wide-body
British Aerospace originally marketed the 146 as an unusually spacious five-abreast airliner. Many operators, however, prefer to use the generous cabin width to accommodate six-abreast seating. Regardless of the seating layout chosen by the customer, all 16 variants had a forward galley and two toilets as standard.

Wing fuel tanks
A single integral fuel tank is contained in each wing, with a third tank installed above the fuselage centre section. Combined capacity is 211,728 litres (,580 Imp gal). An additional 1173 litres)l 258 Imp gal) of fuel can be carried in auxiliary wingroot-fairing tanks.

Airbrake
A large 'petal' airbrake forms the tailcone of the 146. It opens out to either side, forming a powerful airbrake for use in flight, or to shorten the landing roll.

Undercarriage
With its high-set wing, the 146 required only a very short undercarriage. Each Dowty Rotol unit is lightweight but very sturdy in order to withstand the stresses of STOL operations.

Auxiliary power unit
Located in the rear fuselage is a small Garrett GTCP 36-150 gas turbine APU (auxiliary power unit) which provides electrical power while the aircraft is on the ground with its engines shut down.

N406XV

CONTINENTAL EXPRESS

M. Badrocke

146-300 and RJ

Updating its already successful 146 series as the RJ family – with standard five-abreast seating, glass cockpits and uprated engines – BAe (now trading in the regional airliner market as Avro) was guaranteed to find success.

The 146 entered service during 1983, initially as the 88-seat 146-100 with Dan-Air, followed by the 100-seat Series 200 for Air Wisconsin. Both versions used a six-abreast seating standard which, with a reasonable load factor, enabled the aircraft to offer a sound return.

As Pacific Southwest Airlines (PSA) built up its fleet from mid-1984 onwards, it became apparent that this layout was too tight for generously built Californians and the airline decided to adopt five-abreast seating, offering a much larger seat and enhanced comfort. BAe, which had been considering a stretched version of the aircraft, quickly recognized the need to restore 100-seat capability as

soon as possible, believing that, in many parts of the world, a fare structure to support a maximum of 85 seats would be untenable. Initial project studies showed that a significant stretch could be achieved with only minor changes to the basic structure and that the existing engines would not require an upgrade.

To reduce the development costs of what would become the 146-300, aircraft 1001 was withdrawn from service and its nose and rear fuselage were separated from its centre section and moved out to allow two fuselage drums to be inserted. The 2.46-m (8 ft 1-in) forward plug and 2.34-m (7 ft 8-in) rear plug resulted in an increase in length to 30.99 m (101 ft 8 in). This more than restored the seating capacity; 103 passengers could be accommodated in five-abreast comfort, while (subject to the insertion of additional emergency exits) high-density seating could be

The shortest of the RJs, the RJ70, fell by the wayside as operators realized the limitations of its smaller capacity. Many RJ customers continue the tradition of the 146, by flying into inner-city airports.

provided for a maximum of 128 passengers.

Fears that increased maximum weight would erode short-field performance – so much a selling point for the type – proved groundless. The new version soon joined the earlier series in

gaining approval to operate from London City Airport.

The first order for the longer aircraft came from the airline that had initially put the type into service in the United States – Air Wisconsin. Five aircraft were delivered between December

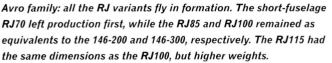

Avro family: all the RJ variants fly in formation. The short-fuselage RJ70 left production first, while the RJ85 and RJ100 remained as equivalents to the 146-200 and 146-300, respectively. The RJ115 had the same dimensions as the RJ100, but higher weights.

SPECIFICATION

BAe 146-300
Type: regional jet airliner
Powerplant: four 31.0-kN (6,970-lb-thrust) Textron Lycoming ALF 502R-5 turbofan engines
Maximum speed: Mach 0.73
Cruising speed: 790 km/h (491 mph)
Range: 2817 km (1750 miles) with standard fuel; 1927 km (1197 miles) with maximum payload
Weights: operating empty

24,878 kg (54,848 lb), maximum take-off 44,225 kg (97,500 lb)
Dimensions: wing span 26.21 m (86 ft); length 30.99 m (101 ft 8 in); height 8.61 m (28 ft 3 in); wing area 77.3 m² (832.0 sq ft)
Accommodation: flight crew of two, plus 100 passengers in standard layout; 116 passengers at six abreast; maximum of 128 passengers in high-density layout

1988 and November 1989, and all are still in service with the airline today.

Avro RJ series

The first Woodford-built 146 emerged in March 1988, intended at first to bolster the Hatfield (Hertfordshire) assembly line, although it would later supplant it. The last Hatfield-built aircraft was the prototype that was to lead to the RJ series.

Hatfield had extensive experience of glass cockpits through its work on the BAe 125 executive jet, and applied this knowledge to the 146 in stages. Honeywell supplied the complete avionics suite.

European regional carriers were now becoming customers, with Crossair and Sabena DAT in the lead; the RJ was turning into the aircraft of choice for major airlines seeking its capacity.

Improvements

With this new emerging market, Avro concentrated on further improving cabin comfort. An irritating 'hoot' that accompanied the up or down movement of the flaps was eliminated by sealing the wingroot flap tracks, extra width was found inside the cabin by reaming the fuselage frames, the overhead bins were refined and changes were made to the cabin lighting – all these improvements allowed the aircraft to offer the most comfortable ride available in regional air transport.

While the RJ specification was firming up, another outstanding

Freighter variants

In March 1986, airframe c/n E2056 left Hatfield, in Hertfordshire, as a 'green' airframe for Dothan, Alabama, where Pemco carried out the first 146 conversion to freighter standard. Rather than just cutting a large door in the rear fuselage, this involved the installation of a heavy-duty floor with built-in rollers, crash protection for the flight-deck (preventing the intrusion of cargo) and a comprehensive fire-detection system. The aircraft's operating weight turned out to be around 907 kg)2,000 lb) less than that of a comparable passenger aircraft. The Series 200QT (QT – Quiet Trader) could carry a 10,206-kg (22,500-lb) payload; the Series 300QT (below) increased this to 11,512 kg (25,380 lb).

The prototype returned to the United Kingdom just in time to appear at the 1986 Farnborough Air Show

where it excited the interest of the TNT Group, then in the throes of setting up an overnight operation centred on Birmingham. A highly successful two-night trial led to the optimistic announcement of an order for 72 freighters from TNT for worldwide use. While this did not materialize in full, the type was used for a sophisticated overnight European network, taking advantage of its quietness to operate where other aircraft were excluded by curfews.

One Series 100 was converted as a possible military variant, but this was not accepted and the aircraft was later sold on the civil market. Several were made into QCs (Quickly Convertible) – able to make a rapid transition from the freighter to the passenger-carrying role. The QCs retain cabin trim and have seats mounted on pallets for quick installation.

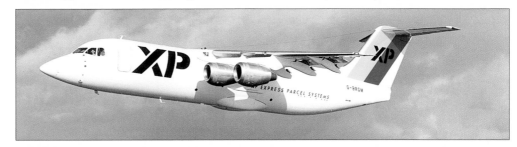

irritant was being dealt with. Right from the first flight, it had been apparent that neither the APU nor control of the cabin air-conditioning were up to the task. The result had been that passengers would occasionally be faced with an oily smell in the cabin. A new APU supplier

was found, and the air-conditioning and pressurization programmes were rescheduled.

Performance enhancements were achieved in two ways. A weight-saving programme resulted in improvements to both payload and range, but of greater significance to most

operators was a redesign of the engine to incorporate full-authority digital engine control (FADEC) and an additional supercharger stage, resulting in the engine running cooler, so retaining performance at higher altitudes. The new engine was designated LF507.

Above: Turkey's national airline, Turkish Airlines, was one of the first carriers to receive the RJ100. The airline ordered nine RJ100s and four RJ70s, of which six and three, respectively, remain in service.

Left: Ansett New Zealand received nine 146-300s (illustrated) and one 146-200QC. The quietness of the 146 was appreciated by both Queenstown and Wellington airports, which have noise restrictions.

British Aerospace ATP/Jetstream 61
Underachieving turboprop

The ATP is widely regarded as an unsuccessful aircraft – a mid-1980s regional turboprop airliner that was killed off by heavy competition and its own unremarkable performance. Just over 60 aircraft were built before the production line was closed down, but today demand for the surviving ATPs remains strong, with freighter conversions the way for the future.

BAe announced its intention to develop a larger advanced turboprop (ATP) regional transport, to succeed the Super 748 (HS.748), on 1 March 1984. The BAe ATP design that emerged had the same cabin cross-section as the Super 748, but a longer fuselage to accommodate 64 passengers in a standard configuration, with up to 72 seats possible. An important change was the aircraft's longer nose gear, which effectively raised the sill-height of the main cabin door and allowed it to be used with conventional airport jetways. New, fuel-efficient, 2,150-hp (1604-kW) Pratt & Whitney Canada PW124 turboprops, driving slow-turning propellers with six composite blades were fitted, but later replaced by the more powerful PW126A engine.

Other significant improvements included installation of the most modern equipment, including an advanced flight deck with a four-screen Smiths SDS-201 EFIS cockpit. The ATP also introduced separate forward and rear passenger doors, with integral airstairs in the forward door, and separate forward and rear baggage doors.

Maiden flight
The prototype ATP flew for the first time on 6 August 1986 and was joined in the air by the first production aircraft on 20 February 1987. The ATP obtained its European JAR 25 certification in March 1988 and US FAR 25 certification in August 1988. The launch customer for the type was the Airlines of Britain (AoB) group and British Midland Airways put the first ATP into revenue service on 9 May 1988. The AoB ATP order was initially for eight aircraft, but was later increased to 13. Other early ATP customers included Air Wisconsin (14), Biman Bangladesh (two), British Airways (14), Merpati Nusantara (five), SATA (three) and THT (four).

In spite of good operating economics and figures showing the ATP to be the quietest aircraft in its class, its slow speed and repeated early technical reliability problems kept sales sluggish. By December 1993 just 58 had been ordered and prospects were virtually nonexistent. In

Launched in March 1984 as a modern, quiet, fuel-efficient development of the HS.748, the Advanced Turboprop (ATP) first flew in prototype form on 6 August 1986.

SATA Air Açores owns two ATPs and leases a further two examples. The aircraft are operated on inter-island services in the Azores and are configured to carry 64 passengers.

a last-ditch attempt to stimulate interest in the ATP, on 26 April 1993 BAe announced an improved version which it dubbed the Jetstream 61. Adopting the Jetstream name neatly removed the unpopularity associated with the ATP and aligned the new aircraft with the more successful Jetstream 31/41 family.

The Jetstream 61 was powered by more powerful 2051-kW (2,750-hp) Pratt & Whitney PW127D engines, giving improved airfield performance, especially in 'hot-and-high' conditions.

Manx Airlines became one of a number of British Airways partner airlines to be absorbed into British Regional Airlines, now British Airways Citiexpress. A fleet of six ATPs remains on strength.

In the early 1990s, BAe proposed the BAe P132 ASW/ASuW variant with equipment to include a 360-degree maritime radar, FLIR, MAD and six weapon hardpoints. No orders were forthcoming.

The ATP was relaunched in 1993 as the Jetstream 61 with G-JLXI being the sole example to fly. It is seen here in promotional livery prior to the 1994 Farnborough Air Show.

A completely new interior with new-style seats, better underseat stowage and larger overhead bins was also added to enhance passenger appeal. The aircraft would also be certified to operate at higher weights. However, the relaunch failed to attract any meaningful new orders and production was finally halted at a total of 65 aircraft. The aircraft dubbed as the first Jetstream 61 was, in fact, the 64th ATP to fly. Both it and the 65th aircraft were later broken up (along with several unfinished aircraft on the production line).

The last ATP customer delivery came in 1995, with an aircraft built in 1993. However, the fortunes of those that remain in service have undergone a renaissance in

Despite an aggressive marketing campaign, the ATP never made the impact on the lucrative North American regional airliner market that it needed to become successful. This example was painted in American Eagle colours, but the airline purchased ATR 42s and 72s instead.

the hands of BAE Systems Asset Management – demand for them is solid, with nearly all are in regular service. Today the aircraft is referred to only as the ATP. ATP operators have included Air Europa Express, British Regional Airways, West Air Sweden, British World Airlines, SATA, Sun Air, Biman Bangladesh and BAE Systems (as a corporate shuttle).

Freighter ATP

On 28 June 2000, BAE Systems and West Air Sweden AB announced a 50:50 joint venture agreement to develop and market a freighter version of the ATP. Together, the two cooperated in the design and development of a side cargo door (SCD) modification. The new sliding door was sized to accommodate a standard LD3 container and mounted on the port rear fuselage. Up to eight LD3s can be carried, plus one additional LD346 (the cut-down version used by the Airbus A320). In this configuration the ATP freighter has a range of approximately 1,000 nm (1850 km; 1,150 miles). With BAE introducing an increased maximum weight limit for the basic ATP, the freighter has a maximum gross structural payload of 18,560 lb (8237 kg).

West Air (which already had a fleet of 11 HS.748 freighters), acquired six of the nine ATPs formerly operated by United Feeder Services in the United States, and placed options on the others. The first aircraft was immediately operated in the all-freight role – the first time that ATPs had been used in this way. The SCD modification was then planned to produce the first ATP freighter proper, with West Air initially having the capacity to undertake four conversions per year, with a maximum of six possible. By August 2005, the carrier had five ATP freight conversions in service, alongside nine unconverted aircraft.

SPECIFICATION	
BAe ATP	**Weights:** operating empty 14,193 kg (31,290 lb); maximum take-off 22,930 kg (50,550 lb)
Type: turboprop-powered regional airliner	
Powerplant: two 1978-kW (2653-shp) Pratt & Whitney Canada PW126A turboprops driving six-blade constant speed BAe/Hamilton Standard propellers	**Dimensions:** wing span 30.63 m (100 ft 6 in); length 26.01 m (85 ft 4 in); height 7.59 m (24 ft 11 in); wing area 78.3 m² (842.84 sq ft)
Cruising speed: 437 km/h (272 mph)	**Accommodation:** flight crew of two, plus 64 to 68 passengers in typical one-class seating
Range: 630 km (391 miles) with paximum payload and reserves	

Saab 340 Sweden's feederliner

Shared production

Fairchild took responsibility for wing, nacelle and empennage design, with Saab taking care of the fuselage, as well as production, systems integration, flight test and certification. The aircraft would be legally Swedish, with initial certification by the Swedish Civil Aviation Board.

The existence of the Saab-Fairchild 340 project was revealed at a press conference on 25 January 1980, the same day that the two companies finally signed a formal agreement to produce the new aircraft. Saab built a 24990-m² (269,000-sq ft) factory for production of the new aircraft, taking a SwKr350 million loan from the Swedish government, which would be repaid in the form of a royalty on each Saab-Fairchild 340A.

The first of five prototypes and early production aircraft (SE-ISF) made its maiden flight on 25 January 1983; the aircraft received Swedish certification on 30 May 1984. The aircraft entered scheduled service with Switzerland's Crossair (which had placed an order in November 1980) on 14 June 1984, and with Comair of Cincinnati in October 1984. Saab assumed overall control of the programme on 1 November 1985, and in 1987 took over wing and empennage construction from the 110th aircraft onwards. The aircraft was thereafter simply known as the Saab 340.

After 159 Saab 340As had been built (including three prototypes), production switched

Although Saab remained disappointed in 340/2000 sales to the end, the manufacturer made significant inroads into the lucrative US market.

Produced initially in cooperation with Fairchild in the United States, the Saab 340 eventually became an all-Swedish project, achieving significant sales and spawning the even more advanced Saab 2000.

The Saab 340 began life as the Saab-Fairchild 340A, a joint venture between the Swedish and US companies responsible for the sales, manufacture and further development of Swearingen's Metro and Merlin. Saab had begun working on a high-winged civil/military twin turboprop (the Saab 1084) some time before, but growing costs led the Swedish company to look for a foreign (and preferably American) partner.

A preliminary agreement was signed with Fairchild Republic in June 1979, and a joint team

(made up of about 50 engineers from each company) began work at Fairchild's Long Island facility. The Saab 1084 was refined into a low-winged, 35- to 37-passenger aircraft for airline use only, with considerable emphasis on use of advanced technology in the airframe, engines and systems to achieve low operating costs. The airframe thus used a high proportion of composites, and even many of the alloy components were bonded rather than conventionally riveted. This gave low weight and better corrosion resistance. Fairchild selected an extremely advanced low-drag aerofoil for the wing, while the engines were 1268-kW (1,700-shp) General

Of these, the first four 340s, SE-ISA was the second completed and was later revised as the first 340B. SE-ISB was the pre-production machine, SE-E04 was the fourth 340 and the first for Comair, while -ISF was the first prototype.

Electric CT7s with composite four-bladed Dowty propellers. The aircraft was fitted with all-digital avionics which have been compared to those used on much larger contemporary airliners such as the Boeing 757 and 767, with a sophisticated autopilot and flight director.

While extremely advanced in its details, the Saab-Fairchild 340A was entirely conventional in its overall appearance, with only its swept tailfin distinguishing it from much older aircraft such as the BAe 748 or NAMC YS-11.

Left: This Saab 340A was delivered to Formosa Airlines in August 1988 as one of the first of the type configured with 37 seats. The revised cabin layout was designated as the Generation II interior by Saab.

Below: This Mesaba Airlines Saab 340B Plus was the 300th aircraft of the 340 family to be built and it was flown for the first time on 22 April 1992. The basic 340B marked a considerable improvement over the 340A and, as such, Saab made the modifications included in the new standard available as a retrofit.

to the 'hot-and-high' Saab 340B, with more powerful CT7-9B engines and increased tailplane span. The prototype 340B made its maiden flight in April 1989, and deliveries began in September 1989. A stretched, scaled-up, 50- to 58-passenger derivative with 3096-kW (4,152-shp) Allison AE2100A turboprops was launched at the end of 1988 as the Saab 2000, with Westland, CASA and Valmet as major subcontractors. The prototype first flew on 26 March 1992.

Latest variant

The next variant was the Saab 340B Plus, which introduced some of the high-technology features developed for the Saab 2000, including a new interior, active noise suppression and optional extended wingtips. The first was delivered to AMR Eagle/Wings West in April 1994.

The 340B Plus is available specially equipped for gravel runway operation, with strengthening and special coatings on parts of the undersides. Like all 340 variants, the B Plus carries 35 (or 37) passengers as standard, with eleven rows of three seats (two to starboard, one to port), plus two rear-facing seats one behind the other at the forward end of the cabin on the starboard side. Alternatively, the aircraft can carry 19 passengers in a combi passenger/freight layout.

More than 450 Saab 340s were delivered (at least 290 of these being Saab 340Bs or Saab 340B Pluses). The biggest 340 operators were US regionals, principally members of the American Eagle and Northwest Airlink groups of companies which, between them, operated more than 250 aircraft. By comparison, Crossair's total of 14 aircraft seems modest, although the Swiss carrier became the largest operator of the Saab 2000, with 32 aircraft.

These sales figures are regarded as 'disappointing' by Saab, and efforts were made to sell the Saab 2000 production tooling (most notably to the Shanghai Aircraft Manufacturing Company). Saab reportedly views its future in civil aviation as lying in collaborative projects with much larger companies such as Airbus or Boeing, and currently builds components for the Airbus A320 series, A340-500/-600 and A380. Saab also maintains a leasing arm for the 340/2000 range and conducts maintenance and modification work, the latter including 340 freighter conversion.

SPECIFICATION	
Saab 340B	with 45-minute reserves and 30 passengers
Type: regional commercial and corporate transport	**Service ceiling:** 7620 m (25,000 ft)
Powerplant: two 1394-kW (1,870-hp) General Electric CT79B turboprop engines	**Weights:** maximum take-off 12,927 kg (28,439 lb)
Maximum speed: 522 km/h (324 mph)	**Dimensions:** wing span 21.44 m (70 ft 4 in); length 19.72 m (64 ft 8 in); height 6.91 m (22 ft 8 in); wing area 41.81 m² (450 sq ft)
Initial climb rate: 624 m/min (2,048 fpm)	**Accommodation:** 33, 35 or 37 passengers seated three abreast
Range: 2414 km (1,500 miles)	

Saab 2000

Saab is no longer an airliner manufacturer. After 16 years at the top, the Swedish company was forced to call it a day when sales slumped and the regional airliner market moved on. Saab had pinned its hopes on the 2000, a revolutionary high-speed turboprop, which it hoped would take over from where the smaller, slower Saab 340 had left off.

Saab had ridden the crest of a wave with the 340 during the 1980s but, as the 1990s unfolded, the 340 was seen as too small and too slow. To counter this, the Saab 2000 was conceived as a super-fast 50-seat regional aircraft that would link city pairs at jet-like speeds, but at a fraction of the operating costs.

Like the 340 before it, the Saab 2000 concept was driven largely by Crossair, which signed up as the launch customer when the programme was launched in December 1988. The Saab 2000 had all the appearance of a stretched 340, but there were many subtle and important differences. The fuselage had the same cross-section as the

Saab 340, but was 7.55 m (24 ft 10 in) longer. It could carry up to 58 passengers, seated in rows of three. The standard layout was for 50.

A six-screen Collins Pro Line 4 avionics system was selected for the cockpit and the radical reduction of cabin noise became a major design goal. To this end, a pair of 3096-kW (4,152-shp) Allison GMA 2100 turboprops (now AE2100) was selected, each driving slow-speed Dowty R381 propellers with six swept blades. The engines were set out from the cabin to reduce noise, but Saab also developed an active noise reduction system which effectively 'switched off' cabin noise.

Records and delays

Saab spread the development burden of its new aircraft, entering into agreements with CASA to build the wing, Valmet to build the tail unit and elevators, Hispano-Suiza to supply the engine cowlings and Westland Engineering to build the rear fuselage. The prototype

Above: Crossair was the launch customer for the earlier Saab 340 and the 2000. This is the fourth Saab 2000 built and the first for Crossair, seen prior to delivery.

flew for the first time on 26 March 1992. Early on in the test programme all Saab's performance requirements were met or exceeded. Underlining this, a Saab 2000 set a new time-to-climb record of 9000 m (29,527 ft) in 8 minutes 8 seconds, bettering that set previously by an E-2 Hawkeye.

The certification timetable, however, was set back by problems with the aircraft's high-speed longitudinal stability, and a new powered elevator control system had to be initiated in late 1993. First delivery dates were thus delayed into the fourth quarter of 1994 – 18 months behind schedule.

The family resemblance is obvious in this shot of the third Saab 2000 and a Saab 340B (actually the 340th built). As outstanding as the Saab 2000 was, it failed to sell in a market that had become fixated on regional jets.

Above: When first flown in March 1992, the 2000 was at the forefront of glass cockpit technology.

Above: Deutsche BA received five Saab 2000s and held options for a further five examples, which it did not exercise. This aircraft was passed on to Regional Airlines, which today, as Regional, uses six.

The Swedish division of Scandinavian Airlines Commuter, Swelink, used six Saab 2000s. Gerd Viking was the fourth delivered.

SE-001, fitted with a flight-test nose probe, was the first prototype Saab 2000, making its maiden flight on 26 March 1992. It was scrapped in mid-June 1996.

Into service

European certification of the Saab 2000 was achieved on 31 March 1994. FAA certification was achieved on 29 April 1994. Deliveries to Crossair finally began on 30 September 1994. These were followed by the first aircraft for Deutsche BA on 17 March 1995. Other customers included Air Marshall Islands, Med Airlines, Regional Air and SAS.

Saab had proposed using the 2000 as a platform for the Ericsson Erieye AEW radar, carried by Saab 340s in Swedish air force service, but no Saab 2000s ever entered service in this role. The modified Saab 340s (known in Sweden as the S 100B Argus) do, however, incorporate the rear fuselage section of a Saab 2000, as the latter features an auxiliary power unit which is needed by the AEW&C aircraft.

In airline service, the Saab 2000 suffered from additional early teething troubles, but these were nothing compared to the explosive arrival of competing regional jets, which emerged just as the 2000 was trying to find its feet. EMBRAER and Bombardier forged ahead to create an enormous new market that conventional wisdom had always decreed did not, and

could not, exist. It was too much for Saab. Saab announced that the 340 and 2000 production lines would close in 1999.

End of the line

Saab 2000 production ceased at 63, although a 64th airframe was laid down on the Linköping line. Crossair was very happy with its aircraft and gave them the nickname 'Concordino', to reflect their impressive performance. Despite having left the manufacturing business – its final airliner was completed in 1998 – Saab finds that there is still demand for its aircraft.

To meet that demand Saab Aerospace established Saab Aircraft Leasing (SAL) to manage its worldwide fleet.

SPECIFICATION	
Saab 2000	1525 m (5,000 ft)
Type: twin-turboprop regional transport	**Service ceiling:** 9450 m (31,000 ft)
Powerplant: two 3906-kW (4,150-hp) (flat rating) Allison AE 2100A turboprop engines	**Weights:** operating empty 13,800 kg (30,360 lb); maximum take-off 22,800 kg (50,160 lb)
Maximum speed: 682 km/h (423 mph)	**Dimensions:** wing span 24.75 m (81 ft 3 in); length 27.28 m (89 ft 6 in); height 7.73 m (25 ft 4 in); wing area 55.64 m² (600 sq ft)
Cruising speed: 594 km/h (369 mph) at 9450 m (31,000 ft)	
Range: 2222 km (1,375 miles) at maximum cruising speed with 50 passengers and reserves at	**Accomodation:** flight crew of three or four, plus 50 passengers ('European' configuration) or 58 (high-density configuration)

One of the early Saab 2000s is put through its paces over typical Swedish terrain. The majority of the surviving 2000s are based in Europe.

Raytheon 1900 King Air-based commuterliner

A conventional machine of efficient design, the Beech 1900 was cleverly produced to fill a recognized gap in the market place. With its King Air twin-turboprop executive aircraft well established, Beech decided that a new market existed for turboprop commuter airliners. The company's first move was to reintroduce its Model 99 Airliner into production during 1980. It was soon apparent that the large number of airlines now feeding passengers into the services of the main US carriers could use an aircraft of greater capacity, and to fill this requirement Beech developed the Model 1900.

The new aircraft used a wing based on that of the Model 200 Super King Air, while its tail section, cockpit and nose section were lifted directly from the Super King Air.

New fuselage

Quite clearly, the Model 1900 would need a new fuselage with cabin space for a maximum of 19 passengers and their baggage. The pressurized fuselage was of aluminium construction and featured a small vortex generator ahead of each wing root leading

*Regular orders from feederlines such as **Continental Express** allowed Model 1900D deliveries to reach almost 700.*

edge. Initially installed as retractable surfaces, these vortex generators are among a number of aerodynamic 'tweaks' that have been applied to the 1900 airframe during its evolution and add to the type's distinctive if somewhat untidy overall appearance. The flight deck was comprehensively equipped with Honeywell EFIS as standard, while avionics included a Bendix RDR-160 weather radar. A pair of Pratt & Whitney Canada PT6A-65B

turboprops flat rated at 820 kW (1,100 shp) powered the aircraft.

Prototypes

Three flying prototypes were constructed, along with one aircraft for static test and another for fuselage pressure cycle testing. The first of the fliers completed its successful first flight on 3 September 1982, and FAA certification was gained on 22 November 1983.

The first of the production models was the Model 1900C

Above: Of the three flying Model 1900 prototypes, the third was used for an range of systems and reliability testing, as well as acting as the type demonstrator.

Right: Thanks to its standard cargo door, the 1900C makes an ideal basis for freighter conversion. This machine has its cabin windows blanked off.

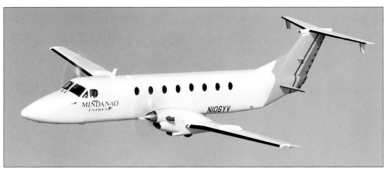

Above: Additional aerodynamic surfaces sported by 1900C-series aircraft include 'tail-lets' beneath the tailplanes and large horizontal 'stabilons' either side of the rear fuselage.

Below: This view of the Model 1900D prototype emphasizes the type's increased fuselage depth, especially when compared to the 1900C pictured left. Note also the aircraft's winglets and prominent ventral strakes.

SPECIFICATION

Raytheon Model 1900D
Type: twin-turboprop commuter airliner
Powerplant: two 954-kW (1,280-hp) Pratt & Whitney Canada PT6A-7D turboprop engines
Maximum cruising speed: 533 km/h (331 mph) at 4875 m (16,000 ft) and 6804 kg (15,000 lb)
Range: 2778 km (1,726 miles) at 1525 m (5,000 ft) at long-range cruise power with reserves
and 10 passengers
Service ceiling: 10,058 m (33,000 ft)
Weights: empty 4815 kg (10,615 lb); maximum take-off 7688 kg (16,949 lb)
Dimensions: wing span 17.67 m (58 ft); length 17.63 m (57 ft 10 in); height 4.72 m (15 ft 6 in); wing area 28.80 m² (310 sq ft)
Accommodation: two pilots on flight dec; maximum of 19 passengers and 939 kg (2070 lb) of baggage

Airliner, the first example of which was delivered in February 1984. The 1900C's versatility was improved by the addition, as standard, of a 1.32-m (52-in) square cargo door. In addition, both the forward and rear cabin doors featured integral airstairs, and there were baggage compartments situated in the rear fuselage and in the nose. Drawing on its extensive experience with executive aircraft, Beech also offered an executive version of the 1900C as the Model 1900 Exec-Liner.

Construction of both models of the 1900C finally reached 72 in total, with production slowing from October 1991 after the withdrawal of the special conditions under which the aircraft had been certified.

'Wet-wing' 1900C-1

The most successful of the 1900Cs was the 1900C-1, however, an aircraft which was built to a total of 173 before production ended in 1993. The C-1 has a 'wet-wing' – its internal wing structure is sealed to act as an integral fuel tank – giving a total capacity of 92,593 litres (685 US gallons).

This model also formed the basis for the 1900C's limited military sales. In March 1986 the US Air Force ordered six 1900C-1s, extending its C-12 designation system for the King Air to include the 1900C-1 as the C-12J. The C-12Js initially replaced Convair C-131 Samaritans with the Air National Guard, but two were later transferred to the US Army.

Egypt purchased six 1900C-1s for the electronic surveillance and maritime patrol roles. Two of the machines were equipped for maritime reconnaissance. The final military customer was the Republic of China Air Force, which took 12 aircraft from early 1988. They are primarily employed on utility transport duties, although two were modified for radar/navigational aid calibration duties.

High-roof 1900D

At the March 1989 US Regional Airlines Association meeting, Beech announced its intention to produce a new Model 1900 variant. By virtue of a 0.36-m (1-ft 2-in) increase in fuselage depth, the cabin could now be made obstruction free, as the wing mainspar now passed beneath the cabin floor. On all previous 1900's passengers had been forced to step over the spar as they walked through the cabin. The higher roof line of the new aircraft gave the machine a decidedly odd look, but increased the cabin volume by 28.5 per cent. Externally, winglets were added to improve 'hot-and-high' performance, while large ventral strakes were added beneath the aircraft's rear fuselage to improve directional stability and turbulence penetration. Powered by 953-kW (1,279-shp) PT6A-67D turboprops, the first Model 1900D prototype made its maiden flight on 1 March 1990. Certification was granted in March 1991 and the first aircraft was delivered to Mesa Airlines in November 1991.

Since 15 February 1994, Beech has traded under the name of its owner Raytheon and in summer 2005 this company had a dedicated used Model 1900 sales facility. A Model 1900D Executive aircraft was also offered and could be configured either as a business aircraft or corporate shuttle.

Military deliveries were restricted to a single 1900D received by the US Army in March 1997 for use by its Chemical and Biological Defense Command. Model 1900D airline orders included a 16-aircraft contract for Air New Zealand subsidiary Eagle Airways.

A number of export orders have been won by the 1900, this 1900D flying with Canada's Air Creebec. The design is made more attractive by an optional UltraQuiet system for the cabin.

Swearingen Merlin/Metro Fleet feederliner

Above: North America was by far the most lucrative market for the 19-20 seat Metro III. This example has been operated by Bearskin Airlines of Canada since March 1992.

Left: Scenic Airlines of Las Vegas, Nevada, utilized both Merlins and Metros in the 1980s and early 1990s. The aircraft were mainly utilised for sightseeing trips over the Grand Canyon.

Designed in the early 1960s, the Merlin/Metro series of light transport aircraft remained in production into the late 1990s.

The spindly fuselage of the Metro has been a regular sight at most US airports, sizeable fleets of the aircraft hurrying between large fields and smaller ports of call to bring passengers into the main hub centres. This commuter traffic constitutes the bulk of the Metro's operations, although an increasing number has been used for cargo carriage, albeit operating in a similar fashion by feeding a central hub from outlying airfields.

Edward J. Swearingen started his little company at San Antonio, Texas, over 35 years ago. His first major work was to build prototypes for others, and to fit more powerful engines to

Beech Twin Bonanza and Queen Air aircraft, but he yearned to produce aircraft of his own design. To start with, he took a modified Queen Air wing and Twin-Bonanza landing gear and added twin turboprop engines and a completely new fuselage and tail. Called the Merlin IIA, the new aircraft first flew on 13 April 1965 and was a winner from the start. It needed few changes, and deliveries began soon after certification in August 1966. This was the starting point for the entire Merlin/Metro family.

Structurally, the original Merlin IIA was a completely traditional all-metal stressed-skin machine, with a smooth, flush-riveted exterior. The engines were 410-kW (550-hp) Pratt & Whitney Canada PT6A-20 turboprops, fed from integral tanks in the wing

and with bleed-air anti-icing of the inlets. The retractable tricycle landing gear had a single wheel on each leg and, like the flaps, was operated electrically, the only hydraulic item being the wheel brakes. The cabin was fully air-conditioned with a Freon-cycle system, and pressurized by engine bleed. Normal accommodation was provided for two people on the flight deck and six more (three pairs) in the cabin, with a bulkhead with a sliding door behind the flight deck. Easy access was gained by an airstair door on the left side.

In 1968, when 36 aircraft had been produced, the engines were changed to the 496-kW (665-shp) Garrett TPE331-1-151G. The inlets were located above the spinners of the Hartzell three-bladed propellers, the latter being feathering and reversing, and fitted with a synchrophasing system to reduce noise and 'beat' vibration. Although there have been projects to use PT6A engines, all subsequent production versions of the Merlin/Metro family used various sub-types of Garrett (now Honeywell) TPE331.

Merlin IIB production continued to 1972, but back in 1968 work had begun on a completely redesigned aircraft known as the Merlin III. It had a longer fuselage, and totally new wings with a different aerofoil profile and fractionally greater span, and new landing gears with two small wheels on each leg. The new, more-tapered wing had double-slotted flaps, and both these and the forward-retracting landing gears were operated hydraulically. Thanks to the use of 626-kW (840-shp) TPE331-303G engines, the all-round flight performance was considerably enhanced. The Merlin III was certificated in July 1970, and was followed in production by the IIIA, IIIB and IIIC, incorporating numerous – mostly minor – improvements, among the most important being the introduction of 671-kW (900-shp) TPE331-IOU-501G or -503G engines, driving four-bladed propellers, giving cruising speeds of up to 355 mph (571 km/h).

In parallel with the Merlin III, the growing Swearingen engineering staff designed the SA-226TC Metro. In most

SPECIFICATION	
Fairchild Metro III	
Type: twin-engined regional airliner	**Weights:** empty operational 3963 kg (8,710 lb); maximum take-off 6350 kg (13,970 lb)
Powerplant: two 746-kW (1,000-hp) Garrett Air Research TPE331-11U-601G turboprops	**Dimensions:** wing span 17.37 m (57 ft); length 18.09 m (59 ft 4 in); height 5.08 m (16 ft 8 in); wing area 28.71 m² (309 sq ft)
Cruising speed: 513 km/h (318 mph)	**Accommodation:** two flight crew and 19 passengers
Initial climb rate: 743 m/min (2,440 fpm)	
Range: 1149 km (712 miles)	

Below: This SA-226TC Metro II was converted from SA-226AT Merlin IV standard and commenced service with US operator Tejas Airlines in September 1977.

respects, the two aircraft were identical, but the Metro was considerably longer, to seat 19 or 20 passengers. One might have thought such cramped dimensions would have made the long, tube-like Metro unsaleable, but airlines all over the world queued to build up fleets of these aircraft, which were cheap to buy, relatively fast and, once passengers are in their seats, comfortable.

The development and marketing of the new aircraft was a joint venture with what was then Fairchild Hiller, and the new wings and various other parts were made at Fairchild's plant at Hagerstown, Maryland. The first Metro flew on 26 August 1969 and, as with previous Swearingen designs, it proved virtually right first time.

Early upgrades

Sales were certainly enhanced by the early switch of production to the Metro II, still designated SA-226TC. This greatly improved the psychological comfort of the cabin by replacing the tiny portholes with upright rectangular windows every bit as large as those found in typical jetliners. The 'corporate Metro' was replaced with the Merlin IVA, first delivered in 1970. This introduced a modified fuselage with two fewer windows on

each side, the interior being normally configured for 12 to 15 passengers, with a toilet and baggage compartment. In 1979 Swearingen became a wholly owned subsidiary of Fairchild Industries, but the work remained centred at San Antonio and the company operated as the Fairchild Aircraft Corporation.

It was partly the obvious desire to increase the weights of the Metro/Merlin family that led, in 1981, to a major upgrade. The chief change in this new Metro III version was a dramatic 3.05-m (10-ft) increase in span, providing an increase in useful load of 672 kg (1,480 lb).

While the Metro III was entering production, the design team at San Antonio continued the product improvement process by upgrading the smaller Merlin III into the SA-227/TT41 Merlin 300. In 1983, development began of the Merlin 300, and deliveries of this began at the beginning of 1985. The most obvious change was the addition of 0.76-m (2-ft 5-in) wingtip fences, or winglets.

The corporate version of the Metro III was the Merlin IVC, which included, among other upgrades, certification of a Bendix electronic flight instrument system. Fitted with a luxurious interior which included reclining seats, a couch and sophisticated

refreshment and entertainment centres, the Merlin IVC can accommodate between 11 and 14 persons.

Able to seat 25 passengers, the Metro 25 – a higher gross weight modification of the Metro III – had the cargo door deleted, but featured an increased number of windows in the rear of the cabin; here, the extra passengers were accommodated

in what was the baggage area. Luggage is housed in a large underfuselage pannier. A rebuilt Metro III incorporating Metro 25 features began flight tests on 25 September 1989 to assess design features prior to a full production decision. Deliveries began in 1992 and production continued into the late 1990s. In total, over 1000 of the Merlin/Metro family was produced.

Special missions

Fairchild has offered a number of Special Mission Aircraft based on the Metro III and, subsequently, the Metro 23. These have included the maritime patrol variant with a 360-degree Litton radar in an underbelly blister and an endurance of more than 10 hours, and the anti-submarine variant offered with sonobuoys and a MAD tailboom. In response to a Swedish air force requirement, a Metro III was fitted with an Ericsson PS-890 Erieye AEW radar (below). The aircraft underwent flight trials from 1986, but the Saab 340 was eventually chosen as the mount for the radar. Launched in 1993, the Multi-Mission Surveillance Aircraft (MMSA) (bottom) is capable of performing multiple missions, while maintaining the ability to return quickly to passenger or cargo configuration. Equipment can include a centreline-mounted surveillance pod, mission radar and electronic reconnaissance systems.

The Expediter I is a dedicated cargo version of the Metro III family, with a payload of more than 2268 kg (5,000 lb) and a reinforced floor. The first deliveries were made to DHL Worldwide Courier Express in April 1985.

Antonov An-24 'Coke' family Versatile turboprop

Tough, simple and easy to maintain, Antonov's An-24 was the Soviets' answer to the Fokker F27. Since entering service in the early 1960s, the 'Coke' and its derivatives have served with both military and civil operators around the world.

After World War II the 'DC-3 replacement' question bothered the Soviet Union as much as it did the rest of the world, as the Lisunov Li-2s on Aeroflot routes were licence-built DC-3s. Ilyushin provided the first-generation replacements in the form of Il-12s and Il-14s, but by 1955 the GUGVF, the chief administration of the civil air fleet, had begun to study requirements for a replacement for all these piston-engined aircraft. For longer-range routes the An-10 and Il-18 were eventually ordered. Settling the requirement for the true mass market on the short-haul routes was more difficult.

The main reason for the delay had been uncertainty over engine type; there was great reluctance to abandon piston power.

Turboprop power

The specification drawn up did not demand a turboprop, but it was significant that a special engine, the AI-24, had in 1955 been ordered from the Ivchenko

bureau. A massive single-shaft engine, it was scaled down from the established AI-20 to reduce power from 2983 kW (4,000 hp) to 1864 kW (2,500 hp). It was deliberately conservative in design so that it would withstand the often brutish treatment to which Soviet hardware was sometimes subjected, and still run without trouble.

From the start Antonov decided on a high-wing monoplane in order to put the cabin floor near the ground and the engines and propellers well above it, to avoid slush, stones and other material. In 1955 he had expected to use four piston engines, but with great reluctance he followed the thinking at Handley Page for the Herald and changed to two of the new turboprops. From the operating point of view this was considered retrograde: reliability was probably going to be poorer (at least initially) and costs would be slightly higher. What tipped the scales was that in the USSR almost everything had a military angle. It was considered highly desirable, first, to train the personnel of the gigantic GVF (civil air fleet) in the rudiments of gas turbines, and to familiarize them with this type of powerplant on a daily basis, and, secondly, to get high-

Of the six species of multi-bladed propellers developed in the Soviet Union in the 1980s, two were tested on An-24s. The technology has since been integrated on the An-70 and Il-114.

The Russian Ministry of Defence operates this An-30 'Clank' in civilian markings. The aircraft is used in the survey/mapping role and has been in service since 1977.

octane petrol replaced by standard turbine fuel, so that warplanes could, if necessary, refuel at all civil airports.

Thus, to Antonov's delight, the new transport was designed in 1958 as a truly modern machine, with a large, almost circular fuselage and two of Ivchenko's new AI-24 turboprops. By this time the possibility of substantial exports was also obvious.

Antonov pulled out all the stops to make the An-24, as it was designated, totally modern and efficient. Very curiously, the

aircraft's wing was made quite small in relation to the fuselage size and aircraft gross weight. Reasonable field length was achieved by powerful, slotted, area-increasing flaps.

Thanks to the new engine, which initially gave 1902 kW (2,550 ehp), Antonov was able to exceed the specification and provide a cabin big enough for 50, even with the typically Soviet four-place flight deck. At first, however, Antonov hardly mentioned this possibility, and the first brochures did not go

Formerly part of Aeroflot's Arkhangelsk directorate, Arkhangelskie Vozdushnye Linii (AVL) is now a subsidiary of Aeroflot Russian Airlines as Aeroflot-Nord. It operates a mixture of An-24RVs (seen here), An-26Bs, An-26RBLs, Tu-134s and Tu-154s.

Below: CAAC of China operated a fleet of An-24RVs, 17 of which were delivered by Antonov, with subsequent examples being constructed by the Xian factory as Y-7s.

Above: Cuban airline Aero Caribbean was typical of the many carriers of Soviet-aligned countries that ordered examples of the An-24 family. Note the open air inlet on the starboard engine for the 7.85-kN (1,765-lb st) RU-19A-300 auxiliary turbojet on this An-26.

beyond a 40-seat 'all-tourist' version, as required. The prototype was flown at Kiev on 20 December 1959. There were no major problems, but on the second aircraft vertical tail area was increased and the engine nacelles were extended.

First delivery, to Aeroflot's Ukrainian Directorate, took place in April 1962. Flight testing was announced as complete in September, by which time regular cargo services were being flown in the Ukraine. Passenger service opened in October 1962, usually with 32 seats but from spring 1963 with nine instead of eight passenger windows on each side and 40 seats. A 44-seat version began flying from Moscow in September 1963. These initial versions were designated An-24V Srs I (NATO codename 'Coke').

By 1965 the fact that shorter field length was needed was obvious, especially in hot-and-high conditions. The An-24V

Series II replaced the Srs I in production, with 2103-kW (2,820-ehp) AI-24T engines, with water injection, and with the inboard flaps extended in chord and slightly in span. Later in 1967 a further boost was added in the form of a Tumanskii RU-19-300 turbojet/APU in the rear of the right nacelle. This could give 8.93 kN (1,985 lb) of extra thrust, but was normally used to give about 2.16 kN (480 lb) of thrust and also provide all electric power, thus putting more power into the propellers. Jet-equipped aircraft were designated An-24RV. A third 1967 prototype was the An-24TV (later An-24T), with the passenger door replaced by a broader rear fuselage with twin canted ventral fins and an upward-hinging cargo door.

Now Antonov designed a complex cargo ramp door and in 1970 the An-24 so equipped was redesignated An-26 ('Curl'). As well as being fully pressurized

(which the An-24T was not), it was restressed for operation at increased weight, and had two additional fuel cells.

After 1981, production centred on the An-26B freighter. There were many special variants and over 1000 An-24s were built.

'Clank' and 'Cline'

A variant so different that it was given a new designation was the An-30 ('Clank'), first flown in 1974. The fuselage was redesigned to accommodate a giant glazed nose for the navigator and a darkroom in the main cabin. The navigator has special precision

aids for accurate positioning of the aircraft. If required, equipment for many kinds of geophysical duties can be carried.

Last of the production-derived versions, the An-32 ('Cline') achieved a dramatic improvement in the payload that can be carried in extremely adverse hot-and-high conditions. Much more powerful AI-20 engines are fitted extraordinarily high, either the 3128-kW (4,195-ehp) AI-20M for 'normal' conditions, or the 3863-kW (5,180-ehp) AI-20DM for the most severe conditions.

Soviet production of the An-24 ended in 1978.

SPECIFICATION	
Antonov An-24T	**Weights:** empty 13,300 kg
Type: regional airliner and freighter	(29,320 lb); maximum take-off
Powerplant: two 1670-ekW (2250-ehp) ZMDB Progress (Ivchenko) AI-24A turboprop engines	21,000 kg (49,297 lb)
	Dimensions: wing span 29.20m (95 ft 9.5 in); length 23.53 m (77 ft 2.5 in); height 8.32 m (27 ft 3.5 in; wing area 72.46 m² (779.98 sq ft)
Maximum cruising speed: 450 km/h (279 mph)	
Range: 640 km (397 miles) with maximum payload	**Accommodation:** 44 to 52 passengers or 5700 kg (12,566 lb freight)
Service ceiling: 8400 m (27,560 ft)	

Turboprop family

The An-24 family has been built in huge numbers and in a wide variety of variants. Modern in appearance, the aircraft was one of the first Soviet airliners to be successfully exported. Low construction costs ensured that the unit price was far cheaper than that of its Western counterparts.

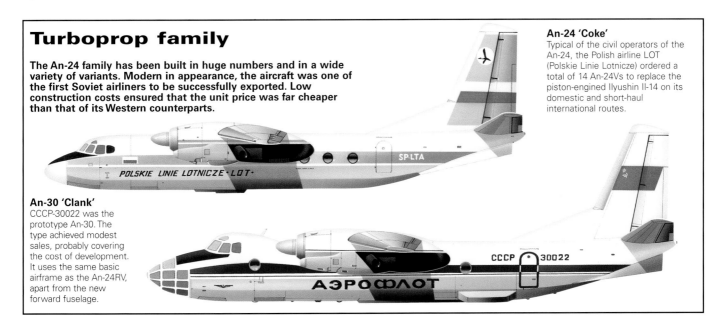

An-24 'Coke'
Typical of the civil operators of the An-24, the Polish airline LOT (Polskie Linie Lotnicze) ordered a total of 14 An-24Vs to replace the piston-engined Ilyushin Il-14 on its domestic and short-haul international routes.

An-30 'Clank'
CCCP-30022 was the prototype An-30. The type achieved modest sales, probably covering the cost of development. It uses the same basic airframe as the An-24RV, apart from the new forward fuselage.

Ilyushin Il-114 Turboprop hope

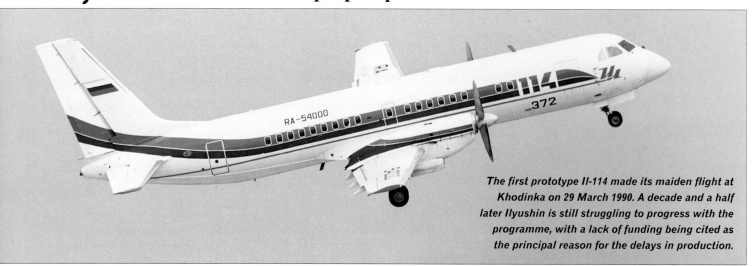

The first prototype Il-114 made its maiden flight at Khodinka on 29 March 1990. A decade and a half later Ilyushin is still struggling to progress with the programme, with a lack of funding being cited as the principal reason for the delays in production.

The Il-114 was an advanced regional turboprop designed to meet Russia's domestic air transport needs during the late 1980s. Developments of the aircraft saw the addition of Western engines and avionics to improve its chances in the export market. However, drastic funding shortfalls have imposed severe delays on the development programme and the Il-114 is barely in airline service.

In the former USSR travelling by air was the quickest (and sometimes the only) way to gain access to the huge number of remote destinations scattered across the country's interior. Aeroflot had a major responsibility to serve these airfields, over what would generally be described as 'regional routes'. What it needed was a tough passenger and freight aircraft that could operate in austere conditions from unprepared airfields. This came in the form of the Antonov An-24, an unrefined aircraft that

fulfilled its function admirably, but was never designed with passenger appeal in mind.

During the early 1980s several Soviet design bureaux drew up plans for an An-24 replacement. The equivalent Western aircraft were several generations further advanced in terms of their technology, design functionality, operating economics and simple comfort – all of which were becoming increasingly important factors for Aeroflot. Despite its lack of experience in designing small turboprop airliners, Ilyushin emerged as the competition's front-runner with its twin-engined Il-114. However, even though the design was finalized as early as 1986, the prototype did not make its maiden flight until March 1990.

ATP lookalike

The Il-114 closely resembles the BAe ATP in outline. It is a conventional low-wing design, with a swept fin and rudder.

This Il-114 was one of two pre-series aircraft purchased by Uzbekistan Airways in 1994. After each had flown 300 hours, both were grounded pending the establishment of an overhaul plant.

Power is provided by a pair of 1839-kW (2,466-shp) Klimov TV7-117S turboprops driving six-bladed Stupino SV-34 low-noise propellers. For the first time in such a Russian-designed aircraft, the Il-114 makes substantial use of composite materials. The flight deck is fitted with a five-screen EFIS, featuring colour CRT displays and two data input panels. In the passenger version, the main cabin is configured for 64 seats. The Il-114 was produced in cooperation with the TAPO

plant in Tashkent, Uzbekistan. The first prototype was built at Ilyushin's Khodinka facility, in Moscow, and made its maiden flight on 29 March 1990. The first production aircraft flew on 7 August 1992 and a flight test schedule involving the first five series production Il-114s was drawn up. Unfortunately, the second prototype was lost in an accident on 5 July 1993, which brought about the withdrawal of all Russian government funding.

As a result of this loss, a major delay was suffered and, coupled with problems in the TV7 engine development programme, the Il-114 did not receive its Russian type certification until 26 April 1997. A pair of TV7-engined aircraft was received by Vyborg North-West Air Transport in 2002/03 and remains in service.

Cargo variants

Ilyushin hoped to build several versions of the Il-114. The basic passenger version was joined by

In passenger configuration, the Il-114 is designed to carry 64 passengers at 76 cm (30 in) seat pitch. Overwing emergency exits are provided along with a galley, cloakroom and toilet at the rear of the cabin and overhead baggage racks on either side of the central aisle.

Just as the ATP is receiving a new lease of life as a freighter, the Il-144's best hope of commercial success may lie in its freighter versions.

for use in civil emergencies and has a projected endurance of some 10 hours.

Announced in 1996, the Il-114FK is intended as a replacement for the An-30 in Russian military service and resembles the older Antonov in its redesigned glass nose. The Il-114FK would also be capable of carrying a podded SLAR radar and Elint systems.

To date, Ilyushin's progress with the Il-114 has been slow and only a handful of aircraft has been built. Two Il-114Ps were 'ordered' by Uzbekistan Airlines, and entered service in 1998. These aircraft had to be withdrawn from service once the 300-hour overhaul limit had been reached on their engines – as no proper maintenance procedure was in place.

Ilyushin/TAPO and Iran's national aircraft manufacturing company at Isfahan had discussed the establishment of a licence-production line at Isfahan for the Il-114, but these plans apparently stalled.

the Il-114T freighter. This all-cargo version has already been ordered by Uzbekistan Airways and is fitted with a 3.31-m x 1.78-m (10-ft 10¼-in x 5-ft 10-in) cargo door in the rear fuselage. The cabin has a removable roller floor, maximum take-off weight is set at 23,500 kg (51,805 lb) and the first aircraft flew on 14 September 1996. Ilyushin and Pratt & Whitney Canada signed a joint-venture agreement in 1997 to develop and market the aircraft. Customer deliveries were due to begin in 1998 and Uzbekistan Airways began operating two examples on service trials during the latter part of the year, but none has yet entered official revenue service.

A second cargo version – designated Il-114N200S – incorporating a rear-loading ramp has also been designed, but none of this variant was built.

Ilyushin also developed the Il-114-100 (known until 1997 as the Il-114PC) – a Westernized version powered by two Pratt & Whitney Canada PW127H turboprops driving Hamilton

Standard propellers and equipped with Sextant avionics. This export-dedicated version was initiated by a joint venture between Ilyushin and Pratt & Whitney in June 1997, and the first aircraft in an order for 10 from Uzbekistan Airways were delivered in December 2002. Subsequent problems with the supply of Russian components delayed further deliveries until late 2004. The ninth production Il-114 was converted to act as the -100 demonstrator and it first flew on 26 January 1999. The Il-114-100 has increased range and performance, when compared to the TV7-powered version, and Ilyushin has discussed a freighter version designated Il-114-100T. Ilyushin has also proposed a PW127-powered version with 74 seats, dubbed the Il-114MA. It has additionally drawn up plans for the Il-114M, powered by uprated TV7M-117 turboprops. These would permit an increased maximum take-off weight, comparable to that of the -100 version, but without the hard currency expenditure on foreign-supplied engines.

Military applications

Plans for two dedicated military versions have also been drawn up – the Il-114P maritime patrol aircraft and the Il-114FK survey/reconnaissance platform. The Il-114P would be built around the Leninetz Sea Dragon mission system and drawings of the aircraft reveal a revised nosecone to accommodate a sea-search radar, an optional MAD tailboom and bulged observation windows in the rear cabin. It is intended that two underfuselage and two underwing hardpoints would carry a variety of stores. Like the Il-114T, the Il-114P is fitted with a large port-side freight door. The aircraft is intended for military or paramilitary duties or

SPECIFICATION	
Ilyushin Il-114	1500-kg (3300-lb) payload
Type: turboprop regional airliner	**Weights:** operating empty
Powerplant: two 1840-kW (2466-shp) Klimov TV7117S turboprop engines driving six-blade constant-speed SV-34 propellers	15,000 kg (33,070 lb); maximum take-off 23,500 kg (50,045 lb)
	Dimensions: wing span 30.00 m (98 ft 5 in); length 26.88 m (88 ft 2 in); height 9.32 m (30 ft 7 in); wing area 81.9 m² (881.6 sq ft)
Cruising speed: 470 km/h (292 mph)	
Range: 1000 km (621 miles) with 64 passengers and reserves; 4800 km (2983 miles) with a	**Accommodation:** flight crew of two, plus 64 passengers (four abreast)

The introduction of PW127H engines improves the Il-114-100's range and economy, but also leads to a significant increase in price.

Antonov An-12 Civilian 'Cubs'

As with many Soviet-era aircraft, it was often difficult to discern exactly where the An-12's civil role ended and its military duties began. In Aeroflot hands, the big transport looked like a commercial freighter, but it also had military masters, and this was true of other operators around the world.

Oleg Antonov revolutionized the design of Soviet transport aircraft. It was his creations, the An-8, An-10 and An-12, which helped to establish many of the features now seen as most desirable in a 'go-anywhere' cargo aircraft – a high wing, beaver tail, rear ramp, on-board APU (auxiliary power unit) and even rough-field capability. Certainly, all these ingredients were part of the recipe for a successful military tactical airlifter, and that was Antonov's primary design goal. The same aircraft could also serve civil needs; one had only to look at Lockheed's C-130 to see the truth in that. But the great restraint on the Antonov Design Bureau was that its primary, in many ways sole, customer was the military, and no allowances were made to exploit the civil market. Outside the Soviet Union, an aircraft such as the An-12 should have carved its own furrow in the airline and air cargo market (as the Hercules did). However, as a product of the Soviet military, the An-12 entered civil service almost by default, only in limited numbers and only to very controlled customers. It took the collapse of the Soviet Union and the liberalization of its air transport industry to place the An-12 truly on the world stage in the twilight years of its career.

Based at Vnukovo 3 in Moscow, this An-12TB is operated by Kosmos, one of the many fledgling companies to emerge in Russia since 1992. Kosmos also operates an Antonov An-12 and three Tupolev Tu-134s.

The predecessors of the An-12, the An-8 transport of 1955 and 1957's An-10 Ukraina ('Cat') airliner, did serve the civil market. The An-12, on the other hand, was a military freighter. The PV-23U gun turret mounted in its tail underlined its military origins yet, like most other Soviet-era transports, it first appeared wearing the colours and civil registrations of Aeroflot. There is no doubt that Aeroflot An-12s performed many essential civil tasks – the red-painted aircraft of Aeroflot's Polar Division were just one notable group – but Aeroflot's primary purpose was to serve in the wartime transport role for the Soviet air force.

Aeroflot An-12s were seen around the world on military tasks, Aeroflot's civil identity giving it safe passage into the world's trouble spots.

Pseudo-military 'Cubs'

The cloak of respectability worn by Aeroflot's aircraft was adopted by several other 'civil' users of the An-12, including Yugoslavia, Poland, Indonesia, Iraq, Egypt and Sudan. Indeed, prior to the 1990s, only a handful of legitimate airlines took delivery of An-12s, and these were all largely operating within the Soviet sphere of influence. Such customers included Air Guinea, Balkan Bulgarian and Ghana Airlines.

China and new operators

In China, things were a little different. The Chinese aviation industry worked closely with that of the Soviet Union until links were cut by Mao after the Cultural Revolution. A few An-12s had already been supplied by Antonov along with

Antonov's An-12 has built its reputation on being able to deliver a hefty payload to remote regions in inhospitable conditions. Here, a tractor is unloaded from the rear ramp on a snow-covered landing strip.

Above: Vast and often inaccessible, Russia relies heavily on its air-freight network. Avial Aviation operated An-12BPs from all three of Moscow's major civilian airports until 2004.

Below: Two An-12BKs were extensively modified as An-12BKT aircraft for meteorological research. The aircraft featured a nose-mounted instrumentation boom and pylon-mounted samplers and sensors.

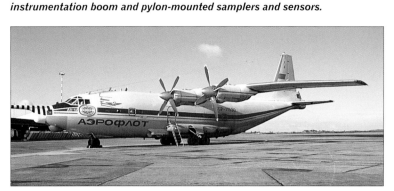

Operated in the 1980s by Balkan Bulgarian Airlines, LZ-BAB was used as a freighter, transporting goods to destinations in both Eastern and Western Europe. The airline latterly used three An-12s in this role.

SPECIFICATION

Antonov An-12
Type: mid-sized turboprop freighter
Powerplant: four 2490-kW (3495-shp) Ivchenko AI-20K turboprops driving AV68 four-blade constant-speed propellers
Maximum speed: 777 km/h (483 mph)
Maximum cruising speed: 670 km/h (416 mph)
Range: 3600 km (2237 miles) with maximum payload; 5700 km (3542 miles) with maximum fuel
Weights: empty 28,000 kg

(61,730 lb), maximum take-off 61,000 kg (134,480 lb)
Dimensions: wing span 38.00 m (124 ft 8 in); length 33.10 m (108 ft 7 in), height 10.53m (34ft 7in); wing area 121.7 m² (1,310 sq ft)
Accommodation: flight crew of two pilots, flight engineer, radio operator and navigator; can be arranged to accommodate 14 passengers plus freight, with military versions carrying up to 90 troops; maximum payload 20,000 kg (44,090 lb)

technical drawings and details. From this basis, the Chinese went on to develop a whole family of aircraft based on the An-12, as the Shaanxi Y-8 series. The first Y-8 flew in 1975, some 18 years after the An-12 had made its maiden flight, and the basic aircraft closely resembled its Antonov counterpart. Shaanxi developed the Y-8A which incorporated an extended glass nose. Shaanxi then produced the dedicated passenger/freight

Y-8B for CAAC, the monolithic state civil aviation enterprise.

Y-8Bs can be distinguished from their military counterparts only by their paint scheme, some retaining the tail turret. AVIC II SAC (previously Shaanxi) still builds Y-8 variants, a further improved version with a redesigned rear ramp and a fully pressurized fuselage.

One uniquely Chinese aircraft is the Y-8F, which first flew in 1990. This aircraft is a livestock

transporter, capable of carrying up to 350 sheep and goats.

The collapse of the Soviet Union allowed the many regional divisions of Aeroflot to set themselves up as independent airlines, together with hundreds of new start-up carriers – established, in many cases, with whatever aircraft could be found lying around.

The An-12 was perfectly suited to operations in far-flung regions of Russia and the CIS states, but also started to appear elsewhere in the world, particularly in the Middle East and Africa. It had the advantage

of being available in sizeable numbers and was cheap to hire (if not to operate). The low-cost of aviation fuel during the mid-1990s helped the An-12 to become established in the marketplace. At one time, there were over 30 airlines or brokers in Russia and the CIS offering An-12s for cargo charters and grabbing a portion of the lucrative if quicksilver 'tramp' freighter market by being affordable and available. The Russian economic crash of 1998 took many of these aircraft off the market and their numbers are now much diminished.

Above: The An-10 'Cat' was the passenger-carrying forerunner of the An-12. It incorporated a pressurized fuselage, capable of carrying 84 passengers and, on entering service in 1959, was claimed by Antonov to be the most economic transport in the world.

Right: Classic transport aircraft features abound on the An-12. Clearly visible in this view are the type's rugged, wide track undercarriage and upswept beaver tail. Both attributes are equally valuable to civil and military operators.

SATIC A300-600ST Beluga Super Transporter

Airbus components were airlifted between plants by the Aerospacelines Super Guppy for many years. While they were reliable workhorses, and the only aircraft available that could carry large airframe sub-assemblies, they were old and expensive to operate. To solve these difficulties Airbus decided to build its own 'Super Transporter'.

By the late 1980s it was becoming clear that Airbus Industrie's fleet of four Model 377SG Super Guppies – modified from Boeing Stratocruisers by Aerospacelines in the United States – would need replacing. For most of their careers the Guppies were irreplaceable, as they carried Airbus parts from factories in the United Kingdom, Germany and Spain to the central production line in France. But despite its Allison 501 turboprops, the Super Guppy was still an aircraft of the 1950s. It was not very fast, it was complicated to operate and its costs increased year by year.

Beluga is born

In 1990 Airbus proposed a modification of its own A300 airliner to replace the Super Guppies, using the A300B4 as a baseline. On 22 August 1991 Airbus Industrie's executive committee gave the project its

The Beluga (foreground) was developed to replace the ageing Super Guppy (behind). Seen here shortly before its initial flight in September 1994, the first Beluga (c/n 655) underwent 12 months of flight trials before entering service in October 1995.

go-ahead, approving the purchase of four 'Super Transporters', with an option on a fifth. Several European and US companies tendered for the development contract, but the successful bid came, in May 1992, from an Aérospatiale/DASA consortium dubbed SATIC (Super Airbus Transport International Company).

SPECIFICATION
SATIC A300-600ST **Super Transporter** **Type:** Oversize cargo freighter **Powerplant:** two 262.4-kN (59,000-lb-thrust) class General Electric CF6-80C2A8 turbofans **Maximum cruising speed:** 780km/h (463 mph) **Range:** 2400 km (1491 miles) with a 40-tonne (88,185-lb) payload; 4000 km (2485 miles) with a	30-tonne (66,150-lb) payload **Weights:** maximum take-off 155,000 kg (341,700 lb) **Dimensions:** wing span 44.84 m (147 ft); length 56.16 m (184 ft 3 in); height 17.23 m (56 ft 6 in); wing area 260 m² (2798.7 sq ft) **Accommodation:** maximum payload of 47 tonnes (103,615 lb) **Cargo hold volume:** 1400 m³ (49,442 cu ft)

The plan to use older A300 airframes was dropped in favour of the slightly larger and more advanced A300-600R structure, which also has a more sophisticated wing. The new aircraft's configuration was the subject of much debate. A front-loading design was preferred by the users, but in the Super Guppy this had imposed the need to disconnect all electrical, hydraulic and flight control systems each time the swing nose was opened.

Beluga '2' is seen arriving at Filton, United Kingdom, on its inaugural visit in June 1996. BAE Systems' Filton factory produces Airbus wings, which are transported by Beluga to the final assembly plants in Toulouse and Hamburg.

Left: The Beluga's upward-hinging cargo door and cavernous hold allow the aircraft to carry the fuselage sections or wings of any current Airbus products except the A380, including, as demonstrated here, a pair of Airbus A330 wings.

Below: The Beluga's immense fuselage cross-section disturbs airflow to the tail control surfaces. To counter the problem, the Beluga incorporates an A340 tail section and large endplate fins to give adequate lateral stability.

This increased the chance of system failure and led to lengthy recalibrations before each flight. A side-loading door was the easiest option, but no door large enough to accommodate an A340 wing section could be made, and complicated offset loading positions would have to be developed. The elegant solution was to build a 'dropped' flight deck, below the level of the cargo hold floor, and install a large but conventional upward-opening cargo door that allowed direct access to the hold. As a result, the Beluga can be loaded and unloaded in as little as 45 minutes.

Beluga described

The enlarged cargo hold of the A300-600ST has a usable length of 37.70 m (123 ft 8 in). It is capable of carrying an entire A330/A340 fuselage section. The cargo deck is 7.40 m (24 ft 3 in) wide. Total volume of the cargo hold is 1400 m³ (49,440 cu ft). The A300-600ST is fitted with an A340 tail section, extended by a 1.20-m (4-ft) plug, to which is attached the CASA-built

horizontal tail. This has distinctive endplate fins for improved lateral stability. In all, the Super Transporter can carry a load twice that of the Super Guppy – 45500 kg (105,310 lb) over a range of 900 nm (1666 km; 1,035 miles). Power is supplied by two 262.4-kN (59,000-lb) General Electric CF6-80C2A8 turbofans, engines more usually found on the A310. It has the standard EFIS two-crew cockpit of the A300-600R.

The aircraft destined for modification were taken straight off the A300 production line, at the wing/central fuselage mating stage. The first airframe entered the modification stage in 1992 and was rolled out on 23 June 1994. The maiden flight occurred on 13 September 1994 and certification was achieved in September 1995. The A300-600ST entered service for Airbus in October 1996. The second aircraft flew in March 1996, the third on 21 April 1997 and the fourth was handed over in July 1998. A fifth aircraft was subsequently delivered. Airbus christened the

aircraft Beluga – an appropriate for this great white whale.

The Belugas were built primarily for Airbus's own needs, but the possibility of leasing them out to other operators, when their schedule allowed, was raised from the beginning. In October 1996 Airbus Transport International (ATI) was established to market the Beluga's unique capabilities commercially. The

acquisition of a fifth aircraft allowed ATI to offer a dedicated aircraft for cargo charters. The first customer was the European Space Agency, which used the Beluga to carry a 40-ton section of the Alpha Space Station in November 1996.

SATIC has latterly considered a Beluga development of the A340 to provide even greater lift capability over longer ranges.

Right: The Beluga utilizes standard A300-600R wings, engines and landing gear, which helped to keep development and production costs to a minimum.

Below: The A300-600ST (Super Transporter) has been actively marketed to companies looking to lease an outsize cargo aircraft. A fifth Beluga has been acquired to facilitate more charter work.

Ilyushin Il-76 'Candid' Multi-role transport

The Il-76 is the most versatile airlifter to emerge from the Soviet Union. It combines outstanding rough field capability with jet performance, while carrying a substantial payload.

When the Il-76 (ASCC code name 'Candid') first emerged in the early 1970s, it was dismissed as yet another Soviet copy of a Western aircraft. In this case, the Il-76 bore a striking resemblance to the C-141 StarLifter; however, the truth was not quite as straightforward. For a start, the undercarriage gave true rough-field capability, which was routinely used in military service. Under the glazed navigator's station in the nose the Il-76 had a ground-mapping radar, allowing it to operate autonomously, by day or night, and well outside controlled airspace. The cargo hold was equipped with four overhead hoists and the rear ramp could lift a load of up to 30 tonnes, allowing the maximum hold volume to be exploited. The Il-76 could carry a load of

40 tonnes from a normal runway and 33 tonnes off a grass, dirt or packed-snow strip.

The Il-76 was the Soviet Union's first truly strategic airlifter, but it was never portrayed as such. When the aircraft made its Western debut at the Paris Air Show of 1971, and again in 1973, it was presented as a purely commercial aircraft. By 1973, Il-76s in Soviet service had begun to adopt Aeroflot markings, but there was no question that the big freighter was intended 'simply to resupply remote areas of the USSR where there are no runways', as one Ilyushin representative put it. More so

Although carrying Aeroflot markings, this line-up of Il-76s was used for military purposes. The second and fourth aircraft from the camera are Be-976 missile-tracking aircraft, the third machine is an Il-76VPK command post, and the nearest aircraft is a standard Il-76T.

than any of its predecessors, the Il-76 had a primary military role. However, Ilyushin did develop civilian versions of the aircraft, Il-76s that were not as obviously militarized as their siblings. These aircraft were seen on Aeroflot services around the

world, mostly on resupply flights to friendly nations, but so, too, were the military versions, and

Seen prior to the break-up of the Soviet Union, this Il-76TD is painted in an Arctic-support Aeroflot scheme.

SPECIFICATION

Ilyushin Il-76T
Type: medium- to long-range freighter
Powerplant: four 117.7-kN (26,455-lb-st) Aviadvigatel (Soloviev) D30KP turbofan engines
Cruising speed: 750–800 km/h (466–497 mph)
Range: 6700 km (4163 miles) maximum range with reserves; 5000 km (3107 miles) with

40-tonne (88,185-lb) payload
Weights: 170,000 kg (374,785 lb) maximum take-off
Dimensions: wing span 50.50 m (165 ft 8 in); length 46.59 m (152 ft 10 in); height 14.76 m (48 ft 5 in); wing area 300.0 m² (3229.2 sq ft)
Accommodation: Flight crew of five including two pilots, flight engineer, navigator and radio operator, plus two freight handlers

the line between the two is almost nonexistent.

The basic military version of the 'Candid' was quickly followed by the Il-76M 'Candid-B'. This version had more fuel and a higher gross weight, but retained obvious military features such as the rear gun turret and para-dropping equipment in the hold.

At the same time, Ilyushin did develop a nominally civil version of the basic aircraft, the Il-76T 'Candid-A' (T meaning *trahnsportnyy* – transport). This aircraft had no gun turret, no rear paratroop doors, an extra fuel tank and a maximum payload of 48 tonnes. Ilyushin next produced an increased-weight/extended-range version of the Il-76T, the Il-76TD 'Candid-A', which had uprated D-30KP Srs 2 engines, yet more fuel and a maximum payload of 50 tonnes. The wings and landing gear were strengthened and the prototype first flew in 1982.

What is noteworthy about the Il-76TD is that it flew before the similarly improved military equivalent, the Il-76MD 'Candid-B'. And, despite the seemingly clear division between 'armed' military Il-76M/MDs and unarmed Il-76T/TDs, Ilyushin went on to confuse matters completely by building Il-76T/TDs with gun turrets and Il-76M/MDs without.

False identities

The origin of these aircraft, which have become known as 'falsies', is unclear. It is thought that the Il-76T/TD 'falsies' were a convenient way of concealing the military mission of export aircraft – most of the civil 'falsies' served with Iraq, in the colours of Iraqi Airways. On the other hand, no explanation has yet been offered as to why 'falsie' Il-76M/MDs were built without gun turrets. Several of these aircraft were exported, to Cuba and Iraq, and it is the Il-76's

Intended to compete with the Antonov An-70 for sales to CIS and foreign customers, the Il-76MF incorporates new engines, a front and rear fuselage stretch and modern avionics.

export customers who have led the way in placing the type into 'civil' service. Most have a military role, but wear civilian colour schemes. In Cuba, two Il-76MDs wore full Cubana colours, but were operated on behalf of the air force. In Iraq, most of the 38 Il-76T/TD/M/MDs had Iraqi Airways markings. North Korea's three 'falsie' Il-76MDs are operated by the national airline, Air Koryo. Perversely, Libya's Il-76Ms were painted in Libyan Arab Airlines markings, while its Il-76TDs were

not. Syria's Il-76Ms have always worn Syrian Air markings, or at least a quasi-civil scheme.

Countries such as Azerbaijan, Belarus and the Ukraine took over substantial numbers of Il-76s after the break-up of the Soviet Union. Although these were all originally military aircraft, many are now operated by commercial firms; some are even operated by the commercial 'arms' of air force units and several Western companies have leased Il-76s from Russian brokers.

Il-76TD 'Candid-B'

The Il-76 has no direct Western equivalent (although comparisons with the C-141 are inevitable). Aeroflot's Il-76s were used for both civilian and military tasks, on both internal and worldwide operations. The aircraft were capable of being fitted with comprehensive infra-red countermeasures to deter heat-seeking missiles.

Powerplant
The Il-76TD is powered by four Aviadvigatel D-30KP-2 turbofans, each delivering up to 117.7 kN (26,455 lb st), housed in individual pods beneath the wings. Each engine has a service life of 6500 hours, with an intermediate service after 3000 hours. All the engines are fitted with a clamshell-type thrust reverser, giving a minimum landing run of 900 m (2,950 ft). A new version of the Il-76TD, the Il-76TD-90VD, flew for the first time on 5 August 2005. Powered by PS-90A76 turbofans, the new machine is the subject of two orders from Volga-Dnepr for delivery later in the year. The new engines can also be retrofitted to older airframes, and while Silk Way plans to re-engine at least one Il-76TD, Volga-Dnepr may re-engine its whole fleet.

Tail section
The variable-incidence tailplane has aerodynamically balanced tabbed elevators and is set in a T-tail arrangement. The rudder is also aerodynamically balanced and, like all flight controls, is hydraulically boosted with emergency manual revision.

Wing structure
The wing is constructed in five sections with the centre section being the width of the fuselage. The other four sections of the wing are set at 4 degrees anhedral.

Cargo hold
The hold has an available volume of 235.3 m³ (8,310 cu ft) and is available with a reinforced titanium floor or folding roller conveyor panels. Access is through two outward-opening clamshell doors, with an upward-hinged ramp able to lift a 30-tonne load.

Flight crew
The Il-76's standard crew of seven includes pilot and co-pilot in side-by-side seating in the cockpit, navigator in the glazed nose section, radio operator, supernumerary and two freight handlers.

Undercarriage
The steerable nosewheel has two pairs of wheels attached to a central oleo and retracts forward into the fuselage. The main landing gear has two units in tandem on each side, each unit with four wheels on a single axle. During retraction, the mainwheel axles rotate around the leg to lie parallel to the fuselage axis.

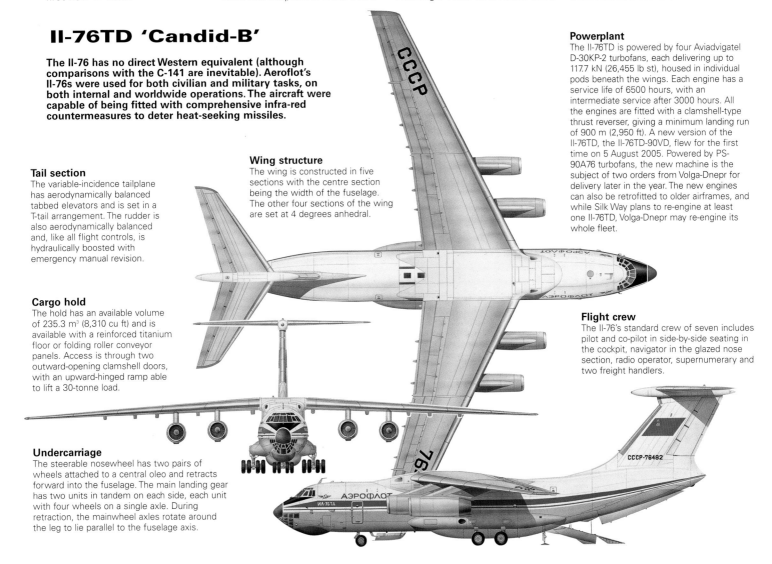

Antonov An-124 Ruslan 'Condor' Cargo superstar

The largest series production aircraft yet built, Antonov's colossal An-124 began life as a strategic military freighter, before finding further success in the post-Cold War era commercial heavylift market.

Designed to a specification issued following the cessation of An-22 production in 1974, the An-40 project was intended to result in an aircraft 'in the class of the C-5 Galaxy'. Revealed in 1977, Antonov's aircraft was now its designated An-400. The first prototype for the new long-range heavylift freighter made its maiden flight on 26 December 1982. Prior to the second prototype, named *Ruslan* after a character from Russian folklore, being flown to the 1985 Paris Air Show, the aircraft's designation changed again, to An-124.

Military operations

The Soviet V-TA (Military Transport Aviation), announced the specification of the An-124 during the developmental phase, and the resulting aircraft featured loading doors, and a fuselage cross-section and titanium floor suitable for typical military loads, together with landing gear for use from unpaved airstrips. A further stipulation insisted that the An-124 be able to fly 8000 fully loaded flights without fatigue problems.

Powered by four Lotarev D-18T turbofans equipped with thrust-reversal, the An-124 emerged as a world-beating aircraft, with aerodynamics superior to those of its American rivals. It also had an advanced supercritical wing. The gross weight of the An-124 is also almost 77,112 kg (170,000 lb) greater than that of the C-5A, and the aircraft boasts hydraulically powered full-span leading-edge flaps, Fowler flaps, ailerons, inboard airbrakes and outboard spoilers. Within the wing itself, the An-124 (appropriately assigned the ASCC/NATO code name 'Condor') has capacity for 230,004 kg

(507,063 lb) of fuel. The An-124's flight controls are fully fly-by-wire, with hydraulic back-up. Further advanced features include the widespread use of carbon and glass composites in construction, the engine nacelles and pylons being composed entirely of these materials.

Internal capacity

The pear-shaped fuselage section gives the An-124 a main cargo hold which is 4.40 m (14 ft 5 in) high and 6.40 m (21 ft) wide, originally designed to be capable of accepting the the currently outlawed SS-20 'Saber' mobile IRBM (intermediate-range ballistic missile) in V-TA service. Entry to the capacious 36-m (118-ft 1-in) long hold is via a rear ramp door. In order to cope with the heaviest internal loads, the hold is equipped with twin 3000-kg (6,614-lb) winches and two 10,000-kg (22,049-lb) travelling cranes. A pressurized upper deck area provides seating for up to 88 personnel. In order to cope with internal payloads of around 150,000 kg (330,668 lb), the An-124's robust

This HeavyLift/Volga-Dnepr An-124 was used to deploy helicopters such as this No. 78 Sqn, RAF, Sea King HAR.Mk 3 from the United Kingdom to the Falkland Islands.

Limited availability of outsize freighters has led to the An-124 having been used by a number of Western operators, including Air Foyle at Luton and Stansted's HeavyLift Cargo Airlines (pictured).

landing gear comprises twin two-wheel independent steerable nose gear, and Hydromash main gear with five twin-wheel units retracting into low-drag fairings on each side, both of which incorporate an APU for inflight or ground auxiliary power. The wheel units can be collapsed in order to gain a nose-up or nose-down attitude during loading or unloading.

Production of the An-124 began at Ulyanovsk after the seventh production airframe had been completed at Kiev in late 1985. Following a temporary interruption to Kiev production during the

upheavals of 1991, both sites continued low-rate production until 1995, by which date 55 aircraft had been completed or substantially built (19 at Kiev and 36 at Ulyanovsk). By 1999, it was reported that three further examples had been built at Ulyanovsk and in 2005 Antonov and Volga-Dnepr unveiled plans to build 50 modernized An-124M-150 aircraft by 2008.

On 26 July 1985 an An-124 set a new record by lifting a payload of 171,222 kg (377,473 lb) to a height of 10,750 m (35,269 ft). Twenty more records followed, including

Commercial An-124 operators included Ajax (the freight subsidiary of ARIA), Polet (pictured), Titan and Trans Charter. In addition, Aviaobshchemash and Transaero both occasionally chartered examples from the Russian air force.

a closed-circuit record which was established in May 1987 when an An-124 flew 20,151 km (12,521 miles) in 25 hours 30 minutes. In January 1986 the An-124 began to be accepted into the V-TA and Aeroflot inventories.

One of the first tasks for the 'Condor' was the transportation of units of 154-tonne Euclid dumper trucks for Yakut diamond miners. Since this date, the An-124's achievements have tended to be more humanitarian-oriented.

Civil applications

The An-124-100 was granted civil certification by the Russian Interstate Aviation Committee on 30 December 1992, with civil-operated aircraft either being built to, or converted to, this new standard. The maximum take-off weight is lower than that of the standard military An-124, at 392,000 kg (864,200 lb), and maximum payload is reduced to 120,000 kg (264,550 lb).

The first civilian customer for the An-124 was Air Foyle. Further civil derivatives of the baseline An-124 have been offered, comprising the An-124-100M with Western avionics. The flight crew of the An-124-100M is reduced to four, with the removal of the radio operator and the navigator. The first prototype was completed in late 1995 (the 34th Ulyanovsk aircraft), and Ajax was announced as the first customer for the derivative.

The An-124-102 would feature a crew reduced to just three, and the incorporation of an EFIS-equipped flight deck and dual sets of CRTs. The An-124-130 proposal would have been powered by General Electric CF6-80 turbofans. A further proposed propulsion modification would have seen the An-124 Turboprop retrofit re-equipped with four Aviadvigatel NK-93 propfans.

More radical proposals have included the An-124FFR water-bomber conversion project, able to drop up to 200 tonnes (440,917 lb) of fire retardants, including 70 tonnes (154,321 lb) from the centre fuel tank; and the An-124 Satellite Launcher, with, at one time, up to four An-124s earmarked for conversion in order to carry the Vozdushny Start booster, capable of placing a 2000-kg (4,409-lb) satellite into a 200-km (124-mile) orbit.

SPECIFICATION	
Antonov An-124 Ruslan	405,000 kg (892,875 lb)
Type: heavylift freighter	**Dimensions:** wing span 73.30 m
Powerplant: four 229.5-kN (51,590-lb-thrust) ZMKB Progress (Lotarev) D18T turbofan	(240 ft 6 in); length 69.10 m (226 ft 9in); height 20.78 m (68 ft 2 in); wing area 628.0 m² (6,760 sq ft)
Cruising speed: 800–850 km/h (497–528 mph)	**Accommodation:** flight crew of two pilots, two flight engineers,
Range: 4500 km (2796 miles) with maximum payload; 16,500 km (10,253 miles) with maximum fuel	navigator and communications operator; upper deck area behind the wing can accommodate up to
Weights: operating empty 175,000 kg (385,800 lb), maximum take-off	88 passengers; maximum payload 150 tonnes (330,695 lb)

An An-124-100 touches down at the Farnborough Air Show, United Kingdom, September 1988. The AN-124's sheer size and versatility has made it popular amongst aviation enthusiasts throughout the world.

Antonov An-225 Mriya 'Cossack' Ukrainian giant

With a maximum payload of some 600 tonnes and a wing span of more than 80 m (260 ft), the mighty 'Cossack' lands at the Farnborough Air Show in 1990.

The largest aircraft in the world, the An-225 could have played an important role in Russia's space programme and the country's industrial expansion. Despite its capabilities, however, the sole 'Cossack' has long languished in the Ukraine, although there may be renewed interest in the type.

Despite making a number of appearances at international air shows and setting a collection of world records, the An-225 Mriya (Dream) remains an enigma to the West. It was originally thought to have been designed to carry the Soviet space shuttle and, indeed, it did fly with *Buran* on 13 May 1989. It made its Western debut at the Paris Air Show later that year, and visited Farnborough in 1990. Since then, however, the An-225 has apparently languished in storage, with many of its

components being scavenged to service An-124s.

The 'Cossack' design is firmly rooted in that of its predecessor, the An-124. Antonov had been assigned the task of designing an airframe able to carry, as a 'piggy-back' load, such enormous items as the *Buran* manned space orbiter, the Energiya space launch vehicle, and various gigantic structures needed by the expanding oil, gas and petrochemical industries, especially those in the isolation of Siberia.

The main changes to the An-124 were the addition of a new wing centre section with two extra engines, the lengthening of the fuselage, and the fitting of a new twin-finned tail to a modified rear fuselage. Much consideration was given to the length of the An-225's

fuselage, especially in view of the aircraft's 'piggy-back' role. The first aircraft was earmarked to carry *Buran*, and two large axial beams raised above the fuselage were fitted to serve as the main load pylons.

The An-225 was rolled out at the end of November 1988 and first flew on 21 December of the same year.

Record-breaker

Crowds at the Paris Air Show were impressed by Mriya's slick handling. Also impressive were details of a single flight on

22 March 1989 which broke no fewer than 106 world and class records. Taking off from Kiev at 508350 kg (1,126,370 lb), Mriya carried a payload of 156,300 kg (344,576 lb) around a 2000-km (1,243-mile) circuit, at an average speed of 813 km/h (505 mph), reaching a cruise height of 12,340 m (40,485 ft).

A second 'Cossack' began to take shape in the early 1990s, but it remains unfinished. There was recently talk of completing this aircraft and building more, but the 'Cossack' trail seems to have once again gone cold.

SPECIFICATION	
Antonov An-225 Mriya **Type:** extra-large cargo aircraft **Powerplant:** six 229.50-kN (51,590-lb-thrust) ZMKB Progress Lotarev D-18T turbofans **Maximum speed:** 850 km/h (528 mph) **Cruising speed:** 800km/h (497 mph) **Range:** 4500 km (2796 miles) with maximum payload; 15,400 km (9569 miles) with no cargo	**Weights:** 600,000 kg (1,322,750 lb) maximum take-off **Dimensions:** wing span 88.4 m (290 ft); length 84.00 m (275 ft 8 in); height 18.10 m (59 ft 5 in) **Accommodation:** maximum load of 250,000kg (551,150 lb) **Cargo hold:** length: 43.32 m (142 ft); width 6.4 m (21 ft); height 4.39 m (14 ft 4 in)

An-225 Mriya 'Cossack'

The *Buran*-carrying An-225 Cossack is one of the most impressive aircraft ever to fly. Despite its load-carrying performance and record-breaking achievements, however, only one was completed and it is unlikely that there will be any more unless a new customer can be found.

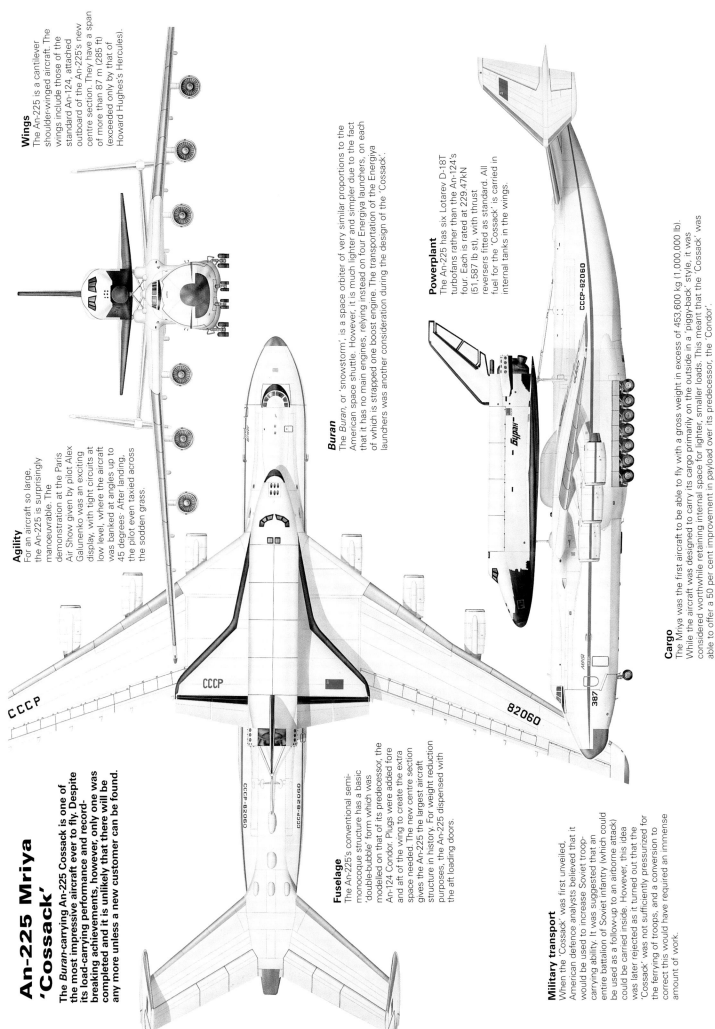

Wings

The An-225 is a cantilever shoulder-winged aircraft. The wings include those of the standard An-124, attached outboard of the An-225's new centre section. They have a span of more than 87 m (285 ft) (exceeded only by that of Howard Hughes's Hercules).

Agility

For an aircraft so large, the An-225 is surprisingly manoeuvrable. The demonstration at the Paris Air Show given by pilot Alex Galunenko was an exciting display, with tight circuits at low level, where the aircraft was banked at angles up to 45 degrees. After landing, the pilot even taxied across the sodden grass.

Buran

The *Buran*, or 'snowstorm', is a space orbiter of very similar proportions to the American space shuttle. However, it is much lighter and simpler due to the fact that it has no main engines, relying instead on four Energiya launchers, on each of which is strapped one boost engine. The transportation of the Energiya launchers was another consideration during the design of the 'Cossack'.

Powerplant

The An-225 has six Lotarev D-18T turbofans rather than the An-124's four. Each is rated at 229.47kN (51,587 lb st), with thrust reversers fitted as standard. All fuel for the 'Cossack' is carried in internal tanks in the wings.

Fuselage

The An-225's conventional semi-monocoque structure has a basic 'double-bubble' form which was modelled on that of its predecessor, the An-124 Condor. Plugs were added fore and aft of the wing to create the extra space needed. The new centre section gives the An-225 the largest aircraft structure in history. For weight reduction purposes, the An-225 dispensed with the aft loading doors.

Military transport

When the 'Cossack' was first unveiled, American defence analysts believed that it would be used to increase Soviet troop-carrying ability. It was suggested that an entire battalion of Soviet infantry (which could be used as a follow-up to an airborne attack) could be carried inside. However, this idea was later rejected as it turned out that the 'Cossack' was not sufficiently pressurized for the ferrying of troops, and a conversion to correct this would have required an immense amount of work.

Cargo

The Mriya was the first aircraft to be able to fly with a gross weight in excess of 453,600 kg (1,000,000 lb). While the aircraft was designed to carry its cargo primarily on the outside in a 'piggy-back' style, it was considered worthwhile retaining internal space for lighter, smaller loads. This meant that the 'Cossack' was able to offer a 50 per cent improvement in payload over its predecessor, the 'Condor'.

439

Long-lived Douglas DC-8

Although its passenger-carrying days are over, the DC-8 remains a hard-working freighter that is still in service, albeit in dwindling numbers, around the world. Most surviving aircraft are late-production Series 60s or the re-engined, CFM56-powered Series 70, introduced during the 1980s. As a result of several overhaul and upgrade programmes, the worldwide DC-8 fleet still has many active years ahead of it.

Douglas built six basic versions of the DC-8, in three fuselage lengths. By the time production ended in 1972 the final DC-8-60 versions – launched as the 'Super Sixty Series' – were more than 10.97 m (36 ft) longer than the basic aircraft, accommodating up to 250 passengers. It was this ability to stretch the DC-8, a feature which had been built into its design from day one, that contributed to its longevity. The DC-8 will probably outlive its great rival, the Boeing 707, because it has proved to be so adaptable. Today, however, apart from a handful of military and VIP aircraft, there are no DC-8s in (regular) passenger service. Instead, the DC-8 family has carved an important niche for itself as a freighter, and many operators have spent a lot of

money on upgrading and improving their ageing aircraft.

In all, McDonnell Douglas built a total of 556 DC-8s. The first major changes to the standard aircraft were driven by the arrival of new noise and environmental regulations, which took force in the early 1980s. McDonnell Douglas looked at re-engining options for the DC-8, which included fitting Pratt & Whitney's JT8D-209 engines as used on the MD-80, or completely new CFM56 turbofans. In March 1979 United Airlines launched the first DC-8 re-engining programme, opting to fit the CFM56 to its fleet of 30 DC-8-60s, at a cost of $400 million. In fact, the CFM56 became the only new engine option and McDonnell Douglas announced that the modified aircraft would be known as the Series 70. Only Series 60 DC-8s were selected for conversion, and so re-engined DC-8-61s became DC-8-71s, -62s became -72s and -63s became -73s.

A new joint venture company called Cammacorp was established by McDonnell Douglas, CFM International and Grumman (Grumman built the

new engine nacelles), charged with gaining a new FAA Supplemental Type Certificate (STC) for the DC-8-70 Series and began work on its first conversion, a DC-8-61. This aircraft was redelivered to United Airlines, as a DC-8-71, on 10 May 1981 and made its first revenue flight on 16 May.

A number of conversions (44) was handled at the Douglas facility, in Tulsa, Oklahoma. Three customers – Delta, UTA and Air Canada – opted to undertake the work themselves, under agreement with Cammacorp.

The 98.12-kN (22,000-lb-st) CFM56-2 engines brought the DC-8 into full compliance not only with the Stage 2/Chapter 2 noise regulations of the mid-1980s, but also with the far more stringent Stage 3/Chapter 3 standards, which were brought into full effect in mid-2000. Hand-in-hand with this came a substantial increase in performance and a 25 per cent reduction in overall fuel burn. Over a 3,000-nm (5552-km;

Not all of the passenger DC-8s saw out their days with airlines. A40-HMQ served with the Oman Royal Flight. It was built as a DC-8-63CF and converted to -73CF standard (illustrated) in 1982.

3,450-mile) sector, McDonnell Douglas claimed that a DC-8-71 burned 7711 kg (17,000 lb) less fuel than a DC-8-61. More power and greater economy pushed the range of a Series 70 to a maximum of 10,138 km (6,300 miles), or about 25 per cent more than a Series 60. The CFM56-2 turbofan provided 17 per cent more power than a JT3D-7 engine and 22 per cent more power than a JT3D-3B. The new engines also reduced take-off roll by about 10 per cent and improved climb performance by 16 per cent.

The last of 110 Series 70 conversions was a DC-8-72, delivered to NASA in April 1986. Major customers included United Airlines, Delta Air Lines, Flying Tiger, UPS, Air Canada and UTA.

To these airlines the DC-8-70 Series offered low acquisition and running costs, coupled with the ability to fly into noise-sensitive airports around the clock thanks to the Stage 3/Chapter 3 compliance. On top of

Preparations for the the 1991 Gulf War saw the US Civil Reserve Air Fleet mobilized, with the result that a number of DC-8 cargo conversions saw active service as strategic airlifters. This aircraft is a Hawaiian Airlines DC-8-62F.

Emery Worldwide Airlines maintained a large fleet of DC-8 freighters. This included examples of the DC-8-54F, -62F, -63F, -71F and -73F (illustrated).

this, for those aircraft not already configured as freighters, the cargo conversion process was straightforward and several companies began to offer DC-8 freighter modifications.

Freighters and hush-kits

McDonnell Douglas developed its own freighter conversion in the mid-1970s. This involved the removal of all seating and passenger facilities, fitting a strengthened cargo floor, with rollers, and adding an 2.15- x 3.55-m (85- x 140-in) main cargo door in the forward port fuselage. All windows were removed and replaced with blank plugs. The US firm later sold its design to Italy's Aeronavali (now part of Alenia). Aeronavali's Venice facility became the main centre for cargo conversions, which included a major contract for 25, placed by lessors GPA in the early 1990s. A handful of other cargo conversions was carried out by firms such as Zantop, PSA and Stambaugh Aviation.

For DC-8 operators who cannot meet the cost of re-engining their aircraft, but who still need to meet today's noise rules, several hush-kit options have been developed for the JT3D engine. These include the 'SilentKnight' hush-kit designed by the Aeronautical Development Corp., plus Stage

For the long-range transport of passengers and cargo, the French air force flies three Airbus A310s and two DC-8-72s.

3/Chapter 3 solutions developed by the Burbank Aeronautical Corp. and Quiet Technology Venture (previously Quiet Nacelle Corp.). In 1990 US charter operator MGM Grand Air became the launch customer for the BAC hush-kit, while the QTV hush-kit was first fitted to Fine Air DC-8s in 1997.

Another engine-related modification was conducted by Page AvJet for Airborne Express, in the United States. In 1991 Airborne Express started to have the long-duct engine pylons and nacelles of the DC-8-62/63 refitted to all its DC-8-61 freighters, allowing them to accommodate the BAC Stage 3 hush kit.

Today, the largest operator of DC-8s is United Parcel Service (UPS), which has a fleet of 47 DC-8-70 freighters. UPS launched an ambitious upgrade for all its DC-8s and Boeing 727s, adding a four-screen EFIS cockpit, INS, colour weather radar, autopilot and complete electrical re-wiring. By 1995, work on all its DC-8s had been completed, bringing what had previously been 14 different levels of equipment up to a common standard. Other major DC-8 operators include ATI-Air Transport International (six DC-8-60s and 13 DC-8-70s), ABX Air (23 DC-8-60s), Arrow Air (seven DC-8-60s) and Astar Air Cargo (nine DC-8-70s). All of these airlines are pure cargo-carriers.

By summer 2005, the DC-8 population was approximately 200 aircraft worldwide.

SPECIFICATION
Douglas DC-8 Super 70 series **Type:** long-range medium-capacity airliner and freighter **Powerplant:** four 97.9-kN (22,000-lb-st) CFM International CFM562C5 turbofans **Maximum cruising speed:** 887km/h (551 mph) **Economical cruising speed:** 850km/h (528 mph) **Range:** (Super 73) 8950km (5561 miles) with maximum payload **Weights:** (Super 73) operating empty 75,500 kg (166,500 lb),	maximum take-off 162,025 kg (355,000 lb) **Dimensions:** (Super 73) wing span 45.23 m (148 ft 5 in); length 57.12 m (187 ft 5 in); height 12.92 m (45 ft 5 in); wing area 271.9 m² (2,927 sq ft) **Accommodation:** flight crew of three, plus between 180 and 220 passengers in standard layout for Series 71 & 73 (259 passengers maximum); 189 passengers in standard layout for Series 72; Super 60 and 70 freighters payload between 40,405 kg (89,000 lb) and 49,585 kg (109,217 lb)

As one of the world's leading parcel movement companies, UPS uses the DC-8 to fill the gap in its cargo capacity between the smaller Boeing 727 and 757, and the larger A300, MD-11, 767 and 747.

Glossary

AAM: Air-to-Air Missile.

ADP: Automatic Data Processing.

ADV: Air Defence Variant (of the Tornado).

Aeronautics: The science of travel through the Earth's atmosphere.

AEW: Airborne Early Warning.

Afterburning (reheat): Method of increasing the thrust of a gas turbine aircraft engine by injecting additional fuel into the hot exhaust duct between the engine and the tailpipe, where it ignites to provide a short-term increase of power.

Aileron: An aerofoil used for causing an aircraft to roll around its longitudinal axis, usually fitted near the wingtips. Ailerons are controlled by use of the pilot's control column.

ALARM: Air-Launched Anti-Radiation Missile.

All-Up Weight: The total weight of an aircraft in operating condition. Normal maximum AUW is the maximum at which an aircraft is permitted to fly within normal design restrictions, while overload weight is the maximum AUW at which an aircraft is permitted to fly subject to ultimate flying restrictions.

Altimeter: Instrument that measures altitude, or height above sea level.

AMRAAM: Advanced Medium-Range Air-to-Air Missile.

ASV: Air to Surface Vessel – airborne detection radar for locating ships and submarines.

ASW: Anti-Submarine Warfare.

ATF: Advanced Tactical Fighter.

Autogiro: Heavier-than-air craft which supports itself in the air by means of a rotary wing (rotor), forward propulsion being provided by a conventional engine.

Automatic Pilot (Autopilot): Automatic device that keeps an aircraft flying on a set course at a set speed and altitude.

AWACS: Airborne Warning and Control System.

Basic Weight: The tare weight of an aircraft plus the specified operational load.

Centre of Gravity: Point in a body through which the sum of the weights of all its parts passes. A body suspended from this point is said to be in a state of equilibrium.

Centre of Pressure: Point through which the lifting force of a wing acts.

Chord: Cross-section of a wing from leading edge to trailing edge.

Circular Error Probable (CEP): A measure of the accuracy attributable to ballistic missiles, bombs and shells. It is the radius of a circle into which 50 per cent of the missiles aimed at the centre of the circle are expected to fall.

Clutter: A term used in radar parlance to describe reflected echoes on a cathode ray tube caused by the ground, sea or bad weather.

Convertiplane: Vertical take-off and landing craft with wing-mounted rotors that act as helicopter rotors for take-off, then tilt to act as conventional propellers for forward flight.

Delta Wing: Aircraft shaped like the Greek letter delta.

Disposable Load: The weight of crew and consumable load (fuel, missiles etc.).

Electronic Combat Reconnaissance (ECR): A variant of the Panavia Tornado optimized for electronic warfare.

Electronic Countermeasures (ECM): Systems designed to confuse and disrupt enemy radar equipment.

Electronic Counter-Countermeasures (ECCM): Measures taken to reduce the effectiveness of ECM by improving the resistance of radar equipment to jamming.

Elevator: A horizontal control surface used to control the upward or downward inclination of an aircraft in flight. Elevators are usually hinged to the trailing edge of the tailplane.

ELF: Extremely Low Frequency. A radio frequency used for communication with submarines.

ELINT: Electronic Intelligence. Information gathered through monitoring enemy electronic transmissions by specially equipped aircraft, ships or satellites.

EW: Electronic Warfare.

FAC: Forward Air Controller. A battlefront observer who directs strike aircraft on to their targets near the front line.

FAE: Fuel-Air Explosive. A weapon that disperses fuel into the atmosphere in the form of an aerosol cloud. The cloud is ignited to produce intense heat and heat effects.

FGA: Fighter Ground Attack.

FLIR: Forward-Looking Infra-Red. Heat-sensing equipment fitted in an aircraft that scans the path ahead to detect heat from objects such as vehicle engines.

FRS: Fighter Reconnaissance Strike.

Gas turbine: Engine in which burning fuel supplies hot gas to spin a turbine.

GPS: Global Positioning System. A system of navigational satellites.

HUD: Head-Up Display. A system in which essential information is projected on to a cockpit windscreen so that the pilot has no need to look down at his instrument panel.

IFF: Identification Friend or Foe. An electronic pulse emitted by an aircraft to identify it as friendly on a radar screen.

INS: Inertial Navigation System. An on-board guidance system that steers an aircraft or missile over a pre-determined course by measuring factors such as the distance travelled and reference to 'waypoints' (landmarks) en route.

IR: Infra-Red.

Jet propulsion: Method of propulsion in which an object is propelled in one direction by a jet, or stream of gases, moving in the other.

JSTARS: Joint Surveillance and Target Attack Radar System. An airborne command and control system that directs air and ground forces in battle.

LAMPS: Light Airborne Multi-Purpose System. Anti-submarine helicopter equipment, comprising search radar, sonobuoys and other detection equipment.

Landing Weight: The AUW of an aircraft at the moment of landing.

Lantirn: Low-Altitude Navigation and Targeting Infra-Red for Night. An infra-red system fitted to the F-15E Strike Eagle that combines heat sensing with terrain-following radar to enable the pilot to view the ground ahead of the aircraft during low-level night operations. The information is projected on the pilot's head-up display.

Mach: Named after the Austrian Professor Ernst Mach, a Mach number is the ratio of the speed of an aircraft or missile to the local speed of sound. At sea level, Mach One (1.0M) is approximately 1226 km/h (762mph), decreasing to about 1062 km/h (660mph) at 30,000 feet. An aircraft or missile travelling faster than Mach One is said to be supersonic. Mach numbers are dependent on variations in atmospheric temperature and pressure and are registered on a Machmeter in the aircraft's cockpit.

Maximum Landing Weight: The maximum AUW, due to design or operational limitations, at which an aircraft is permitted to land.

Maximum Take-Off Weight: The maximum AUW, due to design or operational limitations, at which an aircraft is permitted to take off.

Megaton: Thermonuclear weapon yield, one megaton (mT) being roughly equal to 1,000,000 tons of TNT.

MG: Machine gun (*Maschinengewehr* in German, hence MG 15).

Mk: Mark (of aircraft).

Muzzle Velocity: The speed at which a bullet or shell leaves a gun barrel.

NATO: North Atlantic Treaty Organization.

NBC: Nuclear, Biological and Chemical (warfare).

Operational Load: The weight of equipment necessarily carried by an aircraft for a particular role.

Payload: The weight of passengers and/or cargo.

PPLSS: Precision Location Strike System. A battlefield surveillance system installed in the Lockheed TR-1 that detects the movement of enemy forces and directs air and ground attacks against them.

Ramjet: Simple form of jet engine which is accelerated to high speed causing air to be forced into the combustion chamber, into which fuel is sprayed and then ignited. The Pulse Jet engine, used in the V-1 flying bomb, is a form of ramjet.

Rudder: Movable vertical surface or surfaces forming part of the tail unit, by which the yawing of an aircraft is controlled.

RWR: Radar Warning Receiver. A device mounted on an aircraft that warns the pilot if he is being tracked by an enemy missile guidance or intercept radar.

SAM: Surface-to-Air Missile.

SHF: Super High Frequency (radio waves).

SIGINT: Signals Intelligence. Information on enemy intentions gathered by monitoring electronic transmissions from his command, control and communications network.

SLAM: Stand-off Land Attack Missile – a missile that can be air-launched many miles from its target.

Sound Barrier: Popular name for the concept that the speed of sound (see Mach) constitutes a limit to to flight through the atmosphere to all aircraft except those specially designed to penetrate it. The cone-shaped shock wave created by an aircraft breaking the 'barrier' produces a 'sonic boom' when it passes over the ground.

Spin: A spin is the result of yawing or rolling an aeroplane at the point of a stall.

SRAM: Short-range Attack Missile.

Stall: Condition that occurs when the smooth flow of the air over an aircraft's wing changes to a turbulent flow and the lift decreases to the point where control is lost.

Stealth Technology: Technology applied to aircraft or fighting vehicles to reduce their radar signatures. Examples of stealth aircraft are the Lockheed F-117 and the Northrop B-2.

STOVL: Short Take-off, Vertical Landing.

TADS: Target Acquisition/Designation System. A laser sighting system fitted to the AH-64 Apache attack helicopter.

Take-Off Weight: The AUW of an aircraft at the moment of take-off.

Thermal Imager: Equipment fitted to an aircraft or fighting vehicle which typically comprises a telescope to collect and focus infra-red energy emitted by objects on a battlefield, a mechanism to scan the scene across an array of heat-sensitive detectors, and a processor to turn the signals from these detectors into a 'thermal image' displayed on a TV screen.

TIALD: Thermal Imaging/Airborne Laser Designator. Equipment fitted to the Panavia Tornado IDS enabling it to locate and attack precision targets at night.

Turbofan engine: Type of jet engine fitted with a very large front fan that not only sends air into the engine for combustion but also around the engine to produce additional thrust. This results in faster and more fuel-efficient propulsion.

Turbojet engine: Jet engine that derives its thrust from a stream of hot exhaust gases.

Turboprop engine: Jet engine that derives its thrust partly from a jet of exhaust gases, but mainly from a propeller powered by a turbine in the jet exhaust.

Variable-Geometry Wing: A type of wing whose angle of sweep can be altered to suit a particular flight profile. Popularly called a Swing Wing.

VHF: Very High Frequency.

VLF: Very Low Frequency.

V/STOL: Vertical/Short Take-off and Landing.

Index Page numbers in *italics* refer to illustrations.